THE NEW TESTAMENT

Journal Edition

DESERET
BOOK

SALT LAKE CITY, UTAH

DESERET BOOK is a registered trademark of Deseret Book Company.
Visit us at deseretbook.com

ISBN 978-1-62972-597-0 (hardbound)

Printed in the United States of America
Lake Book Manufacturing Inc., Melrose Park, IL

10   9   8   7   6   5   4   3   2   1

THE
NEW TESTAMENT

OF OUR LORD AND SAVIOUR
JESUS CHRIST

TRANSLATED OUT OF THE
ORIGINAL GREEK: AND WITH THE
FORMER TRANSLATIONS DILIGENTLY COMPARED
AND REVISED, BY HIS MAJESTY'S
SPECIAL COMMAND

AUTHORIZED KING JAMES VERSION
WITH EXPLANATORY NOTES AND
CROSS-REFERENCES TO THE STANDARD WORKS
OF THE CHURCH OF JESUS CHRIST
OF LATTER-DAY SAINTS

ABBREVIATIONS

Old Testament

Gen.	Genesis
Ex.	Exodus
Lev.	Leviticus
Num.	Numbers
Deut.	Deuteronomy
Josh.	Joshua
Judg.	Judges
Ruth	Ruth
1 Sam.	1 Samuel
2 Sam.	2 Samuel
1 Kgs.	1 Kings
2 Kgs.	2 Kings
1 Chr.	1 Chronicles
2 Chr.	2 Chronicles
Ezra	Ezra
Neh.	Nehemiah
Esth.	Esther
Job	Job
Ps.	Psalms
Prov.	Proverbs
Eccl.	Ecclesiastes
Song	Song of Solomon
Isa.	Isaiah
Jer.	Jeremiah
Lam.	Lamentations
Ezek.	Ezekiel
Dan.	Daniel
Hosea	Hosea
Joel	Joel
Amos	Amos
Obad.	Obadiah
Jonah	Jonah
Micah	Micah
Nahum	Nahum
Hab.	Habakkuk
Zeph.	Zephaniah
Hag.	Haggai
Zech.	Zechariah
Mal.	Malachi

New Testament

Matt.	Matthew
Mark	Mark
Luke	Luke
John	John
Acts	Acts
Rom.	Romans
1 Cor.	1 Corinthians
2 Cor.	2 Corinthians
Gal.	Galatians
Eph.	Ephesians
Philip.	Philippians
Col.	Colossians
1 Thes.	1 Thessalonians
2 Thes.	2 Thessalonians
1 Tim.	1 Timothy
2 Tim.	2 Timothy
Titus	Titus
Philem.	Philemon
Heb.	Hebrews
James	James
1 Pet.	1 Peter
2 Pet.	2 Peter
1 Jn.	1 John
2 Jn.	2 John
3 Jn.	3 John
Jude	Jude
Rev.	Revelation

Book of Mormon

1 Ne.	1 Nephi
2 Ne.	2 Nephi
Jacob	Jacob
Enos	Enos
Jarom	Jarom
Omni	Omni
W of M	Words of Mormon
Mosiah	Mosiah
Alma	Alma
Hel.	Helaman
3 Ne.	3 Nephi
4 Ne.	4 Nephi
Morm.	Mormon
Ether	Ether
Moro.	Moroni

Doctrine and Covenants

D&C	Doctrine and Covenants
OD	Official Declaration

Pearl of Great Price

Moses	Moses
Abr.	Abraham
JS—M	Joseph Smith—Matthew
JS—H	Joseph Smith—History
A of F	Articles of Faith

Other Abbreviations and Explanations

JST	Joseph Smith Translation
TG	Topical Guide
BD	Bible Dictionary
HEB	An alternate translation from the Hebrew
GR	An alternate translation from the Greek
IE	An explanation of idioms and difficult wording
OR	Alternate words that clarify the meaning of an archaic expression
HC	History of the Church

Italics in biblical text. Following the traditional format, italics in Bible verses indicate words that are not found in the original text (Hebrew, Aramaic, or Greek) but have been added for clarification in the translation.

ST MATTHEW

CHAPTER 1

Christ is born of Mary—She conceives by the power of the Holy Ghost—Our Lord is named Jesus.

THE book of the generation of Jesus Christ, the son of ªDavid, the son of Abraham.

2 ªAbraham begat Isaac; and Isaac begat Jacob; and Jacob begat ᵇJudas and his brethren;

3 And Judas begat ªPhares and ᵇZara of Thamar; and Phares begat ᶜEsrom; and Esrom begat Aram;

4 And Aram begat Aminadab; and Aminadab begat Naasson; and ªNaasson begat Salmon;

5 And Salmon begat ªBooz of Rachab; and Booz begat Obed of Ruth; and Obed begat Jesse;

6 And Jesse begat David the king; and David the king begat ªSolomon of her *that had been the wife* of Urias;

7 And Solomon begat Roboam; and Roboam begat Abia; and Abia begat Asa;

8 And Asa begat Josaphat; and Josaphat begat Joram; and Joram begat Ozias;

9 And Ozias begat Joatham; and Joatham begat Achaz; and Achaz begat Ezekias;

10 And Ezekias begat Manasses; and Manasses begat Amon; and Amon begat Josias;

11 And Josias begat Jechonias and his brethren, about the time they were carried away to ªBabylon:

12 And after they were brought to Babylon, Jechonias begat Salathiel; and Salathiel begat ªZorobabel;

13 And Zorobabel begat Abiud; and Abiud begat Eliakim; and Eliakim begat Azor;

14 And Azor begat Sadoc; and Sadoc begat Achim; and Achim begat Eliud;

15 And Eliud begat Eleazar; and Eleazar begat Matthan; and Matthan begat Jacob;

16 And Jacob begat ªJoseph the husband of ᵇMary, of whom was born ᶜJesus, ᵈwho is called ᵉChrist.

17 So all the generations from Abraham to David *are* fourteen generations; and from David until the carrying away into Babylon *are* fourteen generations; and from the carrying away into Babylon unto Christ *are* fourteen ªgenerations.

18 ¶ ªNow the ᵇbirth of Jesus Christ was ᶜon this wise: When as his mother Mary was espoused to

---

Title: JST entitles this book "The Testimony of St. Matthew."
1 1a TG Jesus Christ, Davidic Descent of.
2a Gen. 25:19.
  b TG Israel, Judah, People of.
3a Ruth 4:18;
  1 Chr. 2:4 (4–15).
  b Gen. 38:30.
  c 1 Chr. 2:9.
4a Num. 1:7.
5a Ruth 4:21.

6a 2 Sam. 12:24 (24–25);
  1 Chr. 3:5.
11a TG Israel, Bondage of, in Other Lands.
12a 1 Chr. 3:19 (17–19);
  Ezra 2:2 (1–2);
  Hag. 1:1.
16a Luke 3:23 (23–38).
  b 1 Ne. 11:18 (14–21);
  Mosiah 3:8.
  c Luke 20:14;
  D&C 93:14 (3–17).
  d JST Matt. 1:4 . . . *as the prophets have written,*

who is called Christ.
  e The Greek title "Christ" and the Hebrew title "Messiah" are synonymous, meaning "Anointed One."
17a TG Book of Remembrance.
18a JST Matt. 2:1 Now, *as it is written,* the birth of . . .
  b D&C 20:1.
  c GR in this way.

Joseph, before they came together, she was found with child of the Holy Ghost.

19 Then Joseph her husband, being a just *man*, and not willing to make her a publick ªexample, ᵇwas minded to ᶜput her away privily.

20 But while he thought on these things, behold, the angel of the Lord appeared unto him in a ªdream, saying, Joseph, thou son of ᵇDavid, fear not to take unto thee Mary thy wife: for that which is conceived in her is of the ᶜHoly Ghost.

21 And she shall bring forth a son, and thou shalt call his ªname ᵇJESUS: for he shall ᶜsave his people from their sins.

22 Now all this was done, that it might be fulfilled which was spoken of the Lord by the prophet, saying,

23 ªBehold, a ᵇvirgin shall be with child, and shall bring forth a son, and they shall call his ᶜname ᵈEmmanuel, which being interpreted is, God with us.

24 Then Joseph being raised from sleep did as the angel of the Lord had bidden him, and took unto him his ªwife:

25 And knew her not till she had brought forth her ªfirstborn son: and he called his name JESUS.

CHAPTER 2

The wise men are directed by a star to Jesus—Joseph takes the child to Egypt—Herod slays the children in Bethlehem—Jesus is taken to Nazareth to dwell.

NOW when Jesus was ªborn in Bethlehem of Judæa in the days of Herod the king, behold, there came wise men from the east to Jerusalem,

2 Saying, ªWhere is he that is born ᵇKing of the Jews? for we have seen his ᶜstar in the east, and are come to ᵈworship him.

3 When Herod the king had heard *these things*, he was troubled, and all Jerusalem with him.

4 ªAnd when he had gathered all the chief priests and scribes of the people together, he ᵇdemanded of them where Christ should be born.

5 And they said unto him, In Bethlehem of Judæa: for thus it is written by the prophet,

6 And thou ªBethlehem, *in* the land of ᵇJuda, art not the least among the princes of Juda: for out of thee shall come a ᶜGovernor, that shall ᵈrule my people Israel.

7 Then Herod, when he had privily called the wise men, inquired of them diligently what time the star appeared.

8 And he sent them to Bethlehem, and said, Go and search diligently for the young child; and when ye have found *him,* bring me word again, that I may come and worship him also.

9 When they had heard the king, they departed; and, lo, the star, which they saw in the east, went

---

19a TG Example.
  b IE desired to release or divorce her secretly.
  c Deut. 24:1.
20a TG Dream.
  b 2 Ne. 19:7.
  c Luke 1:35;
    Alma 7:10.
21a TG Jesus Christ, Prophecies about.
  b Luke 2:21;
  c TG Forgive;
    Jesus Christ, Atonement through;
    Jesus Christ, Mission of;
    Jesus Christ, Redeemer;
    Jesus Christ, Savior;
    Redemption; Salvation.

23a Isa. 7:14.
  b TG Jesus Christ, Birth of.
  c TG Name.
  d TG Jesus Christ, Prophecies about.
24a Luke 2:5.
25a TG Firstborn.
2 1a TG Jesus Christ, Birth of.
  2a JST Matt. 3:2 . . . Where is *the child* that is born, *the Messiah* of the Jews? . . .
  b Isa. 6:5;
    Jer. 23:5;
    2 Ne. 10:14;
    Alma 5:50;

    D&C 128:22 (22–23);
    Moses 7:53.
  c Hel. 14:5 (1–2, 5);
    3 Ne. 1:21.
  d TG Worship.
4a JST Matt. 3:4–6 (Appendix).
  b GR inquired.
6a TG Jesus Christ, Prophecies about.
  b TG Israel, Judah, People of.
  c 1 Chr. 5:2;
    Micah 5:2;
    John 7:42.
  d GR tend, protect, nurture.

before them, till it came and stood over where the young child was.

10 When they saw the star, they rejoiced with exceeding great joy.

11 ¶ And when they were come into the house, they saw the young child with Mary his mother, and fell down, and worshipped him: and when they had opened their treasures, they presented unto him gifts; gold, and ^afrankincense, and myrrh.

12 And being warned of God in a ^adream that they should not return to Herod, they departed into their own country another way.

13 And when they were departed, behold, the angel of the Lord appeareth to Joseph in a dream, saying, Arise, and take the young child and his mother, and flee into Egypt, and be thou there until I bring thee word: for Herod will seek the young child to destroy him.

14 When he arose, he took the young child and his mother by night, and departed into Egypt:

15 And was there until the death of Herod: that it might be fulfilled which was spoken of the Lord by the prophet, saying, Out of ^aEgypt have I called my son.

16 ¶ Then Herod, when he saw that he was ^amocked of the wise men, ^bwas exceeding wroth, and sent forth, and ^cslew all the children that were in Bethlehem, and in all the ^dcoasts thereof, from two years old and under, according to the time which he had diligently inquired of the wise men.

17 Then was fulfilled that which was spoken by ^aJeremy the prophet, saying,

18 In ^aRama was there a voice heard, lamentation, and weeping, and great ^bmourning, Rachel weeping for her ^cchildren, and would not be comforted, because they are not.

19 ¶ But when Herod was dead, behold, an angel of the Lord appeareth in a ^adream to Joseph in Egypt,

20 Saying, Arise, and take the young child and his mother, and go into the ^aland of Israel: for they are dead which sought the young child's life.

21 And he arose, and took the young child and his mother, and came into the land of Israel.

22 But when he heard that Archelaus did reign in Judæa in the ^aroom of his father Herod, he was afraid to go thither: notwithstanding, being warned of God in a ^bdream, he turned aside into the parts of Galilee:

23 And he came and dwelt in a city called ^aNazareth: that it might be fulfilled which was ^bspoken by the prophets, He shall be called a ^cNazarene.

CHAPTER 3

John the Baptist preaches in Judæa— Jesus is baptized, and the Father acclaims Him as His Beloved Son.

IN those days came ^aJohn the Baptist, preaching in the wilderness of Judæa,

2 And saying, ^aRepent ye: for the ^bkingdom of heaven ^cis at hand.

3 For this is he that was spoken of by the prophet ^aEsaias, saying, The ^bvoice of one crying in the

11a Lev. 2:1.
12a TG Dream.
15a TG Jesus Christ, Prophecies about.
16a GR deceived by.
  b GR became extremely angry.
  c TG Tyranny.
  d GR surrounding regions.
17a IE Jeremiah.
18a Jer. 31:15.
  b TG Mourning.
  c Jer. 40:1.
19a JST Matt. 3:19 . . . vision . . .

    TG Dream.
20a TG Israel, Land of.
22a GR place.
  b TG Dream.
23a 1 Ne. 11:13.
  b TG Scriptures, Lost.
  c JST Matt. 3:24–26 (Appendix).
3 1a JS—H 1:72.
  2a The Greek word denotes "a change of heart or mind," i.e., "a conversion." Alma 7:9; 9:25 (25–26); Hel. 5:32;

    D&C 33:10.
  b Luke 10:9.
    TG Kingdom of God, in Heaven; Kingdom of God, on Earth.
  c GR has come. Isa. 56:1; Matt. 4:17; D&C 39:19.
3a See JST Luke 3:4–11 (Appendix). TG Foreordination.
  b Isa. 40:3; Mark 1:3; Luke 3:4; John 1:23; D&C 65:3; 88:66.

wilderness, ^cPrepare ye the way of the Lord, make his ^dpaths straight.

4 And the same John had his ^araiment of ^bcamel's hair, and a leathern girdle about his loins; and his meat was ^clocusts and wild honey.

5 Then went out to him Jerusalem, and all Judæa, and all the region round about Jordan,

6 And were baptized of him in Jordan, ^aconfessing their sins.

7 ¶ But when he saw many of the Pharisees and Sadducees come to his ^abaptism, he said unto them, O ^bgeneration of vipers, who hath ^cwarned you to flee from the wrath to come?

8 ^aBring forth therefore fruits ^bmeet for ^crepentance:

9 And think not to say within yourselves, We have Abraham ^ato our father: for I say unto you, that God is able of these stones to raise up children unto Abraham.

10 And now also the axe is laid unto the root of the trees: therefore every tree which ^abringeth not forth good fruit is ^bhewn down, and cast into the fire.

11 ^aI indeed ^bbaptize you with water unto ^crepentance: but ^dhe that cometh after me is mightier than I, whose shoes I am not ^eworthy to bear: he shall ^fbaptize you with the Holy Ghost, and with ^gfire:

12 Whose ^afan is in his hand, and he will throughly purge his floor, and gather his wheat into the ^bgarner; but he will burn up the chaff with unquenchable ^cfire.

13 ¶ Then cometh Jesus from Galilee to Jordan unto John, to be ^abaptized of him.

14 But John forbad him, saying, I have need to be baptized of thee, and comest thou to me?

15 ^aAnd Jesus answering said unto him, ^bSuffer it to be so now: for thus it ^cbecometh us to ^dfulfil all ^erighteousness. Then he suffered him.

16 And Jesus, when he was ^abaptized, went up ^bstraightway out of the water: and, lo, the heavens were opened unto him, and he saw the ^cSpirit of God descending like a ^ddove, and lighting upon him:

17 And lo a ^avoice from heaven, saying, This is my ^bbeloved ^cSon, in whom I am well pleased.

CHAPTER 4

Jesus fasts forty days and is tempted— He begins His ministry, calls disciples, and heals the sick.

THEN was Jesus ^aled up of the Spirit into the wilderness ^bto be ^ctempted of the devil.

2 And when he had ^afasted ^bforty

3c 1 Ne. 10:8 (7–10);
  D&C 34:6; 65:1 (1–2); 84:26.
 d Alma 7:19 (9, 19).
4a GR garment. See also
  2 Kgs. 1:8.
 b Zech. 13:4.
 c Lev. 11:22.
6a TG Confession.
7a See JST Matt. 9:18–21
  (Appendix).
  Luke 7:29 (29–30).
 b GR crop of serpents.
  Matt. 12:34; 23:33;
  Alma 9:8; 10:17 (17–25).
 c TG Warn.
8a JST Matt. 3:34–36
  (Appendix).
 b GR appropriate to,
  worthy of.
 c TG Baptism, Qualifications for; Repent.
9a GR as our father.
10a Alma 5:36 (36–41);
  3 Ne. 14:19;
  D&C 52:18; 97:7.

 b Luke 13:7;
  Jacob 5:42 (42–66).
11a JST Matt. 3:38–40
  (Appendix).
 b Acts 19:3 (1–7);
  2 Ne. 31:5 (5–10).
 c TG Baptism, Qualifications for.
 d See JST John 1:27–34
  (Appendix).
 e TG Worthiness.
 f TG Holy Ghost, Baptism of.
 g D&C 19:31.
12a Jer. 51:2.
 b GR storehouse.
 c D&C 43:32; 63:34 (33–34);
  101:66.
13a TG Jesus Christ, Baptism of.
15a JST Matt. 3:43–46
  (Appendix).
 b GR Permit it now.
 c GR is fitting for us.
 d TG Baptism, Essential.
 e TG Jesus Christ, Mission
  of; Righteousness.

16a TG Baptism;
  Baptism, Immersion.
 b GR immediately.
 c TG God, Spirit of.
 d TG Holy Ghost, Dove,
  Sign of.
17a Mark 9:7;
  Luke 9:35 (34–36).
  TG God, Body of,
  Corporeal Nature;
  God, Manifestations of.
 b Matt. 17:5; 3 Ne. 11:7;
  JS—H 1:17.
  TG Witness of the Father.
 c TG Godhead; God the
  Father, Elohim; Jesus
  Christ, Divine Sonship.
4 1a TG Guidance, Divine.
 b JST Matt. 4:1 . . . to be
  with God.
 c TG Jesus Christ, Temptation of; Temptation; Test.
2a Mosiah 3:7.
  TG Fast, Fasting.
 b Ex. 24:18.

days and forty nights, ^{c}he was afterward an hungred.

3 And when the ^{a}tempter came to him, he said, If thou be the Son of God, command that these stones be made ^{b}bread.

4 But he answered and said, It is written, ^{a}Man shall not ^{b}live by ^{c}bread alone, but by every ^{d}word that proceedeth out of the ^{e}mouth of God.

5 ^{a}Then the devil taketh him up into the ^{b}holy city, and setteth him on a pinnacle of the temple,

6 ^{a}And saith unto him, ^{b}If thou be the Son of God, cast thyself down: for it is written, He shall give his angels charge concerning thee: and in *their* hands they shall bear thee up, lest at any time thou dash thy foot against a stone.

7 Jesus said unto him, It is written again, Thou shalt not ^{a}tempt the Lord thy God.

8 ^{a}Again, the devil taketh him up into an exceeding high mountain, and sheweth him all the ^{b}kingdoms of the world, and the glory of them;

9 ^{a}And saith unto him, All these things will I give thee, if thou wilt fall down and worship me.

10 Then saith Jesus unto him, Get thee hence, ^{a}Satan: for it is written, Thou shalt ^{b}worship the Lord thy God, and him only shalt thou serve.

11 Then the devil leaveth him, ^{a}and, behold, ^{b}angels came and ministered unto him.

12 ¶ Now when Jesus had heard that John was cast into prison, he departed into ^{a}Galilee;

13 And leaving Nazareth, he came and dwelt in Capernaum, which is upon the sea coast, in the borders of Zabulon and Nephthalim:

14 That it might be ^{a}fulfilled which was spoken by Esaias the prophet, saying,

15 The land of ^{a}Zabulon, and the land of Nephthalim, *by* the way of the sea, beyond Jordan, Galilee of the Gentiles;

16 The people which sat in ^{a}darkness saw great ^{b}light; and to them which sat in the region and shadow of death light is sprung up.

17 ¶ From that time Jesus began to ^{a}preach, and to say, ^{b}Repent: for the ^{c}kingdom of heaven ^{d}is at hand.

18 ¶ And Jesus, walking by the sea of Galilee, saw two brethren, Simon called Peter, and Andrew his brother, casting a net into the sea: for they were ^{a}fishers.

19 And he saith unto them, ^{a}Follow me, and I will make you ^{b}fishers of men.

2c JST Matt. 4:2 . . . *and had communed with God, he was afterwards an hungered, and was left to be tempted of the devil.*
3a TG Devil.
  b TG Bread.
4a Deut. 8:3;
    D&C 84:44 (43–44).
  b TG Mortality.
  c TG Bread.
  d TG Revelation.
  e TG God, Body of, Corporeal Nature.
5a JST Matt. 4:5 Then *Jesus was taken* up into the holy city, and *the Spirit* setteth him on *the* pinnacle of the temple.
  b Neh. 11:1.
6a JST Matt. 4:6 *Then the devil came unto him and said, If . . .*
  b Matt. 27:40;

D&C 20:22.
7a D&C 10:29; 24:13 (13–14).
    TG Jesus Christ, Temptation of; Test.
8a JST Matt. 4:8 *And again, Jesus was in the Spirit, and it taketh him . . .*
  b D&C 10:19.
    TG Kings, Earthly.
9a JST Matt. 4:9 *And the devil came unto him again, and said, All . . .*
10a TG Devil.
  b TG Worship.
11a JST Matt. 4:11–12 *And now Jesus knew that John was cast into prison, and he sent angels, and, behold, they came and ministered unto him [John]. And Jesus departed into Galilee . . .*
  b TG Angels.

12a Luke 4:14.
14a D&C 24:14.
15a Isa. 9:1 (1–2).
16a D&C 57:10.
  b TG Jesus Christ, Light of the World; Jesus Christ, Prophecies about.
17a TG Preaching.
  b TG Repent.
  c TG Kingdom of God, in Heaven.
  d GR has come. Isa. 56:1; Matt. 3:2.
18a TG Skill.
19a JST Matt. 4:18 . . . *I am he of whom it is written by the prophets; follow me . . .*
    TG Jesus Christ, Exemplar.
  b TG Apostles; Missionary Work.

20 And they straightway left *their* nets, and ^afollowed him.

21 And going on from thence, he saw other two brethren, James *the son* of ^aZebedee, and John his brother, in a ship with Zebedee their father, mending their nets; and he ^bcalled them.

22 And they immediately left the ship and their father, and followed him.

23 ¶ And Jesus went about all ^aGalilee, ^bteaching in their synagogues, and ^cpreaching the gospel of the kingdom, and ^dhealing all manner of ^esickness and all manner of disease among the ^fpeople.

24 And his fame went throughout all Syria: and they brought unto him all sick people that were taken with divers diseases and torments, and those which were possessed with ^adevils, and those which were lunatic, and those that had the ^bpalsy; and he ^chealed them.

25 And there followed him great multitudes of people from Galilee, and *from* Decapolis, and *from* Jerusalem, and *from* Judæa, and *from* beyond Jordan.

CHAPTER 5

Jesus preaches the Sermon on the Mount—Its teachings replace and transcend *some aspects of the law of Moses—All are commanded to be perfect like their Father in Heaven.*

^aAND seeing the multitudes, he went up into a mountain: and when he was set, his disciples came unto him:

2 And he opened his mouth, and taught them, saying,

3 ^aBlessed *are* the ^bpoor in spirit: for theirs is the ^ckingdom of heaven.

4 Blessed *are* they that ^amourn: for they shall be ^bcomforted.

5 Blessed *are* the ^ameek: for they shall inherit the ^bearth.

6 Blessed *are* they which do ^ahunger and thirst after ^brighteousness: for they shall be filled.

7 Blessed *are* the ^amerciful: for they shall obtain mercy.

8 Blessed *are* the ^apure in ^bheart: for they shall ^csee God.

9 Blessed *are* the ^apeacemakers: for they shall be called the ^bchildren of God.

10 Blessed *are* they which are ^apersecuted for ^brighteousness' sake: for ^ctheirs is the kingdom of heaven.

11 Blessed are ye, when *men* shall ^arevile you, and persecute *you*, and shall say all manner of ^bevil against you falsely, ^cfor my sake.

12 ^aRejoice, and be exceeding glad: for great *is* your ^breward in heaven:

20a TG Commitment.
21a John 21:2.
  b TG Called of God.
23a Luke 4:44.
  b Matt. 9:35.
  c D&C 71:1.
  d TG Heal; Miracle.
  e TG Sickness.
  f JST Matt. 4:22 . . . people *which believed on his name.*
24a Matt. 8:16 (16, 28, 33); 9:32 (32–34).
  b GR paralysis.
  c Mosiah 3:5 (5–6).
5 1a 3 Ne. 12:1 (1–48).
  3a The Latin *beatus* is the basis of the English "beatitude," meaning "to be fortunate," "to be happy," or "to be blessed."
   TG Blessing.

b IE poor in pride, humble in spirit;
3 Ne. 12:3 reads ". . . the poor in spirit who come unto me."
James 2:5 (1–9);
D&C 56:18 (18–20); 88:17.
TG Contrite Heart; Humility; Poor in Spirit.
  c TG Kingdom of God, in Heaven.
4a TG Mourning; Sorrow.
  b TG Comfort.
5a GR gentle, forgiving, or benevolent; the Hebrew in Ps. 37:11 characterizes as the humble those who have suffered.
TG Meek.
  b TG Earth, Destiny of.
6a 3 Ne. 12:6.
TG Teachable.

b TG Good Works; Righteousness.
7a TG Mercy.
8a TG Chastity; Cleanliness; Purity.
  b TG Heart.
  c TG God, Presence of; God, Privilege of Seeing.
9a TG Contentment; Peace; Peacemakers.
  b TG Sons and Daughters of God.
10a TG Affliction; Persecution.
  b TG Righteousness.
  c D&C 6:37; 10:55.
11a TG Reviling.
  b TG Backbiting; Slander.
  c GR on account of me.
12a 2 Ne. 9:18.
TG Joy.
  b D&C 84:38.
TG Reward.

for so ^cpersecuted they the prophets which were before you.

13 ¶ Ye are the ^asalt of the earth: but if the salt have lost his savour, wherewith shall it be salted? it is thenceforth good for nothing, but to be cast out, and to be trodden under foot of men.

14 Ye are the ^alight of the world. A city that is set on an hill cannot be hid.

15 Neither do men light a ^acandle, and put it under a bushel, but on a candlestick; and it giveth light unto all that are in the house.

16 Let your ^alight so shine before men, that they may see your good ^bworks, and ^cglorify your Father which is in heaven.

17 ¶ Think not that I am come to ^adestroy the ^blaw, or the prophets: I am not come to destroy, but to fulfil.

18 For verily I say unto you, Till heaven and earth pass, one jot or one tittle shall in no wise pass from the ^alaw, till all be ^bfulfilled.

19 ^aWhosoever therefore shall ^bbreak one of these least commandments, and shall ^cteach men so, he shall be called the least in the kingdom of heaven: but whosoever shall do and ^dteach *them*, the same shall be called great in the kingdom of heaven.

20 For I say unto you, That except your ^arighteousness shall exceed *the righteousness* of the ^bscribes and Pharisees, ye shall in no case enter into the kingdom of heaven.

21 ¶ Ye have heard that it was said by them of old time, Thou ^ashalt not ^bkill; and whosoever shall kill shall be ^cin danger of the judgment:

22 But I say unto you, That whosoever is ^aangry with his brother ^bwithout a cause shall be ^cin danger of the judgment: and whosoever shall say to his brother, ^dRaca, shall be ^ein danger of the council: but whosoever shall say, Thou fool, shall be in danger of hell fire.

23 Therefore if thou bring thy gift to the altar, and there rememberest that thy brother hath ought against thee;

24 Leave there thy gift before the altar, and go thy way; first be ^areconciled to thy brother, and then come and offer thy gift.

25 ^aAgree with thine adversary quickly, whiles thou art in the way with him; lest at any time the adversary deliver thee to the judge, and the judge deliver thee to the officer, and thou be cast into prison.

26 Verily I say unto thee, Thou shalt by no means come out thence, till thou hast paid ^athe uttermost farthing.

27 ¶ Ye have heard that it was said by them of old time, Thou shalt not commit ^aadultery:

28 But I say unto you, That

12c TG Persecution.
13a See Lev. 2:13 and Num. 18:19, where salt is a token of the covenant and was part of sacrificial ritual. TG Salt.
14a TG Mission of Early Saints.
15a Luke 11:33 (33–34).
16a 3 Ne. 18:24. TG Children of Light; Example; Light [noun].
 b 1 Pet. 2:12. TG Good Works.
 c John 15:8.
17a D&C 10:52 (52, 54).
 b TG Law of Moses.
18a TG Law of Moses.

 b D&C 1:38.
19a JST Matt. 5:21 (Appendix).
 b TG Sin.
 c 2 Ne. 28:15 (12, 15).
 d TG Missionary Work.
20a TG Righteousness.
 b TG Scribe.
21a TG Commandments of God.
 b TG Blood, Shedding of; Murder.
 c GR subject to condemnation.
22a Prov. 29:22 (21–23); 3 Ne. 12:22 (21–24). TG Anger; Rashness.
 b JST Matt. 5:24 and 3 Ne. 12:22 omit the

words "without a cause."
 c GR subject to condemnation.
 d A word suggesting contempt or derision in both Aramaic and Greek.
 e IE subject to the Sanhedrin.
24a Matt. 18:15 (15–18). TG Forgive; Reconciliation.
25a GR Quickly have kind thoughts for, or be well disposed toward. TG Communication; Disputations.
26a GR the last penny.
27a D&C 42:22 (22–26).

whosoever ^alooketh on a ^bwoman to ^clust after her hath committed ^dadultery with her already in his heart.

29 And if thy right eye ^aoffend thee, pluck it out, and cast *it* from thee: for it is profitable for thee that one of thy members should perish, and not *that* thy whole body should be cast into ^bhell.

30 And if thy right ^ahand offend thee, cut it off, and cast *it* from thee: for it is profitable for thee that one of thy members should perish, and not *that* thy whole body should be cast into ^bhell.

31 It hath been said, Whosoever shall put away his wife, let him give her a writing of ^adivorcement:

32 But I say unto you, That whosoever shall ^aput away his ^bwife, saving for the cause of ^cfornication, causeth her to commit adultery: and whosoever shall marry her that is divorced committeth adultery.

33 ¶ Again, ye have heard that it hath been said by them of old time, Thou shalt not ^aforswear thyself, but shalt ^bperform unto the Lord thine ^coaths:

34 But I say unto you, ^aSwear not at all; neither by heaven; for it is God's ^bthrone:

35 Nor by the earth; for it is his ^afootstool: neither by Jerusalem; for it is the ^bcity of the great King.

36 Neither shalt thou swear by thy head, because thou canst not make one hair white or black.

37 But let your ^acommunication be, Yea, yea; Nay, nay: for whatsoever is more than these cometh ^bof evil.

38 ¶ Ye have heard that it hath been said, An ^aeye for an eye, and a tooth for a tooth:

39 But I say unto you, That ye resist not ^aevil: but whosoever shall smite thee on thy right ^bcheek, ^cturn to him the other also.

40 And if any man will sue thee at the law, and take away thy coat, let him have *thy* cloak also.

41 And whosoever shall compel thee to go a mile, go with him twain.

42 ^aGive to him that asketh thee, and from him that would ^bborrow of thee turn not thou away.

43 ¶ Ye have heard that it hath been said, Thou shalt ^alove thy ^bneighbour, and hate thine enemy.

44 But I say unto you, ^aLove your ^benemies, ^cbless them that ^dcurse you, do ^egood to them that ^fhate you, and ^gpray for them which despitefully use you, and ^hpersecute you;

45 That ye ^amay be the ^bchildren of your Father which is in heaven: for he maketh his sun to rise on the evil and on the good, and sendeth ^crain on the just and on the unjust.

28a D&C 63:16 (16–17).
 b TG Body, Sanctity of;
   Woman.
 c Mosiah 4:30 (29–30).
   TG Carnal Mind;
   Chastity; Fornication;
   Lust; Motivations;
   Sensuality.
 d TG Adulterer;
   Sexual Immorality.
29a GR cause to stumble; see
   also Matt. 18:6–9.
   TG Offense.
 b TG Damnation; Hell.
30a Matt. 18:8;
   JST Matt. 18:9 (Matt. 18:9
   note *a*).
 b JST Matt. 5:33–34 . . . hell.
   And now this I speak, a
   parable concerning your
   sins; wherefore, cast them
   from you, that ye may not
   be hewn down and cast
   into the fire.

31a TG Divorce.
32a Ezek. 44:22.
 b D&C 42:74.
 c 1 Cor. 7:10 (10–11).
   TG Fornication.
33a GR break your oath, or
   perjure yourself.
   Ps. 139:20.
 b TG Dedication.
 c Deut. 23:21.
   TG Oath.
34a TG Honesty; Profanity;
   Swearing.
 b Isa. 66:1.
35a Isa. 60:13; Ezek. 43:7.
37a TG Communication.
 b GR from the evil one.
38a Lev. 24:20;
   3 Ne. 12:38 (38–40).
   TG Punish.
39a TG Evil.
 b Lam. 3:30.
   TG Patience.

 c TG Forbear.
42a TG Almsgiving;
   Generosity; Poor.
 b TG Borrow; Debt.
43a D&C 112:11.
 b TG Neighbor.
44a TG Love.
 b TG Enemies; Opposition.
 c TG Retribution.
 d TG Curse.
 e TG Benevolence.
 f TG Hate.
 g Job 42:10;
   Acts 7:60 (55–60).
   TG Prayer.
 h TG Persecution.
45a GR may become; see
   Mosiah 5:7.
 b TG Sons and Daughters
   of God.
 c Job 2:10; 2 Ne. 2:11;
   Alma 60:13;
   D&C 5:22; 29:39;
   122:7 (5–9).

46 For if ye *a*love them which love you, what reward have ye? do not even the publicans the same?

47 And if ye salute your brethren only, what do ye more *than others?* do not even the publicans so?

48 *a*Be ye therefore *b*perfect, even as your *c*Father which is in heaven is *d*perfect.

CHAPTER 6

Jesus continues the Sermon on the Mount—He teaches the disciples the Lord's Prayer—They are commanded to seek first the kingdom of God and His righteousness.

*a*TAKE heed that ye do not your *b*alms before men, to be seen of them: otherwise ye have no reward of your Father which is in heaven.

2 Therefore when thou doest *thine* alms, do not sound a trumpet before thee, as the *a*hypocrites do in the synagogues and in the streets, that they may have *b*glory of men. Verily I say unto you, They have their reward.

3 But when thou doest alms, let not thy left hand know what thy right hand doeth:

4 That thine *a*alms may be in secret: and thy Father which seeth in secret himself shall *b*reward thee openly.

5 ¶ And when thou prayest, thou shalt not be as the *a*hypocrites *are:* for they love to pray standing in the synagogues and in the corners of the streets, that they may be seen of men. Verily I say unto you, They have their reward.

6 But thou, when thou prayest, enter into thy *a*closet, and when thou hast *b*shut thy door, *c*pray to thy Father which is in *d*secret; and thy Father which *e*seeth in secret shall *f*reward thee openly.

7 But when ye pray, use not vain *a*repetitions, as the *b*heathen *do:* for they think that they shall be heard for their much speaking.

8 Be not ye therefore like unto them: for your Father *a*knoweth what things ye have *b*need of, before ye ask him.

9 *a*After this manner therefore *b*pray ye: Our *c*Father which art in heaven, *d*Hallowed be thy *e*name.

10 Thy *a*kingdom come. Thy *b*will be done *c*in earth, as *it is* in heaven.

11 Give us this day our daily *a*bread.

12 And forgive us our *a*debts, as we *b*forgive our debtors.

46*a* Prov. 19:6.
48*a* JST Matt. 5:50 Ye are therefore *commanded to be* perfect . . .
  b GR complete, finished, fully developed. D&C 67:13.
  TG God, the Standard of Righteousness; Godliness; Man, New, Spiritually Reborn; Man, Potential to Become like Heavenly Father; Mission of Early Saints; Objectives; Perfection.
  c TG God the Father, Elohim.
  d TG God, Perfection of.
6 1*a* JST Matt. 6:1 *And it came to pass that, as Jesus taught his disciples, he said unto them,* Take heed . . .

3 Ne. 13:1 (1–34).
  b GR righteousness, acts of religious devotion.
  TG Almsgiving; Generosity; Motivations; Poor.
2*a* GR pretenders; the Greek word means "a play actor," or "one who feigns, represents dramatically, or exaggerates a part."
  TG Hypocrisy.
  b D&C 121:35 (34–35).
4*a* TG Welfare.
  b Luke 14:14.
5*a* Alma 31:14 (14–22).
6*a* Alma 33:7 (4–11); 34:26 (17–27).
  b 2 Kgs. 4:33.
  c TG Prayer.
  d TG Meditation.
  e TG God, Omniscience of.
  f TG Reward.
7*a* Eccl. 5:2;

Alma 31:20; 3 Ne. 19:24.
  b TG Heathen.
8*a* D&C 84:83 (81–86).
  TG God, Intelligence of; God, Omniscience of.
  b Ps. 23:1.
9*a* IE It is in this way that you ought to pray.
  b TG Prayer.
  c TG God the Father, Elohim.
  d GR Let Thy name be sanctified.
  e TG Name.
10*a* TG Kingdom of God, on Earth; Millennium.
  b TG God, Will of.
  c GR on earth.
11*a* TG Bread.
12*a* GR debts, offenses, faults, or sins.
  TG Debt.
  b TG Forgive.

13 ^aAnd ^blead us not into ^ctemptation, ^dbut deliver us from evil: For thine is the kingdom, and the power, and the ^eglory, for ever. Amen.

14 For if ye ^aforgive men their trespasses, your heavenly Father will also forgive you:

15 But if ye ^aforgive not men their trespasses, neither will your Father forgive your trespasses.

16 ¶ Moreover when ye fast, be not, as the hypocrites, of a sad countenance: for they disfigure their faces, that they may appear unto men to ^afast. Verily I say unto you, They ^bhave their reward.

17 But thou, when thou fastest, anoint thine head, and wash thy face;

18 That thou appear not unto men to ^afast, but unto thy Father which is in secret: and thy Father, which seeth in secret, shall ^breward thee openly.

19 ¶ Lay not up for yourselves ^atreasures upon earth, where moth and rust doth corrupt, and where thieves ^bbreak through and steal:

20 But lay up for yourselves ^atreasures in heaven, where neither moth nor rust doth corrupt, and where thieves do not break through nor ^bsteal:

21 For where your treasure is, there will your heart be also.

22 The light of the body is the eye: if therefore thine ^aeye be ^bsingle, thy whole body shall be full of ^clight.

23 But if thine eye be evil, thy whole body shall be full of darkness. If therefore the light that is in thee be darkness, how great *is* that ^adarkness!

24 ¶ ^aNo man can ^bserve two ^cmasters: for either he will ^dhate the one, and love the other; or else he will hold to the one, and despise the other. Ye cannot serve God and ^emammon.

25 ^aTherefore I say unto you, Take no ^bthought for your life, what ye shall eat, or what ye shall drink; nor yet for your body, what ye shall put on. Is not the life more than meat, and the body than raiment?

26 Behold the fowls of the air: for they sow not, neither do they reap, nor gather into barns; yet your heavenly Father feedeth them. Are ye not much better than they?

27 Which of you by taking thought can add one cubit unto his stature?

28 And why take ye thought for raiment? ^aConsider the lilies of the field, how they grow; they toil not, neither do they spin:

29 And yet I say unto you, That even Solomon in all his glory was not arrayed like one of these.

30 Wherefore, if God so clothe the grass of the field, which to day is, and to morrow is cast into the oven, ^ashall he not much more *clothe* you, O ye of little ^bfaith?

31 Therefore take no thought, saying, What shall we eat? or, What

---

13a JST Matt. 6:14 And *suffer us not to be led* into temptation . . .
  b Syriac: do not let us enter into temptation.
  c TG Temptation; Test.
  d GR but protect us from the evil one.
    TG Deliver; Evil.
  e 1 Chr. 29:11.
    TG Glory.
14a TG Forbear.
15a TG Forgive.
16a Zech. 7:5 (5–6).
  b GR receive.
18a TG Fast, Fasting; Motivations.
  b TG Reward.
19a TG Family, Managing

Finances in.
  b GR dig through (as an earthen wall).
20a Heb. 10:34;
    1 Pet. 1:4 (1–16).
    TG Treasure.
  b TG Stealing.
22a 3 Ne. 13:22;
    Morm. 8:15;
    D&C 4:5; 59:1 (1–2).
  b GR healthy, sincere, without guile.
    JST Matt. 6:22 . . . single *to the glory of God* . . .
    TG Dedication.
  c D&C 93:28 (28, 36–38).
23a TG Darkness, Spiritual.
24a TG Loyalty.
  b TG Service.

  c Alma 5:39 (39–42).
  d TG Hate.
  e TG Idolatry; Treasure; Worldliness.
25a JST Matt. 6:25–27 (Appendix).
  b GR anxious concern.
    Ps. 55:22; Prov. 16:3;
    Luke 12:22;
    Philip. 4:6;
    3 Ne. 13:25;
    D&C 84:81.
    TG Self-Sacrifice.
28a TG Meditation.
30a JST Matt. 6:34 . . . *how much more will he not provide for you, if ye are not of little faith?*
  b TG Faith.

shall we drink? or, Wherewithal shall we be clothed?

32 (For after all these things do the Gentiles seek:) for your heavenly Father [a]knoweth that ye have need of all these things.

33 [a]But [b]seek ye first the [c]kingdom of God, and his [d]righteousness; and all these [e]things shall be [f]added unto you.

34 Take therefore no thought for the morrow: for the morrow shall take [a]thought for the things of itself. Sufficient unto the day is the evil thereof.

CHAPTER 7

Jesus concludes the Sermon on the Mount—He commands, Judge not; ask of God; beware of false prophets—He promises salvation to those who do the will of the Father.

[a]JUDGE not, that ye be not [b]judged.

2 For with what [a]judgment ye judge, ye shall be judged: and with what [b]measure ye mete, it shall be [c]measured to you again.

3 [a]And why beholdest thou the [b]mote that is in thy brother's eye, but considerest not the [c]beam that is in thine own eye?

4 Or how wilt thou say to thy brother, Let me pull out the mote out of thine eye; and, behold, a beam *is* in thine own eye?

5 Thou [a]hypocrite, first cast out the beam out of thine own eye; and then shalt thou see clearly to cast out the mote out of thy brother's eye.

6 ¶ [a]Give not that which is [b]holy unto the dogs, neither cast ye your [c]pearls before swine, lest they trample them under their feet, and turn again and rend you.

7 ¶ [a]Ask, and it shall be [b]given you; [c]seek, and ye shall find; [d]knock, and it shall be opened unto you:

8 For every one that asketh receiveth; and he that [a]seeketh findeth; and to him that knocketh it shall be opened.

9 Or what man is there of you, whom if his son ask [a]bread, will he give him a stone?

10 Or if he ask a fish, will he give him a serpent?

11 If ye then, [a]being evil, know how to give good gifts unto your children, how much more shall your Father which is in heaven give good things to them that ask him?

12 Therefore all things [a]whatsoever

32a Hel. 8:8; D&C 84:83.
33a JST Matt. 6:38 *Wherefore, seek not the things of this world but seek ye first to build up the kingdom of God, and to establish his righteousness . . .*
  b 1 Kgs. 3:13; Alma 39:14 (12–14); D&C 6:7 (6–7); 11:23; 68:31 (31–32); 106:3. TG Commitment; Dedication; Priesthood, Magnifying Callings within.
  c Col. 3:2. TG Mission of Early Saints; Objectives.
  d Prov. 21:21. TG God, the Standard of Righteousness; Righteousness.
  e Prov. 28:10. TG Blessing.
  f 2 Ne. 5:11 (10–13); Mosiah 2:41.

34a TG Abundant Life.
34a D&C 84:84.
7 1a JST Matt. 7:1–2 *Now these are the words which Jesus taught his disciples that they should say unto the people.* Judge not *unrighteously, that ye be not judged; but judge righteous judgment.* Alma 41:14 (14–15); 3 Ne. 14:1 (1–27); D&C 11:12.
  b TG Accountability.
2a TG Judgment.
  b Prov. 11:25; D&C 1:10.
  c Esth. 7:10; 1 Ne. 14:3; D&C 10:26 (25–27).
3a JST Matt. 7:4–8 (Appendix).
  b GR speck, chip, or splinter. TG Gossip.
  c The Greek word refers to a wooden beam used in constructing houses.

5a TG Hypocrisy.
6a JST Matt. 7:9–11 (Appendix).
  b TG Holiness; Sacred; Sacrilege.
  c Prov. 23:9; Matt. 15:26 (26–28); D&C 6:12 (10–12); 10:37 (36–37); 41:6.
7a JST Matt. 7:12–17 (Appendix). Isa. 58:9 (8–9); Hel. 10:5 (4–11); D&C 6:5. TG Faith; God, Access to; Prayer; Problem-Solving.
  b TG Revelation.
  c TG Meditation; Objectives; Study.
  d TG Learn.
8a TG Education.
9a TG Bread.
11a GR although you are wicked.
12a TG Good Works.

ye would that [b]men should [c]do to you, [d]do ye even so to them: for this is the [e]law and the prophets.

13 ¶ Enter ye in at the [a]strait [b]gate: for wide is the gate, and broad is the way, that leadeth to [c]destruction, and many there be which go in thereat:

14 Because [a]strait is the [b]gate, and narrow is the way, which leadeth unto [c]life, and few there be that find it.

15 ¶ Beware of [a]false prophets, which come to you in [b]sheep's clothing, but [c]inwardly they are ravening [d]wolves.

16 Ye shall [a]know them by their [b]fruits. Do men gather grapes of thorns, or figs of thistles?

17 Even so every good tree bringeth forth [a]good [b]fruit; but a [c]corrupt tree bringeth forth [d]evil fruit.

18 A good tree cannot bring forth evil fruit, neither can a corrupt tree bring forth good fruit.

19 Every tree that bringeth not forth good [a]fruit is [b]hewn down, and cast into the fire.

20 Wherefore by their [a]fruits ye shall know them.

21 ¶ Not every one that [a]saith unto me, [b]Lord, Lord, shall enter into the kingdom of heaven; but he that [c]doeth the [d]will of my Father which is in [e]heaven.

22 Many will say to me in that day, Lord, Lord, have we not [a]prophesied in thy name? and in thy [b]name have cast out devils? and in thy name done many wonderful works?

23 [a]And then will I profess unto them, I never knew you: [b]depart from me, ye that work [c]iniquity.

24 ¶ Therefore whosoever [a]heareth these sayings of mine, and [b]doeth them, [c]I will liken him unto a [d]wise man, which [e]built his house upon [f]a rock:

25 And the [a]rain descended, and the floods came, and the winds blew, and [b]beat upon that house; and it fell not: for it was founded upon a [c]rock.

26 And every one that heareth these sayings of mine, and doeth them not, shall be likened unto a [a]foolish man, which built his house upon the sand:

27 And the rain descended, and

12b TG Marriage, Continuing Courtship in.
  c Deut. 15:15 (12–15); Prov. 24:29. TG Citizenship; Courtesy; Kindness.
  d TG Benevolence.
  e TG Law of Moses.
13a GR narrow; see also 2 Ne. 31:17–21.
  b Luke 13:24; 3 Ne. 27:33; D&C 22:4 (1–4); 43:7.
  c D&C 132:25. TG Hell.
14a Mosiah 3:17.
  b 1 Ne. 8:20 (19–24); 2 Ne. 33:9. TG Baptism, Essential.
  c Jer. 21:8.
15a TG False Prophets.
  b TG Sheep.
  c TG Hypocrisy.
  d TG Guile.
16a GR recognize, detect. TG Discernment, Spiritual.
  b Prov. 20:11; Jer. 28:9 (8–9); Luke 6:44; Moro. 7:6 (5–17).

  TG Good Works.
17a The Greek wording carries the meaning of beautiful, precious fruit without blemish.
  b Matt. 12:33; 3 Ne. 14:20 (17–20).
  c GR decayed, rotten, stale.
  d GR bad, spoiled, degenerate.
19a Luke 3:9; John 15:2 (1–6); Jacob 5:26 (26–60); Alma 5:36; D&C 97:7.
  b Luke 13:7.
20a James 2:18 (14–26); 1 Jn. 3:10 (10–18).
21a Titus 1:16. TG Hypocrisy; Sincere.
  b Hosea 8:2 (1–4); Luke 6:46.
  c Luke 8:21 (9–21); D&C 138:4. TG Duty; Good Works; Obedience.
  d TG God, Will of.
  e JST Matt. 7:30–31 . . . heaven. For the day soon cometh, that men shall come before me to judgment, to be judged

according to their works.
22a Jer. 23:25 (25–32). TG Unrighteous Dominion.
  b D&C 84:67. TG Name.
23a JST Matt. 7:33 And then will I say, Ye never knew me . . . Ps. 101:4; Matt. 25:12; Mosiah 26:27 (23–27); 3 Ne. 14:23.
  b Ps. 119:115. TG Judgment, the Last.
  c GR lawlessness. TG Sin.
24a Mosiah 4:10; Hel. 5:12 (9–12); D&C 41:5.
  b TG Commitment; Obedience.
  c GR he will resemble.
  d TG Wisdom.
  e D&C 6:34; 11:24.
  f GR the rock. 3 Ne. 11:39 (39–40).
25a D&C 90:5.
  b TG Adversity.
  c TG Rock.
26a TG Foolishness.

the floods came, and the winds blew, and beat upon that ^ahouse; and it ^bfell: and great was the fall of it.

28 And it came to pass, when Jesus had ended ^athese sayings, the people were ^bastonished at his ^cdoctrine:

29 For he taught them as *one* having ^aauthority, and not as ^bthe scribes.

CHAPTER 8

Jesus heals a leper, cures the centurion's servant and others, stills the tempest, and casts out devils—The devils enter a herd of swine.

WHEN he was come down from the mountain, great multitudes followed him.

2 And, behold, there came a ^aleper and worshipped him, saying, Lord, if thou wilt, thou canst make me clean.

3 And Jesus put forth *his* hand, and touched him, saying, I will; be thou clean. And immediately his leprosy was ^acleansed.

4 And Jesus saith unto him, See thou tell no man; but go thy way, shew thyself to the priest, and offer the gift that Moses commanded, for a testimony unto them.

5 ¶ And when Jesus was entered into Capernaum, there came unto him a centurion, beseeching him,

6 And saying, Lord, my ^aservant lieth at home sick of the ^bpalsy, grievously tormented.

7 And Jesus saith unto him, I will come and heal him.

8 The centurion answered and said,

Lord, I am not ^aworthy that thou shouldest come under my roof: but speak the word only, and my servant shall be ^bhealed.

9 For I am a man under ^aauthority, having soldiers under me: and I say to this *man*, Go, and he goeth; and to another, Come, and he cometh; and to my servant, Do this, and he doeth *it*.

10 ^aWhen Jesus heard *it*, he marvelled, and said to them that followed, Verily I say unto you, I have not found so great ^bfaith, no, not in Israel.

11 And I say unto you, That ^amany shall come from the east and west, and shall sit down with Abraham, and Isaac, and Jacob, in the kingdom of heaven.

12 But the ^achildren of the kingdom shall be cast out into ^bouter darkness: there shall be ^cweeping and gnashing of teeth.

13 And Jesus said unto the centurion, Go thy way; and as thou hast believed, *so* be it done unto thee. And his servant was healed in the selfsame hour.

14 ¶ And when Jesus was come into Peter's house, he saw his ^awife's mother ^blaid, and sick of a fever.

15 And he ^atouched her hand, and the fever left her: and she arose, and ministered unto them.

16 ¶ When the even was come, they brought unto him many that were possessed with ^adevils: and he cast out the ^bspirits with *his* word, and ^chealed all that were sick:

27*a* Prov. 14:11.
 b TG Apostasy of Individuals.
28*a* JST Matt. 7:36 . . . these sayings *with his disciples*, the people . . .
 b Matt. 13:54.
 c John 7:16; 2 Ne. 31:21.
29*a* JST Matt. 7:37 . . . authority *from God, and not as having authority from the* scribes.
 TG Jesus Christ, Authority of; Jesus Christ, Teaching Mode of; Teaching with the Spirit.
 b GR their scribes.

TG Scribe.
8 2*a* TG Leprosy.
 3*a* TG Miracle.
 6*a* GR child, servant, son; see John 4:43–54.
 b GR paralysis.
 8*a* GR fit, qualified.
 b TG Heal.
 9*a* TG Authority.
10*a* JST Matt. 8:9 *And when they that followed him, heard this, they marveled. And when Jesus* . . .
 b 3 Ne. 17:8 (5–20).
11*a* Luke 13:29 (28–30); Acts 10:45; 2 Ne. 10:18 (9–18);

D&C 45:9.
12*a* 2 Ne. 30:2.
 b Matt. 22:13 (1–14); D&C 77:8; 133:72.
 c Isa. 65:14; Matt. 13:42; Rev. 19:20; D&C 112:24.
14*a* 1 Cor. 9:5; 1 Tim. 4:3.
 b GR lying sick and feverish.
15*a* GR took hold of.
16*a* Matt. 4:24; 9:32 (32–34).
 b TG Spirits, Evil or Unclean.
 c TG Heal.

17 That it might be fulfilled which was spoken by Esaias the prophet, saying, ^aHimself took our ^binfirmities, and bare our ^csicknesses.

18 ¶ Now when Jesus saw great multitudes about him, he gave commandment to depart unto the other side.

19 And a certain scribe came, and said unto him, Master, I will ^afollow thee whithersoever thou goest.

20 And Jesus saith unto him, The foxes have holes, and the birds of the air *have* nests; but the Son of man hath not where to lay *his* head.

21 And another of his disciples said unto him, Lord, ^asuffer me first to go and bury my father.

22 But Jesus said unto him, ^aFollow me; and let the ^bdead bury their dead.

23 ¶ And when he was entered into a ship, his disciples followed him.

24 And, behold, there arose a great ^atempest in the sea, insomuch that the ship was covered with the waves: but he was asleep.

25 And his disciples came to *him*, and awoke him, saying, Lord, save us: we perish.

26 And he saith unto them, Why are ye ^afearful, O ye of little faith? Then he arose, and ^brebuked the winds and the sea; and there was a great calm.

27 But the men marvelled, saying, What manner of man is this, that even the winds and the ^asea obey him!

28 ¶ And when he was come to the other side into the country of the Gergesenes, there met him two possessed with ^adevils, coming out of the tombs, exceeding fierce, so that no man might pass by that way.

29 And, behold, they cried out,

saying, What have we to do with thee, Jesus, thou Son of God? art thou come hither to torment us before ^athe time?

30 And there was a good way off from them an herd of many swine feeding.

31 So the devils besought him, saying, If thou cast us out, suffer us to go away into the herd of swine.

32 And he said unto them, Go. And when they were come out, they went into the herd of swine: and, behold, the whole herd of swine ran violently down a steep place into the sea, and perished in the waters.

33 And they that kept them fled, and went their ways into the city, and told every thing, and what was befallen to the possessed of the devils.

34 And, behold, the whole city came out to ^ameet Jesus: and when they saw him, they besought *him* that he would depart out of their ^bcoasts.

CHAPTER 9

Jesus forgives sins, heals a paralytic, and calls Matthew—Jesus eats with sinners, heals a woman who touches His garments, and raises Jairus's daughter to life—He opens the eyes of the blind, casts out a devil, and preaches the gospel.

AND he entered into a ship, and passed over, and came into his own city.

2 And, behold, they brought to him a man sick of the ^apalsy, lying on a bed: and Jesus seeing their ^bfaith said unto the sick of the palsy; Son, be of good ^ccheer; thy ^dsins be forgiven thee.

3 And, behold, certain of the scribes said within themselves, This *man* blasphemeth.

4 And Jesus ^aknowing their

17a GR He Himself.
  b TG Jesus Christ,
    Atonement through.
  c TG Sickness.
19a Luke 9:57;
    2 Ne. 31:10 (10–13);
    Moro. 7:11;
    D&C 4:3; 56:2.
21a GR let, allow.

22a TG Commitment.
  b TG Death.
24a Jonah 1:4;
    1 Ne. 18:13 (9–13).
26a TG Courage; Fearful.
  b Ps. 65:7; 89:9; 107:29.
    TG God, Power of.
27a Hel. 12:16 (8–17).
28a TG Spirits, Evil or

    Unclean.
29a GR the appointed hour.
34a John 12:18.
  b GR lands, regions.
9 2a GR stroke, paralysis.
  b Luke 7:50.
  c D&C 68:6; 112:4.
  d D&C 25:3; 62:3.
4a TG God, Omniscience of.

thoughts said, Wherefore think ye evil in your hearts?

5 [a]For whether is easier, to say, *Thy* sins be forgiven thee; or to say, Arise, and walk?

6 But that ye may know that the [a]Son of man hath [b]power on earth to [c]forgive sins, (then saith he to the sick of the palsy,) Arise, take up thy bed, and go unto thine house.

7 And he arose, and departed to his house.

8 But when the multitudes saw *it,* they marvelled, and glorified God, which had given such power unto men.

9 ¶ And as Jesus passed forth from thence, he saw a man, named [a]Matthew, sitting at the [b]receipt of custom: and he saith unto him, Follow me. And he arose, and followed him.

10 ¶ And it came to pass, as Jesus sat at meat in the house, behold, many publicans and sinners came and sat down with him and his disciples.

11 And when the Pharisees saw *it,* they said unto his disciples, [a]Why eateth your Master with publicans and sinners?

12 But when Jesus heard *that,* he said unto them, They that be whole need not a physician, but they that are sick.

13 But go ye and learn what *that* meaneth, [a]I [b]will have [c]mercy, and not sacrifice: for I am not come to [d]call the [e]righteous, but sinners to [f]repentance.

14 ¶ Then came to him the disciples of John, saying, Why do we and the Pharisees fast oft, but thy disciples fast not?

15 And Jesus said unto them, Can the children of the bridechamber mourn, as long as the bridegroom is with them? but the days will come, when the bridegroom shall be taken from them, [a]and then shall they fast.

16 [a]No man putteth a piece of [b]new cloth unto an old garment, for that which is put in to fill it up taketh from the garment, and the rent is made worse.

17 Neither do men put new wine into old bottles: else the bottles break, and the wine runneth out, and the bottles perish: but they put new wine into new bottles, and both are preserved.

18 ¶ While he spake these things unto them, behold, there came a certain [a]ruler, and worshipped him, saying, [b]My daughter is even now dead: but come and lay thy [c]hand upon her, and she shall [d]live.

19 And Jesus arose, and followed him, and *so did* his disciples.

20 ¶ And, behold, a woman, which was diseased with an [a]issue of [b]blood twelve years, came behind *him,* and touched the hem of his garment:

21 For she said within herself, If I may but touch his garment, I shall be [a]whole.

22 But Jesus turned him about, and when he saw her, he said, Daughter, be of good comfort; thy faith hath made thee [a]whole. And the woman was made whole from that hour.

23 And when Jesus came into the ruler's house, and saw the minstrels and the people making a noise,

24 He said unto them, Give place: for the maid is not dead, but sleepeth. And they [a]laughed him to scorn.

5a JST Matt. 9:5 For is *it not easier* to say, Thy sins be forgiven thee, *than* to say, Arise and walk?
6a TG Jesus Christ, Son of Man.
  b GR authority. TG Jesus Christ, Authority of.
  c TG Forgive.
9a Luke 5:27 (27–32).
  b GR tax office.
11a See JST Mark 3:21–25 (Appendix).

Isa. 53:3 (1–3); 65:5.
13a Hosea 6:6.
  b GR desire.
  c TG Mercy.
  d 1 Tim. 1:15.
  e TG Righteousness.
  f TG Repent.
15a TG Fast, Fasting.
16a JST Matt. 9:18–21 (Appendix).
  b GR unshrunken.
18a Luke 8:41.
  b JST Matt. 9:24 . . . My

daughter is even now *dying . . .*
  c TG Administrations to the Sick;
    Hands, Laying on of.
  d D&C 66:9.
20a GR hemorrhage.
  b Lev. 15:25.
21a GR free from disease.
22a TG Heal.
24a GR ridiculed Him.
    1 Ne. 8:27 (26–27).
    TG Laughter.

25 But when the people were put forth, he went in, and took her by the hand, and the maid arose.

26 And the fame hereof went abroad into all that land.

27 ¶ And when Jesus departed thence, two blind men followed him, crying, and saying, *Thou* Son of David, have mercy on us.

28 And when he was come into the house, the ^ablind men came to him: and Jesus saith unto them, ^bBelieve ye that I am able to do this? They said unto him, Yea, Lord.

29 Then touched he their eyes, saying, According to your ^afaith be it unto you.

30 And their ^aeyes were ^bopened; and Jesus ^cstraitly charged them, saying, See *that* no man know *it*.

31 But they, when they were departed, ^aspread abroad his ^bfame in all that country.

32 ¶ As they went out, behold, they brought to him a dumb man possessed with a ^adevil.

33 And when the devil was cast out, the dumb spake: and the multitudes marvelled, saying, It was never so seen in Israel.

34 But the Pharisees said, He casteth out devils through the prince of the devils.

35 And Jesus went about all the cities and villages, ^ateaching in their synagogues, and preaching the ^bgospel of the kingdom, and ^chealing every sickness and every disease among the people.

36 ¶ But when he saw the multitudes, he was moved with ^acompassion on them, because ^bthey fainted, and were scattered abroad, as ^csheep having no ^dshepherd.

37 Then saith he unto his disciples, The ^aharvest truly *is* plenteous, but the ^blabourers *are* few;

38 Pray ye therefore the Lord of the harvest, that he will send forth labourers into his harvest.

CHAPTER 10

Jesus instructs and empowers the Twelve Apostles and sends them forth to preach, minister, and heal the sick— Those who receive the Twelve receive the Lord.

AND when he had ^acalled unto *him* his ^btwelve disciples, he gave them ^cpower *against* ^dunclean spirits, to cast them out, and to ^eheal all manner of ^fsickness and all manner of disease.

2 Now the names of the twelve apostles are these; The first, Simon, who is called Peter, and Andrew his brother; James *the son* of Zebedee, and John his brother;

3 Philip, and Bartholomew; Thomas, and Matthew the ^apublican; James *the son* of Alphæus, and Lebbæus, whose surname was Thaddæus;

4 Simon the Canaanite, and Judas Iscariot, who also ^abetrayed him.

5 These twelve Jesus ^asent forth, and commanded them, saying, Go not into the way of the Gentiles, and into *any* city of the ^bSamaritans enter ye not:

28a Matt. 20:30 (30–34);
       John 9:1 (1–4);
       Mosiah 3:5;
       3 Ne. 17:9 (7–10);
       D&C 84:69.
    b GR Do you have faith
       that.
29a TG Faith.
30a Ps. 146:8 (1–10).
    b TG Heal;
       Miracle.
    c GR warned them sternly.
31a Mark 7:36.
    b John 12:19.
32a Matt. 4:24;
       8:16 (16, 28, 33).
35a Matt. 4:23.

    b D&C 84:80 (79–80);
       JS—M 1:31.
    c Mosiah 3:5.
36a TG Compassion.
    b GR they were harassed.
    c TG Sheep.
    d TG Jesus Christ, Good
       Shepherd;
       Shepherd.
37a Luke 10:2.
       TG Harvest.
    b Jacob 5:70.
10 1a 1 Ne. 12:7 (6–7);
       Moro. 2:2 (1–3).
       TG Delegation of
       Responsibility.
    b TG Apostles.

    c GR authority over.
       D&C 50:32.
       TG Authority;
       Jesus Christ, Power of;
       Priesthood, Power of.
    d TG Spirits, Evil or
       Unclean;
       Uncleanness.
    e TG Heal.
    f TG Sickness.
 3a GR tax collector.
 4a TG Jesus Christ,
       Betrayal of.
 5a 3 Ne. 28:34;
       D&C 107:35.
    b Luke 9:52.

6 But go rather to the [a]lost [b]sheep of the house of Israel.

7 And as ye go, preach, saying, The kingdom of heaven [a]is at hand.

8 [a]Heal the sick, cleanse the [b]lepers, raise the dead, [c]cast out devils: [d]freely ye have received, freely [e]give.

9 Provide neither gold, nor silver, nor brass in your [a]purses,

10 Nor [a]scrip for *your* journey, neither two coats, neither shoes, nor yet staves: for the workman is [b]worthy of his [c]meat.

11 And into whatsoever city or town ye shall [a]enter, inquire who in it is worthy; and there abide till ye go thence.

12 And when ye come into an house, salute it.

13 And if the house be worthy, let your peace come upon it: but if it be not worthy, let your peace return to you.

14 And whosoever shall not receive you, nor hear your words, when ye depart out of that house or city, shake off the [a]dust of your [b]feet.

15 Verily I say unto you, It shall be more tolerable for the land of [a]Sodom and Gomorrha in the day of judgment, than for that city.

16 ¶ Behold, I send you forth as [a]sheep in the midst of wolves: be ye therefore [b]wise as serpents, and [c]harmless as doves.

17 But beware of men: for they will deliver you up to the councils, and they will scourge you in their synagogues;

18 And ye shall be brought before governors and [a]kings [b]for my sake, for a [c]testimony against them and the Gentiles.

19 But when they deliver you up, [a]take no thought how or what ye shall speak: for it shall be given you in that same hour what ye shall [b]speak.

20 For it is not ye that speak, but the [a]Spirit of your Father which speaketh in you.

21 And the brother shall deliver up the brother to death, and the father the child: and the children shall rise up against *their* parents, and cause them to be put to death.

22 And ye shall be [a]hated of all *men* [b]for my [c]name's sake: but he that [d]endureth to the end shall be saved.

23 But when they persecute you in this city, flee ye into another: for verily I say unto you, Ye shall not have gone over the cities of Israel, till the Son of man be come.

24 The [a]disciple is not above *his* master, nor the servant above his lord.

25 It is enough for the disciple [a]that he be as his master, and the servant as his lord. If they have called the master of the house Beelzebub, how much more *shall they call* them of his household?

26 Fear them not therefore: for

6a TG Missionary Work.
 b TG Sheep.
7a GR has come.
8a Luke 9:2; D&C 84:68.
 b TG Leprosy.
 c D&C 84:67.
 d GR without payment.
   Isa. 55:1.
 e TG Generosity.
9a Luke 10:4; 22:35 (35–36);
   D&C 24:18; 84:78.
10a GR traveling bag or
   beggar's bag.
   Mark 6:8.
 b 1 Cor. 9:14.
 c Num. 18:31; Luke 10:7.
11a D&C 24:15.
14a Luke 10:11 (11–12);
   Acts 13:51;
   D&C 75:20 (19–22).

 b Acts 18:6 (5–6);
   D&C 60:15;
   84:92 (92–93).
15a Ezek. 16:48.
16a Luke 10:3.
 b Jacob 6:12;
   Alma 18:22;
   Morm. 9:28;
   D&C 111:11.
 c GR guileless.
18a Ps. 119:46;
   Acts 9:15;
   D&C 1:23;
   124:3 (3, 16, 107).
 b GR on account of me.
 c GR witness to.
19a GR do not be anxiously
   concerned.
   Dan. 3:16;
   Acts 20:24.

 b Ex. 4:12 (12–15);
   Mark 13:11;
   Luke 21:15 (14–15);
   D&C 24:6.
   TG Teaching.
20a TG God, Spirit of;
   Teaching with the
   Spirit.
22a 1 Ne. 22:5.
   TG Hate; Martyrdom;
   Persecution.
 b GR because of my name.
 c TG Name.
 d Mark 13:13;
   3 Ne. 15:9;
   D&C 10:4; 53:7.
   TG Perseverance;
   Steadfastness.
24a John 15:20.
25a GR that he become.

there is nothing *a*covered, that shall not be revealed; and hid, that shall not be known.

27 What I tell you in darkness, *that* speak ye in light: and what ye hear in the ear, *that* preach ye upon the housetops.

28 And *a*fear not them which kill the body, but are not able to kill the soul: but rather *b*fear him which is able to *c*destroy both *d*soul and body in *e*hell.

29 Are not two *a*sparrows sold for a farthing? and one of them shall not fall on the ground without your Father.

30 But the very *a*hairs of your head are all numbered.

31 Fear ye not therefore, ye are of more *a*value than many *b*sparrows.

32 Whosoever therefore shall *a*confess me before men, him will I confess also before my Father which is in heaven.

33 But whosoever shall *a*deny me before men, him will I also deny before my Father which is in heaven.

34 Think not that I am come to send *a*peace on earth: I came not to send peace, but a sword.

35 For I am come to set a man at variance against his father, and the daughter against her mother, and the daughter in law against her mother in law.

36 And a man's *a*foes *shall be* they of his own *b*household.

37 He that *a*loveth father or mother *b*more than me is not worthy of me: and he that *c*loveth son or daughter more than me is not worthy of me.

38 And he that taketh not his *a*cross, and followeth after me, is not *b*worthy of me.

39 *a*He that findeth his life shall *b*lose it: and he that *c*loseth his *d*life for my sake shall find it.

40 ¶ He that *a*receiveth you *b*receiveth me, and he that receiveth me receiveth him that sent me.

41 He that *a*receiveth a prophet in the name of a prophet shall receive a prophet's *b*reward; and he that receiveth a righteous man in the name of a righteous man shall receive a righteous man's reward.

42 And whosoever shall give to drink unto one of these little ones a cup of cold *water* only in the *a*name of a disciple, verily I say unto you, he shall in no wise *b*lose his reward.

CHAPTER 11

Jesus acclaims John as more than a prophet—The cities of Chorazin, Bethsaida, and Capernaum are rebuked for unbelief—The Son reveals the Father—The yoke of Christ is easy, and His burden is light.

AND it came to pass, when Jesus had made an end of commanding his twelve disciples, he departed thence to teach and to *a*preach in their cities.

26*a* Morm. 5:8.
28*a* Isa. 51:7; Jer. 1:8 (7–8);
  Luke 12:4 (4–5).
 b Deut. 13:8 (6–11);
  D&C 3:7 (6–8).
 c TG Devil.
 d TG Soul.
 e TG Hell.
29*a* TG God, Omniscience of.
30*a* Luke 21:18 (17–18).
31*a* Gen. 39:3 (1–6);
  Ps. 37:25;
  Rom. 8:39 (35–39);
  1 Ne. 17:3 (1–5, 12–14);
  Mosiah 2:41;
  D&C 121:33.
 b TG Nature, Earth.
32*a* GR solemnly covenant
  with, promise me.

33*a* TG Witness.
33*a* Rom. 1:16 (15–18);
  2 Tim. 2:12 (10–15);
  2 Ne. 31:14 (12–21);
  D&C 101:5 (1–5).
34*a* John 7:43.
  TG Peace.
36*a* TG Persecution.
 b Micah 7:6.
37*a* TG Love.
 b Luke 14:26.
 c 1 Sam. 2:29.
38*a* Matt. 16:24;
  Luke 9:23; 14:27;
  3 Ne. 12:30;
  D&C 23:6.
 b TG Worthiness.
39*a* JST Matt. 10:34 He *who seeketh to save* his life . . .

 b GR sacrifice.
 c Luke 9:24 (23–26).
  TG Loyalty.
 d TG Martyrdom;
  Self-Sacrifice.
40*a* Luke 9:48; 10:16;
  D&C 84:36 (36–38).
  TG Priesthood,
  Magnifying Callings
  within; Teachable.
 b Ex. 16:8.
  TG Hospitality.
41*a* TG Sustaining Church
  Leaders.
 b TG Reward.
42*a* TG Name.
 b Mark 9:41;
  D&C 84:90.
11 1*a* TG Missionary Work.

2 Now when [a]John had heard in the prison the works of Christ, he sent two of his disciples,

3 And said unto him, Art thou he that should come, or do we look for another?

4 Jesus answered and said unto them, Go and shew John again those [a]things which ye do hear and see:

5 The [a]blind receive their [b]sight, and the lame walk, the [c]lepers are cleansed, and the deaf hear, the dead are raised up, and the [d]poor have the gospel preached to them.

6 And blessed is *he,* whosoever shall not be [a]offended in me.

7 ¶ And as they departed, Jesus began to say unto the multitudes concerning John, What went ye out into the wilderness to see? A reed shaken with the wind?

8 But what went ye out for to see? A man clothed in soft raiment? behold, they that wear soft *clothing* are in [a]kings' houses.

9 But what went ye out for to see? A prophet? yea, I say unto you, and more than a [a]prophet.

10 For this is *he,* of whom it is written, Behold, I send my [a]messenger before thy face, which shall [b]prepare thy way before thee.

11 Verily I say unto you, Among them that are born of [a]women there hath not risen a greater than [b]John the Baptist: [c]notwithstanding he that is least in the kingdom of heaven is greater than he.

12 And from the days of John the Baptist until now the kingdom of heaven suffereth violence, and [a]the violent take it by force.

13 [a]For all the [b]prophets and the law [c]prophesied until John.

14 And if ye will receive *it,* this is [a]Elias, which was for to come.

15 He that hath ears to [a]hear, let him hear.

16 ¶ But whereunto shall I liken this generation? It is like unto children sitting in the markets, and calling unto their fellows,

17 And saying, We have piped unto you, and ye have not danced; we have mourned unto you, and ye have not lamented.

18 For John came neither eating nor drinking, and they say, He hath a devil.

19 The Son of man came eating and drinking, and they say, Behold a man gluttonous, and [a]a winebibber, a friend of [b]publicans and sinners. But wisdom is justified [c]of her children.

20 ¶ Then began he to upbraid the [a]cities wherein most of his mighty works were done, because they repented not:

21 Woe unto thee, Chorazin! woe unto thee, Bethsaida! for if the mighty works, which were done in you, had been done in Tyre and Sidon, they would have [a]repented long ago in sackcloth and [b]ashes.

22 But I say unto you, It shall be more [a]tolerable for Tyre and Sidon at the day of judgment, than for you.

23 And thou, Capernaum, which art [a]exalted unto heaven, shalt be brought down to [b]hell: for if the mighty works, which have been done in thee, had been done in

---

2a Luke 7:18 (18–35).
4a John 5:36.
5a Ps. 146:8; Isa. 42:7.
  b TG Sight.
  c TG Leprosy.
  d D&C 35:15.
6a Isa. 8:14 (14–15); Matt. 24:10.
8a TG Kings, Earthly.
9a Matt. 14:5; 21:26; Luke 20:6.
10a Mal. 3:1; Mark 1:2; 1 Ne. 11:27; D&C 35:4; 45:9.
  b Isa. 40:3.

11a TG Woman.
  b John 5:35 (32–35).
  c GR but he who is less important.
    Luke 7:28; D&C 50:26.
12a GR violent men are seizing control of it, or plundering it.
13a JST Matt. 11:13–15 (Appendix).
  b Zech. 7:12; 1 Ne. 3:20; Mosiah 15:13.
    TG Jesus Christ, Prophecies about.
  c IE The law and prophets

foretold such violence.
14a Luke 1:17.
15a Ezek. 33:31 (30–33); Heb. 5:11 (11–14); 2 Ne. 9:31; D&C 1:14.
19a GR a drunkard.
  b GR tax collectors.
  c GR by her deeds, works.
20a Alma 34:31 (31–36); 3 Ne. 9:3; D&C 84:114.
21a Ezek. 3:6.
  b Job 2:8; 42:6.
22a D&C 45:54; 75:22.
23a TG Haughtiness.
  b TG Hell.

Sodom, it would have remained until this day.

24 But I say unto you, That it shall be more tolerable for the land of ^{a}Sodom in the day of judgment, than for thee.

25 ¶ At that time Jesus answered and said, I ^{a}thank thee, O Father, Lord of heaven and earth, because thou hast ^{b}hid these things from the wise and ^{c}prudent, and hast ^{d}revealed them unto ^{e}babes.

26 Even so, Father: for so it seemed good in thy sight.

27 All ^{a}things are delivered unto me of my Father: and no man knoweth the Son, but the Father; neither ^{b}knoweth any man the Father, save the Son, ^{c}and *he* to whomsoever the Son will ^{d}reveal *him*.

28 ¶ ^{a}Come unto me, all *ye* that ^{b}labour and are heavy laden, and I will give you ^{c}rest.

29 Take my ^{a}yoke upon you, and ^{b}learn of me; for I am ^{c}meek and ^{d}lowly in ^{e}heart: and ye shall find ^{f}rest unto your souls.

30 For my yoke *is* ^{a}easy, and my burden is light.

CHAPTER 12

Jesus proclaims Himself Lord of the Sabbath and heals on the Sabbath day—He is accused of casting out devils through the power of Beelzebub—He speaks of blasphemy against the Holy Ghost and says that an evil and adulterous generation seeks signs.

AT that time Jesus went on the ^{a}sabbath day through the ^{b}corn; and his disciples were an hungred, and began to pluck the ^{c}ears of corn, and to eat.

2 But when the Pharisees saw *it*, they said unto him, Behold, thy disciples do that which is not lawful to do upon the sabbath day.

3 But he said unto them, Have ye not ^{a}read what ^{b}David did, when he was an hungred, and they that were with him;

4 How he entered into the house of God, and did eat the ^{a}shewbread, which was not lawful for him to eat, neither for them which were with him, but only for the priests?

5 Or have ye not read in the law, how that on the ^{a}sabbath days the priests in the temple profane the sabbath, and are blameless?

6 But I say unto you, That in this place is *one* greater than the ^{a}temple.

7 But if ye had known what *this* meaneth, I will have ^{a}mercy, and not sacrifice, ye would not have condemned the guiltless.

8 For the Son of man is Lord even of the ^{a}sabbath day.

9 And when he was departed thence, he went into their synagogue:

10 ¶ And, behold, there was a man which had *his* hand withered. And they asked him, saying, Is it lawful to heal on the sabbath days? that they might accuse him.

11 And he said unto them, What man shall there be among you,

24*a* Ezek. 16:48.
25*a* GR praise.
　　Luke 10:21.
　b Matt. 13:11;
　　D&C 6:11 (11–12).
　c TG Prudence.
　d Alma 32:23;
　　D&C 133:58.
　e GR innocent people.
　　2 Ne. 9:42 (42–43);
　　Alma 32:23;
　　3 Ne. 26:16 (14–16);
　　D&C 128:18.
27*a* TG Jesus Christ,
　　Messiah.
　b TG Knowledge.
　c JST Matt. 11:28 . . . and
　　they to *whom* the Son
　　will reveal *himself; they*

shall see the Father also.
　d Luke 10:22;
　　John 14:6 (6–14).
　　TG God, Privilege of
　　Seeing.
28*a* Ps. 55:22;
　　Isa. 55:3;
　　D&C 10:67.
　　TG Problem-Solving.
　b TG Labor.
　c TG Rest.
29*a* 1 Jn. 2:6.
　　TG Jesus Christ, Taking
　　the Name of.
　b D&C 32:1.
　　TG Learn.
　c GR gentle and humble.
　　TG Humility;
　　Meek.

d TG Contrite Heart.
　e TG Heart.
　f Mosiah 2:41;
　　Alma 37:34 (33–34);
　　D&C 54:10; 59:23.
　　TG Comfort.
30*a* 1 Jn. 5:3 (1–5);
　　Alma 37:46 (43–47).
12 1*a* John 5:9.
　b GR grain.
　c Deut. 23:25.
3*a* TG Jesus Christ,
　　Teaching Mode of.
　b 1 Sam. 21:6 (3–6).
4*a* TG Bread, Shewbread.
5*a* Num. 28:9 (9–10).
6*a* TG Temple.
7*a* Hosea 6:6.
8*a* TG Sabbath.

that shall have one sheep, and if it fall into a pit on the sabbath day, will he not lay hold on it, and lift *it* out?

12 How much then is a man better than a sheep? Wherefore it is lawful to do well on the sabbath days.

13 Then saith he to the man, Stretch forth thine hand. And he stretched *it* forth; and it was restored whole, like as the other.

14 ¶ Then the Pharisees went out, and held a council against him, how they might destroy him.

15 But *a*when Jesus knew *it*, he withdrew himself from thence: and great multitudes followed him, and he healed them all;

16 And charged them that they should not make him known:

17 That it might be fulfilled which was spoken by *a*Esaias the prophet, saying,

18 Behold my *a*servant, whom I have *b*chosen; my *c*beloved, in whom my soul is well pleased: I will put my spirit upon him, and he shall shew judgment to the Gentiles.

19 He shall not strive, nor *a*cry; neither shall any man hear his voice in the streets.

20 A bruised reed shall he not break, and smoking flax shall he not quench, till he send forth *a*judgment unto victory.

21 And in his *a*name shall the *b*Gentiles trust.

22 ¶ Then was brought unto him one possessed with a devil, blind, and dumb: and he healed him, insomuch that the blind and dumb both spake and saw.

23 And all the people were amazed, and said, Is not this the son of *a*David?

24 But when the Pharisees heard *it*, they said, This *fellow* doth not cast out devils, but by *a*Beelzebub the prince of the devils.

25 And Jesus knew their *a*thoughts, and said unto them, Every *b*kingdom divided against itself is brought to desolation; and every city or house divided against itself shall not stand:

26 And if *a*Satan cast out Satan, he is divided against himself; how shall then his kingdom stand?

27 And if I by Beelzebub cast out devils, by whom do your children cast *them* out? therefore they shall be your judges.

28 But if I cast out *a*devils by the *b*Spirit of God, then the kingdom of God is come unto *c*you.

29 Or else how can one enter into a strong man's house, and *a*spoil his goods, except he first bind the strong man? and then he will spoil his house.

30 He that is not with me is against me; and he that gathereth not *a*with me scattereth abroad.

31 ¶ Wherefore I say unto you, All manner of sin and blasphemy shall be forgiven *a*unto men: but the *b*blasphemy *against* the Holy Ghost shall *c*not be forgiven unto men.

32 And whosoever speaketh a word against the Son of man, it shall be forgiven him: but whosoever speaketh against the Holy Ghost, it shall not be *a*forgiven him, neither

15a JST Matt. 12:13 . . . *Jesus knew when they took counsel, and he withdrew* . . .
17a Isa. 42:1–3.
18a GR son.
   b TG Jesus Christ, Authority of.
   c TG Witness of the Father.
19a GR cry for help.
20a D&C 52:11.
21a TG Jesus Christ, Taking the Name of; Name.
   b GR nations.

2 Ne. 10:18 (9, 11, 18).
23a TG Jesus Christ, Davidic Descent of.
24a 2 Kgs. 1:2 (2–6).
25a Ps. 139:2; Luke 11:17; John 2:25; Mosiah 24:12; D&C 6:16.
   b TG Governments.
26a TG Spirits, Evil or Unclean.
28a TG Devil.
   b TG God, Spirit of.
   c JST Matt. 12:23 . . . you. *For they also cast out devils by the Spirit of God,*

for unto them is given power over devils, that they may cast them out.
29a GR plunder.
30a Mark 9:40; Luke 9:50; 2 Ne. 10:16.
31a JST Matt. 12:26 . . . unto men *who receive me and repent; but* . . .
   b TG Blaspheme; Holy Ghost, Unpardonable Sin against.
   c TG Holy Ghost, Loss of.
32a TG Death, Spiritual, Second; Forgive.

in this world, neither in the *world* to come.

33 Either make the tree good, and his ^afruit good; or else make the tree corrupt, and his fruit corrupt: for the tree is known by *his* ^bfruit.

34 O ^ageneration of vipers, how can ye, being evil, ^bspeak good things? for out of the abundance of the heart the mouth speaketh.

35 A good man out of the good ^atreasure of the heart bringeth forth good things: and an evil man out of the evil treasure bringeth forth ^bevil things.

36 But I say unto you, That every ^aidle ^bword that men shall ^cspeak, they shall give ^daccount thereof in the day of ^ejudgment.

37 For by thy ^awords thou shalt be justified, and by thy words thou shalt be condemned.

38 ¶ Then certain of the scribes and of the Pharisees answered, saying, Master, we would see a ^asign from thee.

39 But he answered and said unto them, An evil and adulterous generation seeketh after a ^asign; and there shall no sign be given to it, but the sign of the prophet Jonas:

40 For as Jonas was three days and three nights in the whale's belly; so shall the Son of man be ^athree days and three nights in the heart of the earth.

41 The men of ^aNineveh shall rise in judgment with this generation, and shall condemn it: because they ^brepented at the preaching of Jonas;

and, behold, a greater than Jonas *is* here.

42 The ^aqueen of the south shall rise up in the judgment with this generation, and shall condemn it: for she came from the uttermost parts of the earth to hear the wisdom of Solomon; and, behold, a greater than Solomon *is* here.

43 ^aWhen the ^bunclean spirit is gone out of a man, he walketh through dry places, seeking rest, and findeth none.

44 Then he saith, I will return into my house from whence I came out; and when he is come, he findeth *it* empty, swept, and garnished.

45 Then goeth ^ahe, and taketh with himself seven other ^bspirits more wicked than himself, and they enter in and dwell there: and the last ^cstate of that man is ^dworse than the first. Even so shall it be also unto this wicked generation.

46 ¶ While he yet talked to the people, behold, *his* mother and his ^abrethren stood ^bwithout, desiring to speak with him.

47 Then one said unto him, Behold, thy mother and thy brethren stand without, desiring to speak with thee.

48 But he answered and said unto him that told him, Who is my mother? and who are my brethren?

49 And he stretched forth his hand toward his disciples, and said, Behold my ^abrethren and my brethren!

50 For whosoever shall do the ^awill of my Father which is in heaven, the same is my ^bbrother, and sister, and mother.

33a Matt. 7:17 (16–20);
        3 Ne. 14:20 (17–20).
      b Moro. 7:16 (5–19).
34a Matt. 3:7; 23:33;
        D&C 121:23.
      b Luke 6:45;
        James 3:10 (10–12).
35a TG Treasure.
      b TG Evil.
36a Eccl. 5:2;
        Eph. 5:4.
      b TG Gossip.
      c TG Profanity.
      d TG Accountability.
      e Alma 11:43 (43–44).
        TG Judgment, the Last.

37a Prov. 18:21.
38a John 6:30.
39a TG Miracle; Signs;
        Sign Seekers.
40a TG Jesus Christ, Death
        of; Jesus Christ, Types
        of, in Anticipation.
41a Jonah 3:5.
      b TG Repent.
42a 1 Kgs. 10:1 (1–10).
43a JST Matt. 12:37–38
        (Appendix).
      b TG Uncleanness.
45a JST Matt. 12:39 . . . *the*
        evil spirit, and taketh . . .
      b TG Spirits, Evil or

      Unclean.
      c TG Apostasy of
        Individuals.
      d Alma 24:30.
46a John 7:3 (3, 5, 10);
        1 Cor. 9:5.
        TG Jesus Christ,
        Family of.
      b GR outside.
49a Mosiah 5:7.
        TG Marriage,
        Motherhood.
50a Mark 3:35.
        TG God, Will of.
      b TG Brotherhood and
        Sisterhood.

CHAPTER 13

Jesus explains why He teaches with parables—He gives the parables of the sower, the wheat and the tares, the grain of mustard seed, the leaven, the treasure hidden in the field, the pearl of great price, and the net cast into the sea—A prophet is not honored by his own people.

THE same day went Jesus out of the house, and sat by the ᵃsea side.

2 And great multitudes were gathered together unto him, so that he went into a ship, and sat; and the whole multitude stood on the shore.

3 And he spake many things unto them in parables, saying, Behold, a sower went forth to sow;

4 And when he sowed, some *seeds* fell by the way side, and the fowls came and devoured them up:

5 Some fell upon ᵃstony places, where they had not much earth: and forthwith they sprung up, because they had no deepness of earth:

6 And when the sun was up, they were scorched; and because they had no root, they withered away.

7 And some fell among ᵃthorns; and the thorns sprung up, and choked them:

8 But other fell into good ground, and ᵃbrought forth fruit, some an hundredfold, some sixtyfold, some thirtyfold.

9 Who hath ears to hear, let him hear.

10 And the disciples came, and said unto him, Why speakest thou unto them in ᵃparables?

11 He answered and said unto them, Because it is given unto you to know the ᵃmysteries of the kingdom of heaven, but to them it is not given.

12 ᵃFor whosoever hath, to him shall be ᵇgiven, and he shall have more ᶜabundance: but whosoever hath not, from him shall be taken away even that he hath.

13 Therefore speak I to them in parables: because they seeing see not; and hearing they hear not, neither do they understand.

14 And in them is fulfilled the prophecy of Esaias, which saith, By hearing ye shall ᵃhear, and shall not understand; and seeing ye shall see, and shall not perceive:

15 For this people's ᵃheart is waxed gross, and *their* ears are dull of hearing, and their ᵇeyes they have ᶜclosed; lest at any time they should see with *their* eyes, and hear with *their* ears, and should understand with *their* heart, and should be converted, and I should ᵈheal them.

16 But blessed *are* your ᵃeyes, for they see: and your ears, for they hear.

17 For verily I say unto you, That many ᵃprophets and righteous *men* have desired to see *those things* which ye see, and have not seen *them*; and to hear *those things* which ye hear, and have not heard *them*.

18 ¶ ᵃHear ye therefore the parable of the sower.

19 When any one heareth the word of the kingdom, and ᵃunderstandeth *it* not, then cometh the wicked *one*, and ᵇcatcheth away that which was sown in his heart. This is he which received seed by the way side.

---

13 1a Mark 4:1 (1–12).
  5a IE rocky land over which a thin layer of soil is spread.
  7a Jer. 4:3 (3–18).
  8a GR began to bring forth.
  10a Dan. 12:10.
    TG Jesus Christ, Teaching Mode of.
  11a Matt. 11:25; D&C 6:11 (11–12); 19:8.
    TG Mysteries of Godliness.

12a JST Matt. 13:10–11 For whosoever *receiveth*, to him shall be given, and he shall have more abundance; but whosoever *continueth not to receive*, from him shall be taken away even that he hath.
  b Matt. 25:29.
  c Prov. 9:9.
14a Jer. 5:21; Rom. 11:8;

    2 Ne. 9:31; 16:10.
15a TG Apostasy of Israel; Hardheartedness.
  b TG Spiritual Blindness.
  c TG Unbelief.
  d 3 Ne. 9:13; 18:32.
16a Luke 10:23.
17a Heb. 11:13; 1 Pet. 1:10 (10–11).
18a GR Learn, Understand.
19a 1 Ne. 8:23 (20–23).
  b D&C 84:50 (49–53); 93:39 (38–39).

20 But he that received the seed into ᵃstony places, the same is he that heareth the word, and anon with joy receiveth it;

21 Yet hath he not root in himself, but dureth for a while: for when ᵃtribulation or ᵇpersecution ariseth because of the word, by and by ᶜhe is offended.

22 He also that received seed among the thorns is he that heareth the word; and the care of this ᵃworld, and the ᵇdeceitfulness of ᶜriches, choke the word, and he becometh unfruitful.

23 But he that received seed into the good ground is he that ᵃheareth the word, and ᵇunderstandeth it; which also beareth ᶜfruit, and bringeth forth, some an hundredfold, some sixty, some thirty.

24 ¶ Another ᵃparable put he forth unto them, saying, The ᵇkingdom of heaven is likened unto a man which sowed good ᶜseed in his field:

25 But while men slept, his enemy came and sowed ᵃtares among the wheat, and went his way.

26 But when the blade was sprung up, and brought forth fruit, then appeared the tares also.

27 So the servants of the householder came and said unto him, Sir, didst not thou sow good seed in thy field? from whence then hath it tares?

28 He said unto them, An enemy hath done this. The servants said unto him, Wilt thou then that we go and gather them up?

29 But he said, Nay; lest while ye gather up the tares, ye root up also the wheat with them.

30 Let both grow together until the ᵃharvest: and in the time of harvest I will say to the reapers, Gather ye together ᵇfirst the tares, and bind them in bundles to ᶜburn them: but gather the wheat into my barn.

31 ¶ Another parable put he forth unto them, saying, The kingdom of heaven is like to a ᵃgrain of mustard seed, which a man took, and sowed in his field:

32 Which indeed is the least of all seeds: but when it is grown, it is the greatest among herbs, and becometh a tree, so that the ᵃbirds of the air come and lodge in the branches thereof.

33 ¶ Another parable spake he unto them; The kingdom of heaven is like unto ᵃleaven, which a woman took, and hid in three measures of meal, till the whole was leavened.

34 All these things spake Jesus unto the multitude in parables; and without a parable spake he not unto them:

35 That it might be fulfilled which was spoken by the prophet, saying, I will open my mouth in ᵃparables; I will utter things which have been kept ᵇsecret from the foundation of the world.

36 Then Jesus sent the multitude away, and went into the house: and his disciples came unto him, saying, Declare unto us the parable of the ᵃtares of the field.

37 He answered and said unto them, He that soweth the good ᵃseed is the Son of man;

38 The field is the world; the good seed are the children of the kingdom;

20a Zech. 7:12.
21a TG Test; Tribulation.
  b D&C 40:2 (1–3).
    TG Persecution.
  c GR he stumbles, falls away.
    TG Apostasy of Individuals; Offense.
22a Hel. 7:5; D&C 39:9.
    TG Worldliness.
  b TG Deceit.
  c TG Treasure.

23a TG Teachable.
  b JST Matt. 13:21 . . . understandeth and endureth; which . . .
  c Alma 32:42 (41–43).
    TG Good Works.
24a D&C 86:1 (1–11).
  b TG Kingdom of God, on Earth.
  c Matt. 13:37 (36–43).
25a TG Apostasy of the Early Christian Church.
30a TG Harvest.
  b JST Matt. 13:29 . . . first

the wheat into my barn; and the tares are bound in bundles to be burned.
  c D&C 38:12.
31a Isa. 60:22.
32a TG Nature, Earth.
33a GR yeast.
    TG Leaven.
35a Ps. 78:2; Mark 4:11 (11–12).
  b D&C 35:18.
36a D&C 86:1 (1–7); 101:65 (65–67).
37a Matt. 13:24 (24–30).

but the *tares are the children of the wicked *one;*

39 The enemy that sowed them is the devil; *the *harvest is the end of the world; and the reapers are the angels.

40 As therefore the tares are gathered and burned in the fire; so shall it be in the *end of this world.

41 The Son of man shall send forth his *angels, and they shall gather out of his kingdom all things that *offend, and them which do iniquity;

42 And shall cast them into a furnace of fire: there shall be *wailing and *gnashing of teeth.

43 Then shall the *righteous *shine forth as the *sun in the kingdom of their Father. Who hath ears to hear, let him hear.

44 ¶ Again, the kingdom of heaven is like unto *treasure hid in a field; the which when a man hath found, he hideth, and for joy thereof goeth and selleth all that he hath, and buyeth that field.

45 ¶ Again, the kingdom of heaven is like unto a merchant man, seeking goodly pearls:

46 Who, when he had found one *pearl of great price, went and sold *all that he had, and bought it.

47 ¶ Again, the kingdom of heaven is like unto a net, that was cast into the sea, and *gathered of every kind:

48 Which, when it was full, they drew to shore, and sat down, and gathered the good into vessels, but cast the bad away.

49 So shall it be at the *end of the *world: the angels shall come forth, and *sever the wicked from among the *just,

50 *And shall cast them into the furnace of fire: there shall be wailing and gnashing of teeth.

51 Jesus saith unto them, Have ye understood all these things? They say unto him, Yea, Lord.

52 Then said he unto them, Therefore every *scribe *which is instructed unto the kingdom of heaven is like unto a man *that is* an householder, which bringeth forth out of his treasure *things* new and old.

53 ¶ And it came to pass, *that* when Jesus had finished these parables, he departed thence.

54 And when he was come into his own country, he taught them in their synagogue, insomuch that they were *astonished, and said, Whence hath this *man* this *wisdom, and *these* mighty works?

55 Is not this the carpenter's *son? is not his mother called Mary? and his *brethren, James, and Joses, and Simon, and Judas?

56 And his sisters, are they not all with us? Whence then hath this *man* all these things?

57 And they were offended in him. But Jesus said unto them, A prophet is not without *honour, save in his own country, and in his own house.

58 And he did not many mighty works there because of their *unbelief.

38*a* D&C 88:94.
　　TG Devil, Church of.
39*a* JST Matt. 13:39–44
　　(Appendix).
　b TG Harvest.
40*a* TG World, End of.
41*a* TG Angels.
　b TG Offense.
42*a* Matt. 8:12;
　　Rev. 19:20;
　　D&C 19:5; 29:15; 112:24.
　b TG Pain.
43*a* Ps. 68:3;
　　Alma 40:25.
　　TG Righteousness.
　b TG Celestial Glory.

　c D&C 76:70.
44*a* TG Treasure.
46*a* Rev. 3:18.
　b Alma 22:15.
47*a* Matt. 22:10 (1–14).
49*a* TG World, End of.
　b JST Matt. 13:49–51 . . .
　　world. *And the world is
　　the children of the wicked.
　　The angels* . . .
　c GR separate.
　d TG Righteousness.
50*a* JST Matt. 13:51 . . .
　　and shall cast them
　　*out into the world to be
　　burned.* There shall be

　　wailing . . .
52*a* TG Scribe.
　b GR which has become
　　a disciple in.
54*a* Matt. 7:28.
　b TG God, Wisdom of;
　　Jesus Christ, Teaching
　　Mode of.
55*a* Mark 6:3.
　b TG Jesus Christ,
　　Family of.
57*a* TG Prophets,
　　Rejection of.
58*a* Luke 4:23 (23–27);
　　Ether 12:12 (6–19);
　　Moro. 7:37 (33–39).

CHAPTER 14

John the Baptist is beheaded—Jesus feeds the five thousand and walks on the sea—Those who touch the hem of His garment are made whole.

AT that time ^aHerod the tetrarch heard of the fame of Jesus,

2 And said unto his servants, This is John the Baptist; he is risen from the dead; and therefore mighty works do shew forth themselves in him.

3 ¶ For Herod had laid hold on John, and bound him, and put *him* in prison for Herodias' sake, his brother Philip's wife.

4 For John said unto him, It is not ^alawful for thee to have her.

5 And ^awhen he would have put him to death, he feared the multitude, because they counted him as a ^bprophet.

6 But when Herod's birthday was kept, the daughter of Herodias danced before them, and pleased Herod.

7 Whereupon he ^apromised with an oath to give her whatsoever she would ask.

8 And she, being before instructed of her mother, said, Give me here John Baptist's head in a ^acharger.

9 And the king was sorry: nevertheless for the oath's sake, and them which sat with him at meat, he commanded *it* to be given *her*.

10 And he sent, and ^abeheaded John in the prison.

11 And his head was brought in a charger, and given to the damsel: and she brought *it* to her mother.

12 And his disciples came, and took up the body, and buried it, and went and told Jesus.

13 ¶ When Jesus heard *of it,* he departed thence by ship into a desert place apart: and when the people had heard *thereof,* they followed him on foot out of the cities.

14 And Jesus went forth, and saw a great multitude, and was moved with ^acompassion toward them, and he healed their ^bsick.

15 ¶ And when it was evening, his disciples came to him, saying, This is a desert place, and the time is now past; send the multitude away, that they may go into the villages, and buy themselves ^avictuals.

16 But Jesus said unto them, They need not depart; give ye them to eat.

17 And they say unto him, We have here but five loaves, and two fishes.

18 He said, Bring them hither to me.

19 And he commanded the multitude to sit down on the grass, and took the five loaves, and the two fishes, and looking up to heaven, he blessed, and ^abrake, and gave the loaves to *his* disciples, and the disciples to the multitude.

20 And they did all eat, and were filled: and they ^atook up of the fragments that remained twelve baskets full.

21 And they that had eaten were about ^afive thousand men, beside women and children.

22 ¶ And straightway Jesus constrained his disciples to get into a ship, and to go before him unto the other side, while he sent the multitudes away.

23 And when he had sent the multitudes away, he went up into a mountain apart to ^apray: and when the evening was come, he was there alone.

24 But the ship was now in the midst of the sea, tossed with waves: for the wind was contrary.

25 And ^ain the fourth watch of the night Jesus went unto them, walking on the sea.

26 And when the disciples saw

---

14 1a Luke 9:7.
  4a Lev. 18:16; 20:21.
    TG Divorce.
  5a GR although he desired
     to kill him.
   b Matt. 11:9; 21:26;
     Luke 20:6.
  7a TG Vow.

  8a GR platter.
 10a TG Tyranny.
 14a TG Compassion.
   b TG Sickness.
 15a GR food.
 19a 3 Ne. 18:5 (4–5);
     20:6 (6–7).
 20a 2 Kgs. 4:44 (42–44);

     Matt. 15:37 (36–38).
 21a Mark 6:44 (32–44);
     Luke 9:14 (10–17);
     John 6:10 (1–13).
 23a Matt. 26:36;
     Luke 6:12; 9:28.
 25a IE between three and
     six in the morning.

him walking on the sea, they were troubled, saying, It is a spirit; and they cried out for fear.

27 But straightway Jesus spake unto them, saying, Be of good ªcheer; it is I; be not afraid.

28 And Peter answered him and said, Lord, if it be thou, bid me come unto thee on the water.

29 And he said, Come. And when Peter was come down out of the ship, he walked on the water, to go to Jesus.

30 But when he saw the wind boisterous, he was ªafraid; and beginning to sink, he cried, saying, Lord, save me.

31 And immediately Jesus stretched forth *his* hand, and caught him, and said unto him, O thou of little ªfaith, wherefore didst thou ᵇdoubt?

32 And when they were come into the ship, the wind ceased.

33 Then they that were in the ship came and worshipped him, saying, Of a truth thou art the Son of God.

34 ¶ And when they were gone over, they came into the land of Gennesaret.

35 And when the men of that place ªhad knowledge of him, they sent out into all that country round about, and brought unto him all that were diseased;

36 And besought him that they might only touch the ªhem of his garment: and as many as touched were made perfectly ᵇwhole.

CHAPTER 15

The scribes and Pharisees contend against Jesus—He heals the daughter of a gentile woman—He feeds the four thousand.

THEN came to Jesus ªscribes and Pharisees, which were of Jerusalem, saying,

2 Why do thy disciples transgress the ªtradition of the elders? for they wash not their hands when they eat bread.

3 But he answered and said unto them, Why do ye also transgress the commandment of God by your ªtradition?

4 For God commanded, saying, ªHonour thy father and mother: and, He that curseth father or mother, ᵇlet him die the death.

5 But ye say, Whosoever shall say to *his* father or *his* mother, *It is* a ªgift, by whatsoever thou mightest be profited by me;

6 And honour not his father or his mother, *he shall be free.* Thus have ye made the commandment of God of none effect by your tradition.

7 Ye hypocrites, well did Esaias prophesy of you, saying,

8 This people draweth nigh unto me with their ªmouth, and ᵇhonoureth me with *their* lips; but their ᶜheart is far from me.

9 But in vain they do ªworship me, teaching *for* ᵇdoctrines the ᶜcommandments of men.

10 ¶ And he called the multitude, and said unto them, Hear, and understand:

11 Not that which goeth into the mouth ªdefileth a man; but that which cometh out of the ᵇmouth, this defileth a man.

12 Then came his disciples, and said unto him, Knowest thou that the Pharisees were offended, after they heard this saying?

13 But he answered and said, Every ªplant, which my heavenly

27a TG Cheerful.
30a TG Courage; Fearful.
31a Mark 4:40; 16:14;
    Luke 24:25.
   ᵇ TG Doubt.
35a GR recognized Him.
36a Mark 5:27 (25–34).
   ᵇ TG Heal.
15 1a TG Scribe.
2a Alma 24:7;
    D&C 123:7 (7–8).
3a TG Traditions of Men.

4a TG Honor; Honoring
    Father and Mother;
    Respect.
   ᵇ GR he shall surely die.
    TG Capital Punishment.
5a Mark 7:11.
8a Jer. 12:2.
   ᵇ Isa. 29:13;
    Titus 1:16 (15–16);
    2 Ne. 27:25 (24–25).
    TG Hypocrisy.
   ᶜ Ezek. 33:31;

    Alma 34:28;
    D&C 45:29.
9a Isa. 1:13.
   ᵇ Matt. 16:12;
    Col. 2:22 (18–22);
    Titus 1:14 (13–14);
    2 Ne. 28:9.
   ᶜ TG Apostasy of Israel.
11a TG Cleanliness.
   ᵇ TG Gossip; Profanity.
13a John 15:2 (1–2).
    TG Vineyard of the Lord.

Father hath not planted, shall be rooted up.

14 Let them alone: they be *a*blind *b*leaders of the blind. And if the blind lead the blind, both shall fall into the ditch.

15 Then answered Peter and said unto him, Declare unto us this parable.

16 And Jesus said, Are ye also yet without understanding?

17 Do not ye yet understand, that whatsoever entereth in at the mouth goeth into the belly, and is cast out into the draught?

18 But those things which proceed out of the *a*mouth come forth from the heart; and they defile the man.

19 For out of the *a*heart proceed evil thoughts, *b*murders, *c*adulteries, *d*fornications, thefts, *e*false witness, *f*blasphemies:

20 These are *the things* which *a*defile a man: but to eat with unwashen hands defileth not a man.

21 ¶ Then Jesus went thence, and departed into the *a*coasts of Tyre and Sidon.

22 And, behold, a woman of Canaan came out of the same coasts, and cried unto him, saying, Have mercy on me, O Lord, *thou* Son of David; my daughter is grievously vexed with a devil.

23 But he answered her not a word. And his disciples came and besought him, saying, Send her away; for she crieth after us.

24 But he answered and said, I am not *a*sent but unto the lost sheep of the house of *b*Israel.

25 Then came she and worshipped him, saying, Lord, help me.

26 But he answered and said, It is not meet to take the children's bread, and to cast *it* to *a*dogs.

27 And she said, Truth, Lord: yet the dogs eat of the crumbs which fall from their masters' table.

28 Then Jesus answered and said unto her, O woman, great *is* thy *a*faith: be it unto thee even as thou wilt. And her daughter was made whole from that very hour.

29 And Jesus departed from thence, and came nigh unto the sea of Galilee; and went up into a mountain, and sat down there.

30 And great multitudes came unto him, having with them *those that were* lame, blind, dumb, maimed, and many others, and cast them down at Jesus' feet; and he healed them:

31 Insomuch that the multitude wondered, when they saw the dumb to speak, the maimed to be whole, the lame to walk, and the blind to see: and they glorified the God of Israel.

32 ¶ Then Jesus called his disciples *unto him,* and said, I have compassion on the multitude, because they continue with me now three days, and have nothing to eat: and I will not send them away fasting, lest they faint in the way.

33 And his disciples say unto him, Whence should we have so much bread in the wilderness, as to fill so great a multitude?

34 And Jesus saith unto them, How many loaves have ye? And they said, Seven, and a few little fishes.

35 And he commanded the multitude to sit down on the ground.

36 And he took the seven *a*loaves and the fishes, and gave thanks, and brake *them,* and gave to his disciples, and the disciples to the multitude.

37 And they did all eat, and were

14a TG Spiritual Blindness.
  b TG Governments; Leadership.
18a Mosiah 4:30 (29–30).
19a Gen. 6:5; Heb. 3:12; Hel. 12:4.
   TG Chastity.
  b TG Blood, Shedding of; Murder.
  c TG Adulterer;

Sexual Immorality.
  d TG Fornication.
  e Ps. 27:12; Hel. 7:21 (21–22).
  f GR slanderous statements.
   TG Blaspheme.
20a TG Pollution.
21a GR regions.
24a 3 Ne. 15:23.

TG Jesus Christ, Messenger of the Covenant.
  b TG Israel, Scattering of.
26a Prov. 23:9; Matt. 7:6; D&C 6:12 (10–12); 10:37 (36–37); 41:6.
28a James 5:15 (14–15).
36a TG Bread.

filled: and they ªtook up of the ᵇbroken *meat* that was left seven baskets full.

38 And they that did eat were four thousand men, beside women and children.

39 And he sent away the multitude, and took ship, and came into the coasts of Magdala.

CHAPTER 16

Jesus warns against the doctrine of the Pharisees and Sadducees—Peter testifies that Jesus is the Christ and is promised the keys of the kingdom—Jesus foretells His death and resurrection.

THE Pharisees also with the Sadducees came, and tempting desired him that he would shew them a sign from ªheaven.

2 He ªanswered and said unto them, When it is evening, ye say, *It will be* fair weather: for the sky is red.

3 And in the morning, *It will be* foul weather to day: for the sky is red and ªlowring. O *ye* ᵇhypocrites, ye can discern the face of the sky; but can ye not *discern* the ᶜsigns of the ᵈtimes?

4 A wicked and ªadulterous generation seeketh after a ᵇsign; and there shall no sign be given unto it, but the ᶜsign of the prophet ᵈJonas. And he left them, and departed.

5 And when his disciples were come to the other side, they had forgotten to take bread.

6 ¶ Then Jesus said unto them, Take heed and beware of the ªleaven of the Pharisees and of the Sadducees.

7 And they reasoned among themselves, saying, *It is* because we have taken no bread.

8 ªWhich when Jesus perceived, he said unto them, O ye of little faith, why reason ye among yourselves, because ye have brought no bread?

9 Do ye not yet understand, neither remember the five loaves of the five thousand, and how many baskets ye took up?

10 Neither the seven loaves of the four thousand, and how many baskets ye took up?

11 How is it that ye do not understand that I spake *it* not to you concerning bread, that ye should beware of the leaven of the Pharisees and of the Sadducees?

12 Then understood they how that he bade *them* not beware of the leaven of bread, but of the ªdoctrine of the Pharisees and of the ᵇSadducees.

13 ¶ When Jesus came into the coasts of Cæsarea Philippi, he asked his disciples, saying, Whom do men say that I the Son of man am?

14 And they said, Some *say that thou art* John the Baptist: some, ªElias; and others, Jeremias, or one of the prophets.

15 He saith unto them, But whom say ªye that I am?

16 And Simon Peter answered and said, Thou art the ªChrist, the ᵇSon of the ᶜliving God.

17 And Jesus answered and said unto him, Blessed art thou, Simon ªBar-jona: for flesh and blood hath not ᵇrevealed *it* unto thee, but my Father which is in heaven.

18 And I say also unto thee, That

37a 2 Kgs. 4:44 (42–44);
　　Matt. 14:20 (19–21).
　　b GR excess food.
16 1a TG Heaven.
　2a Prov. 26:5.
　3a GR dark, gloomy.
　　b TG Hypocrisy.
　　c 2 Pet. 3:4 (3–10).
　　d Esth. 1:13.
　4a TG Adulterer.
　　b Mark 8:12 (11–21).
　　c Jonah 1:17.
　　d TG Jesus Christ,
　　　Death of.
　6a TG Leaven.
　8a JST Matt. 16:9 *And when they reasoned among themselves*, Jesus perceived *it* . . .
12a Matt. 15:9.
　　b Matt. 22:23 (23–33).
14a IE Elijah.
15a IE The plural pronoun used here in the Greek indicates that Jesus asked this question of all the apostles and not just one of them.
16a TG Loyalty.
　　b TG Jesus Christ, Divine Sonship.
　　c TG God, Body of, Corporeal Nature.
17a IE Son of Jonah.
　　b TG Revelation; Testimony; Witness.

thou art Peter, and upon this ^arock I will build my ^bchurch; and the gates of ^chell shall not ^dprevail against it.

19 And I will ^agive unto thee the ^bkeys of the ^ckingdom of heaven: and whatsoever thou shalt ^dbind on earth shall be bound in heaven: and whatsoever thou shalt loose on earth shall be loosed in heaven.

20 Then charged he his disciples that they should tell no man that he was Jesus the ^aChrist.

21 ¶ From that time forth began Jesus to shew unto his disciples, how that he must go unto Jerusalem, and suffer many things of the elders and chief priests and scribes, and be killed, and be ^araised again the third day.

22 Then Peter took him, and began to rebuke him, saying, Be it far from thee, Lord: this shall not be unto thee.

23 But he turned, and said unto Peter, Get thee behind me, Satan: thou art an offence unto me: for thou ^asavourest not the things that be of God, but those that be of men.

24 ¶ ^aThen said Jesus unto his disciples, If any *man* will come after me, let him ^bdeny himself, and take up his ^ccross, and ^dfollow ^eme.

25 For whosoever will save his life shall lose it: and whosoever will ^alose his life for my sake shall ^bfind it.

26 For what is a man ^aprofited, if he shall ^bgain the whole ^cworld, and ^dlose his own ^esoul? or what shall a man give in exchange for his soul?

27 For the ^aSon of man shall come in the ^bglory of his Father with his angels; and then he shall ^creward every man according to his ^dworks.

28 Verily I say unto you, There be some standing here, which shall not taste of ^adeath, till they see the Son of man coming in his ^bkingdom.

CHAPTER 17

Jesus is transfigured before Peter, James, and John on the mount—Jesus heals a lunatic, tells of His coming death, and pays taxes in a miraculous manner.

AND after six days Jesus taketh ^aPeter, James, and John his brother, and bringeth them up into an high mountain apart,

2 And was ^atransfigured before them: and his face did shine as the sun, and his raiment was white as the light.

18*a* Here is a subtle wordplay upon "Peter" (Greek *petros* = small rock) and "rock" (Greek *petra* = bedrock). Christ is the Stone of Israel. John 1:42; 1 Cor. 3:11 (9–11); 10:4; D&C 50:44; 128:10. TG Rock.
  b TG Church Organization; Jesus Christ, Head of the Church.
  c TG Hell.
  d D&C 17:8; 21:6.
19*a* D&C 7:7; 27:13. TG Delegation of Responsibility; God, Gifts of.
  b TG Apostles; Priesthood; Priesthood, Authority; Priesthood, History of; Priesthood, Keys of.
  c TG Kingdom of God, on Earth.
  d Hel. 10:7 (5–11); D&C 138:58 (58–60).

TG Genealogy and Temple Work; Marriage, Celestial; Salvation for the Dead; Sealing.
20*a* TG Jesus Christ, Messiah.
21*a* TG Jesus Christ, Resurrection.
23*a* Hel. 10:4 (4–5).
24*a* JST Matt. 16:25–29 (Appendix).
  b TG Self-Mastery.
  c Matt. 10:38; 3 Ne. 12:30.
  d Philip. 3:17 (13–21); 2 Ne. 31:12 (12–13).
  e JST Matt. 16:25–26 . . . me. *And now for a man to take up his cross, is to deny himself all ungodliness, and every worldly lust, and keep my commandments.*
25*a* TG Self-Mastery; Self-Sacrifice.
  b TG Abundant Life.
26*a* 1 Sam. 12:21; Prov. 13:7;

Eccl. 1:3 (2–3).
  b Job 27:8. TG Selfishness; Treasure.
  c TG Worldliness.
  d Luke 9:25.
  e TG Mortality; Soul.
27*a* TG Jesus Christ, Son of Man.
  b TG Glory; Jesus Christ, Glory of; Jesus Christ, Second Coming.
  c TG Jesus Christ, Judge; Judgment, the Last; Retribution; Reward.
  d TG Good Works.
28*a* TG Translated Beings.
  b TG Millennium.
17 1*a* D&C 128:20.
  2*a* Mark 9:2 (2–13); Luke 9:29 (28–36); John 1:14; 2 Pet. 1:16 (16–19). TG Jesus Christ, Glory of; Transfiguration.

3 And, behold, there appeared unto them [a]Moses and [b]Elias talking with him.

4 Then answered Peter, and said unto Jesus, Lord, it is good for us to be here: if thou wilt, let us make here three tabernacles; one for thee, and one for Moses, and one for Elias.

5 While he yet spake, behold, a bright [a]cloud overshadowed them: and behold a [b]voice out of the cloud, which said, This is my [c]beloved [d]Son, in whom I am well pleased; hear ye him.

6 And when the disciples heard it, they fell on their face, and were sore [a]afraid.

7 And Jesus came and touched them, and said, Arise, and be not afraid.

8 And when they had lifted up their eyes, they saw no man, save Jesus only.

9 And as they came down from the mountain, Jesus charged them, saying, Tell the [a]vision to no [b]man, until the Son of man be risen again from the [c]dead.

10 And his disciples asked him, saying, Why then say the scribes that Elias must first come?

11 [a]And Jesus answered and said unto them, Elias truly shall first come, and [b]restore all things.

12 But I say unto you, That Elias is come already, and they knew him not, but have done unto him whatsoever they [a]listed. Likewise shall also the Son of man suffer of them.

13 Then the disciples understood that he spake unto them of John the Baptist.

14 ¶ And when they were come to the multitude, there came to him a *certain* man, kneeling down to him, and saying,

15 Lord, have mercy on my son: for he is lunatic, and sore vexed: for ofttimes he [a]falleth into the fire, and oft into the water.

16 And I brought him to thy disciples, and they could not cure him.

17 Then Jesus answered and said, O [a]faithless and [b]perverse generation, how long shall I be with you? how long shall I suffer you? bring him hither to me.

18 And Jesus rebuked the devil; and he departed out of him: and the child was cured from that very hour.

19 Then came the disciples to Jesus apart, and said, Why could not we cast him out?

20 And Jesus said unto them, Because of your [a]unbelief: for verily I say unto you, If ye have [b]faith as a grain of mustard seed, ye shall say unto this [c]mountain, Remove hence to yonder place; and it shall remove; and nothing shall be [d]impossible unto you.

21 Howbeit this [a]kind goeth not out but by prayer and [b]fasting.

22 ¶ And while they abode in Galilee, Jesus said unto them, The Son of man shall be [a]betrayed into the hands of men:

23 And they shall kill him, and the third day he shall be [a]raised again. And they were exceeding sorry.

24 ¶ And when they were come to Capernaum, they that received tribute *money* came to Peter, and said, Doth not your master pay [a]tribute?

3a D&C 63:21; 110:11.
  TG Priesthood, Keys of;
  Translated Beings.
 b IE Elijah.
  1 Kgs. 17:1; Luke 4:25;
  D&C 110:13 (13–16).
5a Ex. 24:15.
 b TG God, Body of,
  Corporeal Nature.
 c Matt. 3:17; 3 Ne. 11:7;
  JS—H 1:17.
  TG Witness of the Father.
 d TG God; Godhead;
  God the Father, Elohim;

Jesus Christ, Divine
  Sonship.
6a Ex. 3:6; Deut. 5:5.
9a TG Vision.
 b Mark 9:9 (9–13).
 c TG Death.
11a JST Matt. 17:10–14
  (Appendix).
 b D&C 27:6; 77:14;
  110:13–16.
  TG Dispensations; Restoration of the Gospel.
12a GR desired.
15a GR throws himself.

17a TG Unbelief.
 b Deut. 32:5.
20a GR little faith.
  TG Doubt.
 b TG Faith.
 c Ether 12:30; Moses 7:13.
 d TG God, Power of.
21a D&C 84:67 (65–73).
 b TG Fast, Fasting.
22a TG Jesus Christ,
  Betrayal of.
23a TG Jesus Christ,
  Resurrection.
24a D&C 58:21 (21–22).

25 He saith, Yes. And when he was come into the house, Jesus ^aprevented him, saying, What thinkest thou, Simon? of whom do the ^bkings of the earth take custom or tribute? of their own children, or of strangers?

26 Peter saith unto him, Of strangers. Jesus saith unto him, Then are the children free.

27 Notwithstanding, lest we should offend them, go thou to the sea, and cast an hook, and take up the fish that first cometh up; and when thou hast opened his mouth, thou shalt find a piece of ^amoney: that take, and ^bgive unto them for me and thee.

CHAPTER 18

Jesus explains how we are to treat our offending brethren—The Son of Man came to save that which was lost—All of the Twelve receive the keys of the kingdom—Jesus explains why we should forgive.

AT the same time came the disciples unto Jesus, saying, Who is the ^agreatest in the kingdom of heaven?

2 And Jesus called a little child unto him, and set him in the midst of them,

3 And said, Verily I say unto you, Except ye be converted, and become as little ^achildren, ye shall not enter into the kingdom of heaven.

4 Whosoever therefore shall ^ahumble himself as this little ^bchild, the same is greatest in the kingdom of heaven.

5 And whoso shall receive one such little child in my ^aname receiveth me.

6 But whoso shall ^aoffend one of these little ones which believe in me, it were better for him that a millstone were hanged about his neck, and *that* he were drowned in the depth of the sea.

7 ¶ Woe unto the world because of ^aoffences! for it must needs be that offences come; but woe to that man by whom the offence cometh!

8 Wherefore if thy hand or thy foot offend thee, cut them off, and cast *them* from thee: it is better for thee to enter into life halt or maimed, rather than having two hands or two feet to be cast into everlasting fire.

9 And if thine eye offend thee, pluck it out, and cast *it* from thee: it is better for thee to enter into life with one eye, rather than having two eyes to be cast into ^ahell fire.

10 Take heed that ye despise not one of these ^alittle ones; for I say unto you, That in heaven their angels do always behold the face of my Father which is in heaven.

11 For the ^aSon of man is come to ^bsave that which was ^clost.

12 How think ye? if a man have an hundred ^asheep, and one of them be gone astray, doth he not leave the ninety and nine, and goeth into the mountains, and seeketh that which is gone astray?

13 And if so be that he find it, verily I say unto you, he rejoiceth more of that *sheep,* than of the ninety and nine which went not astray.

14 Even so it is not the will of your Father which is in heaven, that one of these ^alittle ones should ^bperish.

25a GR spoke to him first.
  b TG Kings, Earthly.
27a Ex. 30:13; 38:26.
  b TG Citizenship.
18 1a Luke 9:46.
  3a 1 Cor. 14:20;
    Mosiah 3:19.
    TG Children; Salvation
    of Little Children.
  4a TG Humility; Meek.
  b TG Children.
  5a TG Name.
  6a GR cause to stumble.

D&C 121:19 (19–22).
  TG Offense.
7a TG Sin.
9a JST Matt. 18:8–9 . . .
  hellfire. *And a man's
  hand is his friend, and
  his foot also; and a man's
  eye, are they of his own
  household.*
10a TG Children;
  Family, Children, Re-
  sponsibilities toward.
11a TG Jesus Christ,

Son of Man.
  b TG Jesus Christ, Mission
    of; Life, Sanctity of;
    Worth of Souls.
  c JST Matt. 18:11 . . . lost,
    *and to call sinners to
    repentance; but these
    little ones have no need of
    repentance, and I will save
    them.*
12a TG Sheep.
14a TG Children.
  b Mosiah 28:3.

15 ¶ Moreover if thy brother shall ªtrespass against thee, go and ᵇtell him his ᶜfault between thee and him alone: if he shall hear thee, thou hast gained thy brother.

16 But if he will not hear *thee, then* take with thee one or two more, that in the mouth of two or three ªwitnesses every word may be established.

17 And if he shall neglect to hear them, tell *it* unto the ªchurch: but if he ᵇneglect to hear the ᶜchurch, let him be unto thee as an heathen man and a publican.

18 Verily I ªsay unto you, Whatsoever ye shall ªbind on earth shall be bound in heaven: and whatsoever ye shall loose on earth shall be loosed in heaven.

19 Again I say unto you, That if two of you shall ªagree on earth as ᵇtouching any thing that they shall ᶜask, it shall be done for them of my Father which is in heaven.

20 For where two or three are ªgathered ᵇtogether in my ᶜname, there am I in the ᵈmidst of them.

21 ¶ Then came Peter to him, and said, Lord, how oft shall my brother sin against me, and I ªforgive him? till seven times?

22 Jesus saith unto him, I say not unto thee, Until seven times: but, Until ªseventy times seven.

23 ¶ Therefore is the kingdom of heaven likened unto a certain king, which would ªtake account of his ᵇservants.

24 And when he had begun to reckon, one was brought unto him, which owed him ten thousand talents.

25 But forasmuch as he had not to pay, his lord commanded him to be ªsold, and his wife, and children, and all that he had, and payment to be made.

26 The servant therefore fell down, and worshipped him, saying, Lord, have patience with me, and I will pay thee all.

27 Then the lord of that servant was moved with compassion, and loosed him, and forgave him the debt.

28 But the same servant went out, and found one of his fellowservants, which owed him ªan hundred pence: and he laid hands on him, and took *him* by the throat, saying, Pay me that thou owest.

29 And his fellowservant fell down at his feet, and besought him, saying, Have patience with me, and I will pay thee all.

30 And he would not: but went and cast him into prison, till he should pay the debt.

31 So when his fellowservants saw what was done, they were very ªsorry, and came and told unto their lord all that was done.

32 Then his lord, after that he had called him, said unto him, O thou wicked servant, I forgave thee all that ªdebt, because thou desiredst me:

33 ªShouldest not thou also have had ᵇcompassion on thy fellowservant, even as I had ᶜpity on thee?

34 And his lord was wroth, and delivered him to the tormentors, till he should pay all that was due unto him.

35 So likewise shall my heavenly

15*a* TG Offense.
  b TG Reproof.
  c Matt. 5:24 (23–24);
     Luke 17:3 (3–4);
     D&C 42:88 (88–92).
16*a* 2 Ne. 29:8.
     TG Witness.
17*a* 1 Cor. 6:1;
     D&C 42:81.
  b Titus 3:10.
  c TG Church.
18*a* TG Apostles;
     Priesthood, Keys of;

     Sealing.
19*a* TG Common Consent.
  b D&C 6:32; 42:3.
  c TG Prayer.
20*a* TG Church.
  b TG Unity.
  c TG Name.
  d D&C 29:5; 32:3;
     45:59; 49:27.
21*a* TG Forbear.
22*a* D&C 98:40 (39–48).
     TG Patience.
23*a* GR settle accounts with.

     TG Accountability;
     Stewardship.
  b TG Servant.
25*a* 2 Kgs. 4:1.
28*a* IE approximately three
     months' wages of a poor
     working man.
31*a* GR distressed.
32*a* TG Debt.
33*a* TG Ingratitude.
  b TG Compassion;
     Mercy.
  c GR compassion.

Father do also unto you, if ye from your hearts ᵃforgive not every one his brother their trespasses.

CHAPTER 19

Jesus teaches about marriage and divorce—Eternal life is for those who keep the commandments—The Twelve Apostles will judge the house of Israel.

AND it came to pass, *that* when Jesus had finished these sayings, he departed from Galilee, and came into the coasts of Judæa beyond Jordan;

2 And great multitudes followed him; and he healed them there.

3 ¶ The Pharisees also came unto him, tempting him, and saying unto him, Is it lawful for a man to ᵃput away his wife for every cause?

4 And he answered and said unto them, Have ye not read, that he which ᵃmade *them* at the beginning made them male and female,

5 And said, For this cause shall a man leave father and mother, and shall ᵃcleave to his wife: and they twain shall be one flesh?

6 Wherefore they are no more twain, but one flesh. What therefore God hath ᵃjoined together, let not man ᵇput asunder.

7 They say unto him, Why did Moses then command to give a ᵃwriting of ᵇdivorcement, and to put her away?

8 He saith unto them, Moses because of the ᵃhardness of your hearts suffered you to put away your ᵇwives: but from the beginning it was not so.

9 And I say unto you, Whosoever shall put away his wife, except *it* be for ᵃfornication, and shall marry another, committeth ᵇadultery: and whoso marrieth her which is put away doth commit adultery.

10 ¶ His disciples say unto him, If the case of the man be so with *his* wife, it is not good to marry.

11 But he said unto them, All *men* cannot receive this saying, save *they* to whom it is given.

12 For there are some eunuchs, which were so born from *their* mother's womb: and there are some eunuchs, which were made eunuchs of men: and there be eunuchs, which have made themselves eunuchs for the kingdom of heaven's sake. He that is able to receive *it,* let him receive *it.*

13 ¶ Then were there brought unto him little children, that he should put *his* ᵃhands on them, and pray: and the disciples rebuked ᵇthem.

14 But Jesus said, ᵃSuffer little ᵇchildren, and forbid them not, to come unto me: for of such is the kingdom of heaven.

15 And he laid *his* hands on them, and departed thence.

16 ¶ And, behold, one came and said unto him, Good Master, what good thing shall I do, that I may have ᵃeternal life?

17 And he said unto him, Why callest thou me good? *there is* none ᵃgood but one, *that is,* God: but if thou wilt enter into ᵇlife, keep the ᶜcommandments.

18 He saith unto him, Which? Jesus said, Thou shalt do no ᵃmurder, Thou shalt not commit ᵇadultery, Thou shalt not ᶜsteal, Thou shalt not bear ᵈfalse witness,

---

35*a* ᴛɢ Forgive.
19 3*a* ɢʀ divorce.
    4*a* ᴛɢ Man, Physical
      Creation of.
    5*a* ᴛɢ Family, Love
      within;
      Marriage, Celestial.
    6*a* ᴛɢ Marriage, Marry.
    b ɢʀ divide, separate.
    7*a* ɢʀ certificate of
      divorce.
    b ᴛɢ Divorce.

    8*a* ᴛɢ Hardheartedness.
    b ᴛɢ Family, Eternal.
    9*a* ᴛɢ Fornication.
    b ᴛɢ Sexual Immorality.
   13*a* ᴛɢ Hands, Laying
      on of.
    b ᴊsᴛ Matt. 19:13 . . . them,
      saying, There is no need,
      for Jesus hath said, Such
      shall be saved.
   14*a* ɢʀ Allow, Permit.
    b D&C 137:10.

      ᴛɢ Children;
      Salvation of Little
      Children.
   16*a* ᴛɢ Eternity.
   17*a* ᴛɢ God, Perfection of.
    b Prov. 4:22.
    c 1 Ne. 22:31.
   18*a* ᴛɢ Blood, Shedding of;
      Murder.
    b ᴛɢ Adulterer.
    c ᴛɢ Stealing.
    d Prov. 25:18.

19 ^aHonour thy father and *thy* mother: and, Thou shalt ^blove thy ^cneighbour as thyself.

20 The young man saith unto him, All these things have I kept from my youth up: what lack I yet?

21 Jesus said unto him, If thou wilt be ^aperfect, go *and* sell that thou hast, and ^bgive to the ^cpoor, and thou shalt have ^dtreasure in heaven: and come *and* ^efollow me.

22 But when the young man heard that saying, he went away sorrowful: for he had ^agreat possessions.

23 ¶ Then said Jesus unto his disciples, Verily I say unto you, That a ^arich man shall ^bhardly enter into the kingdom of heaven.

24 And again I say unto you, It is easier for a camel to go through the eye of a needle, than for a ^arich man to enter into the kingdom of God.

25 When his disciples heard *it*, they were exceedingly amazed, saying, Who then can be saved?

26 ^aBut Jesus beheld *them,* and said unto them, With men this is impossible; but with God all things are ^bpossible.

27 ¶ Then answered Peter and said unto him, Behold, we have forsaken all, and followed thee; what shall we have therefore?

28 And Jesus said unto them, Verily I say unto you, That ye which have followed me, in the ^aregeneration when the Son of man shall sit in the throne of his glory, ye also shall sit upon twelve thrones, ^bjudging the twelve tribes of Israel.

29 And every one that hath ^aforsaken houses, or brethren, or sisters, or father, or mother, or wife, or children, or lands, for my ^bname's sake, shall receive an hundredfold, and shall inherit ^ceverlasting life.

30 But many *that are* ^afirst shall be last; and the last *shall be* first.

CHAPTER 20

Jesus gives the parable of the laborers in the vineyard—He foretells His crucifixion and resurrection—He came to give His life as a ransom for many.

FOR the kingdom of heaven is like unto a man *that is* an householder, which went out early in the morning to hire ^alabourers into his vineyard.

2 And when he had agreed with the labourers for a penny a day, he sent them into his ^avineyard.

3 And he went out about the third hour, and saw others standing ^aidle in the marketplace,

4 And said unto them; Go ye also into the vineyard, and whatsoever is right I will give you. And they went their way.

5 Again he went out about the sixth and ninth hour, and did likewise.

6 And about the ^aeleventh hour he went out, and found others standing idle, and saith unto them, Why stand ye here all the day idle?

7 They say unto him, Because no man hath hired us. He saith unto them, Go ye also into the vineyard; and whatsoever is right, *that* shall ye receive.

8 So when even was come, the lord

19*a* TG Family, Children, Duties of; Honoring Father and Mother.
 b TG Citizenship; Love.
 c TG Fellowshipping; Neighbor.
21*a* TG Commitment; Perfection.
 b TG Almsgiving; Sacrifice.
 c TG Poor.
 d TG Treasure.
 e Alma 22:15.
22*a* GR many.
23*a* 2 Ne. 9:30; Jacob 2:19 (16–19);

D&C 6:7 (5–7).
 b GR with difficulty.
24*a* Prov. 18:11.
26*a* JST Matt. 19:26 But Jesus beheld *their thoughts,* and said unto them, With men this is impossible; but *if they will forsake all things for my sake,* with God whatsoever things I speak are possible.
 b Job 42:2.
 TG God, Power of.
28*a* JST Matt. 19:28 . . .

resurrection . . .
 b Morm. 3:18 (18–20); D&C 29:12.
 TG Apostles; Judgment, the Last.
29*a* D&C 19:36.
 TG Self-Sacrifice.
 b TG Name.
 c TG Exaltation.
30*a* D&C 29:30.
20 1*a* TG Labor.
 2*a* TG Vineyard of the Lord.
 3*a* Alma 38:12.
 6*a* D&C 33:3 (1–3).

of the vineyard saith unto his steward, Call the *a*labourers, and give them *their* *b*hire, beginning from the last unto the first.

9 And when they came that *were hired* about the eleventh hour, they received every man a penny.

10 But when the first came, they supposed that they should have received more; and they likewise received every man a penny.

11 And when they had received *it,* they murmured against the goodman of the house,

12 Saying, These last have wrought *but* one hour, and thou hast made them equal unto us, which have borne the burden and heat of the day.

13 But he answered one of them, and said, Friend, I do thee no wrong: didst not thou agree with me for a penny?

14 Take *that* thine *is,* and go thy way: I will give unto this last, even as unto thee.

15 Is it not lawful for me to do what I will with mine own? Is thine eye evil, because I am good?

16 So the *a*last shall be first, and the first last: for many be *b*called, but few chosen.

17 ¶ And Jesus going up to Jerusalem took the twelve disciples apart in the way, and said unto them,

18 Behold, we go up to Jerusalem; and the Son of man shall be *a*betrayed unto the chief priests and unto the scribes, and they shall condemn him to *b*death,

19 And shall deliver him to the Gentiles to *a*mock, and to scourge, and to *b*crucify *him:* and the third day he shall *c*rise again.

20 ¶ Then came to him the mother of Zebedee's children with her sons, worshipping *him,* and desiring a certain thing of him.

21 And he said unto her, What wilt thou? She saith unto him, Grant that these my two sons may sit, the one on thy right hand, and the other on the left, in thy kingdom.

22 But Jesus answered and said, Ye know not what ye ask. Are ye able to drink of the cup that I shall drink of, and to be baptized with the baptism that I am baptized with? They say unto him, We are able.

23 And he saith unto them, Ye shall drink indeed of my cup, and be baptized with the baptism that I am baptized with: but to sit on my right hand, and on my left, is not mine to give, but *it shall be given to them* for whom it is prepared of my *a*Father.

24 And when the ten heard *it,* they were moved with indignation against the two brethren.

25 But Jesus called them *unto him,* and said, Ye know that the princes of the Gentiles exercise dominion over them, and they that are great exercise authority upon them.

26 But it shall not be so among you: but whosoever will be *a*great among you, let him be your *b*minister;

27 And whosoever *a*will be chief among you, let him be your *b*servant:

28 Even as the *a*Son of man came not to be ministered unto, but to minister, and to *b*give his life a *c*ransom for many.

29 And as they departed from Jericho, a great multitude followed him.

30 ¶ And, behold, two *a*blind men

8*a* D&C 39:13.
  b TG Wages.
16*a* Jacob 5:63.
  b TG Called of God;
     Foreordination.
18*a* TG Jesus Christ,
     Betrayal of.
  b TG Jesus Christ, Death of.
19*a* TG Mocking.
  b TG Jesus Christ,
     Crucifixion of;
     Martyrdom.

  c TG Jesus Christ,
     Resurrection.
23*a* TG Godhead.
26*a* TG Leadership.
  b TG Priesthood,
     Magnifying Callings
     within.
27*a* GR desires to be.
  b TG Humility;
     Self-Sacrifice; Servant;
     Service.
28*a* Moses 6:57.

  b TG God, Gifts of.
  c D&C 138:2 (2–4).
     TG Jesus Christ,
     Atonement through;
     Jesus Christ, Redeemer;
     Redemption.
30*a* Matt. 9:28 (28–31);
     Mark 10:46 (46–52);
     John 9:1 (1–4);
     Mosiah 3:5;
     3 Ne. 17:9 (7–10);
     D&C 84:69.

sitting by the way side, when they heard that Jesus passed by, cried out, saying, Have mercy on us, O Lord, *thou* Son of David.

31 And the multitude rebuked them, because they should hold their peace: but they cried the more, saying, Have mercy on us, O Lord, *thou* Son of David.

32 And Jesus stood still, and called them, and said, What will ye that I shall do unto you?

33 They say unto him, Lord, that our eyes may be opened.

34 So Jesus had ^acompassion *on them,* and touched their eyes: and immediately their eyes received ^bsight, and they followed him.

CHAPTER 21

Jesus rides in triumph into Jerusalem— He cleanses the temple, curses the fig tree, and discusses authority—He gives the parables of the two sons and the wicked husbandmen.

AND when they drew nigh unto Jerusalem, and were come to Bethphage, unto the mount of Olives, then sent Jesus two disciples,

2 Saying unto them, Go into the village ^aover against you, and straightway ye shall find an ass tied, and a colt with her: loose *them,* and bring *them* unto me.

3 And if any *man* say ought unto you, ye shall say, The Lord hath need of them; and straightway he will send them.

4 All this was done, that it might be fulfilled which was spoken by the prophet, saying,

5 Tell ye the daughter of Sion, Behold, thy ^aKing cometh unto thee, meek, and sitting upon an ass, and a colt the foal of an ass.

6 And the disciples went, and did as Jesus commanded them,

7 ^aAnd brought the ass, and the colt, and put on them their clothes, and they set *him* thereon.

8 And a very great multitude spread their garments in the way; others cut down branches from the trees, and strawed *them* in the way.

9 And the multitudes that went before, and that followed, cried, saying, ^aHosanna to the Son of David: ^bBlessed *is* he that cometh in the name of the Lord; Hosanna in the highest.

10 And when he was come into Jerusalem, all the city was moved, saying, Who is this?

11 And the ^amultitude said, This is Jesus the prophet of Nazareth of Galilee.

12 ¶ And Jesus went into the temple of God, and cast out all them that sold and bought in the temple, and overthrew the tables of the money-changers, and the seats of them that sold doves,

13 And said unto them, It is written, My ^ahouse shall be called the house of ^bprayer; but ye have made it a ^cden of thieves.

14 And the blind and the lame came to him in the temple; and he healed them.

15 And when the chief priests and scribes saw the wonderful things that he did, and the ^achildren crying in the temple, and saying, Hosanna to the Son of David; they were sore displeased,

16 And said unto him, Hearest thou what these say? And Jesus saith unto them, Yea; have ye never read, Out of the mouth of babes and sucklings thou hast perfected praise?

17 ¶ And he left them, and went out of the city into Bethany; and he lodged there.

18 Now in the morning as he returned into the city, he hungered.

34*a* TG Compassion.
  b TG Sight.
21 2*a* GR in front of you.
  5*a* Isa. 62:11;
      Zech. 9:9 (9–11).
  7*a* JST Matt. 21:5 . . . and
      brought the *colt,* and

put on *it* their clothes;
*and Jesus took the colt
and sat* thereon;
and they followed him.
9*a* Luke 19:40.
  b Ps. 118:25–26.
11*a* GR crowds kept saying.

13*a* Ps. 27:4.
    TG Temple.
  b TG Prayer.
  c Jer. 7:11.
15*a* JST Matt. 21:13 . . .
    children *of the kingdom*
    crying . . .

19 And when he saw a fig tree ^ain the way, he came to it, and found nothing thereon, but leaves only, and said unto it, Let no ^bfruit grow on thee henceforward for ever. And ^cpresently the fig tree withered away.

20 And when the disciples saw *it*, they marvelled, saying, How soon is the fig tree withered away!

21 Jesus answered and said unto them, Verily I say unto you, If ye have ^afaith, and ^bdoubt not, ye shall not only do this *which is done* to the fig tree, but also if ye shall say unto this ^cmountain, Be thou removed, and be thou cast into the sea; it shall be done.

22 And all ^athings, whatsoever ye shall ^bask in ^cprayer, believing, ye shall receive.

23 ¶ And when he was come into the temple, the chief priests and the elders of the people came unto him as he was teaching, and said, By what ^aauthority doest thou these things? and who gave thee this authority?

24 And Jesus answered and said unto them, I also will ask you one thing, which if ye tell me, I in like wise will tell you by what ^aauthority I do these things.

25 The baptism of John, whence was it? from heaven, or of men? And they reasoned with themselves, saying, If we shall say, From heaven; he will say unto us, Why did ye not then believe him?

26 But if we shall say, Of men; we fear the people; for all hold John as a ^aprophet.

27 And they answered Jesus, and said, We cannot tell. And he said unto them, Neither tell I you by what authority I do these things.

28 ¶ But what think ye? A *certain* man had two sons; and he came to the first, and said, Son, go ^awork to day in my vineyard.

29 He answered and said, ^aI will not: but afterward he repented, and went.

30 And he came to the second, and said likewise. And he answered and said, I *go*, sir: and ^awent ^bnot.

31 Whether of them twain did the will of *his* father? They say unto him, The first. Jesus saith unto them, Verily I say unto you, That the publicans and the harlots go into the kingdom of God before you.

32 For John came unto you in the way of ^arighteousness, and ye ^bbelieved him not: but the ^cpublicans and the harlots believed him: ^dand ye, when ye had seen *it*, repented not afterward, that ye might believe him.

33 ¶ ^aHear another parable: There was a certain householder, which planted a vineyard, and hedged it round about, and digged a winepress in it, and built a tower, and let it out to ^bhusbandmen, and went into a far country:

34 And when the time of the fruit drew near, he sent his servants to the husbandmen, that they might receive the fruits of it.

19a GR by the road.
  b TG Vineyard of the Lord.
  c GR immediately; see also Mark 11:20–24.
21a TG Faith.
  b TG Doubt.
  c TG God, Power of.
22a TG Blessing.
  b 3 Ne. 18:20; Morm. 9:21.
  c TG Prayer.
23a TG Authority.
24a TG Jesus Christ, Authority of.
26a Matt. 11:9; 14:5;

Luke 20:6.
28a Jacob 5:71 (70–71).
29a GR I don't desire to go.
30a TG Hypocrisy.
  b D&C 41:5.
32a TG Righteousness.
  b TG Unbelief.
  c Luke 3:12; 7:29 (28–30).
  d JST Matt. 21:32–34 . . . and ye, *afterward*, when ye had seen *me*, repented not, that ye might believe him. *For he that believed not John concerning me, cannot*

believe me, except he first repent. And except ye repent, the preaching of John shall condemn you in the day of judgment . . .
33a JST Matt. 21:34–35 . . . *And again*, hear another parable; *for unto you that believe not, I speak in parables; that your unrighteousness may be rewarded unto you. Behold*, there was . . .
  b TG Stewardship; Watchman.

35 And the husbandmen took his ^aservants, and ^bbeat one, and killed another, and stoned another.

36 Again, he sent other servants more than the first: and they did unto them likewise.

37 But last of all he sent unto them his son, saying, They will reverence my son.

38 But when the husbandmen saw the son, they said among themselves, This is the ^aheir; come, let us kill him, and let us seize on his inheritance.

39 And they caught him, and cast *him* out of the vineyard, and slew *him*.

40 When the lord therefore of the vineyard cometh, what will he do unto those husbandmen?

41 They say unto him, He will miserably destroy those wicked men, and will let out *his* ^avineyard unto other husbandmen, which shall render him the fruits in their seasons.

42 Jesus saith unto them, Did ye never read in the scriptures, The ^astone which the builders ^brejected, the same is become the head of the ^ccorner: this is the Lord's doing, and it is marvellous in our eyes?

43 Therefore say I unto you, The ^akingdom of God shall be ^btaken from you, and ^cgiven to a ^dnation bringing forth the fruits thereof.

44 ^aAnd whosoever shall fall on this stone shall be broken: but on whomsoever it shall fall, it will grind him to powder.

45 ^aAnd when the chief priests and Pharisees had heard his parables, they perceived that he spake of them.

46 But when they sought to lay hands on him, they feared the mul-titude, because they took him for a prophet.

CHAPTER 22

Jesus gives the parable of the marriage of the king's son—Pay tribute to Cæsar and to God—Worldly marriages endure in this life only—The first commandment is to love the Lord—Jesus asks, What think ye of Christ?

AND Jesus answered and spake unto them again by parables, and said,

2 The kingdom of heaven is like unto a certain king, which ^amade a ^bmarriage for his son,

3 And sent forth his servants to call them that were bidden to the wedding: and ^athey would not come.

4 Again, he sent forth other servants, saying, Tell them which are bidden, Behold, I have prepared my dinner: my oxen and *my* fatlings *are* killed, and all things *are* ready: come unto the marriage.

5 But they made light of *it,* and went their ways, one to his farm, another to his merchandise:

6 And the remnant took his servants, and entreated *them* spitefully, and slew *them.*

7 But when the king heard *thereof,* he was wroth: and he sent forth his armies, and destroyed those murderers, and burned up their city.

8 Then saith he to his servants, The wedding is ready, but they which were bidden were not worthy.

9 Go ye therefore into the highways, and as many as ye shall find, bid to the marriage.

10 So those servants went out into the highways, and ^agathered together all as many as they found,

35*a* Matt. 23:30 (29–38).
  b TG Prophets,
     Rejection of.
38*a* John 11:53 (47–53);
     Heb. 1:2.
41*a* TG Vineyard of the Lord.
42*a* TG Cornerstone;
     Jesus Christ, Prophecies
     about;
     Rock.
  b Luke 9:22;
     1 Pet. 2:7.

  c Zech. 10:4.
43*a* Isa. 5:5 (1–7);
     Luke 14:24 (21–24);
     Acts 13:46;
     1 Ne. 13:26;
     D&C 90:3 (1–5).
  b Dan. 2:44.
  c Isa. 48:11.
  d TG Nations.
44*a* Isa. 8:14 (13–15);
     Luke 2:34;
     Rom. 9:32 (28–33);

     1 Pet. 2:8 (6–8).
45*a* JST Matt. 21:47–56
     (Appendix).
22 2*a* GR gave a wedding
     celebration.
  b Luke 5:34;
     Rev. 19:7 (7–9); 21:2;
     D&C 65:3.
  3*a* GR they did not want
     to come.
10*a* Matt. 13:47 (47–53).

both bad and good: and the wedding was furnished with guests.

11 ¶ And when the king came in to see the guests, he saw there a man which had not on a wedding *garment:

12 And he saith unto him, Friend, how camest thou in hither not having a wedding garment? And he was speechless.

13 Then said the king to the servants, Bind him hand and foot, and take him away, and cast *him* into *outer darkness; there shall be weeping and gnashing of teeth.

14 For many are *called, but few *are* *chosen.

15 ¶ Then went the Pharisees, and took counsel how they might *entangle him in *his* talk.

16 And they sent out unto him their disciples with the Herodians, saying, Master, we know that thou art true, and teachest the way of God in truth, *neither carest thou for any *man:* for thou *regardest not the person of men.

17 Tell us therefore, What thinkest thou? Is it *lawful to give tribute unto Cæsar, or not?

18 But Jesus perceived their wickedness, and said, Why *tempt ye me, *ye* hypocrites?

19 Shew me the tribute money. And they brought unto him a penny.

20 And he saith unto them, Whose *is* this image and superscription?

21 They say unto him, Cæsar's. Then saith he unto them, *Render therefore unto *Cæsar the things which are Cæsar's; and unto God the things that are God's.

22 When they had heard *these*

words, they marvelled, and left him, and went their way.

23 ¶ The same day came to him the *Sadducees, which say that there is no resurrection, and asked him,

24 Saying, Master, Moses said, If a man die, having no children, his *brother shall *marry his wife, and raise up seed unto his brother.

25 Now there were with us seven brethren: and the first, when he had married a wife, deceased, and, having no issue, left his wife unto his brother:

26 Likewise the second also, and the third, unto the seventh.

27 And last of all the woman died also.

28 Therefore in the resurrection whose wife shall she be of the seven? for they all had her.

29 Jesus answered and said unto them, Ye do err, not knowing the *scriptures, nor the *power of God.

30 For in the *resurrection they neither *marry, nor are given in marriage, but are as the *angels of God in heaven.

31 But as touching the resurrection of the dead, have ye not read that which was spoken unto you by God, saying,

32 I am the *God of Abraham, and the God of Isaac, and the God of Jacob? God is not the God of the dead, but of the living.

33 And when the multitude heard *this,* they were astonished at his doctrine.

34 ¶ But when the Pharisees had heard that he had put the Sadducees to silence, they were gathered together.

11a Rev. 19:8.
13a Matt. 8:12 (11–12); D&C 77:8; 133:72 (71–73).
14a D&C 121:34 (34–40).
  b JST Matt. 22:14 . . . chosen; *wherefore all do not have on the wedding garment.*
15a Mark 12:13 (13–17); Luke 11:54; 20:20 (19–26).
16a IE you court no man's favor.

  b Prov. 24:23.
17a D&C 58:22 (20–23). TG Test.
18a GR are you testing. TG Test.
21a TG Citizenship.
  b TG Governments.
23a Matt. 16:12 (1, 6, 11–12); Acts 23:8.
24a Deut. 25:5; Mark 12:19.
  b Ruth 3:13.
29a D&C 138:1 (1–4). TG Jesus Christ,

Teaching Mode of; Scriptures, Study of.
  b TG God, Power of.
30a TG Resurrection.
  b TG Marriage, Marry; Marriage, Temporal.
  c D&C 131:4 (1–4); 132:16 (15–17).
32a Gen. 32:9; 1 Ne. 19:10; D&C 136:21.

35 Then one of them, *which was a lawyer*, asked *him a question*, ^atempting him, and saying,

36 Master, which *is* the great commandment in the law?

37 Jesus said unto him, Thou shalt ^alove the Lord thy God with all thy ^bheart, and with all thy soul, and with all thy ^cmind.

38 This is the first and great ^acommandment.

39 And the second *is* like unto it, Thou shalt ^alove thy neighbour as thyself.

40 On these two commandments hang all the ^alaw and the prophets.

41 ¶ While the Pharisees were gathered together, Jesus asked them,

42 Saying, What think ye of Christ? whose son is he? They say unto him, *The Son* of ^aDavid.

43 He saith unto them, How then doth David in spirit call him Lord, saying,

44 The Lord said unto my Lord, Sit thou on my right hand, till I make thine enemies thy footstool?

45 If David then call him Lord, how is he his son?

46 And no man was able to answer him a word, neither ^adurst any *man* from that day forth ask him any more *questions*.

CHAPTER 23

Jesus pronounces woes upon the scribes and Pharisees—They will be held responsible for killing the prophets—

They will not escape the damnation of hell.

THEN spake Jesus to the multitude, and to his disciples,

2 Saying, The ^ascribes and the Pharisees sit in Moses' ^bseat:

3 All therefore whatsoever they bid you observe, *that* observe and do; but do not ye after their works: for they say, and do not.

4 For they bind heavy burdens and grievous to be borne, and lay *them* on men's shoulders; but they *themselves* will not move them with one of their fingers.

5 But all their works they do for to be seen of men: they ^amake broad their ^bphylacteries, and enlarge the ^cborders of their garments,

6 And love the ^auppermost rooms at feasts, and the chief seats in the synagogues,

7 And greetings in the markets, and to be called of men, Rabbi, ^aRabbi.

8 But be not ye called ^aRabbi: for one is your ^bMaster, *even* Christ; and all ye are brethren.

9 ^aAnd call no *man* your father upon the earth: for one is your Father, which is in heaven.

10 Neither be ye called masters: for one is your Master, ^aeven Christ.

11 But he that is ^agreatest among you shall be your ^bservant.

12 And whosoever shall ^aexalt himself shall be ^babased; and he that shall ^chumble himself shall be exalted.

35a TG Test.
37a TG Dedication; God, Love of; Love.
  b TG Heart.
  c TG Mind.
38a TG Commandments of God.
39a TG Love.
40a Mark 12:33 (13–37); Rom. 13:10 (8–10). TG Law of Moses.
42a TG Jesus Christ, Davidic Descent of.
46a GR dared.
23 2a TG Scribe.
  b The Greek word connotes a chair of

judgment and instruction.
5a GR enlarge their phylacteries.
  b Ex. 13:9 (9, 16); Deut. 6:8.
  c Num. 15:38.
6a Luke 11:43; 14:7.
7a JST Matt. 23:4 . . . Rabbi, (which is master).
8a Hebrew and Aramaic: Master, or, My master.
  b Col. 4:1 (1–11).
9a JST Matt. 23:6 And call no *one* your *creator* upon the earth, *or your heavenly Father; for one is your creator and*

heavenly Father, *even he who is in heaven.*
10a JST Matt. 23:7 . . . even *he whom your heavenly Father sent, which is Christ; for he hath sent him among you that ye might have life.*
11a Mark 10:44 (42–45); Luke 22:24 (24–30). TG Leadership.
  b TG Servant.
12a TG Haughtiness; Pride.
  b D&C 49:10.
  c James 1:9 (8–16); D&C 112:3; 124:114. TG Humility.

13 ¶ But woe unto you, ᵃscribes and ᵇPharisees, ᶜhypocrites! for ye shut up the kingdom of heaven against men: for ye neither go in *yourselves*, neither suffer ye them that are entering to go in.

14 Woe unto you, scribes and Pharisees, hypocrites! for ye ᵃdevour widows' houses, and for a pretence make long prayer: therefore ye shall receive the greater ᵇdamnation.

15 Woe unto you, scribes and Pharisees, hypocrites! for ye compass sea and land to make one proselyte, and when he is made, ye make him twofold more the child of hell ᵃthan yourselves.

16 Woe unto you, *ye* ᵃblind guides, which say, Whosoever shall swear by the temple, it is nothing; but whosoever shall swear by the gold of the temple, he is a debtor!

17 *Ye* fools and blind: for whether is greater, the gold, or the temple that sanctifieth the gold?

18 And, Whosoever shall swear by the altar, it is nothing; but whosoever sweareth by the gift that is upon it, he is guilty.

19 *Ye* fools and blind: for whether *is* greater, the gift, or the altar that sanctifieth the gift?

20 Whoso therefore shall swear by the altar, sweareth by it, and by all things thereon.

21 And whoso shall swear by the temple, sweareth by it, and by him that dwelleth therein.

22 And he that shall swear by heaven, sweareth by the throne of God, and by him that sitteth thereon.

23 Woe unto you, scribes and Pharisees, ᵃhypocrites! for ye pay ᵇtithe of mint and ᶜanise and cummin, and have ᵈomitted the weightier *matters* of the law, ᵉjudgment, ᶠmercy, and faith: these ought ye to have done, and not to leave the other undone.

24 *Ye* blind guides, which strain at a gnat, and swallow a ᵃcamel.

25 Woe unto you, scribes and Pharisees, hypocrites! for ye make clean the outside of the cup and of the platter, but within they are full of ᵃextortion and ᵇexcess.

26 *Thou* blind Pharisee, ᵃcleanse first that *which is* within the cup and platter, that the outside of them may be clean also.

27 Woe unto you, scribes and Pharisees, hypocrites! for ye are like unto ᵃwhited ᵇsepulchres, which indeed appear ᶜbeautiful outward, but are within full of dead *men's* bones, and of all ᵈuncleanness.

28 Even so ye also outwardly appear ᵃrighteous unto men, but within ye are full of ᵇhypocrisy and iniquity.

29 Woe unto you, scribes and Pharisees, hypocrites! because ye build the tombs of the prophets, and garnish the sepulchres of the righteous,

30 And say, If we had been in the days of our fathers, we would not have been partakers with them in the blood of the ᵃprophets.

31 Wherefore ye be witnesses unto yourselves, that ye are the children of them which ᵃkilled the ᵇprophets.

32 Fill ye up then the ᵃmeasure of your ᵇfathers.

13a TG Scribe.
  b TG Apostasy of Israel.
  c GR actors.
14a TG Injustice.
  b TG Damnation.
15a JST Matt. 23:12 . . . than
    he was before, like unto
    yourselves.
16a TG Spiritual Blindness.
23a TG Hypocrisy.
  b TG Tithing.
  c GR dill.
  d GR abandoned.
  e TG Justice.

f TG Mercy.
24a JST Matt. 23:21 . . .
    camel; *who make
    yourselves appear unto
    men that ye would not
    commit the least sin,
    and yet ye yourselves,
    transgress the whole law.*
25a GR rapacity, greediness.
  b GR self-indulgence,
    lack of self-control.
    TG Temperance.
26a TG Purification;
    Wash.

27a GR whitewashed tombs.
    Acts 23:3.
  b Luke 11:44.
  c TG Beauty.
  d TG Cleanliness.
28a D&C 10:37.
  b TG Guile.
30a Matt. 21:35 (33–42).
31a TG Martyrdom.
  b TG Prophets,
    Rejection of.
32a Judg. 2:19.
  b Acts 7:51 (51–52);
    Hel. 13:25 (25–29).

33 Ye serpents, ye *a*generation of vipers, how can ye escape the *b*damnation of hell?

34 ¶ Wherefore, behold, I send unto you *a*prophets, and wise men, and *b*scribes: and *some* of them ye shall kill and crucify; and *some* of them shall ye scourge in your synagogues, and persecute *them* from city to city:

35 That upon you may come all the righteous *a*blood shed upon the earth, from the blood of *b*righteous Abel unto the blood of Zacharias son of Barachias, whom ye slew between the *c*temple and the altar.

36 Verily I say unto you, All these things shall come upon this *a*generation.

37 O *a*Jerusalem, Jerusalem, *thou* that *b*killest the prophets, and stonest them which are sent unto thee, how often *c*would I have *d*gathered thy children together, even as a hen gathereth her chickens under *her* wings, and ye *e*would not!

38 Behold, your house is left unto you *a*desolate.

39 *a*For I say unto you, Ye shall not see me henceforth, till ye shall say, *b*Blessed *is* he that cometh in the name of the Lord.

CHAPTER 24

Jesus foretells the doom of Jerusalem and the destruction of the temple—Great calamities will precede His Second Coming—He gives the parable of the fig tree.

AND Jesus went out, and departed from the temple: and his disciples came to *him* for to *a*shew him the buildings of the *b*temple.

2 And Jesus said unto them, *a*See ye not all these things? verily I say unto you, There shall not be left here one *b*stone upon another, that shall not be thrown down.

3 ¶ And as he sat upon the mount of Olives, the disciples came unto him privately, saying, Tell us, when shall these things be? and what *shall* be the *a*sign of thy coming, and of the end of the *b*world?

4 And Jesus answered and said unto them, Take heed that no man *a*deceive you.

5 For many shall come in my *a*name, saying, I am *b*Christ; and shall *c*deceive many.

6 And ye shall hear of *a*wars and rumours of wars: see that ye be not *b*troubled: for all *these things* must come to pass, but the end is not yet.

7 For *a*nation shall rise against nation, and kingdom against kingdom: and there shall be *b*famines, and pestilences, and earthquakes, in divers places.

8 All these *are* the beginning of *a*sorrows.

33*a* Matt. 3:7; 12:34.
  b TG Damnation;
    Punish.
34*a* D&C 1:38; 43:25.
  b TG Scribe.
35*a* TG Martyrdom.
  b TG Righteousness.
  c Luke 11:51.
36*a* JST Matt. 23:33–35
    ... generation. Ye
    bear testimony against
    your fathers, when ye,
    yourselves, are partakers
    of the same wickedness.
    Behold your fathers did
    it through ignorance, but
    ye do not; wherefore, their
    sins shall be upon your
    heads.
37*a* TG Jerusalem.
  b TG Prophets,
    Rejection of.

  c GR have I desired to
    gather.
  d 3 Ne. 10:6 (4–6);
    D&C 29:2;
    43:24 (24–25).
    TG Israel, Gathering of.
  e D&C 138:21 (21–22).
    TG Rebellion;
    Stubbornness.
38*a* Ps. 69:25;
    Jer. 12:7; 22:5.
39*a* JS—M 1:1.
  b Ps. 118:26.
24 1*a* JS—M 1:2.
  b D&C 45:20 (15–21).
    TG Temple.
 2*a* D&C 45:18.
  b Luke 19:44 (41–44);
    JS—M 1:3 (1–55).
 3*a* Luke 21:7 (7–36);
    D&C 45:16 (16–75).
  b JS—M 1:4 adds "or

the destruction of the
wicked, which is the end
of the world."
    D&C 45:22.
    TG Last Days;
    World, End of.
 4*a* Col. 2:18 (16–23);
    D&C 49:23 (22–24).
    TG Lying.
 5*a* TG Name.
  b TG False Christs.
  c Mark 13:6.
    TG Apostasy of the Early
    Christian Church.
 6*a* TG War.
  b GR frightened.
    D&C 45:35 (34–35).
 7*a* TG Last Days;
    Nations.
  b TG Drought.
 8*a* TG Sorrow.

9 Then shall they deliver you up to be afflicted, and shall *a*kill you: and ye shall be *b*hated of all nations *c*for my name's sake.

10 And then shall many be *a*offended, and shall betray one another, and shall hate one another.

11 And many *a*false prophets shall rise, and shall deceive many.

12 And because *a*iniquity shall abound, the love of many shall wax *b*cold.

13 But he that shall *a*endure unto the end, the same shall be saved.

14 And this *a*gospel of the *b*kingdom shall be preached in all the world for a witness unto all nations; and then shall the *c*end come.

15 When ye therefore shall see the *a*abomination of desolation, spoken of by Daniel the prophet, stand in the *b*holy place, (whoso readeth, let him *c*understand:)

16 Then let them which be in Judæa *a*flee into the mountains:

17 Let him which is on the housetop not come down to take any thing out of his house:

18 Neither let him which is in the field return back to take his clothes.

19 And *a*woe unto them that are with child, and to them that give suck in those days!

20 But pray ye that your flight be not in the winter, neither on the sabbath day:

21 For then shall be great *a*trib-ulation, such as was not since the beginning of the world to this time, no, nor ever shall be.

22 And except those days should be shortened, there should no flesh be saved: but for the elect's sake those *a*days shall be shortened.

23 Then if any man shall say unto you, Lo, here *is* Christ, or there; *a*believe *it* not.

24 For there shall arise *a*false *b*Christs, and *c*false prophets, and shall shew great *d*signs and wonders; insomuch that, if *it were* possible, they shall *e*deceive the very *f*elect.

25 Behold, I have told you before.

26 Wherefore if they shall say unto you, Behold, he is in the desert; go not forth: behold, *he is* in the *a*secret chambers; believe *it* not.

27 For as the *a*lightning cometh out of the *b*east, and shineth even unto the west; so shall also the coming of the Son of man be.

28 For wheresoever the carcase is, there will the eagles be *a*gathered together.

29 ¶ Immediately after the tribulation of those *a*days shall the *b*sun be *c*darkened, and the moon shall not give her light, and the stars shall fall from heaven, and the powers of the heavens shall be shaken:

30 And then shall appear the *a*sign of the Son of man in *b*heaven: and then shall all the tribes of the earth *c*mourn, and they shall see the *d*Son

---

9a TG Martyrdom.
  b TG Persecution.
  c GR on account of my name.
10a Isa. 8:14 (14–15); Matt. 11:6.
11a TG Apostasy of the Early Christian Church; False Prophets.
12a D&C 45:27.
  b TG Apostasy of Individuals.
13a TG Perseverance; Steadfastness.
14a TG Gospel; Restoration of the Gospel.
  b TG Kingdom of God, on Earth.
  c D&C 29:23; 43:31.

15a TG Abomination of Desolation.
  b TG Jerusalem.
  c D&C 57:9.
16a TG Israel, Scattering of.
19a Luke 23:29.
21a JS—M 1:18.
  TG Tribulation.
22a TG Time.
23a D&C 49:22.
24a TG Apostasy of the Early Christian Church.
  b TG False Christs.
  c TG False Prophets.
  d Rev. 16:14 (13–14). TG Signs; Sign Seekers.
  e Rev. 13:14 (11–18). TG Deceit.
  f D&C 29:7 (7–8); 84:34 (33–34).

26a D&C 49:22 (22–23).
27a D&C 45:36 (36–44).
  b Ezek. 43:2.
28a D&C 29:8 (7–8); JS—M 1:27.
29a TG Day of the Lord.
  b TG Astronomy.
  c Isa. 13:10; Ezek. 32:7; 34:12 (11–19); Joel 2:10; Rev. 6:12.
30a D&C 88:93. TG Jesus Christ, Second Coming.
  b TG Heaven.
  c Zech. 12:12; Rev. 1:7 (7–8).
  d TG Jesus Christ, Son of Man.

of man coming in the clouds of heaven with *e*power and great *f*glory.

31 And he shall send his *a*angels with a great sound of a *b*trumpet, and they shall gather together his *c*elect from the four winds, from one end of *d*heaven to the other.

32 Now learn a parable of the *a*fig tree; When his branch is yet tender, and putteth forth leaves, ye know that summer *is* nigh:

33 So likewise ye, when ye shall see all these things, know that *a*it is near, *even* at the *b*doors.

34 Verily I say unto you, This *a*generation shall not pass, till all these *b*things be *c*fulfilled.

35 Heaven and earth shall *a*pass away, but my *b*words shall not *c*pass away.

36 ¶ But of that *a*day and *b*hour knoweth no *man*, no, not the *c*angels of heaven, but my Father only.

37 But as the days of *a*Noe *were*, so shall also the coming of the Son of man be.

38 For as in the days that were before the *a*flood they were eating and drinking, marrying and giving in marriage, until the day that Noe entered into the ark,

39 And knew not until the flood came, and took them all away; so shall also the coming of the Son of man be.

40 Then shall two be in the field; the one shall be taken, and the other left.

41 Two *women shall be* grinding at the mill; the one shall be taken, and the other left.

42 ¶ *a*Watch therefore: for ye know not what hour your Lord doth come.

43 But know this, that if the goodman of the house had known in what watch the thief would come, he would have watched, and would not have suffered his house to be *a*broken up.

44 Therefore be ye also *a*ready: for in such a *b*hour *c*as ye think not the Son of man cometh.

45 Who then is a *a*faithful and *b*wise *c*servant, whom his lord hath made ruler over his household, to give them meat in due season?

46 Blessed *is* that *a*servant, whom his lord when he cometh shall find so doing.

47 Verily I say unto you, That he shall make him ruler over all his goods.

48 But and if that evil servant shall say in his heart, My lord *a*delayeth his coming;

49 And shall begin to smite *his* fellowservants, and to eat and drink with the drunken;

50 The lord of that servant shall come in a day when he looketh not for *him*, and in an hour that he is not aware of,

51 And shall cut him asunder, and appoint *him* his portion with the hypocrites: there shall be weeping and gnashing of teeth.

CHAPTER 25

Jesus gives the parables of the ten virgins, the talents, and the sheep and the goats.

30*e* TG Jesus Christ, Power of.
   f TG Jesus Christ, Glory of.
31*a* TG Angels.
   b Isa. 27:13;
      1 Thes. 4:16;
      D&C 49:23 (23–28).
   c Ps. 147:2 (1–20);
      JS—M 1:27.
      TG Election.
   d Deut. 30:4.
32*a* D&C 35:16.
33*a* GR He is near.
   b D&C 45:63.
34*a* JS—M 1:34 (31–35).
   b Isa. 10:22 (21–34);
      D&C 1:7.

   c D&C 45:21.
35*a* D&C 29:23 (22–29).
   b D&C 1:38 (37–39).
   c Josh. 21:45;
      1 Kgs. 8:56;
      D&C 45:23.
36*a* D&C 39:21; 49:7.
   b TG Jesus Christ, Second Coming.
   c TG Angels.
37*a* IE Noah.
      Gen. 7:1;
      Luke 17:27 (26–27);
      3 Ne. 22:9.
38*a* TG Worldliness.
42*a* TG Millennium,

Preparing a People for; Watch.
43*a* Ex. 22:2 (1–4).
44*a* TG Procrastination.
   b Luke 12:40;
      D&C 45:2; 51:20.
   c GR when you do not expect Him.
45*a* D&C 51:19.
   b D&C 72:4.
   c D&C 58:26 (26–29);
      84:86 (85–86);
      107:100 (99–100).
      TG Stewardship.
46*a* TG Servant.
48*a* D&C 45:26.

*a*THEN shall the kingdom of heaven be likened unto ten *b*virgins, which took their *c*lamps, and went forth to meet the bridegroom.

2 And five of them were wise, and five *were* foolish.

3 They that *were* foolish took their lamps, and took no oil with them:

4 But the wise took oil in their vessels with their lamps.

5 While the bridegroom tarried, they all *a*slumbered and *b*slept.

6 And at midnight there was a cry made, Behold, the *a*bridegroom cometh; go ye out to meet him.

7 Then all those virgins arose, and trimmed their *a*lamps.

8 And the foolish said unto the wise, Give us of your oil; for our lamps *a*are gone out.

9 But the wise answered, saying, *Not so;* lest there be not enough for us and you: but go ye rather to them that sell, and buy for yourselves.

10 And while they went to buy, the bridegroom came; and they that were *a*ready went in with him to the marriage: and the door was *b*shut.

11 Afterward came also the other virgins, saying, Lord, Lord, open to us.

12 But he answered and said, *a*Verily I say unto you, I *b*know you not.

13 *a*Watch therefore, for ye know neither the day nor the hour wherein the Son of man cometh.

14 ¶ For *the kingdom of heaven is* as a man travelling into a far country, *who* called his own servants, and delivered unto them his goods.

15 And unto one he *a*gave five *b*talents, to another two, and to another one; to every man according to his several ability; and straightway took his journey.

16 Then he that had received the five talents went and traded with the same, and made *them* other five talents.

17 And likewise he that *had received* two, he also gained other two.

18 But he that had received one went and digged in the earth, and hid his lord's money.

19 After a long time the lord of those servants cometh, and *a*reckoneth with them.

20 And so he that had received five talents came and brought other five talents, saying, Lord, thou *a*deliveredst unto me five talents: behold, I have gained beside them five talents more.

21 His lord said unto him, Well done, *thou* good and faithful *a*servant: thou hast been *b*faithful over a few things, I will make thee *c*ruler over many things: enter thou into the *d*joy of thy lord.

22 He also that had received two talents came and said, Lord, thou deliveredst unto me two talents: behold, I have gained two other talents beside them.

23 His lord said unto him, Well done, good and *a*faithful servant; thou hast been faithful over a few things, I will make thee ruler over many things: enter thou into the joy of thy lord.

24 Then he which had received the one talent came and said, Lord, I knew thee that thou art an *a*hard man, reaping where thou hast not sown, and gathering where thou hast not strawed:

25 And I was *a*afraid, and went and

---

25 1*a* JST Matt. 25:1 *And then, at that day, before the Son of man comes,* the kingdom of . . .
  b D&C 45:56 (56–59); 63:54.
  c Lev. 24:2.
5*a* D&C 35:21.
  b TG Sleep.
6*a* D&C 88:92; 133:10.
7*a* Luke 12:35; D&C 33:17.
8*a* GR are going out.
10*a* TG Millennium,

Preparing a People for; Procrastination.
  b GR locked.
12*a* JST Matt. 25:11 . . . Verily I say unto you, Ye know *me* not.
  b Matt. 7:23.
13*a* TG Watch.
15*a* Mark 4:24 (23–25).
  b TG Talents; Work, Value of.
19*a* GR settled accounts. D&C 72:3 (3–5).

20*a* GR entrustedst.
21*a* TG Servant.
  b Luke 16:10; D&C 132:53.
  c Rev. 3:21; D&C 132:20.
  TG Leadership; Stewardship.
  d TG Joy.
23*a* D&C 52:13. TG Trustworthiness.
24*a* GR strict.
25*a* D&C 60:2 (2–3, 13).

hid thy talent in the earth: lo, *there* thou hast *that is* thine.

26 His lord answered and said unto him, *Thou* wicked and ^aslothful servant, thou knewest that I ^breap where I sowed not, and gather where I have not strawed:

27 Thou oughtest therefore to have put my money to the exchangers, and *then* at my coming I should have received mine own with ^ausury.

28 Take therefore the ^atalent from him, and give *it* unto him which hath ten talents.

29 For unto every one that hath shall be ^agiven, and he shall have ^babundance: but from him that hath not shall be ^ctaken away even that which he hath.

30 And cast ye the unprofitable servant into outer darkness: there shall be weeping and gnashing of teeth.

31 ¶ When the ^aSon of man shall come in his ^bglory, and all the holy angels with him, then shall he sit upon the throne of his glory:

32 And before him shall be gathered all ^anations: and he shall ^bseparate them one from another, as a ^cshepherd divideth *his* ^dsheep from the goats:

33 And he shall set the sheep on his ^aright hand, but the goats on the left.

34 Then shall the King say unto them on his ^aright hand, Come, ye ^bblessed of my Father, ^cinherit the ^dkingdom prepared for you from the foundation of the world:

35 For I was an ^ahungred, and ye ^bgave me meat: I was thirsty, and ye gave me drink: I was a ^cstranger, and ye took me in:

36 Naked, and ye clothed me: I was sick, and ye ^avisited me: I was in ^bprison, and ye came unto me.

37 Then shall the righteous answer him, saying, Lord, when saw we thee an hungred, and fed *thee?* or thirsty, and gave *thee* drink?

38 When saw we thee a stranger, and took *thee* in? or naked, and clothed *thee?*

39 Or when saw we thee ^asick, or in prison, and came unto thee?

40 And the King shall answer and say unto them, Verily I say unto you, Inasmuch as ye have ^adone *it* unto one of the ^bleast of these my ^cbrethren, ye have done *it* unto me.

41 Then shall he say also unto them on the ^aleft hand, ^bDepart from me, ye ^ccursed, into everlasting ^dfire, ^eprepared for the devil and his angels:

42 For I was an ^ahungred, and ye gave me no meat: I was thirsty, and ye gave me no drink:

43 I was a stranger, and ye took me not in: naked, and ye clothed me not: sick, and in prison, and ye visited me not.

44 Then shall they also answer him, saying, Lord, when saw we thee an hungred, or athirst, or a stranger, or naked, or sick, or in prison, and did not minister unto thee?

45 Then shall he answer them, saying, Verily I say unto you, Inasmuch

---

26a TG Laziness.
  b TG Harvest.
27a TG Usury.
28a D&C 82:18.
29a Matt. 13:12.
  b D&C 82:3.
  c Alma 12:11 (9–11);
    D&C 1:33; 60:3 (2–3).
31a TG Jesus Christ, Son
    of Man.
  b TG Jesus Christ, Second
    Coming;
    Millennium.
32a TG Nations.
  b TG Jesus Christ, Judge;
    Judgment, the Last;
    Separation.

  c TG Shepherd.
  d TG Sheep.
33a D&C 29:27.
34a Moses 7:56 (56–57).
  b TG Blessing.
  c TG Exaltation;
    Reward.
  d Luke 12:32;
    Rev. 22:5.
35a TG Poor.
  b TG Almsgiving;
    Generosity.
  c TG Hospitality;
    Stranger.
36a GR took care of,
    cared for.
  b Heb. 13:3.

39a TG Health.
40a Mosiah 2:17;
    D&C 42:38.
  b TG Good Works;
    Neighbor; Poor.
  c TG Welfare.
41a D&C 19:5.
  b D&C 29:28.
  c GR who have come
    under a curse. (See also
    2 Ne. 9:16;
    D&C 76:31–38, 43–48.)
    TG Curse.
  d TG Hell.
  e GR which has been
    prepared.
42a Job 22:7 (6–7).

as ye did *it* not to one of the ^aleast of these, ye did *it* not to me.

46 And these shall go away into ^aeverlasting ^bpunishment: but the ^crighteous into ^dlife ^eeternal.

CHAPTER 26

Jesus is anointed—He keeps the Passover and institutes the sacrament—He suffers in Gethsemane, is betrayed by Judas, and is taken before Caiaphas—Peter denies that he knows Jesus.

AND it came to pass, when Jesus had finished all these sayings, he said unto his disciples,

2 Ye know that after two days is *the feast of* the ^apassover, and the Son of man is ^bbetrayed to be ^ccrucified.

3 Then assembled together the chief priests, and the scribes, and the elders of the people, unto the palace of the high priest, who was called ^aCaiaphas,

4 And ^aconsulted that they might take Jesus by ^bsubtilty, and ^ckill *him.*

5 But they said, Not on the feast *day,* lest there be an ^auproar among the people.

6 ¶ Now when Jesus was in Bethany, in the house of Simon the leper,

7 There came unto him a woman having an alabaster box of very precious ^aointment, and poured it on his head, as he sat *at meat.*

8 But when his disciples saw *it,* they had indignation, saying, To what purpose *is* this ^awaste?

9 For this ointment might have been sold for much, and given to the poor.

10 When Jesus understood *it,* he said unto them, Why trouble ye the woman? for she hath ^awrought a good work upon me.

11 For ye have the poor always with you; but me ye have not always.

12 For in that she hath poured this ointment on my body, she did *it* ^afor my burial.

13 Verily I say unto you, Wheresoever this gospel shall be preached in the whole world, *there* shall also this, that this woman hath done, be told for a memorial of her.

14 ¶ Then one of the twelve, called Judas Iscariot, went unto the chief priests,

15 And said *unto them,* What will ye give me, and I will deliver him unto you? And they covenanted with him for ^athirty pieces of silver.

16 And from that time he sought opportunity to ^abetray him.

17 ¶ Now the first *day* of the *feast of* ^aunleavened bread the disciples came to Jesus, saying unto him, Where wilt thou that we prepare for thee to eat the ^bpassover?

18 And he said, Go into the city ^ato such a man, and say unto him, The Master saith, My ^btime is at hand; I will keep the passover at thy house with my disciples.

19 And the disciples did as Jesus had appointed them; and they made ready the ^apassover.

20 Now when the even was come, he sat down with the twelve.

21 And as they did eat, he said, Verily I say unto you, that one of you shall betray me.

22 And they were exceeding sorrowful, and began every one of them to say unto him, Lord, is it I?

23 And he answered and said, He

45*a* Prov. 14:31.
46*a* D&C 19:11 (6–12).
   b TG Damnation;
     Punish.
   c TG Righteousness.
   d TG Resurrection.
   e TG Eternal Life.
26 2*a* TG Passover.
   b TG Jesus Christ,
     Betrayal of.
   c TG Martyrdom.

3*a* John 11:49 (47–52).
4*a* GR plotted.
   b GR treachery, cunning.
     Matt. 27:20 (11–26).
   c Mark 14:1 (1–2).
     Luke 22:2 (1–2).
5*a* TG Rioting and
     Reveling.
7*a* John 11:2.
8*a* TG Waste.
10*a* TG Benevolence.

12*a* GR to prepare me for
     my burial.
15*a* Ex. 21:32 (28–32).
16*a* TG Jesus Christ,
     Betrayal of.
17*a* TG Bread, Unleavened.
   b TG Passover.
18*a* GR to a certain man.
   b John 7:6.
19*a* Ex. 12:27 (1–51).

that dippeth *his* hand with me in the dish, the same shall betray me.

24 The Son of man goeth as it is ^awritten of him: but woe unto that man by whom the ^bSon of man is betrayed! ^cit had been good for that man if he had not been ^dborn.

25 Then Judas, which betrayed him, answered and said, Master, is it I? He said unto him, Thou hast said.

26 ¶ ^aAnd as they were eating, Jesus took ^bbread, ^cand blessed *it*, and brake *it*, and gave *it* to the disciples, and said, Take, eat; this is my ^dbody.

27 And he took the ^acup, and gave thanks, and gave *it* to them, saying, ^bDrink ye all of it;

28 For this is my ^ablood of the new ^btestament, which is shed for many for the ^cremission of sins.

29 But I say unto you, I will not ^adrink henceforth of this fruit of the vine, until that day when I ^bdrink it new with you in my Father's kingdom.

30 And when they had sung an ^ahymn, they went out into the mount of Olives.

31 Then saith Jesus unto them, All ye shall be ^aoffended because of me this night: for it is written, I will ^bsmite the ^cshepherd, and the sheep of the flock shall be scattered abroad.

32 But after I am ^arisen again, I will go before you into Galilee.

33 Peter answered and said unto him, Though all *men* shall be offended because of thee, *yet* will I never be ^aoffended.

34 Jesus said unto him, Verily I say unto thee, That this night, before the cock crow, thou shalt deny me thrice.

35 Peter said unto him, Though I should die with thee, yet will I not deny thee. Likewise also said all the disciples.

36 ¶ Then cometh Jesus with them unto a place called ^aGethsemane, and saith unto the disciples, Sit ye here, while I go and ^bpray yonder.

37 And he took with him Peter and the two sons of Zebedee, and ^abegan to be sorrowful and very heavy.

38 Then saith he unto them, My soul is ^aexceeding sorrowful, even unto death: tarry ye here, and ^bwatch with me.

39 And he went a little further, and fell on his face, and ^aprayed, saying, O my ^bFather, if it be possible, let this ^ccup pass from me: nevertheless not as I ^dwill, but as ^ethou ^fwilt.

40 And he cometh unto the disciples, and findeth them ^aasleep, and

---

24a TG Jesus Christ, Prophecies about.
  b TG Jesus Christ, Son of Man.
  c GR it would have been good.
  d Luke 22:22; Acts 2:23.
26a JST Matt. 26:22, 24–25 (Appendix).
  b TG Bread; Bread of Life; Jesus Christ, Types of, in Memory.
  c JST Matt. 26:22 . . . and *brake* it, and *blessed* it, and gave to *his* disciples, and said, Take, eat; this is *in remembrance of my body which I give a ransom for you.*
  d TG Sacrament.
27a 1 Cor. 10:16 (16–17).
  b GR All of you drink

from it.
  TG Sacrament.
28a Ex. 24:8 (3–8); Deut. 32:14; Heb. 9:16 (15–22).
  TG Jesus Christ, Atonement through.
  b GR covenant.
  TG Covenants.
  c TG Jesus Christ, Redeemer; Remission of Sins.
29a Mark 14:25; Luke 22:18.
  b JST Matt. 26:26 . . . *shall come and* drink it . . . D&C 27:5 (5–14).
30a TG Singing.
31a TG Offense.
  b GR strike, hit, slay.
  c Zech. 13:7.
32a TG Jesus Christ, Resurrection.
33a Luke 22:33–34, 56–62.

36a TG Jesus Christ, Atonement through.
  b Matt. 14:23; Luke 6:12; 9:28.
37a GR began to be distressed and troubled.
38a GR deeply grieved.
  TG Pain; Sorrow.
  b TG stay awake.
39a Heb. 5:7.
  TG Prayer.
  b TG God the Father, Elohim.
  c Mark 14:36 (32–42); Mosiah 3:7; D&C 19:18 (16–19).
  d GR wish, desire. Isa. 50:5.
  TG Agency.
  e TG Godhead.
  f TG Obedience; Self-Mastery.
40a TG Sleep.

saith unto Peter, What, *b*could ye not watch with me one hour?

41 *a*Watch and *b*pray, that ye enter not into *c*temptation: the spirit indeed *is* willing, but the flesh *is* weak.

42 He went away again the second time, and prayed, saying, O my Father, if this cup may not pass away from me, except I drink it, thy *a*will be done.

43 And he came and found them asleep again: for their eyes were heavy.

44 And he left them, and went away again, and prayed the third time, saying the same words.

45 Then cometh he to his disciples, and saith unto them, Sleep on now, and take *your* rest: behold, the hour is at hand, and the Son of man is *a*betrayed into the hands of sinners.

46 Rise, let us be going: behold, he is at hand that doth betray me.

47 ¶ And while he yet spake, lo, Judas, one of the twelve, came, and with him a great multitude with swords and staves, from the chief priests and elders of the people.

48 Now he that betrayed him gave them a sign, saying, Whomsoever I shall kiss, that same is he: hold him fast.

49 And *a*forthwith he came to Jesus, and said, Hail, master; and kissed him.

50 And Jesus said unto him, Friend, wherefore art thou come? Then came they, and laid hands on Jesus, and took him.

51 And, behold, one of them which were with Jesus stretched out *his* hand, and drew his sword, and struck a *a*servant of the high priest's, and smote off his ear.

52 Then said Jesus unto him, Put

up again thy sword into his place: for all they that take the sword shall *a*perish with the sword.

53 Thinkest thou that I cannot now pray to my Father, and he shall presently give me more than twelve legions of angels?

54 But how then shall the *a*scriptures be fulfilled, that thus it must be?

55 In that same hour said Jesus to the multitudes, Are ye come out as against a thief with swords and staves for to take me? I sat daily with you *a*teaching in the temple, and ye laid no hold on me.

56 But all this was done, that the scriptures of the prophets might be fulfilled. Then all the disciples forsook him, and fled.

57 ¶ And they that had laid hold on Jesus led *him* away to *a*Caiaphas the high priest, where the scribes and the elders were assembled.

58 But Peter followed him afar off unto the high priest's palace, and went in, and sat with the servants, to see the end.

59 Now the chief priests, and elders, and all the council, sought false *a*witness against Jesus, *b*to put him to death;

60 But found none: yea, though many false witnesses came, *yet* found they none. At the last came two false *a*witnesses,

61 And said, This *fellow* said, I am able to destroy the *a*temple of God, and to build it in three days.

62 And the high priest arose, and said unto him, Answerest thou nothing? what *is it which* these witness against thee?

63 But Jesus *a*held his *b*peace. And the high priest answered and

---

40*b* GR are you so powerless that you could not stay awake with me . . .
41*a* TG Watch.
　b TG Prayer.
　c TG Temptation.
42*a* Acts 21:14.
　TG God, Will of.
45*a* TG Jesus Christ, Betrayal of.
49*a* GR immediately.

51*a* John 18:10.
52*a* TG Punish; Retribution.
54*a* 2 Ne. 9:7 (5–10); Mosiah 3:15 (11–17).
55*a* Luke 21:37; John 8:2 (1–2). TG Teaching.
57*a* John 18:13 (13, 24). TG Jesus Christ, Trials of.
59*a* TG Slander.

　b GR so that they might put Him to death.
60*a* Deut. 19:15 (15–19).
61*a* Matt. 27:40; Mark 14:58; John 2:19 (18–22).
63*a* GR was silent, "kept silent."
　b Isa. 53:7.

said unto him, I ^cadjure thee by the ^dliving God, that thou tell us whether thou be the Christ, the Son of God.

64 Jesus saith unto him, Thou hast said: nevertheless I say unto you, Hereafter shall ye see the ^aSon of man sitting on the right hand of ^bpower, and ^ccoming in the clouds of heaven.

65 Then the high priest rent his clothes, saying, He hath spoken ^ablasphemy; what further need have we of witnesses? behold, now ye have heard his blasphemy.

66 What think ye? They answered and said, He is ^aguilty ^bof ^cdeath.

67 Then did they ^aspit in his face, and buffeted him; and others smote *him* with the palms of their hands,

68 Saying, Prophesy unto us, thou Christ, Who is he that ^asmote thee?

69 ¶ Now Peter sat without in the palace: and a ^adamsel came unto him, saying, Thou also wast with Jesus of Galilee.

70 But he denied before *them* all, saying, I know not what thou sayest.

71 And when he was gone out into the porch, another *maid* saw him, and said unto them that were there, This *fellow* was also with Jesus of Nazareth.

72 And again he denied with an oath, I do not know the man.

73 And after a while came unto *him* they that stood by, and said to Peter, Surely thou also art *one* of them; for thy speech ^abewrayeth thee.

74 Then began he to curse and to swear, *saying,* I know not the man. And immediately the ^acock crew.

75 And Peter remembered the word of Jesus, which said unto him, Before the cock crow, thou shalt ^adeny me thrice. And he went out, and wept bitterly.

CHAPTER 27

Jesus is accused and condemned before Pilate—Barabbas is released—Jesus is mocked, crucified, and buried in the tomb of Joseph of Arimathæa.

When the morning was come, all the chief priests and elders of the people took counsel against Jesus to put him to death:

2 And when they had bound him, they led *him* away, and delivered him to ^aPontius Pilate the governor.

3 ¶ Then Judas, which had betrayed him, when he saw that he was condemned, repented himself, and brought again the thirty pieces of silver to the chief priests and elders,

4 Saying, I have sinned in that I have ^abetrayed the innocent ^bblood. And they said, What *is that* to us? ^csee thou *to that.*

5 And he cast down the pieces of silver in the temple, and departed, and went ^aand ^bhanged himself.

6 And the chief priests took the silver pieces, and said, It is not lawful for to put them into the treasury, because it is the price of blood.

7 And they took counsel, and bought with them the ^apotter's field, to bury ^bstrangers in.

8 Wherefore that field was called, The field of blood, unto this day.

9 Then was fulfilled that which was spoken by Jeremy the prophet,

63c GR charge (you) under oath ("cause you to swear").
 d TG Oath; Swearing.
64a TG Jesus Christ, Son of Man.
 b TG Celestial Glory.
 c TG Jesus Christ, Second Coming.
65a TG Blaspheme.
66a TG Guilt.
 b JST Matt. 26:67 . . . and worthy of death.

 c TG Jesus Christ, Death of.
67a Isa. 50:6.
68a Luke 22:64.
69a GR servant-girl.
73a GR reveals you.
74a GR rooster crowed.
75a TG Honesty.
27 2a TG Jesus Christ, Trials of.
 4a TG Jesus Christ, Betrayal of.
 b TG Blood, Shedding of.

 c GR that is your affair. JST Matt. 27:5 . . . See thou to *it; thy sins be upon thee.*
 5a JST Matt. 27:6 . . . *and hanged himself on a tree. And straightway he fell down, and his bowels gushed out, and he died.*
 b Acts 1:18 (15–20).
 7a Zech. 11:13 (12–13).
 b TG Stranger.

saying, And they took the [a]thirty pieces of silver, the price of him that was valued, whom they of the children of Israel did value;

10 And gave them for the potter's field, as the Lord appointed me.

11 And Jesus stood before the governor: and the governor asked him, saying, Art thou the King of the Jews? And Jesus said unto him, [a]Thou sayest.

12 And when he was accused of the chief priests and elders, he answered [a]nothing.

13 Then said Pilate unto him, Hearest thou not how many things they witness against thee?

14 And he answered him to never a word; insomuch that the governor marvelled greatly.

15 Now at *that* feast the governor was [a]wont to [b]release unto the people a prisoner, whom they [c]would.

16 And they had then a notable prisoner, called Barabbas.

17 Therefore when they were gathered together, Pilate said unto them, Whom will ye that I release unto you? Barabbas, or Jesus which is called Christ?

18 For he knew that for [a]envy they had [b]delivered him.

19 ¶ When he was set down on the judgment seat, his wife sent unto him, saying, Have thou nothing to do with that just man: for I have suffered many things this day in a [a]dream because of him.

20 But the chief [a]priests and elders [b]persuaded the multitude that they should [c]ask Barabbas, and destroy Jesus.

21 The governor answered and said unto them, Whether of the twain will ye that I release unto you? They said, Barabbas.

22 Pilate saith unto them, What shall I do then with Jesus which is called Christ? *They* all say unto him, Let him be [a]crucified.

23 And the governor said, Why, what evil hath he done? But they cried out [a]the more, saying, Let him be crucified.

24 ¶ When Pilate saw that he [a]could prevail nothing, but *that* rather a [b]tumult was made, he took water, and washed *his* hands before the multitude, saying, I am innocent of the blood of this [c]just person: see ye *to it.*

25 Then answered all the people, and said, His [a]blood *be* on us, and on our children.

26 ¶ Then released he Barabbas unto them: and when he had [a]scourged Jesus, he delivered *him* to be crucified.

27 Then the soldiers of the governor took Jesus into the [a]common hall, and gathered unto him the whole band *of soldiers.*

28 And they stripped him, and put on him a [a]scarlet robe.

29 ¶ And when they had [a]plaited a crown of thorns, they put *it* upon his head, and a [b]reed in his right hand: and they bowed the knee before him, and mocked him, saying, Hail, King of the Jews!

30 And they [a]spit upon him, and took the reed, and smote him on the head.

31 And after that they had mocked him, they took the robe off from him, and put his own raiment on him, and led him away to crucify *him.*

32 And as they came out, they

9a TG Jesus Christ, Betrayal of.
11a JST Matt. 27:12 . . . Thou sayest *truly; for thus it is written of me.*
12a TG Jesus Christ, Trials of.
15a GR accustomed.
  b Luke 23:17.
  c GR desired.
18a TG Envy.
  b TG Jesus Christ, Betrayal of.

19a TG Dream.
20a TG Priestcraft.
  b Matt. 26:4 (3–4); Acts 3:13; 13:28; 2 Ne. 10:5 (3–6).
  c GR request.
22a 2 Ne. 10:3.
23a GR exceedingly, beyond measure.
24a GR was accomplishing.
  b TG Rioting and Reveling.
  c John 18:38 (28–38).

25a Ps. 69:27; Acts 5:28; 2 Ne. 6:10 (8–11).
26a Isa. 50:6. TG Cruelty.
27a GR governor's house, residence.
28a JST Matt. 27:30 . . . *purple* . . .
29a GR woven.
  b GR stalk, staff.
30a 1 Ne. 19:9.

found a man of Cyrene, Simon by name: him they compelled to bear his cross.

33 And when they were come unto a place called Golgotha, that is to say, a place of ªa skull,

34 ¶ They gave him ªvinegar to drink mingled with gall: and when he had tasted *thereof,* he would not drink.

35 And they ªcrucified him, and ᵇparted his garments, casting lots: that it might be fulfilled which was spoken by the prophet, They parted my ᶜgarments among them, and upon my vesture did they cast lots.

36 And sitting down they watched him there;

37 And set up over his head his accusation written, THIS IS JESUS THE KING OF THE JEWS.

38 Then were there two thieves crucified with him, one on the right hand, and another on the left.

39 ¶ And they that passed by ªreviled him, wagging their heads,

40 And saying, Thou that destroyest the ªtemple, and buildest *it* in three days, save thyself. If thou be the ᵇSon of God, come down from the cross.

41 Likewise also the chief priests mocking *him,* with the scribes and elders, said,

42 He saved others; himself he cannot save. If he be the King of Israel, let him now come down from the cross, and we will believe him.

43 He ªtrusted in God; let him ᵇdeliver him now, if he will have him: for he said, I am the ᶜSon of God.

44 The thieves also, which were crucified with him, ªcast the same in his teeth.

45 Now from the sixth hour there was ªdarkness over all the land unto the ninth hour.

46 And about the ninth hour Jesus cried with a loud voice, saying, Eli, Eli, lama sabachthani? that is to say, ªMy God, my God, why hast thou ᵇforsaken me?

47 Some of them that stood there, when they heard *that,* said, This *man* calleth for ªElias.

48 And straightway one of them ran, and took a sponge, and filled *it* with ªvinegar, and put *it* on a reed, and gave him to drink.

49 The rest said, Let be, let us see whether Elias will come to save him.

50 ¶ Jesus, when he had cried again with ªa loud voice, yielded up the ghost.

51 And, behold, the ªveil of the temple was ᵇrent in twain from the top to the bottom; and the earth did ᶜquake, and the rocks rent;

52 And the ªgraves were opened; and many ᵇbodies of the ᶜsaints ᵈwhich slept ᵉarose,

53 And came out of the graves after his resurrection, and went into the ªholy city, and appeared unto many.

54 Now when the centurion, and they that were with him, watching Jesus, saw the earthquake, and those things that were done, they feared greatly, saying, Truly this was the Son of God.

55 And many ªwomen were there beholding afar off, which followed

---

33 a JST Matt. 27:35 . . .
　　 burial . . .
34 a Ps. 69:21.
35 a TG Jesus Christ,
　　 Crucifixion of.
　 b IE they divided
　　 His clothes among
　　 themselves.
　 c Ps. 22:18.
39 a TG Reviling.
40 a Matt. 26:61;
　　 Mark 14:58;
　　 John 2:19 (18–22).
　 b Matt. 4:6;
　　 D&C 20:22.

43 a Ps. 22:8.
　 b TG Deliver.
　 c TG Jesus Christ, Divine
　　 Sonship.
44 a GR insulted, reproached
　　 Him.
45 a TG Darkness, Physical.
46 a Ps. 22:1.
　 b D&C 121:1 (1–8).
47 a IE Elijah.
48 a TG Jesus Christ,
　　 Prophecies about.
50 a JST Matt. 27:54 . . . a loud
　　 voice, *saying, Father, it is*
　　 finished, thy will is done,

　　 yielded up the ghost.
51 a TG Jesus Christ, Types
　　 of, in Anticipation;
　　 Veil.
　 b GR torn into two pieces.
　 c 3 Ne. 8:6 (5–12);
　　 Moses 7:56 (55–56).
52 a TG Jesus Christ,
　　 Prophecies about.
　 b D&C 129:1.
　 c TG Saints.
　 d GR who had died.
　 e TG Resurrection.
53 a Neh. 11:1.
55 a TG Woman.

Jesus from Galilee, ministering unto him:

56 Among which was Mary Magdalene, and Mary the mother of James and *Joses, and the mother of Zebedee's children.

57 When the even was come, there came a rich man of Arimathæa, named *Joseph, who also himself was Jesus' *disciple:

58 He went to Pilate, and *begged the body of Jesus. Then Pilate commanded the body to be delivered.

59 And when Joseph had taken the body, he wrapped it in a clean linen cloth,

60 And laid it in his own new tomb, which he had hewn out in the rock: and he rolled a great *stone to the door of the *sepulchre, and departed.

61 And there was Mary Magdalene, and the other Mary, sitting *over against the sepulchre.

62 ¶ Now the next day, that followed the day of the *preparation, the chief priests and Pharisees came together unto Pilate,

63 Saying, Sir, we remember that that *deceiver said, while he was yet alive, After three days I will rise again.

64 Command therefore that the sepulchre be made sure until the third day, lest his disciples come by night, and steal him away, and say unto the people, He is risen from the dead: so the last *error shall be worse than the first.

65 Pilate said unto them, Ye have a watch: go your way, make it as sure as ye can.

66 So they went, and made the sepulchre sure, sealing the stone, and setting a watch.

CHAPTER 28

Christ the Lord is risen—He appears to many—He has all power in heaven and earth—He sends the Apostles to teach and baptize all nations.

*IN the end of the *sabbath, as it began to dawn toward the first *day* of the week, came Mary Magdalene and the other Mary to see the sepulchre.

2 And, behold, there was a great earthquake: for *the *angel of the Lord descended from heaven, and came and rolled back the stone from the door, and sat upon it.

3 *His *countenance was like lightning, and his raiment white as snow:

4 And for fear of him the keepers did shake, and became as dead *men*.

5 *And the angel answered and said unto the women, Fear not ye: for I know that ye seek Jesus, which was crucified.

6 He is not here: for he is *risen, as he said. Come, see the place where the *Lord lay.

7 And go quickly, and tell his disciples that he is risen from the dead; and, behold, he goeth before you into Galilee; there shall ye see him: lo, I have told you.

8 And they departed quickly from the sepulchre with fear and great joy; and did run to bring his disciples word.

9 ¶ And as they went to tell his disciples, behold, *Jesus met them, saying, All hail. And they came and held him by the feet, and worshipped him.

10 Then said Jesus unto them, Be not afraid: go tell my brethren that they go into Galilee, and there shall they see me.

56a GR Joseph.
57a John 19:38.
  b John 8:31.
58a GR asked for, requested.
60a John 11:38 (37–40); 20:1.
  b 1 Ne. 19:10.
61a GR in front of, before.
62a TG Passover.
63a John 2:19.
64a GR deception.
28 1a GR After the sabbath.

  b TG Sabbath.
2a JST Matt. 28:2 . . . *two angels* . . .
  b TG Angels.
3a JST Matt. 28:3 *And their* countenance was like lightning, and *their* raiment white as snow . . .
  b D&C 20:6.
5a JST Matt. 28:4 And the

angels answered and said unto the women, Fear not ye; for *we* know . . .
6a TG Jesus Christ, Resurrection; Resurrection.
  b TG Jesus Christ, Lord.
9a TG Jesus Christ, Appearances, Postmortal.

11 ¶ Now when they were going, behold, some of the ªwatch came into the city, and ᵇshewed unto the chief priests all the things that were done.

12 And when they were assembled with the elders, and had taken counsel, they gave ªlarge money unto the soldiers,

13 Saying, Say ye, His disciples came by night, and stole him *away* while we slept.

14 And if this come to the governor's ears, we will persuade him, and ªsecure you.

15 So they took the money, and did as they were taught: and this saying is commonly reported among the Jews until this day.

16 ¶ Then the eleven disciples went away into Galilee, into a mountain where Jesus had appointed them.

17 And when they saw him, they worshipped him: but some ªdoubted.

18 And ªJesus came and spake unto them, saying, All ᵇpower is given unto me in heaven and in earth.

19 ¶ Go ye therefore, and ªteach all ᵇnations, ᶜbaptizing them in the name of the ᵈFather, and of the Son, and of the Holy Ghost:

20 ªTeaching them to ᵇobserve all things whatsoever I have ᶜcommanded you: and, lo, ᵈI am with you alway, *even* unto the ᵉend of the world. Amen.

THE GOSPEL ACCORDING TO
ST MARK

CHAPTER 1

Jesus is baptized by John—He preaches the gospel, calls disciples, casts out devils, heals the sick, and cleanses a leper.

THE beginning of the ªgospel of Jesus Christ, the Son of God;

2 As it is written in the prophets, Behold, I send my ªmessenger before thy face, which shall prepare thy way before thee.

3 The ªvoice of one crying in the wilderness, Prepare ye the way of the Lord, make his paths straight.

4 John did baptize in the wilderness, and ªpreach the ᵇbaptism of

---

11a GR guard.
  b GR reported.
12a GR much money.
14a GR keep you out of trouble.
17a TG Doubt.
18a TG Jesus Christ, Appearances, Postmortal.
  b Heb. 2:8;
    1 Ne. 9:6.
    TG God, Power of;
    Jesus Christ, Messiah;
    Jesus Christ, Power of;
    Priesthood, Power of.
19a GR preach to, make disciples of (meaning "make Christians in all nations").

TG Apostles;
Israel, Mission of;
Missionary Work;
Mission of Early Saints;
Mission of Latter-day Saints; Teaching.
  b TG Nations.
  c TG Baptism;
    Baptism, Essential.
  d TG Godhead.
20a The Greek text suggests this would be post-baptismal teaching.
    TG Prophets, Mission of.
  b TG Baptism, Qualifications for.
  c Jer. 1:7 (7–10).
  d D&C 30:11; 31:13;

61:10; 62:9.
    TG Guidance, Divine;
    Protection, Divine.
  e D&C 24:8; 132:49.
    TG World, End of.

[MARK]
Title: JST entitles this book "The Testimony of St. Mark."
1 1a TG Gospel.
  2a Mal. 3:1;
    Matt. 11:10.
  3a Matt. 3:3;
    Luke 3:4;
    John 1:23.
  4a TG Missionary Work.
  b TG Baptism.

^crepentance for the ^dremission of sins.

5 And there went out unto him all the land of Judæa, and they of Jerusalem, and were all ^abaptized of him in the river of Jordan, ^bconfessing their sins.

6 And John was ^aclothed with ^bcamel's hair, and with a girdle of a skin about his loins; and he did eat ^clocusts and wild honey;

7 And preached, saying, There cometh one mightier than I after me, the latchet of whose shoes I am not worthy to stoop down and unloose.

8 I indeed have baptized you with water: ^abut he shall baptize you with the Holy Ghost.

9 And it came to pass in those days, that Jesus came from Nazareth of Galilee, and was ^abaptized of John in Jordan.

10 And straightway coming ^aup out of the water, he saw the heavens opened, and the Spirit like a ^bdove descending upon him:

11 And there came a voice from heaven, *saying,* Thou art my beloved Son, in whom I am well pleased.

12 ^aAnd immediately the Spirit driveth him into the ^bwilderness.

13 And he was there in the wilderness forty days, tempted of Satan; and was with the wild beasts; and the angels ministered unto him.

14 Now after that John was put in prison, Jesus came into Galilee, ^apreaching the gospel of the kingdom of God,

15 And saying, The ^atime is fulfilled, and the ^bkingdom of God ^cis at hand: ^drepent ye, and ^ebelieve the gospel.

16 Now as he walked by the sea of Galilee, he saw Simon and Andrew his brother casting a net into the sea: for they were fishers.

17 And Jesus said unto them, Come ye after me, and I will make you to become ^afishers of men.

18 And straightway they forsook their nets, and followed him.

19 And when he had gone a little further thence, he saw James the *son* of Zebedee, and John his brother, who also were in the ship mending their nets.

20 And straightway he called them: and they left their father Zebedee in the ship with the hired servants, and went after him.

21 And they went into Capernaum; and straightway on the sabbath day he entered into the synagogue, and ^ataught.

22 And they were astonished at his doctrine: for he taught them as one that had ^aauthority, and not as the ^bscribes.

23 And there was in their synagogue a man with an ^aunclean spirit; and he cried out,

24 Saying, Let *us* alone; ^awhat have we to do with thee, thou Jesus of Nazareth? art thou come to destroy us? I know thee who thou art, the ^bHoly One of God.

25 And Jesus ^arebuked him, saying, Hold thy peace, and come out of him.

4c TG Repent.
  d TG Remission of Sins.
5a TG Baptism, Immersion.
  b TG Baptism,
      Qualifications for.
6a TG Clothing.
  b 2 Kgs. 1:8.
  c Lev. 11:22.
8a JST Mark 1:6 . . . but he
      shall *not only* baptize
      you with *water, but with
      fire, and* the Holy Ghost.
9a TG Baptism;
      Baptism, Essential;
      Jesus Christ, Baptism of.
10a TG Baptism, Immersion.
  b TG Holy Ghost, Dove,

Sign of.
12a JST Mark 1:10–11 And
      immediately the Spirit
      took him into the
      wilderness. And he was
      there in the wilderness
      forty days, *Satan seeking
      to tempt him;* and was
      with . . .
  b GR desert.
14a TG Jesus Christ,
      Teaching Mode of.
15a TG Time.
  b D&C 33:10 (1–18).
      TG Kingdom of God, in
      Heaven.
  c GR has arrived.

d TG Repent.
  e TG Faith.
17a TG Apostles;
      Missionary Work.
21a TG Jesus Christ,
      Teaching Mode of.
22a TG Authority;
      Jesus Christ,
      Authority of.
  b TG Scribe.
23a TG Spirits, Evil or
      Unclean.
24a GR what business do
      you have with us . . .
  b TG Holiness.
25a TG Heal.

26 And when the unclean spirit had ^atorn him, and cried with a loud voice, he came out of him.

27 And they were all amazed, insomuch that they questioned among themselves, saying, What thing is this? what new doctrine *is* this? for with ^aauthority commandeth he even the unclean spirits, and they do obey him.

28 And immediately his fame spread abroad throughout all the region round about Galilee.

29 And forthwith, when they were come out of the synagogue, they entered into the house of Simon and Andrew, with James and John.

30 But Simon's wife's mother lay sick of a fever, and ^aanon they tell him of her.

31 And he came and took her by the hand, and ^alifted her up; and immediately the fever left her, and she ministered unto them.

32 And at even, when the sun did set, they brought unto him all that were diseased, and them that were possessed with devils.

33 And all the city was gathered together at the door.

34 And he ^ahealed many that were sick of divers diseases, and cast out many ^bdevils; and ^csuffered not the devils to speak, because they knew him.

35 And in the morning, rising up a great while before day, he went out, and departed into a solitary place, and there prayed.

36 And Simon and they that were with him followed after him.

37 And when they had found him, they said unto him, All *men* seek for thee.

38 And he said unto them, Let us go into the next towns, that I may ^apreach there also: for therefore came I forth.

39 And he preached in their synagogues throughout all Galilee, and cast out ^adevils.

40 And there came a ^aleper to him, beseeching him, and kneeling down to him, and saying unto him, If thou wilt, thou canst make me ^bclean.

41 And Jesus, moved with ^acompassion, put forth *his* hand, and touched him, and saith unto him, I will; be thou clean.

42 And as soon as he had spoken, immediately the leprosy departed from him, and he was cleansed.

43 And he ^astraitly charged him, and forthwith sent him away;

44 And saith unto him, See thou say nothing to any man: but go thy way, shew thyself to the priest, and offer for thy cleansing those things which Moses commanded, for a testimony unto them.

45 But he went out, and began to publish *it* much, and to ^ablaze abroad the matter, insomuch that Jesus could no more openly enter into the city, but was without in desert places: and they came to him from every quarter.

CHAPTER 2

Jesus forgives sins, heals a paralytic, eats with tax gatherers and sinners, and announces that He is Lord of the Sabbath.

AND again he entered into Capernaum after *some* days; and it was noised that he was ^ain the house.

2 And straightway many were gathered together, insomuch that there was no room to receive *them*, no, not so much as about the door: and he ^apreached the word unto them.

3 And they come unto him, bringing one sick of the palsy, which was ^aborne of four.

26*a* Mark 9:20 (14–29).
27*a* TG Authority; Jesus Christ, Authority of.
30*a* GR immediately.
31*a* TG Heal.
34*a* TG Heal; Miracle.
    b Mosiah 3:6 (5–6).

    TG Spirits, Evil or Unclean.
  c GR did not allow.
38*a* TG Jesus Christ, Mission of; Teaching.
39*a* Luke 4:36 (31–37); D&C 35:9 (6–12).
40*a* TG Leprosy.

  b GR pure.
41*a* TG Compassion.
43*a* GR warned him sternly.
45*a* GR spread widely.
2 1*a* OR at home.
   2*a* TG Jesus Christ, Teaching Mode of.
   3*a* GR carried.

4 And when they could not come nigh unto him for the press, they uncovered the roof where he was: and when they had broken *it* up, they let down the bed wherein the sick of the palsy lay.

5 When Jesus saw their faith, he said unto the sick of the palsy, Son, thy sins be *a*forgiven thee.

6 But there were certain of the scribes sitting there, and reasoning in their hearts,

7 Why doth this *man* thus speak *a*blasphemies? who can forgive sins but God only?

8 And immediately when Jesus perceived in his spirit that they so reasoned within themselves, he said unto them, Why reason ye these things in your hearts?

9 Whether is it easier to say to the sick of the palsy, *Thy* sins be forgiven thee; or to say, Arise, and take up thy bed, and walk?

10 But that ye may know that the *a*Son of man hath power on earth to forgive sins, (he saith to the sick of the palsy,)

11 I say unto thee, *a*Arise, and take up thy *b*bed, and go thy way into thine house.

12 And immediately he arose, took up the bed, and went forth before them all; insomuch that they were all amazed, and glorified God, saying, We never saw it on this fashion.

13 And he went forth again by the sea side; and all the multitude resorted unto him, and he taught them.

14 And as he passed by, he saw Levi the *son* of Alphæus sitting at the *a*receipt of custom, and said unto him, Follow me. And he arose and followed him.

15 And it came to pass, that, as Jesus sat at meat in his house, many publicans and sinners sat also together with Jesus and his disciples: for there were many, and they followed him.

16 And when the scribes and Pharisees saw him eat with *a*publicans and sinners, they said unto his disciples, How is it that he eateth and drinketh with publicans and sinners?

17 When Jesus heard *it,* he saith unto them, They that are *a*whole have no need of the physician, but they that are sick: I came not to call the righteous, but sinners to repentance.

18 And the disciples of John and of the Pharisees used to *a*fast: and they come and say unto him, Why do the disciples of John and of the Pharisees fast, but thy disciples fast not?

19 And Jesus said unto them, Can the children of the bridechamber fast, while the *a*bridegroom is with them? as long as they have the *b*bridegroom with them, they cannot fast.

20 But the days will come, when the bridegroom shall be taken away from them, and then shall they fast in those days.

21 No man also seweth a piece of *a*new cloth on an old garment: else the new piece that filled it up taketh away from the old, and the rent is made worse.

22 And no man putteth new wine into old bottles: else the new wine doth burst the bottles, and the wine is spilled, and the bottles will be marred: but new wine must be put into new bottles.

23 And it came to pass, that he went through the corn fields on the sabbath day; and his disciples began, as they went, *a*to pluck the ears of corn.

24 And the Pharisees said unto him, Behold, why do they on the sabbath day that which is not lawful?

5*a* Luke 7:48;
  James 5:15 (14–15).
7*a* TG Blaspheme.
10*a* TG Jesus Christ,
  Son of Man.
11*a* Alma 15:10 (4–11);

  3 Ne. 9:13 (10–22).
  b 3 Ne. 7:22.
14*a* GR tax office.
16*a* Luke 15:1 (1–2).
17*a* Moro. 8:8 (8–27).
18*a* Luke 5:33 (33–38).

19*a* Luke 5:35.
  b D&C 65:3.
21*a* GR unshrunken or
  unsized.
23*a* GR occasionally picking
  some grain.

25 And he said unto them, Have ye never read what David did, when he had need, and was an hungred, he, and they that were with him?

26 How he went into the house of God in the days of Abiathar the high priest, and did eat the shewbread, which is not lawful to eat but for the priests, and gave also to them which were with him?

27 And he said unto them, The ^asabbath was made for man, and not man for the sabbath:

28 ^aTherefore the ^bSon of man is Lord also of the sabbath.

CHAPTER 3

Jesus heals on the Sabbath day—He chooses and ordains the Twelve Apostles—He asks, Can Satan cast out Satan?—Jesus speaks of blasphemy against the Holy Ghost and identifies those who believe as being members of His family.

AND he entered again into the synagogue; and there was a man there which had a withered hand.

2 And they ^awatched him, whether he would heal him on the sabbath day; that they might accuse him.

3 And he saith unto the man which had the withered hand, Stand forth.

4 And he saith unto them, Is it lawful to do good on the ^asabbath days, or to do evil? to save life, or to kill? But they ^bheld their peace.

5 And when he had looked round about on them with ^aanger, being grieved for the ^bhardness of their hearts, he saith unto the man, Stretch forth thine hand. And he stretched *it* out: and his hand was restored whole as the other.

6 And the Pharisees went forth, and straightway took ^acounsel with the Herodians against him, how they might destroy him.

7 But Jesus withdrew himself with his disciples to the sea: and a great multitude from Galilee followed him, and from Judæa,

8 And from Jerusalem, and from Idumæa, and *from* beyond Jordan; and they about Tyre and Sidon, a great multitude, when they had heard what great things he did, came unto him.

9 And he spake to his disciples, that a small ^aship should wait on him because of the multitude, lest they should throng him.

10 For he had healed many; insomuch that they ^apressed upon him for to touch him, as many as had plagues.

11 And ^aunclean spirits, when they saw him, fell down before him, and cried, saying, Thou art the Son of God.

12 And he straitly charged them that they should not make him known.

13 And he goeth up into a mountain, and calleth *unto him* whom he ^awould: and they came unto him.

14 And he ^aordained twelve, that they should be with him, and that he might send them forth to ^bpreach,

15 And to have ^apower to heal ^bsicknesses, and to cast out ^cdevils:

16 And Simon he surnamed Peter;

17 And James the *son* of Zebedee, and John the brother of James; and he surnamed them Boanerges, which is, The sons of ^athunder:

18 And Andrew, and Philip, and Bartholomew, and Matthew, and Thomas, and James the *son* of Alphæus, and Thaddæus, and Simon the Canaanite,

---

27a TG Sabbath.
28a JST Mark 2:26–27 (Appendix).
   b TG Jesus Christ, Son of Man.
3 2a GR watched carefully, maliciously.
  4a TG Sabbath.
   b GR remained silent.
  5a TG God, Indignation of.
   b GR insensibility,

dullness.
   TG Cruelty.
  6a TG Counsel.
  9a GR boat.
 10a GR impetuously rushed at Him.
 11a TG Spirits, Evil or Unclean.
 13a GR desired.
 14a TG Apostles; Jesus Christ,

Authority of;
   Priesthood, Authority;
   Priesthood, History of;
   Priesthood, Ordination.
   b TG Missionary Work.
 15a GR authority.
   TG Priesthood;
   Priesthood, Power of.
   b TG Sickness.
   c TG Devil.
 17a Luke 9:54.

19 And Judas Iscariot, which also betrayed him: and they ^awent into an house.

20 And the multitude cometh together again, so that they could not so much as ^aeat bread.

21 And when his friends heard *of it,* they went out to lay hold on him: for they said, He is ^abeside himself.

22 ¶ And the scribes which came down from Jerusalem said, He hath Beelzebub, and by the prince of the devils casteth he out devils.

23 And he called them *unto him,* and said unto them in parables, How can Satan cast out Satan?

24 And if a kingdom be divided against itself, that kingdom cannot stand.

25 And if a house be divided against itself, that house cannot stand.

26 And if Satan rise up against himself, and be divided, he cannot stand, but hath an end.

27 No man can enter into a strong man's house, and spoil his goods, except he will first bind the strong man; and then he will spoil his house.

28 ^aVerily I say unto you, All sins shall be forgiven unto the sons of men, and blasphemies ^bwherewith soever they shall blaspheme:

29 But he that shall ^ablaspheme against the Holy Ghost hath never ^bforgiveness, but is in danger of ^ceternal damnation:

30 Because they said, He hath an unclean spirit.

31 ¶ There came then his ^abrethren and his mother, and, standing ^bwithout, sent unto him, calling him.

32 And the multitude sat about him, and they said unto him, Behold, thy mother and thy brethren without seek for thee.

33 And he answered them, saying, Who is my mother, or my brethren?

34 And he looked round about on them which sat about him, and said, Behold my mother and my brethren!

35 For whosoever shall do the ^awill of God, the same is my brother, and my sister, and mother.

CHAPTER 4

Jesus gives the parables of the sower, the candle under a bushel, the seed growing secretly, and the mustard seed—He stills the tempest.

AND he began again to teach by the ^asea side: and there was gathered unto him a great multitude, so that he entered into a ship, and sat in the sea; and the whole multitude was by the sea on the land.

2 And he taught them many things by parables, and said unto them in his ^adoctrine,

3 Hearken; Behold, there went out a ^asower to sow:

4 And it came to pass, as he sowed, some fell by the way side, and the fowls of the air came and devoured it up.

5 And some fell on stony ground, where it had not much earth; and immediately it sprang up, because it had no depth of earth:

6 But when the sun was up, it was scorched; and because it had no root, it withered away.

7 And some fell among thorns, and the thorns grew up, and choked it, and it yielded no fruit.

8 And other fell on good ground, and did yield fruit that sprang up and increased; and brought forth, some thirty, and some sixty, and some an hundred.

9 And he said unto them, He that hath ears to hear, let him hear.

19a OR went home.
20a Mark 6:31 (30–36).
21a GR out of his senses.
28a JST Mark 3:21–25 (Appendix).
  b GR however so many.
29a TG Holy Ghost,

Unpardonable Sin against.
  b TG Forgive.
  c TG Damnation; Eternity; Punish.
31a TG Jesus Christ,

Family of.
  b OR outside.
35a Matt. 12:50.
4 1a Matt. 13:1.
 2a 3 Ne. 11:39 (31–41).
 3a D&C 86:2 (2–3).

10 And when he was ^aalone, they that were about him with the twelve asked of him the parable.

11 And he said unto them, Unto you it is given to know the ^amystery of the kingdom of God: but unto them that are without, all *these* things are done in ^bparables:

12 That seeing they may see, and not ^aperceive; and hearing they may hear, and not understand; lest at any time they should be converted, and *their* sins should be ^bforgiven them.

13 And he said unto them, Know ye not this parable? and how then will ye know all parables?

14 ¶ The sower soweth the word.

15 And these are they by the way side, where the word is sown; but when they have heard, ^aSatan cometh immediately, and taketh away the word that was sown in their hearts.

16 And these are they likewise which are sown on stony ground; who, when they have heard the word, immediately ^areceive it with gladness;

17 And have no root in themselves, and so endure but for a time: afterward, when ^aaffliction or ^bpersecution ariseth for the word's sake, immediately they are offended.

18 And these are they which are sown among thorns; such as hear the word,

19 And the cares of this world, and the deceitfulness of ^ariches, and the ^blusts of other things entering in, choke the word, and it becometh unfruitful.

20 And these are they which are sown on good ground; such as hear the word, and receive *it*, and bring forth fruit, some thirtyfold, some sixty, and some an hundred.

21 ¶ And he said unto them, Is a ^acandle brought to be put under a bushel, or under a bed? and not to be set on a candlestick?

22 For there is nothing hid, which shall not be manifested; neither was any thing kept secret, but that it should come abroad.

23 ^aIf any man have ears to hear, let him hear.

24 And he said unto them, Take heed what ye hear: with what measure ye mete, it shall be measured to you: ^aand unto you that hear shall more be ^bgiven.

25 ^aFor he that hath, to him shall be given: and he that hath not, from him shall be ^btaken even that which he hath.

26 ¶ And he said, So is the kingdom of God, as if a man should cast seed into the ground;

27 And should sleep, and rise night and day, and the seed should spring and ^agrow up, he knoweth not how.

28 For the earth bringeth forth ^afruit of herself; first the blade, then the ear, after that the full corn in the ear.

29 But when the fruit is brought forth, immediately he putteth in the sickle, because the ^aharvest is come.

30 ¶ And he said, Whereunto shall we liken the kingdom of God? or with what comparison shall we compare it?

31 *It is* like a grain of mustard seed, which, when it is sown in the earth, is less than all the seeds that be in the earth:

32 But when it is sown, it groweth up, and becometh greater than

---

10*a* JST Mark 4:9 . . . alone
  with the twelve, and they
  that believed in him, they
  that were . . .
11*a* TG Mysteries of
  Godliness.
  b Matt. 13:35 (34–35);
  Luke 8:10.
  TG Jesus Christ,
  Teaching Mode of.
12*a* TG Spiritual Blindness.
  b TG Forgive.

15*a* TG Devil.
16*a* D&C 40:2.
17*a* 1 Ne. 8:28 (24–28).
  TG Affliction.
  b TG Persecution.
19*a* TG Treasure.
  b TG Lust.
21*a* 3 Ne. 18:24.
23*a* See JST Isa. 42:19–23
  (Appendix).
24*a* JST Mark 4:20 . . . and
  unto you that *continue*

  to receive, shall more be
  given . . .
  b Matt. 25:15; Luke 8:18.
25*a* JST Mark 4:20 . . . for
  he that *receiveth,* to him
  shall be given; *but* he
  that *continueth not to re-*
  ceive, from him shall . . .
  b D&C 43:10; 60:3.
27*a* 1 Cor. 3:6 (6–7).
28*a* TG Nature, Earth.
29*a* TG Harvest.

all herbs, and shooteth out great branches; so that the fowls of the air may lodge under the shadow of it.

33 And with many such parables spake he the word unto them, as they were *able to hear *it*.

34 But without a parable spake he not unto them: and when they were alone, he expounded all things to his disciples.

35 And the same day, when the even was come, he saith unto them, Let us pass over unto the other side.

36 And when they had sent away the multitude, they took him even as he was in the ship. And there were also with him other little ships.

37 And there arose a great storm of wind, and the waves beat into the ship, so that it was now full.

38 And he was in the hinder part of the ship, asleep on a pillow: and they awake him, and say unto him, Master, carest thou not that we perish?

39 And he arose, and rebuked the wind, and said unto the sea, *Peace, be still. And the wind ceased, and there was a great *calm.

40 And he said unto them, Why are ye so *fearful? how is it that ye have no *faith?

41 And they feared exceedingly, and said one to another, What manner of man is this, that even the wind and the sea obey him?

CHAPTER 5

Jesus casts out a legion of devils, who then enter the swine—A woman is healed by touching Jesus' clothes—He raises Jairus's daughter from the dead.

AND they came over unto the other side of the sea, into the country of the Gadarenes.

2 And when he was come out of the ship, immediately there met him out of the tombs a man with an unclean spirit,

3 Who had *his* dwelling among the tombs; and no man could bind him, no, not with chains:

4 Because that he had been often bound with fetters and chains, and the chains had been *plucked asunder by him, and the fetters broken in pieces: neither *could any *man* tame him.

5 And always, night and day, he was in the mountains, and in the tombs, crying, and cutting himself with stones.

6 But when he saw Jesus afar off, he ran and worshipped him,

7 And cried with a loud voice, and said, What have I to do with thee, Jesus, *thou* Son of the most high God? I *adjure thee by God, that thou torment me not.

8 For he said unto him, Come out of the man, *thou* *unclean *spirit.

9 And he asked him, What *is* thy name? And he answered, saying, My name *is* Legion: for we are many.

10 And he besought him much that he would not send them away out of the country.

11 Now there was there nigh unto the mountains a great herd of swine feeding.

12 And all the devils besought him, saying, Send us into the swine, that we may enter into them.

13 And forthwith Jesus gave them leave. And the unclean spirits went out, and entered into the swine: and the herd ran violently down a steep place into the sea, (they were about two thousand;) and were *choked in the sea.

14 And they that fed the swine fled, and told *it* in the city, and in the country. And they went out to see what it was that was done.

15 And they come to Jesus, and see him that was possessed with the

---

33a JST Mark 4:26 . . . able to
   bear; but without . . .
39a TG Peace.
   b Ps. 89:9.
40a Matt. 14:31;
   Mark 16:14;

Luke 24:25.
   b Alma 44:4 (1–5);
     D&C 4:5 (1–7).
5 4a GR broken, taken apart.
   b GR was any man strong
     enough to tame him.

7a OR implore.
8a TG Spirits, Evil or
   Unclean.
   b TG Heal.
13a OR drowned.

*a*devil, and had the legion, sitting, and clothed, and in his right *b*mind: and they were afraid.

16 And they that saw *it* told them how it befell to him that was possessed with the devil, and *also* concerning the swine.

17 And they began to pray him to depart out of their coasts.

18 And when he was come into the ship, he that had been possessed with the devil prayed him that he might be with him.

19 Howbeit Jesus suffered him not, but saith unto him, Go home to thy friends, and tell them how great things the Lord hath done for thee, and hath had *a*compassion on thee.

20 And he departed, and began to *a*publish in Decapolis how great things Jesus had done for him: and all *men* did marvel.

21 And when Jesus was passed over again by ship unto the other side, much people gathered unto him: and he was nigh unto the sea.

22 And, behold, there cometh one of the rulers of the synagogue, Jairus by name; and when he saw him, he fell at his feet,

23 And besought him greatly, saying, My little daughter lieth at the point of death: *I pray thee,* come and lay thy *a*hands on her, that she may be healed; and she shall live.

24 And *Jesus* went with him; and much people followed him, and thronged him.

25 And a certain woman, which had an *a*issue of blood twelve years,

26 And had suffered many things of many physicians, and had spent all that she had, and was nothing bettered, but rather grew worse,

27 When she had heard of Jesus, came in the press behind, and touched his *a*garment.

28 For she said, If I may touch but his clothes, I shall be whole.

29 And straightway the fountain of her blood was dried up; and she felt in *her* body that she was healed of that plague.

30 And Jesus, immediately knowing in himself that *a*virtue had gone out of him, turned him about in the press, and said, Who touched my clothes?

31 And his disciples said unto him, Thou seest the multitude thronging thee, and sayest thou, Who touched me?

32 And he looked round about to see her that had done this thing.

33 But the woman fearing and trembling, knowing what was done in her, came and fell down before him, and told him all the truth.

34 And he said unto her, Daughter, thy *a*faith hath made thee whole; go in *b*peace, and be whole of thy plague.

35 While he yet spake, there came from the ruler of the synagogue's *house certain* which said, Thy daughter is dead: why troublest thou the Master any further?

36 As soon as Jesus heard the word that was spoken, he saith unto the ruler of the synagogue, Be not afraid, only *a*believe.

37 And he suffered no man to follow him, save Peter, and James, and John the brother of James.

38 And he cometh to the house of the ruler of the synagogue, and seeth the tumult, and them that wept and wailed greatly.

39 And when he was come in, he saith unto them, Why make ye this *a*ado, and weep? the damsel is not dead, but sleepeth.

40 And they *a*laughed him to scorn. But when he had put them all out, he taketh the father and the mother of the damsel, and them that were with him, and entereth in where the damsel was lying.

15*a* 1 Ne. 11:31; Morm. 9:24.
  b TG Mind.
19*a* TG Compassion.
20*a* Luke 8:39.
23*a* TG Administrations to the Sick;

Hands, Laying on of.
25*a* OR hemorrhage.
27*a* Matt. 14:36.
30*a* GR power, strength.
  Luke 6:19 (17–19);
  8:46 (41–48).

34*a* Hel. 15:9 (9–10);
  D&C 46:19.
  b TG Peace of God.
36*a* GR exercise faith.
39*a* OR uproar, tumult.
40*a* OR ridiculed Him.

41 And he took the damsel by the hand, and said unto her, Talitha cumi; which is, being interpreted, Damsel, I say unto thee, *a*arise.

42 And straightway the damsel *a*arose, and walked; for she was *of the age* of twelve years. And they were astonished with a great astonishment.

43 And he *a*charged them straitly that no man should know it; and commanded that something should be given her to eat.

CHAPTER 6

Jesus sends forth the Twelve—John the Baptist is beheaded by Herod—Our Lord feeds the five thousand, walks on the water, and heals multitudes.

AND he went out from thence, and came into his own country; and his disciples follow him.

2 And when the sabbath day was come, he began to teach in the synagogue: and many hearing *him* were astonished, saying, From whence hath this *man* these things? and what *a*wisdom *is* this which is given unto him, that even such mighty works are wrought by his hands?

3 Is not this the *a*carpenter, the son of Mary, the *b*brother of James, and Joses, and of Juda, and Simon? and are not his sisters here with us? And they were offended at him.

4 But Jesus said unto them, A prophet is not without honour, but in his own country, and among his own kin, and in his own house.

5 And he could there do no *a*mighty work, save that he *b*laid his *c*hands upon a few sick folk, and healed *them.*

6 And he marvelled because of their *a*unbelief. And he went round about the villages, teaching.

7 ¶ And he called *unto him* the *a*twelve, and began to send them forth by *b*two and two; and gave them power over unclean spirits;

8 And commanded them that they should take nothing for *their* journey, save a staff only; no *a*scrip, no bread, no money in *their* purse:

9 But *be* shod with sandals; and not put on two coats.

10 And he said unto them, In what place soever ye enter into an house, there abide till ye depart from that place.

11 And whosoever shall not receive you, nor hear you, when ye depart thence, shake off the *a*dust under your feet for a testimony against them. Verily I say unto you, It shall be more tolerable for Sodom and Gomorrha in the day of judgment, than for that city.

12 And they went out, and *a*preached that men should repent.

13 And they cast out many devils, and *a*anointed with oil many that were sick, and healed *them.*

14 And king *a*Herod heard *of him;* (for his name was spread abroad:) and he said, That John the Baptist was risen from the dead, and therefore mighty works do shew forth themselves in him.

15 Others said, That it is Elias. And others said, That it is a prophet, or as one of the prophets.

16 But when Herod heard *thereof,* he said, It is John, whom I beheaded: he is risen from the dead.

17 For Herod himself had sent forth and laid hold upon John, and bound him in prison for Herodias' sake, his brother Philip's wife: for he had married her.

18 For John had said unto Herod, It is not lawful for thee to have thy brother's wife.

19 Therefore Herodias had a

41*a* TG Death, Power over.
42*a* TG Heal.
43*a* GR strongly warned them.
6 2*a* Eccl. 9:16.
   3*a* Matt. 13:55.
    b TG Jesus Christ, Family of.

5*a* Morm. 9:18 (18–21).
   b TG Hands, Laying on of.
   c TG Administrations to the Sick.
6*a* OR lack of faith.
7*a* TG Apostles.
   b Luke 10:1; D&C 42:6.

8*a* Matt. 10:10 (9–11).
11*a* Luke 10:11; D&C 24:15.
12*a* TG Preaching.
13*a* Ex. 31:11.
     TG Administrations to the Sick; Anointing.
14*a* Luke 9:7 (7–9).

quarrel against him, and would have killed him; but she could not:

20 For Herod feared John, knowing that he was a *a*just man *b*and an holy, and *c*observed him; and when he heard him, he did many things, and heard him gladly.

21 And when a convenient day was come, that Herod on his birthday made a supper to his *a*lords, high captains, and chief *estates* of Galilee;

22 And when the daughter of the said Herodias came in, and danced, and pleased Herod and them that sat with him, the king said unto the damsel, Ask of me whatsoever thou wilt, and I will give *it* thee.

23 And he *a*sware unto her, Whatsoever thou shalt ask of me, I will give *it* thee, unto the *b*half of my kingdom.

24 And she went forth, and said unto her mother, What shall I ask? And she said, The head of John the Baptist.

25 And she came in straightway with *a*haste unto the king, and asked, saying, I will that thou give me *b*by and by in a *c*charger the head of *d*John the Baptist.

26 And the king was exceeding sorry; *yet* for his *a*oath's sake, and for their sakes which sat with him, *b*he would not reject her.

27 And immediately the king sent an executioner, and commanded his head to be brought: and he went and beheaded him in the prison,

28 And brought his head in a charger, and gave it to the damsel: and the damsel gave it to her mother.

29 And when his disciples heard *of* *it*, they came and took up his corpse, and laid it in a tomb.

30 And the apostles gathered themselves together unto Jesus, and told him all things, both what they had done, and what they had taught.

31 And he said unto them, Come ye yourselves apart into a *a*desert place, and rest a while: for there were many coming and going, and they had no *b*leisure so much as to eat.

32 And they departed into a *a*desert place by ship privately.

33 And the people saw them departing, and many knew him, and ran afoot thither out of all cities, and outwent them, and came together unto him.

34 And Jesus, when he came out, saw much people, and was moved with *a*compassion toward them, because they were as sheep not having a *b*shepherd: and he began to *c*teach them many things.

35 And when the day was now far spent, his disciples came unto him, and said, *a*This is a desert place, and now the time *is* far passed:

36 Send them away, that they may go into the country round about, and into the villages, and buy themselves bread: for they have nothing to eat.

37 He answered and said unto them, Give ye them to eat. And they say unto him, Shall we go and buy two hundred *a*pennyworth of bread, and give them to eat?

38 He saith unto them, How many loaves have ye? go and see. And when they knew, they say, Five, and two fishes.

39 And he commanded them to

20*a* GR righteous and holy man.
  b JST Mark 6:21 . . . and a holy *man, and one who feared God* and observed *to worship* him; and when he heard him he did many things *for him,* and heard . . .
  c GR protected.
21*a* GR nobles, military commanders, and prominent men.

23*a* TG Swearing.
  b Esth. 5:3.
25*a* TG Haste.
  b GR at once.
  c OR platter.
  d TG Martyrdom.
26*a* TG Vow.
  b GR he did not desire to refuse.
31*a* JST Mark 6:32 . . . solitary . . .
  b Mark 3:20.
32*a* JST Mark 6:33 . . .

    solitary . . .
34*a* TG Compassion.
  b TG Shepherd.
  c TG Jesus Christ, Teaching Mode of.
35*a* JST Mark 6:36 . . . This is a *solitary* place, and now the time *for departure* is *come* . . .
37*a* GR *denarii;* one *denarius* was a workman's daily wage.

make all sit down by companies upon the green grass.

40 And they sat down in ranks, by hundreds, and by fifties.

41 And when he had taken the five loaves and the two fishes, he looked up to heaven, and blessed, and brake the loaves, and gave *them* to his disciples to set before them; and the two fishes divided he among them all.

42 And they did all eat, and were filled.

43 And they took up twelve baskets full of the fragments, and of the fishes.

44 And they that did eat of the loaves were about ªfive thousand men.

45 And straightway he constrained his disciples to get into the ship, and to go to the other side before unto Bethsaida, while he sent away the people.

46 And when he had ªsent them away, he departed into a mountain to pray.

47 And when even was come, the ship was in the midst of the sea, and he alone on the land.

48 And he saw them ªtoiling in rowing; for the wind was contrary unto them: and about the fourth watch of the night he cometh unto them, walking upon the sea, and would have passed by them.

49 But when they saw him walking upon the sea, they supposed it had been a spirit, and cried out:

50 For they all saw him, and were ªtroubled. And immediately he talked with them, and saith unto them, Be of good cheer: it is I; be not afraid.

51 And he went up unto them into the ship; and the wind ceased: and they were sore amazed in themselves beyond measure, and wondered.

52 For they ªconsidered not *the miracle* of the loaves: for their heart was ᵇhardened.

53 And when they had passed over, they came into the land of Gennesaret, and drew to the shore.

54 And when they were come out of the ship, straightway they knew him,

55 And ran through that whole region round about, and began to carry about in beds those that were sick, where they heard he was.

56 And whithersoever he entered, into villages, or cities, or country, they laid the sick in the streets, and besought him that they might touch if it were but the border of his garment: and as many as touched him were made whole.

CHAPTER 7

Jesus reproves the Pharisees for their false traditions and ceremonies—He casts a devil out of the daughter of a Greek woman—He opens the ears and loosens the tongue of a person with an impediment.

THEN came together unto him the Pharisees, and certain of the scribes, which came from Jerusalem.

2 And when they saw some of his disciples eat bread with defiled, that is to say, with unwashen, hands, they found fault.

3 For the Pharisees, and all the Jews, except they ªwash *their* hands oft, eat not, holding the tradition of the elders.

4 And *when they come* from the market, except they wash, they eat not. And many other things there be, which they have received to hold, *as* the washing of cups, and pots, brasen vessels, and of tables.

5 Then the Pharisees and scribes asked him, Why walk not thy disciples according to the tradition of the elders, but eat bread with ªunwashen hands?

6 He answered and said unto them, Well hath Esaias prophesied of you hypocrites, as it is written,

---

44a Matt. 14:21 (13–21);
    Luke 9:14 (10–17);
    John 6:10 (1–13).
46a GR bid them farewell.

48a GR struggling at their
    oars.
50a OR terrified.
52a OR did not understand.

1 Cor. 2:11.
  b TG Hardheartedness.
7 3a TG Purification.
  5a TG Wash.

This people *a*honoureth me with *their* lips, but their heart is far from me.

7 Howbeit in vain do they worship me, teaching *for* doctrines the commandments of men.

8 For laying aside the commandment of God, ye hold the *a*tradition of men, *as* the washing of pots and cups: and many other such like things ye do.

9 And he said unto them, Full well ye reject the commandment of God, that ye may keep your own tradition.

10 *a*For Moses said, Honour thy father and thy mother; and, Whoso *b*curseth father or mother, let him die the death:

11 But ye say, If a man shall say to his father or mother, It is *a*Corban, that is to say, a gift, by whatsoever thou mightest be profited by me; *he shall be free.*

12 And ye suffer him no more to do ought for his father or his mother;

13 Making the word of God of none effect through your tradition, which ye have delivered: and many such like things do ye.

14 ¶ And when he had called all the people *unto him,* he said unto them, Hearken unto me every one *of you,* and understand:

15 There is nothing from without a man, that entering into him can *a*defile him: but the things which come out of him, those are they that *b*defile the man.

16 If any man have ears to hear, let him hear.

17 And when he was entered into the house from the people, his disciples asked him concerning the parable.

18 And he saith unto them, Are ye so without understanding also? Do ye not perceive, that whatsoever thing from without entereth into the man, *it* cannot defile him;

19 Because it entereth not into his heart, but into the belly, and goeth out into the draught, purging all meats?

20 And he said, That which cometh out of the man, that *a*defileth the man.

21 For from within, out of the *a*heart of men, proceed evil thoughts, *b*adulteries, fornications, murders,

22 *a*Thefts, *b*covetousness, *c*wickedness, *d*deceit, lasciviousness, an evil eye, blasphemy, pride, foolishness:

23 All these *a*evil things come from within, and *b*defile the man.

24 ¶ And from thence he arose, and went into the borders of Tyre and Sidon, and entered into an house, *a*and would have no man know *it:* but he could not be hid.

25 For a *certain* woman, whose young daughter had an unclean spirit, heard of him, and came and fell at his feet:

26 The woman was a Greek, a Syrophenician by nation; and she besought him that he would cast forth the devil out of her daughter.

27 But Jesus said unto her, Let the *a*children first be filled: for it is not meet to take the children's bread, and to cast *it* unto the *b*dogs.

28 And she answered and said unto him, Yes, Lord: yet the dogs under the table eat of the children's crumbs.

6*a* TG Apostasy of Israel;
    Hypocrisy.
8*a* TG Traditions of Men.
10*a* JST Mark 7:10–12
    (Appendix).
  b TG Curse; Honoring
    Father and Mother.
11*a* Matt. 15:5.
15*a* JST Mark 7:15 . . . defile
    him, *which is food;* but
    the things which come
    out of him; those are
    they that defile the

man, *that proceedeth forth
    out of the heart.*
  b Titus 1:15;
    2 Ne. 19:17;
    D&C 93:35.
20*a* James 3:6;
    D&C 88:121.
21*a* 1 Jn. 2:16.
  b TG Adulterer.
22*a* TG Stealing.
  b TG Covet.
  c TG Wickedness.
  d TG Deceit;

Fraud.
23*a* TG Motivations.
  b Mosiah 4:30.
24*a* JST Mark 7:22–23 . . .
    and would *that* no
    man *should come unto
    him.* But he could not
    deny them; *for he had
    compassion upon all men.*
27*a* JST Mark 7:26 . . .
    children *of the kingdom*
    first . . .
  b D&C 41:6.

29 And he said unto her, For this saying go thy way; the devil is gone out of thy daughter.

30 And when she was come to her house, she found the ^adevil gone out, and her daughter laid upon the bed.

31 ¶ And again, departing from the coasts of Tyre and Sidon, he came unto the sea of Galilee, through the midst of the coasts of Decapolis.

32 And they bring unto him one that was deaf, and had an impediment in his speech; and they beseech him to put his ^ahand upon him.

33 And he took him aside from the multitude, and put his fingers into his ears, and he spit, and touched his tongue;

34 And looking up to heaven, he sighed, and saith unto him, Ephphatha, that is, Be opened.

35 And straightway his ears were ^aopened, and the string of his tongue was loosed, and he spake plain.

36 And he charged them that they should tell no man: but the more he charged them, so much the more a great deal they ^apublished it;

37 And were beyond measure astonished, saying, He hath done all things well: he maketh both the deaf to hear, and the dumb to speak.

CHAPTER 8

Jesus feeds the four thousand—He counsels, Beware of the leaven of the Pharisees—He heals a blind man in Bethsaida—Peter testifies that Jesus is the Christ.

IN those days the multitude being very great, and having nothing to eat, Jesus called his disciples *unto him,* and saith unto them,

2 I have compassion on the multitude, because they have now been with me three days, and have nothing to eat:

3 And if I send them away fasting to their own houses, they will faint by the way: for ^adivers of them came from far.

4 And his disciples answered him, From whence can a man satisfy these *men* with bread here in the wilderness?

5 And he asked them, How many loaves have ye? And they said, Seven.

6 And he commanded the people to sit down on the ground: and he took the seven loaves, and gave thanks, and brake, and gave to his disciples to set before *them;* and they did set *them* before the people.

7 And they had a few small fishes: and he blessed, and commanded to set them also before *them.*

8 So they did eat, and were filled: and they took up of the broken *meat* that was left seven baskets.

9 And they that had eaten were about four thousand: and he sent them away.

10 ¶ And straightway he entered into a ship with his disciples, and came into the parts of Dalmanutha.

11 And the Pharisees came forth, and began to question with him, seeking of him a ^asign from heaven, tempting him.

12 And he sighed deeply in his spirit, and saith, Why doth this generation seek after a ^asign? verily I say unto you, There shall no sign be given unto this generation.

13 And he left them, and entering into the ship again departed to the other side.

14 ¶ Now the disciples had forgotten to take bread, neither had they in the ship with them more than one loaf.

15 And he charged them, saying, Take heed, beware of the leaven of the Pharisees, and *of* the leaven of Herod.

16 And they reasoned among themselves, saying, *It is* because we have no bread.

17 And when Jesus knew *it,* he saith unto them, Why reason ye, because

---

30a 1 Ne. 11:31.
32a TG Administrations
    to the Sick;

Hands, Laying on of.
35a TG Miracle.
36a Matt. 9:31.

8 3a GR some.
11a D&C 46:9; 63:7 (7–11).
12a Matt. 16:4 (1–12).

ye have no bread? perceive ye not yet, neither understand? *a*have ye your heart yet *b*hardened?

18 Having eyes, see ye not? and having ears, hear ye not? and do ye not remember?

19 When I brake the five loaves among five thousand, how many baskets full of fragments took ye up? They say unto him, Twelve.

20 And when the seven among four thousand, how many baskets full of fragments took ye up? And they said, Seven.

21 And he said unto them, How is it that ye do not understand?

22 ¶ And he cometh to Bethsaida; and they bring a blind man unto him, and besought him to touch him.

23 And he took the blind man by the hand, and led him out of the town; and when he had spit on his eyes, and put his *a*hands upon him, he asked him if he saw *b*ought.

24 And he looked up, and said, I see men as trees, walking.

25 After that he put *his* hands again upon his eyes, and made him look up: and he was restored, and saw *a*every man clearly.

26 And he sent him away to his house, saying, Neither go into the town, nor tell *it* to any in the town.

27 ¶ And Jesus went out, and his disciples, into the towns of Cæsarea Philippi: and by the way he asked his disciples, saying unto them, Whom do men say that I am?

28 And they answered, John the Baptist: but some *say,* Elias; and others, One of the prophets.

29 And he saith unto them, But whom say ye that I am? And Peter answereth and saith unto him, Thou art the *a*Christ.

30 And he charged them that they should *a*tell no man of him.

31 And he began to *a*teach them, that the Son of man must suffer many things, and be rejected of the elders, and *of* the chief priests, and scribes, and be killed, and after three days rise again.

32 And he spake that saying openly. And Peter took him, and began to rebuke him.

33 But when he had turned about and looked on his disciples, he rebuked Peter, saying, Get thee behind me, *a*Satan: for *b*thou savourest not the things that be of God, but the things that be of men.

34 ¶ And when he had called the people *unto him* with his disciples also, he said unto them, Whosoever will come after me, let him *a*deny himself, and take up his cross, and *b*follow me.

35 *a*For whosoever will save his life shall lose it; but whosoever shall *b*lose his *c*life for my sake and the gospel's, the same shall save it.

36 For what shall it profit a man, if he shall *a*gain the whole world, and lose his own soul?

37 Or what shall a man give in exchange for his *a*soul?

38 Whosoever therefore shall be *a*ashamed of me and of my words in this adulterous and sinful generation; of him also shall the *b*Son of man be ashamed, when he cometh in the glory of his Father with the holy *c*angels.

17*a* GR do you still have hardened hearts?
  b TG Hardheartedness.
23*a* TG Administrations to the Sick; Hands, Laying on of.
  b OR anything.
25*a* OR everything.
29*a* TG Jesus Christ, Messiah.
30*a* Luke 9:21.
31*a* TG Jesus Christ, Teaching Mode of.
33*a* Alma 12:5 (5–6, 34).

  b GR you do not consider, cherish.
34*a* TG Self-Mastery.
  b TG Jesus Christ, Exemplar.
35*a* JST Mark 8:37–38 (Appendix).
  b Luke 9:24; JST Luke 9:24–25 (Appendix).
  c Heb. 11:35; JST Heb. 11:35 (Heb. 11:35 note *b*);

    D&C 103:28 (27–28).
    TG Martyrdom.
36*a* Jer. 45:5.
37*a* JST Mark 8:39–40 . . . soul? *Therefore deny yourselves of these, and be not ashamed of me.*
38*a* 1 Ne. 8:28 (24–28).
    TG Shame.
  b TG Jesus Christ, Son of Man.
  c JST Mark 8:42–43 (Appendix).

CHAPTER 9

Jesus is transfigured on the moun-
tain—He casts out an unclean spirit—
He teaches concerning His death and
resurrection, who will be greatest, and
the condemnation of those who offend
His little ones.

AND he said unto them, Verily I say unto you, That there be some of them that stand here, which shall not taste of death, till they have seen the kingdom of God come with power.

2 ¶ And after ªsix days Jesus taketh *with him* Peter, and James, and John, ᵇand leadeth them up into an high mountain apart by themselves: and he was ᶜtransfigured before them.

3 And his raiment became shining, exceeding white as snow; so as no fuller on earth can white them.

4 And there appeared unto them Elias with ªMoses: and they were talking with Jesus.

5 And Peter answered and said to Jesus, Master, it is good for us to be here: and let us make three tabernacles; one for thee, and one for Moses, and one for Elias.

6 For he wist not what to say; for they were sore afraid.

7 And there was a cloud that overshadowed them: and a ªvoice came out of the cloud, saying, This is my ᵇbeloved Son: hear him.

8 And suddenly, when they had looked round about, they saw no man any more, save Jesus only with themselves.

9 And as they came down from the mountain, he charged them that they should tell no ªman what things they had seen, till the Son of man were risen from the dead.

10 And they kept that saying with themselves, questioning one with another what the ªrising from the dead should mean.

11 ¶ And they asked him, saying, Why say the scribes that Elias must first come?

12 And he answered and told them, Elias verily cometh first, ªand ᵇrestoreth all things; and how it is written of the ᶜSon of man, that he must ᵈsuffer many things, and be set at ᵉnought.

13 But I say unto you, That Elias is indeed come, and they have done unto him whatsoever they ªlisted, as it is written of ᵇhim.

14 ¶ And when he came to *his* disciples, he saw a great multitude about them, and the scribes questioning with them.

15 And straightway all the people, when they beheld him, were greatly amazed, and running to *him* saluted him.

16 And he asked the scribes, What question ye with them?

17 And one of the multitude answered and said, Master, I have brought unto thee my son, which hath a dumb spirit;

18 And wheresoever he taketh him, he ªteareth him: and he foameth, and gnasheth with his teeth, and pineth away: and I spake to thy disciples that they should cast him out; and they could not.

19 He answereth him, and saith, O faithless generation, how long shall I be with you? how long shall I suffer you? bring him unto me.

20 And they brought him unto

9 2*a* Luke 9:28 (28–36).
  b JST Mark 9:1 . . . *who*
    asked him many questions
    concerning his sayings;
    and *Jesus* leadeth
    them . . .
  c Matt. 17:2 (1–13);
    Luke 9:29 (28–36).
 4*a* JST Mark 9:3 . . . *Moses,*
    or in other words, John the
    Baptist and Moses . . .
 7*a* TG God, Manifesta-

tions of.
  b Matt. 3:17;
    Luke 9:35 (34–36).
 9*a* Matt. 17:9 (9–12).
10*a* John 20:9.
12*a* JST Mark 9:10 . . . *and*
    prepareth all things;
    and teacheth you of the
    prophets; how . . .
  b TG Dispensations.
  c TG Jesus Christ,
    Prophecies about.

  d TG Jesus Christ,
    Crucifixion of.
  e Isa. 53:3.
13*a* GR willed, chose,
    intended.
  b JST Mark 9:11 . . . *him;*
    and he bore record of me,
    and they received him not.
    Verily this was Elias.
18*a* GR dashes on the
    ground, convulses,
    lacerates.

him: and when he saw him, straight-way the spirit ªtare him; and he fell on the ground, and wallowed foaming.

21 And he asked his father, How long is it ago since this came unto him? And he said, Of a child.

22 And ofttimes it hath cast him into the fire, and into the waters, to destroy him: but if thou canst do any thing, have ªcompassion on us, and help us.

23 Jesus said unto him, If thou canst believe, all things *are* ªpossible to him that ᵇbelieveth.

24 And straightway the father of the child cried out, and said with tears, Lord, I believe; help thou mine ªunbelief.

25 When Jesus saw that the peo-ple came running together, he ªre-buked the ᵇfoul spirit, saying unto him, *Thou* dumb and deaf spirit, I charge thee, come out of him, and enter no more into him.

26 And *the spirit* cried, and rent him sore, and came out of him: and he was as one dead; insomuch that many said, He is dead.

27 But Jesus took him by the hand, and ªlifted him up; and he arose.

28 And when he was come into the house, his disciples asked him privately, Why could not we cast him out?

29 And he said unto them, This kind can come forth by nothing, but by prayer and ªfasting.

30 ¶ And they departed thence, and passed through Galilee; and he would not that any man should know *it*.

31 For he taught his disciples, and said unto them, The ªSon of man is delivered into the hands of men, and they shall kill him; and after that he is killed, he shall ᵇrise the third day.

32 But they understood not that saying, and were afraid to ask him.

33 ¶ And he came to Capernaum: and being in the house he asked them, What was it that ye ªdisputed among yourselves by the way?

34 But they held their peace: for by the way they had ªdisputed among themselves, who *should be* the ᵇgreatest.

35 And he sat down, and called the twelve, and saith unto them, If any man desire to be ªfirst, *the same* shall be last of all, and ᵇservant of all.

36 And he took a child, and set him in the midst of them: and when he had taken him in his arms, he said unto them,

37 ªWhosoever shall receive one of such ᵇchildren in my name, re-ceiveth me: and whosoever shall receive me, receiveth not me, but him that sent me.

38 ¶ And John answered him, say-ing, Master, we saw one ªcasting out devils in thy name, and he followeth not us: and we forbad him, because he followeth not us.

39 But Jesus said, Forbid him not: for there is no man which shall do a ªmiracle in my ᵇname, that can lightly speak evil of me.

40 For he that is not against us is ªon our part.

41 For whosoever shall give you a cup of water to drink in my name,

---

20ª Mark 1:26.
22ª TG Compassion.
23ª Dan. 3:29.
    TG God, Power of.
  b TG Faith.
24ª TG Doubt.
25ª TG Heal.
  b TG Spirits, Evil or Unclean.
27ª Acts 3:7.
29ª TG Problem-Solving.
31ª TG Jesus Christ, Son of Man.
  b TG Jesus Christ,

Resurrection.
33ª GR reasoned, disputed, pondered.
34ª TG Disputations.
  b Luke 9:46.
35ª Prov. 18:17.
  b TG Meek.
37ª JST Mark 9:34–35 *Whosoever shall humble himself like one of these children, and receiveth me, ye shall receive in my name. And whosoever shall receive me,*

receiveth not me only, but him that sent me, even the Father.
  b TG Children; Salvation of Little Children.
38ª Luke 11:19; Acts 19:13.
39ª TG Miracle.
  b TG Name.
40ª Matt. 12:30; Luke 9:50.

because ye belong to Christ, verily I say unto you, he shall not *a*lose his *b*reward.

42 And whosoever shall *a*offend one of *these* little ones that believe in me, it is better for him that a millstone were hanged about his neck, and he were cast into the sea.

43 *a*And if thy hand offend thee, *b*cut it off: it is better for thee to enter into life maimed, than having two hands to go into *c*hell, into the fire that never shall be quenched:

44 Where their worm dieth not, and the fire is not quenched.

45 And if thy foot *a*offend thee, cut it off: it is better for thee to enter halt into life, than having two feet to be cast into hell, into the fire that never shall be quenched:

46 Where their worm dieth not, and the fire is not quenched.

47 And if thine eye offend thee, pluck it out: it is better for thee to enter into the kingdom of God with one eye, than having two eyes to be cast into hell fire:

48 Where their *a*worm dieth not, and the fire is not quenched.

49 For every one shall be *a*salted with fire, and every sacrifice shall be salted with salt.

50 Salt *is* good: but if the salt have lost his saltness, wherewith will ye season it? Have salt in yourselves, and have *a*peace one with another.

CHAPTER 10

Jesus teaches the higher law of marriage—He blesses little children—Jesus counsels the rich young man, foretells His own death, and heals blind Bartimæus.

AND he arose from thence, and cometh into the coasts of Judæa by the farther side of Jordan: and the people resort unto him again; and, as he was wont, he taught them again.

2 ¶ And the Pharisees came to him, and asked him, Is it lawful for a man to put away *his* wife? tempting him.

3 And he answered and said unto them, What did Moses command you?

4 And they said, Moses suffered to write a bill of divorcement, and to put *her* away.

5 And Jesus answered and said unto them, For the hardness of your heart he wrote you this precept.

6 But from the beginning of the creation God made them male and female.

7 For this cause shall a *a*man leave his father and mother, and cleave to his *b*wife;

8 And they twain shall be one flesh: so then they are no more twain, but one flesh.

9 What therefore God hath *a*joined together, let not man put *b*asunder.

10 And in the house his disciples asked him again of the same *matter.*

11 And he saith unto them, Whosoever shall put away his wife, and marry another, committeth adultery against her.

12 And if a woman shall put away her husband, and be married to another, she committeth adultery.

13 ¶ And they brought young children to him, that he should touch them: and *his* disciples rebuked those that brought *them.*

14 But when Jesus saw *it,* he was much displeased, and said unto them, Suffer the little *a*children to come unto me, and forbid them not: for of such is the kingdom of God.

15 Verily I say unto you, Whosoever shall not receive the kingdom of God as a little *a*child, he shall not enter therein.

41*a* Matt. 10:42; D&C 84:90.
  b TG Reward.
42*a* TG Offense.
43*a* JST Mark 9:40–48 (Appendix).
  b TG Self-Mastery.
  c TG Hell.
45*a* GR cause thee to stumble.
48*a* Isa. 66:24; D&C 76:44.
49*a* TG Salt.
50*a* 1 Thes. 5:13. TG Peace.
10 7*a* TG Marriage, Husbands.
  b TG Marriage, Wives.
9*a* TG Family, Eternal; Genealogy and Temple Work; Marriage, Marry.
  b TG Divorce.
14*a* Moro. 8:8 (5–9). TG Example.
15*a* TG Meek.

16 And he took them up in his arms, put *his* hands upon them, and *a*blessed them.

17 ¶ And when he was gone forth into the way, there came one running, and kneeled to him, and asked him, Good Master, what shall I do that I may inherit eternal life?

18 And Jesus said unto him, Why callest thou me good? *there is* none *a*good but one, *that is,* God.

19 Thou knowest the commandments, Do not commit *a*adultery, Do not *b*kill, Do not *c*steal, Do not bear false witness, *d*Defraud not, *e*Honour thy father and mother.

20 And he answered and said unto him, Master, all these have I observed from my youth.

21 Then Jesus beholding him loved him, and said unto him, One thing thou lackest: go thy way, sell whatsoever thou hast, and *a*give to the poor, and thou shalt have treasure in heaven: and come, take up the cross, and *b*follow me.

22 And he was sad at that saying, and went away grieved: for he had great possessions.

23 ¶ And Jesus looked round about, and saith unto his disciples, How hardly shall they that have riches enter into the kingdom of God!

24 And the disciples were astonished at his words. But Jesus answereth again, and saith unto them, Children, how hard is it for them that *a*trust in *b*riches to enter into the kingdom of God!

25 It is easier for a camel to go through the eye of a needle, than for a rich man to enter into the kingdom of God.

26 And they were astonished out of measure, saying among themselves, Who then can be saved?

27 And Jesus looking upon them saith, *a*With men *it is* impossible, but not with God: for with God all things are *b*possible.

28 ¶ Then Peter began to say unto him, Lo, we have left all, and have followed thee.

29 And Jesus answered and said, Verily I say unto you, There is no man that hath left house, or brethren, or sisters, or father, or mother, or wife, or children, or lands, for my sake, and the gospel's,

30 But he shall receive an *a*hundredfold now in this time, houses, and brethren, and sisters, and mothers, and children, and lands, with persecutions; and in the world to come eternal life.

31 *a*But many *that are b*first shall be last; and the last first.

32 ¶ And they were in the way going up to Jerusalem; and Jesus went before them: and they were amazed; and as they followed, they were afraid. And he took again the twelve, and began to tell them what things should happen unto him,

33 *Saying,* Behold, we go up to Jerusalem; and the *a*Son of man shall be delivered unto the chief priests, and unto the *b*scribes; and they shall condemn him to death, and shall deliver him to the Gentiles:

34 And they shall *a*mock him, and shall scourge him, and shall spit

---

16*a* 3 Ne. 17:21.
     TG Salvation of Little Children.
18*a* Ether 4:12 (11–12).
19*a* D&C 66:10.
   b TG Murder.
   c TG Stealing.
   d TG Fraud.
   e TG Honoring Father and Mother.
21*a* TG Charity; Generosity.
   b TG Jesus Christ, Exemplar.
24*a* Jacob 2:18 (17–19).
   b TG Treasure.
27*a* JST Mark 10:26 . . . With men *that trust in riches, it is impossible; but not impossible with men who trust in God and leave all for my sake, for with such all these things are possible.*
   b TG God, Power of.
30*a* TG Reward.
31*a* JST Mark 10:30–31 But *there are* many *who make themselves* first, *that* shall be last, and the last first. *This he said, rebuking Peter . . .*
   b Jacob 5:63; Ether 13:12 (10–12).
33*a* TG Jesus Christ, Son of Man.
   b TG Scribe.
34*a* TG Mocking.

upon him, and shall kill him: and the third day he shall ᵇrise again.

35 ¶ And James and John, the sons of Zebedee, come unto him, saying, Master, we would that thou shouldest do for us whatsoever we shall desire.

36 And he said unto them, What would ye that I should do for you?

37 They said unto him, Grant unto us that we may sit, one on thy right hand, and the other on thy left hand, in thy glory.

38 But Jesus said unto them, Ye know not what ye ask: can ye drink of the cup that I drink of? and be baptized with the ᵃbaptism that I am baptized with?

39 And they said unto him, We can. And Jesus said unto them, Ye shall indeed drink of the cup that I drink of; and with the baptism that I am baptized withal shall ye be baptized:

40 But to sit on my right hand and on my left hand is not mine to give; but *it shall be given to them* for whom it is prepared.

41 And when the ten heard *it*, they began to be much displeased with James and John.

42 But Jesus called them *to him*, and saith unto them, Ye know that they which are accounted to rule over the Gentiles exercise lordship over them; and their great ones exercise authority upon them.

43 But so shall it not be among you: but whosoever will be ᵃgreat among you, shall be your minister:

44 And whosoever of you will be the ᵃchiefest, shall be servant of all.

45 For even the Son of man came not to be ministered unto, but to minister, and to give his life a ᵃransom for many.

46 ¶ And they came to Jericho: and as he went out of Jericho with his disciples and a great number of people, blind ᵃBartimæus, the son

of Timæus, sat by the highway side begging.

47 And when he heard that it was Jesus of Nazareth, he began to cry out, and say, Jesus, *thou* Son of David, have mercy on me.

48 And many charged him that he should hold his peace: but he cried the more a great deal, *Thou* Son of David, have mercy on me.

49 And Jesus stood still, and commanded him to be called. And they call the ᵃblind man, saying unto him, Be of good comfort, rise; he calleth thee.

50 And he, casting away his garment, rose, and came to Jesus.

51 And Jesus answered and said unto him, What wilt thou that I should do unto thee? The blind man said unto him, Lord, that I might receive my sight.

52 And Jesus said unto him, Go thy way; thy faith hath ᵃmade thee whole. And immediately he received his sight, and followed Jesus in the way.

CHAPTER 11

Jesus rides into Jerusalem amid shouts of hosanna—He curses a fig tree, drives the money changers from the temple, and confounds the scribes on the matter of authority.

AND when they came nigh to Jerusalem, unto Bethphage and Bethany, at the mount of Olives, he sendeth forth two of his disciples,

2 And saith unto them, Go your way into the village over against you: and as soon as ye be entered into it, ye shall find a colt tied, whereon never man sat; loose him, and bring *him*.

3 And if any man say unto you, Why do ye this? say ye that the Lord hath need of him; and straightway he will send him hither.

4 And they went their way, and found the colt tied by the door

34b TG Jesus Christ, Resurrection.
38a TG Jesus Christ, Baptism of.
43a D&C 50:26 (26–27).
44a Matt. 23:11; Luke 22:24 (24–30); 2 Ne. 9:5.
45a Rom. 4:25.
46a Matt. 20:30 (29–34).
49a 1 Ne. 17:51.
52a GR saved, preserved, healed thee.

without in a place where two ways met; and they loose him.

5 And certain of them that stood there said unto them, What do ye, loosing the colt?

6 And they said unto them even as Jesus had commanded: and they let them go.

7 And they brought the [a]colt to Jesus, and cast their garments on him; and he sat upon him.

8 And many spread their garments in the way: and others cut down branches off the trees, and strawed *them* in the way.

9 And they that went before, and they that followed, cried, saying, Hosanna; [a]Blessed *is* he that cometh in the name of the Lord:

10 [a]Blessed *be* the kingdom of our father David, that cometh in the name of the Lord: Hosanna in the highest.

11 And Jesus entered into Jerusalem, and into the temple: and when he had looked round about upon all things, and now the eventide was come, he went out unto Bethany with the twelve.

12 ¶ And on the morrow, when they were come from Bethany, he was hungry:

13 And seeing a fig tree afar off having leaves, he came, if haply he might find any thing thereon: and when he came to it, he found nothing but leaves; for the time of figs was not *yet.*

14 And Jesus answered and said unto it, No man eat fruit of thee hereafter for ever. And his disciples heard *it.*

15 ¶ And they come to Jerusalem: and Jesus went into the temple, and began to cast out them that sold and bought in the temple, and overthrew the tables of the moneychangers, and the seats of them that sold doves;

16 And would not suffer that any man should carry *any* vessel through the temple.

17 And he taught, saying unto them, Is it not written, My house shall be called of all nations the house of prayer? but ye have made it a den of thieves.

18 And the scribes and chief priests heard *it,* and sought how they might [a]destroy him: for they feared him, because all the people was astonished at his doctrine.

19 And when even was come, he went out of the city.

20 ¶ And in the morning, as they passed by, they saw the fig tree dried up from the roots.

21 And Peter calling to remembrance saith unto him, Master, behold, the fig tree which thou cursedst is withered away.

22 And Jesus answering saith unto them, Have [a]faith in God.

23 For verily I say unto you, That whosoever shall say unto this mountain, Be thou removed, and be thou cast into the sea; and shall not [a]doubt in his heart, but shall believe that those things which he saith shall come to pass; he shall have whatsoever he saith.

24 Therefore I say unto you, What things soever ye desire, when ye [a]pray, [b]believe that ye receive *them,* and ye shall have *them.*

25 And when ye stand [a]praying, forgive, if ye have ought against any: that your Father also which is in heaven may [b]forgive you your trespasses.

26 But if ye do not [a]forgive, neither will your Father which is in heaven forgive your trespasses.

27 ¶ And they come again to Jerusalem: and as he was walking in the temple, there come to him the chief priests, and the scribes, and the elders,

---

11 7*a* Zech. 9:9.
  9*a* Ps. 118:26.
  10*a* JST Mark 11:11–12 *That bringeth* the kingdom of our father David; *Blessed is he* that

cometh in the name of the Lord . . .
18*a* TG Jesus Christ, Betrayal of.
22*a* TG Faith.
23*a* TG Doubt.

24*a* TG Prayer.
  b 3 Ne. 18:20; D&C 29:6.
25*a* TG Prayer.
  b TG Forgive.
26*a* D&C 64:9 (7–10).

28 And say unto him, By what *authority doest thou these things? and who gave thee this authority to do these things?

29 And Jesus answered and said unto them, I will also ask of you one question, and answer me, and I will tell you by what authority I do these things.

30 The baptism of John, was *it* from heaven, or of men? answer me.

31 And they reasoned with themselves, saying, If we shall say, From heaven; he will say, Why then did ye not believe him?

32 But if we shall say, Of men; they feared the people: for all *men* counted John, that he was a prophet indeed.

33 And they answered and said unto Jesus, We cannot tell. And Jesus answering saith unto them, Neither do I tell you by what authority I do these things.

CHAPTER 12

Jesus gives the parable of the wicked husbandmen—He speaks of paying taxes, celestial marriage, the two great commandments, the divine sonship of Christ, and the widow's mites.

AND he began to speak unto them by parables. A *certain* man planted a vineyard, and set an hedge about *it,* and digged *a place for* the winefat, and built a tower, and let it out to husbandmen, and went into a far country.

2 And at the season he sent to the husbandmen a servant, that he might receive from the husbandmen of the fruit of the vineyard.

3 And they caught *him,* and beat him, and sent *him* away empty.

4 And again he sent unto them another servant; and at him they cast stones, and wounded *him* in the head, and sent *him* away shamefully handled.

5 And again he sent another; and

him they killed, and many others; beating some, and killing some.

6 Having yet therefore one son, his wellbeloved, he sent him also last unto them, saying, They will reverence my son.

7 But those husbandmen said among themselves, This is the heir; come, let us kill him, and the inheritance shall be ours.

8 And they took him, and killed *him, and cast him* out of the vineyard.

9 What shall therefore the lord of the vineyard do? he will come and destroy the husbandmen, and will give the *vineyard unto others.

10 And have ye not read this scripture; The *stone which the builders rejected is become the head of the corner:

11 This was the Lord's doing, and it is marvellous in our eyes?

12 And they sought to lay hold on him, but feared the people: for they knew that he had spoken the parable against them: and they left him, and went their way.

13 ¶ And they send unto him certain of the Pharisees and of the Herodians, to *catch him in *his* words.

14 And when they were come, they say unto him, Master, we know that thou art true, and carest for no man: for thou regardest not the person of men, but teachest the way of God in truth: Is it lawful to give tribute to Cæsar, or not?

15 Shall we give, or shall we not give? But he, knowing their hypocrisy, said unto them, Why *tempt ye me? bring me a penny, that I may see *it.

16 And they brought *it.* And he saith unto them, Whose *is* this image and superscription? And they said unto him, Cæsar's.

17 And Jesus answering said unto them, Render to Cæsar the things that are Cæsar's, and to God the things that are God's. And they marvelled at him.

28*a* TG Priesthood, Authority.
12 9*a* TG Vineyard of the

Lord.
10*a* TG Cornerstone.
13*a* Matt. 22:15 (15–22);

Luke 11:54 (53–54); 20:20 (19–26).
15*a* TG Test.

18 ¶ Then come unto him the Sadducees, which say there is no resurrection; and they asked him, saying,

19 Master, Moses wrote unto us, If a man's brother die, and leave *his* wife *behind him,* and leave no children, that his *a*brother should take his wife, and raise up seed unto his brother.

20 Now there were seven brethren: and the first took a wife, and dying left no seed.

21 And the second took her, and died, neither left he any seed: and the third likewise.

22 And the seven had her, and left no seed: last of all the woman died also.

23 In the resurrection therefore, when they shall rise, whose wife shall she be of them? for the seven had her to wife.

24 And Jesus answering said unto them, *a*Do ye not therefore err, because ye know not the scriptures, neither the power of God?

25 For when they shall rise from the dead, they neither *a*marry, nor are given in marriage; but are as the angels which are in heaven.

26 And as touching the dead, that they *a*rise: have ye not read in the book of Moses, how in the bush God *b*spake unto him, saying, I *am* the *c*God of Abraham, and the God of Isaac, and the God of Jacob?

27 *a*He is not the God of the dead, but the God of the living: ye therefore do greatly err.

28 ¶ And one of the *a*scribes came, and having heard them reasoning together, and perceiving that he had answered them well, asked him, Which is the first commandment of all?

29 And Jesus answered him, The first of all the commandments *is,* *a*Hear, O Israel; The Lord our God is one Lord:

30 And thou shalt *a*love the Lord thy God with all thy *b*heart, and with all thy soul, and with all thy mind, and with all thy *c*strength: this *is* the first commandment.

31 And the second *is* like, *namely* this, Thou shalt love thy neighbour as thyself. There is none other commandment greater than these.

32 And the scribe said unto him, Well, Master, thou hast said the truth: for there is one God; and there is none other but he:

33 And to love him with all the heart, and with all the understanding, and with all the soul, and with all the strength, and to love *his* neighbour as himself, is more than all whole burnt *a*offerings and sacrifices.

34 And when Jesus saw that he answered discreetly, he said unto him, Thou art not far from the kingdom of God. And no man after that durst ask him *any question.*

35 ¶ And Jesus answered and said, while he taught in the temple, How say the scribes that Christ is the Son of David?

36 For David himself said by the Holy Ghost, The *a*LORD said to my Lord, Sit thou on my right hand, till I make thine enemies thy footstool.

37 David therefore himself calleth him Lord; and whence is he *then* his son? And the common people heard him gladly.

38 ¶ And he said unto them in his doctrine, Beware of the *a*scribes, which love to go in long clothing, and *love* *b*salutations in the marketplaces,

19*a* Deut. 25:5;
        Matt. 22:24;
        Luke 20:28.
24*a* JST Mark 12:28 . . . *Ye do err therefore,* because ye know not, *and understand not* the scriptures . . .
25*a* TG Marriage, Marry.
26*a* TG Resurrection.

      b TG God, Manifestations of.
      c Ex. 3:6.
27*a* JST Mark 12:32 He is not *therefore* the God of the dead, but the God of the living; *for he raiseth them up out of their graves.* Ye therefore . . .
28*a* TG Scribe.

29*a* Deut. 6:4.
30*a* Deut. 6:5.
      b TG Commitment.
      c TG Strength.
33*a* Matt. 22:40 (15–40).
      TG Sacrifice.
36*a* Ps. 110:1.
38*a* TG Pride.
      b John 12:43 (42–43).

39 And the chief seats in the synagogues, and the uppermost rooms at feasts:

40 Which devour widows' houses, and for a pretence make long prayers: these shall receive greater ªdamnation.

41 ¶ And Jesus sat over against the treasury, and beheld how the people cast money into the treasury: and many that were rich cast in much.

42 And there came a certain ªpoor widow, and she threw in two ᵇmites, which make a farthing.

43 And he called *unto him* his disciples, and saith unto them, Verily I say unto you, That this ªpoor widow hath cast more in, than all they which have cast into the treasury:

44 For all *they* did cast in of their ªabundance; but she of her ᵇwant did ᶜcast in ᵈall that she had, *even* all her living.

CHAPTER 13

Jesus tells of the calamities and signs preceding the Second Coming—There will be false Christs and false prophets—He gives the parable of the fig tree.

ªAND as he went out of the temple, one of his disciples saith unto him, Master, see what manner of stones and what buildings *are here!*

2 And Jesus answering said unto him, Seest thou these great buildings? there shall not be left one stone upon another, that shall not be thrown down.

3 And as he sat upon the mount of Olives over against the temple, Peter and James and John and Andrew asked him privately,

4 Tell us, when shall these things be? and what *shall be* the ªsign when all these things shall be fulfilled?

5 And Jesus answering them began to say, Take heed lest any *man* deceive you:

6 For many shall come in my name, saying, I am *Christ*; and shall ªdeceive many.

7 And when ye shall hear of wars and rumours of wars, be ye not troubled: for *such things* must needs be; but the end *shall* not *be* yet.

8 For ªnation shall rise against nation, and kingdom against kingdom: and there shall be earthquakes in divers places, and there shall be famines and troubles: these *are* the beginnings of sorrows.

9 ¶ But take heed to yourselves: for they shall deliver you up to councils; and in the synagogues ye shall be beaten: and ye shall be brought before rulers and ªkings for my sake, for a testimony against them.

10 And the ªgospel must first be ᵇpublished among all nations.

11 But when they shall lead *you*, and deliver you up, take no thought beforehand what ye shall speak, neither do ye premeditate: but whatsoever shall be given you in that hour, that ªspeak ye: for it is not ye that speak, but the ᵇHoly Ghost.

12 Now the brother shall betray the brother to death, and the father the son; and children shall rise up against *their* parents, and shall cause them to be put to death.

13 And ye shall be ªhated of all *men* for my name's sake: but he that shall ᵇendure unto the end, the same shall be saved.

14 ¶ But when ye shall see the abomination of desolation, spoken of by Daniel the prophet, standing where it ought not, (let him that readeth understand,) then let them that be in Judæa flee to the mountains:

40a TG Damnation.
42a TG Poor.
  b Deut. 16:17.
43a TG Almsgiving.
44a TG Treasure.
  b 2 Cor. 8:2 (2–12).
  c Mosiah 4:24 (16–27).
  d TG Generosity.
13 1a The text of JST Mark 13
   is the same as

JST Matthew 24. See
Pearl of Great Price,
JS—M.
 4a TG Signs.
 6a Matt. 24:5.
 8a 1 Ne. 14:15;
   D&C 87:6.
 9a TG Kings, Earthly.
10a TG Gospel;
  b 1 Ne. 13:37;

3 Ne. 20:40;
   D&C 19:29.
11a Matt. 10:19 (19–20).
  b TG Holy Ghost,
   Mission of.
13a 1 Ne. 11:34.
  b Matt. 10:22 (22–33);
   3 Ne. 15:9.

15 And let him that is on the house-top not go down into the house, neither enter *therein,* to take any thing out of his house:

16 And let him that is in the field not turn back again for to take up his garment.

17 But woe to them that are with child, and to them that give suck in those days!

18 And pray ye that your flight be not in the winter.

19 For *in* those days shall be ᵃaf-fliction, such as was not from the beginning of the creation which God created unto this time, neither shall be.

20 And except that the Lord had shortened those days, no flesh should be saved: but for the ᵃelect's sake, whom he hath chosen, he hath shortened the days.

21 And then if any man shall say to you, Lo, here *is* Christ; or, lo, *he is* there; believe *him* not:

22 For ᵃfalse Christs and ᵇfalse prophets shall rise, and shall shew ᶜsigns and wonders, to seduce, if *it were* possible, even the elect.

23 But take ye heed: behold, I have foretold you all things.

24 ¶ But in those days, after that tribulation, the sun shall be dark-ened, and the moon shall not give her light,

25 And the ᵃstars of heaven shall fall, and the powers that are in heaven shall be shaken.

26 And then shall they see the ᵃSon of man coming in the clouds with great power and glory.

27 And then shall he send his angels, and shall gather together his elect from the four winds, from the uttermost part of the earth to the uttermost part of heaven.

28 Now learn a parable of the ᵃfig tree; When her branch is yet tender,

and putteth forth leaves, ye know that summer is near:

29 So ye in like manner, when ye shall see these things come to pass, know that it is nigh, *even* at the doors.

30 Verily I say unto you, that this ᵃgeneration shall not pass, till all these things be done.

31 Heaven and earth shall pass away: but my ᵃwords shall not pass away.

32 ¶ But of that ᵃday and *that* hour knoweth no man, no, not the angels which are in heaven, neither the Son, but the Father.

33 Take ye heed, ᵃwatch and ᵇpray: for ye know not when the time is.

34 *For the Son of man is* as a man taking a far journey, who left his house, and gave ᵃauthority to his servants, and to every man his work, and commanded the porter to watch.

35 Watch ye therefore: for ye know not when the master of the house cometh, at even, or at midnight, or at the cockcrowing, or in the morning:

36 Lest coming suddenly he find you ᵃsleeping.

37 And what I say unto you I say unto all, Watch.

CHAPTER 14

Jesus is anointed with oil—He eats the Passover, institutes the sacrament, suffers in Gethsemane, and is betrayed by Judas—Jesus is falsely accused, and Peter denies that he knows Him.

AFTER two days was *the feast of* the passover, and of unleavened bread: and the chief priests and the ᵃscribes sought how they might take him by craft, and put *him* to ᵇdeath.

2 But they said, Not on the feast *day,* lest there be an uproar of the people.

19a TG Affliction.
20a D&C 29:7; 84:34.
22a TG False Christs.
  b TG False Prophets.
  c TG Signs.
25a TG World, End of.
26a TG Jesus Christ, Son of Man.
28a D&C 45:37.
30a D&C 45:21.
31a D&C 64:31.
32a TG Day of the Lord.
33a See JST Luke 12:41–57 (Appendix).
  D&C 45:44.
  TG Watch.
  b TG Prayer.
34a TG Authority.
36a TG Procrastination; Sleep.
14 1a TG Scribe.
  b Matt. 26:4 (2–5); Luke 22:2 (1–2).

3 ¶ And being in Bethany in the house of Simon the leper, as he sat at meat, there came a woman having an alabaster box of ointment of spikenard very precious; and she brake the box, and poured *it* on his head.

4 And there were some that had indignation within themselves, and said, Why was this ᵃwaste of the ointment made?

5 For it might have been sold for more than three hundred pence, and have been given to the poor. And they murmured against her.

6 And Jesus said, Let her alone; why trouble ye her? she hath wrought a good work on me.

7 For ye have the ᵃpoor with you always, and whensoever ye will ye may do them good: but me ye have not always.

8 She hath done what she could: ᵃshe is come aforehand to anoint my body to the burying.

9 Verily I say unto you, Wheresoever this gospel shall be preached throughout the whole world, *this* also that ᵃshe hath done shall be spoken of for a memorial of her.

10 ¶ And Judas Iscariot, one of the twelve, went unto the chief priests, ᵃto betray him unto them.

11 And when they heard *it*, they were glad, and promised to give him money. And he sought how he might conveniently betray him.

12 ¶ And the first day of unleavened bread, when they killed the passover, his disciples said unto him, Where wilt thou that we go and prepare that thou mayest eat the ᵃpassover?

13 And he sendeth forth two of his ᵃdisciples, and saith unto them, Go ye into the city, and there shall meet you a man bearing a pitcher of water: follow him.

14 And wheresoever he shall go in, say ye to the goodman of the house, The Master saith, Where is the guestchamber, where I shall eat the passover with my disciples?

15 And he will shew you a large upper room furnished *and* prepared: there make ready for us.

16 And his disciples went forth, and came into the city, and found as he had said unto them: and they made ready the passover.

17 And in the evening he cometh with the twelve.

18 And as they sat and did eat, Jesus said, Verily I say unto you, One of you which eateth with me shall betray me.

19 And they began to be sorrowful, and to say unto him one by one, *Is* it I? and another *said, Is* it I?

20 And he answered and said unto them, *It is* one of the twelve, that dippeth with me in the dish.

21 The Son of man indeed goeth, as it is written of him: but woe to that man by whom the Son of man is betrayed! good were it for that man if he had never been born.

22 ¶ ᵃAnd as they did eat, Jesus took ᵇbread, and blessed, and brake *it*, and gave to them, and said, Take, eat: this is my ᶜbody.

23 And he took the cup, and when he had given ᵃthanks, he gave *it* to them: and they all drank of it.

24 And he said unto them, This is my blood of the new testament, which is shed for many.

25 Verily I say unto you, I will ᵃdrink no more of the fruit of the vine, until that day that I drink it new in the kingdom of God.

26 ¶ And when they had sung an hymn, they went out into the mount of Olives.

27 And Jesus saith unto them, All ye shall be offended because of me

---

4a D&C 117:4 (4–7).
7a TG Poor.
8a JST Mark 14:8 . . . *and this which she has done unto me, shall be had in remembrance in generations to come, wheresoever my gospel shall be preached; for verily she* has come *beforehand* . . .
9a John 12:7 (7–8).
10a JST Mark 14:31 . . . *to* betray *Jesus* unto them; *for he turned away from him, and was offended because of his words.*
12a TG Passover.
13a Luke 22:8 (7–13).
22a JST Mark 14:20–26 (Appendix).
b TG Bread, Unleavened; Jesus Christ, Types of, in Memory; Passover.
c Luke 22:19; John 6:53.
23a TG Thanksgiving.
25a Matt. 26:29; Luke 22:18; D&C 27:5.

this night: for it is written, I will smite the [a]shepherd, and the sheep shall be scattered.

28 But after that I am risen, I will go before you into Galilee.

29 But Peter said unto him, Although all shall be offended, yet *will* not I.

30 And Jesus saith unto him, Verily I say unto thee, That this day, *even* in this night, before the cock crow twice, thou shalt deny me thrice.

31 But he spake the more vehemently, If I should die with thee, I will not deny thee in any wise. Likewise also said they all.

32 [a]And they came to a place which was named Gethsemane: and he saith to his disciples, Sit ye here, while I shall pray.

33 And he taketh with him Peter and James and John, and began to be [a]sore amazed, and to be [b]very [c]heavy;

34 And saith unto them, My soul is exceeding sorrowful unto death: tarry ye here, and watch.

35 And he went forward a little, and fell on the ground, and prayed that, if it were possible, the hour might pass from him.

36 And he said, Abba, Father, all things *are* possible unto thee; [a]take away this [b]cup from me: nevertheless not what I will, but what thou wilt.

37 And he cometh, and findeth them sleeping, and saith unto Peter, Simon, sleepest thou? couldest not thou watch one [a]hour?

38 [a]Watch ye and pray, lest ye enter into [b]temptation. The spirit truly *is* ready, but the flesh *is* weak.

39 And again he went away, and prayed, and spake the same words.

40 And when he returned, he found them asleep again, (for their eyes were heavy,) neither wist they what to answer him.

41 And he cometh the third time, and saith unto them, Sleep on now, and take *your* rest: it is enough, the hour is come; behold, the Son of man is betrayed into the hands of sinners.

42 Rise up, let us go; lo, he that betrayeth me is at hand.

43 ¶ And immediately, while he yet spake, cometh Judas, one of the twelve, and with him a great multitude with swords and staves, from the chief priests and the scribes and the elders.

44 And he that [a]betrayed him had given them a token, saying, Whomsoever I shall kiss, that same is he; take him, and lead *him* away safely.

45 And as soon as he was come, he goeth straightway to him, and saith, Master, master; and kissed him.

46 ¶ And they laid their hands on him, and took him.

47 And one of them that stood by drew a sword, and smote a servant of the high priest, and cut off his ear.

48 And Jesus answered and said unto them, Are ye come out, as against a thief, with swords and *with* staves to take me?

49 I was daily with you in the temple teaching, and ye took me not: but the scriptures must be fulfilled.

50 And they all forsook him, and fled.

51 And there followed him a certain young man, [a]having a linen cloth cast about *his* naked *body*; and the young men laid hold on him:

52 And he left the linen cloth, and fled from them naked.

53 ¶ And they led Jesus away to the high priest: and with him were assembled all the chief priests and the elders and the scribes.

54 And Peter followed him afar off, even into the palace of the high priest: and he sat with the servants, and warmed himself at the fire.

55 And the chief priests and all the council sought for witness against

27a Zech. 13:7.
32a JST Mark 14:36–38
     (Appendix).
33a GR amazed, awestruck,
     astonished.
  b GR depressed, dejected,
     in anguish.
  c Ps. 69:20.
36a 3 Ne. 11:11.
  b Matt. 26:39 (36–46);
     D&C 19:17 (13–20).
37a D&C 76:107; 122:8 (7–8).
38a TG Watch.
  b D&C 20:33; 23:1; 31:12.
44a TG Jesus Christ,
     Betrayal of.
51a JST Mark 14:57 . . . a
     disciple, having . . .

Jesus to put him to *death; and found none.

56 For many bare *false witness against him, but their witness agreed not together.

57 And there arose certain, and bare false witness against him, saying,

58 We heard him say, I will destroy this *temple that is made with hands, and within three days I will build another made without hands.

59 But neither so did their witness agree together.

60 And the high priest stood up in the midst, and asked Jesus, saying, Answerest thou nothing? what *is it which* these witness against thee?

61 But he held his peace, and *answered nothing. Again the high priest asked him, and said unto him, Art thou the *Christ, the Son of the Blessed?

62 And Jesus said, I am: and ye shall see the *Son of man sitting on the right hand of power, and coming in the clouds of heaven.

63 Then the high priest rent his clothes, and saith, What need we any further witnesses?

64 Ye have heard the blasphemy: what think ye? And they all *condemned him to be *guilty of death.

65 And some began to spit on him, and to cover his face, and to buffet him, and to say unto him, Prophesy: and the servants did strike him with the palms of their hands.

66 ¶ And as Peter was beneath in the palace, there cometh one of the maids of the high priest:

67 And when she saw Peter warming himself, she looked upon him, and said, And thou also wast with Jesus of Nazareth.

68 But he denied, saying, I know not, neither understand I what thou sayest. And he went out into the porch; and the cock crew.

69 And a maid saw him again, and began to say to them that stood by, This is *one* of them.

70 And he denied it again. And a little after, they that stood by said again to Peter, Surely thou art *one* of them: for thou art a Galilæan, and thy speech agreeth *thereto.*

71 But he began to curse and to swear, *saying,* I know not this man of whom ye speak.

72 And the second time the cock crew. And Peter called to mind the word that Jesus said unto him, Before the cock crow twice, thou shalt deny me thrice. And when he thought thereon, he wept.

CHAPTER 15

Pilate decrees the death of Jesus—Jesus is mocked and crucified between two thieves—He dies and is buried in the tomb of Joseph of Arimathœa.

AND straightway in the morning the chief priests held a consultation with the elders and scribes and the whole council, and bound Jesus, and carried *him* away, and delivered *him* to Pilate.

2 And *Pilate asked him, Art thou the King of the Jews? And he answering said unto him, *Thou sayest *it.*

3 And the chief priests accused him of many things: but he *answered nothing.

4 And Pilate asked him again, saying, Answerest thou nothing? behold how many things they witness against thee.

5 But Jesus yet answered nothing; so that Pilate marvelled.

6 Now at *that* feast he *released unto them one prisoner, whomsoever they desired.

55a TG Jesus Christ, Death of.
56a TG Lying.
58a Matt. 26:61; 27:40;
　　John 2:19 (18–22);
　　Heb. 9:11.
61a Isa. 53:7 (7–8).
　b TG Jesus Christ,

Messiah.
62a TG Jesus Christ,
　　Son of Man.
64a TG Jesus Christ,
　　Trials of.
　b TG Guilt.
15 2a TG Jesus Christ,

Trials of.
　b JST Mark 15:4 . . . I am,
　even as thou sayest.
3a Isa. 53:7 (7–8);
　　Mosiah 14:7 (6–8).
6a GR usually released.

7 And there was *one* named Barabbas, *which lay* bound with them that had made insurrection with him, who had committed murder in the insurrection.

8 And the multitude crying aloud began to desire *him to do* as he had ever done unto them.

9 But Pilate answered them, saying, Will ye that I release unto you the ªKing of the Jews?

10 For he knew that the chief priests had delivered him for ªenvy.

11 But the chief priests moved the people, that he should rather release Barabbas unto them.

12 And Pilate answered and said again unto them, What will ye then that I shall do *unto him* whom ye call the King of the Jews?

13 And they cried out again, Crucify him.

14 Then Pilate said unto them, Why, what evil hath he done? And they cried out the more exceedingly, Crucify him.

15 ¶ And *so* Pilate, willing to content the people, released Barabbas unto them, and delivered Jesus, when he had scourged *him,* to be crucified.

16 And the soldiers led him away into the hall, called Prætorium; and they call together the whole band.

17 And they clothed him with purple, and plaited a crown of ªthorns, and put it about his *head,*

18 And began to salute him, Hail, King of the Jews!

19 And they ªsmote him on the head with a reed, and did spit upon him, and bowing *their* knees worshipped him.

20 And when they had ªmocked him, they took off the purple from him, and put his own clothes on him, and led him out to crucify him.

21 And they compel one Simon a Cyrenian, who passed by, coming out of the country, the father of Alexander and Rufus, to bear his cross.

22 And they bring him unto the place Golgotha, which is, being interpreted, The place of a skull.

23 And they gave him to drink wine mingled with myrrh: but he received *it* not.

24 And when they had crucified him, they parted his ªgarments, casting lots upon them, what every man should take.

25 And it was the third hour, and they crucified him.

26 And the superscription of his accusation was written over, THE KING OF THE JEWS.

27 And with him they crucify two ªthieves; the one on his right hand, and the other on his left.

28 And the scripture was ªfulfilled, which saith, And he was numbered with the transgressors.

29 And they that passed by railed on him, wagging their heads, and saying, Ah, thou that destroyest the temple, and buildest *it* in three days,

30 Save thyself, and come down from the cross.

31 Likewise also the chief priests mocking said among themselves with the scribes, He saved others; himself he cannot save.

32 Let Christ the King of Israel descend now from the cross, that we may see and believe. And they that were crucified with him ªreviled him.

33 And when the sixth hour was come, there was ªdarkness over the whole land until the ninth hour.

34 And at the ninth hour Jesus cried with a loud voice, saying, ªEloi, Eloi, lama sabachthani? which is, being interpreted, My God, my God, why hast thou ᵇforsaken me?

35 And some of them that stood by, when they heard *it,* said, Behold, he calleth Elias.

9ª Luke 23:22 (17–25).
10ª TG Envy.
17ª TG Jesus Christ, Trials of.
19ª 1 Ne. 11:32.
20ª TG Mocking.
24ª Ps. 22:18.
27ª Mosiah 14:9.
28ª Isa. 53:12.
32ª TG Malice; Reviling.
33ª TG Darkness, Physical.
34ª Aramaic: My God, my God, why hast thou forsaken me?
  ᵇ TG Jesus Christ, Crucifixion of.

36 And one ran and filled a sponge full of [a]vinegar, and put *it* on a reed, and gave him to drink, saying, Let alone; let us see whether Elias will come to take him down.

37 And Jesus cried with a loud voice, and gave up the [a]ghost.

38 And the veil of the temple was rent in twain from the top to the bottom.

39 ¶ And when the centurion, which stood over against him, saw that he so cried out, and gave up the ghost, he said, Truly this man was the Son of God.

40 There were also women looking on afar off: among whom was Mary Magdalene, and Mary the mother of James the less and of Joses, and Salome;

41 (Who also, when he was in Galilee, followed him, and ministered unto him;) and many other women which came up with him unto Jerusalem.

42 ¶ And now when the even was come, because it was the [a]preparation, that is, the day before the sabbath,

43 Joseph of Arimathæa, an honourable [a]counsellor, which also waited for the kingdom of God, came, and went in boldly unto Pilate, and [b]craved the body of Jesus.

44 And Pilate marvelled if he were already dead: and calling *unto him* the centurion, he asked him whether he had been any while dead.

45 And when he knew *it* of the centurion, he gave the body to Joseph.

46 And he bought fine linen, and took him down, and wrapped him in the linen, and laid him in a [a]sepulchre which was hewn out of a rock, and rolled a stone unto the door of the sepulchre.

47 And Mary Magdalene and Mary *the mother* of Joses beheld where he was laid.

CHAPTER 16

Christ is risen—He appears to Mary Magdalene, then to others—He sends the Apostles to preach and promises that signs will follow faith—He ascends into heaven.

AND when the sabbath was past, Mary Magdalene, and Mary the *mother* of James, and Salome, had bought sweet spices, that they might come and anoint him.

2 And very early in the morning the [a]first *day* of the week, they came unto the sepulchre at the [b]rising of the sun.

3 And they said among themselves, Who shall roll us away the stone from the door of the sepulchre?

4 [a]And when they looked, they saw that the stone was rolled away: for it was very great.

5 And entering into the sepulchre, they saw a young man sitting on the right side, [a]clothed in a long white garment; and they were [b]affrighted.

6 And he saith unto them, Be not affrighted: Ye seek Jesus of Nazareth, which was crucified: he is [a]risen; he is not here: behold the place where they laid him.

7 But go your way, tell his disciples and Peter that he goeth before you into Galilee: there shall ye see him, as he said unto you.

8 And they went out quickly, and fled from the sepulchre; for they trembled and were amazed: neither said they any thing to any *man*; for they were afraid.

9 ¶ Now when *Jesus* was [a]risen early the first *day* of the week, [b]appeared first to [c]Mary Magdalene, out of whom he had cast seven devils.

10 *And* she went and told them that had been with him, as they mourned and wept.

11 And they, when they had heard

36a Ps. 69:21.
37a TG Spirits,
    Disembodied.
42a TG Passover.
43a TG Counselor.
  b GR requested, desired.
46a Mosiah 14:9.

16 2a TG Jesus Christ, Types
      of, in Memory.
    b John 20:1.
  4a JST Mark 16:3–6
      (Appendix).
  5a TG Clothing.
    b GR amazed, astonished.

6a TG Immortality.
9a TG Jesus Christ,
    Resurrection.
  b TG Jesus Christ,
    Appearances,
    Postmortal.
  c Luke 8:2.

that he was alive, and had been seen of her, believed not.

12 ¶ After that he appeared in another form unto two of them, as they walked, and went into the country.

13 And they went and told *it* unto the residue: neither believed they them.

14 ¶ Afterward he appeared unto the *a*eleven as they sat at meat, and upbraided them with their *b*unbelief and *c*hardness of heart, because they believed not them which had seen him after he was risen.

15 And he said unto them, Go ye into all the world, and *a*preach the *b*gospel to every *c*creature.

16 He that *a*believeth and is *b*bap-

tized shall be saved; but he that believeth not shall be *c*damned.

17 And these *a*signs shall *b*follow them that believe; In my *c*name shall they *d*cast out *e*devils; they shall speak with new *f*tongues;

18 They shall take up *a*serpents; and if they drink any deadly thing, it shall not *b*hurt them; they shall lay *c*hands on the *d*sick, and they shall recover.

19 ¶ So then after the *a*Lord had spoken unto them, he was received up into heaven, and sat on the right hand of God.

20 And they went forth, and preached every where, the Lord working with *them*, and confirming the word with signs following. Amen.

THE GOSPEL ACCORDING TO

ST LUKE

CHAPTER 1

Gabriel promises Zacharias that Elisabeth will bear a son, whom they will name John—He also tells Mary that she will be the mother of the Son of God—Mary visits Elisabeth and utters a psalm of praise—John the Baptist is born—Zacharias prophesies of John's mission.

*a*F ORASMUCH as *b*many have taken in hand to set forth in order a declaration of those things *c*which are most surely believed among us,

2 Even as they delivered them unto us, which from the beginning were *a*eyewitnesses, and ministers of the word;

3 It seemed good to me also, having

14a TG Apostles.
  b Matt. 14:31; Mark 4:40;
    Luke 24:25.
  c TG Stiffnecked.
15a John 20:21 (19–31);
    Acts 6:4 (1–4);
    D&C 66:5.
    TG Israel, Mission of.
  b TG Gospel.
  c Acts 11:18 (1–18);
    D&C 68:8; 124:128.
    TG Missionary Work.
16a TG Baptism, Qualifications for; Faith.
  b TG Baptism;
    Baptism, Essential.

  c TG Damnation.
17a D&C 84:65 (64–73).
    TG Holy Ghost, Gifts of;
    Miracle; Signs.
  b D&C 63:9.
  c TG Name.
  d D&C 24:13; 35:9.
  e TG Spirits, Evil or
    Unclean.
  f TG Language.
18a Acts 28:3.
  b TG Protection, Divine.
  c TG Administrations
    to the Sick;
    Hands, Laying on of.
  d TG Heal.

19a TG Jesus Christ, Lord.
[LUKE]
Title: JST entitles this book
    "The Testimony of
    St. Luke."
1 1a JST Luke 1:1 *As I am a
    messenger of Jesus Christ,
    and knowing that many
    have . . .*
  b 2 Tim. 4:13;
    1 Ne. 13:26 (24–26).
  c GR which have been
    fulfilled.
2a John 1:14;
    Acts 5:32; 26:16.

had perfect understanding of all things from the very first, to write unto thee in order, most excellent ^aTheophilus,

4 That thou mightest ^aknow the certainty of those things, wherein thou hast been instructed.

5 ¶ THERE was in the days of Herod, the king of Judæa, a certain priest named ^aZacharias, of the course of ^bAbia: and his wife *was* of the daughters of Aaron, and her name *was* Elisabeth.

6 And they were both righteous before God, walking in all the commandments and ^aordinances of the Lord blameless.

7 And they had no child, because that Elisabeth was ^abarren, and they both were *now* well ^bstricken in years.

8 And it came to pass, that while he executed the ^apriest's office before God in the order of his ^bcourse,

9 According to the custom of the ^apriest's office, his lot was to burn incense when he went into the temple of the Lord.

10 And the whole multitude of the people were praying without at the time of incense.

11 And there appeared unto him an angel of the Lord standing on the right side of the altar of incense.

12 And when Zacharias saw *him,* he was troubled, and fear fell upon him.

13 But the angel said unto him, ^aFear not, Zacharias: for thy prayer is heard; and thy wife Elisabeth shall bear thee a ^bson, and thou shalt call his name John.

14 And thou shalt have joy and gladness; and many shall rejoice at his birth.

15 For he shall be great in the sight of the Lord, and shall drink neither ^awine nor strong drink; and he shall be ^bfilled with the ^cHoly Ghost, even from his mother's womb.

16 And many of the children of Israel shall he turn to the Lord their God.

17 And he shall go before him in the spirit and power of ^aElias, to turn the hearts of the ^bfathers to the children, and the ^cdisobedient to the wisdom of the just; to make ready a people ^dprepared for the Lord.

18 And Zacharias said unto the angel, Whereby shall I ^aknow this? for I am an ^bold man, and my wife well ^cstricken in years.

19 And the ^aangel answering said unto him, I am ^bGabriel, that stand in the presence of God; and am sent to speak unto thee, and to shew thee these glad tidings.

20 And, behold, thou shalt be ^adumb, and not able to speak, until the day that these things shall be performed, because thou ^bbelievest not my words, which shall be fulfilled in their season.

21 And the people waited for Zacharias, and marvelled that he tarried so long in the temple.

22 And when he came out, he could not speak unto them: and they perceived that he had seen a vision in the temple: for he beckoned unto them, and remained speechless.

23 And it came to pass, that, as soon as the ^adays of his ministration

3a Acts 1:1.
4a John 20:31 (30–31); 1 Ne. 6:4.
5a TG Priesthood, Aaronic.
b 1 Chr. 24:10 (5, 10, 19); Neh. 12:4.
6a TG Ordinance.
7a TG Barren.
b GR advanced.
8a TG Priest, Aaronic Priesthood. BD Priests.
b JST Luke 1:8 . . . priesthood,
9a Lev. 7:35.
13a Dan. 10:12.
b TG Foreordination.
15a Num. 6:3 (2–8); D&C 89:7 (5, 7).
b D&C 84:27.
c TG Holy Ghost, Gift of; Holy Ghost, Mission of.
17a This is the Greek form of the Hebrew name, Elijah. Matt. 11:14; D&C 27:7 (6–8).
b TG Salvation for the Dead.
c TG Disobedience.
d Luke 1:76.
18a Gen. 15:8 (7–9).
b Gen. 18:13.
c GR advanced.
19a TG Angels.
b Dan. 8:16; D&C 27:7; 128:21.
20a Dan. 10:15; Mosiah 27:19; Alma 30:49 (47–52).
b Luke 12:29; 24:25; Morm. 9:11 (9–11, 27).
23a Lev. 8:33.

were accomplished, he departed to his own house.

24 And after those days his wife Elisabeth conceived, and hid herself five months, saying,

25 Thus hath the Lord dealt with me in the days wherein he looked on *me*, to take away my *a*reproach among men.

26 And in the sixth month the *a*angel Gabriel was sent from God unto a city of Galilee, named Nazareth,

27 To a *a*virgin espoused to a man whose name was Joseph, of the house of David; and the virgin's name *was* Mary.

28 And the angel came in unto her, and said, Hail, *thou that art* highly favoured, the Lord *is* with thee: blessed *art* thou among *a*women.

29 And when she saw *him,* she was troubled at his saying, and cast in her mind what manner of salutation this should be.

30 And the angel said unto her, *a*Fear not, Mary: for thou hast found favour with God.

31 And, behold, thou shalt conceive in thy womb, and bring forth a son, and shalt call his name *a*JESUS.

32 He shall be great, and shall be called the *a*Son of the Highest: and the Lord God shall give unto him the *b*throne of his father *c*David:

33 And he shall *a*reign over the house of Jacob for ever; and of his kingdom there shall be no *b*end.

34 Then said Mary unto the angel, How shall this be, seeing I *a*know not a man?

35 And the angel answered and said unto her, The *a*Holy Ghost shall come upon thee, and the power of the Highest shall overshadow thee: therefore also that holy thing which shall be born of thee shall be called the *b*Son of God.

36 And, behold, thy *a*cousin Elisabeth, she hath also conceived a son in her *b*old age: and this is the sixth month with her, who was called barren.

37 For with God nothing shall be *a*impossible.

38 And Mary said, Behold the handmaid of the Lord; be it unto me according to thy word. And the angel departed from her.

39 And Mary arose in those days, and went into the hill country with haste, into a city of Juda;

40 And entered into the house of Zacharias, and *a*saluted Elisabeth.

41 And it came to pass, that, when Elisabeth heard the salutation of Mary, the babe leaped in her womb; and Elisabeth was *a*filled with the Holy Ghost:

42 And she spake out with a loud voice, and said, Blessed *art* thou among *a*women, and blessed *is* the fruit of thy womb.

43 And *a*whence *is* this to me, that the mother of my Lord should come to me?

44 For, lo, as soon as the voice of thy salutation sounded in mine ears, the babe leaped in my womb for joy.

45 And blessed *is* she that believed: for there shall be a performance of those things which were told her from the Lord.

46 And Mary *a*said, My soul doth *b*magnify the Lord,

47 And my spirit hath *a*rejoiced in God my *b*Saviour.

25a TG Barren;
    Reproach.
26a Moro. 7:29 (29–32).
27a 1 Ne. 11:13.
28a TG Woman.
30a TG Courage;
    Fearful.
31a TG Jesus Christ, Birth of.
32a TG Godhead;
    Jesus Christ, Divine
    Sonship.
  b TG Jesus Christ,
    Millennial Reign.

c TG Jesus Christ, Davidic
    Descent of.
33a Micah 4:7.
    TG Jesus Christ,
    Mission of.
  b 2 Sam. 7:16;
    Isa. 9:7 (6–7).
34a 1 Ne. 11:18 (15–20);
    Alma 7:10 (7–12).
35a Matt. 1:20.
  b 2 Cor. 1:19.
36a GR relative (not
    necessarily a cousin).

b TG Old Age.
37a Gen. 18:14;
    Rom. 4:21.
    TG God, Power of.
40a GR greeted.
41a TG Holy Ghost, Gifts of.
42a TG Woman.
43a GR how.
46a TG Singing.
  b 1 Sam. 2:1 (1–10).
47a TG Thanksgiving.
  b TG Jesus Christ, Savior;
    Salvation.

48 For he hath regarded the low estate of his [a]handmaiden: for, behold, from henceforth all generations shall call me [b]blessed.

49 For he that is mighty hath done to me great [a]things; and [b]holy *is* his name.

50 And his mercy *is* on them that fear him from generation to generation.

51 He hath shewed strength with his arm; he hath scattered the [a]proud in the imagination of their hearts.

52 He hath put down the mighty from *their* seats, and exalted them of [a]low degree.

53 He hath filled the hungry with good things; and the rich he hath sent empty away.

54 He hath [a]holpen his servant Israel, in remembrance of *his* mercy;

55 As he spake to our [a]fathers, to Abraham, and to his [b]seed for ever.

56 And Mary abode with her about three months, and returned to her own house.

57 Now Elisabeth's full time came that she should be delivered; and she brought forth a son.

58 And her neighbours and her [a]cousins heard how the Lord had shewed great [b]mercy upon her; and they rejoiced with her.

59 And it came to pass, that on the [a]eighth day they came to [b]circumcise the child; and they called him Zacharias, after the name of his father.

60 And his mother answered and said, Not *so*; but he shall be called John.

61 And they said unto her, There is none of thy kindred that is called by this name.

62 And they made signs to his father, how he would have him called.

63 And he asked for a [a]writing table, and wrote, saying, His name is John. And they marvelled all.

64 And his mouth was opened immediately, and his tongue *loosed,* and he spake, and praised God.

65 And fear came on all that dwelt round about them: and all these sayings were [a]noised abroad throughout all the hill country of Judæa.

66 And all they that heard *them* laid *them* up in their hearts, saying, What manner of child shall this be! And the hand of the Lord was with him.

67 And his father Zacharias was filled with the Holy Ghost, and [a]prophesied, saying,

68 [a]Blessed *be* the Lord God of Israel; for he hath [b]visited and [c]redeemed his people,

69 And hath raised up an horn of salvation for us in the house of his servant David;

70 As he [a]spake by the mouth of his holy [b]prophets, which have been since the world began:

71 That we should be saved from our enemies, and from the hand of all that hate us;

72 To perform the mercy [a]promised to our fathers, and to remember his holy [b]covenant;

73 The [a]oath which he sware to our [b]father Abraham,

74 That he would grant unto us, that we being delivered out of the hand of our enemies might serve him without [a]fear,

75 In [a]holiness and righteousness before him, all the days of our life.

76 And thou, child, shalt be called the prophet of the Highest: for thou

48a 1 Sam. 1:11.
  b Ps. 72:17;
    Luke 11:27 (27–28).
49a Ps. 126:2.
  b Ps. 99:3; Isa. 57:15.
51a Ex. 18:11.
52a Ezek. 21:26.
54a OR helped.
55a Ps. 132:11; Micah 7:20;
    Luke 1:72;
    Gal. 3:16.

  b TG Seed of Abraham.
58a GR relatives.
  b TG God, Mercy of.
59a D&C 84:28 (27–28).
  b TG Circumcision.
63a IE writing tablet.
65a GR discussed.
67a TG Holy Ghost, Gifts of.
68a TG Thanksgiving.
  b Luke 7:16.
  c TG Jesus Christ,

    Redeemer.
70a TG Prophets, Mission of.
  b TG Jesus Christ,
    Prophecies about.
72a Micah 7:20;
    Luke 1:55 (54–55).
  b TG Covenants.
73a TG Oath; Vow.
  b TG Family, Patriarchal.
74a Philip. 1:14 (12–17).
75a TG Holiness.

shalt go before the face of the Lord to [a]prepare his ways;

77 To give [a]knowledge of salvation unto his people by the [b]remission of their sins,

78 Through the [a]tender mercy of our God; whereby the [b]dayspring from on high hath visited us,

79 To give [a]light to them that sit in [b]darkness and in the shadow of [c]death, to guide our feet into the way of peace.

80 And the child grew, and waxed strong in spirit, and was in the deserts till the day of his shewing unto Israel.

CHAPTER 2

Heavenly messengers herald the birth of Jesus in Bethlehem—He is circumcised, and Simeon and Anna prophesy of His mission—At twelve years of age, He goes about His Father's business.

AND it came to pass in those days, that there went out a decree from Cæsar Augustus, that all [a]the world should be [b]taxed.

2 (And this [a]taxing was first made when Cyrenius was governor of Syria.)

3 And all went to be taxed, every one into his own city.

4 And Joseph also went up from Galilee, out of the city of Nazareth, into Judæa, unto the city of David, which is called [a]Bethlehem; (because he was of the house and lineage of David:)

5 To be taxed with Mary his [a]espoused wife, being great with child.

6 And so it was, that, while they were there, the days were accomplished that she should be delivered.

7 And she brought forth her [a]firstborn son, and wrapped him in swaddling clothes, and laid him in a manger; because there was no room for them in the [b]inn.

8 And there were in the same country shepherds abiding in the field, keeping watch over their flock by night.

9 And, lo, the angel of the Lord came upon them, and the [a]glory of the Lord shone round about them: and they were sore afraid.

10 And the angel said unto them, Fear not: for, behold, I bring you [a]good tidings of great [b]joy, which shall be to all people.

11 For unto you is [a]born this day in the city of David a [b]Saviour, which is Christ the [c]Lord.

12 And this *shall be* a [a]sign unto you; Ye shall find the babe wrapped in swaddling clothes, lying in a manger.

13 And suddenly there was with the angel a multitude of the heavenly host praising God, and saying,

14 [a]Glory to God in the highest, and on earth [b]peace, good will toward men.

15 And it came to pass, as the angels were gone away from them into heaven, the shepherds said one to another, Let us now go even unto Bethlehem, and see this thing which is come to pass, which the Lord hath made known unto us.

16 And they came with [a]haste, and found Mary, and Joseph, and the babe lying in a manger.

17 And when they had seen *it,* they made known abroad the saying which was told them concerning this child.

76a Luke 1:17.
77a Luke 11:52.
   b TG Remission of Sins.
78a 1 Ne. 1:20.
   b GR dawn; see Mal. 4:2.
79a TG Jesus Christ,
      Light of the World;
      Jesus Christ,
      Prophecies about.
   b 1 Pet. 3:19 (18–20).
      TG Darkness, Spiritual.
   c D&C 45:17 (16–17);

138:50 (50–51).
2 1a JST Luke 2:1 . . . *his
      empire* should be taxed.
   b GR enrolled, registered
      (also vv. 3, 5).
  2a GR enrollment.
  4a 1 Sam. 16:1;
      Micah 5:2 (1–2);
      John 7:42 (41–44);
      Alma 7:10.
  5a Matt. 1:24 (20–25).
  7a TG Firstborn.

   b JST Luke 2:7 . . . *inns.*
  9a TG God, Glory of.
 10a TG Gospel.
   b TG Joy.
 11a TG Jesus Christ,
      Birth of.
   b TG Jesus Christ, Savior.
   c TG Jesus Christ, Lord.
 12a TG Signs.
 14a Luke 19:38.
   b TG Peace.
 16a TG Haste.

18 And all they that heard it ªwondered at those things which were told them by the shepherds.

19 But Mary kept all these things, and ªpondered *them* in her heart.

20 And the shepherds returned, glorifying and praising God for all the things that they had heard and seen, as it was told unto them.

21 And when eight days were accomplished for the ªcircumcising of the child, his name was called ᵇJESUS, which was so ᶜnamed of the angel before he was conceived in the womb.

22 And when the days of her ªpurification according to the law of Moses were accomplished, they brought him to Jerusalem, to present *him* to the Lord;

23 (As it is written in the law of the Lord, Every male that openeth the ªwomb shall be called holy to the Lord;)

24 And to offer a sacrifice according to that which is said in the law of the Lord, A pair of ªturtledoves, or two young pigeons.

25 And, behold, there was a man in Jerusalem, whose name *was* Simeon; and the same man *was* just and devout, waiting for the consolation of Israel: and the Holy Ghost was upon him.

26 And it was revealed unto him by the Holy Ghost, that he should not see death, before he had seen the Lord's Christ.

27 And he came by the Spirit into the temple: and when the parents brought in the child Jesus, to do for him after the custom of the law,

28 Then took he him up in his arms, and blessed God, and said,

29 Lord, now lettest thou thy servant depart in peace, according to thy word:

30 For mine eyes have seen thy ªsalvation,

31 Which thou hast prepared before the face of all people;

32 A ªlight ᵇto lighten the Gentiles, and the glory of thy people Israel.

33 And Joseph and his mother marvelled at those things which were spoken of him.

34 And Simeon blessed them, and said unto Mary his mother, Behold, this *child* is ªset for the ᵇfall and rising again of many in Israel; and for a sign which shall be spoken against;

35 (Yea, a sword shall ªpierce through thy own soul also,) that the thoughts of many hearts may be revealed.

36 And there was one Anna, a ªprophetess, the daughter of Phanuel, of the tribe of Aser: she was of a great age, and had lived with an husband seven years from her virginity;

37 And she *was* a widow of about fourscore and four years, which departed not from the temple, but served *God* with ªfastings and prayers night and day.

38 And she coming in that instant gave thanks likewise unto the Lord, and spake of him to all them that looked for ªredemption in Jerusalem.

39 And when they had performed all things according to the law of the Lord, they returned into Galilee, to their own city Nazareth.

40 And the child grew, and ªwaxed strong in spirit, filled with wisdom: and the ᵇgrace of God was upon him.

41 Now his parents went to Jerusalem every year at the ªfeast of the passover.

42 And when he was twelve years

18a OR marveled.
19a TG Meditation.
21a TG Circumcision.
  b Matt. 1:21.
  c TG Jesus Christ, Prophecies about.
22a TG Purification.
23a Ex. 13:2; 34:19.
24a Lev. 1:14; 5:7.
30a Ps. 67:2.

32a TG Jesus Christ, Light of the World.
  b GR for revelation to.
34a OR appointed.
  b Isa. 8:14 (13–15);
    Matt. 21:44 (43–45);
    Rom. 9:32 (28–33);
    2 Ne. 18:14;
    Alma 11:40 (40–41).
35a John 19:25.

36a TG Woman.
37a TG Fast, Fasting.
38a D&C 29:42.
40a OR became.
    See JST Matt. 3:24–26 (Appendix).
  b TG Grace.
41a Deut. 16:1.

old, they went up to Jerusalem after the custom of the feast.

43 And when they had fulfilled the days, as they returned, the child Jesus tarried behind in Jerusalem; and Joseph and his mother knew not *of it.*

44 But they, supposing him to have been in the company, went a day's journey; and they sought him among *their* kinsfolk and acquaintance.

45 And when they found him not, they turned back again to Jerusalem, seeking him.

46 And it came to pass, that after three days they found him in the ^atemple, sitting in the midst of the ^bdoctors, ^cboth hearing them, and ^dasking them questions.

47 And all that heard him were astonished at his ^aunderstanding and answers.

48 And when they saw him, they were amazed: and his mother said unto him, Son, why hast thou thus dealt with us? behold, thy father and I have sought thee sorrowing.

49 And he said unto them, How is it that ye sought me? ^awist ye not that I must be about my ^bFather's business?

50 And they understood not the saying which he spake unto them.

51 And he went down with them, and came to Nazareth, and was ^asubject unto them: but his mother kept all these sayings in her ^bheart.

52 And Jesus ^aincreased in ^bwisdom and stature, and in ^cfavour with God and man.

CHAPTER 3

John the Baptist preaches and baptizes— Jesus is baptized, and God acclaims Him as His Son—Jesus' genealogy back to Adam is given.

Now in the fifteenth year of the reign of Tiberius Cæsar, Pontius Pilate being governor of Judæa, and ^aHerod being tetrarch of Galilee, and his brother Philip tetrarch of Ituræa and of the region of Trachonitis, and Lysanias the tetrarch of Abilene,

2 ^aAnnas and Caiaphas being the ^bhigh priests, the word of God came unto John the son of Zacharias in the wilderness.

3 And he came into all the country about Jordan, preaching the ^abaptism of repentance for the ^bremission of sins;

4 ^aAs it is written in the book of the words of Esaias the prophet, saying, The ^bvoice of one crying in the wilderness, Prepare ye the way of the Lord, make his paths straight.

5 Every ^avalley shall be filled, and every mountain and hill shall be brought low; and the crooked shall be made straight, and the rough ways *shall be* made smooth;

6 And all flesh shall see the ^asalvation of God.

7 Then said he to the multitude that came forth to be baptized of him, O ^ageneration of vipers, who hath warned you to flee from the wrath to come?

8 Bring forth therefore ^afruits ^bworthy of ^crepentance, and begin

---

46a TG Temple.
  b GR teachers.
  c JST Luke 2:46 . . . *and they were* hearing *him,* and asking *him* questions.
  d John 7:15 (14–15).
47a TG Understanding.
49a OR knew.
  b John 4:34; 6:39 (38–39). TG God the Father, Elohim.
51a TG Family, Children, Duties of; Self-Mastery.

  b TG Heart.
52a 1 Sam. 2:26; 3:19.
  b TG God, Wisdom of; Study.
  c D&C 93:13 (12–14). TG Jesus Christ, Relationships with the Father.
3 1a Luke 9:7.
2a John 18:13 (13–24).
  b TG Priesthood, Aaronic.
3a TG Baptism.
  b TG Remission of Sins.
4a JST Luke 3:4–11 (Appendix).

  b Matt. 3:3; Mark 1:3; John 1:23; D&C 84:28 (26–28); JS—H 1:72 (70–73).
5a Isa. 40:4; Hel. 14:23; D&C 109:74.
6a TG Salvation.
7a GR offspring.
8a Alma 13:13 (10–13). TG Baptism, Qualifications for.
  b TG Worthiness.
  c TG Repent.

not to say within yourselves, [d]We have [e]Abraham to *our* father: for I say unto you, That God is able of these stones to raise up children unto Abraham.

9 And now also the [a]axe is laid unto the root of the trees: every tree therefore which bringeth not forth good [b]fruit is hewn down, and cast into the fire.

10 And the people asked him, saying, What shall we do then?

11 He answereth and saith unto them, He that hath two [a]coats, let him [b]impart to him that hath none; and he that hath meat, let him do likewise.

12 Then came also [a]publicans to be baptized, and said unto him, Master, what shall we do?

13 [a]And he said unto them, Exact no more than that which is appointed you.

14 And the soldiers likewise demanded of him, saying, And what shall we do? And he said unto them, Do violence to no man, neither accuse *any* [a]falsely; and be [b]content with your [c]wages.

15 And as the people were in expectation, and all men [a]mused in their hearts of [b]John, whether he were the Christ, or not;

16 John answered, saying unto *them* all, I indeed baptize you with water; but one mightier than I cometh, the latchet of whose shoes I am not worthy to unloose: he shall [a]baptize you with the Holy Ghost and with fire:

17 Whose [a]fan *is* in his hand, and he will throughly purge his floor, and will gather the wheat into his [b]garner; but the [c]chaff he will burn with fire unquenchable.

18 And many other things in his exhortation preached he unto the people.

19 But [a]Herod the tetrarch, being reproved by him for Herodias his brother Philip's wife, and for all the evils which Herod had done,

20 Added yet this above all, that he shut up John in prison.

21 Now when all the people were baptized, it came to pass, that Jesus also being [a]baptized, and praying, the heaven was opened,

22 And the [a]Holy Ghost descended in a bodily shape like a [b]dove upon him, and a voice came from heaven, which said, Thou art my beloved Son; in thee I am well pleased.

23 And [a]Jesus himself began to be about [b]thirty years of age, being (as was supposed) the son of [c]Joseph, which was *the son* of Heli,

24 Which was *the son* of Matthat, which was *the son* of Levi, which was *the son* of Melchi, which was *the son* of Janna, which was *the son* of Joseph,

25 Which was *the son* of Mattathias, which was *the son* of Amos, which was *the son* of Naum, which was *the son* of Esli, which was *the son* of Nagge,

26 Which was *the son* of Maath, which was *the son* of Mattathias, which was *the son* of Semei, which was *the son* of Joseph, which was *the son* of Juda,

27 Which was *the son* of Joanna, which was *the son* of Rhesa, which

---

8d JST Luke 3:13 . . .
Abraham *is* our father;
*we have kept the
commandments of God,
and none can inherit the
promises but the children of
Abraham;* for I say . . .
 e TG Abrahamic Covenant.
9a Alma 5:52 (51–52);
D&C 97:7.
 b Matt. 7:19 (15–20);
John 15:2 (1–6);
Jacob 5:46 (1–77).
11a Mosiah 4:16;

D&C 104:18 (14–18).
 b James 2:16 (14–17);
1 Jn. 3:17 (14–23).
TG Generosity.
12a Matt. 21:32 (28–32);
Luke 7:29 (28–30).
13a JST Luke 3:19–20
(Appendix).
14a GR for extortion.
 b TG Contentment.
 c TG Wages.
15a TG Meditation.
 b John 1:19 (19–27).
16a TG Holy Ghost, Gift of.

17a OR winnowing fork.
 b GR storehouse, granary.
 c 2 Ne. 15:24;
Mosiah 7:30 (29–31).
19a Luke 13:31 (31–34).
21a TG Baptism, Essential;
Jesus Christ, Baptism of.
22a TG Godhead.
 b TG Holy Ghost, Dove,
Sign of.
23a TG Jesus Christ, Davidic
Descent of.
 b Num. 4:3 (3, 47).
 c Matt. 1:16.

was *the son* of Zorobabel, which was *the son* of Salathiel, which was *the son* of Neri,

28 Which was *the son* of Melchi, which was *the son* of Addi, which was *the son* of Cosam, which was *the son* of Elmodam, which was *the son* of Er,

29 Which was *the son* of Jose, which was *the son* of Eliezer, which was *the son* of Jorim, which was *the son* of Matthat, which was *the son* of Levi,

30 Which was *the son* of Simeon, which was *the son* of Juda, which was *the son* of Joseph, which was *the son* of Jonan, which was *the son* of Eliakim,

31 Which was *the son* of Melea, which was *the son* of Menan, which was *the son* of Mattatha, which was *the son* of Nathan, which was *the son* of David,

32 Which was *the son* of Jesse, which was *the son* of Obed, which was *the son* of Booz, which was *the son* of Salmon, which was *the son* of Naasson,

33 Which was *the son* of Amina-dab, which was *the son* of Aram, which was *the son* of Esrom, which was *the son* of ᵃPhares, which was *the son* of ᵇJuda,

34 Which was *the son* of Jacob, which was *the son* of Isaac, which was *the son* of ᵃAbraham, which was *the son* of Thara, which was *the son* of Nachor,

35 Which was *the son* of Saruch, which was *the son* of Ragau, which was *the son* of Phalec, which was *the son* of Heber, which was *the son* of Sala,

36 Which was *the son* of Cainan, which was *the son* of Arphaxad, which was *the son* of ᵃSem, which

was *the son* of Noe, which was *the son* of Lamech,

37 Which was *the son* of Mathusala, which was *the son* of Enoch, which was *the son* of Jared, which was *the son* of Maleleel, which was *the son* of Cainan,

38 Which was *the* ᵃson of Enos, which was *the son* of Seth, which was *the son* of ᵇAdam, ᶜwhich was *the* ᵈson of God.

CHAPTER 4

Jesus fasts forty days and is tempted by the devil—Jesus announces His divine sonship in Nazareth and is rejected—He casts out a devil in Capernaum, heals Peter's mother-in-law, and preaches and heals throughout Galilee.

AND Jesus being full of the Holy Ghost returned from Jordan, and was ᵃled by the Spirit into the wilderness,

2 ᵃBeing forty days ᵇtempted of the ᶜdevil. And in those days he did eat nothing: and when they were ended, he afterward hungered.

3 And the devil said unto him, If thou be the Son of God, command this stone that it be made bread.

4 And Jesus answered him, saying, It is written, That ᵃman shall not live by bread alone, but by every word of God.

5 ᵃAnd the devil, taking him up into an high mountain, shewed unto him all the kingdoms of the world in a moment of time.

6 And the devil said unto him, All this ᵃpower will I give thee, and the glory of them: for that is delivered unto me; and to whomsoever I will I give it.

7 If thou therefore wilt worship me, all shall be thine.

33a Gen. 38:29 (1–30); Ruth 4:18 (18–22).
  b TG Israel, Judah, People of.
34a Gen. 11:26 (10–26).
36a Gen. 5:32 (3–32).
38a TG Family, Patriarchal.
  b TG Adam.
  c JST Luke 3:45 . . . *who was formed* of God, *and the first man upon*

  the earth.
  d Moses 6:22.
    TG Man, Physical Creation of.
4 1a Ezek. 37:1 (1–2).
    TG Holy Ghost, Mission of.
  2a JST Luke 4:2 *And after forty days, the devil came unto him, to tempt him. And in those . . .*

  b Mosiah 15:5 (4–7); D&C 62:1; Moses 7:24 (24–27).
  c TG Devil.
4a Deut. 8:3.
5a JST Luke 4:5 And the *Spirit taketh* him up into a high mountain, *and he beheld* all the kingdoms . . .
6a Rev. 13:2.

8 And Jesus answered and said unto him, Get thee behind me, Satan: for it is written, Thou shalt *a*worship the Lord thy God, and him only shalt thou *b*serve.

9 *a*And he brought him to Jerusalem, and set him on a pinnacle of the temple, and said unto him, If thou be the Son of God, cast thyself down from hence:

10 For it is written, He shall give his *a*angels charge over thee, to keep thee:

11 And in *their* hands they shall bear thee up, lest at any time thou dash thy foot against a stone.

12 And Jesus answering said unto him, It is said, Thou shalt not *a*tempt the Lord thy God.

13 And when the devil had ended all the temptation, he departed from him for a season.

14 ¶ And Jesus returned in the *a*power of the Spirit into *b*Galilee: and there went out a fame of him through all the region round about.

15 And he taught in their synagogues, being glorified of all.

16 ¶ And he came to Nazareth, where he had been brought up: and, as his custom was, he went into the synagogue on the sabbath day, and stood up for to read.

17 And there was delivered unto him the book of the prophet Esaias. And when he had opened the book, he found the place where it was written,

18 The *a*Spirit of the Lord *is* upon me, because he hath *b*anointed me to *c*preach the *d*gospel to the *e*poor; he hath sent me to heal the brokenhearted, to *f*preach *g*deliverance to the *h*captives, and recovering of sight to the blind, to set at *i*liberty them that are bruised,

19 *a*To preach the acceptable year of the Lord.

20 And he closed the book, and he gave *it* again to the minister, and sat down. And the eyes of all them that were in the synagogue were fastened on him.

21 And he began to say unto them, This day is this scripture *a*fulfilled in your ears.

22 And all bare him witness, and *a*wondered at the *b*gracious words which proceeded out of his mouth. And they said, Is not this *c*Joseph's son?

23 And he said unto them, Ye will surely say unto me this proverb, Physician, heal thyself: whatsoever we have heard done in *a*Capernaum, *b*do also here in thy country.

24 And he said, Verily I say unto you, No prophet is *a*accepted in his own country.

25 But I tell you of a truth, many *a*widows were in Israel in the days of *b*Elias, when the heaven was shut up three years and six months, when great famine was throughout all the land;

26 But unto none of them was Elias sent, save unto Sarepta, *a city* of Sidon, unto a woman *that was* a widow.

27 And many *a*lepers were in Israel in the time of Eliseus the prophet; and none of them was *b*cleansed, saving Naaman the Syrian.

8a TG Worship.
  b TG Commitment.
9a JST Luke 4:9 And *the Spirit* brought him to Jerusalem, and set him on a pinnacle of the temple. *And the devil came unto him, and said . . .*
10a Ps. 91:11 (11–12).
12a Deut. 6:16.
14a TG Jesus Christ, Power of.
  b Matt. 4:12.
18a Isa. 61:1 (1–2).
  TG God, Spirit of.
  b TG Anointing; Jesus Christ, Messiah.

  c TG Teaching.
  d D&C 137:7.
  TG Gospel.
  e TG Poor.
  f TG Jesus Christ, Mission of; Preaching.
  g GR remission.
  TG Deliver; Remission of Sins.
  h D&C 138:8 (5–10).
  TG Bondage, Spiritual; Salvation for the Dead; Spirits in Prison.
  i TG Liberty.
19a John 12:47.
21a TG Jesus Christ,

  Prophecies about.
22a OR marveled.
  b Ps. 45:2.
  c John 6:42.
23a John 4:46 (43–54).
  b Matt. 13:58.
24a TG Prophets, Rejection of.
25a 1 Kgs. 17:9 (1, 8–10).
  TG Widows.
  b IE Elijah.
  1 Kgs. 17:1;
  Matt. 17:3 (1–4);
  D&C 110:13 (13–16).
27a TG Leprosy.
  b 2 Kgs. 5:14.

28 And all they in the synagogue, when they heard these things, were filled with wrath,

29 And rose up, and thrust him out of the city, and led him unto the brow of the hill whereon their city was built, that they might cast him down headlong.

30 But he *passing through the midst of them went his way,

31 And came down to Capernaum, a city of Galilee, and taught them on the sabbath days.

32 And they were astonished at his doctrine: for his word was with *power.

33 ¶ And in the synagogue there was a man, which had a spirit of an unclean devil, and cried out with a loud voice,

34 Saying, Let *us* alone; what have we to do with thee, *thou* Jesus of Nazareth? art thou come to destroy us? I know thee who thou art; the Holy One of God.

35 And Jesus rebuked him, saying, Hold thy peace, and come out of him. And when the devil had thrown him in the midst, he came out of him, and hurt him not.

36 And they were all amazed, and spake among themselves, saying, What a word *is* this! for with authority and power he commandeth the *unclean spirits, and they come out.

37 And the fame of him went out into every place of the country round about.

38 ¶ And he arose out of the synagogue, and entered into Simon's house. And Simon's wife's mother was taken with a great fever; and they besought him for her.

39 And he stood over her, and *rebuked the fever; and it left her: and immediately she arose and ministered unto them.

40 ¶ Now when the sun was set-

ting, all they that had any sick with *divers diseases brought them unto him; and he *laid his *hands on every one of them, and healed them.

41 And devils also came out of many, crying out, and saying, Thou art *Christ the Son of God. And he rebuking *them* suffered them not to speak: for they knew that he was Christ.

42 And when it was day, he *departed and went into a *desert place: and the people sought him, and came unto him, and *stayed him, that he should not depart from them.

43 And he said unto them, I must *preach the kingdom of God to other cities also: for therefore am I *sent.

44 And he preached in the synagogues of *Galilee.

CHAPTER 5

Peter, the fisherman, is called to catch men—Jesus heals a leper—He forgives sins and heals a paralytic—Matthew is called—The sick need a physician—New wine must be put in new bottles.

AND it came to pass, that, as the people pressed upon him to hear the word of God, he stood by the lake of Gennesaret,

2 And saw two ships standing by the lake: but the fishermen were gone out of them, and were washing *their* nets.

3 And he entered into one of the ships, which was Simon's, and prayed him that he would thrust out a little from the land. And he sat down, and taught the people out of the ship.

4 Now when he had left speaking, he said unto Simon, Launch out into the deep, and let down your nets for a *draught.

5 And Simon answering said unto

30a John 8:59.
32a GR authority.
 TG Jesus Christ, Authority of; Jesus Christ, Teaching Mode of; Teaching with the Spirit.
36a Mark 1:39 (21–45).

39a D&C 84:68 (64–73).
40a GR various.
 b TG Hands, Laying on of.
 c TG Administrations to the Sick.
41a TG Jesus Christ, Messiah.
42a Luke 5:16; 6:12.

 b JST Luke 4:42 . . . solitary . . .
 c GR detained Him.
43a TG Preaching.
 b TG Jesus Christ, Messenger of the Covenant.
44a Matt. 4:23 (23–25).
5 4a GR catch, haul.

him, Master, we have ^atoiled all the night, and have taken nothing: nevertheless at thy word I will let down the net.

6 And when they had this done, they inclosed a great multitude of fishes: and their net ^abrake.

7 And they beckoned unto *their* partners, which were in the other ship, that they should come and help them. And they came, and filled both the ships, so that they began to sink.

8 When Simon Peter saw *it,* he fell down at Jesus' knees, saying, Depart from me; for I am a sinful man, O Lord.

9 For he was astonished, and all that were with him, at the draught of the fishes which they had taken:

10 And so *was* also James, and John, the sons of Zebedee, which were partners with Simon. And Jesus said unto Simon, Fear not; from henceforth thou shalt ^acatch men.

11 And when they had brought their ships to land, they ^aforsook all, and ^bfollowed him.

12 ¶ And it came to pass, when he was in a certain city, behold a man full of ^aleprosy: who seeing Jesus fell on *his* face, and besought him, saying, Lord, if thou wilt, thou canst make me clean.

13 And he put forth *his* hand, and touched him, saying, I will: be thou clean. And immediately the leprosy departed from him.

14 And he charged him to tell no man: but go, and shew thyself to the ^apriest, and offer for thy cleansing, according as Moses commanded, for a testimony unto them.

15 But so much the more went there a fame abroad of him: and great multitudes came together to hear, and to be healed by him of their infirmities.

16 ¶ And he ^awithdrew himself into the wilderness, and prayed.

17 And it came to pass on a certain day, as he was teaching, that there were Pharisees and doctors of the law sitting by, which were come out of every town of Galilee, and Judæa, and Jerusalem: and the power of the Lord was *present* to heal them.

18 ¶ And, behold, men brought in a bed a man which was ^ataken with a palsy: and they sought *means* to bring him in, and to lay *him* before him.

19 And when they could not find by what *way* they might bring him in because of the multitude, they went upon the housetop, and let him down through the tiling with *his* couch into the midst before Jesus.

20 And when he saw their faith, he said unto him, Man, thy sins are ^aforgiven thee.

21 And the scribes and the Pharisees began to reason, saying, Who is this which speaketh ^ablasphemies? Who can ^bforgive sins, but God alone?

22 But when Jesus ^aperceived their thoughts, he answering said unto them, What reason ye in your hearts?

23 ^aWhether is easier, to say, Thy sins be forgiven thee; or to say, Rise up and walk?

24 But that ye may know that the Son of man hath power upon earth to ^aforgive sins, (he said unto the sick of the palsy,) I say unto thee, Arise, and take up thy couch, and go into thine house.

25 And immediately he rose up before them, and took up that whereon he lay, and departed to his own house, ^aglorifying God.

26 And they were all amazed, and they glorified God, and were filled

---

5a TG Industry.
6a OR was breaking.
10a GR capture, take alive.
  TG Missionary Work.
11a Luke 14:33 (28–33).
  b TG Apostles.
12a TG Leprosy.
14a Lev. 14:2 (1–32).

16a Luke 4:42; 6:12.
18a GR paralyzed.
20a TG Forgive.
21a TG Blaspheme.
  b D&C 64:3 (1–5);
    110:5 (4–6).
  TG Remission of Sins.
22a TG Jesus Christ,

Teaching Mode of.
23a JST Luke 5:23 *Does it require more power to forgive sins than to make the sick rise up and walk?*
24a TG Remission of Sins.
25a Luke 18:43.

with fear, saying, We have seen strange things to day.

27 ¶ And after these things he went forth, and saw a publican, named *a*Levi, sitting at the receipt of custom: and he said unto him, Follow me.

28 And he left all, rose up, and followed him.

29 And Levi made him a great feast in his own house: and there was a great company of publicans and of others that sat down with them.

30 But their scribes and Pharisees murmured against his disciples, saying, Why do ye eat and drink with publicans and sinners?

31 And Jesus answering said unto them, They that are whole need not a physician; but they that are sick.

32 I came not to call the righteous, but *a*sinners to repentance.

33 ¶ And they said unto him, Why do the disciples of John *a*fast often, and make prayers, and likewise *the disciples* of the Pharisees; but thine eat and drink?

34 And he said unto them, Can ye make the children of the *a*bridechamber fast, while the bridegroom is with them?

35 But the days will come, when the *a*bridegroom shall be taken away from them, and then shall they *b*fast in those days.

36 ¶ And he spake also a parable unto them; No man putteth a piece of a new garment upon an old; if otherwise, then both the new maketh a rent, and the piece that was *taken* out of the new *a*agreeth not with the old.

37 And no man putteth new wine into old bottles; else the new wine will burst the *a*bottles, and be spilled, and the bottles shall perish.

38 But new wine must be put into new bottles; and both are preserved.

39 No man also having drunk old *wine* *a*straightway desireth new: for he saith, The old is better.

CHAPTER 6

Jesus heals on the Sabbath—He chooses the Twelve Apostles—He pronounces blessings upon the obedient and woes upon the wicked.

AND it came to pass on the second sabbath after the first, that he went through the corn fields; and his disciples plucked the ears of corn, and did eat, rubbing *them* in *their* hands.

2 And certain of the Pharisees said unto them, Why do ye that which is not lawful to do on the *a*sabbath days?

3 And Jesus answering them said, Have ye not read so much as this, what David did, when himself was an hungred, and they which were with him;

4 How he went into the house of God, and did take and eat the *a*shewbread, and gave also to them that were with him; which it is not lawful to eat but for the priests alone?

5 And he said unto them, That the Son of man is Lord also of the *a*sabbath.

6 And it came to pass also on another sabbath, that he entered into the synagogue and taught: and there was a man whose right hand was withered.

7 And the scribes and Pharisees watched him, whether he would heal on the sabbath day; that they might find an accusation against him.

8 But he *a*knew their thoughts, and said to the man which had the withered hand, Rise up, and stand forth in the midst. And he arose and stood forth.

9 Then said Jesus unto them, I will ask you one thing; Is it lawful on the

---

27a Matt. 9:9 (9–13).
32a John 9:39 (39–41);
    1 Tim. 1:15.
33a Mark 2:18 (18–22).
34a Matt. 22:2 (2–14);
    Rev. 19:7 (7–9); 21:2.
35a Mark 2:19;

       John 16:5 (4–7).
  b Acts 13:2 (2–3).
36a GR fits, accords.
37a GR leather bags or
    wineskins.
39a GR immediately.
6 2a John 5:10 (10–16).

4a Ex. 29:33 (32–33);
    Lev. 24:9 (5–9);
    1 Sam. 21:6 (1–6).
5a TG Sabbath.
8a John 2:24 (23–25).

sabbath days to do good, or to do evil? to save life, or to destroy *it?*

10 And looking round about upon them all, he said unto the man, Stretch forth thy hand. And he did so: and his hand was restored whole as the other.

11 And they were filled with madness; and communed one with another what they might do to Jesus.

12 And it came to pass in those days, that he ªwent out into a mountain to ᵇpray, and continued all night in prayer to God.

13 ¶ And when it was day, he called *unto him* his disciples: and of them he ªchose ᵇtwelve, whom also he named ᶜapostles;

14 Simon, (whom he also named ªPeter,) and Andrew his brother, James and John, Philip and Bartholomew,

15 Matthew and Thomas, James the *son* of Alphæus, and Simon called Zelotes,

16 And Judas *the brother* of James, and Judas ªIscariot, which also was the traitor.

17 ¶ And he came down with them, and stood in the plain, and the company of his disciples, and a great multitude of people out of all Judæa and Jerusalem, and from the sea coast of Tyre and Sidon, which came to hear him, and to be healed of their diseases;

18 And they that were vexed with ªunclean spirits: and they were healed.

19 And the whole multitude sought to touch him: for there went ªvirtue out of him, and ᵇhealed *them* all.

20 ¶ And he lifted up his eyes on his disciples, and said, Blessed *be* ye ªpoor: for yours is the ᵇkingdom of God.

21 Blessed *are ye* that ªhunger now: for ye shall be filled. Blessed *are ye* that weep now: for ye shall ᵇlaugh.

22 Blessed are ye, when men shall ªhate you, and when they shall ᵇseparate you *from their company,* and shall ᶜreproach *you,* and ᵈcast out your name as evil, for the Son of man's sake.

23 ªRejoice ye in that day, and leap for ᵇjoy: for, behold, your ᶜreward *is* great in heaven: for in the like manner did their fathers unto the prophets.

24 But woe unto you that are ªrich! for ye have ᵇreceived your consolation.

25 Woe unto you that are full! for ye shall hunger. Woe unto you that laugh now! for ye shall mourn and weep.

26 Woe unto you, when all ªmen shall speak ᵇwell of you! for so did their fathers to the false prophets.

27 ¶ But I say unto you which hear, ªLove your enemies, do good to them which hate you,

28 Bless them that curse you, and ªpray for them which despitefully use you.

29 ªAnd unto him that ᵇsmiteth thee on the *one* cheek offer also the other; and him that ᶜtaketh away thy cloak forbid not *to take thy* coat also.

30 ªGive to every man that ᵇasketh of thee; and of him that taketh away thy goods ask *them* not again.

12a Luke 4:42; 5:16.
  b Matt. 14:23; 26:36;
    Luke 9:28.
13a 1 Ne. 12:7 (6–7).
    TG Called of God.
  b TG Apostles.
  c TG Church Organization.
14a John 1:42.
16a Josh. 15:25.
18a TG Spirits, Evil or
    Unclean;
    Uncleanness.
19a GR power.
    Mark 5:30 (25–34);
    Luke 8:46 (41–48).

  b TG Heal.
20a James 2:5 (1–9).
  b D&C 38:9.
21a Isa. 55:1 (1–2).
  b TG Laughter.
22a 1 Pet. 3:14.
  b TG Persecution.
  c TG Reproach.
  d Isa. 66:5.
23a Acts 5:41.
  b TG Joy.
  c TG Reward.
24a TG Treasure.
  b Luke 16:25 (19–25).
26a TG Trust Not in the

    Arm of Flesh.
  b John 15:19 (18–19);
    1 Ne. 22:23;
    Alma 1:3.
27a TG Reconciliation.
28a Luke 23:34 (33–34);
    Acts 7:60 (53–60).
29a JST Luke 6:29–30
    (Appendix).
  b Alma 43:46 (46–47);
    D&C 98:23 (22–48).
  c 1 Cor. 6:7 (6–8).
30a TG Generosity.
  b Prov. 3:27 (27–28);
    21:26 (25–26).

31 And as ye would that men should do to you, do ye also to them likewise.

32 For if ye love them which love you, what thank have ye? for sinners also love those that love them.

33 And if ye do good to them which do good to you, what thank have ye? for sinners also do even the same.

34 And if ye lend *to them* of whom ye hope to receive, what thank have ye? for sinners also lend to sinners, to receive as much again.

35 But *ᵃ*love ye your enemies, and do good, and *ᵇ*lend, hoping for nothing again; and your *ᶜ*reward shall be great, and ye shall be the *ᵈ*children of the Highest: for he is kind unto the *ᵉ*unthankful and *to* the evil.

36 Be ye therefore *ᵃ*merciful, as your Father also is *ᵇ*merciful.

37 *ᵃ*Judge not, and ye shall not be judged: *ᵇ*condemn not, and ye shall not be condemned: forgive, and ye shall be *ᶜ*forgiven:

38 *ᵃ*Give, and it shall be given unto you; good measure, pressed down, and shaken together, and running over, shall men give into your bosom. For with the same *ᵇ*measure that ye mete withal it shall be measured to you again.

39 And he spake a parable unto them, Can the *ᵃ*blind *ᵇ*lead the blind? shall they not both fall into the *ᶜ*ditch?

40 The disciple is not above his master: but every one *ᵃ*that is perfect shall be as his master.

41 And why beholdest thou the *ᵃ*mote that is in thy brother's eye,

but perceivest not the beam that is in thine own eye?

42 Either how canst thou say to thy brother, Brother, let me pull out the mote that is in thine eye, when thou thyself beholdest not the beam that is in thine own eye? Thou hypocrite, cast out first the beam out of thine own eye, and then shalt thou see clearly to pull out the mote that is in thy brother's eye.

43 For a good tree bringeth not forth corrupt *ᵃ*fruit; neither doth a corrupt tree bring forth good fruit.

44 For every tree is known by his own *ᵃ*fruit. For of thorns men do not gather figs, nor of a bramble bush gather they grapes.

45 A good man out of the good treasure of his *ᵃ*heart bringeth forth that which is good; and an evil man out of the evil treasure of his heart bringeth forth that which is evil: for of the abundance of the *ᵇ*heart his *ᶜ*mouth *ᵈ*speaketh.

46 ¶ And why *ᵃ*call ye me, *ᵇ*Lord, Lord, and *ᶜ*do not the things which I say?

47 Whosoever cometh to me, and heareth my sayings, and *ᵃ*doeth them, I will shew you to whom he is like:

48 He is like a man which built an house, and digged deep, and laid the foundation on a rock: and when the flood arose, the stream beat vehemently upon that house, and could not shake it: for it was founded upon a rock.

49 But he that *ᵃ*heareth, and doeth not, is like a man that without a foundation built an house upon the

---

35a TG Charity.
   b TG Generosity.
   c TG Reward.
   d D&C 76:58 (50–62).
   e TG Ingratitude.
36a TG Mercy.
   b TG God, Mercy of.
37a Moro. 7:18 (12–19).
   TG Retribution.
   b TG Gossip.
   c TG Forgive.
38a TG Generosity;
   Kindness.
   b D&C 1:10 (9–10).

39a TG Trust Not in the
   Arm of Flesh.
   b TG Leadership.
   c GR pit, well, cistern.
40a GR having been
   perfectly prepared.
   TG Perfection.
41a GR chip, splinter.
43a 3 Ne. 14:20 (14–20).
44a Matt. 7:16 (15–16);
   Alma 7:24 (23–24);
   D&C 84:58 (54–58);
   97:7 (6–8).
45a TG Motivations.

   b TG Heart.
   c TG Gossip.
   d Matt. 12:34;
   James 3:10 (10–12).
46a 1 Ne. 17:41 (40–41);
   Alma 37:46 (44–47).
   b Ezek. 33:31 (30–33);
   Hosea 8:2 (1–4);
   Matt. 7:21 (21–23);
   D&C 112:26;
   JS—H 1:19.
   c TG Disobedience.
47a TG Commitment.
49a James 1:23 (22–25).

earth; against which the stream did beat vehemently, and immediately it fell; and the ruin of that house was great.

CHAPTER 7

Jesus heals the centurion's servant—Jesus raises from death the son of the widow of Nain—He praises John the Baptist as more than a prophet—A woman anoints Jesus' feet, and He forgives her sins.

Now when he had ended all his sayings in the audience of the people, he entered into Capernaum.

2 And a certain centurion's servant, who was dear unto him, was sick, and ready to die.

3 And when he heard of Jesus, he sent unto him the elders of the Jews, beseeching him that he would come and heal his servant.

4 And when they came to Jesus, they besought him *a*instantly, saying, That he was worthy for whom he should do this:

5 For he loveth our nation, and he hath built us a synagogue.

6 Then Jesus went with them. And when he was now not far from the house, the centurion sent friends to him, saying unto him, Lord, trouble not thyself: for I am not worthy that thou shouldest enter under my roof:

7 Wherefore neither thought I myself worthy to come unto thee: but say in a word, and my servant shall be healed.

8 For I also am a man set under authority, having under me soldiers, and I say unto one, Go, and he goeth; and to another, Come, and he cometh; and to my servant, Do this, and he doeth *it*.

9 When Jesus heard these things, he marvelled at him, and turned him about, and said unto the people that followed him, I say unto you, I have not found so great faith, no, not in *a*Israel.

10 And they that were sent, returning to the house, found the servant whole that had been sick.

11 ¶ And it came to pass the day after, that he went into a city called Nain; and many of his disciples went with him, and much people.

12 Now when he came nigh to the gate of the city, behold, there was a dead man carried out, the only son of his mother, and she was a widow: and much people of the city was with her.

13 And when the Lord saw her, he had *a*compassion on her, and said unto her, Weep not.

14 And he came and touched the bier: and they that bare *him* stood still. And he said, Young man, I say unto thee, Arise.

15 And he that was *a*dead sat up, and began to speak. And he delivered him to his mother.

16 And there came a *a*fear on all: and they glorified God, saying, That a great prophet is risen up among us; and, That God hath *b*visited his people.

17 And this rumour of him went forth throughout all Judæa, and throughout all the region round about.

18 And the disciples of *a*John shewed him of all these things.

19 ¶ And John calling *unto him* two of his disciples sent *them* to Jesus, saying, Art thou he that should come? or look we for another?

20 When the men were come unto him, they said, John Baptist hath sent us unto thee, saying, Art thou he that should come? or look we for another?

21 And in that same hour he *a*cured many of *their* infirmities and plagues, and of evil spirits; and unto many *that were* blind he gave *b*sight.

22 Then Jesus answering said unto them, Go your way, and tell John what things ye have seen and heard; how that the blind see, the lame walk, the lepers are cleansed, the

---

7 4*a* GR earnestly.
　9*a* Alma 19:10.
　13*a* TG Compassion; Mercy.
　15*a* TG Death, Power over.

16*a* Alma 19:25 (24–27);
　　Moses 6:39 (37–40).
　b Ex. 3:16;
　　Luke 1:68;

D&C 110:7.
18*a* Matt. 11:2 (2–19).
21*a* TG Heal.
　b TG Sight.

deaf hear, the dead are raised, to the *a*poor the gospel is preached.

23 And blessed is *he*, whosoever shall not be *a*offended in me.

24 ¶ And when the messengers of John were departed, he began to speak unto the people concerning John, What went ye out into the wilderness for to see? A reed shaken with the wind?

25 But what went ye out for to see? A man clothed in soft raiment? Behold, they which are gorgeously *a*apparelled, and live delicately, are in kings' courts.

26 But what went ye out for to see? A prophet? Yea, I say unto you, and much more than a prophet.

27 This is *he*, of whom it is written, Behold, I send my *a*messenger before thy face, which shall prepare thy way before thee.

28 For I say unto you, Among those that are born of women there is not a greater prophet than John the Baptist: but he that is *a*least in the kingdom of God is greater than he.

29 And all the people that heard *him*, and the *a*publicans, justified God, being baptized with the *b*baptism of John.

30 But the Pharisees and lawyers *a*rejected the counsel of God *b*against themselves, being not *c*baptized of him.

31 ¶ And the Lord said, Whereunto then shall I liken the men of this generation? and to what are they like?

32 They are like unto children sitting in the marketplace, and calling one to another, and saying, We have piped unto you, and ye have not danced; we have *a*mourned to you, and ye have not wept.

33 For John the Baptist came neither eating bread nor drinking wine; and ye say, He hath a devil.

34 The Son of man is come eating and drinking; and ye say, Behold a gluttonous man, and a winebibber, a friend of publicans and sinners!

35 But wisdom is justified of all her children.

36 ¶ And one of the Pharisees desired him that he would eat with him. And he went into the Pharisee's house, and sat down to meat.

37 And, behold, a *a*woman in the city, which was a sinner, when she knew that *Jesus* sat at meat in the Pharisee's house, brought an alabaster *b*box of ointment,

38 And stood at his feet behind *him* weeping, and began to wash his feet with tears, and did wipe *them* with the hairs of her head, and kissed his feet, and *a*anointed *them* with the ointment.

39 Now when the Pharisee which had bidden him saw *it*, he spake within himself, saying, This man, if he were a prophet, would have known who and what manner of woman *this is* that toucheth him: for she is a sinner.

40 And Jesus answering said unto him, Simon, I have somewhat to say unto thee. And he saith, Master, say on.

41 There was a certain creditor which had two debtors: the one owed five hundred *a*pence, and the other fifty.

42 And when they had nothing to pay, he frankly *a*forgave them both. *b*Tell me therefore, which of them will love him most?

43 Simon answered and said, I suppose that *he*, to whom he forgave most. And he said unto him, Thou hast rightly judged.

44 And he turned to the woman, and said unto Simon, Seest thou this woman? I entered into thine house, thou gavest me no water for my feet:

22*a* Alma 32:2 (2–6).
23*a* 2 Ne. 18:14 (13–15).
25*a* TG Apparel.
27*a* D&C 45:9.
28*a* Matt. 11:11; D&C 50:26.
29*a* Matt. 21:32 (28–32); Luke 3:12.

b Matt. 3:7 (1–8).
30*a* Alma 5:41.
b GR for.
c TG Baptism, Essential.
32*a* TG Mourning.
37*a* TG Woman.
b GR flask.

38*a* TG Anointing.
41*a* GR *denarii*; one *denarius* was a workman's daily wage.
42*a* TG Forgive.
b TG Jesus Christ, Teaching Mode of.

but she hath washed my feet with tears, and wiped *them* with the hairs of her head.

45 Thou gavest me no kiss: but this woman since the time I came in hath not ceased to kiss my feet.

46 My head with oil thou didst not anoint: but this woman hath anointed my feet with ointment.

47 Wherefore I say unto thee, Her sins, which are many, are *a*forgiven; for she loved much: but to whom little is forgiven, *the same* loveth little.

48 And he said unto her, Thy sins are *a*forgiven.

49 And they that sat at meat with him began to say within themselves, Who is this that *a*forgiveth sins also?

50 And he said to the woman, Thy *a*faith hath saved thee; go in *b*peace.

CHAPTER 8

Jesus gives and interprets the parable of the sower—He stills the tempest; casts out a legion of devils, who then enter the swine; heals a woman of an issue of blood; and raises Jairus's daughter from death.

AND it came to pass afterward, that he went throughout every *a*city and village, preaching and shewing the glad *b*tidings of the kingdom of God: *c*and the twelve *were* with him,

2 And certain women, which had been healed of evil spirits and infirmities, *a*Mary called Magdalene, out of whom went seven devils,

3 And Joanna the wife of Chuza Herod's steward, and Susanna, and many others, which ministered unto him of their substance.

4 ¶ And when much people were gathered together, and were come to him out of every city, he spake by a parable:

5 A sower went out to sow his seed:

and as he sowed, some fell by the way side; and it was trodden down, and the fowls of the air devoured it.

6 And some fell upon a rock; and as soon as it was sprung up, it withered away, because it lacked moisture.

7 And some fell among thorns; and the thorns sprang up with it, and choked it.

8 And other fell on good ground, and sprang up, and bare fruit an hundredfold. And when he had said these things, he cried, He that hath ears to hear, let him hear.

9 And his disciples asked him, saying, What might this parable be?

10 And he said, Unto you it is given to know the *a*mysteries of the kingdom of God: but to others in *b*parables; that seeing they might not see, and hearing they might not *c*understand.

11 Now the parable is this: The *a*seed is the word of God.

12 Those by the way side are they that hear; then cometh the devil, and taketh away the word out of their hearts, lest they should believe and be saved.

13 They on the rock *are they*, which, when they hear, receive the word with joy; and these have no root, which for a while believe, and in time of *a*temptation fall away.

14 And that which fell among thorns are they, which, when they have heard, go forth, and are *a*choked with *b*cares and *c*riches and *d*pleasures of *this* life, and bring no fruit to *e*perfection.

15 But that on the good ground are they, which in an *a*honest and good *b*heart, having heard the word, keep *it*, and bring forth *c*fruit with patience.

16 ¶ No man, when he hath lighted

47*a* TG Forgive.
48*a* Mark 2:5.
49*a* TG Remission of Sins.
50*a* Matt. 9:2;
    Ether 12:4.
  b Mosiah 15:18.
8 1*a* Alma 23:4;
    D&C 66:5; 75:18.
  b D&C 76:40.
  c JST Luke 8:1 . . . and the

twelve *who were ordained of him*, were with him,
 2*a* Mark 16:9 (1, 9).
10*a* Alma 26:22.
  b Ps. 78:2;
    Mark 4:11 (11–12).
  c Isa. 6:9.
11*a* Alma 32:28 (27–28).
13*a* 1 Ne. 8:28 (24–28).
    TG Temptation.

14*a* Gal. 6:9 (8–10).
  b TG Worldliness.
  c TG Treasure.
  d TG Pleasure.
  e TG Perfection.
15*a* D&C 11:10.
  b TG Heart.
  c Alma 12:30 (29–30).

a ^acandle, covereth it with a vessel, or putteth *it* under a bed; but setteth *it* on a candlestick, that they which enter in may see the light.

17 For nothing is ^asecret, that shall not be made manifest; neither *any thing* hid, that shall not be known and come abroad.

18 Take heed therefore how ye hear: for whosoever ^ahath, to him shall be ^bgiven; and whosoever hath not, from him shall be taken even that which he seemeth to have.

19 ¶ Then came to him *his* mother and his ^abrethren, and could not come at him for the ^bpress.

20 And it was told him *by certain* which said, Thy mother and thy brethren stand without, desiring to see thee.

21 And he answered and said unto them, My ^amother and my brethren are these which hear the word of God, and ^bdo it.

22 ¶ Now it came to pass on a certain day, that he went into a ship with his disciples: and he said unto them, Let us go over unto the other side of the lake. And they launched forth.

23 But as they sailed he fell asleep: and there came down a storm of wind on the lake; ^aand they were filled *with water*, and were in jeopardy.

24 And they came to him, and awoke him, saying, Master, master, we perish. Then he arose, and rebuked the wind and the raging of the water: and they ceased, and there was a calm.

25 And he said unto them, Where is your faith? And they being afraid wondered, saying one to another, What manner of man is this! for he commandeth even the ^awinds and water, and they obey him.

26 ¶ And they arrived at the country of the Gadarenes, which is ^aover against Galilee.

27 And when he went forth to land, there met him out of the city a certain man, which had devils long time, and ware no clothes, neither abode in *any* house, but in the tombs.

28 When he saw Jesus, he cried out, and fell down before him, and with a loud voice said, What have I to do with thee, ^aJesus, *thou* Son of God most high? I beseech thee, torment me not.

29 (For he had commanded the unclean spirit to come out of the man. For oftentimes it had caught him: and he was kept bound with chains and in fetters; and he brake the bands, and was driven of the devil into the wilderness.)

30 And Jesus asked him, saying, What is thy name? And he said, ^aLegion: because many devils were entered into him.

31 And they besought him that he would not command them to go out into the ^adeep.

32 And there was there an herd of many swine feeding on the mountain: and they besought him that he would suffer them to enter into them. And he suffered them.

33 Then went the devils out of the man, and entered into the swine: and the herd ran violently down a steep place into the lake, and were choked.

34 When they that fed *them* saw what was done, they fled, and went and told *it* in the city and in the country.

35 Then they went out to see what was done; and came to Jesus, and found the man, out of whom the devils were departed, sitting at the feet of Jesus, clothed, and in his right mind: and they were afraid.

36 They also which saw *it* told them

16*a* 3 Ne. 12:15 (14–16);
    D&C 60:2 (2–3).
17*a* D&C 1:3.
18*a* 2 Ne. 28:30 (29–31).
  b Mark 4:24.
19*a* TG Jesus Christ,
    Family of.

  b GR crowd.
21*a* 3 Ne. 9:17 (13–18).
  b Matt. 7:21 (21–23).
23*a* JST Luke 8:23 . . . and
    they were filled with
    fear, and were in *danger*.
25*a* TG Nature, Earth.

26*a* GR on the other side of.
28*a* James 2:19 (19–20).
30*a* D&C 29:36 (36–38).
31*a* GR abyss. (See also
    Rev. 9:1; 20:3.)

by what means he that was possessed of the devils was healed.

37 ¶ Then the whole multitude of the country of the Gadarenes round about besought him to depart from them; for they were taken with great fear: and he went up into the ship, and returned back again.

38 Now the man out of whom the devils were departed besought him that he might be with him: but Jesus sent him away, saying,

39 Return to thine own house, and shew how great things God hath done unto thee. And he went his way, and *published throughout the whole city how great things Jesus had done unto him.

40 And it came to pass, that, when Jesus was returned, the people *gladly* received him: for they were all waiting for him.

41 ¶ And, behold, there came a man named *Jairus, and he was a ruler of the synagogue: and he fell down at Jesus' feet, and besought him that he would come into his house:

42 For he had one only daughter, about twelve years of age, and she lay a dying. But as he went the people thronged him.

43 ¶ And a woman having an issue of *blood twelve years, which had spent all her living upon physicians, neither could be healed of any,

44 Came behind *him,* and touched the *border of his garment: and immediately her issue of blood *stanched.

45 And Jesus said, Who touched me? When all denied, Peter and they that were with him said, Master, the multitude throng thee and press *thee,* and sayest thou, Who touched me?

46 And Jesus said, Somebody hath touched me: for I perceive that *virtue is gone out of me.

47 And when the woman saw that she was not hid, she came trembling, and falling down before him, she declared unto him before all the people for what cause she had touched him, and how she was *healed immediately.

48 And he said unto her, Daughter, be of good *comfort: thy faith hath made thee whole; go in peace.

49 ¶ While he yet spake, there cometh one from the ruler of the synagogue's *house,* saying to him, Thy daughter is dead; trouble not the Master.

50 But when Jesus heard *it,* he answered him, saying, Fear not: believe only, and she shall be made whole.

51 And when he came into the house, he suffered no man to go in, save Peter, and James, and John, and the father and the mother of the *maiden.

52 And all wept, and bewailed her: but he said, Weep not; she is not dead, but sleepeth.

53 And they *laughed him to scorn, knowing that she was dead.

54 And he put them all out, and took her by the hand, and called, saying, Maid, arise.

55 And her spirit came again, and she arose straightway: and he commanded to give her meat.

56 And her parents were astonished: but he charged them that they should tell no man what was done.

CHAPTER 9

The Twelve are sent out—Jesus feeds the five thousand—Peter testifies of Christ—Jesus foretells His death and resurrection—He is transfigured on the mount—He heals and teaches.

THEN he called his *twelve disciples together, and gave them power and *authority over all devils, and to cure diseases.

39a Mark 5:20.
41a Matt. 9:18 (18–26).
43a Lev. 15:25.
44a Acts 5:15; 19:12 (11–12).
  b GR ceased.
46a GR power.

Mark 5:30 (25–34);
  Luke 6:19 (17–19).
47a TG Heal.
48a GR courage, cheer.
51a GR child.
53a 2 Chr. 30:10;

Alma 26:23.
9 1a TG Apostles.
  b TG Authority;
     Priesthood, Authority.

2 And he sent them to ^apreach the kingdom of God, and to ^bheal the sick.

3 And he said unto them, Take nothing for *your* journey, neither staves, nor scrip, neither bread, neither money; neither have two coats apiece.

4 And whatsoever house ye enter into, there abide, and thence depart.

5 And whosoever will not receive you, when ye go out of that city, ^ashake off the very ^bdust from your feet for a testimony against them.

6 And they departed, and went through the towns, preaching the ^agospel, and healing every where.

7 ¶ Now ^aHerod the tetrarch heard of all that was done by him: and he was perplexed, because that it was said of some, that John was risen from the dead;

8 And of some, that Elias had appeared; and of others, that one of the old prophets was risen again.

9 And Herod said, John have I beheaded: but who is this, of whom I hear such things? And he desired to see him.

10 ¶ And the apostles, when they were returned, told ^ahim all that they had done. And he took them, and went aside privately into a ^bdesert place belonging to the city called Bethsaida.

11 And the people, when they knew *it,* followed him: and he received them, and spake unto them of the kingdom of God, and healed them that had need of healing.

12 And when the day began to wear away, then came the twelve, and said unto him, Send the multitude away, that they may go into the towns and country round about,

and lodge, and get victuals: for we are here in a desert place.

13 But he said unto them, Give ye them to eat. And they said, We have no more but five loaves and two fishes; except we should go and buy meat for all this people.

14 For they were about ^afive thousand men. And he said to his disciples, Make them sit down by fifties in a company.

15 And they did so, and made them all sit down.

16 Then he took the five loaves and the two fishes, and looking up to heaven, he blessed them, and brake, and gave to the disciples to set before the multitude.

17 And they did eat, and were all filled: and there was taken up of fragments that remained to them twelve baskets.

18 ¶ And it came to pass, as he was alone praying, his disciples were with him: and he asked them, saying, Whom say the people that I am?

19 They answering said, John the Baptist; but some *say,* Elias; and others *say,* that one of the old prophets is risen again.

20 He said unto them, But whom say ye that I am? Peter answering said, The ^aChrist of God.

21 And he straitly charged them, and commanded *them* to ^atell no man that thing;

22 Saying, The Son of man must suffer many things, and be ^arejected of the elders and chief priests and scribes, and be slain, and be raised the third day.

23 ¶ And he said to *them* all, If any *man* will come after me, let him deny himself, and take up his ^across daily, and ^bfollow me.

24 ^aFor whosoever will save his life

---

2 a TG Missionary Work;
     Preaching.
  b Matt. 10:8 (7–8).
5 a D&C 60:15.
  b Luke 10:11 (11–12);
     D&C 84:92.
6 a TG Gospel.
7 a Matt. 14:1 (1–3);
     Mark 6:14 (14–29);
     Luke 3:1.

10 a JST Luke 9:10 . . .
      Jesus . . .
   b JST Luke 9:10 . . .
      solitary . . .
14 a Matt. 14:21 (13–21);
      Mark 6:44 (32–44);
      John 6:10 (1–13).
20 a TG Testimony.
21 a Mark 8:30.
22 a Matt. 21:42 (42–46);

1 Pet. 2:7.
23 a See JST Matt. 16:25–26
      (Appendix).
      Matt. 10:38;
      3 Ne. 12:30 (29–30).
   b TG Jesus Christ,
      Exemplar.
24 a JST Luke 9:24–25
      (Appendix).

shall *b*lose it: but whosoever will lose his life for my sake, the same shall save it.

25 For what is a man advantaged, if he gain the whole world, and *a*lose himself, or be cast away?

26 For whosoever shall be *a*ashamed of me and of my words, of him shall the *b*Son of man be ashamed, *c*when he shall come in his own glory, and *in his* Father's, and of the holy angels.

27 But I tell you of a truth, there be some standing here, which shall not taste of *a*death, till they see the kingdom of God.

28 ¶ And it came to pass about an *a*eight days after these sayings, he took Peter and John and James, and went up into a *b*mountain to *c*pray.

29 And as he prayed, the fashion of his countenance was *a*altered, and his raiment *was* white *and* *b*glistering.

30 And, behold, there talked with him two men, which were Moses and Elias:

31 Who appeared in glory, *a*and spake of his *b*decease which he should accomplish at Jerusalem.

32 But Peter and they that were with him were heavy with sleep: and when they were awake, they saw his *a*glory, and the two men that stood with him.

33 And it came to pass, as they departed from him, Peter said unto Jesus, Master, it is good for us to be here: and let us make three tabernacles; one for thee, and one for Moses, and one for Elias: not knowing what he said.

34 While he thus spake, there came a cloud, and overshadowed them:

and they feared as they entered into the cloud.

35 And there came a voice out of the cloud, saying, This is my *a*beloved Son: hear him.

36 And when the voice was past, Jesus was found alone. And they kept *it* close, and told no man in those days any of those things which they had seen.

37 ¶ And it came to pass, that on the next day, when they were come down from the hill, much people met him.

38 And, behold, a man of the company cried out, saying, Master, I beseech thee, look upon my son: for he is mine only child.

39 And, lo, a spirit taketh him, and he suddenly crieth out; and it teareth him that he foameth again, and bruising him hardly departeth from him.

40 And I besought thy disciples to cast him out; and they could not.

41 And Jesus answering said, O faithless and perverse generation, how long shall I be with you, and suffer you? Bring thy son hither.

42 And as he was yet a coming, the devil threw him down, and tare *him*. And Jesus rebuked the unclean spirit, and healed the child, and delivered him again to his father.

43 ¶ And they were all amazed at the *a*mighty power of God. But while they wondered every one at all things which Jesus did, he said unto his disciples,

44 Let these sayings sink down into your ears: for the Son of man shall be *a*delivered into the hands of men.

45 But they *a*understood not this saying, and it was hid from them,

24*b* Matt. 10:39 (34–39);
   Mark 8:35;
   D&C 98:13 (13–14);
   103:27 (27–28).
25*a* Matt. 16:26.
26*a* D&C 3:7 (6–8).
  b TG Jesus Christ,
   Son of Man.
  c JST Luke 9:26 . . . when
   he shall come in his
   own *kingdom, clothed in*
   the glory of his Father,

   with the holy angels.
27*a* John 21:23 (21–23);
   3 Ne. 28:7 (4–10);
   D&C 7:2 (1–8).
28*a* Mark 9:2 (2–8).
  b 2 Pet. 1:18 (10–19).
  c Matt. 14:23; 26:36;
   Luke 6:12.
29*a* Matt. 17:2 (1–13);
   Mark 9:2 (2–13).
  b OR brilliant, glistening.
31*a* JST Luke 9:31 . . . and

   spake of his *death, and*
   also his resurrection,
   which he . . .
  b GR departure.
   TG Jesus Christ,
   Death of.
32*a* TG Glory.
35*a* Matt. 3:17; Mark 9:7.
43*a* GR majesty, glory.
44*a* 1 Ne. 11:32;
   3 Ne. 27:14.
45*a* John 12:16.

that they perceived it not: and they feared to ask him of that saying.

46 ¶ Then there arose a reasoning among them, which of them should be ªgreatest.

47 And Jesus, perceiving the thought of their heart, took a child, and set him by him,

48 And said unto them, Whosoever shall receive this child in my ªname receiveth me: and whosoever shall ᵇreceive me receiveth him that sent me: for he that is least among you all, the same shall be ᶜgreat.

49 ¶ And John answered and said, Master, we saw one casting out devils in thy name; and we forbad him, because he followeth not with us.

50 And Jesus said unto him, Forbid *him* not: for he that is not against us is ªfor us.

51 ¶ And it came to pass, when the time was come that he should be received up, he steadfastly set his face to go to Jerusalem,

52 And sent messengers before his face: and they went, and entered into a village of the ªSamaritans, to make ready for him.

53 And they did not receive him, because his face was as though he would go to Jerusalem.

54 And when his disciples ªJames and John saw *this*, they said, Lord, wilt thou that we command ᵇfire to come down from heaven, and consume them, even as Elias did?

55 But he turned, and rebuked them, and said, Ye know not what manner of ªspirit ye are of.

56 For the ªSon of man is not come to ᵇdestroy men's ᶜlives, but to ᵈsave *them*. And they went to another village.

57 ¶ And it came to pass, that, as they went in the way, a certain *man* said unto him, Lord, I will ªfollow thee whithersoever thou goest.

58 And Jesus said unto him, Foxes have holes, and birds of the air *have* nests; but the Son of man hath not where to lay *his* head.

59 And he said unto another, ªFollow me. But he said, Lord, suffer me first to go and bury my father.

60 Jesus said unto him, Let the dead bury their dead: but go thou and preach the kingdom of God.

61 And another also said, Lord, I will ªfollow thee; but let me first go bid them farewell, which are at home at my house.

62 And Jesus said unto him, No man, having put his hand to the ªplough, and ᵇlooking back, is fit for the kingdom of God.

CHAPTER 10

Jesus calls, empowers, and instructs the Seventy—They preach and heal—Those who receive Christ's disciples receive Christ—The Father is revealed by the Son—Jesus gives the parable of the good Samaritan.

AFTER these things the Lord ªappointed other ᵇseventy also, and sent them ᶜtwo and two before his face into every city and place, whither he himself would come.

2 Therefore said he unto them, The ªharvest truly *is* great, but the labourers *are* few: pray ye therefore the Lord of the harvest, that he would send forth labourers into his harvest.

3 Go your ways: behold, I send you forth as ªlambs among wolves.

46a Matt. 18:1 (1–5);
    Mark 9:34 (34–37).
48a TG Name.
  b Matt. 10:40.
  c Ether 12:27 (26–27).
50a Matt. 12:30;
    Mark 9:40.
52a Matt. 10:5.
54a Mark 3:17.
  b 2 Kgs. 1:10 (9–16).
55a TG Spirits, Evil or
    Unclean.

56a TG Jesus Christ,
    Son of Man.
  b John 3:17 (16–17).
  c TG Mortality.
  d TG Life, Sanctity of;
    Worth of Souls.
57a Matt. 8:19.
59a 2 Ne. 31:12 (12–13).
    TG Called of God.
61a 1 Kgs. 19:20.
62a TG Commitment.
  b Luke 14:18 (16–24);

    D&C 133:15.
10 1a TG Authority;
      Called of God;
      Priesthood, Authority.
   b TG Church
      Organization;
      Missionary Work;
      Seventy.
   c Mark 6:7.
 2a Matt. 9:37.
 3a Matt. 10:16.

4 Carry neither ^apurse, nor scrip, nor shoes: and ^bsalute no man by the way.

5 And into whatsoever house ye enter, first say, ^aPeace *be* to this house.

6 And if the son of peace be there, your peace shall rest upon it: if not, it shall turn to you again.

7 And in the same house remain, eating and drinking such things as they give: for the ^alabourer is worthy of his ^bhire. Go not from house to house.

8 And into whatsoever city ye enter, and they ^areceive you, eat such things as are set before you:

9 And heal the sick that are therein, and say unto them, The ^akingdom of God is come nigh unto you.

10 But into whatsoever city ye enter, and they receive you not, go your ways out into the streets of the same, and say,

11 Even the very ^adust of your city, which cleaveth on us, we do wipe off against you: notwithstanding be ye sure of this, that the kingdom of God is come nigh unto you.

12 But I say unto you, that it shall be more tolerable in that day for Sodom, than for that city.

13 Woe unto thee, Chorazin! woe unto thee, Bethsaida! for if the mighty works had been done in Tyre and Sidon, which have been done in you, they had a great while ago repented, sitting in sackcloth and ashes.

14 But it shall be more tolerable for Tyre and Sidon at the judgment, than for you.

15 And thou, Capernaum, which art exalted to heaven, shalt be thrust down to hell.

16 ^aHe that ^bheareth you heareth me; and he that ^cdespiseth you ^ddespiseth me; and he that ^edespiseth me despiseth him that sent me.

17 ¶ And the ^aseventy returned again with joy, saying, Lord, even the devils are subject unto us through thy name.

18 And he said unto them, I beheld ^aSatan as lightning fall from heaven.

19 Behold, I give unto you ^apower to ^btread on serpents and scorpions, and over all the power of the enemy: and nothing shall by any means ^churt you.

20 Notwithstanding in this ^arejoice not, that the spirits are subject unto you; but rather ^brejoice, because your names are ^cwritten in heaven.

21 ¶ In that hour Jesus ^arejoiced in spirit, and said, I thank thee, O Father, Lord of heaven and earth, that thou hast hid these things ^bfrom the wise and ^cprudent, and hast revealed them unto ^dbabes: even so, Father; for so it seemed good in thy sight.

22 All things are ^adelivered to me of my Father: and no man knoweth ^bwho the Son is, but the Father; and who the Father is, but the Son, and *he* to whom the Son will ^creveal *him*.

23 ¶ And he turned him unto his

4a Matt. 10:9.
 b 2 Kgs. 4:29.
5a 1 Sam. 25:6.
 TG Peace of God.
7a D&C 31:5 (3–7).
 TG Labor.
 b Num. 18:31;
 Matt. 10:10.
 TG Wages.
8a TG Teachable.
9a Matt. 3:2.
11a Matt. 10:14 (12–14);
 Mark 6:11;
 Luke 9:5;
 Acts 13:51 (44–52);
 D&C 24:15;
 75:20 (19–22).
16a JST Luke 10:17 And he

said unto his disciples, He that heareth . . .
 b Matt. 10:40;
 Mosiah 15:11.
 c GR rejects.
 D&C 84:36 (35–39).
 d 1 Thes. 4:8.
 e John 5:23.
17a TG Seventy.
18a TG Council in Heaven;
 Devil.
19a TG Priesthood, Power of.
 b Ps. 91:13.
 c Acts 28:5.
20a D&C 50:33 (30–34).
 b TG Joy.
 c Ex. 32:32;
 Heb. 12:23.

21a Matt. 11:25 (25–27).
 b JST Luke 10:22 . . . from them who think they are wise and prudent . . .
 c TG Prudence.
 d Alma 32:23;
 3 Ne. 26:14 (14–16);
 D&C 128:18.
22a TG Jesus Christ, Authority of.
 b JST Luke 10:23 . . . that the Son is the Father, and the Father is the Son, but him to whom the Son will reveal it.
 c Matt. 11:27;
 John 1:18; 14:6 (6–14).

disciples, and said privately, Blessed *are* the [a]eyes which see the things that ye see:

24 For I tell you, that many [a]prophets and [b]kings have desired to see those things which ye see, and have not seen *them;* and to hear those things which ye hear, and have not heard *them.*

25 ¶ And, behold, a certain lawyer stood up, and tempted him, saying, Master, what shall I do to inherit [a]eternal life?

26 He said unto him, What is written in the law? how readest thou?

27 And he answering said, Thou shalt love the Lord thy God with all thy [a]heart, and with all thy soul, and with all thy strength, and with all thy mind; and thy neighbour as thyself.

28 And he said unto him, Thou hast answered right: this do, and thou shalt [a]live.

29 But he, willing to [a]justify himself, said unto Jesus, And who is my [b]neighbour?

30 And Jesus answering said, A certain *man* went down from Jerusalem to Jericho, and fell among thieves, which stripped him of his raiment, and [a]wounded *him,* and departed, leaving *him* half dead.

31 And by chance there came down a certain priest that way: and when he saw him, he passed by on the other side.

32 And likewise a Levite, when he was at the place, came and looked *on him,* and passed by on the other side.

33 But a certain [a]Samaritan, as he journeyed, came where he was: and when he saw him, he had [b]compassion *on him,*

34 And went to *him,* and bound up his wounds, pouring in oil and wine, and set him on his own beast, and brought him to an inn, and took [a]care of him.

35 And on the morrow when he departed, he took out two pence, and gave *them* to the [a]host, and said unto him, Take care of him; and whatsoever thou spendest more, when I come again, I will repay thee.

36 Which now of these three, thinkest thou, was neighbour unto him that fell among the thieves?

37 And he said, He that shewed mercy on him. Then said Jesus unto him, Go, and do thou likewise.

38 ¶ Now it came to pass, as they went, that he entered into a certain village: and a certain woman named [a]Martha received him into her house.

39 And she had a sister called Mary, which also sat at Jesus' feet, and heard his word.

40 But Martha was cumbered about much serving, and came to him, and said, Lord, dost thou not care that my sister hath left me to serve alone? bid her therefore that she help me.

41 And Jesus answered and said unto her, Martha, Martha, thou art [a]careful and troubled about many things:

42 But one thing is needful: and Mary hath [a]chosen that good part, which shall not be taken away from her.

CHAPTER 11

Jesus gives the Lord's Prayer—He discusses the casting out of devils—He acclaims Himself as greater than Jonah and Solomon—He rebukes the Pharisees and says that the blood of all the prophets may be required of their generation.

AND it came to pass, that, as he was praying in a certain place, when he ceased, one of his disciples said unto him, Lord, [a]teach us to [b]pray, as John also taught his disciples.

2 And he said unto them, When ye pray, say, Our [a]Father which art in

23a Matt. 13:16.
24a 2 Ne. 25:26 (24–27).
  b TG Kings, Earthly.
25a Luke 18:18.
27a TG Apathy.
28a Lev. 18:5.
29a Luke 16:15.
  b TG Neighbor.
30a TG Cruelty.
33a John 4:9.
  b TG Benevolence; Compassion; Kindness.
34a TG Charity; Welfare.
35a GR innkeeper.
38a John 11:1 (1, 5); 12:2.
41a GR worried.
42a TG Agency.
11 1a TG Teaching.
  b TG Prayer.
2a TG God the Father, Elohim.

heaven, Hallowed be thy [b]name. Thy kingdom come. Thy will be done, as in heaven, so in earth.

3 Give us day by day our daily bread.

4 And [a]forgive us our sins; for we also forgive every one that is [b]indebted to us. [c]And lead us not into temptation; but deliver us from evil.

5 [a]And he said unto them, Which of you shall have a friend, and shall go unto him at midnight, and say unto him, Friend, lend me three loaves;

6 For a friend of mine in his journey is come to me, and I have nothing to set before him?

7 And he from within shall answer and say, Trouble me not: the door is now shut, and my children are with me in bed; I cannot rise and give thee.

8 I say unto you, Though he will not rise and give him, because he is his [a]friend, yet because of his importunity he will rise and give him as many as he needeth.

9 And I say unto you, Ask, and it shall be given you; seek, and ye shall find; knock, and it shall be opened unto you.

10 For every one that asketh receiveth; and he that seeketh findeth; and to him that knocketh it shall be opened.

11 If a son shall ask bread of any of you that is a father, will he give him a stone? or if *he ask* a fish, will he for a fish give him a serpent?

12 Or if he shall ask an egg, will he offer him a scorpion?

13 If ye then, being evil, know how to give good gifts unto your children: how much more shall *your* heavenly Father give [a]the Holy Spirit to them that ask him?

14 ¶ And he was casting [a]out a devil, and it was dumb. And it came to pass, when the devil was gone out, the dumb spake; and the people wondered.

15 But some of them said, He casteth out devils through [a]Beelzebub the chief of the devils.

16 And others, tempting *him*, sought of him a [a]sign from heaven.

17 But he, knowing their [a]thoughts, said unto them, Every kingdom divided against itself is brought to desolation; and a house *divided* against a house falleth.

18 If Satan also be divided against himself, how shall his kingdom stand? because ye say that I cast out devils through Beelzebub.

19 And if I by Beelzebub cast out devils, by whom do your sons [a]cast *them* out? therefore shall they be your judges.

20 But if I with the [a]finger of God cast out devils, no doubt the kingdom of God is come upon you.

21 When a strong man armed keepeth his palace, his goods are in peace:

22 But when a stronger than he shall come upon him, and overcome him, he taketh from him all his armour wherein he trusted, and divideth his spoils.

23 He that is not with me is [a]against me: and he that gathereth not with me scattereth.

24 When the [a]unclean spirit is gone out of a man, [b]he walketh through dry places, seeking rest; and finding

---

2b TG Name.
4a TG Forgive.
　b TG Debt.
　c JST Luke 11:4 . . . And let us not be led unto temptation; but deliver us from evil; *for thine is the kingdom and power. Amen.*
5a JST Luke 11:5–6 And he said unto them, *Your heavenly Father will not fail to give unto you*

whatsoever ye ask of him. And he spake a parable, saying, Which . . .
8a TG Brotherhood and Sisterhood; Friendship.
13a JST Luke 11:14 . . . *good gifts, through* the Holy Spirit . . .
14a JST Luke 11:15 . . . a devil *out of a man, and he* was dumb . . .
15a Mosiah 3:9 (9–12);

Hel. 13:26 (26–27).
16a TG Sign Seekers.
17a Matt. 12:25; John 2:25.
19a Matt. 12:27–28; Mark 9:38 (38–49); Acts 19:13.
20a Ex. 8:19; John 3:2; Acts 2:22; 10:38.
23a D&C 10:68 (67–68).
24a D&C 50:31 (31–33).
　b JST Luke 11:25 . . . *it* . . .

none, ^{c}he saith, I will return unto my house whence I came out.

25 ^{a}And when he cometh, he findeth *it* swept and ^{b}garnished.

26 Then goeth he, and taketh *to him* seven other spirits more wicked than himself; and they enter in, and dwell there: and the last *state* of that man is worse than the first.

27 ¶ And it came to pass, as he spake these things, a certain woman of the company lifted up her voice, and said unto him, ^{a}Blessed *is* the womb that bare thee, and the paps which thou hast sucked.

28 But he said, Yea rather, ^{n}blessed *are* they that hear the word of God, and ^{b}keep it.

29 ¶ And when the people were gathered thick together, he began to say, This is an evil generation: they seek a ^{a}sign; and there shall no sign be given it, but the sign of Jonas the prophet.

30 For as Jonas was a sign unto the Ninevites, so shall also the Son of man be to this generation.

31 The ^{a}queen of the south shall rise up in the judgment with the men of this generation, and condemn them: for she came from the utmost parts of the earth to hear the wisdom of Solomon; and, behold, a greater than Solomon *is* here.

32 The men of Nineve shall rise up in the judgment with this generation, and shall condemn it: for they repented at the preaching of Jonas; and, behold, a greater than Jonas *is* here.

33 No man, when he hath lighted a ^{a}candle, putteth *it* in a secret place,

neither under a bushel, but on a candlestick, that they which come in may see the light.

34 The light of the body is the ^{a}eye: therefore when thine eye is ^{b}single, thy whole body also is full of light; but when *thine eye* is evil, thy body also *is* full of ^{c}darkness.

35 Take heed therefore that the light which is in thee be not darkness.

36 If thy whole body therefore *be* full of light, having no part dark, the whole shall be full of light, as when the bright shining of a candle doth give thee light.

37 ¶ And as he spake, a certain Pharisee besought him to dine with him: and he went in, and sat down to meat.

38 And when the Pharisee saw *it,* he marvelled that he had not first washed before dinner.

39 And the Lord said unto him, Now do ye Pharisees make ^{a}clean the outside of the cup and the platter; but your ^{b}inward part is full of ^{c}ravening and ^{d}wickedness.

40 *Ye* fools, did not he that made that which is without make that which is within also?

41 ^{a}But rather ^{b}give ^{c}alms of such things as ye have; and, behold, all things are ^{d}clean unto you.

42 But woe unto you, Pharisees! for ye tithe mint and rue and all manner of herbs, and pass over judgment and the ^{a}love of God: these ought ye to have done, and not to leave the other undone.

43 Woe unto you, Pharisees! for ye love the ^{a}uppermost seats in the

---

24*c* JST Luke 11:25 . . . *it* . . .
25*a* JST Luke 11:26–27 And when *it* cometh, *it* findeth *the house* swept and garnished. Then goeth *the evil spirit,* and taketh seven other spirits . . .
  b GR put in order.
27*a* Luke 1:48.
28*a* TG Blessing.
  b Prov. 19:16; 29:18.
   TG Obedience.
29*a* TG Sign Seekers.

31*a* 1 Kgs. 10:1.
33*a* Matt. 5:15 (15–16); 3 Ne. 18:24.
34*a* D&C 88:68 (67–68).
  b Morm. 8:15 (13–15); JS—H 1:46.
  c TG Darkness, Spiritual.
39*a* TG Purification.
  b Titus 1:15 (15–16).
   TG Hypocrisy.
  c GR plunder, spoil.
  d TG Wickedness.
41*a* JST Luke 11:42 But *if ye would* rather give alms

of such things as ye have; and *observe to do all things which I have commanded you, then would your inward parts be clean also.*
  b TG Generosity.
  c TG Almsgiving; Charity.
  d TG Cleanliness.
42*a* TG Love.
43*a* Matt. 23:6; Luke 20:46.

synagogues, and greetings in the markets.

44 Woe unto you, *a*scribes and Pharisees, hypocrites! for ye are as *b*graves which appear not, and the men that walk over *them* are not aware *of them.*

45 ¶ Then answered one of the lawyers, and said unto him, Master, thus saying thou *a*reproachest us also.

46 And he said, Woe unto you also, ye *a*lawyers! for ye lade men with burdens grievous to be borne, and ye yourselves touch not the burdens with one of your fingers.

47 Woe unto you! for ye build the sepulchres of the prophets, and your fathers killed them.

48 Truly ye bear witness that ye *a*allow the deeds of your fathers: for they indeed killed them, and ye build their sepulchres.

49 Therefore also said the wisdom of God, I will send them prophets and apostles, and *some* of them they shall slay and persecute:

50 That the *a*blood of all the prophets, which was *b*shed from the foundation of the world, may be required of this generation;

51 From the blood of Abel unto the blood of Zacharias, which perished between the altar and the *a*temple: verily I say unto you, It shall be required of this generation.

52 Woe unto you, *a*lawyers! for ye have taken away the *b*key of *c*knowledge: ye entered not in yourselves, and them that were entering in ye *d*hindered.

53 And as he said these things unto them, the scribes and the Pharisees began to *a*urge *him* vehemently, and to *b*provoke him to speak of many things:

54 Laying wait for him, and seeking to *a*catch something out of his mouth, that they might accuse him.

CHAPTER 12

Jesus teaches, Beware of hypocrisy; lay up treasures in heaven rather than on earth; prepare for the coming of the Lord; where much is given, much is required; preaching the gospel causes division.

In the mean time, when there were gathered together an innumerable multitude of people, insomuch that they trode one upon another, he began to say unto his disciples first of all, Beware ye of the *a*leaven of the Pharisees, which is *b*hypocrisy.

2 For there is nothing covered, that shall not be revealed; neither *a*hid, that shall not be known.

3 Therefore whatsoever ye have spoken in *a*darkness shall be heard in the light; and that which ye have *b*spoken in the ear in *c*closets shall be proclaimed upon the housetops.

4 And I say unto you my *a*friends, Be not *b*afraid of them that kill the body, and after that have no more that they can do.

5 But I will forewarn you whom ye shall *a*fear: Fear him, which after he hath killed hath power to cast into *b*hell; yea, I say unto you, Fear him.

6 Are not five sparrows sold for two farthings, and not one of them is *a*forgotten before God?

44a TG Scribe.
  b Ps. 5:9 (9–10);
    Matt. 23:27; Acts 23:3.
45a TG Reproach.
46a Alma 10:27 (12–32).
48a GR agree, accord with.
    Acts 22:20.
50a TG Martyrdom.
  b TG Prophets,
    Rejection of.
51a Matt. 23:35.
52a Alma 10:27 (13–27);
    11:20 (20–22).
  b Moses 1:23 (23, 41).
  c JST Luke 11:53 . . .

knowledge, *the fullness of the scriptures; ye enter not in yourselves into the kingdom; and those who* were entering in, ye hindered.
    Luke 1:77.
  d Acts 13:45 (45, 50);
    1 Thes. 2:16.
53a GR be angry with, be exasperated against.
  b TG Provoking.
54a Matt. 22:15;
    Mark 12:13 (13–17);
    2 Ne. 27:32 (31–32).

12 1a TG Leaven.
  b TG Hypocrisy.
2a Prov. 28:13.
3a D&C 1:3.
  b TG Gossip.
  c GR places of privacy.
4a John 15:15 (13–15).
  b Matt. 10:28.
    TG Peer Influence.
5a D&C 122:9 (4–9).
  b TG Death, Spiritual,
    Second;
    Devil.
6a TG God, Omniscience of.

7 But even the very hairs of your head are all numbered. Fear not therefore: ye are of more value than many sparrows.

8 Also I say unto you, Whosoever shall ªconfess me before men, him shall the Son of man also confess before the ᵇangels of God:

9 ªBut he that denieth me before men shall be denied before the angels of God.

10 And whosoever shall speak a word against the Son of man, it shall be forgiven him: but unto him that ªblasphemeth against the Holy Ghost it shall not be forgiven.

11 And when they bring you unto the synagogues, and unto magistrates, and ªpowers, ᵇtake ye no thought how or what thing ye shall answer, or what ye shall ᶜsay:

12 For the ªHoly Ghost shall ᵇteach you in the same hour what ye ought to say.

13 ¶ And one of the company said unto him, Master, speak to my brother, that he divide the inheritance with me.

14 And he said unto him, Man, who made me a judge or a divider over you?

15 And he said unto them, Take heed, and beware of ªcovetousness: for a man's life consisteth not in the abundance of the things which he possesseth.

16 And he spake a parable unto them, saying, The ground of a certain rich man brought forth plentifully:

17 And he thought within himself, saying, What shall I do, because I have no room where to ªbestow my fruits?

18 And he said, This will I do: I will pull down my barns, and build greater; and there will I bestow all my fruits and my goods.

19 And I will say to my soul, ªSoul, thou hast much goods laid up for many years; take thine ease, ᵇeat, drink, and be merry.

20 But God said unto him, Thou fool, this night thy ªsoul shall be required of thee: then whose shall those things be, which thou hast provided?

21 So is he that layeth up ªtreasure for ᵇhimself, and is not rich toward God.

22 ¶ And he said unto his disciples, Therefore I say unto you, ªTake no ᵇthought for your life, what ye shall eat; neither for the body, what ye shall put on.

23 The life is more than meat, and the body is more than raiment.

24 Consider the ªravens: for they neither sow nor reap; which neither have storehouse nor barn; and God feedeth them: how much more are ye better than the fowls?

25 And which of you with taking thought can add to his stature one cubit?

26 If ye then be not able to do that thing which is least, why take ye thought for the rest?

27 Consider the ªlilies how they grow: they toil not, they spin not; and yet I say unto you, that Solomon in all his glory was not arrayed like one of these.

28 If then God so clothe the grass, which is to day in the field, and to morrow is cast into the oven; ªhow much more will he clothe you, O ye of little faith?

8a Moro. 7:44 (44–48);
  D&C 62:3.
 b TG Angels.
9a JST Luke 12:9–12
  (Appendix).
10a TG Apostasy of
  Individuals;
  Holy Ghost,
  Unpardonable Sin
  against.
11a GR authorities.
 b GR don't worry; don't

be anxious about.
 c D&C 84:85.
12a Ex. 4:12;
  D&C 24:6.
 b TG Holy Ghost,
  Mission of.
15a Ps. 62:10; 119:36.
  TG Covet.
17a GR gather.
19a Eccl. 2:24.
 b Isa. 22:13;
  1 Cor. 15:32.

20a TG Soul.
21a TG Treasure.
 b Hosea 10:1.
22a GR Don't worry.
 b Matt. 6:25;
  D&C 84:81.
24a Job 38:41.
27a TG Nature, Earth.
28a JST Luke 12:30 . . . how
  much more will he
  provide for you, if ye are
  not of little faith?

29 And seek not ye what ye shall eat, or what ye shall drink, neither be ye of ᵃdoubtful mind.

30 For all these things do the nations of the world seek after: and your Father knoweth that ye have need of these things.

31 ¶ ᵃBut rather seek ye the ᵇkingdom of God; and ᶜall these things shall be added unto you.

32 Fear not, little ᵃflock; for it is your Father's good pleasure to give you the ᵇkingdom.

33 Sell that ye have, and give ᵃalms; provide yourselves bags which wax not old, a ᵇtreasure in the heavens that ᶜfaileth not, where no thief approacheth, neither moth corrupteth.

34 For where your ᵃtreasure is, there will your heart be also.

35 Let your loins be girded about, and *your* ᵃlights burning;

36 And ye yourselves like unto men that wait for their lord, when he will return from the wedding; that when he cometh and knocketh, they may open unto him immediately.

37 ᵃBlessed *are* those servants, whom the lord when he cometh shall find ᵇwatching: verily I say unto you, that he shall gird himself, and make them to sit down to meat, and will come forth and serve them.

38 And if he shall come in the second watch, or come in the third watch, and find *them* so, blessed are those servants.

39 And this know, that if the ᵃgoodman of the house had known what hour the thief would come, he would have watched, and not have ᵇsuffered his house to be broken through.

40 Be ye therefore ready also: for the Son of man ᵃcometh at an ᵇhour when ye think not.

41 ¶ Then Peter said unto him, Lord, speakest thou this parable unto us, or even to all?

42 And the Lord said, Who then is that ᵃfaithful and wise ᵇsteward, whom *his* lord shall make ruler over his household, to give *them their* portion of meat in due season?

43 Blessed *is* that servant, whom his lord when he cometh shall find so ᵃdoing.

44 Of a truth I say unto you, that he will make him ᵃruler over ᵇall that he hath.

45 But and if that servant say in his heart, My lord delayeth his coming; and shall begin to beat the menservants and ᵃmaidens, and to eat and drink, and to be drunken;

46 The lord of that servant will come in a day when he looketh not for *him*, and at an hour when he is not aware, and will cut him in sunder, and will appoint him his ᵃportion with the unbelievers.

47 And that ᵃservant, which knew his lord's ᵇwill, and ᶜprepared not *himself*, neither did according to his will, shall be beaten with many *stripes*.

48 But he that ᵃknew not, and did commit things worthy of stripes, shall be ᵇbeaten with few *stripes*. For unto whomsoever ᶜmuch is ᵈgiven, of him shall be much ᵉrequired: and to

29a Luke 1:20 (19–20); 24:25.
     TG Doubt.
31a JST Luke 12:34 *Therefore
     seek ye to bring forth* the
     kingdom of God . . .
   b 1 Tim. 4:8;
     Jacob 2:18 (18–19);
     3 Ne. 13:33 (25–34);
     D&C 29:5.
   c Deut. 28:8;
     D&C 24:3 (3–4).
32a D&C 35:27.
   b Matt. 25:34.
     TG Kingdom of God,
     on Earth.
33a TG Almsgiving.
   b TG Treasure.

   c TG Dependability.
34a 2 Ne. 9:30;
     Hel. 13:22 (20–23).
35a Matt. 25:7 (7–8).
37a JST Luke 12:41–57
     (Appendix).
   b TG Watch.
39a GR master.
   b GR allowed, permitted.
40a D&C 133:11.
   b Matt. 24:44.
42a TG Trustworthiness.
   b TG Stewardship.
43a TG Commitment.
44a 1 Pet. 5:4.
   b Rom. 8:17 (14–18);
     1 Cor. 3:22 (21–23);

     D&C 76:59 (58–59);
     84:38 (35–38).
45a GR maidservants.
46a TG Punish.
47a James 4:17.
     TG Apostasy of
     Individuals.
   b 2 Ne. 9:27 (25–27).
   c TG Accountability;
     Procrastination.
48a Rom. 2:12.
   b Deut. 25:2.
   c TG Talents.
   d TG Stewardship.
   e TG Accountability;
     Duty;
     Judgment.

whom men have committed much, of him they will ask the more.

49 ¶ I am come to send fire on the earth; and what will I, if it be already kindled?

50 But I have a *a*baptism to be baptized with; and how am I *b*straitened till it be accomplished!

51 Suppose ye that I am come to give peace on earth? I tell you, Nay; but rather division:

52 For from henceforth there shall be five in one house divided, three against two, and two against three.

53 The father shall be divided against the son, and the son *a*against the father; the mother against the daughter, and the daughter against the mother; the mother in law against her daughter in law, and the daughter in law against her mother in law.

54 ¶ And he said also to the people, When ye see a cloud rise out of the west, straightway ye say, There cometh a shower; and so it is.

55 And when *ye see* the south wind blow, ye say, There will be heat; and it cometh to pass.

56 *Ye* hypocrites, ye can discern the face of the sky and of the earth; but how is it that ye do not discern this time?

57 Yea, and why even of yourselves judge ye not what is right?

58 ¶ When thou goest with thine adversary to the magistrate, *as thou art* in the way, give diligence that thou mayest be delivered from him; lest he hale thee to the judge, and the judge deliver thee to the officer, and the officer cast thee into prison.

59 I tell thee, thou shalt not depart thence, till thou hast paid the very last *a*mite.

CHAPTER 13

Jesus teaches, Repent or perish—He gives the parable of the barren fig tree, *heals a woman on the Sabbath, and likens the kingdom of God to a mustard seed—He discusses whether few or many are saved and laments over Jerusalem.*

THERE were present at that season some that told him of the Galilæans, whose blood Pilate had mingled with their sacrifices.

2 And Jesus answering said unto them, Suppose ye that these Galilæans were *a*sinners above all the Galilæans, because they suffered such things?

3 I tell you, Nay; but, except ye *a*repent, ye shall all likewise *b*perish.

4 Or those eighteen, upon whom the tower in Siloam fell, and slew them, think ye that they were sinners above all men that dwelt in Jerusalem?

5 I tell you, Nay: but, except ye repent, ye shall all likewise perish.

6 ¶ He spake also this parable; A certain *man* had a fig tree planted in his *a*vineyard; and he came and sought fruit thereon, and found none.

7 Then said he unto the dresser of his vineyard, Behold, these three years I come seeking fruit on this fig tree, and find none: *a*cut it down; why cumbereth it the ground?

8 And he answering said unto him, Lord, let it alone this year also, till I shall dig about it, and dung *it:*

9 And if it bear fruit, *well:* and if not, *then* after that thou shalt cut it down.

10 And he was teaching in one of the synagogues on the sabbath.

11 ¶ And, behold, there was a woman which had a spirit of infirmity eighteen years, and was bowed together, and could in no wise lift up *herself.*

12 And when Jesus saw her, he called *her to him,* and said unto her,

50*a* Mosiah 3:7.
  b GR distressed, hardpressed.
53*a* Micah 7:6.
59*a* IE the smallest Jewish coin, worth less than half a penny.
13 2*a* TG Suffering.
  3*a* D&C 3:11.
     TG Repent.
   b Ether 8:23 (21–24); D&C 19:4.
6*a* TG Vineyard of the Lord.
7*a* Matt. 3:10; 7:19 (19–20); Hel. 14:18 (17–19).

Woman, thou art loosed from thine infirmity.

13 And he ᵃlaid *his* ᵇhands on her: and immediately she was made straight, and glorified God.

14 And the ruler of the synagogue answered with indignation, because that Jesus had healed on the sabbath day, and said unto the people, There are six days in which men ought to ᵃwork: in them therefore come and be healed, and not on the sabbath day.

15 The Lord then answered him, and said, *Thou* hypocrite, doth not each one of you on the sabbath loose his ox or *his* ass from the stall, and lead *him* away to watering?

16 And ought not this woman, being a daughter of Abraham, whom Satan hath bound, lo, these eighteen years, be loosed from this bond on the ᵃsabbath day?

17 And when he had said these things, all his adversaries were ashamed: and all the people rejoiced for all the glorious things that were done by him.

18 ¶ Then said he, Unto what is the kingdom of God like? and whereunto shall I ᵃresemble it?

19 It is like a grain of mustard seed, which a man took, and cast into his garden; and it grew, and ᵃwaxed a great tree; and the fowls of the air lodged in the branches of it.

20 And again he said, Whereunto shall I liken the kingdom of God?

21 It is like leaven, which a woman took and hid in three measures of meal, till the whole was leavened.

22 And he went through the cities and villages, teaching, and journeying toward Jerusalem.

23 Then said one unto him, Lord, are there ᵃfew that be saved? And he said unto them,

24 ¶ Strive to enter in at the ᵃstrait ᵇgate: for many, I say unto you, will ᶜseek to enter in, and shall not be able.

25 When once the master of the house is risen up, and hath shut to the door, and ye begin to stand without, and to knock at the door, saying, Lord, ᵃLord, open unto us; and he shall answer and say unto you, I know you not whence ye are:

26 Then shall ye begin to say, We have eaten and drunk in thy presence, and thou hast taught in our streets.

27 But he shall say, I tell you, I know you not whence ye are; ᵃdepart from me, all *ye* workers of iniquity.

28 There shall be ᵃweeping and gnashing of teeth, when ye shall see Abraham, and Isaac, and Jacob, and all the prophets, in the ᵇkingdom of God, and you *yourselves* thrust out.

29 And ᵃthey shall come from the east, and *from* the west, and from the north, and *from* the south, and shall sit down in the kingdom of God.

30 And, behold, there are last which shall be first, and there are ᵃfirst which shall be last.

31 ¶ The same day there came certain of the Pharisees, saying unto him, Get thee out, and depart hence: for ᵃHerod will kill thee.

32 And he said unto them, Go ye, and tell that fox, Behold, I cast out devils, and I do cures to day and to

13a TG Hands, Laying on of.
  b TG Administrations to the Sick.
14a TG Industry.
16a TG Sabbath.
18a GR compare.
19a GR became.
23a 3 Ne. 27:33;
    D&C 121:34.
24a GR narrow.
    2 Ne. 9:41;
    Alma 37:13 (13, 44–46);

  3 Ne. 14:13 (13–14);
    D&C 132:22 (22–25).
  b Matt. 7:13 (13–14);
    3 Ne. 27:33;
    D&C 22:4 (1–4).
  c 1 Ne. 12:17.
25a Isa. 55:6.
27a Mosiah 26:27 (24–27);
    3 Ne. 14:23 (21–23);
    D&C 29:28 (27–28).
28a Mosiah 16:2 (1–2);
    D&C 133:73 (72–73).

  b Alma 5:24 (14–24).
    TG Exaltation; Kingdom of God, in Heaven.
29a Matt. 8:11 (11–12);
    Acts 10:45;
    2 Ne. 10:18 (9–18);
    D&C 45:9 (7–30).
30a 1 Ne. 13:42;
    Jacob 5:63 (1–77);
    Ether 13:12 (10–12);
    D&C 29:30 (30–32).
31a Luke 3:19.

morrow, and the third *day* I shall be ᵃperfected.

33 Nevertheless I must walk to day, and to morrow, and the *day* following: for it cannot be that a ᵃprophet perish out of ᵇJerusalem.

34 O Jerusalem, Jerusalem, which ᵃkillest the prophets, and stonest them that are sent unto thee; how often would I have gathered thy children together, as a ᵇhen *doth gather* her brood under *her* wings, and ye would not!

35 Behold, your house is left unto you ᵃdesolate: and verily I say unto you, ᵇYe shall not see me, until *the time* come when ye shall say, ᶜBlessed *is* he that cometh in the name of the Lord.

CHAPTER 14

Jesus again heals on the Sabbath—He teaches humility and gives the parable of the great supper—Those who follow Him must forsake all else.

AND it came to pass, as he went into the house of one of the chief Pharisees to eat bread on the sabbath day, that they watched him.

2 And, behold, there was a certain man before him which had the dropsy.

3 And Jesus answering spake unto the lawyers and Pharisees, saying, Is it lawful to heal on the sabbath day?

4 And they held their peace. And he took *him*, and healed him, and let him go;

5 And answered them, saying, Which of you shall have an ass or an ox fallen into a pit, and will not straightway pull him out on the ᵃsabbath day?

6 And they could not answer him again to these things.

7 ¶ And he put forth a parable to those which were bidden, when he marked how they chose out the ᵃchief rooms; saying unto them,

8 When thou art ᵃbidden of any *man* to a wedding, sit not down in the highest room; lest a more honourable man than thou be bidden of him;

9 And he that bade thee and him come and say to thee, Give this man place; and thou begin with shame to take the lowest room.

10 But when thou art bidden, go and sit down in the ᵃlowest room; that when he that bade thee cometh, he may say unto thee, Friend, go up ᵇhigher: then shalt thou have ᶜworship in the presence of them that sit at meat with thee.

11 For whosoever ᵃexalteth himself shall be ᵇabased; and he that ᶜhumbleth himself shall be exalted.

12 ¶ Then said he also to him that bade him, When thou makest a dinner or a supper, call not thy friends, nor thy brethren, neither thy kinsmen, nor *thy* rich neighbours; lest they also bid thee again, and a recompence be made thee.

13 But when thou makest a feast, call the ᵃpoor, the maimed, the lame, the blind:

14 And thou shalt be ᵃblessed; for they cannot recompense thee: for thou shalt be ᵇrecompensed at the ᶜresurrection of the just.

15 ¶ And when one of them that sat at meat with him heard these

---

32*a* TG Perfection.
33*a* TG Prophets,
    Rejection of.
  b JST Luke 13:33–34 . . .
    Jerusalem. *This he spake,*
    signifying of his death.
    And in this very hour
    he began to weep over
    Jerusalem,
34*a* TG Persecution.
  b D&C 10:65 (63–65);
    43:24 (24–25).
35*a* Jer. 12:7; 22:5;

D&C 84:115 (114–15).
  b JST Luke 13:36 . . . Ye
    shall not *know me, until*
    ye have received from the
    hand of the Lord a just
    recompense for all your
    sins; until the time . . .
  c Ps. 118:26.
14 5*a* TG Sabbath.
  7*a* GR first places.
    Matt. 23:6.
  8*a* GR invited.
  10*a* TG Humility.

  b Prov. 25:7 (6–8).
  c GR honor, glory, respect.
11*a* TG Haughtiness.
  b D&C 101:42.
    TG Shame.
  c D&C 104:82.
    TG Contrite Heart.
13*a* TG Generosity;
    Poor.
14*a* TG Blessing.
  b Matt. 6:4.
  c TG Resurrection.

things, he said unto him, Blessed *is* he that shall ᵃeat ᵇbread in the kingdom of God.

16 Then said he unto him, A certain man made a great supper, and bade many:

17 And sent his servant at supper time to say to them that were bidden, Come; for all things are now ready.

18 And they all with one *consent* began to make ᵃexcuse. The first said unto him, I have bought a piece of ground, and I must needs go and see it: I pray thee have me excused.

19 And another said, I have bought five yoke of oxen, and I go to prove them: I pray thee have me excused.

20 And another said, I have married a wife, and therefore I cannot come.

21 So that servant came, and shewed his lord these things. Then the master of the house being angry said to his servant, Go out quickly into the streets and lanes of the city, and bring in hither the poor, and the maimed, and the ᵃhalt, and the blind.

22 And the servant said, Lord, it is done as thou hast commanded, and yet there is room.

23 And the ᵃlord said unto the servant, Go out into the highways and ᵇhedges, and ᶜcompel *them* to come in, that my house may be filled.

24 For I say unto you, That ᵃnone of those men which were bidden shall taste of my supper.

25 ¶ And there went great multi-tudes with him: and he turned, and said unto them,

26 If any *man* come to me, and ᵃhate not his father, and mother, and wife, and children, and brethren, and sisters, ᵇyea, and his own ᶜlife also, he cannot be my ᵈdisciple.

27 And whosoever doth not bear his ᵃcross, and come after me, cannot be my ᵇdisciple.

28 For which of you, intending to build a tower, sitteth not down first, and ᵃcounteth the ᵇcost, whether he have *sufficient* to ᶜfinish *it*?

29 Lest ᵃhaply, after he hath laid the foundation, and is not able to finish *it*, all that behold *it* begin to mock him,

30 Saying, This man began to build, and was not able to ᵃfinish.

31 Or what king, going to make war against another king, sitteth not down first, and ᵃconsulteth whether he be able with ten thousand to meet him that cometh against him with twenty thousand?

32 Or else, while the other is yet a great way off, he sendeth an ᵃambassage, and desireth conditions of peace.

33 So likewise, whosoever he be of you that ᵃforsaketh not all that he hath, he cannot be my ᵇdisciple.

34 ¶ ᵃSalt *is* good: but if the ᵇsalt have lost his savour, wherewith shall it be seasoned?

35 It is neither fit for the land, nor yet for the dunghill; *but* men cast it out. He that hath ears to hear, let him hear.

15a Luke 22:30; Rev. 19:9.
  b TG Bread.
18a Luke 9:62 (57–62);
    D&C 121:35 (34–35).
21a GR lame.
23a 2 Cor. 5:20.
  b GR hedged pathways.
  c GR urge.
24a Matt. 21:43;
    Acts 13:46.
26a Matt. 10:37.
  b JST Luke 14:26 . . . *or
    husband,* yea and his
    own life also; *or in other
    words, is afraid to lay
    down his life for my sake,
    he cannot be* . . .

  c TG Martyrdom.
  d TG Self-Mastery.
27a See JST Matt. 16:25–26
    (Appendix).
    Matt. 10:38;
    John 19:17;
    2 Ne. 9:18; Jacob 1:8;
    3 Ne. 12:30;
    D&C 56:2.
  b JST Luke 14:27–28 . . .
    disciple. *Wherefore, settle
    this in your hearts, that ye
    will do the things which I
    shall teach, and command
    you.*
28a Prov. 24:27.
    TG Self-Mastery.

  b TG Problem-Solving.
  c TG Commitment.
29a GR perhaps.
30a JST Luke 14:31 . . .
    finish. *And this he said,
    signifying there should
    not any man follow him,
    unless he was able to
    continue; saying,*
31a Prov. 20:18.
32a OR embassy.
33a Luke 5:11;
    D&C 103:27 (27–28).
  b D&C 132:50 (49–51).
34a JST Luke 14:35–37
    (Appendix).
  b TG Salt.

CHAPTER 15

Jesus gives the parables of the lost sheep, the piece of silver, and the prodigal son.

THEN drew near unto him all the ªpublicans and sinners for to hear him.

2 And the Pharisees and scribes murmured, saying, This man receiveth sinners, and eateth with them.

3 ¶ And he spake this parable unto them, saying,

4 What man of you, having an hundred sheep, if he lose one of them, doth not leave the ninety and nine ªin the wilderness, and go after that which is ᵇlost, until he find it?

5 And when he hath found *it,* he layeth *it* on his shoulders, rejoicing.

6 And when he cometh home, he calleth together *his* friends and neighbours, saying unto them, Rejoice with me; for I have found my sheep which was lost.

7 I say unto you, that likewise ªjoy shall be in heaven over one ᵇsinner that ᶜrepenteth, more than over ninety and nine just persons, which need no repentance.

8 ¶ Either what woman having ten pieces of silver, if she lose one ªpiece, doth not light a candle, and sweep the house, and seek diligently till she find *it?*

9 And when she hath found *it,* she calleth *her* friends and *her* neighbours together, saying, Rejoice with me; for I have found the piece which I had lost.

10 Likewise, I say unto you, there is joy in the presence of the ªangels of God over one ᵇsinner that repenteth.

11 ¶ And he said, A certain man had two sons:

12 And the younger of them said to *his* father, Father, give me the portion of ªgoods that falleth *to me.* And he divided unto them *his* living.

13 And not many days after the younger son gathered all together, and took his journey into a far country, and there ªwasted his ᵇsubstance with ᶜriotous living.

14 And when he had spent all, there arose a mighty famine in that land; and he began to be in want.

15 And he went and joined himself to a citizen of that country; and he sent him into his fields to feed swine.

16 And he ªwould fain have filled his belly with the ᵇhusks that the swine did eat: and no man gave unto him.

17 And when he ªcame to himself, he said, How many hired servants of my father's have bread enough and to spare, and I perish with hunger!

18 I will ªarise and go to my father, and will say unto him, Father, I have ᵇsinned against heaven, and before thee,

19 And am no more worthy to be called thy son: make me as one of thy hired servants.

20 And he arose, and came to his father. But when he was yet a great way off, his father saw him, and had ªcompassion, and ran, and fell on his neck, and kissed him.

21 And the son said unto him, Father, I have sinned against heaven, and in thy sight, and am no more ªworthy to be called thy ᵇson.

22 But the father said to his servants, Bring forth the best robe, and

---

15 1ª Mark 2:16 (15–16).
4ª JST Luke 15:4 . . . *and go into* the wilderness after that which is lost . . .
 ᵇ Ezek. 34:16 (11–12, 16).
7ª TG Joy.
 ᵇ TG Missionary Work.
 ᶜ TG Repent.
8ª GR *drachma* (a silver coin equal to the Roman *denarius*— a workman's daily

wage).
10ª TG Angels.
 ᵇ TG Worth of Souls.
12ª GR property.
13ª TG Waste.
 ᵇ GR property.
 ᶜ Prov. 28:7.
  TG Rioting and Reveling.
16ª GR desired, set the heart upon.
 ᵇ GR pods (of the carob tree).

17ª Ps. 119:59.
  TG Repent.
18ª Lam. 3:40.
 ᵇ TG Confession.
20ª TG Benevolence; Compassion; Family, Love within; Mercy.
21ª TG Contrite Heart; Worthiness.
 ᵇ TG Family, Patriarchal.

put *it* on him; and put a ring on his hand, and shoes on *his* feet:

23 And bring hither the fatted calf, and kill *it*; and let us eat, and be merry:

24 For this my son was dead, and is alive again; he was lost, and is found. And they began to be merry.

25 Now his elder son was in the field: and as he came and drew nigh to the house, he heard musick and dancing.

26 And he called one of the servants, and asked what these things meant.

27 And he said unto him, Thy brother is come; and thy father hath killed the fatted calf, because he hath received him safe and sound.

28 And he was angry, and would not go in: therefore came his father out, and entreated him.

29 And he answering said to *his* father, Lo, these many years do I serve thee, neither transgressed I at any time thy commandment: and yet thou never gavest me a kid, that I might make merry with my friends:

30 But as soon as this thy son was come, which hath devoured thy living with harlots, thou hast killed for him the fatted calf.

31 And he said unto him, [a]Son, thou art ever with me, and [b]all that I have is thine.

32 It was [a]meet that we should make merry, and be glad: for this thy brother was dead, and is alive again; and was lost, and is found.

CHAPTER 16

Jesus gives the parable of the unjust steward—He teaches of service and condemns divorce—He gives the parable of the rich man and Lazarus.

AND he said also unto his disciples, There was a certain rich man, which had a steward; and the same was accused unto him that he had [a]wasted his goods.

2 And he called him, and said unto him, How is it that I hear this of thee? give an [a]account of thy [b]stewardship; for thou mayest be no longer steward.

3 Then the steward said within himself, What shall I do? for my lord taketh away from me the stewardship: I cannot dig; to beg I am ashamed.

4 I am resolved what to do, that, when I am put out of the stewardship, they may receive me into their houses.

5 So he called every one of his lord's debtors *unto him,* and said unto the first, How much owest thou unto my lord?

6 And he said, An hundred measures of oil. And he said unto him, Take thy bill, and sit down quickly, and write fifty.

7 Then said he to another, And how much owest thou? And he said, An hundred measures of wheat. And he said unto him, Take thy bill, and write fourscore.

8 And the lord commended the unjust steward, because he had done wisely: for the children of this world are in their generation wiser than the [a]children of [b]light.

9 And I say unto you, Make to yourselves friends of the [a]mammon of unrighteousness; that, when ye fail, they may receive you into everlasting habitations.

10 He that is [a]faithful in that which is least is faithful also in much: and he that is unjust in the least is unjust also in much.

11 If therefore ye have not been faithful in the unrighteous mammon, who will commit to your [a]trust the true [b]riches?

12 And if ye have not been faithful in that which is another man's, who shall give you that which is your own?

31*a* TG Family, Love within.
  b D&C 84:38.
32*a* GR necessary.
16 1*a* TG Waste.

2*a* TG Accountability.
  b TG Stewardship.
8*a* TG Children of Light.
  b TG Light [noun].
9*a* D&C 82:22.

10*a* Matt. 25:21;
    D&C 51:19;
    132:44, 53.
11*a* TG Trustworthiness.
  b TG Treasure.

13 ¶ No servant can serve two ^amasters: for either he will hate the one, and love the other; or else he will hold to the one, and despise the other. Ye cannot serve God and mammon.

14 And the Pharisees also, who were ^acovetous, heard all these things: and they derided him.

15 And he said unto them, Ye are they which ^ajustify yourselves before men; but God ^bknoweth your ^chearts: for that which is highly esteemed among ^dmen is ^eabomination in the sight of God.

16 ^aThe law and the prophets *were* until John: since that time the kingdom of God is preached, and every man presseth into it.

17 And it is easier for heaven and earth to pass, than one tittle of the ^alaw to fail.

18 Whosoever ^aputteth away his wife, and marrieth another, committeth adultery: and whosoever marrieth her that is put away from *her* husband committeth adultery.

19 ¶ There was a certain rich man, which was clothed in purple and fine linen, and fared sumptuously every day:

20 And there was a certain ^abeggar named Lazarus, which was laid at his gate, full of sores,

21 And desiring to be fed with the crumbs which fell from the rich man's table: moreover the dogs came and licked his sores.

22 And it came to pass, that the beggar died, and was carried by the ^aangels into ^bAbraham's bosom: the rich man also died, and was buried;

23 And in ^ahell he lift up his eyes, being in torments, and seeth Abraham afar off, and Lazarus in his bosom.

24 And he cried and said, Father Abraham, have mercy on me, and send Lazarus, that he may dip the tip of his finger in water, and cool my tongue; for I am tormented in this flame.

25 But Abraham said, Son, remember that thou in thy lifetime ^areceivedst thy good things, and likewise Lazarus evil things: but now he is comforted, and thou art tormented.

26 And beside all this, between us and you there is a great ^agulf fixed: so that they which would pass from hence to you cannot; neither can they pass to us, that *would come* from thence.

27 Then he said, I pray thee therefore, father, that thou wouldest send him to my father's house:

28 For I have five brethren; that he may testify unto them, lest they also come into this place of torment.

29 Abraham saith unto him, They have ^aMoses and the prophets; let them hear them.

30 And he said, Nay, father Abraham: but if one went unto them from the ^adead, they will repent.

31 And he said unto him, If they ^ahear not Moses and the ^bprophets, neither will they be ^cpersuaded, though one rose from the dead.

CHAPTER 17

Jesus speaks of offenses, forgiveness, and faith—Even the faithful are unprofitable servants—Ten lepers are healed—Jesus discourses on the Second Coming.

THEN said he unto the disciples, It is impossible but that ^aoffences will

---

13a Alma 5:39 (38–39).
14a Alma 11:24 (20, 24).
15a Luke 10:29.
  b TG God, Intelligence of; God, Omniscience of.
  c Prov. 21:2.
  d 2 Ne. 9:28 (28–30).
  e TG Man, Natural, Not Spiritually Reborn.
16a JST Luke 16:16–23 (Appendix).

17a TG Law of Moses.
18a TG Divorce.
20a TG Poor.
22a TG Angels.
  b Alma 40:11 (11–21).
23a TG Hell;
  Spirits in Prison.
25a Luke 6:24.
26a 1 Ne. 15:28 (28–30).
  TG Separation.
29a TG Scriptures, Value of.

30a Alma 32:18 (17–18);
  Ether 12:12 (12, 18);
  D&C 5:7 (5–10).
31a TG Scriptures,
  Study of;
  Unbelief.
  b 2 Ne. 33:11 (10–14);
  Hel. 13:26 (24–30).
  c D&C 5:8 (7–10); 133:71.
17 1a TG Offense.

come: but woe *unto him,* through whom they come!

2 It were better for him that a millstone were hanged about his neck, and he cast into the sea, than that he should ^aoffend one of these little ones.

3 ¶ Take heed to yourselves: If thy brother ^atrespass against thee, rebuke him; and if he repent, ^bforgive him.

4 And if he trespass against thee seven times in a day, and seven times in a day turn again to thee, saying, I ^arepent; thou shalt forgive him.

5 And the apostles said unto the Lord, Increase our faith.

6 And the Lord said, If ye had ^afaith as a grain of mustard seed, ye might say unto this sycamine tree, Be thou plucked up by the root, and be thou planted in the sea; and it should obey you.

7 But which of you, having a servant plowing or ^afeeding cattle, will say unto him ^bby and by, when he is come from the field, Go and sit down to meat?

8 And will not rather say unto him, Make ready wherewith I may sup, and gird thyself, and serve me, till I have eaten and drunken; and afterward thou shalt eat and drink?

9 Doth he thank that servant because he did the things that were commanded him? I ^atrow not.

10 So likewise ye, when ye shall have done all those things which are commanded you, say, We are ^aunprofitable servants: we have done that which was our ^bduty to do.

11 ¶ And it came to pass, as he went to Jerusalem, that he passed through the midst of Samaria and Galilee.

12 And as he entered into a certain village, there met him ten men that were ^alepers, which stood afar off:

13 And they lifted up *their* voices, and said, Jesus, Master, have mercy on us.

14 And when he saw *them,* he said unto them, Go shew yourselves unto the ^apriests. And it came to pass, that, as they went, they were cleansed.

15 And one of them, when he saw that he was healed, turned back, and with a loud voice glorified God,

16 And fell down on *his* face at his feet, giving him ^athanks: and he was a Samaritan.

17 And Jesus answering said, Were there not ten ^acleansed? but where *are* the ^bnine?

18 There are not found that returned to give glory to God, save this stranger.

19 And he said unto him, Arise, go thy way: thy faith hath made thee whole.

20 ¶ And when he was demanded of the Pharisees, when the ^akingdom of God should come, he answered them and said, The kingdom of God cometh not with observation:

21 Neither shall they say, Lo here! or, lo there! for, behold, the ^akingdom of God ^bis ^cwithin you.

22 And he said unto the disciples, The days will come, when ye shall desire to see one of the days of the Son of man, and ye shall not see *it.*

23 And they shall say to you, See here; or, ^asee there: go not after *them,* nor follow *them.*

24 For as the lightning, that lighteneth out of the one *part* under heaven, shineth unto the other *part* under heaven; so shall also the Son of man be in his ^aday.

2a TG Sin.
3a Matt. 18:15 (15–17).
  b TG Forgive.
4a TG Repent.
6a Moses 7:13.
7a GR tending a flock.
  b GR immediately.
9a GR think.
10a Rom. 3:12;
    Mosiah 2:21 (20–26).

  TG Humility;
    Ingratitude.
  b TG Duty.
12a TG Leprosy.
14a Lev. 13:49.
16a TG Thanksgiving.
17a TG Purification.
  b TG Ingratitude.
20a TG Kingdom of God,
    on Earth.

21a D&C 65:2.
  b JST Luke 17:21 . . . *has
    already come unto* you.
  c Many translations read
    "among" because the
    pronoun "you" is plural
    here in Greek.
23a TG False Christs.
24a Luke 21:34;
    1 Thes. 5:4.

25 But first must he suffer many things, and be rejected of this generation.

26 And as it was in the days of ^aNoe, so shall it be also in the days of the Son of man.

27 They did eat, they drank, they married wives, they were given in marriage, until the day that Noe entered into the ark, and the ^aflood came, and destroyed them all.

28 Likewise also as it was in the days of Lot; they did eat, they drank, they bought, they sold, they planted, they builded;

29 But the same day that Lot went out of ^aSodom it rained fire and brimstone from heaven, and destroyed *them* all.

30 Even thus shall it be in the day when the Son of man is revealed.

31 In that day, he which shall be upon the housetop, and his stuff in the house, let him not come down to take it away: and he that is in the field, let him likewise not return back.

32 Remember ^aLot's wife.

33 Whosoever shall seek to save his life shall lose it; and whosoever shall ^alose his life shall preserve it.

34 I tell you, in that night there shall be two *men* in one bed; the one shall be taken, and the other shall be left.

35 Two *women* shall be grinding together; the one shall be taken, and the other left.

36 Two *men* shall be in the field; the one shall be taken, and the other left.

37 ^aAnd they answered and said unto him, Where, Lord? And he said unto them, Wheresoever the body *is*, thither will the eagles be gathered together.

CHAPTER 18

Jesus gives the parables of the unjust judge and the Pharisee and publican—He invites little children to come unto Him and teaches how to gain eternal life—He tells of His coming death and resurrection and gives sight to a blind man.

AND he spake a parable unto them *to this end*, that men ought ^aalways to ^bpray, and not to ^cfaint;

2 Saying, There was in a city a judge, which feared not God, neither regarded man:

3 And there was a widow in that city; and she came unto him, saying, Avenge me of mine adversary.

4 And he would not for a while: but afterward he said within himself, Though I fear not God, nor regard man;

5 Yet because this widow troubleth me, I will avenge her, lest by her continual coming she weary me.

6 And the Lord said, Hear what the ^aunjust judge saith.

7 And shall not God ^aavenge his own elect, which cry day and night unto him, though he bear long with ^bthem?

8 ^aI tell you that he will ^bavenge them speedily. Nevertheless when the Son of man cometh, shall he find faith on the earth?

9 And he spake this parable unto certain which ^atrusted in themselves that they were righteous, and ^bdespised others:

10 Two men went up into the temple to ^apray; the one a Pharisee, and the other a publican.

11 The Pharisee stood and prayed thus with himself, God, I thank thee, that I am ^anot as other men *are,* extortioners, unjust, adulterers, or even as this publican.

26a TG Earth, Cleansing of; Flood.
27a Matt. 24:37 (36–38).
29a Gen. 19:24.
32a Gen. 19:26.
33a TG Sacrifice.
37a JST Luke 17:36–40 (Appendix).
18 1a TG Perseverance.

b TG Prayer.
c D&C 75:11.
6a TG Injustice.
7a Num. 31:2; Alma 1:13; D&C 121:5.
b JST Luke 18:7 . . . *men?*
8a JST Luke 18:8 I tell you that *he will come, and when he does*

come, he will avenge *his saints* speedily. Nevertheless . . .
b TG Justice.
9a John 5:44.
b Alma 32:3 (3–5).
10a TG Prayer.
11a Isa. 65:5; Alma 31:16 (14–18).

12 I ^afast twice in the week, I give ^btithes of all that I ^cpossess.

13 And the publican, standing afar off, would not lift up so much as *his* eyes unto heaven, but smote upon his breast, saying, God be merciful to me a ^asinner.

14 I tell you, this man went down to his house justified *rather* than the other: for every one that ^aexalteth himself shall be abased; and he that ^bhumbleth himself shall be exalted.

15 And they brought unto him also infants, that he would touch them: but when *his* disciples saw *it*, they rebuked them.

16 But Jesus called them *unto him*, and said, Suffer little ^achildren to come unto me, and forbid them not: for of such is the kingdom of God.

17 Verily I say unto you, Whosoever shall not receive the kingdom of God as a little child shall in no wise enter therein.

18 And a certain ruler asked him, saying, Good Master, what shall I do to inherit ^aeternal life?

19 And Jesus said unto him, Why callest thou me good? none *is* ^agood, save one, *that is,* God.

20 Thou knowest the commandments, Do not commit ^aadultery, Do not ^bkill, Do not steal, Do not bear ^cfalse witness, ^dHonour thy father and thy mother.

21 And he said, All these have I kept from my youth up.

22 Now when Jesus heard these things, he said unto him, Yet lackest thou one thing: sell all that thou hast, and distribute unto the ^apoor, and

thou shalt have treasure in heaven: and come, follow me.

23 And when he heard this, he was very sorrowful: for he was very rich.

24 And when Jesus saw that he was very sorrowful, he said, How hardly shall they that have riches enter into the kingdom of God!

25 For it is easier for a camel to go through a needle's eye, than for a rich man to enter into the kingdom of God.

26 And they that heard *it* said, Who then can be saved?

27 ^aAnd he said, The things which are impossible with men are ^bpossible with God.

28 Then Peter said, Lo, we have left all, and followed thee.

29 And he said unto them, Verily I say unto you, There is no man that hath left house, or parents, or brethren, or wife, or children, for the kingdom of God's sake,

30 Who shall not ^areceive ^bmanifold more in this present time, and in the world to come life everlasting.

31 ¶ Then he took *unto him* the twelve, and said unto them, Behold, we go up to Jerusalem, and all things that are ^awritten by the prophets concerning the Son of man shall be accomplished.

32 For he shall be delivered unto the Gentiles, and shall be ^amocked, and spitefully entreated, and spitted on:

33 And they shall scourge *him*, and put him to death: and the third day he shall ^arise again.

34 And they ^aunderstood none of these things: and this saying was hid

12a Ex. 34:28.
  b TG Tithing.
  c GR acquire, gain, or
    possess.
13a Alma 38:14 (13–14).
    TG Contrite Heart.
14a 2 Cor. 10:18.
    TG Haughtiness.
  b Ether 12:27;
    D&C 101:42; 124:114.
16a Moro. 8:19 (10–26).
18a Luke 10:25.
19a TG God, Perfection of.
20a D&C 42:24 (23–25).

  b D&C 42:79.
  c D&C 42:21.
  d TG Honoring Father
    and Mother.
22a Mosiah 4:26;
    Alma 1:27;
    D&C 42:30 (29–31).
27a JST Luke 18:27 And
    he said *unto them,* It is
    impossible for them who
    trust in riches, to enter
    into the kingdom of God;
    but he who forsaketh the
    things which are of this

    world, it is possible
    with God, that he
    should enter in.
  b TG God, Power of.
30a D&C 132:55.
  b D&C 104:2.
31a 1 Ne. 11:33;
    2 Ne. 10:3;
    Mosiah 3:9 (9–10).
32a TG Jesus Christ, Trials
    of; Mocking.
33a TG Jesus Christ,
    Resurrection.
34a John 12:16.

from them, neither knew they the things which were spoken.

35 ¶ And it came to pass, that as he was come nigh unto Jericho, a certain blind man sat by the way side begging:

36 And hearing the multitude pass by, he asked what it meant.

37 And they told him, that Jesus of Nazareth passeth by.

38 And he cried, saying, Jesus, *thou* Son of David, have mercy on me.

39 And they which went before rebuked him, that he should hold his peace: but he cried so much the more, *Thou* Son of David, have mercy on me.

40 And Jesus stood, and commanded him to be brought unto him: and when he was come near, he asked him,

41 Saying, What wilt thou that I shall do unto thee? And he said, Lord, that I may receive my sight.

42 And Jesus said unto him, Receive thy *a*sight: thy *b*faith hath saved thee.

43 And immediately he received his sight, and followed him, *a*glorifying God: and all the people, when they saw *it*, gave praise unto God.

CHAPTER 19

Jesus came to save souls—He gives the parable of the pounds—He rides in triumph into Jerusalem, weeps over the city, and cleanses the temple again.

AND *Jesus* entered and passed through Jericho.

2 And, behold, *there was* a man named Zacchæus, which was the chief among the publicans, and he was rich.

3 And he sought to see Jesus who he was; and could not for the *a*press, because he was little of stature.

4 And he ran before, and climbed up into a sycomore tree to see him: for he was to pass that *way*.

5 And when Jesus came to the place, he looked up, and saw him, and said unto him, Zacchæus, make haste, and come down; for to day I must abide at thy house.

6 And he made haste, and came down, and *a*received him joyfully.

7 And when they saw *it*, they all murmured, saying, That he was gone to be guest with a man that is a sinner.

8 And Zacchæus stood, and said unto the Lord; Behold, Lord, the half of my goods I give to the poor; and if I have taken any thing from any man by false accusation, I restore *him* *a*fourfold.

9 And Jesus said unto him, This day is salvation come to this house, forsomuch as he also is a son of Abraham.

10 For the Son of man is come to seek and to *a*save that which was *b*lost.

11 And as they heard these things, he added and spake a parable, because he was nigh to Jerusalem, and because they thought that the kingdom of God should *a*immediately appear.

12 He said therefore, A certain nobleman went into a far country to receive for himself a kingdom, and to return.

13 And he called his ten servants, and delivered them ten *a*pounds, and said unto them, *b*Occupy till I come.

14 But his *a*citizens hated him, and sent a *b*message after him, saying, We will not have this *man* to reign over us.

15 And it came to pass, that when he was returned, having received the kingdom, then he commanded these *a*servants to be called unto him, to whom he had given the money, that

---

42a TG Sight.
  b 3 Ne. 17:8;
    D&C 42:48; 58:43.
43a Luke 5:25.
19 3a GR crowd, multitude.
  6a TG Hospitality.

8a 2 Sam. 12:6.
10a TG Life, Sanctity of.
  b Ezek. 34:16;
    2 Ne. 26:25 (23–29).
11a 2 Thes. 2:2 (1–6).
13a TG Talents.

  b GR Do business.
14a TG Citizenship.
  b GR ambassador.
15a D&C 72:3 (3–4).

he might know how much every man had gained by trading.

16 Then came the first, saying, Lord, thy pound hath gained ten pounds.

17 And he said unto him, Well, thou good servant: because thou hast been *faithful in a very little, have thou *authority over ten cities.

18 And the second came, saying, Lord, thy pound hath gained five pounds.

19 And he said likewise to him, Be thou also over five cities.

20 And another came, saying, Lord, behold, *here is* thy pound, which I have kept laid up in a napkin:

21 For I *feared thee, because thou art an *austere man: thou takest up that thou layedst not down, and reapest that thou didst not sow.

22 And he saith unto him, Out of thine own mouth will I judge thee, *thou* wicked servant. Thou knewest that I was an austere man, taking up that I laid not down, and reaping that I did not sow:

23 Wherefore then gavest not thou my money into the bank, that at my coming I might have *required mine own with *usury?

24 And he said unto them that stood by, Take from him the pound, and give *it* to him that hath ten pounds.

25 (And they said unto him, Lord, he hath ten pounds.)

26 For I say unto you, That unto every one *which hath shall be given; and from him that hath not, even that he hath shall be taken away from him.

27 But those mine enemies, which would not that I should reign over them, bring hither, and slay *them* before me.

28 ¶ And when he had thus spoken, he went before, ascending up to Jerusalem.

29 And it came to pass, when he was come nigh to Bethphage and Bethany, at the mount called *the mount* of Olives, he sent two of his disciples,

30 Saying, Go ye into the village over against *you;* in the which at your entering ye shall find a colt tied, whereon yet never man sat: loose him, and bring *him hither.*

31 And if any man ask you, Why do ye loose *him?* thus shall ye say unto him, Because the Lord hath need of him.

32 And they that were sent went their way, and found even as he had said unto them.

33 And as they were loosing the colt, the owners thereof said unto them, Why loose ye the colt?

34 And they said, The Lord hath need of him.

35 And they brought him to Jesus: and they cast their garments upon the *colt, and they set Jesus thereon.

36 And as he went, they spread their clothes in the way.

37 And when he was come nigh, even now at the descent of the mount of Olives, the whole multitude of the disciples began to rejoice and praise God with a loud voice for all the mighty works that they had seen;

38 Saying, Blessed *be* the King that cometh in the name of the Lord: peace in heaven, and *glory in the highest.

39 And some of the Pharisees from among the multitude said unto him, Master, rebuke thy disciples.

40 And he answered and said unto them, I tell you that, if these should hold their peace, the *stones would immediately cry out.

41 ¶ And when he was come near, he beheld the city, and wept over it,

42 Saying, If thou hadst known, even thou, at least in this thy day,

---

17a TG Stewardship.
  b TG Authority.
21a TG Courage;
     Fearful.
  b GR harsh, ungenerous.
23a GR collected.

  b TG Usury.
26a JST Luke 19:25 . . . *who occupieth,* shall be given; and from him *who occupieth* not, even that he hath *received* shall be

taken away from him.
35a Zech. 9:9.
38a Luke 2:14.
40a Matt. 21:9.

the things *which belong* unto thy peace! but now they are hid from thine eyes.

43 For the days shall come upon thee, that thine ªenemies shall cast a ᵇtrench about thee, and ᶜcompass thee round, and keep thee in on every side,

44 And shall ªlay thee even with the ground, and thy children within thee; and they shall not leave in thee one ᵇstone upon another; because thou knewest not the time of thy ᶜvisitation.

45 And he went into the temple, and began to cast out them that sold therein, and them that bought;

46 Saying unto them, It is written, My house is the ªhouse of prayer: but ye have made it a ᵇden of thieves.

47 And he taught daily in the temple. But the chief priests and the scribes and the chief of the people sought to destroy him,

48 And could not find what they might do: for all the people were very attentive to hear him.

CHAPTER 20

The chief priests oppose Jesus—He gives the parable of the wicked husbandmen—Render unto Cæsar and God that which is theirs—Jesus teaches the law of marriage.

AND it came to pass, *that* on one of those days, as he taught the people in the temple, and preached the gospel, the chief priests and the scribes came upon *him* with the elders,

2 And spake unto him, saying, Tell us, by what authority doest thou these things? or who is he that gave thee this authority?

3 And he answered and said unto them, I will also ask you one thing; and answer me:

4 The baptism of John, was it from heaven, or of men?

5 And they reasoned with themselves, saying, If we shall say, From heaven; he will say, Why then believed ye him not?

6 But and if we say, Of men; all the people will stone us: for they be persuaded that John was a ªprophet.

7 And they answered, that they could not tell whence *it was.*

8 And Jesus said unto them, Neither tell I you by what authority I do these things.

9 Then began he to speak to the people this parable; A certain man planted a ªvineyard, and let it forth to ᵇhusbandmen, and went into a far country for a long time.

10 And at the season he sent a servant to the husbandmen, that they should give him of the fruit of the vineyard: but the husbandmen beat him, and sent *him* away empty.

11 And again he sent another servant: and they beat him also, and entreated *him* shamefully, and sent *him* away empty.

12 And again he sent a third: and they wounded him also, and cast *him* out.

13 Then said the lord of the vineyard, What shall I do? I will send my beloved son: it may be they will reverence *him* when they see him.

14 But when the husbandmen saw him, they reasoned among themselves, saying, This is the heir: come, let us kill him, that the inheritance may be ours.

15 So they cast him out of the vineyard, and killed *him.* What therefore shall the lord of the vineyard do unto them?

16 He shall come and destroy these husbandmen, and shall give the vineyard to others. And when they heard *it,* they said, ªGod forbid.

17 And he beheld them, and said,

43*a* Luke 21:20.
 b GR fortification, rampart.
   Isa. 37:33.
 c Deut. 28:52.
44*a* Dan. 9:26.

 b Matt. 24:2 (1–51);
   JS—M 1:3 (1–55).
 c Isa. 10:3.
46*a* Isa. 56:7.
 b Jer. 7:11;
   D&C 94:8 (8–9);

   109:20 (19–20).
20 6*a* Matt. 11:9; 14:5; 21:26.
 9*a* TG Vineyard of the Lord.
 b GR farmers.
16*a* GR May it not be.

What is this then that is written, The *a*stone which the builders rejected, the same is become the head of the corner?

18 Whosoever shall fall upon that stone shall be broken; but on whomsoever it shall fall, it will *a*grind him to powder.

19 ¶ And the chief priests and the scribes the same hour sought to lay hands on him; and they feared the people: for they perceived that he had spoken this parable against them.

20 And they watched *him,* and sent forth spies, which should feign themselves just men, that they might *a*take hold of his words, that so they might deliver him unto the power and authority of the governor.

21 And they asked him, saying, Master, we know that thou sayest and teachest rightly, neither acceptest thou the person *of any,* but teachest the way of God truly:

22 Is it lawful for us to give *a*tribute unto Cæsar, or no?

23 But he perceived their *a*craftiness, and said unto them, Why tempt ye me?

24 Shew me a penny. Whose image and superscription hath it? They answered and said, Cæsar's.

25 And he said unto them, Render therefore unto *a*Cæsar the things which be Cæsar's, and unto God the things which be God's.

26 And they could not take hold of his words before the people: and they marvelled at his answer, and held their peace.

27 ¶ Then came to *him* certain of the Sadducees, which deny that there is any resurrection; and they asked him,

28 Saying, Master, Moses wrote unto us, If any man's *a*brother die, having a wife, and he die without children, that his *b*brother should take his wife, and raise up seed unto his brother.

29 There were therefore seven brethren: and the first took a wife, and died without children.

30 And the second took her to wife, and he died childless.

31 And the third took her; and in like manner the seven also: and they left no children, and died.

32 Last of all the woman died also.

33 Therefore in the resurrection whose wife of them is she? for seven had her to wife.

34 And Jesus answering said unto them, The children of this world *a*marry, and are given in marriage:

35 But they which shall be accounted worthy to obtain *a*that world, and the *b*resurrection from the dead, neither marry, nor are given in *c*marriage:

36 Neither can they die any more: for they are equal unto the *a*angels; and are the *b*children of God, being the children of the resurrection.

37 Now that the dead are raised, even Moses shewed at the *a*bush, when he calleth the Lord the God of Abraham, and the God of Isaac, and the God of Jacob.

38 For he is not a God of the *a*dead, but of the living: for all live unto him.

39 ¶ Then certain of the scribes answering said, Master, thou hast well said.

40 And after that they durst not ask him any *a*question at all.

41 And he said unto them, How say they that Christ is David's *a*son?

42 And David himself saith in the book of Psalms, The LORD said

17*a* TG Rock.
18*a* GR scatter like chaff.
20*a* Matt. 22:15 (15–22);
    Mark 12:13 (13–17).
22*a* GR taxes.
    D&C 58:21 (21–22);
    98:9 (4–10).
23*a* Alma 10:17;
    D&C 10:25 (21–27).
25*a* D&C 58:22 (21–23);
    63:26 (25–29).

28*a* Deut. 25:5.
  b Mark 12:19.
34*a* TG Marriage, Marry;
    Marriage, Temporal.
35*a* JST Luke 20:35 . . .
    that world, *through*
    resurrection from . . .
  b TG Objectives;
    Resurrection.
  c D&C 132:16 (7–39).
36*a* D&C 131:2 (1–4);

    132:17 (5–17).
    TG Angels.
  b TG Sons and Daughters
    of God.
37*a* Ex. 3:2 (2–6).
38*a* Rom. 14:9.
    TG Spirits,
    Disembodied.
40*a* D&C 84:116.
41*a* Matt. 1:16 (1–16);
    D&C 93:14 (3–17).

unto my ªLord, Sit thou on my right hand,

43 Till I make thine enemies thy footstool.

44 David therefore calleth him Lord, how is he then his son?

45 ¶ Then in the audience of all the people he said unto his disciples,

46 Beware of the ªscribes, which desire to walk in long robes, and love greetings in the markets, and the ᵇhighest seats in the synagogues, and the chief rooms at feasts;

47 Which devour widows' houses, and for a shew make long prayers: the same shall receive greater damnation.

CHAPTER 21

Jesus foretells the destruction of the temple and of Jerusalem—He tells of the signs to precede His Second Coming and gives the parable of the fig tree.

AND he looked up, and saw the ªrich men casting their gifts into the treasury.

2 And he saw also a certain poor widow casting in thither two ªmites.

3 And he said, Of a truth I say unto you, that this poor widow hath cast in more than they all:

4 For all these have of their abundance cast in unto the offerings of God: but she of her penury hath cast in all the living that she had.

5 ¶ And as some spake of the temple, how it was adorned with goodly stones and gifts, he said,

6 *As for* these things which ye behold, the days will come, in the which there shall not be left one ªstone upon another, that shall not be thrown down.

7 And they asked him, saying,

Master, but when shall these things be? and what ªsign *will there be* when these things shall come to pass?

8 And he said, Take heed that ye be not deceived: for many shall come in my name, saying, I am *Christ;* and the time draweth near: go ye not therefore after them.

9 But when ye shall hear of wars and commotions, be not terrified: for these things must first come to pass; but the end *is* not by and by.

10 Then said he unto them, ªNation shall rise against nation, and kingdom against kingdom:

11 And great earthquakes shall be in divers places, and famines, and ªpestilences; and fearful sights and great signs shall there be from heaven.

12 But before all these, they shall lay their hands on you, and ªpersecute *you,* delivering *you* up to the synagogues, and into prisons, being brought before kings and rulers for my name's sake.

13 And it shall turn to you for a testimony.

14 Settle *it* therefore in your hearts, not to ªmeditate before what ye shall ᵇanswer:

15 For I will give you a mouth and ªwisdom, which all your adversaries shall not be able to ᵇgainsay nor resist.

16 And ye shall be betrayed both by parents, and brethren, and kinsfolks, and friends; and *some* of you shall they cause to be put to death.

17 And ye shall be hated of all *men* for my name's ªsake.

18 But there shall not an ªhair of your head perish.

19 In your ªpatience ᵇpossess ye your souls.

42a Ps. 110:1.
46a 2 Ne. 28:16;
　　 Alma 10:27.
　 b GR first or most
　　 honorable.
　　 Luke 11:43.
21 1a Mosiah 4:23;
　　 D&C 56:16.
　 2a D&C 64:34 (22, 34).
　 6a D&C 45:20.
　 7a Matt. 24:3 (3–46);

D&C 45:16 (16–75);
　 JS—M 1:4 (4–55).
10a 1 Ne. 22:14 (13–14).
11a 2 Ne. 6:15; Mosiah 12:4;
　　 D&C 97:26 (22–26).
12a TG Persecution.
14a GR practice, prepare.
　　 TG Meditation.
　 b D&C 84:85.
15a Isa. 50:4;
　　 Matt. 10:19 (16–20);

Acts 6:10; D&C 11:21.
　 TG Wisdom.
　 b GR speak against,
　　 oppose, contradict.
17a D&C 98:13; 101:35.
18a Matt. 10:30 (29–31);
　　 Alma 40:23;
　　 D&C 29:25.
19a TG Patience.
　 b GR preserve, win
　　 mastery over.

20 And when ye shall see ^aJerusalem compassed with ^barmies, then know that the ^cdesolation thereof is nigh.

21 Then let them which are in Judæa flee to the mountains; and let them which are in the midst of it depart out; and let not them that are in the ^acountries enter thereinto.

22 For these be the days of vengeance, that all things which are written may be fulfilled.

23 But woe unto them that are with child, and to them that give suck, in those days! for there shall be great distress in the land, and wrath upon this people.

24 And they shall fall by the edge of the sword, and shall be ^aled away ^bcaptive into all ^cnations: and Jerusalem shall be ^dtrodden down of the ^eGentiles, until the times of the Gentiles be fulfilled.

25 ¶ ^aAnd there shall be signs in the sun, and in the ^bmoon, and in the stars; and upon the earth distress of nations, with perplexity; the sea and the waves roaring;

26 Men's hearts ^afailing them for fear, and for looking after those things which are coming on the earth: for the powers of heaven shall be ^bshaken.

27 And then shall they see the Son of man coming in a ^acloud with power and great glory.

28 And when these things begin to come to pass, then look up, and lift up your heads; for your ^aredemption draweth nigh.

29 And he spake to them a parable; Behold the ^afig tree, and all the trees;

30 When they now shoot forth, ye see and know of your own selves that summer is now nigh at hand.

31 So likewise ye, when ye see these things come to pass, know ye that the kingdom of God is nigh at hand.

32 Verily I say unto you, ^aThis generation shall not pass away, till all be fulfilled.

33 Heaven and earth shall pass away: but my words shall not pass away.

34 ¶ And take heed to yourselves, lest at any time your hearts be overcharged with ^asurfeiting, and drunkenness, and ^bcares of this life, and so that ^cday come upon you ^dunawares.

35 For as a ^asnare shall it come on all them that dwell on the face of the whole earth.

36 ^aWatch ye therefore, and ^bpray always, ^cthat ye may be accounted ^dworthy to escape all these things that shall come to pass, and to stand before the ^eSon of man.

37 And in the day time he was ^ateaching in the temple; and at night he went out, and abode in the mount that is called *the mount* of Olives.

38 And all the people came early in the morning to him in the temple, for to hear him.

20a Luke 19:43.
  b Ezek. 38:16 (15–16);
    Rev. 16:16.
  c D&C 45:19 (18–21).
    TG Abomination of
    Desolation.
21a GR districts or regions.
24a Dan. 12:7.
    TG Israel, Scattering of.
  b TG Israel, Bondage of,
    in Other Lands.
  c TG Israel, Twelve
    Tribes of.
  d Dan. 9:27 (24–27).
  e D&C 45:25.
    TG Gentiles.
25a JST Luke 21:24–26
    (Appendix).

  b TG Astronomy.
26a D&C 45:26; 88:91.
  b Isa. 34:4.
27a Dan. 7:13;
    D&C 34:7.
28a D&C 35:26.
29a D&C 35:16 (15–16);
    45:37 (34–38).
32a JST Luke 21:32 . . .
    this generation, *the*
    generation when the times
    of the Gentiles be fulfilled,
    shall not . . .
34a GR debauchery.
    TG Rioting and
    Reveling.
  b TG Worldliness.
  c Luke 17:24;

    1 Thes. 5:4.
  d TG Procrastination.
35a Rev. 3:3; 16:15;
    D&C 63:15.
36a TG Watch.
  b TG Prayer.
  c JST Luke 21:36 . . . *and*
    keep my commandments,
    that ye . . .
  d TG Worthiness.
  e JST Luke 21:36 . . . Son
    of man *when he shall*
    come clothed in the glory
    of his Father.
37a Matt. 26:55;
    John 8:2 (1–2).

CHAPTER 22

Jesus institutes the sacrament—He suffers in Gethsemane and is betrayed and arrested—Peter denies knowing Him—Jesus is smitten and mocked.

Now the feast of unleavened bread drew nigh, which is called the ^aPassover.

2 And the chief ^apriests and ^bscribes sought how they might ^ckill him; for they feared the people.

3 ¶ Then entered Satan into Judas surnamed Iscariot, being of the number of the twelve.

4 And he went his way, and ^acommuned with the chief priests and captains, how he might betray him unto them.

5 And they were glad, and covenanted to give him ^amoney.

6 And he promised, and sought opportunity to betray him unto them in the absence of the multitude.

7 ¶ Then came the day of ^aunleavened bread, when the ^bpassover must be killed.

8 And he sent ^aPeter and John, saying, Go and prepare us the passover, that we may eat.

9 And they said unto him, Where wilt thou that we prepare?

10 And he said unto them, Behold, when ye are entered into the city, there shall a man meet you, bearing a pitcher of water; follow him into the house where he entereth in.

11 And ye shall say unto the ^agoodman of the house, The Master saith unto thee, Where is the guestchamber, where I shall eat the passover with my disciples?

12 And he shall shew you a large upper room furnished: there make ready.

13 And they went, and found as he had said unto them: and they made ready the passover.

14 And when the hour was come, he sat down, and the twelve apostles with him.

15 And he said unto them, With desire I have desired to eat this passover with you before I suffer:

16 For I say unto you, I will not any more eat thereof, ^auntil it be fulfilled in the kingdom of God.

17 And he took the cup, and gave thanks, and said, Take this, and divide *it* among yourselves:

18 For I say unto you, I will not ^adrink of the fruit of the vine, until the kingdom of God shall come.

19 ¶ And he took ^abread, and gave thanks, and brake *it,* and gave unto them, saying, This is my ^bbody which is ^cgiven for you: this do in ^dremembrance of me.

20 Likewise also the ^acup after supper, saying, This cup *is* the new ^btestament in my blood, which is shed for you.

21 ¶ But, behold, the hand of him that betrayeth me *is* with me on the table.

22 And truly the Son of man goeth, as it was ^adetermined: but woe unto that man by whom he is ^bbetrayed!

23 And they began to inquire among themselves, which of them it was that should do this thing.

24 ¶ And there was also a ^astrife among them, which of them should be accounted the ^bgreatest.

25 And he said unto them, The

---

22 1a TG Passover.
2a 2 Ne. 10:5.
   TG Priestcraft.
  b TG Scribe.
  c Matt. 26:4 (2–5);
    Mark 14:1 (1–2);
    2 Ne. 10:3 (3–6).
4a GR talked, conferred.
5a Zech. 11:12.
7a TG Bread, Unleavened.
  b TG Passover.
8a Mark 14:13 (12–16).
11a GR master; i.e., head of house or family.

16a JST Luke 22:16 . . . until it be fulfilled *which is written in the prophets concerning me. Then I will partake with you, in* the . . .
18a Matt. 26:29;
    Mark 14:25;
    D&C 27:5.
19a D&C 20:77.
  b Mark 14:22;
    JST Mark 14:20–25 (Appendix); John 6:53.
    TG Jesus Christ,

Atonement through.
  c TG Jesus Christ, Redeemer.
  d TG Jesus Christ, Types of, in Memory.
20a D&C 20:78.
  b GR covenant.
22a GR appointed, decreed.
    TG Foreordination.
  b Matt. 26:24; Acts 2:23.
24a TG Strife.
  b Matt. 23:11;
    Mark 10:44 (42–45);
    D&C 50:26.

^akings of the Gentiles exercise lordship over them; and they that exercise authority upon them are called benefactors.

26 But ye *shall* not *be* so: but he that is greatest among you, let him be as the younger; and he that is chief, as he that doth ^aserve.

27 For whether *is* greater, he that sitteth at meat, or he that serveth? *is* not he that sitteth at meat? but I am among you as he that ^aserveth.

28 Ye are they which have ^acontinued with me in my ^btemptations.

29 And I appoint unto you a kingdom, as my Father hath ^aappointed unto me;

30 That ye may ^aeat and drink at my table in my kingdom, and sit on thrones ^bjudging the twelve tribes of Israel.

31 ¶ And the Lord said, Simon, Simon, behold, ^aSatan hath desired *to* ^bhave you, that he may sift *you* as wheat:

32 But I have ^aprayed for thee, that thy faith fail not: and when thou art ^bconverted, ^cstrengthen thy brethren.

33 And he said unto him, Lord, I am ^aready to go with thee, both into prison, and to death.

34 And he said, I tell thee, Peter, the cock shall not crow this day, before that thou shalt ^athrice deny that thou knowest me.

35 And he said unto them, When I sent you without ^apurse, and scrip, and shoes, lacked ye any thing? And they said, Nothing.

36 Then said he unto them, But now, he that hath a purse, let him take *it*, and likewise *his* scrip: and he that hath no sword, let him sell his garment, and buy one.

37 For I say unto you, that this that is written must yet be accomplished in me, And he was reckoned among the ^atransgressors: for the things concerning me have an end.

38 And they said, Lord, behold, here *are* two swords. And he said unto them, It is enough.

39 ¶ And he came out, and went, as he was ^awont, to the mount of Olives; and his disciples also followed him.

40 And when he was at the place, he said unto them, Pray that ye enter not into ^atemptation.

41 And he was withdrawn from them about a stone's cast, and kneeled down, and prayed,

42 Saying, Father, if thou be willing, ^aremove this cup from me: nevertheless not my ^bwill, but thine, be done.

43 And there appeared an ^aangel unto him from heaven, strengthening him.

44 And being in an ^aagony he prayed more earnestly: ^band his sweat was as it were great drops of ^cblood falling down to the ground.

45 And when he rose up from prayer, and was come to his disciples, he found them sleeping for sorrow,

46 And said unto them, Why sleep ye? rise and pray, lest ye enter into temptation.

47 ¶ And while he yet spake, behold a multitude, and he that was

---

25a TG Kings, Earthly.
26a Mosiah 2:18 (14, 18–19).
27a TG Meek; Self-Sacrifice.
28a TG Perseverance.
  b TG Jesus Christ,
    Temptation of; Test.
29a TG Authority.
30a Luke 14:15;
    Rev. 19:9.
  b Morm. 3:18 (18–20);
    D&C 29:12.
    TG Apostles.
31a JST Luke 22:31 . . . Satan
    hath desired you, that
    he may sift *the children*

of the kingdom as wheat.
    TG Devil.
  b TG Test.
32a TG Prayer.
  b Mosiah 3:19.
    TG Conversion.
  c D&C 108:7.
    TG Fellowshipping;
    Missionary Work;
    Sustaining Church
    Leaders.
33a Matt. 26:33.
34a Matt. 26:34 (30–35).
35a Matt. 10:9 (9–10);
    D&C 84:78.

37a Isa. 53:12.
39a GR accustomed.
40a TG Temptation.
42a D&C 19:18.
  b Moses 4:2 (1–4).
    TG God, Will of.
43a TG Angels.
44a TG Pain.
  b JST Luke 22:44 . . . and
    he sweat as it were great
    drops of blood . . .
  c Mosiah 3:7;
    D&C 19:18.
    TG Jesus Christ,
    Atonement through.

called Judas, one of the twelve, went before them, and drew near unto Jesus to kiss him.

48 But Jesus said unto him, ^aJudas, ^bbetrayest thou the Son of man with a ^ckiss?

49 When they which were about him saw what would follow, they said unto him, Lord, shall we smite with the sword?

50 ¶ And one of them smote the servant of the high priest, and cut off his right ear.

51 And Jesus answered and said, Suffer ye thus far. And he touched his ear, and ^ahealed him.

52 Then Jesus said unto the chief priests, and captains of the temple, and the elders, which were come to him, Be ye come out, as against a thief, with swords and staves?

53 When I was daily with you in the temple, ye stretched forth no hands against me: but this is your hour, and the power of ^adarkness.

54 ¶ Then took they him, and led *him,* and brought him into the high priest's house. And Peter followed afar off.

55 And when they had kindled a fire in the midst of the ^ahall, and were set down together, Peter sat down among them.

56 But a certain maid beheld him as he sat by the fire, and earnestly looked upon him, and said, This man was also with him.

57 And he denied him, saying, Woman, I know him not.

58 And after a little while another saw him, and said, Thou art also of them. And Peter said, Man, I am not.

59 And about the space of one hour after another confidently affirmed, saying, Of a truth this *fellow* also was with him: for he is a Galilæan.

60 And Peter said, Man, I know not what thou sayest. And immediately, while he yet spake, the cock crew.

61 And the ^aLord turned, and looked upon Peter. And Peter remembered the word of the Lord, how he had said unto him, Before the cock crow, thou shalt deny me thrice.

62 And Peter went out, and wept bitterly.

63 ¶ And the men that held Jesus ^amocked him, and smote *him.*

64 And when they had ^ablindfolded him, they struck him on the face, and asked him, saying, Prophesy, who is it that smote thee?

65 And many other things blasphemously spake they against him.

66 ¶ And as soon as it was day, ^athe elders of the people and the chief priests and the scribes came together, and led him into their council, saying,

67 Art thou the ^aChrist? tell us. And he said unto them, If I tell you, ye will not believe:

68 And if I also ask *you,* ye will not answer me, nor let *me* go.

69 ^aHereafter shall the ^bSon of man sit on the right hand of the power of God.

70 Then said they all, Art thou then the Son of God? And he said unto them, Ye say that I am.

71 And they said, What need we any further ^awitness? for we ourselves have heard of his own mouth.

CHAPTER 23

Jesus is taken before Pilate, then to Herod, and then to Pilate again—Barabbas is released—Jesus is crucified between two thieves—He is buried in the tomb of Joseph of Arimathæa.

AND the whole multitude of them arose, and led him unto Pilate.

2 And they began to accuse him,

48a Acts 1:16.
  b TG Jesus Christ, Betrayal of.
  c Prov. 27:6.
51a TG Heal.
53a TG Darkness, Spiritual.
55a GR courtyard.

61a TG Jesus Christ, Lord.
63a TG Jesus Christ, Trials of; Mocking.
64a Matt. 26:68.
66a IE the Sanhedrin.
67a TG Jesus Christ,

Trials of.
69a GR From now on.
  b TG Jesus Christ, Son of Man.
71a TG Jesus Christ, Trials of.

saying, We found this *fellow* perverting the nation, and forbidding to give tribute to ªCæsar, saying that he himself is Christ a ᵇKing.

3 And Pilate asked him, saying, Art thou the King of the Jews? And he answered him and said, Thou sayest *it*.

4 Then said Pilate to the chief priests and *to* the people, I find no ªfault in this man.

5 And they were the more fierce, saying, He stirreth up the people, teaching throughout all Jewry, beginning from Galilee to this place.

6 When Pilate heard of Galilee, he asked whether the man were a Galilæan.

7 And as soon as he knew that he belonged unto Herod's jurisdiction, he sent him to Herod, who himself also was at Jerusalem at that time.

8 ¶ And when Herod saw Jesus, he was exceeding glad: for he was desirous to see him of a long *season*, because he had heard many things of him; and he hoped to have seen some ªmiracle done by him.

9 Then he questioned with him in many words; but he ªanswered him nothing.

10 And the chief priests and ªscribes stood and vehemently accused him.

11 And Herod with his men of war set him at nought, and ªmocked *him*, and arrayed him in a gorgeous robe, and sent him again to Pilate.

12 ¶ And the same day Pilate and Herod were made friends together: for before they were at enmity between themselves.

13 ¶ And Pilate, when he had called together the chief priests and the rulers and the people,

14 Said unto them, Ye have brought this man unto me, as one that perverteth the people: and, behold, I, having examined *him* before you, have found no fault in this man

touching those things whereof ye accuse him:

15 No, nor yet Herod: for I sent you to him; and, lo, nothing worthy of death is done ªunto him.

16 I will therefore chastise him, and release *him*.

17 (For of necessity he must ªrelease one unto them at the feast.)

18 And they cried out all at once, saying, Away with this *man*, and release unto us Barabbas:

19 (Who for a certain sedition made in the city, and for ªmurder, was cast into prison.)

20 Pilate therefore, willing to release Jesus, spake again to them.

21 But they cried, saying, ªCrucify *him*, crucify him.

22 And he said unto them the third time, Why, what evil hath he done? I have found ªno cause of death in him: I will therefore chastise him, and let *him* go.

23 And they were ªinstant with loud voices, ᵇrequiring that he might be ᶜcrucified. And the voices of them and of the chief priests prevailed.

24 And Pilate gave sentence that it should be as they ªrequired.

25 And he released unto them him that for sedition and ªmurder was cast into prison, whom they had desired; but he delivered Jesus to their will.

26 And as they led him away, they laid hold upon one Simon, a Cyrenian, coming out of the country, and on him they laid the cross, that he might bear *it* after Jesus.

27 ¶ And there followed him a great company of people, and of women, which also bewailed and lamented him.

28 But Jesus turning unto them said, Daughters of ªJerusalem, weep not for me, but weep for yourselves, and for your children.

23 2*a* D&C 63:26.
   b Alma 5:50.
  4*a* TG Jesus Christ,
     Trials of.
  8*a* TG Miracle;
     Sign Seekers.
  9*a* Mosiah 14:7; 15:6.

10*a* TG Scribe.
11*a* TG Mocking.
15*a* GR by.
17*a* Matt. 27:15 (15–26).
19*a* John 18:40.
21*a* TG Jesus Christ,
     Trials of.

22*a* Mark 15:9 (6–15).
23*a* GR urging.
  b GR demanding.
  c 2 Ne. 10:3 (3–6).
24*a* GR demanded.
25*a* Acts 3:14.
28*a* TG Jerusalem.

29 For, behold, the days are coming, in the which they shall say, Blessed *are* the *a*barren, and the wombs that never bare, and the paps which never gave suck.

30 Then shall they begin to say to the *a*mountains, Fall on us; and to the hills, Cover us.

31 For if they do these things in a *a*green tree, what shall be done in the *b*dry?

32 And there were also two other, *a*malefactors, led with him to be put to death.

33 And when they were come to the place, which is called Calvary, there they crucified him, and the malefactors, one on the right hand, and the other on the left.

34 ¶ Then *a*said Jesus, Father, *b*forgive them; for they know not what *c*they do. And they parted his *d*raiment, and cast lots.

35 And the people stood beholding. And the rulers also with them *a*derided *him,* saying, He saved others; let him save himself, if he be Christ, the *b*chosen of God.

36 And the soldiers also *a*mocked him, coming to him, and offering him *b*vinegar,

37 And saying, If thou be the king of the Jews, save thyself.

38 And a superscription also was written over him in letters of Greek, and Latin, and Hebrew, THIS IS THE *a*KING OF THE *b*JEWS.

39 ¶ And one of the malefactors which were hanged *a*railed on him, saying, If thou be Christ, save thyself and us.

40 But the other answering rebuked him, saying, Dost not thou fear God, seeing thou art in the same condemnation?

41 And we indeed justly; for we receive the due *a*reward of our deeds: but this man hath done nothing amiss.

42 And he said unto Jesus, Lord, remember me when thou comest into thy kingdom.

43 And Jesus said unto him, Verily I say unto thee, To day shalt thou be with me in *a*paradise.

44 And it was about the *a*sixth hour, and there was a *b*darkness over all the *c*earth until the ninth hour.

45 And the sun was darkened, and the veil of the temple was rent in the *a*midst.

46 ¶ And when Jesus had cried with a loud voice, he said, Father, into thy hands I *a*commend my *b*spirit: and having said thus, he *c*gave up the *d*ghost.

47 Now when the centurion saw what was done, he glorified God, saying, Certainly this was a *a*righteous man.

48 And all the people that came together to that sight, beholding the things which were done, smote their breasts, and returned.

49 And all his acquaintance, and the women that followed him from Galilee, stood afar off, beholding these things.

29a Matt. 24:19.
30a Hosea 10:8;
    Rev. 6:16 (14–17).
31a D&C 135:6.
  b JST Luke 23:31–32 . . .
    dry *tree? This he spake,*
    signifying the scattering of
    Israel, and the desolation
    of the heathen, or in other
    words, the Gentiles.
32a GR criminals.
    Isa. 53:9.
34a Luke 6:28;
    Acts 7:60 (53–60).
  b TG Benevolence;
    Forgive;
    Mercy.
  c JST Luke 23:35 . . . they

do (*Meaning the soldiers*
    who crucified him,) . . .
  d Ps. 22:18.
35a Ps. 22:7.
  b TG Jesus Christ,
    Relationships with
    the Father.
36a TG Mocking.
  b GR sour wine.
    Ps. 69:21.
38a D&C 45:53 (51–53).
  b Mosiah 15:5.
39a GR blasphemed,
    reproached.
41a TG Reward.
43a John 20:17;
    Alma 40:21 (11–14, 21).
    TG Immortality;

Paradise;
    Spirits, Disembodied.
44a 3 Ne. 8:19.
  b Amos 8:9;
    Hel. 14:20.
    TG Darkness, Physical.
  c GR earth, region, land,
    or country.
45a GR middle.
46a TG Commitment.
  b Ps. 31:5;
    John 10:18 (17–18).
    TG Man, a Spirit Child
    of Heavenly Father.
  c GR expired, ceased
    breathing, or died.
  d TG Death.
47a TG Righteousness.

50 ¶ And, behold, *there was* a man named Joseph, a *a*counsellor; *and he was* a good man, and a just:

51 (The same had not consented to the counsel and deed of them;) *he was* of Arimathæa, a city of the Jews: who also himself waited for the kingdom of God.

52 This *man* went unto Pilate, and *a*begged the body of Jesus.

53 And he took it down, and wrapped it in linen, and laid it in a *a*sepulchre that was hewn in stone, wherein never man before was laid.

54 And that day was the *a*preparation, and the sabbath drew on.

55 And the women also, which came with him from Galilee, followed after, and beheld the *a*sepulchre, and how his body was laid.

56 And they returned, and prepared spices and ointments; and *a*rested the sabbath day according to the commandment.

CHAPTER 24

Angels announce the resurrection of Christ—He walks on the Emmaus road—He appears with a body of flesh and bones, eats food, testifies of His divinity, and promises the Holy Ghost— He ascends into heaven.

Now upon the first *day* of the week, very early in the morning, they came unto the *a*sepulchre, bringing the spices which they had prepared, and certain *others* with them.

2 *a*And they found the stone rolled away from the sepulchre.

3 And they entered in, and found not the body of the Lord Jesus.

4 And it came to pass, as they were much perplexed thereabout, behold, two men stood by them in shining garments:

5 And as they were afraid, and bowed down *their* faces to the earth, they said unto them, Why seek ye the living among the dead?

6 He is not here, but is *a*risen: remember how he spake unto you when he was yet in Galilee,

7 Saying, The Son of man must be delivered into the hands of sinful men, and be crucified, and the third day rise again.

8 And they remembered his words,

9 And returned from the sepulchre, and told all these things unto the eleven, and to all the rest.

10 It was Mary Magdalene, and Joanna, and Mary *the mother* of James, and other *women that were* with them, which told these things unto the apostles.

11 And their words seemed to them as idle tales, and they believed them not.

12 Then arose Peter, and ran unto the sepulchre; and stooping down, he beheld the linen clothes laid by themselves, and departed, wondering in himself at that which was come to pass.

13 ¶ And, behold, two of them went that same day to a village called Emmaus, which was from Jerusalem *a*about threescore furlongs.

14 And they talked together of all these things which had happened.

15 And it came to pass, that, while they *a*communed *together* and reasoned, *b*Jesus himself drew near, and went with them.

16 But their eyes were *a*holden that they should not know him.

17 And he said unto them, What manner of communications *are* these that ye have one to another, as ye walk, and are sad?

18 And the one of them, whose name was *a*Cleopas, answering said unto him, Art thou only a stranger in Jerusalem, and hast not known

---

50a IE member of the
    Sanhedrin, senator.
52a GR requested.
53a John 19:41; 1 Ne. 19:10;
    2 Ne. 25:13.
54a TG Passover.
55a Luke 24:1 (1–3).
56a TG Rest.

24 1a Luke 23:55.
    2a JST Luke 24:2–4
        (Appendix).
    6a TG Jesus Christ,
        Resurrection.
   13a The distance here
        indicated is about 7½
        miles or 12 kilometers.

15a OR talked.
  b TG Jesus Christ,
    Appearances,
    Postmortal.
16a GR restrained.
    Heb. 13:2; Ether 3:25;
    D&C 25:4.
18a John 19:25.

the things which are come to pass there in these days?

19 And he said unto them, What things? And they said unto him, Concerning Jesus of Nazareth, which was a prophet mighty in deed and word before God and all the people:

20 And how the chief priests and our rulers delivered him to be condemned to death, and have crucified him.

21 But we trusted that it had been he which should have redeemed Israel: and beside all this, to day is the third day since these things were done.

22 Yea, and certain women also of our company made us astonished, which were early at the sepulchre;

23 And when they found not his body, they came, saying, that they had also seen a vision of angels, which said that he was alive.

24 And certain of them which were with us went to the sepulchre, and found *it* even so as the women had said: but him they saw not.

25 Then he said unto them, O *a*fools, and slow of *b*heart to *c*believe all that the prophets have spoken:

26 Ought not Christ to have suffered these things, and to enter into his glory?

27 And beginning at *a*Moses and all the *b*prophets, he *c*expounded unto them in all the *d*scriptures the things concerning himself.

28 And they drew nigh unto the village, whither they went: and he made as though he would have gone further.

29 But they constrained him, saying, Abide with us: for it is toward evening, and the day is far spent. And he went in to tarry with them.

30 And it came to pass, as he sat at meat with them, he took bread, and blessed *it,* and brake, and gave to them.

31 And their eyes were opened, and they knew him; and he vanished out of their sight.

32 And they said one to another, Did not our *a*heart *b*burn within us, while he *c*talked with us by the way, and while he opened to us the scriptures?

33 And they rose up the same hour, and returned to Jerusalem, and found the eleven gathered together, and them that were with them,

34 Saying, The Lord is risen indeed, and hath *a*appeared to *b*Simon.

35 And they told what things *were done* in the way, and how he was known of them in breaking of bread.

36 ¶ And as they thus spake, Jesus himself *a*stood in the midst of them, and saith unto them, *b*Peace *be* unto you.

37 But they were terrified and affrighted, and supposed that they had seen a spirit.

38 And he said unto them, Why are ye troubled? and why do *a*thoughts arise in your hearts?

39 Behold my hands and my feet, that it is I myself: *a*handle me, and see; for a *b*spirit hath not *c*flesh and bones, as ye *d*see me have.

40 And when he had thus spoken, he shewed them *his* hands and *his* feet.

41 And while they yet believed not for joy, and *a*wondered, he said unto them, Have ye here any meat?

25a GR unwise.
  b Matt. 14:31;
    Mark 4:40; 16:14.
  c Luke 1:20 (19–20); 12:29;
    Alma 22:7.
27a John 5:46.
  b Acts 3:18 (18–21);
    1 Pet. 1:10 (1–16).
  c TG Scriptures, Study of.
  d TG Jesus Christ,
    Prophecies about.
32a D&C 9:8.
    TG Heart.

  b TG Teaching with the
    Spirit.
  c TG Jesus Christ,
    Teaching Mode of.
34a TG Jesus Christ, Appearances, Postmortal.
  b 1 Cor. 15:5 (3–8).
36a TG Jesus Christ,
    Appearances,
    Postmortal.
  b D&C 19:23.
38a OR doubts, hesitations.
39a 3 Ne. 11:14 (12–15).

  b TG Man, Potential to
    Become like Heavenly
    Father;
    Spirits, Disembodied.
  c D&C 129:2.
    TG God, Body of,
    Corporeal Nature;
    Jesus Christ, Appearances, Postmortal;
    Resurrection.
  d TG God, Knowledge
    about.
41a GR marveled.

42 And they gave him a piece of a broiled fish, and of an honeycomb.

43 And he took *it,* and did eat before them.

44 And he said unto them, These *are* the words which I spake unto you, while I was yet with you, that all things must be *ª*fulfilled, which were written in the law of Moses, and *in* the prophets, and *in* the psalms, concerning me.

45 Then opened he their *ª*understanding, that they might understand the scriptures,

46 And said unto them, Thus it is written, and thus it *ª*behoved Christ to suffer, and to *ᵇ*rise from the dead the third day:

47 And that *ª*repentance and *ᵇ*remission of sins should be *ᶜ*preached in his name among all nations, beginning at Jerusalem.

48 And ye are *ª*witnesses of these things.

49 ¶ And, behold, I send the *ª*promise of my Father upon you: but tarry ye in the city of Jerusalem, until ye be *ᵇ*endued with power from on high.

50 ¶ And he led them out as far as to Bethany, and he lifted up his hands, and blessed them.

51 And it came to pass, while he blessed them, he was parted from them, and *ª*carried up into heaven.

52 And they worshipped him, and returned to Jerusalem with great joy:

53 And were continually in the *ª*temple, praising and blessing God. Amen.

THE GOSPEL ACCORDING TO

ST JOHN

CHAPTER 1

Christ is the Word of God—He created all things and was made flesh—John baptizes Jesus and testifies that He is the Lamb of God—John, Andrew, Simon, Philip, and Nathanael believe in Christ and follow Him.

*ª*IN the *ᵇ*beginning was the Word, and the *ᶜ*Word was with God, and the *ᵈ*Word was *ᵉ*God.

2 The same was in the *ª*beginning with God.

3 All things were *ª*made by him; and without him was not any thing made that was made.

44*a* TG Jesus Christ, Prophecies about.
45*a* TG Understanding.
46*a* GR was necessary for, proper for.
  b TG Resurrection.
47*a* TG Repent.
  b D&C 137:6. TG Forgive; Remission of Sins.
  c TG Apostles; Mission of Early Saints.
48*a* Acts 1:8; 22:15 (14–16); D&C 27:12. TG Witness.
49*a* TG Promise.
  b OR clothed, invested.

D&C 20:8; 38:32 (32, 38).
51*a* TG Jesus Christ, Ascension of.
53*a* Acts 2:46.

[JOHN]
Title: JST entitles this book "The Testimony of St. John."
1 1*a* JST John 1:1–34 (Appendix).
  b D&C 76:39. TG Jesus Christ, Firstborn; Jesus Christ, Foreordained.
  c TG Jesus Christ,

Messenger of the Covenant; Jesus Christ, Relationships with the Father.
  d TG Jesus Christ, Jehovah.
  e TG Jesus Christ, Authority of.
2*a* 1 Jn. 1:1. TG Man, Antemortal Existence of.
3*a* TG Creation; God, Power of; Jesus Christ, Creator; Jesus Christ, Mission of; Jesus Christ, Power of.

4 In him was ^alife; and the life was the ^blight of men.

5 And the ^alight shineth in ^bdarkness; and the darkness ^ccomprehended it not.

6 ¶ There was a man sent from God, whose name *was* ^aJohn.

7 The same came for a ^awitness, to bear ^bwitness of the Light, that all *men* through him might ^cbelieve.

8 He was not that Light, but *was* sent to bear witness of that Light.

9 *That* was the true ^aLight, which ^blighteth ^cevery man that cometh into the world.

10 He was in the ^aworld, and the ^bworld was ^cmade by him, and the world ^dknew him not.

11 He came unto his own, and his own ^areceived him not.

12 But as many as ^areceived him, to them gave he ^bpower to become the ^csons of God, *even* to them that believe on his ^dname:

13 Which were ^aborn, not of blood, nor of the will of the flesh, nor of the will of man, but of God.

14 And the Word was made ^aflesh, and ^bdwelt among us, (and we ^cbeheld his ^dglory, the glory as of the ^eonly ^fbegotten of the Father,) full of ^ggrace and truth.

15 ¶ John bare ^awitness of him, and cried, saying, This was he of whom I spake, He that cometh after me is preferred before me: for he was before me.

16 And of his ^afulness have all we received, and ^bgrace for grace.

17 ^aFor the ^blaw was given by Moses, *but* ^cgrace and ^dtruth came by Jesus Christ.

18 No ^aman hath ^bseen God ^cat any time; the only begotten Son, which is in the bosom of the Father, he hath ^ddeclared *him*.

19 ¶ And this is the record of ^aJohn, when the Jews sent priests and Levites from Jerusalem to ask him, Who art thou?

20 And he confessed, and denied not; but confessed, I am not the Christ.

21 And they asked him, What then? Art thou ^aElias? And he saith, I am not. Art thou that prophet? And he answered, No.

22 Then said they unto him, Who art thou? that we may give an answer to them that sent us. What sayest thou of thyself?

23 He said, I *am* the ^avoice of one crying in the wilderness, Make ^bstraight the ^cway of the Lord, as said the prophet Esaias.

24 And they which were sent were of the Pharisees.

25 And they asked him, and said

4*a* 1 Jn. 5:11 (10–21).
  b TG Jesus Christ, Light of the World; Light [noun].
5*a* D&C 6:21; 34:2; 45:7.
  b TG Darkness, Spiritual.
  c 1 Cor. 2:11 (10–14); D&C 45:29.
6*a* 1 Ne. 11:27.
7*a* John 19:35 (35–37).
  b D&C 66:7.
  c John 20:31 (30–31).
9*a* John 12:46.
  TG Intelligence; Jesus Christ, Light of the World; Light of Christ.
  b TG Discernment, Spiritual.
  c D&C 84:46.
10*a* TG World.
  b TG Creation.
  c TG Jesus Christ, Creator.
  d Isa. 53:3.
11*a* 3 Ne. 9:16; D&C 6:21.
12*a* D&C 25:1.
  TG Teachable.

b GR authority, right, privilege. D&C 11:30.
  TG Jesus Christ, Power of.
c D&C 39:4 (3–6).
  TG Sons and Daughters of God.
d TG Name.
13*a* TG Holy Ghost, Baptism of.
14*a* TG Flesh and Blood; God, Manifestations of; Jesus Christ, Birth of; Jesus Christ, Condescension of.
  b TG God, Presence of.
  c Matt. 17:2 (1–9); Luke 1:2; John 19:35; 21:24; Acts 5:32; 26:16; 2 Pet. 1:16 (16–19); D&C 93:11.
  d Heb. 1:3. TG Glory; Jesus Christ, Glory of.
  e TG Jesus Christ, Divine Sonship.

f D&C 76:23.
g D&C 66:12.
15*a* John 5:33.
16*a* Col. 2:10.
  b D&C 93:12.
17*a* JST John 1:17–18 (Appendix).
  b TG Law of Moses.
  c TG Grace.
  d TG Truth.
18*a* D&C 67:11; 84:22.
  b TG God, Privilege of Seeing.
  c JST John 1:19 . . . at any time, *except he hath borne record of the Son; for except it is through him no man can be saved.*
  d Luke 10:22.
19*a* Luke 3:15 (15–16).
21*a* Mal. 4:5 (5–6).
23*a* Matt. 3:3; Mark 1:3; Luke 3:4.
  b D&C 84:28.
  c D&C 65:1.

unto him, Why baptizest thou then, if thou be not that Christ, nor Elias, neither that prophet?

26 John answered them, saying, I baptize with ^awater: but there standeth one among you, whom ye know not;

27 ^aHe it is, who coming after me is preferred before me, whose ^bshoe's latchet I am not worthy to unloose.

28 These things were done in ^aBethabara beyond Jordan, where John was baptizing.

29 ¶ The next day John seeth Jesus coming unto him, and saith, Behold the ^aLamb of God, which taketh away the ^bsin of the world.

30 This is he of whom I said, After me cometh a man which is preferred before me: for he was before me.

31 And I knew him not: but that he should be made manifest to Israel, therefore am I come baptizing with water.

32 And John ^abare record, saying, I saw the ^bSpirit descending from heaven like a ^cdove, and it abode upon him.

33 ^aAnd I knew him not: but he that sent me to baptize with water, the same said unto me, Upon whom thou shalt see the Spirit descending, and remaining on him, the same is he which baptizeth with the ^bHoly Ghost.

34 And I saw, and bare ^arecord that this is the Son of God.

35 ¶ Again the next day after John stood, and two of his disciples;

36 And looking upon Jesus as he walked, he saith, Behold the ^aLamb of God!

37 And the two disciples heard him speak, and they followed Jesus.

38 Then Jesus turned, and saw them following, and saith unto them, What seek ye? They said unto him, Rabbi, (which is to say, being interpreted, Master,) where dwellest thou?

39 He saith unto them, Come and see. They came and saw where he dwelt, and abode with him that day: for it was about the tenth hour.

40 One of the two which heard John *speak*, and ^afollowed him, was Andrew, Simon Peter's brother.

41 He first findeth his own brother Simon, and saith unto him, We have found the ^aMessias, which is, being interpreted, the Christ.

42 And he brought him to Jesus. And when Jesus beheld him, he said, Thou art Simon the son of Jona: thou shalt be called ^aCephas, which is by interpretation, A stone.

43 ¶ The day following Jesus would go forth into Galilee, and findeth Philip, and saith unto him, Follow me.

44 Now Philip was of Bethsaida, the city of Andrew and Peter.

45 Philip findeth Nathanael, and saith unto him, We have found him, of whom ^aMoses in the law, and the prophets, did ^bwrite, Jesus of Nazareth, the son of Joseph.

46 And Nathanael said unto him, Can there any good thing come out of Nazareth? Philip saith unto him, Come and see.

47 Jesus saw ^aNathanael coming to him, and saith of him, Behold an Israelite indeed, in whom is no ^bguile!

48 Nathanael saith unto him, Whence knowest thou me? Jesus

26a D&C 52:10.
27a JST John 1:28 (Appendix).
  b GR sandal strap.
28a 1 Ne. 10:9.
29a TG Jesus Christ,
    Lamb of God;
    Jesus Christ, Redeemer;
    Jesus Christ, Types of, in
    Anticipation;
    Passover.
  b TG Jesus Christ,
    Atonement through;
    Redemption;
    Sin.
32a D&C 93:11.

  b TG Jesus Christ,
    Baptism of.
  c TG Holy Ghost, Dove,
    Sign of.
33a JST John 1:32 And I knew
    him; *for* he who sent
    me . . .
  b TG Holy Ghost,
    Baptism of.
34a TG Testimony.
36a TG Passover.
40a TG Apostles.
41a TG Jesus Christ, Messiah.
42a GR Stone, Pebble.
    JST John 1:42 . . . Cephas,

    which is, by interpretation, *a seer, or a stone.
    And they were fishermen.
    And they straightway left
    all, and followed Jesus.*
    Matt. 16:18;
    Luke 6:14;
    Gal. 2:9.
45a TG Jesus Christ,
    Prophecies about.
  b TG Record Keeping.
47a D&C 41:11.
  b GR deceit, fraud.
    TG Guile.

answered and said unto him, Before that Philip called thee, when thou wast under the fig tree, I saw thee.

49 Nathanael answered and saith unto him, Rabbi, thou art the ^aSon of God; thou art the ^bKing of Israel.

50 Jesus answered and said unto him, Because I said unto thee, I saw thee under the fig tree, believest thou? thou shalt see greater things than these.

51 And he saith unto him, Verily, verily, I say unto you, Hereafter ye shall see heaven open, and the angels of God ascending and descending upon the Son of man.

CHAPTER 2

Jesus turns water into wine in Cana— He attends the Passover, cleanses the temple, foretells His death and resurrection, and performs miracles.

AND the ^athird day there was a marriage in Cana of Galilee; and the mother of Jesus was there:

2 And both Jesus was called, and his disciples, to the marriage.

3 And when they wanted wine, the mother of Jesus saith unto him, They have no wine.

4 Jesus saith unto her, ^aWoman, what have I to do with thee? mine hour is not yet come.

5 His mother saith unto the servants, Whatsoever he saith unto you, do *it*.

6 And there were set there six waterpots of stone, after the manner of the ^apurifying of the Jews, containing two or three firkins apiece.

7 Jesus saith unto them, Fill the waterpots with water. And they filled them up to the brim.

8 And he saith unto them, Draw out now, and bear unto the governor of the feast. And they bare *it*.

9 When the ruler of the feast had tasted the water that was made wine, and knew not whence it was: (but the servants which drew the water knew;) the governor of the feast called the bridegroom,

10 And saith unto him, Every man at the beginning doth set forth good wine; and when men have well drunk, then that which is worse: *but* thou hast kept the good wine until now.

11 This ^abeginning of ^bmiracles did Jesus in Cana of Galilee, and manifested forth his glory; and his disciples believed on him.

12 ¶ After this he went down to Capernaum, he, and his mother, and his ^abrethren, and his disciples: and they continued there not many days.

13 ¶ And the Jews' passover was at hand, and Jesus went up to Jerusalem,

14 And found in the temple those that sold oxen and sheep and doves, and the changers of ^amoney sitting:

15 And when he had made a ^ascourge of small cords, he drove them all out of the temple, and the sheep, and the oxen; and poured out the changers' money, and overthrew the tables;

16 And said unto them that sold doves, Take these things hence; make not my Father's house an house of merchandise.

17 And his disciples remembered that it was written, The ^azeal of thine house hath ^beaten me up.

18 ¶ Then answered the Jews and said unto him, What ^asign shewest thou unto us, seeing that thou doest these things?

19 Jesus answered and said unto them, Destroy this ^atemple, and in three days I will ^braise it up.

49a TG God, Body of, Corporeal Nature.
  b TG Jesus Christ, Messiah.
2 1a JST John 2:1 . . . third day *of the week* . . .
  4a JST John 2:4 . . . Woman, what *wilt thou have me to do* for *thee? that will I do; for* mine hour is not

yet come.
  TG Woman.
6a TG Purification.
11a John 4:54.
  b TG Miracle.
12a TG Jesus Christ, Family of.
14a Ps. 69:9.
15a GR whip.

Matt. 21:12–16.
17a TG Zeal.
  b GR consumed me.
18a TG Sign Seekers.
19a Matt. 26:61; 27:40, 63 (62–66); Mark 14:58.
  b TG Jesus Christ, Resurrection; Resurrection.

20 Then said the Jews, Forty and six years was this ªtemple in building, and wilt thou rear it up in three days?

21 But he spake of the temple of his body.

22 When therefore he was risen from the dead, his disciples remembered that he had said this unto them; and they believed the scripture, and the word which Jesus had said.

23 ¶ Now when he was in Jerusalem at the ªpassover, in the feast *day*, many believed in his ᵇname, when they saw the ᶜmiracles which he did.

24 But Jesus did not ªcommit himself unto them, because he ᵇknew all ᶜ*men*,

25 And needed not that any should testify of man: for he ªknew what was in ᵇman.

CHAPTER 3

Jesus tells Nicodemus that men must be born again—God so loved the world that He sent His Only Begotten Son to save men—John the Baptist testifies that he that believes on the Son has everlasting life.

THERE was a man of the Pharisees, named ªNicodemus, a ᵇruler of the Jews:

2 The same came to Jesus by night, and said unto him, Rabbi, we know that thou art a teacher come from God: for no man can do these ªmiracles that thou doest, except ᵇGod be with him.

3 Jesus answered and said unto him, Verily, verily, I say unto thee, Except a man be ªborn ᵇagain, he cannot ᶜsee the kingdom of God.

4 Nicodemus saith unto him, How can a man be born when he is old? can he enter the second time into his mother's womb, and be born?

5 Jesus answered, Verily, verily, I say unto thee, Except a man be ªborn of ᵇwater and *of* the ᶜSpirit, he cannot ᵈenter into the kingdom of God.

6 That which is born of the flesh is flesh; and that which is born of the Spirit is spirit.

7 Marvel not that I said unto thee, Ye must be ªborn again.

8 The ªwind bloweth where it listeth, and thou hearest the sound thereof, but canst not tell whence it cometh, and whither it goeth: so is every one that is born of the ᵇSpirit.

9 Nicodemus answered and said unto him, How can these things be?

10 Jesus answered and said unto him, Art thou a master of Israel, and knowest not these things?

11 ªVerily, verily, I say unto thee, We speak that we do know, and ᵇtestify that we have seen; and ye receive not our witness.

12 If I have told you earthly things, and ye ªbelieve not, how shall ye believe, if I tell you *of* heavenly things?

13 And no man hath ªascended up to heaven, but he that ᵇcame down from heaven, *even* the ᶜSon of man which is in heaven.

14 ¶ And as Moses lifted up the

20a TG Temple.
23a TG Passover.
    b TG Name.
    c TG Miracle;
       Signs.
24a GR entrust.
    b Luke 6:8.
    c JST John 2:24 . . . *things,*
25a Matt. 12:25;
       Luke 11:17;
       John 6:61.
    b D&C 62:1.
3 1a John 7:50; 19:39.
    b John 7:26.
2a TG Miracle.
    b Ex. 8:19;

Luke 11:20;
   Acts 2:22; 10:38.
3a TG Man, New,
       Spiritually Reborn.
    b GR from above, anew.
    c D&C 56:18.
5a TG Holy Ghost,
       Baptism of.
    b TG Baptism;
       Baptism, Essential.
    c TG Holy Ghost,
       Mission of.
    d 1 Cor. 6:9; 15:50.
7a TG Man, Natural, Not
       Spiritually Reborn.
8a GR wind, spirit.

    b Eccl. 11:5.
11a The Greek construction
       suggests that verses
       11–21 contain a direct
       quotation. This testimony of Jesus was
       given to a member of
       the Sanhedrin.
    b TG Testimony.
12a TG Faith.
13a TG Jesus Christ,
       Ascension of.
    b John 6:62.
       TG Jesus Christ,
       Condescension of.
    c Moses 6:57.

*a*serpent in the wilderness, even so must the *b*Son of man be lifted up:

15 That whosoever believeth in him should not perish, but have eternal life.

16 ¶ For *a*God so *b*loved the *c*world, that he *d*gave his *e*only begotten *f*Son, that whosoever *g*believeth in him should not perish, but have *h*everlasting *i*life.

17 For God *a*sent not his Son into the world to *b*condemn the world; but that the world through him might be *c*saved.

18 ¶ He that believeth on him is not condemned: but he that *a*believeth not is condemned already, because he hath not believed in the *b*name of the only begotten *c*Son of God.

19 And this is the condemnation, that *a*light is come into the world, and men loved *b*darkness rather than light, because their *c*deeds were evil.

20 For every one that doeth *a*evil *b*hateth the light, neither cometh to the light, lest his deeds should be reproved.

21 But he that *a*doeth *b*truth cometh to the *c*light, that his deeds may be made manifest, that they are wrought in God.

22 ¶ After these things came Jesus and his disciples into the land of Judæa; and there he tarried with them, and *a*baptized.

23 ¶ And John also was baptizing in Ænon near to Salim, because there was much *a*water there: and they came, and were *b*baptized.

24 For John was not yet cast into prison.

25 ¶ Then there arose a question between *some* of John's disciples and the Jews about purifying.

26 And they came unto John, and said unto him, Rabbi, he that was with thee beyond Jordan, to whom thou barest witness, behold, the same baptizeth, *a*and all *men* come to him.

27 John answered and said, A man can *a*receive nothing, except it be given him from heaven.

28 Ye yourselves bear me witness, that I said, I am not the Christ, but that I am sent before him.

29 He that hath the bride is the bridegroom: but the friend of the bridegroom, which standeth and heareth him, rejoiceth greatly because of the bridegroom's voice: this my joy therefore is fulfilled.

30 He must increase, but I *must* decrease.

31 He that cometh from *a*above is above all: he that is of the earth is earthly, and speaketh of the earth: he that cometh from heaven is above all.

32 And what he hath seen and heard, that he *a*testifieth; and no man receiveth his testimony.

33 He that hath received his

14*a* 2 Ne. 25:20.
   TG Jesus Christ,
   Prophecies about;
   Jesus Christ, Types
   of, in Anticipation;
   Symbolism.
  b TG Jesus Christ, Son of
   Man.
16*a* TG God the Father,
   Elohim.
  b TG God, Love of;
   Love;
   Mercy;
   Worth of Souls.
  c TG World.
  d TG God, Gifts of;
   Jesus Christ, Redeemer.
  e Gen. 22:2 (1–14);
   Jacob 4:5.
  f TG Jesus Christ, Divine

Sonship.
  g TG Faith.
  h D&C 45:5.
  i 1 Jn. 4:9.
17*a* D&C 49:5; 132:24 (24, 59).
   TG Jesus Christ, Messenger of the Covenant.
  b Luke 9:56 (54–56).
  c TG Jesus Christ,
   Atonement through.
18*a* TG Unbelief.
  b TG Name.
  c JST John 3:18 . . . Son of God, *which before was preached by the mouth of the holy prophets; for they testified of me.*
19*a* TG Light [noun];
   Light of Christ.
  b TG Darkness, Spiritual;

Secret Combinations.
  c D&C 10:21; 29:45.
20*a* TG Evil.
  b TG Hate.
21*a* TG Good Works.
  b TG Truth.
  c TG Discernment,
   Spiritual.
22*a* John 4:2 (1–2);
   JST John 4:1–4
   (Appendix).
23*a* TG Baptism, Immersion.
  b TG Baptism.
26*a* JST John 3:27 . . . and *he receiveth of* all *people who* come unto him.
27*a* James 1:17 (17–18).
31*a* John 8:23.
32*a* TG Testimony.

testimony hath *set to his *seal that God is true.

34 For he whom God hath sent *speaketh the words of God: *for God giveth not the Spirit by measure *unto him*.

35 The Father loveth the *Son, and hath *given all *things into his hand.

36 *He that believeth on the Son hath *everlasting life: and he that *believeth not the Son shall not see life; but the *wrath of God abideth on him.

CHAPTER 4

Jesus teaches a woman of Samaria— All must worship the Father in spirit and truth—Those who harvest souls gain eternal life—Many Samaritans believe—Jesus heals a nobleman's son.

*WHEN therefore the Lord knew how the Pharisees had heard that Jesus made and baptized more disciples than John,

2 (Though Jesus himself *baptized not, but his disciples,)

3 He left Judæa, and departed again into Galilee.

4 And he must needs go through Samaria.

5 Then cometh he to a city of Samaria, which is called Sychar, near to the parcel of ground that Jacob gave to his son *Joseph.

6 Now Jacob's well was there. Jesus therefore, being wearied with *his* journey, sat thus on the well: *and it was about the sixth hour.

7 There cometh a woman of Samaria to draw water: Jesus saith unto her, Give me to drink.

8 (For his disciples were gone away unto the city to buy meat.)

9 Then saith the woman of Samaria unto him, How is it that thou, being a Jew, askest drink of me, which am a woman of Samaria? for the Jews have no dealings with the *Samaritans.

10 Jesus answered and said unto her, If thou knewest the *gift of God, and who it is that saith to thee, Give me to drink; thou wouldest have asked of him, and he would have given thee *living water.

11 The woman saith unto him, Sir, thou hast nothing to draw with, and the well is deep: from whence then hast thou that living water?

12 Art thou greater than our father Jacob, which gave us the well, and drank thereof himself, and his children, and his cattle?

13 Jesus answered and said unto her, Whosoever drinketh of this water shall thirst again:

14 But whosoever drinketh of the water that I shall give him shall never *thirst; but the water that I shall give him shall be in him a well of water *springing up into *everlasting life.

15 The woman saith unto him, Sir, give me this water, that I thirst not, neither come hither to draw.

16 Jesus saith unto her, Go, call thy husband, and come hither.

17 The woman answered and said, I have no husband. Jesus said unto her, Thou hast well said, I have no husband:

18 For thou hast had five husbands; and he whom thou now hast

---

33a OR declared that, certified that.
  b TG Seal.
34a Isa. 61:1.
     TG Jesus Christ, Teaching Mode of.
  b JST John 3:34 . . . for God giveth *him* not the Spirit by measure, *for he dwelleth in him, even the fullness.*
35a TG Jesus Christ, Divine Sonship.
  b TG Jesus Christ, Authority of.

  c TG Jesus Christ, Power of.
36a JST John 3:36 *And he who believeth on the Son hath everlasting life; and shall receive of his fullness. But he who believeth not the Son, shall not receive of his fullness; for the wrath of God is upon him.*
  b TG Eternal Life.
  c GR disbelieves, disobeys, is uncompliant to.
  d TG God, Indignation of.

4 1a JST John 4:1–4 (Appendix).
  2a John 3:22 (22, 26).
  5a TG Israel, Joseph, People of.
  9a 2 Kgs. 17:29; Luke 10:33.
 10a TG God, Gifts of.
  b TG Living Water.
 14a Ps. 42:2 (1–3); 143:6 (5–12); Isa. 55:1 (1–3); John 6:35; 7:37 (37–39).
  b D&C 63:23.
  c TG Immortality.

is not thy husband: in that saidst thou truly.

19 The woman saith unto him, Sir, I perceive that thou art a ªprophet.

20 Our fathers worshipped in ªthis mountain; and ye say, that in Jerusalem is the place where men ought to worship.

21 Jesus saith unto her, Woman, believe me, the hour cometh, when ye shall neither in this mountain, nor yet at Jerusalem, worship the Father.

22 Ye worship ye ªknow not what: we know what we worship: for salvation is of the Jews.

23 But the hour cometh, and now is, when the true worshippers shall ªworship the Father in spirit and in ᵇtruth: for the Father seeketh such to worship him.

24 ªGod is a ᵇSpirit: and they that worship him must worship him in spirit and in ᶜtruth.

25 The woman saith unto him, I know that ªMessias cometh, which is called Christ: when he is come, he will ᵇtell us all things.

26 Jesus saith unto her, ªI that speak unto thee am he.

27 ¶ And upon this came his disciples, and marvelled that he talked with the woman: yet no man said, What seekest thou? or, Why talkest thou with her?

28 The woman then left her waterpot, and went her way into the city, and saith to the men,

29 Come, see a man, which told me all things that ever I did: is not this the Christ?

30 Then they went out of the city, and came unto him.

31 ¶ In the mean while his disciples prayed him, saying, Master, eat.

32 But he said unto them, I have meat to eat that ye know not of.

33 Therefore said the disciples one to another, Hath any man brought him *ought* to eat?

34 Jesus saith unto them, My meat is to do the ªwill of him that sent me, and to finish his ᵇwork.

35 Say not ye, There are yet four months, and *then* cometh harvest? behold, I say unto you, Lift up your eyes, and look on the ªfields; for they are white already to ᵇharvest.

36 And he that reapeth receiveth ªwages, and gathereth fruit unto life eternal: that both he that soweth and he that reapeth may ᵇrejoice together.

37 And herein is that saying true, One ªsoweth, and another reapeth.

38 I sent you to ªreap that whereon ye bestowed no labour: ᵇother men laboured, and ye are entered into their labours.

39 ¶ And many of the Samaritans of that city believed on him for the saying of the woman, which testified, He told me all that ever I did.

40 So when the Samaritans were come unto him, they besought him that he would tarry with them: and he abode there two days.

41 And many more believed because of his own word;

42 And said unto the woman, Now we believe, not because of thy saying: for we have heard *him* ourselves, and know that this is indeed the ªChrist, the ᵇSaviour of the world.

19ª 1 Ne. 22:20.
20ª Deut. 11:29.
22ª D&C 93:19 (1–20).
　 TG Ignorance.
23ª TG Worship.
　 b Ps. 145:18 (1–21).
24ª JST John 4:26 *For unto such hath* God *promised his* Spirit. And they *who* worship him, must worship in spirit and in truth.
　 b D&C 93:33; 130:22.
　 c TG Truth.

25ª TG Jesus Christ, Messiah.
　 b Deut. 18:18.
26ª The term I AM used here in the Greek is identical with the Septuagint usage in Ex. 3:14 which identifies Jehovah. John 8:58.
　 TG Jesus Christ, Jehovah.
34ª Luke 2:49; John 6:38–39; 8:29; see JST Matt. 27:54 . . . *Father, it is finished, thy will is done . . .*

　 TG God, Will of.
　 b John 9:4 (1–4).
35ª Alma 26:5; D&C 4:4; 33:3.
　 b TG Missionary Work.
36ª TG Wages.
　 b D&C 18:16 (13–16); 50:22 (17–22).
37ª 1 Cor. 3:6 (5–8).
38ª TG Harvest.
　 b JST John 4:40 . . . *the prophets have* labored . . .
42ª TG Jesus Christ, Messiah.
　 b D&C 66:1.

43 ¶ Now after two days he departed thence, and went into Galilee.

44 For Jesus himself testified, that a prophet hath no honour in his own country.

45 Then when he was come into Galilee, the Galilæans received him, having seen all the things that he did at Jerusalem at the feast: for they also went unto the feast.

46 So Jesus came again into Cana of Galilee, where he made the water wine. And there was a certain nobleman, whose son was sick at ªCapernaum.

47 When he heard that Jesus was come out of Judæa into Galilee, he went unto him, and besought him that he would come down, and heal his son: for he was at the point of death.

48 Then said Jesus unto him, Except ye see ªsigns and wonders, ye will not believe.

49 The nobleman saith unto him, Sir, come down ere my child die.

50 Jesus saith unto him, Go thy way; thy son ªliveth. And the man believed the word that Jesus had spoken unto him, and he went his way.

51 And as he was now going down, his servants met him, and told him, saying, Thy son liveth.

52 Then inquired he of them the hour when he began to amend. And they said unto him, Yesterday at the seventh hour the fever left him.

53 So the father knew that it was at the same hour, in the which Jesus said unto him, Thy son liveth: and ªhimself believed, and his whole house.

54 This is again the ªsecond miracle that Jesus did, when he was come out of Judæa into Galilee.

CHAPTER 5

Jesus heals an invalid on the Sabbath—He explains why men must honor the Son—Jesus promises to take the gospel to the dead—Man is resurrected, judged, and assigned his glory by the Son—Jesus obeys the divine law of witnesses.

AFTER this there was ªa feast of the Jews; and Jesus went up to Jerusalem.

2 Now there is at Jerusalem by the sheep *market* a pool, which is called in the Hebrew tongue Bethesda, having five porches.

3 In these lay a great multitude of impotent folk, of blind, halt, withered, waiting for the moving of the water.

4 For an angel went down at a certain season into the pool, and troubled the water: whosoever then first after the troubling of the water stepped in was made whole of whatsoever disease he had.

5 And a certain man was there, which had an infirmity thirty and eight years.

6 When Jesus saw him lie, and knew that he had been now a long time *in that case,* he saith unto him, Wilt thou be made whole?

7 The impotent man answered him, Sir, I have no man, when the water is troubled, to put me into the pool: but while I am coming, another steppeth down before me.

8 Jesus saith unto him, ªRise, take up thy bed, and walk.

9 And immediately the man was made ªwhole, and took up his bed, and walked: and on the same day was the ᵇsabbath.

10 ¶ The Jews therefore said unto him that was cured, It is the ªsabbath day: it is not lawful for thee to carry *thy* bed.

11 He answered them, He that made me whole, the same said unto me, Take up thy bed, and walk.

46a Luke 4:23 (23–24).
48a TG Sign Seekers.
50a TG Heal.
53a GR he himself.
54a John 2:11.
5 1a The *Koine* Greek manuscripts of the

Gospels (Byzantine) read "the feast," implicitly the Passover. See also Matt. 26:5. Some earlier manuscripts do not make this

identification.
  TG Passover.
8a John 7:23.
9a TG Heal.
  b Matt. 12:1 (1–14).
10a Luke 6:2.
  TG Sabbath.

12 Then asked they him, What man is that which said unto thee, Take up thy bed, and walk?

13 And he that was healed ^awist not who it was: for Jesus had conveyed himself away, a multitude being in *that* place.

14 Afterward Jesus findeth him in the temple, and said unto him, Behold, thou art made whole: sin no more, lest a worse thing come unto thee.

15 The man departed, and told the Jews that it was Jesus, which had made him whole.

16 And therefore did the Jews ^apersecute Jesus, and ^bsought to slay him, because he had done these things on the sabbath day.

17 ¶ But Jesus answered them, My Father ^aworketh hitherto, and I ^bwork.

18 Therefore the Jews sought the more to kill him, because he not only had broken the sabbath, but said also that God was his ^aFather, making himself ^bequal with God.

19 Then answered Jesus and said unto them, Verily, verily, I say unto you, The Son can do nothing of himself, but what he ^aseeth the ^bFather do: for what things soever he doeth, these also doeth the Son likewise.

20 For the Father loveth the Son, and sheweth him all things that himself doeth: and he will shew him greater works than these, that ye may marvel.

21 For as the Father ^araiseth up the dead, and ^bquickeneth *them*; even so the Son quickeneth whom he will.

22 For the Father judgeth no man, but hath ^acommitted all ^bjudgment unto the Son:

23 That all *men* should ^ahonour the Son, even as they honour the Father. He that ^bhonoureth not the Son honoureth not the Father which hath sent him.

24 Verily, verily, I say unto you, He that heareth my word, and ^abelieveth on him that sent me, hath everlasting ^blife, and shall not come into ^ccondemnation; but is passed from ^ddeath unto ^elife.

25 Verily, verily, I say unto you, The hour is coming, and now is, when the ^adead shall ^bhear the voice of the Son of God: and they that hear shall ^clive.

26 For as the Father hath life in himself; so hath he given to the ^aSon to have ^blife in himself;

27 And hath given him ^aauthority to execute ^bjudgment also, because he is the ^cSon of man.

28 Marvel not at this: for the hour is coming, in the which all that are in the ^agraves shall ^bhear his voice,

29 And shall ^acome forth; ^bthey that have done good, unto the ^cresurrection of life; and they that have done ^devil, unto the resurrection of ^edamnation.

30 I can of mine own self do

13*a* GR knew.
16*a* TG Persecution.
  b John 7:1.
17*a* TG God, Works of.
  b John 9:4.
18*a* TG God, Body of,
    Corporeal Nature.
  b John 10:33; 19:7;
    D&C 88:107.
    TG Jesus Christ,
    Relationships with
    the Father.
19*a* John 8:28.
  b TG Godhead.
21*a* TG Resurrection.
  b GR causes to become
    alive.
    1 Cor. 15:45.
    TG God, Power of.
22*a* TG Jesus Christ,

Authority of.
  b TG Judgment;
    Judgment, the Last.
23*a* TG Honor; Respect.
  b Luke 10:16.
24*a* TG Faith.
  b John 20:31.
  c D&C 20:15.
  d John 8:51; 11:26;
    D&C 63:49.
  e 1 Jn. 3:14.
25*a* TG Death; Genealogy and
    Temple Work;
    Salvation for the Dead;
    Spirits, Disembodied.
  b Isa. 24:22; 61:1.
  c TG Immortality.
26*a* TG Jesus Christ, Divine
    Sonship.
  b John 6:57.

27*a* TG Authority;
    Delegation of
    Responsibility;
    Jesus Christ,
    Authority of.
  b TG Jesus Christ, Judge.
  c TG Jesus Christ,
    Son of Man.
28*a* Dan. 12:2.
  b D&C 76:16 (16–17).
29*a* D&C 29:26.
  b JST John 5:29 . . . they *who*
    have done good, *in the*
    resurrection of *the just*;
    and they *who* have done
    evil, *in the* resurrection of
    the unjust.
  c TG Resurrection.
  d TG Sin.
  e TG Damnation; Hell.

nothing: as I hear, I judge: and my judgment is *just; because I seek not mine own *will, but the *will of the Father which hath sent me.

31 If I bear witness of myself, my witness is not true.

32 ¶ There is another that beareth *witness of me; and I know that the *witness which he witnesseth of me is true.

33 Ye sent unto *John, and he bare *witness unto the truth.

34 *But I receive not testimony from man: but these things I say, that ye might be saved.

35 He was a burning and a shining *light: and ye were willing for a season to rejoice in his *light.

36 ¶ *But I have *greater witness than *that* of John: for the *works which the Father hath given me to finish, the same *works that I do, bear witness of me, that the Father hath *sent me.

37 And the Father himself, which hath sent me, hath borne *witness of me. Ye have neither heard his voice at any time, nor *seen his shape.

38 And ye have not his word abiding in you: for whom he hath sent, him ye *believe not.

39 ¶ *Search the scriptures; for in them ye think ye have eternal life: and they are they which *testify of me.

40 And ye will not come to me, that ye might have *life.

41 I receive not *honour from men.

42 But I know you, that ye have not the *love of God in you.

43 I am come in my *Father's *name, and ye *receive me not: if another shall come in his own name, him ye will receive.

44 How can ye believe, which receive *honour one of another, and seek not the *honour that *cometh* from God only?

45 Do not think that I will accuse you to the Father: there is *one* that accuseth you, *even* Moses, in whom ye trust.

46 For had ye believed *Moses, ye would have believed me: for he *wrote of me.

47 But if ye believe not his *writings, how shall ye believe my words?

CHAPTER 6

Jesus feeds the five thousand—He walks on the sea—He is the living manna sent from God—Salvation is gained by eating living bread—Jesus explains how men eat His flesh and drink His blood—Peter testifies that Jesus is the Messiah.

AFTER these things Jesus went over the sea of Galilee, which is *the sea of Tiberias.

2 And a great multitude followed him, because they saw his miracles which he did on them that were diseased.

3 And Jesus went up into a

30a TG God, Justice of.
  b 2 Ne. 31:7 (7–10).
    TG Agency.
  c TG God, Will of.
32a TG Holy Ghost, Source of Testimony.
  b TG Witness.
33a D&C 35:4; 84:27 (27–28).
  b John 1:15 (7, 15, 19).
34a JST John 5:35 *And he received* not *his testimony of man, but of God, and ye yourselves say that he is a prophet, therefore ye ought to receive his testimony. These things I say . . .*
35a Matt. 11:11 (7–15).
  b TG Light [noun].

36a JST John 5:37 *But I have a greater witness than the testimony* of John . . .
  b GR the greater witness than John's.
  c TG God, Works of.
  d Matt. 11:4; John 10:25.
  e TG Jesus Christ, Messenger of the Covenant.
37a TG Witness of the Father.
  b TG God, Privilege of Seeing.
38a TG Unbelief.
39a TG Education; Learn; Scriptures, Study of; Study.

  b TG Scriptures, Value of; Testimony.
40a D&C 66:2.
41a John 7:18.
    TG Honor.
42a TG God, Love of; Love.
43a TG Jesus Christ, Authority of.
  b TG Authority; Name.
  c D&C 132:25.
44a Luke 18:9; 1 Thes. 2:6; D&C 76:61.
  b TG God, the Standard of Righteousness.
46a Luke 24:27.
  b TG Jesus Christ, Prophecies about.
47a TG Scriptures, Study of.

mountain, and there he sat with his disciples.

4 And the *a*passover, a feast of the Jews, was nigh.

5 ¶ When Jesus then lifted up *his* eyes, and saw a great company come unto him, he saith unto Philip, Whence shall we buy bread, that these may eat?

6 And this he said to prove him: for he himself knew what he would do.

7 Philip answered him, Two hundred pennyworth of bread is not sufficient for them, that every one of them may take a little.

8 One of his disciples, Andrew, Simon Peter's brother, saith unto him,

9 There is a lad here, which hath five barley loaves, and two small fishes: but what are they among so many?

10 And Jesus said, Make the men sit down. Now there was much grass in the place. So the men sat down, in number about *a*five thousand.

11 And Jesus took the loaves; and when he had given *a*thanks, he distributed to the disciples, and the disciples to them that were set down; and likewise of the fishes as much as they would.

12 When they were filled, he said unto his disciples, Gather up the fragments that remain, that nothing be *a*lost.

13 Therefore they gathered *them* together, and filled twelve baskets with the fragments of the five barley loaves, which remained over and above unto them that had eaten.

14 Then those men, when they had seen the *a*miracle that Jesus did, said, This is of a truth that *b*prophet that should come into the world.

15 ¶ When Jesus therefore perceived that they would come and take him by force, to make him a *a*king, he departed again into a mountain himself alone.

16 And when even was *now* come, his disciples went down unto the sea,

17 And entered into a ship, and went over the sea toward Capernaum. And it was now dark, and Jesus was not come to them.

18 And the sea arose by reason of a great wind that blew.

19 So when they had rowed about five and twenty or thirty furlongs, they see Jesus walking on the sea, and drawing nigh unto the ship: and they were *a*afraid.

20 But he saith unto them, It is I; be not afraid.

21 Then they willingly received him into the ship: and immediately the ship was at the land whither they went.

22 ¶ The day following, when the people which stood on the other side of the sea saw that there was none other boat there, save that one whereinto his disciples were entered, and that Jesus went not with his disciples into the boat, but *that* his disciples were gone away alone;

23 (Howbeit there came other boats from Tiberias nigh unto the place where they did eat bread, after that the Lord had given thanks:)

24 When the people therefore saw that Jesus was not there, neither his disciples, they also took shipping, and came to Capernaum, seeking for Jesus.

25 And when they had found him on the other side of the sea, they said unto him, Rabbi, when camest thou hither?

26 Jesus answered them and said, Verily, verily, I say unto you, Ye seek me, *a*not because ye saw the miracles, but because ye did eat of the loaves, and were filled.

27 *a*Labour not for the meat which

---

6 4*a* TG Passover.
10*a* Matt. 14:21 (13–21);
       Mark 6:44 (32–44);
       Luke 9:14 (10–17).
11*a* D&C 46:32; 59:7.
12*a* TG Waste.
14*a* 3 Ne. 8:1; 20:7 (1–9);

Morm. 9:18 (18–19).
  b TG Jesus Christ,
       Prophecies about.
15*a* John 18:36 (33, 36–37).
19*a* D&C 67:3.
26*a* JST John 6:26 . . . not
       because ye *desire to*

*keep my sayings, neither
because ye saw the
miracles . . .*
27*a* TG Labor;
       Objectives.

perisheth, but for that meat which endureth unto everlasting life, which the *b*Son of man shall give unto you: for him hath God the Father *c*sealed.

28 Then said they unto him, What shall we do, that we might work the works of God?

29 Jesus answered and said unto them, This is the work of God, that ye *a*believe on him whom he hath sent.

30 They said therefore unto him, What *a*sign shewest thou then, that we may see, and believe thee? what dost thou work?

31 Our fathers did eat manna in the desert; as it is written, He gave them *a*bread from heaven to eat.

32 Then Jesus said unto them, Verily, verily, I say unto you, Moses gave you not that bread from heaven; but my Father giveth you the true bread from heaven.

33 For the bread of God is he which cometh down from heaven, and giveth life unto the world.

34 Then said they unto him, Lord, evermore give us this bread.

35 And Jesus said unto them, I am the *a*bread of life: he that cometh to me shall never hunger; and he that believeth on me shall never *b*thirst.

36 But I said unto you, That ye also have seen me, and believe not.

37 All that the Father *a*giveth me shall come to me; and him that cometh to me I will in no wise *b*cast out.

38 For I *a*came down from heaven, not to do mine own *b*will, but the *c*will of him that sent me.

39 And this is the *a*Father's *b*will which hath sent me, that of all which he hath given me I should lose *c*nothing, but should *d*raise it up again at the last day.

40 And this is the will of him that sent me, that every one which seeth the Son, and *a*believeth on him, may have *b*everlasting life: and I will raise him up *c*at the last day.

41 The Jews then murmured at him, because he said, I am the bread which came down from heaven.

42 And they said, Is not this Jesus, the son of *a*Joseph, whose father and mother we know? how is it then that he saith, I came down from heaven?

43 Jesus therefore answered and said unto them, *a*Murmur not among yourselves.

44 *a*No man can *b*come to me, except the Father which hath sent me *c*draw him: and I will raise him up at the last day.

45 It is written in the prophets, And they shall be all *a*taught of God. Every man therefore that hath heard, and hath learned of the *b*Father, cometh unto me.

46 Not that any man hath seen the Father, save he which is of God, he hath *a*seen the Father.

47 Verily, verily, I say unto you, He that *a*believeth on me hath *b*everlasting life.

48 I am that bread of life.

49 Your fathers did eat *a*manna in the wilderness, and are dead.

50 This is the bread which cometh

27b TG Jesus Christ, Son of Man.
  c TG Sealing.
29a TG Faith.
30a Matt. 12:38; Jacob 7:13 (13–21); Alma 30:43 (43–60); D&C 46:9 (8–9).
31a Ps. 78:24.
35a TG Bread of Life.
  b John 4:14; 7:37 (37–39).
37a 3 Ne. 15:24; D&C 27:14; 50:41 (41–42); 84:63.
  b John 17:2.
38a TG Jesus Christ, Condescension of.

  b TG Jesus Christ, Mission of.
  c TG God, Will of.
39a Luke 2:49.
  b 3 Ne. 27:13 (13–16).
  c John 17:12; 18:9.
  d 3 Ne. 15:1; D&C 5:35.
40a TG Faith.
  b TG Eternal Life.
  c JST John 6:40 . . . in the resurrection of the just at the last day.
42a Luke 4:22.
43a TG Murmuring.
44a JST John 6:44 (Appendix).

  b Isa. 55:3.
  c 1 Cor. 12:3; 1 Pet. 1:2; 3 Ne. 27:14; D&C 29:7.
45a 1 Thes. 4:9; 1 Jn. 2:27 (20, 27).
  b TG Witness of the Father.
46a TG God, Manifestations of; God, Privilege of Seeing; Revelation.
47a TG Faith.
  b TG Eternal Life; Exaltation.
49a 1 Ne. 17:28; Mosiah 7:19.

down from heaven, that a man may eat thereof, and not die.

51 I am the living ªbread which came down from heaven: if any man eat of this bread, he shall live for ever: and the ᵇbread that I will give is my ᶜflesh, which I will ᵈgive for the ᵉlife of the world.

52 The Jews therefore strove among themselves, saying, How can this man give us *his* flesh to eat?

53 Then Jesus said unto them, Verily, verily, I say unto you, Except ye ªeat the flesh of the ᵇSon of man, and drink his blood, ye have no life in you.

54 Whoso eateth my ªflesh, and drinketh my ᵇblood, hath eternal life; ᶜand I will ᵈraise him up at the last day.

55 For my flesh is meat indeed, and my blood is drink indeed.

56 He that eateth my flesh, and drinketh my blood, ªdwelleth in me, and I in him.

57 As the living Father hath ªsent me, and I live by the Father: so he that eateth me, even he shall ᵇlive by me.

58 This is that bread which came down from heaven: not as your fathers did eat manna, and are dead: he that eateth of this bread shall live for ever.

59 These things said he in the synagogue, as he taught in Capernaum.

60 Many therefore of his disciples, when they had heard *this*, said, This is an hard saying; who can hear it?

61 When Jesus ªknew in himself that his disciples murmured at it,

he said unto them, Doth this ᵇoffend you?

62 *What* and if ye shall see the ªSon of man ᵇascend up where he was before?

63 It is the ªspirit that quickeneth; the flesh profiteth nothing: the words that I speak unto you, *they* are spirit, and *they* are life.

64 But there are some of you that believe not. For Jesus knew from the beginning who they were that believed not, and who should ªbetray him.

65 And he said, Therefore said I unto you, that no man can come unto me, ªexcept it were given unto him of my Father.

66 ¶ From that *time* many of his ªdisciples went back, and ᵇwalked no more with him.

67 Then said Jesus unto the twelve, Will ye also go away?

68 Then Simon Peter answered him, Lord, to whom shall we go? thou hast the ªwords of eternal life.

69 And ªwe believe and are sure that thou art that Christ, the ᵇSon of the living God.

70 Jesus answered them, Have not I ªchosen you twelve, and one of you is a devil?

71 He spake of Judas Iscariot *the son* of Simon: for he it was that should betray him, being one of the twelve.

CHAPTER 7

Jesus' kinsmen do not believe—He teaches His Father's doctrine and proclaims His divine sonship—Truth may be known through obedience—

51*a* TG Jesus Christ, Types of, in Anticipation.
　b TG Bread of Life;
　　Jesus Christ, Types of, in Memory.
　c Heb. 10:10.
　d TG God, Gifts of.
　e TG Jesus Christ, Atonement through.
53*a* Mark 14:22;
　　Luke 22:19.
　b TG Jesus Christ, Son of Man.
54*a* TG Sacrament.
　b TG Blood, Symbolism of.
　c JST John 6:54 . . . and I

will raise him up *in the resurrection of the just* at the last day.
　d TG Resurrection.
56*a* 1 Jn. 3:24.
57*a* TG Jesus Christ, Messenger of the Covenant.
　b John 5:26.
61*a* John 2:25.
　b TG Offense.
62*a* TG Jesus Christ, Son of Man.
　b John 3:13.
　　TG Jesus Christ, Ascension of.
63*a* 2 Cor. 3:6.

64*a* John 13:11.
65*a* JST John 6:65 . . . except *he doeth the will of my Father who hath sent me.*
66*a* TG Apostasy of Individuals.
　b TG Apostasy of the Early Christian Church.
68*a* John 17:8;
　　Acts 5:20;
　　Moses 6:59.
69*a* GR we have had faith and have known that.
　b TG God, Body of, Corporeal Nature.
70*a* 1 Ne. 12:7 (6–7).

Jesus offers living water to all people—
The people have various opinions con-
cerning Him.

AFTER these things Jesus walked in Galilee: for he would not walk in Jewry, because the Jews ^asought to ^bkill him.

2 Now the Jews' ^afeast of tabernacles was at hand.

3 His ^abrethren therefore said unto him, Depart hence, and go into Judæa, that thy disciples also may see the works that thou doest.

4 For *there is* no man *that* doeth any thing in secret, and he himself seeketh to be known openly. If thou do these things, shew thyself to the world.

5 For neither did his brethren believe in him.

6 Then Jesus said unto them, My ^atime is not yet come: but your time is alway ready.

7 The world cannot hate you; but me it ^ahateth, because I testify of it, that the works thereof are ^bevil.

8 Go ye up unto this feast: I go not up yet unto this feast; for my time is not yet full come.

9 When he had said these words unto them, he abode *still* in Galilee.

10 ¶ But when his brethren were gone up, then went he also up unto the feast, not openly, but as it were in secret.

11 Then the Jews sought him at the feast, and said, Where is he?

12 And there was much murmuring among the people concerning him: for some said, He is a good man: others said, Nay; but he deceiveth the people.

13 Howbeit no man spake openly of him for ^afear of the Jews.

14 ¶ Now about the midst of the feast Jesus went up into the temple, and taught.

15 And the Jews ^amarvelled, saying, How knoweth this man letters, having never learned?

16 Jesus answered them, and said, My ^adoctrine is not mine, but his that ^bsent me.

17 If any man will ^ado his ^bwill, he shall ^cknow of the doctrine, whether it be of God, or *whether* I speak of myself.

18 He that speaketh of himself seeketh his own ^aglory: but he that seeketh his ^bglory that sent him, the same is true, and no unrighteousness is in him.

19 Did not Moses give you the law, and *yet* none of you keepeth the law? Why go ye about to kill me?

20 The people answered and said, Thou hast a devil: who goeth about to kill thee?

21 Jesus answered and said unto them, I have done one work, and ye all marvel.

22 Moses therefore gave unto you ^acircumcision; (not because it is of Moses, but of the fathers;) and ye on the sabbath day circumcise a man.

23 If a man on the ^asabbath day receive circumcision, that the law of Moses should not be broken; are ye angry at me, because I have made a man every whit ^bwhole on the sabbath day?

24 ^aJudge not according to ^bthe ^cappearance, but judge righteous judgment.

25 Then said some of them of Jerusalem, Is not this he, whom they seek to kill?

26 But, lo, he speaketh boldly, and

---

7 1a John 5:16 (16, 18).
  b John 11:53 (53–54).
  2a Lev. 23:34 (34–43).
  3a Matt. 12:46; 1 Cor. 9:5.
  6a Matt. 26:18.
  7a 1 Ne. 16:2 (1–3).
  b TG Evil.
  13a John 19:38.
  15a Luke 2:46 (46–47).
  16a Matt. 7:28; John 8:28;
    2 Ne. 31:21.

  TG Gospel; Jesus Christ,
    Teaching Mode of.
  b TG Jesus Christ,
    Authority of;
    Jesus Christ, Messenger
    of the Covenant.
  17a TG Good Works;
    Obedience.
  b TG God, Will of.
  c TG Discernment,
    Spiritual; Testimony;

    Truth.
  18a John 5:41 (41–43).
  b John 8:50; D&C 88:67;
    Moses 4:2 (1–3).
  22a TG Circumcision.
  23a TG Sabbath.
  b John 5:8 (8–9).
  24a TG Judgment.
  b JST John 7:24 . . . *your*
    traditions, but judge . . .
  c Isa. 11:3.

they say nothing unto him. Do the ^arulers know indeed that this is the very Christ?

27 Howbeit we know this man whence he is: but when Christ cometh, no man knoweth whence he is.

28 Then cried Jesus in the temple as he taught, saying, Ye both know me, and ye know whence I am: and I am not come of myself, but he that sent me is ^atrue, whom ye know not.

29 But I know him: for I am from him, and he hath ^asent me.

30 Then they ^asought to take him: but no man laid hands on him, because his ^bhour was not yet come.

31 And many of the people believed on him, and said, When Christ cometh, will he do more miracles than these which this *man* hath done?

32 ¶ The Pharisees heard that the people murmured such things concerning him; and the Pharisees and the chief priests sent officers to take him.

33 Then said Jesus unto them, Yet a little while am I with you, and *then* I go unto him that sent me.

34 Ye shall ^aseek me, and shall not find *me*: and ^bwhere I am, ^c*thither* ye ^dcannot come.

35 Then said the Jews among themselves, Whither will he go, that we shall not find him? will he go unto the dispersed among the ^aGentiles, and teach the Gentiles?

36 What *manner of* saying is this that he said, Ye shall seek me, and shall not find *me*: and where I am, *thither* ye cannot come?

37 In the last day, that great *day*

of the feast, Jesus stood and cried, saying, If any man ^athirst, let him come unto me, and ^bdrink.

38 He that believeth on me, as the scripture hath said, out of his belly shall flow rivers of living water.

39 (But this spake he of the ^aSpirit, which they that believe on him should receive: ^bfor the Holy Ghost was not yet *given*; because that Jesus was not yet glorified.)

40 ¶ Many of the people therefore, when they heard this saying, said, Of a truth this is the ^aProphet.

41 Others said, This is the Christ. But some said, Shall Christ come out of Galilee?

42 Hath not the scripture said, That ^aChrist cometh of the seed of ^bDavid, and out of the town of ^cBethlehem, where David was?

43 So there was a ^adivision among the people because of him.

44 And some of them would have taken him; but no man laid hands on him.

45 ¶ Then came the officers to the chief priests and Pharisees; and they said unto them, Why have ye not brought him?

46 The officers answered, Never man ^aspake like this man.

47 Then answered them the Pharisees, Are ye also ^adeceived?

48 Have any of the rulers or of the Pharisees believed on him?

49 But this people who knoweth not the law are ^acursed.

50 ^aNicodemus saith unto them, (he that came to Jesus by night, being one of them,)

51 Doth our law judge *any* man,

26*a* John 3:1 (1–2).
28*a* TG Truth.
29*a* John 13:3.
  TG Jesus Christ, Authority of; Jesus Christ, Messenger of the Covenant.
30*a* John 10:39.
  b John 12:23 (23–27).
34*a* John 13:33 (33, 36).
  b D&C 29:29; 76:112 (51–112).
  c 1 Pet. 3:22.
  d D&C 25:15.

35*a* GR Greeks.
37*a* Ps. 42:2 (1–3); 143:6 (5–12); Isa. 55:1 (1–3); John 4:14 (13–15); 6:35.
  b TG Living Water.
39*a* TG Holy Ghost, Gift of.
  b JST John 7:39 . . . for the Holy Ghost was *promised unto them who believe, after that* Jesus was glorified.)
40*a* John 9:17; 1 Ne. 22:20 (20–21).

42*a* 1 Chr. 5:2; Matt. 2:6.
  b TG Jesus Christ, Davidic Descent of.
  c 1 Sam. 16:1; Micah 5:2; Luke 2:4. TG Jesus Christ, Prophecies about.
43*a* Matt. 10:34.
46*a* TG Teaching with the Spirit.
47*a* Jacob 4:14 (13–14).
49*a* TG Curse.
50*a* John 3:1.

before it hear him, and know what he doeth?

52 They answered and said unto him, Art thou also of Galilee? Search, and look: for out of Galilee ariseth no prophet.

53 And every man went unto his own house.

CHAPTER 8

The woman taken in adultery is brought before Christ—Christ is the Light of the world—He again proclaims that He is the Messiah—The true children of Abraham believe in Christ—Jesus says, Before Abraham was I, Jehovah.

JESUS went unto the mount of Olives.

2 And early in the morning he came again into the ᵃtemple, and all the people came unto him; and he sat down, and taught them.

3 And the scribes and Pharisees brought unto him a ᵃwoman taken in ᵇadultery; and when they had set her in the midst,

4 They say unto him, Master, this woman was taken in adultery, in the very act.

5 Now Moses in the ᵃlaw commanded us, that such should be stoned: but what sayest thou?

6 This they said, tempting him, that they might have to accuse him. But Jesus stooped down, and with his finger ᵃwrote on the ground, *as though he heard them not.*

7 So when they continued asking him, he lifted up himself, and said unto them, He that is without ᵃsin among you, let him ᵇfirst cast a ᶜstone at her.

8 And again he stooped down, and wrote on the ground.

9 And they which heard *it,* being convicted by *their own* ᵃconscience, went out one by one, beginning at the eldest, *even* unto the last: and Jesus was left alone, and the woman standing in the midst.

10 When Jesus had lifted up himself, and saw none but the woman, he said unto her, Woman, where are those thine accusers? hath no man condemned thee?

11 She said, No man, Lord. And Jesus said unto her, Neither do I ᵃcondemn thee: go, and ᵇsin no ᶜmore.

12 ¶ Then spake Jesus again unto them, saying, I am the ᵃlight of the world: he that followeth me shall not ᵇwalk in ᶜdarkness, but shall have the light of life.

13 The Pharisees therefore said unto him, Thou bearest record of thyself; thy record is not true.

14 Jesus answered and said unto them, Though I bear record of myself, *yet* my record is true: for I know ᵃwhence I came, and whither I go; but ye cannot tell ᵇwhence I come, and whither I go.

15 Ye judge after the flesh; I ᵃjudge no man.

16 And yet if I ᵃjudge, my ᵇjudgment is true: for I am not ᶜalone, but I and the Father that sent me.

17 It is also written in your law, that the ᵃtestimony of two men is true.

18 I am one that bear witness of myself, and the ᵃFather that sent me beareth ᵇwitness of me.

19 Then said they unto him, Where is thy Father? Jesus answered, Ye neither know me, nor my Father: if ye had ᵃknown me, ye should have known my Father also.

20 These words spake Jesus in the

---

8 2a Matt. 26:55; Luke 21:37.
3a TG Woman.
   b TG Adulterer.
5a Lev. 20:10.
6a TG Jesus Christ,
   Teaching Mode of.
7a 3 Ne. 14:5 (1–5).
   b Deut. 17:7.
   c TG Gossip.
9a TG Conscience.
11a TG Benevolence;
   Mercy.

b D&C 42:25.
c JST John 8:11 . . . more.
   *And the woman glorified
   God from that hour, and
   believed on his name.*
12a 1 Jn. 1:5.
   TG Jesus Christ, Light of
   the World;
   Light [noun];
   Light of Christ.
   b TG Walking in Darkness.
   c TG Darkness, Spiritual.

14a John 16:28.
   b John 9:29.
15a John 12:47.
16a TG Jesus Christ, Judge.
   b TG Judgment.
   c John 8:29; 16:32.
17a TG Witness.
18a TG Godhead; God the
   Father, Elohim.
   b TG Witness of the
   Father.
19a John 14:7.

treasury, as he taught in the temple: and no man laid hands on him; for his hour was not yet come.

21 Then said Jesus again unto them, I go my way, and ye shall seek me, and shall die in your *a*sins: whither I go, ye cannot come.

22 Then said the Jews, Will he kill himself? because he saith, Whither I go, ye cannot come.

23 And he said unto them, Ye are from *a*beneath; I am from above: ye are of this *b*world; I am not of this world.

24 I said therefore unto you, that ye shall *a*die in your sins: for if ye *b*believe not that I am *he*, ye shall die in your sins.

25 Then said they unto him, Who art thou? And Jesus saith unto them, Even *the same* that I said unto you from the beginning.

26 I have many things to say and to judge of you: but he that sent me is true; and I speak to the world those things which I have *a*heard of him.

27 They understood not that he spake to them of the Father.

28 Then said Jesus unto them, When ye have lifted up the Son of man, then shall ye know that I am *he*, and *that* I do *a*nothing of myself; but as my *b*Father hath *c*taught me, I *d*speak these things.

29 And he that *a*sent me is with me: the Father hath not left me *b*alone; for I *c*do always those things that *d*please him.

30 As he spake these words, many *a*believed on him.

31 Then said Jesus to those Jews which believed on him, If ye *a*continue in my word, *then* are ye my *b*disciples indeed;

32 And ye shall *a*know the *b*truth, and the *c*truth shall make you *d*free.

33 ¶ They answered him, We be *a*Abraham's seed, and were never in bondage to any man: how sayest thou, Ye shall be made free?

34 Jesus answered them, Verily, verily, I say unto you, Whosoever *a*committeth *b*sin is the *c*servant of sin.

35 And the servant abideth not in the house for ever: *but* the Son abideth ever.

36 If the Son therefore shall make you *a*free, ye shall be free indeed.

37 I know that ye are Abraham's seed; but ye seek to kill me, because my word hath no place in you.

38 I speak that which I have seen with my Father: and ye do that which ye have seen with your father.

39 They answered and said unto him, Abraham is our father. Jesus saith unto them, If ye were *a*Abraham's *b*children, ye would do the *c*works of Abraham.

40 But now ye seek to kill me, a man that hath told you the truth, which I have heard of God: this did not Abraham.

41 Ye do the deeds of your father. Then said they to him, We be not born of fornication; we have one Father, *even* God.

42 Jesus said unto them, If God were your Father, ye would love me: for I proceeded forth and *a*came

---

21*a* Moro. 10:26 (24–26).
  TG Sin.
23*a* John 3:31 (13, 31).
  b TG World.
24*a* D&C 138:32 (31–34).
  b TG Faith.
26*a* TG Revelation.
28*a* John 5:19.
  b John 7:16 (16–18).
    TG Authority.
  c TG Delegation of Responsibility.
  d Deut. 18:18.
29*a* TG Jesus Christ, Authority of.
  b John 8:16; 16:32.
    TG Jesus Christ,

Relationships with the Father.
  c TG Obedience.
  d John 4:34.
30*a* John 12:42 (11, 42).
31*a* TG Commitment; Perseverance; Steadfastness.
  b Matt. 27:57.
32*a* TG Conversion; Testimony.
  b D&C 50:25.
    TG Education; Gospel; Truth.
  c Moro. 10:5.
  d 3 Ne. 21:4.
    TG Bondage, Spiritual;

Liberty.
33*a* TG Abrahamic Covenant.
34*a* D&C 29:40.
  b TG Sin.
  c Rom. 6:16; Alma 12:11 (9–11, 17).
    TG Servant.
36*a* TG Bondage, Spiritual; Liberty.
39*a* TG Abrahamic Covenant.
  b TG Seed of Abraham.
  c TG Good Works.
42*a* John 16:28 (27–28, 30); 17:8; Gal. 4:4.

from God; neither came I of myself, but he *b*sent me.

43 Why do ye not understand my speech? *even* because ye cannot *a*hear my word.

44 Ye are of *your* father the *a*devil, and the *b*lusts of your father ye will do. He was a *c*murderer from the beginning, and abode not in the *d*truth, because there is no truth in him. When he speaketh a *e*lie, he speaketh of his own: for he is a *f*liar, and the father of it.

45 And because I tell *you* the truth, ye believe me not.

46 Which of you *a*convinceth me of *b*sin? And if I say the truth, why do ye not believe me?

47 *a*He that is of God *b*heareth God's words: ye therefore hear *them* not, because ye are not of God.

48 Then answered the Jews, and said unto him, Say we not well that thou art a Samaritan, and hast a *a*devil?

49 Jesus answered, I have not a devil; but I *a*honour my Father, and ye do dishonour me.

50 And I seek not mine own *a*glory: there is one that seeketh and judgeth.

51 Verily, verily, I say unto you, If a man keep my saying, he shall never see *a*death.

52 Then said the Jews unto him, Now we know that thou hast a devil. Abraham is dead, and the prophets; and thou sayest, If a man keep

my saying, he shall never *a*taste of death.

53 Art thou greater than our father Abraham, which is dead? and the prophets are dead: whom makest thou thyself?

54 Jesus answered, If I honour myself, my honour is nothing: it is my *a*Father that *b*honoureth me; of whom ye say, that he is your God:

55 Yet ye have not known him; but I know him: and if I should say, I know him not, I shall be a liar like unto you: but I know him, and keep his saying.

56 Your father *a*Abraham *b*rejoiced to *c*see my day: and he saw *it,* and was glad.

57 Then said the Jews unto him, Thou art not yet fifty years old, and hast thou seen Abraham?

58 Jesus said unto them, Verily, verily, I say unto you, *a*Before Abraham was, *b*I am.

59 Then took they up *a*stones to cast at him: but Jesus hid himself, and went out of the temple, going through the midst of them, and so *b*passed by.

CHAPTER 9

Jesus, on the Sabbath, heals a man born blind—The Jews accuse Him of Sabbath violation—He lectures them on spiritual blindness.

AND as *Jesus* passed by, he saw a man which was *a*blind from *his* birth.

42*b* TG Jesus Christ, Messenger of the Covenant.
43*a* JST John 8:43 . . . *bear* . . .
44*a* 1 Jn. 3:10 (10–18).
  TG Devil;
  Devil, Church of.
  b TG Lust.
  c TG Murder.
  d TG Truth.
  e TG Lying.
  f TG Honesty.
46*a* GR convicts, reproves.
  b Heb. 4:15.
47*a* JST John 8:47 He that is of God *receiveth* God's words; ye therefore *receive* them not, because ye are not of God.
  b Dan. 12:10;

1 Jn. 4:6 (5–6);
  2 Ne. 33:10 (10–11).
48*a* Mosiah 3:9.
49*a* TG God, the Standard of Righteousness; Honoring Father and Mother; Respect.
50*a* John 7:18.
51*a* John 5:24; 11:26; D&C 63:49.
  TG Death, Spiritual, First; Death, Spiritual, Second.
52*a* D&C 42:46 (46–47).
54*a* TG God, Body of, Corporeal Nature.
  b TG Honor.
56*a* Gen. 22:8 (8–14); Hel. 8:17 (16–19).
  b TG Joy.

  c TG Jesus Christ, Appearances, Antemortal.
58*a* TG Man, Antemortal Existence of.
  b The term I AM used here in the Greek is identical with the Septuagint usage in Ex. 3:14 which identifies Jehovah. (See also John 4:26.) TG Jesus Christ, Jehovah.
59*a* John 10:31.
  b Luke 4:30.
9 1*a* Matt. 9:28 (28–31); 20:30 (30–34); Mosiah 3:5; 3 Ne. 17:9 (7–10); D&C 84:69.

2 And his disciples asked him, saying, Master, who did sin, this ªman, or his parents, that he was born blind?

3 Jesus answered, Neither hath this man sinned, nor his parents: but that the ªworks of God should be made ᵇmanifest in him.

4 I must ªwork the ᵇworks of him that sent me, ᶜwhile it is ᵈday: the ᵉnight cometh, when no man can work.

5 As long as I am in the world, I am the ªlight of the world.

6 When he had thus spoken, he spat on the ground, and made clay of the spittle, and he anointed the eyes of the blind man with the clay,

7 And said unto him, Go, wash in the pool of ªSiloam, (which is by interpretation, Sent.) He went his way therefore, and washed, and came seeing.

8 ¶ The neighbours therefore, and they which before had seen him that he was blind, said, Is not this he that sat and begged?

9 Some said, This is he: others said, He is like him: but he said, I am he.

10 Therefore said they unto him, How were thine eyes opened?

11 He answered and said, A man that is called Jesus made clay, and anointed mine eyes, and said unto me, Go to the pool of Siloam, and ªwash: and I went and washed, and I received ᵇsight.

12 Then said they unto him, Where is he? He said, I know not.

13 ¶ They brought to the Pharisees him that aforetime was blind.

14 And it was the ªsabbath day when Jesus made the clay, and ᵇopened his eyes.

15 Then again the Pharisees also asked him how he had received his sight. He said unto them, He put clay upon mine eyes, and I washed, and do see.

16 Therefore said some of the Pharisees, This man is not of God, because he keepeth not the sabbath day. Others said, How can a man that is a sinner do such miracles? And there was a division among them.

17 They say unto the blind man again, What sayest thou of him, that he hath opened thine eyes? He said, He is a ªprophet.

18 But the Jews did not believe concerning him, that he had been blind, and received his sight, until they called the parents of him that had received his sight.

19 And they asked them, saying, Is this your son, who ye say was born blind? how then doth he now see?

20 His parents answered them and said, We know that this is our son, and that he was born blind:

21 But by what means he now seeth, we know not; or who hath opened his eyes, we know not: he is of age; ask him: he shall speak for himself.

22 These *words* spake his parents, because they feared the Jews: for the Jews had agreed already, that if any man did confess that he was Christ, he should be put out of the synagogue.

23 Therefore said his parents, He is of age; ask him.

24 Then again called they the man that was blind, and said unto him, Give God the praise: we know that this man is a sinner.

25 He answered and said, Whether he be a sinner *or no,* I know not: one thing I know, that, whereas I was blind, now I see.

26 Then said they to him again,

2a TG Man, Antemortal
  Existence of.
3a TG God, Works of.
  b John 11:4.
4a John 5:17.
  b John 4:34.
  TG Good Works.
  c JST John 9:4 ... while

I am with you; the time
cometh when I shall
have finished my work,
then I go unto the Father.
  d Rom. 13:12 (11–12);
  Alma 34:33.
  e TG Darkness, Spiritual.
5a TG Jesus Christ, Light of

the World;
  Light of Christ.
7a Neh. 3:15; Isa. 8:6.
11a 2 Kgs. 5:10.
  b TG Sight.
14a TG Sabbath.
  b TG Heal.
17a John 7:40 (40–44).

What did he to thee? how opened he thine eyes?

27 He answered them, I have told you already, and ye did not hear: wherefore would ye hear it again? will ye also be his disciples?

28 Then they ªreviled him, and said, Thou art his disciple; but we are Moses' disciples.

29 We know that God spake unto Moses: as for this fellow, we know not from ªwhence he is.

30 The man answered and said unto them, Why herein is a marvellous thing, that ye know not from whence he is, and yet he hath opened mine eyes.

31 Now we know that God heareth not sinners: but if any man be a worshipper of God, and doeth his will, him he heareth.

32 Since the world began was it not heard that any man opened the eyes of one that was born ªblind.

33 If this man were not of ªGod, he could do nothing.

34 They answered and said unto him, Thou wast altogether born in sins, and dost thou teach us? And they cast him out.

35 Jesus heard that they had cast him out; and when he had found him, he said unto him, Dost thou believe on the Son of God?

36 He answered and said, Who is he, Lord, that I might believe on him?

37 And Jesus said unto him, Thou hast both seen him, and it is he that talketh with thee.

38 And he said, Lord, I believe. And he worshipped him.

39 ¶ And Jesus said, For ªjudgment I am come into this world, that they which ᵇsee not might see; and that they which see might be made blind.

40 And some of the Pharisees which were with him heard these words, and said unto him, Are we blind also?

41 Jesus said unto them, If ye were ªblind, ye should have no ᵇsin: but now ye say, We ᶜsee; therefore your ᵈsin remaineth.

CHAPTER 10

Jesus is the Good Shepherd—He gained power over death from His Father—He promises to visit His other sheep—He proclaims, I am the Son of God.

VERILY, verily, I say unto you, He that entereth not by the door into the sheepfold, but climbeth up some other way, the same is a thief and a robber.

2 But he that entereth in by the door is the shepherd of the ªsheep.

3 To him the porter openeth; and the sheep hear his ªvoice: and he calleth his own sheep by name, and ᵇleadeth them out.

4 And when he putteth forth his own sheep, he goeth before them, and the sheep follow him: for they ªknow his ᵇvoice.

5 And a stranger will they not follow, but will flee from him: for they know not the voice of ªstrangers.

6 This parable spake Jesus unto them: but they understood not what things they were which he spake unto them.

7 Then said Jesus unto them again, Verily, verily, I say unto you, I am the ªdoor of the sheep.

8 All that ever came before me ªare thieves and robbers: but the sheep did not hear them.

9 I am the door: by me if any man enter in, he shall be saved, and shall go in and out, and find pasture.

10 The thief cometh not, but for to ªsteal, and to kill, and to destroy: I

28a TG Reviling.
29a John 8:14.
32a JST John 9:32 . . . blind, *except he be of God.*
33a Acts 2:22.
39a TG Jesus Christ, Judge.
  b Luke 5:32;
    1 Tim. 1:13, 15.

41a TG Spiritual Blindness.
  b John 15:22 (19–27).
  c TG Accountability.
  d TG Sin.
10 2a TG Sheep.
  3a D&C 35:21.
  b Isa. 55:4.
  4a TG Discernment,

Spiritual.
  b TG Revelation.
  5a TG Stranger.
  7a John 14:6 (4–7).
  8a JST John 10:8 . . . *who testified not of me* are thieves . . .
  10a TG Stealing.

am come that they might have ᵇlife, and that they might have *it* more ᶜabundantly.

11 I am the good ᵃshepherd: the good ᵇshepherd giveth his life for the sheep.

12 But he that is an hireling, and not the shepherd, whose own the sheep are not, seeth the wolf coming, and ᵃleaveth the sheep, and fleeth: and the wolf catcheth them, and scattereth the sheep.

13 The ᵃhireling fleeth, because he is an hireling, and careth not for the sheep.

14 I am the good ᵃshepherd, and ᵇknow my ᶜ*sheep,* and am known of mine.

15 As the Father knoweth me, even so ᵃknow I the Father: and I lay down my ᵇlife for the sheep.

16 And ᵃother ᵇsheep I have, which are not of this fold: them also I must bring, and they shall hear my voice; and there shall be ᶜone fold, *and* one shepherd.

17 Therefore doth my Father ᵃlove me, because I ᵇlay down my life, that I might ᶜtake it again.

18 No man ᵃtaketh it from me, but I lay it down of myself. I have ᵇpower to lay it down, and I have ᶜpower to take it again. This commandment have I ᵈreceived of my Father.

19 ¶ There was a division therefore again among the Jews for these sayings.

20 And many of them said, He hath a devil, and is mad; why hear ye him?

21 Others said, These are not the words of him that hath a devil. Can a devil open the eyes of the blind?

22 ¶ And it was at Jerusalem the feast of the dedication, and it was winter.

23 And Jesus walked in the temple in Solomon's ᵃporch.

24 Then came the Jews round about him, and said unto him, How long dost thou make us to ᵃdoubt? If thou be the Christ, tell us plainly.

25 Jesus answered them, I told you, and ye ᵃbelieved not: the ᵇworks that I do in my Father's ᶜname, they bear witness of me.

26 But ye believe not, because ye are not of my sheep, as I said unto you.

27 My ᵃsheep hear my voice, and I know them, and they ᵇfollow me:

28 And I give unto them eternal life; and they shall never perish, neither shall any *man* pluck them out of my hand.

29 My Father, which ᵃgave *them* me, is greater than all; and no *man* is able to pluck *them* out of my Father's hand.

30 I and *my* Father are ᵃone.

31 Then the Jews took up ᵃstones again to stone him.

32 Jesus answered them, Many good works have I shewed you from my Father; for which of those works do ye stone me?

33 The Jews answered him, saying,

10ᵇ D&C 66:2.
  ᶜ TG Abundant Life; Happiness.
11ᵃ TG Shepherd.
  ᵇ Ezek. 34:2.
12ᵃ TG Leadership.
13ᵃ TG Wages.
14ᵃ TG Jesus Christ, Good Shepherd.
  ᵇ Ex. 33:12 (12, 17); 1 Cor. 8:3.
  ᶜ 3 Ne. 18:31.
15ᵃ TG Jesus Christ, Relationships with the Father.
  ᵇ 1 Jn. 3:16 (10–18). TG Jesus Christ, Atonement through;

Martyrdom.
16ᵃ 3 Ne. 15:21 (11–24); 16:1 (1–3); D&C 10:59. TG Israel, Scattering of.
  ᵇ TG Book of Mormon; Israel, Joseph, People of; Israel, Ten Lost Tribes of; Sheep.
  ᶜ Ezek. 37:22.
17ᵃ TG God, Love of.
  ᵇ TG Self-Sacrifice.
  ᶜ TG Jesus Christ, Resurrection.
18ᵃ Luke 23:46.
  ᵇ TG Death, Power over; God, Power of.
  ᶜ GR authority, full

power.
  ᵈ TG Jesus Christ, Authority of.
23ᵃ 1 Kgs. 6:3; Acts 3:11.
24ᵃ TG Doubt.
25ᵃ TG Faith; Unbelief.
  ᵇ John 5:36. TG Miracle.
  ᶜ TG Name.
27ᵃ TG Sheep.
  ᵇ D&C 38:22.
29ᵃ John 17:2 (2–12); D&C 50:41.
30ᵃ D&C 93:3 (1–6). TG Godhead; Unity.
31ᵃ John 8:59.

For a good work we stone thee not; but for ^ablasphemy; and because that thou, being a man, makest thyself ^bGod.

34 Jesus answered them, Is it not written in your law, I said, Ye are ^agods?

35 If he called them gods, unto whom the word of God came, and the scripture cannot be broken;

36 Say ye of him, whom the Father hath ^asanctified, and ^bsent into the world, Thou blasphemest; because I said, I am the ^cSon of God?

37 If I do not the works of my Father, believe me not.

38 But if I do, though ye believe not me, ^abelieve the works: that ye may know, and believe, that the ^bFather is in me, and I in him.

39 Therefore they ^asought again to take him: but he escaped out of their hand,

40 And went away again beyond Jordan into the place where John at first baptized; and there he abode.

41 And many resorted unto him, and said, John did no miracle: but all things that John spake of this man were true.

42 And many believed on him there.

CHAPTER 11

Jesus testifies that He is the Resurrection and the Life—Mary and Martha testify of Him—He raises Lazarus from the dead—Caiaphas speaks prophetically of the death of Jesus.

Now a certain *man* was sick, *named* Lazarus, of Bethany, the town of Mary and her sister ^aMartha.

2 ^a(It was *that* Mary which anointed the ^bLord with ^cointment, and wiped his feet with her hair, whose brother Lazarus was sick.)

3 Therefore his sisters sent unto him, saying, Lord, behold, he whom thou lovest is sick.

4 When Jesus heard *that,* he said, This sickness is not unto death, but for the ^aglory of God, that the Son of God might be ^bglorified thereby.

5 Now Jesus loved Martha, and her sister, and Lazarus.

6 When he had heard therefore that he was sick, he abode two days still in the same place where he was.

7 Then after that saith he to *his* disciples, Let us go into Judæa again.

8 *His* disciples say unto him, Master, the Jews of late sought to stone thee; and goest thou thither again?

9 Jesus answered, Are there not twelve hours in the day? If any man ^awalk in the day, he stumbleth not, because he seeth the light of this world.

10 But if a man walk in the night, he stumbleth, because there is no light in him.

11 These things said he: and after that he saith unto them, Our friend Lazarus sleepeth; but I go, that I may ^aawake him out of sleep.

12 Then said his disciples, Lord, if he sleep, he shall ^ado well.

13 Howbeit Jesus spake of his death: but they thought that he had spoken of taking of rest in sleep.

14 Then said Jesus unto them plainly, Lazarus is dead.

15 And I am glad for your sakes that I was not there, to the intent ye may ^abelieve; nevertheless let us go unto him.

16 Then said Thomas, which is called Didymus, unto his fellow-

---

33*a* TG Blaspheme.
　b John 5:18 (17–18); 19:7; 1 Tim. 3:16.
34*a* TG Man, Potential to Become like Heavenly Father; Sons and Daughters of God.
36*a* TG Sanctification.
　b TG Jesus Christ, Messenger of the Covenant.

　c TG Jesus Christ, Divine Sonship.
38*a* TG Faith.
　b TG Godhead.
39*a* John 7:30.
11 1*a* Luke 10:38; John 12:2.
　2*a* JST John 11:2 *And Mary, his sister, who* anointed the Lord with ointment and wiped his feet with her hair, *lived*

with her sister Martha, in whose house her brother Lazarus was sick.
　b TG Jesus Christ, Lord.
　c Matt. 26:7 (6–13).
4*a* 3 Ne. 12:16; Ether 12:4.
　b John 9:3.
9*a* TG Walking with God.
11*a* 2 Kgs. 4:31.
12*a* GR be cured, saved.
15*a* TG Faith.

disciples, Let us also go, that we may die with ^ahim.

17 Then when Jesus came, ^ahe found that he had *lain* in the grave four days already.

18 Now Bethany was nigh unto Jerusalem, about fifteen ^afurlongs off:

19 And many of the Jews came to Martha and Mary, to comfort them concerning their brother.

20 Then Martha, as soon as she heard that Jesus was coming, went and met him: but Mary sat *still* in the house.

21 Then said Martha unto Jesus, Lord, if thou hadst been here, my brother had not died.

22 But I know, that even now, whatsoever thou wilt ask of God, God will ^agive *it* thee.

23 Jesus saith unto her, Thy brother shall rise again.

24 Martha saith unto him, I know that he shall rise again in the resurrection at the last day.

25 Jesus said unto her, I am the ^aresurrection, and the ^blife: he that ^cbelieveth in me, though he were ^ddead, yet shall he ^elive:

26 And whosoever liveth and believeth in me shall never ^adie. Believest thou this?

27 She saith unto him, Yea, Lord: I believe that thou art the Christ, the ^aSon of God, which should come into the world.

28 And when she had so said, she went her way, and called Mary her sister secretly, saying, The Master is come, and calleth for thee.

29 As soon as she heard *that,* she arose quickly, and came unto him.

30 Now Jesus was not yet come into the town, but was in that place where Martha met him.

31 The Jews then which were with her in the house, and comforted her, when they saw Mary, that she rose up hastily and went out, followed her, saying, She goeth unto the grave to weep there.

32 Then when Mary was come where Jesus was, and saw him, she fell down at his feet, saying unto him, Lord, if thou hadst been here, my brother had not died.

33 When Jesus therefore saw her weeping, and the Jews also weeping which came with her, he groaned in the spirit, and was troubled,

34 And said, Where have ye laid him? They said unto him, Lord, come and see.

35 Jesus wept.

36 Then said the Jews, Behold how he ^aloved him!

37 And some of them said, Could not this man, which opened the eyes of the blind, have caused that even this man should not have died?

38 Jesus therefore again groaning in himself cometh to the grave. It was a cave, and a ^astone lay upon it.

39 Jesus said, Take ye away the stone. Martha, the sister of him that was dead, saith unto him, Lord, by this time he stinketh: for he hath been *dead* four days.

40 Jesus saith unto her, Said I not unto thee, that, if thou wouldest believe, thou shouldest see the ^aglory of God?

41 Then they took away the stone *from the place* where the dead was laid. And Jesus lifted up *his* eyes, and said, Father, I ^athank thee that thou hast heard me.

42 And I knew that thou hearest

16a JST John 11:16 . . . him; *for they feared lest the Jews should take Jesus and put him to death, for as yet they did not understand the power of God.*

17a JST John 11:17 . . . *to Bethany, to Martha's house, Lazarus had already been* in the grave four days.

18a GR *stadium*—607 English feet, about 185 meters.

22a TG God, Gifts of.

25a TG Jesus Christ, Resurrection; Resurrection.
 b TG Jesus Christ, Atonement through.
 c TG Faith.
 d TG Death.
 e Alma 37:46 (46–47);

Hel. 8:15;
3 Ne. 15:9.

26a John 5:24; 8:51; D&C 42:46 (44, 46); 63:49.

27a TG God, Body of, Corporeal Nature.

36a D&C 42:45.

38a Matt. 27:60.

40a Ex. 16:7.

41a TG Thanksgiving.

me always: but because of the people which stand by I said *it*, that they may believe that thou hast ᵃsent me.

43 And when he thus had spoken, he cried with a loud voice, ᵃLazarus, come forth.

44 And he that was ᵃdead came forth, bound hand and foot with graveclothes: and his face was bound about with a ᵇnapkin. Jesus saith unto them, Loose him, and let him go.

45 Then many of the Jews which came to Mary, and had seen the things which Jesus did, believed on him.

46 But some of them went their ways to the Pharisees, and told them what things Jesus had done.

47 ¶ Then gathered the chief ᵃpriests and the Pharisees a council, and said, What do we? for this man doeth many ᵇmiracles.

48 If we let him thus alone, all *men* will believe on him: and the Romans shall come and take away both our place and nation.

49 And one of them, *named* ᵃCaiaphas, being the ᵇhigh priest that same year, said unto them, Ye know nothing at all,

50 Nor consider that it is expedient for us, that one man should ᵃdie for the people, and that the whole nation perish not.

51 And this spake he not of himself: but being high priest that year, he prophesied that Jesus should die for that nation;

52 And not for that nation only, but that also he should ᵃgather together in one the ᵇchildren of God that were scattered abroad.

53 Then from that day forth they took ᵃcounsel together for to put him to ᵇdeath.

54 Jesus therefore walked no more openly among the Jews; but went thence unto a country near to the wilderness, into a city called Ephraim, and there continued with his disciples.

55 ¶ And the Jews' passover was nigh at hand: and many went out of the country up to Jerusalem before the passover, to ᵃpurify themselves.

56 Then sought they for Jesus, and spake among themselves, as they stood in the temple, What think ye, that he will not come to the feast?

57 Now both the chief priests and the Pharisees had given a commandment, that, if any man knew where he were, he should shew *it*, that they might take him.

CHAPTER 12

Mary anoints Jesus' feet—His triumphal entry into Jerusalem is recounted—He foretells His death—To receive Christ is to receive the Father.

Tʜᴇɴ Jesus six days before the passover came to Bethany, where Lazarus was which had been dead, whom he raised from the dead.

2 There they made him a supper; and ᵃMartha served: but Lazarus was one of them that sat at the table with him.

3 Then took Mary a pound of ointment of spikenard, very costly, and anointed the feet of Jesus, and wiped his feet with her hair: and the house was filled with the odour of the ointment.

4 Then saith one of his disciples, Judas Iscariot, Simon's *son*, which should betray him,

5 Why was not this ointment sold for three hundred pence, and given to the poor?

6 This he said, not that he cared for the poor; but because he was a

---

42a ᴛɢ Jesus Christ,
    Messenger of the
    Covenant.
43a ᴛɢ God, Power of.
44a 2 Kgs. 8:1.
    ᴛɢ Death, Power over.
  b John 20:7.
47a 2 Ne. 10:5.

  b 3 Ne. 19:35.
49a Matt. 26:3 (3–5).
  b ᴛɢ Priesthood, Aaronic.
50a ᴛɢ Jesus Christ,
    Trials of.
52a ᴛɢ Israel, Gathering of.
  b ᴛɢ Sons and Daughters
    of God.

53a Matt. 21:38 (33–46).
    ᴛɢ Counsel.
  b John 7:1.
55a ᴛɢ Purification.
12 2a Luke 10:38;
    John 11:1 (1, 5).

*a*thief, and had the *b*bag, and bare what was put therein.

7 Then said Jesus, Let her alone: *a*against the day of my burying hath *b*she kept this.

8 For the poor always ye have with you; but me ye have not always.

9 Much people of the Jews therefore knew that he was there: and they came not for Jesus' sake only, but that they might see Lazarus also, whom he had raised from the dead.

10 ¶ But the chief priests consulted that they might put Lazarus also to death;

11 Because that by reason of him many of the Jews went away, and believed on Jesus.

12 ¶ On the next day much people that were come to the feast, when they heard that Jesus was coming to Jerusalem,

13 Took branches of palm trees, and went forth to meet him, and cried, Hosanna: Blessed *is* the King of Israel that cometh in the name of the Lord.

14 And Jesus, when he had found a young ass, sat thereon; as it is written,

15 Fear not, daughter of Sion: behold, thy *a*King cometh, sitting on an ass's colt.

16 These things *a*understood not his disciples at the first: but when Jesus was glorified, then remembered they that these things were written of him, and *that* they had done these things unto him.

17 The people therefore that was with him when he called Lazarus out of his grave, and raised him from the dead, bare record.

18 For this cause the people also *a*met him, for that they heard that he had done this *b*miracle.

19 The Pharisees therefore said among themselves, Perceive ye how ye prevail nothing? behold, the *a*world is gone after him.

20 ¶ And there were certain *a*Greeks among them that came up to *b*worship at the feast:

21 The same came therefore to Philip, which was of Bethsaida of Galilee, and desired him, saying, Sir, we would see Jesus.

22 Philip cometh and telleth Andrew: and again Andrew and Philip tell Jesus.

23 ¶ And Jesus answered them, saying, The *a*hour is come, that the Son of man should be *b*glorified.

24 Verily, verily, I say unto you, Except a *a*corn of wheat fall into the ground and *b*die, it abideth alone: but if it *c*die, it bringeth forth much fruit.

25 He that loveth his *a*life shall lose it; and he that *b*hateth his life in this world shall keep it unto life eternal.

26 If any man serve me, let him *a*follow me; and where I am, there shall also my servant be: if any man serve me, him will *my* Father honour.

27 Now is my soul troubled; and what shall I say? Father, save me from this hour: but for this cause came I unto this hour.

28 Father, glorify thy name. Then came there a *a*voice from heaven, *saying,* I have both *b*glorified *it,* and will glorify *it* again.

29 The people therefore, that stood by, and heard *it,* said that it thundered: others said, An *a*angel spake to him.

30 Jesus answered and said, This voice came not because of me, but for your sakes.

31 Now is the judgment of this

6*a* Mosiah 2:36 (36–39).
  b GR purse, money bag.
     John 13:29.
7*a* JST John 12:7 . . . *for she hath preserved this ointment until now, that she might anoint me in token of my burial.*
  b Mark 14:9.
15*a* Zech. 9:9.
16*a* Luke 9:45; 18:34 (31–34).

18*a* Matt. 8:34.
  b D&C 63:10 (7–12).
19*a* Matt. 9:31 (27–31).
20*a* Acts 17:4 (1–9).
  b Acts 8:27.
23*a* John 7:30.
  b TG Jesus Christ, Mission of.
24*a* GR grain, seed.
  b 1 Cor. 15:36 (35–38).
  c TG Death.

25*a* See JST Luke 9:24–25 (Appendix).
  b TG Hate.
26*a* 2 Ne. 31:12 (12–13).
28*a* TG Godhead; Witness of the Father.
  b D&C 45:4.
29*a* TG Angels.

world: now shall the ^aprince of this world be cast out.

32 And I, if I be ^alifted up from the earth, will ^bdraw all *men* unto me.

33 This he said, signifying what ^adeath he should die.

34 The people answered him, We have heard out of the law that ^aChrist abideth for ever: and how sayest thou, The Son of man must be lifted up? who is this Son of man?

35 Then Jesus said unto them, Yet a little while is the ^alight with you. Walk while ye have the ^blight, lest darkness come upon you: for he that walketh in ^cdarkness knoweth not whither he goeth.

36 While ye have light, ^abelieve in the light, that ye may be the ^bchildren of light. These things spake Jesus, and departed, and did hide himself from them.

37 ¶ But though he had done so many ^amiracles before them, yet they ^bbelieved not on him:

38 That the saying of Esaias the prophet might be fulfilled, which he spake, Lord, who hath ^abelieved our report? and to whom hath the arm of the Lord been revealed?

39 Therefore they could not believe, because that Esaias said again,

40 He hath ^ablinded their eyes, and ^bhardened their heart; that they should not see with *their* eyes, nor understand with *their* heart, and be converted, and I should heal them.

41 These things said Esaias, when he ^asaw his ^bglory, and spake of him.

42 ¶ Nevertheless among the chief

^arulers also many ^bbelieved on him; but because of the Pharisees they did not ^cconfess *him*, lest they should be put out of the synagogue:

43 For they loved the ^apraise of men more than the praise of God.

44 ¶ Jesus cried and said, He that ^abelieveth on me, believeth not on me, but on him that sent me.

45 And he that seeth me seeth him that sent me.

46 I am come a ^alight into the world, that whosoever believeth on me should not abide in darkness.

47 And if any man hear my words, and believe not, I judge him not: for I came not to ^ajudge the world, but to save the world.

48 He that ^arejecteth me, and receiveth not my words, hath one that ^bjudgeth him: the ^cword that I have spoken, the same shall ^djudge him in the last day.

49 For I have not spoken of myself; but the Father which ^asent me, he gave me a commandment, what I should say, and what I should speak.

50 And I know that his commandment is life everlasting: whatsoever I ^aspeak therefore, even as the ^bFather said unto me, so I ^cspeak.

CHAPTER 13

Jesus washes the feet of the Twelve—He identifies Judas as His betrayer—He commands them to love one another.

Now before the feast of the ^apassover, when Jesus knew that his hour was come that he should depart out

---

31 a TG Devil.
32 a TG Jesus Christ,
   Atonement through;
   Jesus Christ,
   Crucifixion of.
   b D&C 18:11.
33 a TG Jesus Christ, Death of.
34 a 2 Sam. 7:16.
35 a TG Light of Christ.
   b TG Light [noun].
   c TG Darkness, Spiritual;
   Walking in Darkness.
36 a TG Faith.
   b TG Children of Light.
37 a TG Miracle;
   Signs.
   b Mosiah 3:9 (9–11).

38 a Isa. 53:1;
   Rom. 10:16.
40 a TG Spiritual Blindness.
   b TG Hardheartedness.
41 a TG Jesus Christ,
   Appearances,
   Antemortal.
   b TG Glory.
42 a Acts 6:7.
   b John 8:30 (30–31).
   c Prov. 29:25;
   John 19:38.
43 a Mark 12:38 (38–40);
   1 Cor. 1:26 (26–31);
   1 Ne. 8:28 (26–28);
   Alma 11:24;
   D&C 3:7 (5–8).

44 a TG Faith.
46 a John 1:9 (4, 9).
47 a Luke 4:19;
   John 8:15.
48 a D&C 39:9.
   b TG Judgment.
   c TG Gospel.
   d TG Judgment, the Last.
49 a TG Jesus Christ,
   Authority of.
50 a Deut. 18:18.
   b 3 Ne. 15:18.
   c TG Jesus Christ,
   Teaching Mode of.
13 1 a Deut. 16:1.

of this world unto the Father, having loved his own which were in the world, he *b*loved them unto the end.

2 And supper being ended, the devil having now put into the *a*heart of Judas Iscariot, Simon's *son*, to betray him;

3 Jesus *a*knowing that the Father had given all *b*things into his hands, and that he was *c*come from God, and went to God;

4 He riseth from supper, and laid aside his garments; and took a towel, and girded himself.

5 After that he poureth water into a basin, and began to *a*wash the disciples' feet, and to wipe *them* with the towel wherewith he was girded.

6 Then cometh he to Simon Peter: and Peter saith unto him, Lord, dost thou wash my feet?

7 Jesus answered and said unto him, What I do thou knowest not now; but thou shalt know hereafter.

8 *a*Peter saith unto him, Thou shalt never wash my feet. Jesus answered him, If I *b*wash thee not, thou hast no part with me.

9 Simon Peter saith unto him, Lord, not my feet only, but also *my* hands and *my* head.

10 Jesus saith to him, He that is washed needeth not save to wash *his* feet, but is *a*clean every whit: and ye are *b*clean, but not all.

11 For he knew who should *a*betray him; therefore said he, Ye are not *b*all clean.

12 So after he had washed their feet, and had taken his garments, and was set down again, he said unto them, Know ye what I have done to you?

13 Ye call me *a*Master and Lord: and ye say well; for *so* I am.

14 If I then, *your* Lord and *a*Master, have *b*washed your feet; ye also ought to *c*wash one another's *d*feet.

15 For I have given you an *a*example, that ye should do as I have done to you.

16 Verily, verily, I say unto you, The servant is not greater than his lord; neither he that is sent greater than he that sent him.

17 If ye know these things, *a*happy are ye if ye do them.

18 ¶ I speak not of you all: I know whom I have chosen: but that the scripture may be fulfilled, He that eateth bread with me hath lifted up his heel against me.

19 Now I tell you before it come, that, when it is come to pass, ye may believe that I am *a*he.

20 Verily, verily, I say unto you, He that receiveth whomsoever I send *a*receiveth me; and he that *b*receiveth me receiveth him that sent me.

21 When Jesus had thus said, he was troubled in spirit, and testified, and said, Verily, verily, I say unto you, that one of you shall *a*betray me.

22 Then the disciples looked one on another, doubting of whom he spake.

23 Now there was leaning on Jesus' bosom one of his *a*disciples, whom Jesus loved.

24 Simon Peter therefore beckoned to him, that he should ask who it should be of whom he spake.

25 He then lying on Jesus' breast saith unto him, Lord, who is it?

1*b* TG God, Love of.
2*a* D&C 10:15 (13, 15); 63:28.
3*a* TG God, Omniscience of.
 b TG Jesus Christ, Power of.
 c John 7:29.
5*a* TG Wash.
8*a* JST John 13:8–10 (Appendix).
 b TG Purification.
10*a* TG Purity.

b D&C 38:10.
11*a* John 6:64.
 b D&C 66:3.
13*a* GR Teacher.
14*a* GR Teacher.
 b TG Courtesy.
 c TG Humility.
 d TG Jesus Christ, Teaching Mode of.
15*a* TG Example; God, the Standard of Righteousness;

Jesus Christ, Exemplar; Leadership.
17*a* TG Happiness.
19*a* JST John 13:19 . . . *the Christ.*
20*a* D&C 39:5; 84:37.
 b 1 Jn. 4:6 (1–6).
21*a* TG Jesus Christ, Betrayal of.
23*a* John 20:2; 21:24 (20–24).

26 Jesus answered, He it is, to whom I shall give a ªsop, when I have dipped *it*. And when he had dipped the sop, he gave *it* to Judas Iscariot, *the son* of Simon.

27 And after the sop ªSatan entered into him. Then said Jesus unto him, That thou doest, do quickly.

28 Now no man at the table knew for what intent he spake this unto him.

29 For some *of them* thought, because Judas had the ªbag, that Jesus had said unto him, Buy *those things* that we have need of against the feast; or, that he should give something to the poor.

30 He then having received the sop went immediately out: and it was night.

31 ¶ Therefore, when he was gone out, Jesus said, Now is the ªSon of man glorified, and God is glorified in him.

32 If God be glorified in him, God shall also glorify him in himself, and shall straightway glorify him.

33 Little children, yet a little while I am with you. Ye shall ªseek me: and as I said unto the Jews, Whither I go, ye cannot come; so now I say to you.

34 A new commandment I give unto you, That ye ªlove one another; as I have loved you, that ye also ᵇlove one another.

35 By this shall all *men* know that ye are my disciples, if ye have ªlove one to another.

36 ¶ Simon Peter said unto him, Lord, whither goest thou? Jesus answered him, Whither I go, thou canst not follow me now; but thou shalt follow me afterwards.

37 Peter said unto him, Lord, why cannot I ªfollow thee now? I will lay down my life for thy sake.

38 Jesus answered him, Wilt thou lay down thy life for my sake? Verily, verily, I say unto thee, The cock shall not crow, till thou hast denied me thrice.

CHAPTER 14

Jesus speaks of many mansions—He says that He is the way, the truth, and the life and that to see Him is to see the Father—He promises the first and second Comforters.

LET not your heart be ªtroubled: ye believe in God, believe also in me.

2 In my Father's ªhouse are many ᵇmansions: if *it were* not *so*, I would have told you. I go to prepare a place for you.

3 And if I go and prepare a place for you, I will ªcome again, and receive you unto myself; that ᵇwhere ᶜI am, *there* ye may be also.

4 And whither I go ye know, and the way ye know.

5 Thomas saith unto him, Lord, we know not whither thou goest; and how can we know the way?

6 Jesus saith unto him, I am the ªway, the ᵇtruth, and the life: no man ᶜcometh unto the Father, but by me.

7 If ye had ªknown me, ye should have known my Father also: and from henceforth ye know him, and have seen him.

8 Philip saith unto him, Lord, shew us the Father, and it sufficeth us.

9 Jesus saith unto him, Have I been so long time with you, and yet hast thou not known me, Philip? he that hath seen me hath seen the ªFather;

26a GR morsel, mouthful.
27a TG Devil.
29a John 12:6.
31a TG Jesus Christ, Son of Man.
33a John 7:34 (33–36).
34a TG Love.
  b TG Family, Love within.
35a TG Fellowshipping; God, Love of.
37a TG Commitment.

14 1a D&C 50:41 (41–42).
  2a TG Heaven.
    b D&C 59:2; 98:18.
      TG Eternal Life; Telestial Glory.
  3a Acts 1:11 (9–11).
    b D&C 27:18; 132:23.
    c 1 Thes. 4:17; Rev. 22:4 (3–5).
  6a Ex. 18:20; 33:13; 1 Sam. 12:23 (16–23);

Ps. 25:4; John 10:7 (1–15).
      TG Example.
    b TG Truth.
    c Matt. 11:27; Luke 10:22.
      TG God, Access to.
  7a John 8:19; 1 Jn. 2:23; D&C 88:50.
  9a TG God, Body of, Corporeal Nature.

and how sayest thou *then,* Shew us the Father?

10 Believest thou not that I am in the *a*Father, and the Father in me? the words that I speak unto you I speak not of myself: but the Father that dwelleth in me, he doeth the works.

11 Believe me that I *am* *a*in the *b*Father, and the Father in me: or else believe me for the very works' sake.

12 Verily, verily, I say unto you, He that *a*believeth on me, the works that I do shall he do also; and greater *works* than these shall he do; because I *b*go unto my *c*Father.

13 And whatsoever ye shall *a*ask in my *b*name, that will I do, that the Father may be glorified in the Son.

14 If ye shall ask any thing in my name, I will do *it.*

15 ¶ If ye *a*love me, *b*keep my *c*commandments.

16 And I will pray the Father, and he shall give you another *a*Comforter, that he may *b*abide with you for ever;

17 *Even* the Spirit of truth; whom the world cannot receive, because it seeth him not, neither knoweth him: but ye know him; for he dwelleth with you, and shall be in you.

18 I will not leave you *a*comfortless: I will *b*come to you.

19 Yet a little while, and the world seeth me no more; but ye see me: because I live, ye shall live also.

20 At that day ye shall know that I *am* in my Father, and ye in me, and I in you.

21 He that hath my commandments, and *a*keepeth them, he it is that loveth me: and he that loveth me shall be *b*loved of my Father, and I will love him, and will *c*manifest myself to him.

22 Judas saith unto him, not Iscariot, Lord, how is it that thou wilt manifest thyself unto us, and not unto the world?

23 Jesus answered and said unto him, If a man love me, he will keep my words: and my Father will *a*love him, and we will come unto him, and make our *b*abode with him.

24 He that loveth me not keepeth not my sayings: and the word which ye hear is not mine, but the Father's which sent me.

25 These things have I spoken unto you, being *yet* present with you.

26 But the *a*Comforter, *which is* the *b*Holy Ghost, whom the Father will send in my *c*name, he shall *d*teach you all things, and bring all things to your remembrance, whatsoever I have said unto you.

27 *a*Peace I leave with you, my *b*peace I give unto you: not as the world giveth, give I unto you. Let not your heart be *c*troubled, neither let it be afraid.

28 Ye have heard how I said unto you, I go away, and come *again* unto you. If ye loved me, ye would rejoice, because I said, I *a*go unto

---

10*a* D&C 93:3.
11*a* D&C 50:43.
  b TG Jesus Christ, Relationships with the Father.
12*a* Acts 9:41 (36–43); 4 Ne. 1:5 (5, 32–33). TG Faith.
  b TG Jesus Christ, Ascension of.
  c TG God the Father, Elohim.
13*a* D&C 6:14; 29:6. TG Prayer.
  b TG Name.
15*a* TG God, Love of; God, the Standard of Righteousness; Love.

  b TG Duty; Obedience.
  c TG Commandments of God; Commitment; Good Works.
16*a* TG Holy Ghost, Comforter.
  b D&C 20:77.
18*a* GR orphans. TG Comfort.
  b John 16:32; 2 Tim. 4:17 (16–17). TG God, Privilege of Seeing.
21*a* TG Obedience.
  b TG God, Love of.
  c TG God, Privilege of Seeing; Revelation.
23*a* TG God, Love of.

  b 1 Jn. 3:24; Rev. 3:20; D&C 130:3.
26*a* TG Holy Ghost, Comforter.
  b TG Guidance, Divine.
  c TG Name.
  d TG God, Omniscience of; Holy Ghost, Gifts of; Holy Ghost, Mission of; Inspiration; Learn; Teaching.
27*a* TG Peace of God.
  b TG Contentment; Peace.
  c TG Sorrow.
28*a* TG Jesus Christ, Ascension of.

the Father: for my *b*Father is greater than I.

29 And now I have told you before it come to pass, that, when it is come to pass, ye might *a*believe.

30 Hereafter I will not talk much with you: *a*for the *b*prince of this *c*world cometh, and hath nothing in me.

31 But that the world may know that I love the Father; and as the Father gave me *a*commandment, even so I do. Arise, let us go hence.

CHAPTER 15

Jesus is the vine; His disciples are the branches—He discourses on the perfect law of love—His servants have been chosen and ordained by Him—The world hates and fights true religion—He promises the Comforter, the Spirit of Truth.

I AM the true *a*vine, and my Father is the husbandman.

2 Every *a*branch in me that beareth not *b*fruit he taketh away: and every *branch* that beareth fruit, he *c*purgeth it, that it may bring forth more fruit.

3 Now ye are clean through the word which I have spoken unto you.

4 *a*Abide in me, and I in you. As the branch cannot bear fruit of itself, except it abide in the vine; no more can ye, except ye abide in me.

5 I am the *a*vine, ye *are* the branches: He that abideth in me, and I in him, the same bringeth forth much fruit: for without *b*me ye can do nothing.

6 If a man *a*abide not in me, he is cast forth as a branch, and is withered; and men gather them, and cast *them* into the fire, and they are burned.

7 If ye *a*abide in me, and my words abide in you, ye shall *b*ask what ye will, and it shall be done unto you.

8 Herein is my Father *a*glorified, that ye bear much fruit; so shall ye be my disciples.

9 As the Father hath *a*loved me, so have I loved you: continue ye in my love.

10 If ye *a*keep my commandments, ye shall abide in my *b*love; even as I have kept my Father's commandments, and abide in his love.

11 These things have I spoken unto you, that my joy might remain in you, and *that* your *a*joy might be full.

12 This is my commandment, That ye *a*love one another, as I have *b*loved you.

13 Greater *a*love hath no man than this, that a man lay down his *b*life for his *c*friends.

14 Ye are my *a*friends, if ye do whatsoever I *b*command you.

15 Henceforth I call you not servants; for the servant knoweth not what his lord doeth: but I have called you *a*friends; for all things that I have *b*heard of my Father I have made *c*known unto you.

16 Ye have not chosen me, but I have *a*chosen you, and *b*ordained

28*b* TG Godhead.
29*a* TG Faith.
30*a* JST John 14:30 . . . for the prince *of darkness, who is* of this world, cometh, *but* hath *no power over me, but he hath power over you.*
  b TG Devil.
  c TG Worldliness.
31*a* TG Jesus Christ, Authority of.
15 1*a* Gen. 49:11; 1 Ne. 15:15.
2*a* Matt. 15:13 (13–14).
  b Matt. 7:19 (15–20); Luke 3:9.
  c GR purifies. TG Test.
4*a* 1 Jn. 2:6;

D&C 35:18; 43:3; 50:24.
5*a* TG Vineyard of the Lord.
  b Philip. 4:13.
6*a* Col. 1:23.
7*a* TG Problem-Solving.
  b TG Prayer.
8*a* Isa. 49:3; Matt. 5:16.
9*a* TG God, Love of.
10*a* 1 Ne. 17:35; Mosiah 2:4; D&C 95:12. TG Obedience.
  b TG Love.
11*a* TG Joy.
12*a* TG Love.
  b D&C 6:20.
13*a* 1 Jn. 3:16 (10–18). TG Love.
  b TG Life, Sanctity of; Martyrdom.

  c TG Brotherhood and Sisterhood; Friendship.
14*a* D&C 84:63.
  b TG Commandments of God.
15*a* Luke 12:4;
  b John 16:12; 3 Ne. 15:16 (13–18).
  c TG Revelation.
16*a* TG Apostles; Called of God; Election; Priesthood, Qualifying for.
  b TG Authority; Church Organization; Priesthood, Authority; Priesthood, History of; Priesthood, Melchizedek.

you, that ye should go and bring forth ^cfruit, and *that* your fruit should remain: that whatsoever ye shall ask of the Father in my ^dname, he may give it you.

17 These things I command you, that ye love one another.

18 If the world ^ahate you, ye know that it hated me before *it hated* you.

19 If ye were of the ^aworld, the world would ^blove his own: but because ye are not of the world, but I have chosen you out of the world, therefore the world hateth you.

20 Remember the word that I said unto you, The ^aservant is not greater than his lord. If they have ^bpersecuted me, they will also persecute you; if they have kept my saying, they will keep yours also.

21 But all these things will they do unto you for my name's sake, because they know not him that sent me.

22 If I had not come and spoken unto them, they had not had ^asin: but now they have no ^bcloak for their sin.

23 He that hateth me hateth my Father also.

24 If I had not done among them the works which none other man did, they had not had ^asin: but now have they both seen and hated both me and my Father.

25 But *this cometh to pass,* that the word might be fulfilled that is written in their law, They ^ahated me without a cause.

26 But when the ^aComforter is come, whom I will send unto you from the Father, *even* the Spirit of truth, which proceedeth from the Father, he shall ^btestify of me:

27 And ye also shall bear ^awitness, because ye have been with me from the beginning.

CHAPTER 16

Jesus discourses on the mission of the Holy Ghost—He tells of His death and resurrection, announces that He is the Son of God, and says that He has overcome the world.

THESE things have I spoken unto you, that ye should not be ^aoffended.

2 They shall put you out of the synagogues: yea, the time cometh, that whosoever ^akilleth you will think that he doeth God service.

3 And these things will they do unto you, because they have not ^aknown the Father, nor me.

4 But these things have I told you, that when the time shall come, ye may remember that I told you of them. And these things I said not unto you at the beginning, because I was with you.

5 But now I ^ago my way to him that sent me; and none of you asketh me, Whither goest thou?

6 But because I have said these things unto you, sorrow hath filled your heart.

7 Nevertheless I tell you the truth; It is ^aexpedient for you that I go away: for if I go not away, the ^bComforter will not come unto you; but if I depart, I will send him unto you.

8 And when he is come, he will ^areprove the world of sin, and of ^brighteousness, and of judgment:

9 Of ^asin, because they believe not on me;

10 Of righteousness, because I go to my Father, and ye see me no more;

16c TG Missionary Work;
      Mission of Early Saints.
   d D&C 18:18.
18a TG Hate.
19a TG World;
      Worldliness.
   b Luke 6:26.
20a Matt. 10:24 (24–25).
   b D&C 6:29.
      TG Persecution.
22a John 9:41 (39–41);
      2 Ne. 9:25 (25–27);

D&C 82:3 (3–4).
   b IE pretext, excuse.
24a Alma 32:19 (17–19).
25a TG Hate.
26a TG Comfort;
      Holy Ghost, Comforter.
   b TG Holy Ghost, Mission
      of; Holy Ghost, Source
      of Testimony.
27a TG Witness.
16 1a TG Offense.
   2a TG Persecution.

3a Moses 4:6.
5a Luke 5:35.
7a GR beneficial,
      profitable,
      advantageous.
   b TG Holy Ghost,
      Comforter.
8a TG Holy Ghost,
      Mission of;
      Reproof.
   b TG Righteousness.
9a TG Sin.

11 Of judgment, because the prince of this world is judged.

12 I have yet many things to ᵃsay unto you, but ye cannot ᵇbear them now.

13 Howbeit when he, the ᵃSpirit of truth, is come, he will ᵇguide you into all ᶜtruth: for he shall not speak of himself; but whatsoever he shall hear, *that* shall he speak: and he will ᵈshew you things to come.

14 He shall ᵃglorify me: for he shall receive of mine, and shall shew *it* unto you.

15 All ᵃthings that the ᵇFather hath are mine: therefore said I, that he shall take of mine, and shall shew *it* unto you.

16 A little while, and ye shall not see me: and again, a little while, and ye shall ᵃsee me, because I go to the Father.

17 Then said *some* of his disciples among themselves, What is this that he saith unto us, A little while, and ye shall not see me: and again, a little while, and ye shall see me: and, Because I go to the Father?

18 They said therefore, What is this that he saith, A little while? we cannot tell what he saith.

19 Now Jesus knew that they were desirous to ask him, and said unto them, Do ye inquire among yourselves of that I said, A little while, and ye shall not see me: and again, a little while, and ye shall see me?

20 Verily, verily, I say unto you, That ye shall weep and lament, but the world shall rejoice: and ye shall be sorrowful, but your ᵃsorrow shall be turned into ᵇjoy.

21 A ᵃwoman when she is in travail hath sorrow, because her hour is come: but as soon as she is delivered of the child, she remembereth no more the anguish, for joy that a man is born into the world.

22 And ye now therefore have ᵃsorrow: but I will see you again, and your heart shall rejoice, and your ᵇjoy no man taketh from you.

23 And in that day ye shall ask me ᵃnothing. Verily, verily, I say unto you, Whatsoever ye shall ᵇask the Father in my name, he will give *it* you.

24 Hitherto have ye asked nothing in my name: ᵃask, and ye shall receive, that your joy may be full.

25 These things have I spoken unto you in ᵃproverbs: but the time cometh, when I shall no more speak unto you in proverbs, but I shall shew you plainly of the Father.

26 At that day ye shall ask in my name: and I say not unto you, that I will pray the Father for you:

27 For the Father himself ᵃloveth you, because ye have loved me, and have ᵇbelieved that I came out from God.

28 I ᵃcame ᵇforth from the ᶜFather, and am come into the world: again, I leave the world, and go to the Father.

29 His disciples said unto him, Lo, now speakest thou plainly, and speakest no proverb.

30 Now are we sure that thou ᵃknowest all things, and needest not that any man should ask thee: by this we believe that thou camest forth from God.

12a John 15:15;
　　3 Ne. 15:16 (13–18).
　b Heb. 5:11 (11–12);
　　3 Ne. 17:2 (2–4);
　　D&C 50:40; 78:18 (17–18).
13a TG Conscience.
　b TG God, Omniscience of;
　　Holy Ghost, Gifts of;
　　Holy Ghost, Mission of;
　　Inspiration; Learn.
　c TG God, Intelligence of;
　　Truth.
　d TG Revelation.
14a Acts 3:13.

　　TG Holy Ghost,
　　Mission of.
15a 3 Ne. 28:10;
　　D&C 76:59; 84:38 (37–38).
　b TG Jesus Christ,
　　Divine Sonship.
16a D&C 35:21; 38:8.
20a TG Pain; Patience.
　b TG Joy.
21a TG Marriage,
　　Motherhood.
22a TG Sorrow.
　b TG Joy.
23a JST John 16:23 . . . *nothing*

but it shall be done unto you.
　　Verily, verily, I say . . .
　b TG Prayer.
24a D&C 66:9.
25a GR figurative discourse,
　　similitudes.
27a TG God, Love of.
　b TG Faith.
28a John 8:42; 17:8; Gal. 4:4.
　b John 8:14.
　c TG Man, Antemortal
　　Existence of.
30a TG God, Omniscience of;
　　God, Perfection of.

31 Jesus answered them, Do ye now believe?

32 Behold, the hour cometh, yea, is now come, that ye shall be scattered, every man to his own, and shall leave me alone: and yet I am not *alone, because the Father is with me.

33 These things I have spoken unto you, that in me ye might have *peace. In the *world ye shall have *tribulation: but be of good *cheer; I have *overcome the world.

CHAPTER 17

Jesus offers the great Intercessory Prayer—He is glorified by gaining eternal life—He prays for His Apostles and all the Saints—He explains how the Father and Son are one.

THESE words spake Jesus, and lifted up his eyes to heaven, and said, Father, the hour is come; glorify thy *Son, that thy Son also may *glorify thee:

2 As thou hast given him *power over all flesh, that he should give *eternal life to as many as thou hast *given him.

3 And this is *life *eternal, that they might *know thee the only true *God, and Jesus Christ, whom thou hast *sent.

4 I have *glorified thee on the earth: I have *finished the work which thou gavest me to do.

5 And now, O Father, glorify thou me with thine own self with the *glory which I had with thee *before the world was.

6 I have manifested thy name unto the men which thou gavest me *out of the world: thine they were, and thou gavest them me; and they have kept thy word.

7 Now they have known that all things whatsoever thou hast *given me are of thee.

8 For I have given unto them the *words which thou gavest me; and they have received *them,* and have known surely that I *came out from thee, and they have *believed that thou didst send me.

9 I *pray for them: I pray not for the world, but for them which *thou hast given me; for they are thine.

10 And all mine are thine, and thine are mine; and I am glorified in them.

11 And now I am no more in the world, but these are in the *world, and I come to thee. Holy Father, keep through thine own name those whom thou hast given me, that they may be *one, as we *are.*

12 While I was with them in the world, I kept them in thy name: those that thou gavest me I have kept, and *none of them is *lost, but the son of *perdition; that the scripture might be fulfilled.

13 And now come I to thee; and

32*a* John 8:16, 29; 14:18.
33*a* TG Peace of God.
 b TG Earth, Purpose of; World; Worldliness.
 c TG Affliction; Test; Tribulation.
 d TG Happiness.
 e Rev. 12:11 (10–12); D&C 50:41; 76:107.
17 1*a* TG Jesus Christ, Divine Sonship.
 b TG Jesus Christ, Mission of.
 2*a* TG Jesus Christ, Authority of; Jesus Christ, Power of.
 b John 6:37.
 c John 10:29 (27–29); D&C 50:41.
 3*a* TG Eternal Life.

 b 1 Jn. 1:2; 2:25; D&C 132:24.
 c Jer. 9:3; Hosea 2:20; 1 Jn. 4:8 (7–8); D&C 101:16.
 TG God, Knowledge about; Objectives; Testimony.
 d TG Godhead.
 e TG Jesus Christ, Messenger of the Covenant.
 4*a* D&C 65:6; 76:43 (40–43).
 b D&C 19:2. TG Jesus Christ, Atonement through.
 5*a* TG Celestial Glory; Jesus Christ, Glory of.
 b TG Jesus Christ, Foreordained; Man, Antemortal Existence of.

 6*a* 1 Kgs. 8:53; 3 Ne. 15:19 (19–20).
 7*a* TG Jesus Christ, Relationships with the Father.
 8*a* Deut. 18:18; John 6:68. TG Revelation.
 b John 8:42; 16:28 (27–28, 30); Gal. 4:4.
 c TG Faith.
 9*a* TG Prayer.
 b D&C 27:14; 84:63.
11*a* TG Earth, Purpose of.
 b TG Unity.
12*a* John 6:39; 18:9.
 b D&C 50:42.
 c 3 Ne. 27:32. TG Damnation; Death, Spiritual, Second; Hell.

these things I speak in the world, that they might have my ᵃjoy fulfilled in themselves.

14 I have given them thy word; and the world hath hated them, because they are not of the world, even as I am not of the world.

15 I pray not that thou shouldest take them out of the ᵃworld, but that thou shouldest ᵇkeep them from the ᶜevil.

16 They are not of the ᵃworld, even as I am not of the world.

17 ᵃSanctify them through thy ᵇtruth: thy word is ᶜtruth.

18 As thou hast ᵃsent me into the world, even so have I also sent them into the world.

19 And for their sakes I ᵃsanctify myself, that they also might be sanctified through the truth.

20 Neither ᵃpray I for these alone, but for them also which shall ᵇbelieve on me through their word;

21 That they all may be ᵃone; as thou, ᵇFather, *art* in me, and I in thee, that they also may be ᶜone in us: that the world may believe that thou hast sent me.

22 And the glory which thou gavest me I have given them; that they may be ᵃone, even as we are ᵇone:

23 I in them, and thou in me, that they may be made ᵃperfect in one; and that the world may know that thou hast sent me, and hast ᵇloved them, as thou hast loved me.

24 Father, I will that they also, whom thou hast given me, be with me where I am; that they may behold my glory, which thou hast given me: for thou lovedst me before the foundation of the world.

25 O righteous Father, the world hath not ᵃknown thee: but I have known thee, and these have known that thou hast sent me.

26 And I have ᵃdeclared unto them thy ᵇname, and will declare *it:* that the ᶜlove wherewith thou hast ᵈloved me may be in them, and I in them.

CHAPTER 18

Jesus is betrayed and arrested—He is examined and maltreated first before Annas, then before Caiaphas—Peter denies knowing Jesus—Jesus is arraigned before Pilate.

WHEN Jesus had spoken these words, he went forth with his disciples over the brook Cedron, where was a garden, into the which he entered, and his disciples.

2 And Judas also, which betrayed him, knew the place: for Jesus ofttimes resorted thither with his disciples.

3 Judas then, having received a band *of men* and officers from the chief priests and Pharisees, cometh thither with lanterns and torches and weapons.

4 Jesus therefore, knowing all things that should come upon him, went forth, and said unto them, Whom seek ye?

5 They answered him, Jesus of Nazareth. Jesus saith unto them, I am *he.* And Judas also, which betrayed him, stood with them.

6 As soon then as he had said unto them, I am *he,* they went backward, and fell to the ground.

7 Then asked he them again, Whom seek ye? And they said, Jesus of Nazareth.

8 Jesus answered, I have told you that I am *he:* if therefore ye seek me, let these go their way:

13a ᴛɢ Joy.
15a ᴛɢ World.
  b ᴛɢ Refuge.
  c ᴛɢ Evil.
16a ᴛɢ Worldliness.
17a ᴛɢ Sanctification.
  b Jacob 4:13.
  c 2 Sam. 7:28;
    Ps. 119:142.
    ᴛɢ Truth.
18a ᴛɢ Jesus Christ,

Authority of.
19a ᴛɢ Jesus Christ,
    Atonement through.
20a ᴛɢ Prayer.
  b D&C 45:5.
21a 4 Ne. 1:17 (15–17);
    D&C 38:27.
  b ᴛɢ Godhead;
    God the Father, Elohim.
  c D&C 35:2; Moses 6:68.
22a Gal. 2:20.

  b D&C 93:3.
23a ᴛɢ Perfection.
  b ᴛɢ God, Love of.
25a ᴛɢ God, Knowledge
    about.
26a ᴛɢ Preaching.
  b ᴛɢ Name.
  c ᴛɢ God, Love of.
  d ᴛɢ Jesus Christ,
    Relationships with
    the Father.

9 That the saying might be fulfilled, which he spake, Of them which thou gavest me have I lost ᵃnone.

10 Then Simon Peter having a sword drew it, and smote the high priest's servant, and ᵃcut off his right ear. The servant's name was ᵇMalchus.

11 Then said Jesus unto Peter, Put up thy sword into the sheath: the ᵃcup which my Father hath given me, shall I not drink it?

12 Then the band and the captain and officers of the Jews took Jesus, and bound him,

13 And led him away to ᵃAnnas first; for he was father in law to Caiaphas, which was the high priest that same year.

14 Now ᵃCaiaphas was he, which gave counsel to the Jews, that it was expedient that one man should die for the people.

15 ¶ And Simon Peter followed Jesus, and *so did* another disciple: that disciple was known unto the high priest, and went in with Jesus into the palace of the high priest.

16 But Peter stood at the door without. Then went out that other disciple, which was known unto the high priest, and spake unto her that kept the door, and brought in Peter.

17 Then saith the damsel that kept the door unto Peter, Art not thou also *one* of this man's disciples? He saith, I am not.

18 And the servants and officers stood there, who had made a fire of coals; for it was cold: and they warmed themselves: and Peter stood with them, and warmed himself.

19 ¶ The high ᵃpriest then asked Jesus of his disciples, and of his doctrine.

20 Jesus answered him, I spake openly to the world; I ever taught in the synagogue, and in the temple, whither the Jews always resort; and in secret have I said nothing.

21 Why askest thou me? ask them which heard me, what I have said unto them: behold, they know what I said.

22 And when he had thus spoken, one of the officers which stood by ᵃstruck Jesus with the palm of his hand, saying, Answerest thou the high priest so?

23 Jesus answered him, If I have spoken evil, bear witness of the evil: but if well, why smitest thou me?

24 Now Annas had sent him bound unto Caiaphas the high priest.

25 And Simon Peter stood and warmed himself. They said therefore unto him, Art not thou also *one* of his disciples? He denied *it,* and said, I am not.

26 One of the servants of the high priest, being *his* kinsman whose ear Peter cut off, saith, Did not I see thee in the garden with him?

27 Peter then denied again: and immediately the cock crew.

28 ¶ Then led they Jesus from Caiaphas unto the hall of judgment: and it was early; and they themselves went not into the judgment hall, lest they should be defiled; but that they might eat the ᵃpassover.

29 ᵃPilate then went out unto them, and said, What accusation bring ye against this man?

30 They answered and said unto him, If he were not a malefactor, we would not have delivered him up unto thee.

31 Then said Pilate unto them, Take ye him, and judge him according to your law. The Jews therefore said unto him, It is not lawful for us to put any man to death:

32 That the saying of Jesus might be fulfilled, which he spake, signifying what death he should die.

33 Then Pilate entered into the judgment hall again, and called

---

18 9a John 6:39; 17:12.
  10a TG Rashness.
    b Matt. 26:51.
  11a 3 Ne. 11:11.
  13a Matt. 26:57;

Luke 3:2.
  TG Jesus Christ,
  Trials of.
  14a John 19:11.
  19a TG Jesus Christ,

Trials of.
  22a Acts 23:2.
  28a John 19:14.
  29a TG Jesus Christ,
    Trials of.

Jesus, and said unto him, Art thou the King of the Jews?

34 Jesus answered him, Sayest thou this thing of thyself, or did others tell it thee of me?

35 Pilate answered, Am I a Jew? Thine own nation and the chief priests have delivered thee unto me: what hast thou done?

36 Jesus answered, My *kingdom is not of this *world: if my kingdom were of this world, then would my servants fight, that I should not be delivered to the Jews: but now is my kingdom not from hence.

37 *Pilate therefore said unto him, Art thou a *king then? Jesus answered, Thou sayest that I am a *king. To this end was I born, and for this cause came I into the world, that I should bear witness unto the *truth. Every one that is of the truth heareth my voice.

38 Pilate saith unto him, What is truth? And when he had *said this, he went out again unto the Jews, and saith unto them, I find in him no *fault at all.

39 But ye have a custom, that I should release unto you one at the passover: will ye therefore that I release unto you the King of the Jews?

40 Then cried they all again, saying, Not this man, but Barabbas. Now *Barabbas was a robber.

CHAPTER 19

Jesus is scourged and crucified—He places His mother in John's care— He dies and His side is pierced with a spear—He is buried in the tomb of Joseph of Arimathæa.

THEN Pilate therefore took Jesus, and *scourged *him*.

2 And the soldiers plaited a crown of thorns, and put *it* on his head, and they put on him a purple robe,

3 And said, Hail, *King of the Jews! and they smote him with their hands.

4 Pilate therefore went forth again, and saith unto them, Behold, I bring him forth to you, that ye may know that I find no *fault in him.

5 Then came Jesus forth, wearing the crown of thorns, and the purple robe. And *Pilate* saith unto them, Behold the man!

6 When the chief priests therefore and officers saw him, they *cried out, saying, Crucify *him,* crucify *him.* Pilate saith unto them, Take ye him, and crucify *him:* for I find no *fault in him.

7 The Jews answered him, We have a *law, and by our law he ought to die, because he made himself the *Son of God.

8 ¶ When Pilate therefore heard that saying, he was the more afraid;

9 And went again into the judgment hall, and saith unto Jesus, Whence art thou? But Jesus gave him no *answer.

10 Then saith Pilate unto him, Speakest thou not unto me? knowest thou not that I have power to crucify thee, and have power to release thee?

11 Jesus answered, Thou couldest have no *power *at all* against me, except it were given thee from above: therefore he that delivered me unto thee hath the greater *sin.

12 And from thenceforth Pilate sought to release him: but the Jews cried out, saying, If thou let this man go, thou art not Cæsar's friend: whosoever maketh himself a *king speaketh against Cæsar.

13 ¶ When Pilate therefore heard

36a John 6:15.
  b TG World.
37a 1 Tim. 6:13.
  b Isa. 55:4.
  c John 19:12 (11–13).
  d 3 Ne. 11:31 (31–41).
  TG Truth.
38a GR said this again.
  b Matt. 27:24 (11–26);

John 19:4.
40a Luke 23:19.
19 1a Mosiah 15:5.
  3a D&C 45:53.
  4a GR cause, crime, case.
    John 18:38;
    Mosiah 14:9.
  6a Acts 3:13.
  b GR cause, crime,

motive.
7a Lev. 24:16.
  b John 5:18 (17–33); 10:33;
    Mosiah 15:2.
9a Mosiah 14:7; 15:6.
11a Rom. 13:1;
    D&C 134:1.
  b John 18:14.
12a John 18:37 (33, 36–37).

that saying, he brought Jesus forth, and sat down in the judgment seat in a place that is called the Pavement, but in the Hebrew, Gabbatha.

14 And it was the preparation of the *a*passover, and about the sixth hour: and he saith unto the Jews, Behold your *b*King!

15 But they cried out, Away with *him*, away with *him*, *a*crucify him. Pilate saith unto them, Shall I crucify your King? The chief priests answered, We have no *b*king but Cæsar.

16 Then delivered he him therefore unto them to be crucified. And they took Jesus, and led *him* away.

17 And he *a*bearing his *b*cross went forth into a place called *the place* of a *c*skull, which is called in the Hebrew Golgotha:

18 Where they crucified him, and two other with him, on either side one, and Jesus in the midst.

19 ¶ And Pilate wrote a title, and put *it* on the cross. And the writing was, JESUS OF NAZARETH THE KING OF THE JEWS.

20 This title then read many of the Jews: for the place where Jesus was crucified was nigh to the city: and it was written in Hebrew, *and* Greek, *and* Latin.

21 Then said the chief priests of the Jews to Pilate, Write not, The King of the Jews; but that he said, I am King of the Jews.

22 Pilate answered, What I have written I have written.

23 ¶ Then the soldiers, when they had crucified Jesus, took his garments, and made four parts, to every soldier a part; and also *his* coat: now the coat was without seam, woven from the top throughout.

24 They said therefore among themselves, Let us not rend it, but cast lots for it, whose it shall be: that the scripture might be fulfilled, which saith, They parted my *a*raiment among them, and for my vesture they did cast lots. These things therefore the soldiers did.

25 ¶ Now there stood by the cross of Jesus his *a*mother, and his mother's sister, Mary the *wife* of *b*Cleophas, and Mary Magdalene.

26 When Jesus therefore saw his mother, and the *a*disciple standing by, whom he loved, he saith unto his mother, *b*Woman, behold thy son!

27 Then saith he to the disciple, Behold thy *a*mother! And from that hour that disciple took her unto his own *home*.

28 ¶ After this, Jesus knowing that all things were now accomplished, that the scripture might be fulfilled, saith, I thirst.

29 Now there was set a vessel full of vinegar: and they filled a sponge with *a*vinegar, and put *it* upon hyssop, and put *it* to his mouth.

30 When Jesus therefore had received the vinegar, he said, It is *a*finished: and he bowed his head, and gave up the ghost.

31 The Jews therefore, because it was the preparation, that the bodies should not remain upon the *a*cross on the sabbath day, (for that *b*sabbath day was an *c*high *d*day,) besought Pilate that their legs might be

---

14*a* John 18:28.
    TG Passover.
  b D&C 45:53.
15*a* TG Jesus Christ,
    Trials of.
  b 2 Ne. 10:14.
17*a* Gen. 22:6.
  b Luke 14:27.
  c JST John 19:17 . . .
    burial . . .
    Heb. 13:12 (11–16).
24*a* Ps. 22:18.
25*a* Luke 2:35 (34–35).
    TG Marriage,

Motherhood.
  b Luke 24:18.
26*a* John 20:2 (2–9);
    D&C 7:1.
  b TG Woman.
27*a* TG Family, Love within;
    Honoring Father and
    Mother;
    Jesus Christ, Family of.
29*a* Ps. 69:21.
30*a* TG Jesus Christ,
    Atonement through.
31*a* TG Jesus Christ,
    Crucifixion of.

  b Ex. 12:16 (15–17).
  c Jesus arose on the first
    day of the week. The
    previous day was the
    weekly Sabbath. The
    day before the Sabbath,
    being also the day after
    the Passover meal,
    could be the "high" day.
    Ex. 12:16;
    Lev. 23:7;
    Mark 15:42.
  d Ex. 12:14 (12–16).

ᵉbroken, and *that* they might be taken away.

32 Then came the soldiers, and brake the legs of the first, and of the other which was crucified with him.

33 But when they came to Jesus, and saw that he was dead already, they ᵃbrake not his legs:

34 But one of the soldiers with a spear pierced his side, and forthwith came there out blood and water.

35 And he that ᵃsaw *it* bare ᵇrecord, and his record is true: and he knoweth that he saith true, that ye might believe.

36 For these things were done, that the scripture should be fulfilled, A ᵃbone of him shall not be broken.

37 And again another scripture saith, They shall look on him whom they ᵃpierced.

38 ¶ And after this ᵃJoseph of Arimathæa, being a disciple of Jesus, but secretly for ᵇfear of the Jews, besought Pilate that he might take away the body of Jesus: and Pilate gave *him* leave. He came therefore, and took the body of Jesus.

39 And there came also ᵃNicodemus, which at the first came to Jesus by night, and brought a mixture of ᵇmyrrh and aloes, about an hundred pound *weight*.

40 Then took they the body of Jesus, and wound it in linen clothes with the spices, as the manner of the Jews is to bury.

41 Now in the place where he was crucified there was a garden; and in the garden a new ᵃsepulchre, wherein was never man yet laid.

42 There laid they Jesus therefore because of the Jews' ᵃpreparation *day*; for the sepulchre was nigh at hand.

CHAPTER 20

Mary Magdalene, Peter, and John find the empty tomb—The risen Christ appears to Mary Magdalene in the garden—He appears to the disciples and shows His resurrected body—Thomas feels the wounds in Jesus' hands, feet, and side—Jesus is the Christ, the Son of God.

THE ᵃfirst *day* of the week cometh Mary Magdalene early, when it was yet ᵇdark, unto the sepulchre, and seeth the ᶜstone taken away from the ᵈsepulchre.

2 Then she runneth, and cometh to Simon Peter, and to the other ᵃdisciple, whom Jesus loved, and saith unto them, They have taken away the ᵇLord out of the sepulchre, and we know not where they have laid him.

3 Peter therefore went forth, and that other disciple, and came to the sepulchre.

4 So they ran both together: and the other disciple did outrun Peter, and came first to the sepulchre.

5 And he stooping down, *and looking in,* saw the linen clothes lying; yet went he not in.

6 Then cometh Simon Peter following him, and went into the sepulchre, and seeth the linen clothes lie,

7 And the ᵃnapkin, that was about his head, not lying with the linen clothes, but wrapped together in a place by itself.

8 Then went in also that other disciple, which came first to the sepulchre, and he saw, and believed.

9 For as yet they knew not the scripture, that he must ᵃrise again from the ᵇdead.

10 Then the disciples went away again unto their own home.

31e Deut. 21:23 (22–23).
33a TG Jesus Christ, Types of, in Anticipation; Passover.
35a John 1:14; 21:24.
  b John 1:7 (6–8).
36a Ex. 12:46; Num. 9:12.
37a TG Jesus Christ, Crucifixion of.
38a Matt. 27:57 (57–61).
  b Prov. 29:25;

     John 7:13; 12:42 (42–43).
39a John 3:1 (1–10).
  b Ps. 45:8.
41a Luke 23:53; 2 Ne. 25:13.
42a TG Passover.
20 1a TG Sabbath.
  b Mark 16:2.
  c Matt. 27:60.
  d JST John 20:1 . . . sepulcher, *and two angels sitting thereon.*

2a John 13:23;
     19:26 (26–27);
     21:24 (20–24);
     1 Ne. 14:27 (18–27);
     D&C 7:1.
  b TG Jesus Christ, Lord.
7a John 11:44.
9a Mark 9:10 (9–10);
     Hel. 14:16 (15–17);
     D&C 18:12 (11–12).
  b Isa. 25:8.

11 ¶ But Mary stood without at the sepulchre weeping: and as she wept, she stooped down, *and looked* into the sepulchre,

12 And seeth two *a*angels in white sitting, the one at the head, and the other at the feet, where the body of Jesus had lain.

13 And they say unto her, Woman, why weepest thou? She saith unto them, Because they have taken away my Lord, and I know not where they have laid him.

14 And when she had thus said, she turned herself back, and *a*saw Jesus standing, and knew not that it was Jesus.

15 Jesus saith unto her, Woman, why weepest thou? whom seekest thou? She, supposing him to be the gardener, saith unto him, Sir, if thou have borne him hence, tell me where thou hast laid him, and I will take him away.

16 Jesus saith unto her, Mary. She turned herself, and saith unto him, Rabboni; which is to say, *a*Master.

17 Jesus saith unto her, *a*Touch me not; for I am not yet *b*ascended to my *c*Father: but go to my brethren, and say unto them, I ascend unto my *d*Father, and your Father; and *to* my God, and your God.

18 Mary Magdalene came and told the disciples that she had seen the Lord, and *that* he had spoken these things unto her.

19 ¶ Then the same day at evening, being the first *day* of the week, when the doors were shut where the disciples were *a*assembled for fear of the Jews, came Jesus and *b*stood in the midst, and saith unto them, *c*Peace *be* unto you.

20 And when he had so said, he shewed unto them *his* *a*hands and his side. Then were the disciples glad, when they *b*saw the Lord.

21 Then said Jesus to them again, Peace *be* unto you: as *my* *a*Father hath *b*sent me, even so *c*send I you.

22 And when he had said this, he breathed on *them*, and saith unto them, Receive ye the Holy Ghost:

23 Whose soever sins ye *a*remit, they are remitted unto them; *and* whose soever *sins* ye retain, they are retained.

24 ¶ But Thomas, one of the twelve, called Didymus, was not with them when Jesus came.

25 The other disciples therefore said unto him, We have seen the Lord. But he said unto them, Except I shall see in his hands the *a*print of the nails, and put my finger into the print of the nails, and thrust my hand into his side, I will not believe.

26 ¶ And after eight days again his disciples were within, and Thomas with them: *then* came Jesus, the doors being shut, and stood in the midst, and said, Peace *be* unto you.

27 Then saith he to Thomas, Reach hither thy finger, and behold my hands; and reach hither thy hand, and *a*thrust *it* into my side: and be not *b*faithless, but *c*believing.

28 And Thomas answered and said unto him, My Lord and my God.

29 Jesus saith unto him, Thomas, because thou hast *a*seen me, thou hast believed: *b*blessed *are* they that have not seen, and *yet* have *c*believed.

12a TG Angels.
14a TG Jesus Christ, Appearances, Postmortal.
16a GR Teacher.
17a JST John 20:17 . . . *Hold me not* . . .
  b Luke 23:43 (39–43); Alma 40:11 (6–15). TG Jesus Christ, Ascension of.
  c TG God the Father, Elohim.
  d TG Godhead.
19a TG Assembly for Worship; Meetings.
  b TG Jesus Christ, Appearances, Postmortal.
  c TG Peace of God.
20a TG Jesus Christ, Resurrection.
  b TG Jesus Christ, Appearances, Postmortal.
21a TG Jesus Christ, Divine Sonship.
  b TG Jesus Christ, Authority of.
  c Mark 16:15 (14–18).
TG Authority.
23a TG Priesthood, Keys of; Remission of Sins.
25a TG Jesus Christ, Crucifixion of.
27a 3 Ne. 11:14.
  b TG Doubt.
  c TG Unbelief.
29a TG Jesus Christ, Appearances, Postmortal.
  b D&C 34:4.
  c 1 Pet. 1:8; Alma 32:21 (17–21). TG Faith.

30 ¶ And many other ^asigns truly did Jesus in the presence of his disciples, which are not ^bwritten in this book:

31 But these are ^awritten, that ye might ^bbelieve that Jesus is the ^cChrist, the Son of God; and that believing ye might have ^dlife through his ^ename.

CHAPTER 21

Jesus appears to the disciples at the sea of Tiberias—He says, Feed my sheep—He foretells Peter's martyrdom and that John will not die.

AFTER these things Jesus ^ashewed himself again to the disciples at the sea of Tiberias; and on this wise shewed he *himself.*

2 There were together Simon Peter, and Thomas called Didymus, and Nathanael of Cana in Galilee, and the *sons* of ^aZebedee, and two other of his disciples.

3 Simon Peter saith unto them, I go a fishing. They say unto him, We also go with thee. They went forth, and entered into a ship immediately; and that night they caught nothing.

4 But when the morning was now come, Jesus ^astood on the shore: but the disciples knew not that it was Jesus.

5 Then Jesus saith unto them, Children, have ye any meat? They answered him, No.

6 And he said unto them, Cast the net on the right side of the ship, and ye shall find. They cast therefore, and now they were not able to draw it for the multitude of fishes.

7 Therefore that disciple whom Jesus loved saith unto Peter, It is the Lord. Now when Simon Peter heard that it was the Lord, he girt

his fisher's coat *unto him,* (for he was naked,) and did cast himself into the sea.

8 And the other disciples came in a little ship; (for they were not far from land, but as it were two hundred cubits,) dragging the net with fishes.

9 As soon then as they were come to land, they saw a fire of coals there, and fish laid thereon, and bread.

10 Jesus saith unto them, Bring of the fish which ye have now caught.

11 Simon Peter went up, and drew the net to land full of great fishes, an hundred and fifty and three: and for all there were so many, yet was not the net broken.

12 Jesus saith unto them, Come *and* dine. And none of the disciples durst ask him, Who art thou? knowing that it was the Lord.

13 Jesus then cometh, and taketh bread, and giveth them, and fish likewise.

14 This is now the ^athird time that Jesus ^bshewed himself to his disciples, after that he was risen from the dead.

15 ¶ So when they had dined, Jesus saith to Simon Peter, Simon, *son* of Jonas, lovest thou me more than these? He saith unto him, Yea, Lord; thou knowest that I love thee. He saith unto him, Feed my lambs.

16 He saith to him again the second time, Simon, *son* of Jonas, lovest thou me? He saith unto him, Yea, Lord; thou knowest that I love thee. He saith unto him, ^aFeed my sheep.

17 He saith unto him the third time, Simon, *son* of Jonas, lovest thou me? Peter was grieved because he said unto him the third time, Lovest thou me? And he said

---

30a TG Signs.
  b John 21:25;
    1 Ne. 14:25 (18–30);
    D&C 93:6 (6, 18).
31a 1 Jn. 5:13 (10–21).
  b Luke 1:4 (3–4);
    John 1:7 (6–8);
    1 Ne. 6:4;

Morm. 5:14.
    TG Faith.
  c TG Jesus Christ, Messiah.
  d John 5:24.
  e TG Jesus Christ, Taking
    the Name of; Name.
21 1a TG Jesus Christ,
    Resurrection.

2a Matt. 4:21.
4a TG Jesus Christ,
    Appearances, Postmortal.
14a 3 Ne. 26:13; 27:2.
  b TG Jesus Christ,
    Appearances, Postmortal.
16a 1 Pet. 5:2;
    D&C 112:14.

unto him, Lord, thou knowest all things; thou knowest that I love thee. Jesus saith unto him, *a*Feed my *b*sheep.

18 Verily, verily, I say unto thee, When thou wast young, thou girdedst thyself, and walkedst whither thou wouldest: but when thou shalt be *a*old, thou shalt stretch forth thy hands, and another shall gird thee, and carry *thee* whither thou wouldest not.

19 This spake he, signifying by what *a*death he should glorify God. And when he had spoken this, he saith unto him, Follow me.

20 Then Peter, turning about, seeth the disciple whom Jesus loved following; which also leaned on his breast at supper, and said, Lord, which is he that betrayeth thee?

21 Peter seeing him saith to Jesus, Lord, and what *shall* this man *do*?

22 Jesus saith unto him, If I will that he *a*tarry till I come, what *is that* to thee? *b*follow thou me.

23 Then went this saying abroad among the brethren, that that disciple should not *a*die: yet Jesus said not unto him, He shall not die; but, If I will that he tarry till I come, what *is that* to thee?

24 This is the *a*disciple which testifieth of these things, and *b*wrote these things: and we know that his testimony is *c*true.

25 And there are also many other things which Jesus did, the which, if they should be *a*written every one, I suppose that even the world itself could not contain the *b*books that should be written. Amen.

THE ACTS
OF THE APOSTLES

CHAPTER 1

Jesus ministers for forty days after His resurrection—The kingdom is to be restored to Israel at a later time—The Twelve are to bear witness in Jerusalem, Judœa, Samaria, and the uttermost parts of the earth—Jesus ascends into heaven—Matthias is chosen to fill the vacancy in the Twelve.

THE former treatise have *a*I made, O *b*Theophilus, of all that Jesus began both to do and teach,

2 Until the day in which he was taken up, after that he through the Holy Ghost had given *a*commandments unto the apostles whom he had chosen:

3 To whom also he *a*shewed himself

17a TG Fellowshipping; Jesus Christ, Teaching Mode of; Missionary Work.
  b TG Sheep.
18a TG Old Age.
19a 2 Pet. 1:14.
22a Rev. 10:11; D&C 7:3 (3–4). TG Translated Beings.

b TG Jesus Christ, Exemplar.
23a Luke 9:27.
24a John 1:14; 13:23; 19:35; 20:2.
  b TG Scriptures, Writing of.
  c 3 Ne. 8:1.
25a John 20:30 (30–31); 1 Ne. 14:25 (18–30).
  b 3 Ne. 26:6.

[ACTS]
1 1a 2 Tim. 4:11 (10–11).
  b Luke 1:3.
2a TG Holy Ghost, Mission of.
3a TG Jesus Christ, Appearances, Postmortal; Jesus Christ, Resurrection.

alive after his [b]passion by many infallible proofs, being seen of them forty days, and speaking of the things [c]pertaining to the kingdom of God:

4 And, being assembled together with *them,* commanded them that they should not depart from Jerusalem, but wait for the [a]promise of the Father, which, *saith he,* ye have heard of me.

5 For John truly baptized with water; but ye shall be [a]baptized with the Holy Ghost not many days hence.

6 When they therefore were come together, they asked of him, saying, Lord, wilt thou at this time [a]restore again the kingdom to Israel?

7 And he said unto them, It is not for you to know the times or the [a]seasons, which the Father hath put in his own power.

8 But ye shall receive [a]power, after that the Holy Ghost is come upon you: and ye shall be [b]witnesses unto me both in Jerusalem, and in all Judæa, and in [c]Samaria, and unto the uttermost part of the earth.

9 And when he had spoken these things, while they beheld, he was [a]taken [b]up; and a cloud received him out of their sight.

10 And while they looked steadfastly toward heaven as he went up, behold, two men stood by them in white apparel;

11 Which also said, Ye men of Galilee, why stand ye gazing up into [a]heaven? this same Jesus, which is [b]taken up from you into heaven, shall so [c]come in like [d]manner as ye have seen him go into heaven.

12 Then returned they unto Jeru-salem from the mount called Olivet, which is from Jerusalem a sabbath day's journey.

13 And when they were come in, they went up into an upper room, where abode both Peter, and James, and John, and Andrew, Philip, and Thomas, Bartholomew, and Matthew, James *the son* of Alphæus, and Simon Zelotes, and Judas *the brother* of James.

14 These all continued with [a]one accord in prayer and [b]supplication, with the women, and Mary the mother of Jesus, and with his [c]brethren.

15 ¶ And in those days Peter stood up in the midst of the disciples, and said, (the number of names together were about an hundred and twenty,)

16 Men *and* brethren, this scripture must needs have been fulfilled, which the Holy Ghost by the mouth of David [a]spake before concerning [b]Judas, which was guide to them that took Jesus.

17 For he was numbered with us, and had obtained part of this ministry.

18 Now this man purchased a field with the reward of iniquity; and falling headlong, he [a]burst asunder in the midst, and all his bowels gushed out.

19 And it was known unto all the dwellers at Jerusalem; insomuch as that field is called in their [a]proper tongue, Aceldama, that is to say, The field of blood.

20 For it is written in the book of Psalms, Let his habitation be [a]desolate, and let no man dwell therein: and his [b]bishoprick let another take.

3b GR suffering.
    JST Acts 1:3 . . .
    sufferings . . .
  c D&C 100:11.
4a D&C 95:9 (8–10).
    TG Promise.
5a TG Holy Ghost, Baptism of; Holy Ghost, Gift of.
6a TG Dispensations.
7a Dan. 2:21 (19–22, 28);
    D&C 68:11 (7–12);
    121:12 (12, 27, 31).
8a 2 Tim. 1:7.
    TG Holy Ghost, Gifts of.

  b Luke 24:48;
    D&C 27:12.
  c Acts 8:5 (5, 14).
9a 3 Ne. 10:18 (18–19);
    11:8 (8–10).
    TG Jesus Christ, Resurrection.
  b Ps. 68:18;
    Eph. 4:8.
11a 1 Thes. 1:10.
  b TG Jesus Christ, Ascension of.
  c John 14:3 (1–4).
  d TG Jesus Christ, Second

    Coming.
14a TG Unity.
  b Moro. 6:5 (1–5).
  c TG Jesus Christ, Family of.
16a TG Holy Ghost, Mission of.
  b Ps. 41:9;
    Luke 22:48 (47–48).
18a Matt. 27:5 (3–10).
19a GR own.
20a Ps. 69:25.
  b GR overseership, office.
    Ps. 109:8; D&C 114:2.

21 Wherefore of these men which have companied with us all the time that the Lord Jesus went in and out among us,

22 Beginning from the baptism of John, unto that same day that he was taken up from us, must one ^abe ordained to be a ^bwitness with us of his ^cresurrection.

23 And they appointed two, Joseph called Barsabas, who was surnamed Justus, and Matthias.

24 And they ^aprayed, and said, Thou, Lord, which ^bknowest the hearts of all *men*, shew ^cwhether of these two thou hast ^dchosen,

25 That he may take part of this ministry and ^aapostleship, from which Judas by transgression ^bfell, that he might go to his own place.

26 And they gave forth their lots; and the lot fell upon ^aMatthias; and he was numbered with the eleven apostles.

CHAPTER 2

The Spirit is poured out on the day of Pentecost—Peter testifies of Jesus' resurrection—He tells how to gain salvation and speaks of the gift of the Holy Ghost—Many believe and are baptized.

AND when the day of ^aPentecost was fully come, they were all with one accord in one place.

2 And suddenly there came a sound from heaven as of a rushing mighty ^awind, and it filled all the house where they were sitting.

3 And there appeared unto them ^acloven tongues like as of fire, and it sat upon each of them.

4 And they were all filled with the ^aHoly Ghost, and began to speak with other ^btongues, as the ^cSpirit gave them utterance.

5 And there were dwelling at Jerusalem Jews, devout men, out of every nation under heaven.

6 Now when this was noised abroad, the multitude came together, and were confounded, because that every man heard them speak in his own ^alanguage.

7 And they were all amazed and marvelled, saying one to another, Behold, are not all these which speak Galilæans?

8 And how hear we every man in our own tongue, wherein we were born?

9 Parthians, and Medes, and Elamites, and the dwellers in Mesopotamia, and in Judæa, and Cappadocia, in Pontus, and Asia,

10 Phrygia, and Pamphylia, in Egypt, and in the parts of Libya about Cyrene, and strangers of Rome, Jews and ^aproselytes,

11 Cretes and Arabians, we do hear them speak in our ^atongues the wonderful works of God.

12 And they were all amazed, and were in doubt, saying one to another, What meaneth this?

13 Others ^amocking said, These men are full of new wine.

14 ¶ But Peter, standing up with the eleven, lifted up his voice, and said unto them, Ye men of Judæa, and all *ye* that dwell at Jerusalem, be this known unto you, and hearken to my words:

15 For these are not drunken, as ye suppose, seeing it is *but* the third hour of the day.

16 But this is that which was spoken by the prophet ^aJoel;

17 And it shall come to pass in the ^alast days, saith God, I will ^bpour out of my ^cSpirit upon all flesh: and your

---

22*a* GR become a witness.
  b TG Witness.
  c TG Resurrection.
24*a* D&C 9:8 (7–9).
  b TG God, Omniscience of.
  c GR which one.
  d TG Called of God.
25*a* TG Church Organization.
  b 1 Cor. 10:12;
     D&C 3:9.
26*a* TG Apostles.

2 1*a* Ex. 23:17;
       34:22 (16, 22);
       Lev. 23:16 (15–16);
       Acts 20:16.
  2*a* D&C 109:37.
  3*a* D&C 109:36.
  4*a* Acts 4:31.
     TG Holy Ghost,
     Baptism of.
  b TG Holy Ghost, Gifts of;
     Holy Ghost, Mission of.

   c D&C 14:8.
  6*a* TG Language.
 10*a* Acts 13:43.
 11*a* 1 Cor. 14:22.
 13*a* 1 Cor. 14:23.
 16*a* JS—H 1:41.
 17*a* TG Last Days.
  b Joel 2:28.
  c Isa. 44:3;
     Ezek. 36:27 (26–27);
     D&C 19:38; 44:2; 95:4.

sons and your daughters shall ^dprophesy, and your young men shall see visions, and your old men shall ^edream dreams:

18 And on my servants and on my handmaidens I will pour out in those days of my Spirit; and they shall ^aprophesy:

19 And I will shew ^awonders in heaven above, and ^bsigns in the earth beneath; blood, and fire, and vapour of smoke:

20 The sun shall be turned into ^adarkness, and the moon into blood, before that great and ^bnotable ^cday of the Lord come:

21 And it shall come to pass, *that* whosoever shall call on the name of the Lord shall be ^asaved.

22 Ye men of Israel, hear these words; Jesus of Nazareth, a man ^aapproved of God among you by ^bmiracles and wonders and signs, which ^cGod did by him in the midst of you, as ye yourselves also know:

23 Him, being delivered by the ^adeterminate counsel and ^bforeknowledge of God, ye have taken, and by wicked hands have ^ccrucified and slain:

24 Whom God hath ^araised up, having loosed the ^bpains of ^cdeath: because it was not possible that he should be holden of it.

25 For David speaketh concerning him, I foresaw the ^aLord always before my face, for he is on my right hand, that I should not be moved:

26 Therefore did my heart rejoice, and my tongue was glad; moreover also my flesh shall rest in hope:

27 Because thou wilt not leave my soul in ^ahell, neither wilt thou suffer thine Holy One to see ^bcorruption.

28 Thou hast made known to me the ways of life; thou shalt make me full of joy with thy countenance.

29 Men *and* brethren, let me freely speak unto you of the ^apatriarch David, that he is both dead and ^bburied, and his sepulchre is with us unto this day.

30 Therefore being a prophet, and knowing that God had sworn with an ^aoath to him, that of the fruit of his loins, according to the flesh, he would raise up ^bChrist to sit on his throne;

31 He seeing this before spake of the resurrection of Christ, that his soul was not left in hell, neither his flesh did see corruption.

32 This Jesus hath God ^araised up, whereof we all are ^bwitnesses.

33 Therefore being ^aby the ^bright hand of God ^cexalted, and having received of the Father the promise of the Holy Ghost, he hath ^dshed forth this, which ye now see and hear.

34 For ^aDavid is not ^bascended into the heavens: but he saith himself, The LORD said unto my ^cLord, Sit thou on my right hand,

35 Until I make thy foes thy footstool.

36 Therefore let all the house of Israel know assuredly, that God hath made that same Jesus, whom ye

17d Acts 21:9.
  TG Holy Ghost, Gifts of.
  e TG Dream.
18a Acts 11:28 (27–28);
  21:11 (4, 10–11).
19a TG Last Days.
  b TG Signs.
20a TG Darkness, Physical.
  b GR glorious.
  c TG Day of the Lord.
21a TG Jesus Christ, Savior;
  Salvation.
22a John 9:33 (31–33).
  b Mosiah 3:5 (5–6).
  c Ex. 8:19;
  Luke 11:20;

John 3:2;
  Acts 10:38.
23a GR appointed plan,
  purpose.
  b TG Foreordination;
  God, Foreknowledge of.
  c Matt. 26:24;
  Luke 22:22.
  TG Jesus Christ,
  Crucifixion of.
24a TG Resurrection.
  b TG Pain.
  c TG Jesus Christ, Death of.
25a Ps. 16:8 (8–11).
27a JST Acts 2:27 . . . prison . . .
  b Acts 13:37 (34–37).

29a TG Patriarch.
  b 1 Kgs. 2:10.
30a TG Oath.
  b TG Jesus Christ, Davidic
  Descent of.
32a Eph. 1:20.
  TG Jesus Christ,
  Resurrection.
  b TG Witness.
33a GR to, at.
  b TG Godhead.
  c Heb. 2:9.
  d D&C 53:2.
34a D&C 132:39.
  b Ps. 30:3; 86:13.
  c Ps. 110:1.

have ^acrucified, both ^bLord and Christ.

37 ¶ Now when they heard *this*, they were ^apricked in their ^bheart, and said unto Peter and to the rest of the apostles, Men *and* brethren, ^cwhat shall we do?

38 Then Peter ^asaid unto them, ^bRepent, and be ^cbaptized every one of you in the ^dname of Jesus Christ for the ^eremission of sins, and ye shall receive the ^fgift of the ^gHoly Ghost.

39 For the ^apromise is unto you, and to your children, and to all that are ^bafar off, *even* as many as the Lord our God shall call.

40 And with many other words did he testify and exhort, saying, ^aSave yourselves from this ^buntoward generation.

41 ¶ Then they that gladly ^areceived his ^bword were baptized: and the same day there were added *unto them* about ^cthree thousand souls.

42 And they continued ^asteadfastly in the apostles' doctrine and ^bfellowship, and in breaking of ^cbread, and in prayers.

43 And ^afear came upon every soul: and many wonders and ^bsigns were done by the apostles.

44 And all that believed were together, and had all things ^acommon;

45 And sold their possessions and goods, and parted them to all *men*, as every man had ^aneed.

46 And they, continuing daily with one accord in the ^atemple, and breaking bread from house to house,

did eat their meat with gladness and ^bsingleness of heart,

47 Praising God, and having favour with all the people. And the Lord ^aadded to the ^bchurch daily such as should be saved.

CHAPTER 3

Peter and John heal a man lame since birth—Peter preaches repentance—He also speaks of the age of restoration preceding the Second Coming—He identifies Christ as the prophet of whom Moses spoke.

Now Peter and John went up together into the temple at the hour of prayer, *being* the ninth *hour*.

2 And a certain man ^alame from his mother's womb was carried, whom they laid daily at the gate of the temple which is called Beautiful, to ask alms of them that entered into the temple;

3 Who seeing Peter and John about to go into the temple asked an ^aalms.

4 And Peter, fastening his eyes upon him with John, said, Look on us.

5 And he gave heed unto them, expecting to receive something of them.

6 Then Peter said, Silver and gold have I none; but such as I have ^agive I thee: In the ^bname of Jesus Christ of Nazareth rise up and walk.

7 And he took him by the right hand, and ^alifted *him* up: and immediately his feet and ankle bones received strength.

36a TG Jesus Christ, Crucifixion of.
b TG Jesus Christ, Lord; Jesus Christ, Power of.
37a Alma 22:3 (3–11). TG Conscience; Holy Ghost, Mission of; Holy Ghost, Source of Testimony.
b TG Conversion.
c Alma 22:15.
38a D&C 49:11 (11–14).
b TG Baptism, Qualifications for; Repent; Salvation.
c TG Baptism; Baptism, Essential.
d TG Name.

e TG Remission of Sins.
f TG Holy Ghost, Gift of.
g Acts 8:17 (14–17). TG Holy Ghost, Baptism of.
39a TG Promise.
b Isa. 57:19.
40a D&C 36:6.
b GR crooked.
41a TG Teachable.
b TG Baptism, Qualifications for.
c Acts 4:4.
42a TG Commitment; Steadfastness; Sustaining Church Leaders.
b TG Fellowshipping.

c TG Bread; Sacrament.
43a TG Courage; Fearful.
b TG Signs.
44a TG Consecration.
45a Acts 4:35 (32–35); D&C 51:3.
46a Luke 24:53.
b D&C 36:7.
47a Acts 5:14.
b TG Church.
3 2a Acts 14:8 (8–10).
3a TG Almsgiving.
6a TG Benevolence; Generosity.
b Acts 4:10; Jacob 4:6; 3 Ne. 8:1.
7a Mark 9:27. TG Heal.

8 And he leaping up stood, and walked, and entered with them into the temple, walking, and leaping, and praising God.

9 And all the people *saw him walking and praising God:

10 And they knew that it was he which sat for alms at the Beautiful gate of the temple: and they were filled with wonder and amazement at that which had happened unto him.

11 And as the lame man which was healed held Peter and John, all the people ran together unto them in the *porch that is called Solomon's, greatly wondering.

12 ¶ And when Peter saw *it*, he answered unto the people, Ye men of Israel, why marvel ye at this? or why look ye so earnestly on us, as though by our *own power or holiness we had made this man to walk?

13 The God of Abraham, and of Isaac, and of Jacob, the God of our fathers, hath *glorified his Son Jesus; whom ye *delivered up, and *denied him in the presence of Pilate, when he was determined to let *him* go.

14 But ye denied the Holy One and the Just, and desired a *murderer to be granted unto you;

15 And killed the *Prince of life, whom God hath *raised from the dead; whereof we are *witnesses.

16 And his *name through faith in his name hath made this man strong, whom ye see and know: yea,

the *faith which is by him hath given him this perfect soundness in the presence of you all.

17 And now, brethren, *I *wot that through *ignorance ye did *it*, as *did* also your rulers.

18 But those things, which God before had *shewed by the mouth of all his *prophets, that Christ should *suffer, he hath so fulfilled.

19 ¶ *Repent ye therefore, and be *converted, that your sins may be *blotted out, when the times of re-freshing shall come from the *pres-ence of the Lord;

20 And he shall send *Jesus Christ, which before was preached unto *you:

21 Whom the heaven must receive until the times of *restitution of all things, which God hath *spoken by the mouth of all his holy prophets since the world began.

22 For Moses truly said unto the fathers, A *prophet shall the Lord your God raise up unto you of your brethren, like unto me; him shall ye hear in all things whatsoever he shall say unto you.

23 And it shall come to pass, *that* every soul, which will not hear that prophet, shall be *destroyed from among the people.

24 Yea, and all the prophets from Samuel and those that follow after, as many as have spoken, have like-wise *foretold of these days.

25 Ye are the *children of the prophets, and of the *covenant which

9a Acts 4:16.
11a 1 Kgs. 6:3; John 10:23.
12a Gen. 41:16; Dan. 2:30.
13a John 16:14; 1 Pet. 1:21 (17–21).
  b Matt. 27:20; Acts 13:28.
  c John 19:6.
14a Luke 23:25 (17–19, 25).
15a TG Jesus Christ, Messiah.
  b Acts 10:40.
  c TG Witness.
16a TG Name.
  b TG Faith.
17a JST Acts 3:17 . . . I *know* that through ignorance

ye *have done this*, as also your rulers.
  b OR know.
  c D&C 6:21.
18a TG Foreordination.
  b Luke 24:27; Acts 28:23; Alma 18:36.
  c 1 Cor. 15:3.
19a TG Repent.
  b TG Conversion.
  c Ps. 51:1; Mosiah 26:30; Alma 5:14 (11–15, 21).
  d TG God, Presence of.
20a TG Jesus Christ, Second Coming.
  b JST Acts 3:20 . . . you,

whom ye have crucified;
21a TG Dispensations; Restoration of the Gospel.
  b TG Prophets, Mission of.
22a Deut. 18:15 (15–19); Acts 7:37; 1 Ne. 22:20 (20–22); JS—H 1:40.
23a D&C 1:14 (14–16); 133:63.
24a TG Jesus Christ, Prophecies about.
25a TG Seed of Abraham.
  b TG Abrahamic Covenant; Mission of Early Saints.

God made with our fathers, saying unto Abraham, And in thy seed shall all the kindreds of the earth be ^cblessed.

26 Unto you first God, having raised up his ^aSon Jesus, sent him to bless you, in turning away every one of you from his iniquities.

CHAPTER 4

Peter and John are arrested and brought before the council—Peter testifies that salvation comes because of Christ—The Sadducees strive to silence Peter and John—The Saints glory in the testimony of Jesus—They have all things in common.

AND as they spake unto the people, the priests, and the captain of the temple, and the Sadducees, came upon them,

2 Being grieved that they taught the people, and preached through Jesus the ^aresurrection from the dead.

3 And they laid hands on them, and put *them* in hold unto the next day: for it was now eventide.

4 Howbeit many of them which heard the word believed; and the number of the men was about ^afive thousand.

5 ¶ And it came to pass on the morrow, that their rulers, and elders, and ^ascribes,

6 And Annas the high priest, and Caiaphas, and John, and Alexander, and as many as were of the kindred of the high ^apriest, were gathered together at Jerusalem.

7 And when they had set them in the midst, they asked, By what ^apower, or by what ^bname, have ye done this?

8 Then Peter, filled with the ^aHoly Ghost, said unto them, Ye rulers of the people, and elders of Israel,

9 If we this day be examined of the good deed done to the impotent man, by what means he is made whole;

10 Be it known unto you all, and to all the people of Israel, that by the ^aname of Jesus Christ of Nazareth, whom ye crucified, whom God raised from the dead, *even* by him doth this man stand here before you whole.

11 This is the ^astone which was set at nought of you builders, which is become the head of the corner.

12 Neither is there ^asalvation in any other: for there is none other ^bname under heaven given among men, whereby we must be ^csaved.

13 ¶ Now when they saw the boldness of Peter and John, and perceived that they were ^aunlearned and ^bignorant men, they marvelled; and they took knowledge of them, that they had been with Jesus.

14 And beholding the man which was healed standing with them, they could say nothing against it.

15 But when they had commanded them to go aside out of the council, they conferred among themselves,

16 Saying, What shall we do to these men? for that indeed a notable ^amiracle hath been done by them *is* manifest to all them that dwell in Jerusalem; and we cannot deny *it*.

17 But that it spread no further among the people, let us straitly threaten them, that they speak henceforth to no man in this name.

18 And they called them, and ^acommanded them not to speak at all nor teach in the name of Jesus.

19 But Peter and John answered and said unto them, Whether it be

---

25c TG Israel, Mission of.
26a TG God, Body of, Corporeal Nature.
4 2a Acts 23:8.
  4a Acts 2:41.
  5a TG Scribe.
  6a TG Priestcraft.
  7a TG Priesthood, Power of.
  b TG Name.
  8a TG Teaching with the Spirit.

10a Acts 3:6.
11a TG Cornerstone; Rock.
12a TG Gospel.
  b Ps. 9:10; Hosea 13:4; 1 Jn. 2:12; 2 Ne. 25:20; Mosiah 4:8. TG Jesus Christ, Taking the Name of.

  c TG Jesus Christ, Atonement through; Jesus Christ, Savior; Salvation; Salvation, Plan of.
13a D&C 1:19; 35:13.
  b GR ordinary, plain.
16a Acts 3:9 (6–9).
18a Acts 5:28 (27–28).

right in the sight of God to *a*hearken unto you more than unto God, judge ye.

20 For we cannot but *a*speak the things which we have *b*seen and heard.

21 So when they had further threatened them, they let them go, finding nothing how they might punish them, because of the people: for all *men* glorified God for that which was done.

22 For the man was above forty years old, on whom this miracle of healing was shewed.

23 ¶ And being let go, they went to their own company, and reported all that the chief priests and elders had said unto them.

24 And when they heard that, they lifted up their voice to God with one accord, and said, Lord, thou *art* God, which hast made heaven, and *a*earth, and the sea, and all that in them is:

25 Who by the mouth of thy servant David hast said, Why did the heathen rage, and the people imagine vain things?

26 The *a*kings of the earth stood up, and the rulers were gathered together against the Lord, and against his Christ.

27 For of a truth against thy holy child Jesus, whom thou hast *a*anointed, both Herod, and Pontius Pilate, with the Gentiles, and the people of Israel, were gathered together,

28 For to do whatsoever thy hand and thy counsel determined before to be done.

29 And now, Lord, behold their threatenings: and grant unto thy servants, that with all boldness they may speak thy word,

30 By stretching forth thine hand to heal; and that signs and wonders may be done by the name of thy holy child Jesus.

31 ¶ And when they had prayed, the place was shaken where they were *a*assembled together; and they were all filled with the *b*Holy Ghost, and they spake the word of God with boldness.

32 And the multitude of them that believed were of *a*one heart and of one soul: neither said any *of them* that *b*ought of the things which he *c*possessed was his own; but they had all things *d*common.

33 And with great power gave the apostles *a*witness of the resurrection of the Lord Jesus: and great *b*grace was upon them all.

34 Neither was there any among them that lacked: for as many as were possessors of lands or houses *a*sold them, and brought the prices of the things that were sold,

35 And laid *them* down at the apostles' feet: and *a*distribution was made unto every man according as he had *b*need.

36 And Joses, who by the apostles was surnamed *a*Barnabas, (which is, being interpreted, The son of consolation,) a Levite, *and* of the country of Cyprus,

37 Having land, sold *it,* and brought the *a*money, and laid *it* at the apostles' feet.

CHAPTER 5

Ananias and Sapphira lie to the Lord and lose their lives—The Apostles continue the miracles of Jesus—Peter and John are arrested, an angel delivers them from prison, and they testify of Christ—Gamaliel counsels moderation.

19*a* D&C 3:7.
20*a* Jer. 20:9;
    Amos 3:8.
  b TG Witness.
24*a* D&C 14:9.
26*a* Ps. 2:2 (1–2).
27*a* TG Anointing;
    Jesus Christ,
    Authority of;
    Jesus Christ, Messiah.
31*a* TG Assembly for

Worship;
Meetings.
  b Acts 2:4 (2–4);
    D&C 68:4 (3–4).
32*a* 1 Cor. 1:10 (10–13);
    3 Ne. 11:28 (28–30);
    Moses 7:18.
    TG Unity.
  b GR any.
  c D&C 49:20.
  d TG Consecration.

33*a* 1 Cor. 15:15.
    TG Witness.
  b TG Grace.
34*a* Acts 5:1 (1–11).
35*a* Acts 6:1;
    D&C 83:6 (1–6).
  b Acts 2:45.
    TG Welfare.
36*a* Acts 11:22 (22–24);
    Gal. 2:1.
37*a* D&C 19:34.

BUT a certain man named Ananias, with Sapphira his wife, ªsold a possession,

2 And ªkept back ᵇ*part* of the price, his wife also being privy *to it,* and brought a certain ᶜpart, and laid *it* at the apostles' feet.

3 But Peter said, Ananias, why hath Satan filled thine heart to ªlie to the Holy Ghost, and to ᵇkeep back *part* of the price of the land?

4 Whiles it remained, was it not thine own? and after it was sold, was it not in thine own power? why hast thou conceived this thing in thine heart? thou hast not ªlied unto men, but unto ᵇGod.

5 And Ananias hearing these words fell down, and ªgave up the ghost: and great fear came on all them that heard these things.

6 And the young men arose, wound him up, and carried *him* out, and buried *him.*

7 And it was about the space of three hours after, when his wife, not knowing what was done, came in.

8 And Peter answered unto her, Tell me whether ye sold the land for so much? And she said, Yea, for so much.

9 Then Peter said unto her, How is it that ye have agreed together to ªtempt the Spirit of the Lord? behold, the feet of them which have buried thy husband *are* at the door, and shall carry thee out.

10 Then fell she down ªstraightway at his feet, and yielded up the ghost: and the young men came in, and found her dead, and, carrying *her* forth, buried *her* by her husband.

11 And great fear came upon all the church, and upon as many as heard these things.

12 ¶ And by the hands of the apostles were many ªsigns and wonders wrought among the people; (and they were all with one accord in Solomon's porch.

13 And of the ªrest durst no man join himself to them: but the people magnified them.

14 And believers were the more ªadded to the Lord, multitudes both of men and women.)

15 Insomuch that they brought forth the sick into the streets, and laid *them* on beds and couches, that at the least the ªshadow of Peter passing by might overshadow some of them.

16 There came also a multitude *out* of the cities round about unto Jerusalem, bringing sick folks, and them which were vexed with unclean spirits: and they were ªhealed every one.

17 ¶ Then the high priest rose up, and all they that were with him, (which is the sect of the Sadducees,) and were filled with ªindignation,

18 And laid their hands on the apostles, and put them in the common prison.

19 But the ªangel of the Lord by night opened the ᵇprison doors, and brought them forth, and said,

20 Go, stand and speak in the temple to the people all the ªwords of this life.

21 And when they heard *that,* they entered into the temple early in the morning, and taught. But the high priest came, and they that were with him, and called the council together, and all the senate of the children of Israel, and sent to the prison to have them brought.

22 But when the officers came, and found them not in the prison, they returned, and told,

23 Saying, The prison truly found we shut with all safety, and the keepers standing without before the

---

5 1ª Acts 4:34 (32, 34–35); D&C 19:26 (25–26).
  2ª TG Selfishness.
   b Josh. 7:21 (1–26); D&C 105:3 (2–10).
   TG Consecration.
   c TG Welfare.
  3ª TG Honesty.
   b TG Selfishness.

4ª TG Lying.
  b Josh. 7:20.
  5ª Lev. 10:2.
  9ª TG Test.
10ª OR immediately.
12ª Heb. 2:4.
   TG Signs.
13ª JST Acts 5:13 . . . *rulers* . . .
14ª Acts 2:47.

15ª Luke 8:44 (43–48); Acts 19:12 (11–12).
16ª TG Heal.
17ª GR envy, malice.
19ª Acts 12:7; Moro. 7:29 (29–33).
   TG Angels.
   b Acts 16:26.
20ª John 6:68 (63, 68).

doors: but when we had opened, we found no man within.

24 Now when the high priest and the captain of the temple and the chief priests heard these things, they doubted of them whereunto this would grow.

25 Then came one and told them, saying, Behold, the men whom ye put in prison are standing in the temple, and teaching the people.

26 Then went the captain with the officers, and brought them without violence: for they feared the people, lest they should have been stoned.

27 And when they had brought them, they set *them* before the council: and the high priest asked them,

28 Saying, Did not we straitly *a*command you that ye should not teach in this *b*name? and, behold, ye have filled Jerusalem with your doctrine, and intend to bring this man's *c*blood upon us.

29 ¶ Then Peter and the *other* apostles answered and said, We ought to *a*obey God rather than men.

30 The God of our fathers raised up Jesus, whom ye slew and *a*hanged on a tree.

31 Him hath God exalted *a*with his right hand *to be* a *b*Prince and a *c*Saviour, for to give repentance to Israel, and *d*forgiveness of sins.

32 And we are his *a*witnesses of these things; and *so is* also the *b*Holy Ghost, whom God hath *c*given to them that obey him.

33 ¶ When they heard *that,* they were *a*cut *to the heart,* and took counsel to slay them.

34 Then stood there up one in the council, a Pharisee, named *a*Gamaliel, a doctor of the law, had in reputation among all the people, and commanded to put the apostles forth a little space;

35 And said unto them, Ye men of Israel, take heed to yourselves what ye intend to do as touching these men.

36 For before these days rose up Theudas, boasting himself to be somebody; to whom a number of men, about four hundred, joined themselves: who was slain; and all, as many as *a*obeyed him, were scattered, and brought to nought.

37 After this man rose up Judas of Galilee in the days of the taxing, and drew away much people after him: he also perished; and all, *even* as many as obeyed him, were dispersed.

38 And now I say unto you, *a*Refrain from these men, and let them alone: for if this counsel or this work be of *b*men, it will come to nought:

39 But if it be of God, ye cannot overthrow it; *a*lest haply ye be found even to *b*fight against God.

40 And to him they agreed: and when they had called the apostles, and beaten *them,* they commanded that they should not speak in the name of Jesus, and let them go.

41 ¶ And they departed from the presence of the council, *a*rejoicing that they were counted worthy to *b*suffer *c*shame for his *d*name.

42 And daily in the temple, and in every house, they ceased not to teach and *a*preach Jesus Christ.

28a Acts 4:18 (15–18).
  b TG Name.
  c Matt. 27:25.
29a Ex. 1:17 (16–17);
    D&C 30:1.
    TG Courage; Duty.
30a TG Jesus Christ,
    Crucifixion of.
31a GR at.
  b TG Jesus Christ,
    Messiah.
  c TG Jesus Christ,
    Atonement through.
  d TG Forgive.
32a Luke 1:2;
    John 1:14;
    Acts 26:16.
    TG Holy Ghost,
    Mission of;
    Witness.
  b TG Holy Ghost, Source
    of Testimony.
  c TG Holy Ghost, Gift of.
33a 1 Ne. 16:2.
34a Acts 22:3.
36a GR were persuaded by,
    believed him.
38a Acts 19:35 (35–41).
  b D&C 3:3;
    JS—H 1:23 (22–23).
39a JST Acts 5:39 . . . *be
    careful, therefore,* lest ye
    be . . .
  b Acts 23:9.
41a Luke 6:23 (22–23);
    Col. 1:11;
    1 Thes. 1:6;
    1 Pet. 4:13.
  b TG Persecution;
    Self-Sacrifice;
    Suffering.
  c TG Shame.
  d TG Jesus Christ, Taking
    the Name of.
42a TG Missionary Work.

CHAPTER 6

The Apostles choose seven to assist them—Stephen is tried before the council.

AND in those days, when the number of the disciples was multiplied, there arose a murmuring of the Grecians against the Hebrews, because their ^awidows were ^bneglected in the daily ^cministration.

2 Then the twelve called the multitude of the disciples *unto them,* and said, It is not reason that we should leave the word of God, and serve tables.

3 Wherefore, brethren, look ye out among you seven men of ^ahonest ^breport, full of the Holy Ghost and ^cwisdom, whom we may appoint over this ^dbusiness.

4 But we will give ourselves continually to prayer, and to the ^aministry of the word.

5 ¶ And the saying pleased the whole multitude: and they ^achose Stephen, a man full of faith and of the ^bHoly Ghost, and ^cPhilip, and Prochorus, and Nicanor, and Timon, and Parmenas, and Nicolas a proselyte of Antioch:

6 Whom they set before the apostles: and when they had prayed, they ^alaid *their* ^bhands on them.

7 And the word of God increased; and the number of the disciples multiplied in Jerusalem greatly; and a great company of the ^apriests were obedient to the faith.

8 And Stephen, full of faith and ^apower, did great wonders and ^bmiracles among the people.

9 ¶ Then there arose certain of the synagogue, which is called *the synagogue* of the ^aLibertines, and Cyrenians, and Alexandrians, and of them of Cilicia and of Asia, ^bdisputing with Stephen.

10 And they were not able to resist the ^awisdom and the spirit by which he spake.

11 Then they suborned men, which said, We have heard him speak ^ablasphemous words against Moses, and *against* God.

12 And they stirred up the people, and the elders, and the scribes, and came upon *him,* and caught him, and brought *him* to the council,

13 And set up ^afalse witnesses, which said, This man ceaseth not to speak blasphemous words against this holy place, and the law:

14 For we have heard him say, that this Jesus of Nazareth shall destroy this place, and shall change the ^acustoms which Moses delivered us.

15 And all that sat in the council, looking steadfastly on him, saw his face as it had been the ^aface of an ^bangel.

CHAPTER 7

Stephen recounts the history of Israel and names Moses as a prototype of Christ—He testifies of the apostasy in Israel—He sees Jesus on the right hand of God—Stephen's testimony is rejected, and he is stoned to death.

THEN said the high priest, Are these things so?

2 And he said, Men, brethren, and fathers, hearken; The God of glory appeared unto our father ^aAbraham, when he was in Mesopotamia, before he dwelt in ^bCharran,

3 And said unto him, Get thee out of thy ^acountry, and from thy kindred,

---

6 1a TG Widows.
  b TG Apathy; Welfare.
  c Acts 4:35.
  3a TG Honesty; Priesthood,
     Qualifying for.
  b 1 Tim. 3:7.
  c TG Holy Ghost, Gifts of.
  d D&C 107:68 (14, 68).
  4a Mark 16:15 (15–19);
     D&C 107:8.
  5a TG Called of God.
  b TG Holy Ghost, Gifts of.

  c Acts 21:8.
  6a TG Church Organization;
     Hands, Laying on of;
     Priesthood;
     Priesthood, Authority.
  b TG Setting Apart.
  7a John 12:42.
     TG Priest, Aaronic
     Priesthood.
     BD Priests.
  8a TG Priesthood, Power of.
  b TG Miracle.

  9a GR Freed-men.
  b TG Disputations.
  10a Isa. 54:17; Luke 21:15;
     D&C 100:5 (5–6).
  11a TG Blaspheme.
  13a TG Slander.
  14a Acts 21:21.
  15a TG Angels.
  b TG Angels.
  7 2a Gen. 12:1; Abr. 2:3 (3–4).
  b Gen. 11:31 (31–32).
  3a Abr. 1:1 (1, 5).

and come into the land which I shall shew thee.

4 Then came he out of the land of the ^aChaldæans, and dwelt in Charran: and from thence, when his father was dead, he removed him into this land, wherein ye now dwell.

5 And he gave him none inheritance in it, no, not *so much as* to set his foot on: yet he ^apromised that he would give it to him for a possession, and to his seed after him, when *as yet* he had no child.

6 And God spake on this wise, That his seed should ^asojourn in a strange land; and that they should bring them into ^bbondage, and entreat *them* evil four hundred years.

7 And the nation to whom they shall be in bondage will I judge, said God: and after that shall they come forth, and serve me in this place.

8 And he gave him the covenant of ^acircumcision: and so *Abraham* begat Isaac, and circumcised him the eighth day; and Isaac *begat* Jacob; and Jacob *begat* the twelve ^bpatriarchs.

9 And the patriarchs, moved with ^aenvy, sold ^bJoseph into Egypt: but God was with him,

10 And ^adelivered him out of all his ^bafflictions, and gave him favour and wisdom in the sight of Pharaoh king of Egypt; and he made him governor over Egypt and all his house.

11 Now there came a ^adearth over all the land of Egypt and Chanaan, and great affliction: and our fathers found no sustenance.

12 But when Jacob heard that there was ^acorn in Egypt, he sent out our fathers first.

13 And at the second *time* ^aJoseph was made known to his brethren; and Joseph's kindred was made known unto ^bPharaoh.

14 Then sent ^aJoseph, and called his ^bfather ^cJacob to *him,* and all his kindred, threescore and fifteen souls.

15 So Jacob went down into Egypt, and died, he, and our fathers,

16 And were carried over into Sychem, and laid in the sepulchre that Abraham ^abought for a sum of money of the sons of Emmor *the father* of Sychem.

17 But when the time of the promise drew nigh, which God had sworn to Abraham, the people grew and multiplied in Egypt,

18 Till another ^aking arose, which knew not Joseph.

19 The same dealt subtilly with our kindred, and evil entreated our fathers, so that they cast out their young children, to the end they might not live.

20 In which time Moses was born, and was ^aexceeding fair, and nourished up in his father's house ^bthree months:

21 And when he was cast out, Pharaoh's daughter took him up, and nourished him for her own ^ason.

22 And Moses was ^alearned in all the wisdom of the Egyptians, and was mighty in words and in deeds.

23 And when he was full ^aforty years old, it came into his heart to visit his ^bbrethren the children of Israel.

24 And seeing one *of them* suffer wrong, he defended *him,* and avenged him that was ^aoppressed, and ^bsmote the Egyptian:

25 For he supposed his brethren would have ^aunderstood how that

4*a* Gen. 11:31.
5*a* TG Promised Lands.
6*a* Gen. 26:3.
   b TG Israel, Bondage of, in Egypt.
8*a* TG Circumcision.
   b TG Patriarch.
9*a* TG Envy.
   b Alma 46:24.
10*a* D&C 24:1.
   b TG Affliction.
11*a* OR famine.

TG Drought; Famine.
12*a* Gen. 42:1.
13*a* Gen. 45:3.
   b Gen. 47:2.
14*a* TG Israel, Joseph, People of.
   b Gen. 45:13.
   c TG Israel, Origins of.
16*a* Gen. 23:17.
18*a* Ex. 1:8.
20*a* GR comely, beautiful

to God.
   b Ex. 2:2.
21*a* Ex. 2:10.
22*a* TG Education.
23*a* Ex. 7:7;
   Deut. 31:2 (1–2); 34:7.
   b Ex. 2:11 (11–15);
   Heb. 11:25 (24–27).
24*a* TG Oppression.
   b Ex. 2:12 (11–12).
25*a* Ex. 2:14;
   3:13 (13–15); 4:1.

God by his hand would *b*deliver them: but they understood not.

26 And the next day he shewed himself unto them as they strove, and would have set them at one again, saying, Sirs, ye are brethren; why do ye *a*wrong one to another?

27 But he that did his neighbour wrong thrust him away, saying, Who made thee a *a*ruler and a judge over us?

28 Wilt thou kill me, as thou diddest the Egyptian yesterday?

29 Then *a*fled Moses at this saying, and was a stranger in the land of Madian, where he begat two *b*sons.

30 And when forty years were expired, there appeared to him in the wilderness of mount Sina an *a*angel of the Lord in a flame of fire in a bush.

31 When Moses saw *it,* he wondered at the *a*sight: and as he drew near to behold *it,* the *b*voice of the Lord came unto him,

32 *Saying,* I *am* the *a*God of thy fathers, the God of Abraham, and the God of Isaac, and the God of Jacob. Then Moses trembled, and durst not behold.

33 Then said the Lord to him, Put off thy shoes from thy feet: for the place where thou standest is holy ground.

34 I have seen, I have seen the affliction of my people which is in Egypt, and I have heard their groaning, and am come down to deliver them. And now come, I will send thee into Egypt.

35 This Moses whom they refused, saying, Who made thee a ruler and a judge? the same did God send *to be* a ruler and a *a*deliverer by the hand of the angel which appeared to him in the bush.

36 He *a*brought them out, after that he had shewed wonders and signs in the land of Egypt, and in the Red sea, and in the wilderness forty years.

37 ¶ This is that Moses, which said unto the children of Israel, A *a*prophet shall the Lord your God raise up unto you of your brethren, like unto me; him shall ye hear.

38 This is he, that was in the church in the wilderness with the angel which spake to him in the mount Sina, and *with* our fathers: who received the lively *a*oracles to give unto us:

39 To whom our fathers would not *a*obey, but thrust *him* from them, and in their hearts turned back again into Egypt,

40 Saying unto Aaron, Make us *a*gods to go before us: for *as for* this Moses, which brought us out of the land of Egypt, we wot not what is become of him.

41 And they made a *a*calf in those days, and offered sacrifice unto the idol, and rejoiced in the works of their own hands.

42 Then God turned, and *a*gave them up to worship the host of heaven; as it is written in the book of the prophets, O ye house of Israel, have ye offered to me slain beasts and sacrifices *by the space of* forty years in the wilderness?

43 Yea, ye took up the tabernacle of Moloch, and the star of your god Remphan, figures which ye made to worship them: and I will carry you away beyond Babylon.

44 Our fathers had the tabernacle of witness in the wilderness, as he had appointed, speaking unto Moses, that he should make it according to the *a*fashion that he had seen.

45 Which also our fathers that came after brought in with *a*Jesus

25*b* TG Deliver.
26*a* Ex. 2:13.
    TG Injustice.
27*a* 1 Ne. 17:26 (23–37).
29*a* Ex. 2:15.
    b Ex. 2:22; 18:3.
30*a* Ex. 3:2.
31*a* OR vision.
    b Ex. 3:4 (3–6).

32*a* Ex. 3:15.
35*a* TG Deliver; Jesus Christ,
    Savior; Salvation.
36*a* Ex. 12:51.
37*a* Deut. 18:15 (15–19);
    Acts 3:22 (22–23);
    JS—H 1:40.
    TG Jesus Christ,
    Prophecies about.

38*a* Rom. 3:2; D&C 90:5.
39*a* TG Disobedience.
40*a* Ex. 32:1, 23.
41*a* Ex. 32:4; Hosea 8:5 (5–7).
42*a* Ps. 81:12; Rom. 1:24.
44*a* 1 Chr. 28:19 (11, 19);
    Heb. 8:5.
45*a* IE Joshua.
    Heb. 4:8.

into the possession of the Gentiles, whom God drave out before the face of our fathers, unto the days of David;

46 Who found favour before God, and desired to find a tabernacle for the God of Jacob.

47 But Solomon built him an house.

48 Howbeit the most High ªdwelleth not in temples made with hands; as saith the prophet,

49 Heaven *is* my ªthrone, and earth *is* my footstool: what house will ye build me? saith the Lord: or what *is* the place of my rest?

50 Hath not my hand ªmade all these things?

51 ¶ Ye ªstiffnecked and ᵇuncircumcised in heart and ears, ye do always ᶜresist the ᵈHoly Ghost: as your ᵉfathers *did*, so *do* ye.

52 Which of the prophets have not your fathers ªpersecuted? and they have slain them which shewed before of the coming of the Just One; of whom ye have been now the betrayers and murderers:

53 Who have received the law by the disposition of ªangels, and have not ᵇkept *it*.

54 ¶ When they heard these things, they were ªcut to the heart, and they gnashed on him with *their* teeth.

55 But he, being full of the ªHoly Ghost, looked up steadfastly into heaven, and saw the ᵇglory of ᶜGod,

and ᵈJesus ᵉstanding on the ᶠright hand of God,

56 And said, Behold, I ªsee the heavens ᵇopened, and the ᶜSon of man standing on the right ᵈhand of ᵉGod.

57 Then they cried out with a loud voice, and stopped their ears, and ran upon him with one accord,

58 And cast *him* out of the city, and stoned *him*: and the witnesses laid down their ªclothes at a ᵇyoung man's feet, whose name was Saul.

59 And they ªstoned ᵇStephen, ᶜcalling upon ᵈGod, and saying, Lord Jesus, receive my ᵉspirit.

60 And he kneeled down, and ªcried with a loud voice, ᵇLord, lay not this sin to their ᶜcharge. And when he had said this, he fell asleep.

CHAPTER 8

Saul persecutes the Church—Philip's ministry in Samaria is described—Philip performs miracles and baptizes men and women—Peter and John come to Samaria and confer the gift of the Holy Ghost by the laying on of hands—Simon seeks to buy this gift and is rebuked by Peter—Philip preaches about Christ and baptizes an Ethiopian eunuch.

AND Saul was consenting unto his death. And at that time there was a great ªpersecution against the ᵇchurch which was at Jerusalem; and they were all scattered abroad

---

48*a* Acts 17:24.
49*a* TG Kingdom of God, in Heaven.
50*a* TG Jesus Christ, Creator.
51*a* TG Stiffnecked.
   b Jer. 6:10;
      Rom. 2:29 (28–29).
   c TG Rebellion.
   d Neh. 9:30.
   e Mal. 3:7;
      Matt. 23:32;
      Hel. 13:25 (25–29).
52*a* TG Apostasy of Israel;
      Prophets, Rejection of.
53*a* Moses 5:58.
   b TG Disobedience.
54*a* 1 Ne. 16:2 (1–4).
55*a* TG Holy Ghost,
      Comforter;
      Holy Ghost, Gifts of.
   b TG Jesus Christ,

Glory of.
   c TG Godhead.
   d D&C 137:3.
   e TG Jesus Christ,
      Appearances,
      Postmortal.
   f Heb. 1:3.
      TG Jesus Christ,
      Relationships with
      the Father.
56*a* TG God, Presence of;
      God, Privilege of
      Seeing.
   b Ezek. 1:1;
      D&C 50:45.
   c TG Jesus Christ,
      Son of Man.
   d TG God, Body of,
      Corporeal Nature.
   e TG God, Manifestations of;

God the Father, Elohim.
58*a* Acts 22:20.
   b The Greek word used
      identifies a man who
      is younger than forty
      years of age.
59*a* TG Persecution.
   b TG Martyrdom.
   c JST Acts 7:59 . . . *and
      he*, calling upon God,
      said . . .
   d 3 Ne. 19:22 (18–36).
   e TG Man, a Spirit Child
      of Heavenly Father;
      Spirits, Disembodied.
60*a* Luke 6:28; 23:34 (33–34).
   b Matt. 5:44 (44–47).
   c 2 Tim. 4:16;
      3 Ne. 12:44.
8 1*a* TG Persecution.
   b TG Church.

throughout the regions of Judæa and Samaria, except the apostles.

2 And devout men carried Stephen *to his burial,* and made great *a*lamentation over him.

3 As for Saul, he made *a*havoc of the church, entering into every house, and haling men and women committed *them* to *b*prison.

4 Therefore they that were scattered abroad went every where preaching the word.

5 Then Philip went down to the city of *a*Samaria, and preached Christ unto them.

6 And the people with one accord gave heed unto those things which Philip *a*spake, hearing and seeing the miracles which he did.

7 For *a*unclean spirits, crying with loud voice, came out of many that were possessed *with them:* and many *b*taken with palsies, and that were lame, were *c*healed.

8 And there was great joy in that city.

9 But there was a certain man, called Simon, which beforetime in the same city used *a*sorcery, and *b*bewitched the people of Samaria, giving out that himself was some *c*great one:

10 To whom they all gave heed, from the least to the greatest, saying, This man is the great power of God.

11 And to him they had regard, because that of long time he had bewitched them with sorceries.

12 But when they believed Philip *a*preaching the things concerning the kingdom of God, and the *b*name

of Jesus Christ, they were *c*baptized, both men and women.

13 Then Simon himself believed also: and when he was baptized, he continued with Philip, and *a*wondered, beholding the miracles and signs which were done.

14 Now when the apostles which were at Jerusalem heard that Samaria had received the *a*word of God, they sent unto them Peter and John:

15 Who, when they were come down, prayed for them, that they might receive the Holy Ghost:

16 (For as yet he was fallen upon none of them: only they were baptized in the name of the Lord Jesus.)

17 Then *a*laid they *their* hands on them, and they received the *b*Holy Ghost.

18 And when Simon saw that through *a*laying on of the apostles' hands the Holy Ghost was given, he offered them money,

19 Saying, Give me also this *a*power, that on whomsoever I lay hands, he may receive the Holy Ghost.

20 But Peter said unto him, Thy money perish with thee, because thou hast thought that the *a*gift of God may be *b*purchased with money.

21 Thou hast neither part nor lot in this matter: for thy heart is not *a*right in the sight of God.

22 Repent therefore of this thy *a*wickedness, and pray God, if perhaps the *b*thought of thine *c*heart may be forgiven thee.

23 For I perceive that thou art in the *a*gall of bitterness, and *in* the *b*bond of iniquity.

2*a* TG Mourning.
3*a* Acts 22:4;
     1 Cor. 15:9;
     1 Tim. 1:13;
     Mosiah 27:10 (9–11).
  b Acts 22:19;
     4 Ne. 1:30.
5*a* Acts 1:8.
6*a* TG Counsel.
7*a* TG Spirits, Evil or
     Unclean.
  b GR paralytic and lame.
  c 3 Ne. 7:22.
9*a* TG Sorcery.

  b TG Superstitions.
  c 2 Ne. 26:29.
12*a* TG Missionary Work;
     Preaching.
  b TG Name.
  c TG Baptism, Essential.
13*a* OR was amazed,
     astonished.
14*a* Acts 11:1 (1–18).
17*a* TG Hands, Laying on of.
  b Acts 2:38.
18*a* TG Priesthood,
     Authority.
19*a* TG Priesthood,

     Power of;
     Selfishness;
     Unrighteous Dominion.
20*a* TG God, Gifts of.
  b TG Bribe.
21*a* D&C 49:2.
22*a* TG Wickedness.
  b TG Motivations.
  c 3 Ne. 12:29.
23*a* Alma 41:11;
     Morm. 8:31.
  b TG Bondage, Spiritual.

24 Then answered Simon, and said, Pray ye to the Lord for me, that none of these things which ye have spoken come upon me.

25 And they, when they had testified and preached the word of the Lord, returned to Jerusalem, and preached the gospel in many villages of the Samaritans.

26 And the ^aangel of the Lord spake unto Philip, saying, Arise, and go toward the south unto the way that goeth down from Jerusalem unto Gaza, which is desert.

27 And he arose and went: and, behold, a man of Ethiopia, an eunuch of great authority under Candace queen of the Ethiopians, who had the charge of all her treasure, and had come to Jerusalem for to ^aworship,

28 Was returning, and sitting in his chariot read Esaias the prophet.

29 Then the ^aSpirit said unto Philip, Go near, and join thyself to this chariot.

30 And Philip ran thither to *him*, and heard him read the prophet Esaias, and said, Understandest thou what thou readest?

31 And he said, How can I, except some man should guide me? And he desired Philip that he would come up and sit with him.

32 The place of the scripture which he read was this, He was led as a sheep to the slaughter; and like a ^alamb dumb before his shearer, so opened he not his mouth:

33 In his humiliation his judgment was taken away: and who shall declare his generation? for his life is taken from the earth.

34 And the eunuch answered Philip, and said, I pray thee, of whom speaketh the prophet this? of himself, or of some other man?

35 Then Philip opened his mouth, and began at the same scripture, and preached unto him ^aJesus.

36 And as they went on *their* way, they came unto a certain water: and the eunuch said, See, *here is* water; what doth hinder me to be baptized?

37 And Philip said, If thou ^abelievest with all thine heart, thou mayest. And he answered and said, I believe that Jesus Christ is the Son of God.

38 And he commanded the chariot to stand still: and they went down both into the water, both Philip and the eunuch; and he ^abaptized him.

39 And when they were come up out of the water, the ^aSpirit of the Lord caught away Philip, that the eunuch saw him no more: and he went on his way rejoicing.

40 But Philip was found at Azotus: and passing through he preached in all the cities, till he came to ^aCæsarea.

CHAPTER 9

Jesus appears to Saul—Saul is a chosen vessel—Ananias restores Saul's sight—Saul is baptized and begins his ministry—Peter heals Æneas and raises Dorcas from death.

AND Saul, yet breathing out ^athreatenings and slaughter against the disciples of the Lord, went unto the high priest,

2 And desired of him ^aletters to Damascus to the synagogues, that if he found any of this way, whether they were men or women, he might bring them bound unto Jerusalem.

3 And as he journeyed, he came near Damascus: and suddenly there shined round about him a ^alight from heaven:

4 And he ^afell to the earth, and heard a voice saying unto him, ^bSaul, Saul, why persecutest thou me?

26a TG Angels.
27a John 12:20.
29a TG Holy Ghost, Gifts of.
32a TG Jesus Christ, Lamb of God;
    Jesus Christ, Trials of.
35a Gal. 3:14 (13–14).

37a TG Baptism, Qualifications for.
38a TG Baptism; Baptism, Immersion.
39a TG God, Spirit of.
40a Acts 21:8.
9 1a Acts 26:10.

2a Acts 22:5.
3a TG Light [noun].
4a Ezek. 1:28;
    Ether 3:6 (6–8);
    Moses 1:9.
  b Acts 22:7 (6–16);
    26:14 (9–17).

5 And he said, Who art thou, Lord? And the Lord said, I am ^aJesus whom thou persecutest: *it is* hard for thee to ^bkick against the pricks.

6 And he trembling and astonished said, Lord, ^awhat wilt thou have me to do? And the Lord *said* unto him, Arise, and go into the city, and it shall be told thee what thou must do.

7 ^aAnd the men which journeyed with him stood speechless, hearing a ^bvoice, but seeing ^cno man.

8 And Saul arose from the earth; and when his eyes were opened, he saw no man: but they led him by the hand, and brought *him* into Damascus.

9 And he was three days without sight, and neither did eat nor drink.

10 ¶ And there was a certain disciple at Damascus, named ^aAnanias; and to him said the Lord in a ^bvision, Ananias. And he said, Behold, I *am here*, Lord.

11 And the Lord *said* unto him, Arise, and go into the street which is called Straight, and inquire in the house of Judas for *one* called Saul, of Tarsus: for, behold, he prayeth,

12 And hath seen in a vision a man named Ananias coming in, and putting *his* hand on him, that he might receive his sight.

13 Then Ananias answered, Lord, I have heard by many of this man, how much ^aevil he hath done to thy saints at Jerusalem:

14 And here he hath authority from the chief priests to bind all that call on thy name.

15 But the Lord said unto him, Go thy way: for he is a ^achosen vessel unto me, to ^bbear my ^cname before the ^dGentiles, and ^ekings, and the children of Israel:

16 For I will shew him how great things he must ^asuffer for my name's sake.

17 And Ananias went his way, and entered into the house; and putting his ^ahands on him said, Brother Saul, the Lord, *even* Jesus, that ^bappeared unto thee in the way as thou camest, hath ^csent me, that thou mightest receive thy sight, and be filled with the ^dHoly Ghost.

18 And immediately there fell from his eyes as it had been scales: and he received ^asight forthwith, and arose, and was ^bbaptized.

19 And when he had received meat, he was strengthened. Then was Saul certain days with the disciples which were at Damascus.

20 And straightway he preached Christ in the synagogues, that he is the Son of God.

21 But all that heard *him* were amazed, and said; Is not this he that ^adestroyed them which called on this name in Jerusalem, and came hither for that intent, that he might bring them ^bbound unto the chief priests?

22 But Saul increased the more in strength, and confounded the Jews which dwelt at Damascus, proving that this is very Christ.

23 ¶ And after that many days were fulfilled, the Jews took counsel to ^akill him:

24 But their ^alaying await was

5a TG Jesus Christ, Appearances, Postmortal.
  b D&C 121:38.
6a TG Conversion.
7a JST Acts 9:7 And *they who were journeying* with him *saw indeed the light, and were afraid; but they heard not the voice of him who spake to him.*
  b Acts 22:9.
  c Dan. 10:7; Alma 36:11 (6–11).
10a Acts 22:12.

  b TG Jesus Christ, Appearances, Postmortal.
13a Acts 26:10.
15a 1 Thes. 3:3.
  b Acts 22:15; 26:16.
  c TG Name.
  d Rom. 15:10 (8–21); 1 Tim. 2:7.
  e Ps. 119:46; Matt. 10:18; D&C 1:23; 124:3 (3, 16, 107). TG Kings, Earthly.
16a TG Self-Sacrifice.

17a TG Administrations to the Sick; Hands, Laying on of.
  b 1 Cor. 9:1.
  c TG Called of God; Delegation of Responsibility.
  d TG Holy Ghost, Gift of.
18a TG Sight.
  b TG Baptism, Essential.
21a Gal. 1:13.
  b Acts 26:10.
23a 2 Cor. 11:32.
24a GR plot, conspiracy was known.

known of Saul. And they watched the gates day and night to kill him.

25 Then the disciples took him by night, and let *him* down by the wall in a ^abasket.

26 And when Saul was come to ^aJerusalem, he assayed to join himself to the disciples: but they were all afraid of him, and believed not that he was a disciple.

27 But Barnabas took him, and brought *him* to the apostles, and declared unto them how he had ^aseen the Lord in the way, and that he had spoken to him, and how he had preached boldly at Damascus in the name of Jesus.

28 And he was with them coming in and going out at Jerusalem.

29 And he spake boldly in the name of the Lord Jesus, and ^adisputed against the Grecians: but they went about to slay him.

30 *Which* when the brethren knew, they brought him down to Cæsarea, and sent him forth to Tarsus.

31 Then had the churches rest throughout all Judæa and Galilee and Samaria, and were ^aedified; and walking in the fear of the Lord, and in the ^bcomfort of the Holy Ghost, were multiplied.

32 ¶ And it came to pass, as Peter passed throughout all *quarters,* he came down also to the ^asaints which dwelt at Lydda.

33 And there he found a certain man named Æneas, which had kept his bed eight years, and was ^asick of the palsy.

34 And Peter said unto him, Æneas, Jesus Christ maketh thee whole: arise, and make thy bed. And he arose immediately.

35 And all that dwelt at Lydda and Saron saw him, and turned to the Lord.

36 ¶ Now there was at Joppa a certain disciple named Tabitha, which

by interpretation is called Dorcas: this ^awoman was full of good works and almsdeeds which she did.

37 And it came to pass in those days, that she was sick, and died: whom when they had washed, they laid *her* in an upper chamber.

38 And forasmuch as Lydda was nigh to Joppa, and the disciples had heard that Peter was there, they sent unto him two men, desiring *him* that he would not delay to come to them.

39 Then Peter arose and went with them. When he was come, they brought him into the upper chamber: and all the widows stood by him weeping, and shewing the coats and garments which Dorcas made, while she was with them.

40 But Peter put them all forth, and kneeled down, and prayed; and turning *him* to the body said, Tabitha, ^aarise. And she opened her eyes: and when she saw Peter, she sat up.

41 And he gave her *his* hand, and lifted her up, and when he had called the ^asaints and widows, presented her ^balive.

42 And it was known throughout all Joppa; and many believed in the Lord.

43 And it came to pass, that he tarried many days in Joppa with one Simon a tanner.

CHAPTER 10

An angel ministers to Cornelius—Peter, in a vision, is commanded to take the gospel to the Gentiles—The gospel is taught by witnesses—The Holy Ghost falls upon the Gentiles.

THERE was a certain man in Cæsarea called Cornelius, a centurion of the band called the Italian *band,*

2 A devout *man,* and one that feared God with all his house, which

25 *a* Josh. 2:15.
26 *a* Gal. 1:18 (15–18).
27 *a* TG Jesus Christ, Appearances, Postmortal.
29 *a* TG Disputations.
31 *a* TG Edification.
   b TG Comfort; Holy Ghost, Comforter; Holy Ghost, Gifts of.
32 *a* TG Saints.
33 *a* GR paralyzed.
36 *a* TG Woman.
40 *a* TG Death, Power over.
41 *a* TG Saints.
   b John 14:12 (12–14).

gave much ^aalms to the people, and prayed to God alway.

3 He saw in a ^avision ^bevidently about the ninth hour of the day an ^cangel of God coming in to him, and saying unto him, Cornelius.

4 And when he looked on him, he was afraid, and said, What is it, Lord? And he said unto him, Thy prayers and thine alms are come up for a memorial before God.

5 And now send men to Joppa, and call for *one* Simon, whose surname is Peter:

6 He lodgeth with one Simon a tanner, whose house is by the sea side: he shall tell thee what thou oughtest to do.

7 And when the angel which spake unto Cornelius was departed, he called two of his household servants, and a devout soldier of them that waited on him continually;

8 And when he had declared all *these* things unto them, he sent them to Joppa.

9 ¶ On the morrow, as they went on their journey, and drew nigh unto the city, Peter went up upon the ^ahousetop to pray about the sixth hour:

10 And he became very hungry, and would have eaten: but while they made ready, he fell into a ^atrance,

11 And saw ^aheaven opened, and a certain vessel descending unto him, as it had been a great sheet ^bknit at the four corners, and let down to the earth:

12 Wherein were all manner of fourfooted beasts of the earth, and wild beasts, and creeping things, and fowls of the air.

13 And there came a voice to him, Rise, Peter; kill, and eat.

14 But Peter said, Not so, Lord; for I have never eaten any thing that is common or ^aunclean.

15 And the voice *spake* unto him again the second time, What God hath ^acleansed, *that* call not thou ^bcommon.

16 This was done thrice: and the vessel was received up again into heaven.

17 Now while Peter doubted in himself what this vision which he had seen should mean, behold, the men which were sent from Cornelius had made inquiry for Simon's house, and stood before the gate,

18 And called, and asked whether Simon, which was surnamed Peter, were lodged there.

19 ¶ While Peter thought on the vision, the ^aSpirit said unto him, Behold, three men seek thee.

20 Arise therefore, and get thee down, and ^ago with them, doubting nothing: for I have sent them.

21 Then Peter went down to the men which were sent unto him from Cornelius; and said, Behold, I am he whom ye seek: what *is* the cause wherefore ye are come?

22 And they said, Cornelius the centurion, a just man, and one that feareth God, and of good report among all the nation of the Jews, was ^awarned from God by an holy angel to send for thee into his house, and to hear words of thee.

23 Then called he them in, and lodged *them*. And on the morrow Peter went away with them, and certain brethren from Joppa accompanied him.

24 And the morrow after they entered into Cæsarea. And Cornelius waited for them, and had called together his kinsmen and near friends.

25 And as Peter was coming in, Cornelius met him, and fell down at his feet, and worshipped *him*.

26 But Peter took him up, saying, Stand up; I myself also am a ^aman.

---

10 2*a* TG Almsgiving.
    3*a* TG Vision.
      b GR clearly, distinctly.
      c 2 Ne. 32:3;
          Moro. 7:22 (22–38).
    9*a* 1 Sam. 9:25 (25–27).
  10*a* Acts 22:17.

11*a* D&C 107:19.
    b GR bound.
14*a* Lev. 11:2 (2–47).
15*a* Lev. 20:25.
    TG Cleanliness;
    Purification.
    b Acts 11:9;

    1 Ne. 17:35 (32–41).
19*a* TG Holy Ghost, Gifts of.
20*a* Acts 15:7.
22*a* TG Warn.
26*a* Rev. 19:10;
    D&C 20:19.

27 And as he talked with him, he went in, and found many that were come together.

28 And he said unto them, Ye know how that it is an unlawful thing for a man that is a Jew to keep company, or come unto one of another nation; but God hath shewed me that I should not call any man ªcommon or ᵇunclean.

29 Therefore came I *unto you* without gainsaying, as soon as I was sent for: I ask therefore for what intent ye have sent for me?

30 And Cornelius said, Four days ago I was ªfasting until this hour; and at the ninth hour I prayed in my house, and, behold, a ᵇman stood before me in bright clothing,

31 And said, Cornelius, thy prayer is heard, and thine alms are had in remembrance in the sight of God.

32 Send therefore to Joppa, and call hither Simon, whose surname is Peter; he is lodged in the house of *one* Simon a tanner by the sea side: who, when he cometh, shall speak unto thee.

33 Immediately therefore I sent to thee; and thou hast well done that thou art come. Now therefore are we all here present before God, to hear all things that are commanded thee of God.

34 ¶ Then Peter opened *his* mouth, and said, Of a truth I perceive that God is no ªrespecter of persons:

35 But in every ªnation he that ᵇfeareth him, and ᶜworketh ᵈrighteousness, is ᵉaccepted with him.

36 The ªword which *God* sent unto the children of Israel, preaching peace by Jesus Christ: (he is Lord of all:)

37 That word, *I say,* ye know, which was published throughout all Judæa, and began from Galilee, after the baptism which John preached;

38 How God ªanointed Jesus of Nazareth with the ᵇHoly Ghost and with power: who went about doing good, and healing all that were ᶜoppressed of the devil; for ᵈGod was with him.

39 And we are ªwitnesses of all things which he did both in the land of the Jews, and in Jerusalem; whom they slew and hanged on a tree:

40 Him God ªraised up the third day, and ᵇshewed him openly;

41 ªNot to all the people, but unto witnesses chosen before of God, *even* to us, who did eat and drink with him after he rose from the dead.

42 And he commanded us to ªpreach unto the people, and to testify that it is he which was ᵇordained of God *to be* the ᶜJudge of quick and dead.

43 To him give all the prophets ªwitness, that through his ᵇname whosoever ᶜbelieveth in him shall receive ᵈremission of sins.

44 ¶ While Peter yet spake these words, the Holy Ghost fell on all them which heard the word.

45 And they of the circumcision which believed were astonished, as many as came with Peter, because

---

28a 2 Ne. 26:33;
  Hel. 3:28 (27–30).
  b TG Uncleanness.
30a TG Fast, Fasting.
  b TG Angels.
34a Acts 15:9; 17:26 (25–26);
  Rom. 2:11;
  1 Ne. 17:35;
  D&C 1:35; 38:16.
  TG Judgment.
35a Rom. 10:12 (12–13);
  Alma 26:37 (36–37).
  TG Nations.
  b TG Reverence.
  c TG Good Works.

  d TG Righteousness.
  e 1 Sam. 2:30.
36a 3 Ne. 27:13 (13–22).
38a TG Anointing;
  Jesus Christ, Messiah.
  b TG Holy Ghost, Gifts of.
  c TG Oppression.
  d Ex. 8:19;
  Luke 11:20;
  John 3:2;
  Acts 2:22.
39a Acts 13:31 (29–33).
  TG Witness.
40a Acts 3:15 (15, 26); 17:31.
  TG Jesus Christ,

  Resurrection;
  Resurrection.
  b TG Jesus Christ,
  Appearances,
  Postmortal.
41a Ether 12:7.
42a TG Missionary Work.
  b TG Jesus Christ,
  Authority of;
  Priesthood, Authority.
  c TG Jesus Christ, Judge.
43a TG Prophets, Mission of.
  b TG Name.
  c TG Faith.
  d TG Remission of Sins.

that on the ^aGentiles also was poured out the ^bgift of the Holy Ghost.

46 For they heard them speak with ^atongues, and magnify God. Then answered Peter,

47 Can any man forbid water, that these should not be baptized, which have received the ^aHoly Ghost as well as we?

48 And he commanded them to be ^abaptized in the name of the Lord. Then prayed they him to tarry certain days.

CHAPTER 11

God grants the gift of repentance to the Gentiles—The disciples are first called Christians at Antioch—The Church is guided by revelation.

AND the apostles and brethren that were in Judæa heard that the ^aGentiles had also received the ^bword of God.

2 And when Peter was come up to Jerusalem, they that were of the ^acircumcision ^bcontended with him,

3 Saying, Thou wentest in to men uncircumcised, and didst eat with them.

4 But Peter rehearsed *the matter* from the beginning, and expounded *it* by order unto them, saying,

5 I was in the city of Joppa praying: and in a ^atrance I saw a vision, A certain vessel descend, as it had been a great sheet, let down from heaven by four corners; and it came even to me:

6 Upon the which when I had fastened mine eyes, I considered, and saw fourfooted beasts of the earth, and wild beasts, and creeping things, and fowls of the air.

7 And I heard a voice saying unto me, Arise, Peter; slay and eat.

8 But I said, Not so, Lord: for noth-

ing common or unclean hath at any time entered into my mouth.

9 But the voice answered me again from heaven, What God hath ^acleansed, *that* call not thou ^bcommon.

10 And this was done three times: and all were drawn up again into heaven.

11 And, behold, immediately there were three men already come unto the house where I was, sent from Cæsarea unto me.

12 And the Spirit bade me go with them, nothing doubting. Moreover these six brethren accompanied me, and we entered into the man's house:

13 And he shewed us how he had seen an angel in his house, which stood and said unto him, Send men to Joppa, and call for Simon, whose surname is Peter;

14 Who shall tell thee words, whereby thou and all thy house shall be saved.

15 And as I began to speak, the Holy Ghost fell on them, as on us at the beginning.

16 Then remembered I the word of the Lord, how that he said, John indeed baptized with water; but ye shall be baptized with the Holy Ghost.

17 Forasmuch then as God gave them the like ^agift as *he did* unto us, who believed on the Lord Jesus Christ; what was I, that I could withstand God?

18 When they heard these things, they held their peace, and glorified God, saying, Then hath God also to the ^aGentiles granted ^brepentance unto life.

19 ¶ Now they which were scattered abroad upon the ^apersecution that arose about Stephen travelled

45*a* Matt. 8:11 (11–12);
    Luke 13:29 (28–30);
    2 Ne. 10:18 (9–18);
    D&C 45:9 (7–30).
    TG Gentiles.
 b TG Holy Ghost, Gift of.
46*a* TG Holy Ghost, Gifts of.
47*a* TG Holy Ghost, Baptism of.

48*a* TG Baptism, Essential.
11 1*a* D&C 109:60.
  b Acts 8:14 (14–20).
 2*a* TG Circumcision.
  b TG Contention.
 5*a* Acts 22:17.
 9*a* TG Purification;
    Uncleanness.

 b Acts 10:15 (3, 15).
17*a* TG Holy Ghost, Gift of;
    Holy Ghost, Gifts of.
18*a* Mark 16:15 (15–16);
    Acts 21:19;
    D&C 84:62 (62–64).
  b TG Repent.
19*a* TG Persecution.

as far as Phenice, and Cyprus, and Antioch, preaching the word to none but unto the Jews only.

20 And some of them were men of Cyprus and Cyrene, which, when they were come to Antioch, spake unto the Grecians, preaching the Lord Jesus.

21 And the hand of the Lord was with them: and a great number believed, and turned unto the Lord.

22 ¶ Then tidings of these things came unto the ears of the church which was in Jerusalem: and they sent forth *Barnabas, that he should go as far as Antioch.

23 Who, when he came, and had seen the grace of God, was glad, and exhorted them all, that with purpose of heart they would cleave unto the Lord.

24 For he was a good man, and full of the Holy Ghost and of faith: and much people was added unto the Lord.

25 Then departed Barnabas to Tarsus, for to seek Saul:

26 And when he had found him, he brought him unto Antioch. And it came to pass, that a whole year they *assembled themselves with the church, and taught much people. And the disciples were called *Christians first in *Antioch.

27 ¶ And in these days came *prophets from Jerusalem unto Antioch.

28 And there stood up one of them named Agabus, and signified by the *Spirit that there should be great *dearth throughout all the world: which came to pass in the days of Claudius Cæsar.

29 Then the disciples, every man according to his ability, determined to send *relief unto the brethren which dwelt in Judæa:

30 Which also they did, and sent it to the *elders by the hands of Barnabas and Saul.

CHAPTER 12

The martyrdom of James is described— An angel frees Peter from prison—The Lord slays Herod by disease —The Church grows.

Now about that time Herod the king stretched forth *his* hands to vex certain of the church.

2 And he *killed *James the brother of John with the sword.

3 And because he saw it pleased the Jews, he proceeded further to take Peter also. (Then were the days of *unleavened bread.)

4 And when he had apprehended him, he put *him* in *prison, and delivered *him* to four *quaternions of soldiers to keep him; intending after *Easter to bring him forth to the people.

5 Peter therefore was kept in prison: but prayer was made without ceasing of the church unto God for him.

6 And when Herod would have brought him forth, the same night Peter was sleeping between two soldiers, bound with two chains: and the keepers before the door kept the prison.

7 And, behold, the *angel of the Lord came upon *him,* and a light shined in the prison: and he smote Peter on the side, and raised him up, saying, Arise up quickly. And his chains fell off from *his* hands.

8 And the angel said unto him, Gird thyself, and bind on thy sandals. And so he did. And he saith unto him, Cast thy garment about thee, and follow me.

9 And he went out, and followed

22a Acts 4:36.
26a TG Assembly for
　　Worship; Meetings.
　b Acts 26:28; 1 Pet. 4:16;
　　Mosiah 5:8 (8–11);
　　Alma 46:15 (13–15).
　　TG Jesus Christ, Taking
　　the Name of.
　c Acts 14:26.

27a Acts 13:1 (1–13).
28a Acts 2:18;
　　21:11 (4, 10–11).
　b OR famine.
　　TG Drought.
29a TG Almsgiving; Welfare.
30a TG Elder, Melchizedek
　　Priesthood.
12 2a TG Tyranny.

　b TG Martyrdom.
3a TG Bread, Unleavened.
4a Alma 14:27 (22–29);
　　Hel. 5:21 (21–50).
　b GR squads; i.e.,
　　detachments of four
　　men each.
　c IE Passover.
7a Acts 5:19.

him; and *wist not that it was true which was done by the angel; but thought he saw a vision.

10 When they were past the first and the second ward, they came unto the iron gate that leadeth unto the city; which opened to them of his own accord: and they went out, and passed on through one street; and forthwith the angel departed from him.

11 And when Peter was come to himself, he said, Now I know of a surety, that the Lord hath sent his angel, and hath delivered me out of the hand of Herod, and *from* all the expectation of the people of the Jews.

12 And when he had considered *the thing,* he came to the house of Mary the mother of John, whose surname was Mark; where many were gathered together praying.

13 And as Peter knocked at the door of the gate, a damsel came to hearken, named Rhoda.

14 And when she knew Peter's voice, she opened not the gate for gladness, but ran in, and told how Peter stood before the gate.

15 And they said unto her, Thou art mad. But she constantly affirmed that it was even so. Then said they, It is his angel.

16 But Peter continued knocking: and when they had opened *the door,* and saw him, they were astonished.

17 But he, *beckoning unto them with the hand to hold their peace, declared unto them how the Lord had brought him out of the prison. And he said, Go shew these things unto James, and to the brethren. And he departed, and went into another place.

18 Now as soon as it was day, there was no small stir among the soldiers, what was become of Peter.

19 And when Herod had sought for him, and found him not, he examined the keepers, and commanded that *they* should be put to *death. And he went down from Judæa to Cæsarea, and *there* abode.

20 ¶ And Herod was highly displeased with them of Tyre and Sidon: but they came with one accord to him, and, having made Blastus the king's chamberlain their friend, desired peace; because their country was nourished by the king's *country.*

21 And upon a set day Herod, arrayed in royal apparel, sat upon his throne, and made an oration unto them.

22 And the people gave a shout, *saying, It is* the voice of a god, and not of a man.

23 And immediately the *angel of the Lord smote him, because he gave not God the glory: and he was eaten of worms, and gave up the ghost.

24 ¶ But the word of God grew and multiplied.

25 And Barnabas and Saul returned from Jerusalem, when they had fulfilled *their *ministry, and took with them John, whose surname was Mark.

CHAPTER 13

Saul and Barnabas are called to missionary service—Saul, now called Paul, curses a sorcerer—Christ is a descendant of David—Paul offers the gospel to Israel, then to the Gentiles.

Now there were in the church that was at Antioch certain *prophets and teachers; as Barnabas, and Simeon that was called Niger, and Lucius of Cyrene, and Manaen, which had been brought up with Herod the tetrarch, and Saul.

2 As they ministered to the Lord, and *fasted, the *Holy Ghost said, *Separate me Barnabas and Saul for the work whereunto I have *called them.

3 And when they had fasted and

9*a* OR knew.
17*a* Acts 21:40.
19*a* TG Persecution.
23*a* TG Angels.
25*a* Acts 15:36 (36–37).

13 1*a* Acts 11:27.
TG Church Organization.
2*a* Luke 5:35.
TG Fast, Fasting.

b TG Holy Ghost, Gifts of.
c TG Setting Apart.
d TG Called of God.

prayed, and ^alaid *their* ^bhands on them, they sent *them* away.

4 ¶ So they, being sent forth by the Holy Ghost, departed unto Seleucia; and from thence they sailed to Cyprus.

5 And when they were at Salamis, they preached the word of God in the synagogues of the Jews: and they had also John to *their* minister.

6 And when they had gone through the isle unto Paphos, they found a certain ^asorcerer, a false prophet, a Jew, whose name *was* Bar-jesus:

7 Which was with the deputy of the country, Sergius Paulus, a ^aprudent man; who called for Barnabas and Saul, and desired to hear the word of God.

8 But Elymas the sorcerer (for so is his name by interpretation) withstood them, seeking to turn away the deputy from the faith.

9 Then Saul, (who also *is called* Paul,) filled with the ^aHoly Ghost, set his eyes on him,

10 And said, O full of all subtilty and all mischief, *thou* ^achild of the devil, *thou* ^benemy of all ^crighteousness, wilt thou not cease to pervert the right ways of the Lord?

11 And now, behold, the hand of the Lord *is* upon thee, and thou ^ashalt be ^bblind, not seeing the sun for a season. And immediately there fell on him a mist and a darkness; and he went about seeking some to lead him by the hand.

12 Then the deputy, when he saw what was done, believed, being astonished at the doctrine of the Lord.

13 Now when Paul and his company loosed from Paphos, they came to Perga in Pamphylia: and ^aJohn departing from them returned to Jerusalem.

14 ¶ But when they departed from Perga, they came to Antioch in Pisidia, and went into the synagogue on the sabbath day, and sat down.

15 And after the reading of the law and the prophets the rulers of the synagogue sent unto them, saying, Ye men *and* brethren, if ye have any word of exhortation for the people, say on.

16 Then Paul stood up, and beckoning with *his* hand said, Men of Israel, and ye that ^afear God, give audience.

17 The God of this people of Israel chose our fathers, and exalted the people when they dwelt as ^astrangers in the land of Egypt, and with an high arm brought he them out of it.

18 And about the time of forty years suffered he their manners in the wilderness.

19 And when he had ^adestroyed seven nations in the ^bland of Chanaan, he divided their land to them by lot.

20 And after that he gave *unto them* judges about the space of four hundred and fifty years, until Samuel the prophet.

21 And afterward they desired a king: and God gave unto them Saul the son of Cis, a man of the tribe of Benjamin, by the space of forty years.

22 And when he had removed him, he raised up unto them David to be their king; to whom also he gave testimony, and said, I have found David the *son* of Jesse, a man after mine own ^aheart, which shall fulfil all my will.

23 Of this man's ^aseed hath God according to *his* ^bpromise raised unto Israel a ^cSaviour, Jesus:

3a TG Authority;
       Priesthood, Authority.
   b TG Hands, Laying on of;
       Priesthood, Ordination.
6a TG Sorcery.
7a TG Prudence.
9a TG Holy Ghost, Gifts of.
10a 1 Jn. 3:10 (10–18);

       Alma 11:23.
    b TG Enemies.
    c TG Righteousness.
11a Gen. 19:11.
    b Alma 30:49 (48–60).
13a Acts 15:37 (36–40).
16a Moro. 7:3 (3–4).
17a TG Stranger.

19a Num. 21:3 (1–3);
       Ps. 80:8 (8–10).
    b TG Israel, Land of.
22a TG Heart.
23a TG Jesus Christ, Davidic
       Descent of.
    b TG Promise.
    c TG Jesus Christ, Savior.

24 When John had first preached before his coming the baptism of repentance to all the people of Israel.

25 And as John fulfilled his course, he said, Whom think ye that I am? I am not *he*. But, behold, there cometh one after me, whose shoes of *his* feet I am not worthy to loose.

26 Men *and* brethren, children of the stock of *a*Abraham, and whosoever among you feareth God, to you is the word of this salvation sent.

27 For they that dwell at Jerusalem, and their rulers, because they knew him not, nor yet the voices of the prophets which are read every sabbath day, they have fulfilled *them* in condemning *him*.

28 And though they found no cause of death *in him,* yet desired they Pilate that he should be *a*slain.

29 And when they had fulfilled all that was written of him, they took *him* down from the tree, and laid *him* in a sepulchre.

30 But God raised him from the dead:

31 And he was *a*seen many days of them which came up with him from Galilee to Jerusalem, who are his *b*witnesses unto the people.

32 And we declare unto you glad tidings, how that the promise which was made unto the *a*fathers,

33 God hath fulfilled the same unto us their children, in that he hath raised up Jesus again; as it is also written in the second psalm, Thou art my *a*Son, this day have I begotten thee.

34 And as concerning that he raised him up from the dead, *now* no more to return to corruption, he said on this wise, I will give you the *a*sure mercies of David.

35 Wherefore he saith also in another *psalm*, Thou shalt not suffer thine Holy One to see corruption.

36 For David, after he had served his own generation by the will of God, fell on sleep, and was laid unto his fathers, and saw corruption:

37 But he, whom God *a*raised again, saw no *b*corruption.

38 ¶ Be it known unto you therefore, men *and* brethren, that through this man is preached unto you the *a*forgiveness of sins:

39 And by him all that believe are *a*justified from all things, from which ye could not be *b*justified by the *c*law of Moses.

40 Beware therefore, lest that come upon you, which is spoken of in the prophets;

41 Behold, ye despisers, and wonder, and perish: for I work a work in your days, a *a*work which ye shall in no wise believe, though a man declare it unto you.

42 And when the Jews were gone out of the synagogue, the Gentiles besought that these words might be preached to them the next *a*sabbath.

43 Now when the congregation was broken up, many of the Jews and religious *a*proselytes followed Paul and Barnabas: who, speaking to them, persuaded them to continue in the grace of God.

44 ¶ And the next sabbath day came almost the whole city together to hear the word of God.

45 But when the Jews saw the multitudes, they were filled with *a*envy, and spake *b*against those things which were spoken by Paul, contradicting and *c*blaspheming.

46 Then Paul and Barnabas waxed bold, and said, It was necessary that

26a Abr. 2:9 (9–10).
28a Matt. 27:20;
　　Acts 3:13.
31a TG Jesus Christ,
　　Appearances,
　　Postmortal.
　b Acts 10:39 (39–43);
　　22:15 (14–16).
32a TG Family, Patriarchal.
33a TG Jesus Christ, Divine
　　Sonship.

34a Isa. 55:3.
37a TG Jesus Christ,
　　Resurrection.
　b Acts 2:27 (27, 31).
38a TG Forgive;
　　Jesus Christ, Atonement
　　through;
　　Jesus Christ, Redeemer;
　　Remission of Sins.
39a TG Justification.
　b Rom. 2:13.

　c TG Law of Moses.
41a Hab. 1:5;
　　3 Ne. 21:9 (9–11).
42a TG Sabbath.
43a Acts 2:10.
45a TG Envy.
　b Luke 11:52;
　　1 Thes. 2:16.
　c TG Blaspheme.

the word of God should first have been spoken to you: but seeing ye put it from you, and judge yourselves unworthy of everlasting life, lo, we turn to the ^aGentiles.

47 For so hath the Lord commanded us, *saying,* I have set thee to be a ^alight of the Gentiles, that thou shouldest be for ^bsalvation unto the ends of the earth.

48 And when the Gentiles heard this, they were glad, and glorified the word of the Lord: ^aand as many as were ordained to eternal life believed.

49 And the word of the Lord was ^apublished throughout all the region.

50 But the Jews ^astirred up the devout and honourable ^bwomen, and the chief men of the city, and raised ^cpersecution against Paul and Barnabas, and expelled them out of their coasts.

51 But they shook off the ^adust of their feet against them, and came unto Iconium.

52 And the disciples were filled with joy, and with the Holy Ghost.

CHAPTER 14

Persecution attends the spread of the gospel—Paul heals a crippled man; Paul and Barnabas are hailed as gods—Paul is stoned and revived; he preaches—Elders are ordained.

AND it came to pass in Iconium, that they went both together into the synagogue of the Jews, and so spake, that a great multitude both of the Jews and also of the Greeks believed.

2 But the unbelieving Jews stirred up the Gentiles, and made their minds evil affected against the brethren.

3 Long time therefore abode they speaking boldly in the Lord, which gave ^atestimony unto the word of his ^bgrace, and granted signs and wonders to be done by their hands.

4 But the multitude of the city was divided: and part held with the Jews, and part with the apostles.

5 And when there was an assault made both of the Gentiles, and also of the ^aJews with their rulers, to use *them* despitefully, and to stone them,

6 They were ware of *it,* and fled unto Lystra and Derbe, cities of Lycaonia, and unto the region that lieth round about:

7 And there they preached the gospel.

8 ¶ And there sat a certain man at Lystra, impotent in his feet, being a ^acripple from his mother's womb, who never had walked:

9 The same heard Paul speak: who steadfastly beholding him, and perceiving that he had ^afaith to be ^bhealed,

10 Said with a loud voice, Stand upright on thy feet. And he leaped and walked.

11 And when the people saw what Paul had done, they lifted up their voices, saying in the speech of Lycaonia, The ^agods are come down to us in the likeness of men.

12 And they called Barnabas, ^aJupiter; and Paul, ^bMercurius, because he was the chief speaker.

13 Then the priest of Jupiter, which was before their city, brought oxen and garlands unto the gates, and would have done sacrifice with the people.

14 *Which* when the ^aapostles, Barnabas and Paul, heard *of,* they rent their clothes, and ran in among the people, crying out,

---

46a Matt. 21:43;
  Luke 14:24 (21–24);
  Acts 28:28 (27–28).
47a TG Example.
  b TG Jesus Christ, Savior;
  Salvation.
48a JST Acts 13:48 . . . and as
  many as *believed* were
  ordained unto eternal
  life.

49a D&C 1:6.
50a Alma 27:2 (2, 12).
  b Acts 17:4 (4, 12).
  c TG Persecution.
51a Matt. 10:14 (14–15);
  Luke 10:11;
  Acts 18:6 (5–6);
  D&C 24:15;
  60:15 (13–15).
14 3a TG Testimony.

  b TG Grace.
5a 2 Cor. 11:26.
8a Acts 3:2 (1–10).
9a TG Faith.
  b TG Heal.
11a Acts 28:6 (3–6).
12a GR Zeus.
  b GR Hermes.
14a TG Apostles.

15 And saying, Sirs, why do ye these things? We also are ªmen of like ᵇpassions with you, and preach unto you that ye should turn from these ᶜvanities unto the living God, which ᵈmade heaven, and earth, and the sea, and all things that are therein:

16 Who in times past suffered all nations to ªwalk in their own ᵇways.

17 Nevertheless he left not himself without ªwitness, in that he did good, and gave us ᵇrain from heaven, and fruitful seasons, filling our hearts with ᶜfood and gladness.

18 And with these sayings scarce restrained they the people, that they had not done sacrifice unto them.

19 ¶ And there came thither *certain* Jews from Antioch and Iconium, who persuaded the people, and, having ªstoned Paul, drew *him* out of the city, supposing he had been dead.

20 Howbeit, as the disciples stood round about him, he rose up, and came into the city: and the next day he departed with Barnabas to Derbe.

21 And when they had preached the gospel to that city, and had taught many, they returned again to Lystra, and *to* Iconium, and Antioch,

22 Confirming the souls of the disciples, *and* exhorting them to continue in the faith, and that we must through much ªtribulation enter into the kingdom of God.

23 And when they had ªordained them ᵇelders in every church, and had prayed with ᶜfasting, they commended them to the Lord, on whom they believed.

24 And after they had passed throughout Pisidia, they came to Pamphylia.

25 And when they had preached the word in Perga, they went down into Attalia:

26 And thence sailed to ªAntioch, from whence they had been recommended to the grace of God for the work which they fulfilled.

27 And when they were come, and had gathered the church together, they rehearsed all that God had done with them, and how he had opened the ªdoor of faith unto the Gentiles.

28 And there they abode long time with the disciples.

CHAPTER 15

Great dissension arises at Antioch concerning circumcision—The Apostles at Jerusalem decide the issue—Paul chooses Silas as his companion.

AND certain men which came down from Judæa taught the brethren, *and said*, Except ye be ªcircumcised after the manner of Moses, ye cannot be saved.

2 When therefore Paul and Barnabas had no small dissension and ªdisputation with them, they determined that Paul and Barnabas, and certain other of them, should go up to Jerusalem unto the ᵇapostles and elders about this question.

3 And being brought on their way by the church, they passed through Phenice and Samaria, declaring the ªconversion of the Gentiles: and they caused great joy unto all the brethren.

4 And when they were come to Jerusalem, they were received of the church, and *of* the apostles and elders, and they declared all things that God had done with them.

5 But there rose up certain of the

15a Dan. 2:46;
    James 5:17 (17–18);
    1 Ne. 17:55.
  b TG Lust.
  c TG Vanity.
  d TG Jesus Christ, Creator.
16a TG Walking in
    Darkness.
  b Acts 17:30 (27–30).
17a Rom. 1:20.

  b Lev. 26:4 (3–4).
  c TG Food.
19a TG Persecution.
22a TG Adversity;
    Test;
    Tribulation.
23a TG Authority;
    Priesthood, History of;
    Priesthood, Ordination.
  b TG Church Organization;

    Elder, Melchizedek
    Priesthood.
  c TG Fast, Fasting.
26a Acts 11:26 (25–26).
27a 2 Cor. 2:12.
15 1a TG Circumcision.
  2a TG Disputations.
  b Gal. 2:1.
  3a TG Conversion.

sect of the Pharisees which believed, saying, That it was needful to circumcise them, and to command *them* to keep the *a*law of Moses.

6 ¶ And the *a*apostles and *b*elders came together for to consider of this matter.

7 And when there had been much *a*disputing, *b*Peter rose up, and said unto them, Men *and* brethren, ye know how that a good while ago God made choice among us, that the *c*Gentiles by my mouth should hear the word of the *d*gospel, and believe.

8 And God, which *a*knoweth the hearts, bare them witness, giving them the Holy Ghost, even as *he did* unto us;

9 And put no *a*difference between us and them, *b*purifying their hearts by faith.

10 Now therefore why *a*tempt ye God, to put a yoke upon the neck of the disciples, which neither our fathers nor we were able to bear?

11 But we believe that through the *a*grace of the Lord Jesus Christ we shall be saved, even as they.

12 ¶ Then all the multitude kept silence, and gave audience to Barnabas and Paul, declaring what miracles and wonders God had wrought among the Gentiles by them.

13 ¶ And after they had held their peace, James answered, saying, Men *and* brethren, hearken unto me:

14 Simeon hath declared how God at the first did visit the *a*Gentiles, to take out of them a people for his *b*name.

15 And to this agree the words of the prophets; as it is written,

16 After this I will return, and will build again the *a*tabernacle of David, which is fallen down; and I will build again the ruins thereof, and I will set it up:

17 That the *a*residue of men might seek after the Lord, and all the Gentiles, upon whom my name is called, saith the Lord, who doeth all these things.

18 *a*Known unto God are all his works from the beginning of the world.

19 Wherefore my sentence is, that we trouble not them, which from among the Gentiles are turned to God:

20 But that we write unto them, that they *a*abstain from *b*pollutions of idols, and *from* *c*fornication, and *from* things strangled, and *from* *d*blood.

21 For Moses of old time hath in every city them that preach him, being *a*read in the synagogues every sabbath day.

22 Then pleased it the apostles and elders, with the whole church, to send chosen men of their own company to Antioch with Paul and Barnabas; *namely,* Judas surnamed Barsabas, and Silas, chief men among the brethren:

23 And they *a*wrote *b*letters by them after this manner; The apostles and elders and brethren *send* greeting unto the brethren which are of the Gentiles in Antioch and Syria and Cilicia:

24 Forasmuch as we have heard, that certain which went out from us have troubled you with words, subverting your souls, saying, Ye *must* be *a*circumcised, and keep the law: to whom we gave no *such* commandment:

25 It seemed good unto us, being

5*a* Gal. 5:18 (16–18).
6*a* TG Church Organization.
  b TG Elder, Melchizedek Priesthood.
7*a* TG Disputations.
  b D&C 7:7 (5–7); JS—H 1:72.
  c Acts 10:20 (9–48).
  d TG Gospel.
8*a* TG God, Omniscience of.
9*a* Acts 10:34 (34–35);

17:26 (25–26).
  b TG Purification; Purity.
10*a* TG Test.
11*a* TG Grace.
14*a* Abr. 2:10 (9–10).
  b TG Name.
16*a* Amos 9:11 (11–12).
17*a* Moro. 7:32.
18*a* TG God, Omniscience of.
20*a* Acts 21:25.

TG Abstain.
  b TG Pollution.
  c TG Fornication; Sexual Immorality.
  d TG Blood, Eating of.
21*a* 2 Cor. 3:14 (14–15).
23*a* TG Scriptures, Writing of.
  b Acts 16:4.
24*a* Gen. 17:11 (10–27); Moro. 8:8.

assembled with ªone accord, to send chosen men unto you with our beloved Barnabas and Paul,

26 Men that have ªhazarded their lives for the name of our Lord Jesus Christ.

27 We have sent therefore Judas and Silas, who shall also tell *you* the same things by mouth.

28 For it seemed good to the Holy Ghost, and to us, to lay upon you no greater burden than these necessary things;

29 That ye abstain from meats offered to ªidols, and from blood, and from things strangled, and from fornication: from which if ye keep yourselves, ye shall do well. Fare ye well.

30 So when they were dismissed, they came to Antioch: and when they had gathered the multitude together, they delivered the epistle:

31 *Which* when they had read, they rejoiced for the ªconsolation.

32 And Judas and Silas, being prophets also themselves, exhorted the brethren with many words, and confirmed *them.*

33 And after they had tarried *there* a space, they were let go in peace from the brethren unto the apostles.

34 Notwithstanding it pleased ªSilas to abide there still.

35 Paul also and Barnabas continued in Antioch, teaching and preaching the word of the Lord, with many others also.

36 ¶ And some days after Paul said unto Barnabas, Let us go again and ªvisit our ᵇbrethren in every city where we have preached the word of the Lord, *and see* how they do.

37 And Barnabas determined to take with them ªJohn, whose surname was ᵇMark.

38 But Paul thought not good to take him with them, who departed from them from Pamphylia, and went not with them to the work.

39 And the ªcontention was so sharp between them, that they departed asunder one from the other: and so Barnabas took Mark, and sailed unto Cyprus;

40 And Paul chose Silas, and departed, being recommended by the brethren unto the grace of God.

41 And he went through Syria and Cilicia, ªconfirming the churches.

CHAPTER 16

Paul is directed in a vision to preach in Macedonia—He casts an evil spirit out of a woman—He and Silas are imprisoned, and they convert the jailor—They admonish all to believe on the Lord Jesus and be saved.

THEN came he to Derbe and Lystra: and, behold, a certain disciple was there, named ªTimotheus, the son of a certain woman, which was a ᵇJewess, and believed; but his father *was* a Greek:

2 Which was well reported of by the brethren that were at Lystra and Iconium.

3 Him would Paul have to go forth with him; and took and ªcircumcised him because of the Jews which were in those quarters: for they knew all that his father was a Greek.

4 And as they went through the cities, they delivered them the ªdecrees for to keep, that were ordained of the apostles and elders which were at Jerusalem.

5 And so were the churches ªestablished in the faith, and increased in number daily.

6 Now when they had gone throughout Phrygia and the region of Galatia, and were forbidden of the

25ª ᴛɢ Common Consent.
26ª 2 Tim. 3:11.
29ª 1 Cor. 8:1.
31ª ɢʀ consolation, exhortation, solace, persuasion.
34ª 2 Cor. 1:19;
     1 Thes. 1:1;
     1 Pet. 5:12.

36ª Acts 12:25 (20–25).
    b ᴛɢ Brotherhood and Sisterhood.
37ª Acts 13:13.
    b Col. 4:10;
       2 Tim. 4:11.
39ª ᴛɢ Contention.
41ª D&C 24:9.

16 1ª Acts 17:14 (14–15); 20:4;
       1 Cor. 4:17;
       1 Thes. 1:1; 3:2 (2, 6);
       1 Tim. 1:2.
    b 2 Tim. 1:5.
3ª ᴛɢ Circumcision.
4ª Acts 15:23 (23–29).
5ª Moro. 7:32 (31–32).

^aHoly Ghost to preach the word in Asia,

7 After they were come to Mysia, they assayed to go into Bithynia: but the Spirit suffered them not.

8 And they passing by Mysia came down to Troas.

9 And a ^avision appeared to Paul in the night; There stood a man of Macedonia, and prayed him, saying, Come over into Macedonia, and help us.

10 And after he had seen the vision, immediately we endeavoured to go into Macedonia, assuredly gathering that the Lord had called us for to preach the gospel unto them.

11 Therefore loosing from Troas, we came with a straight course to Samothracia, and the next *day* to Neapolis;

12 And from thence to Philippi, which is the chief city of that part of Macedonia, *and* a colony: and we were in that city abiding certain days.

13 And on the sabbath we went out of the city by a river side, where prayer was wont to be made; and we sat down, and spake unto the women which resorted *thither*.

14 ¶ And a certain woman named ^aLydia, a seller of purple, of the city of Thyatira, which worshipped God, heard *us:* whose ^bheart the Lord opened, that she attended unto the things which were spoken of Paul.

15 And when she was baptized, and her household, she besought *us,* saying, If ye have judged me to be faithful to the Lord, come into my house, and ^aabide *there.* And she constrained us.

16 ¶ And it came to pass, as we went to prayer, a certain damsel possessed with a spirit of divination met us, which brought her masters much gain by ^asoothsaying:

17 The same followed Paul and us,

and cried, saying, ^aThese men are the servants of the most high God, which shew unto us the way of salvation.

18 And this did she many days. But Paul, being grieved, turned and said to the ^aspirit, I command thee in the name of Jesus Christ to come out of her. And he came out the same hour.

19 ¶ And when her masters saw that the hope of their gains was gone, they caught Paul and Silas, and drew *them* into the marketplace unto the rulers,

20 And brought them to the magistrates, saying, These men, being Jews, do exceedingly trouble our city,

21 And teach customs, which are not lawful for us to receive, neither to observe, being Romans.

22 And the multitude rose up together against them: and the magistrates rent off their clothes, and commanded to ^abeat *them.*

23 And when they had laid many ^astripes upon them, they cast *them* into prison, charging the jailor to keep them safely:

24 Who, having received such a charge, thrust them into the inner prison, and made their feet fast in the stocks.

25 ¶ And at ^amidnight Paul and Silas prayed, and ^bsang praises unto God: and the prisoners heard them.

26 And suddenly there was a great earthquake, so that the foundations of the prison were shaken: and immediately all the ^adoors were opened, and every one's bands were loosed.

27 And the keeper of the prison awaking out of his sleep, and seeing the prison doors open, he drew out his sword, and would have killed himself, supposing that the prisoners had been fled.

28 But Paul cried with a loud voice,

6*a* Alma 21:16 (16–17);
  22:1 (1–4).
9*a* 2 Cor. 2:12.
  TG Vision.
14*a* Acts 16:40.
  b Alma 16:16.
15*a* 1 Tim. 5:10.

16*a* TG Sorcery.
17*a* James 2:19.
18*a* TG Spirits, Evil or
  Unclean.
22*a* 2 Cor. 11:25;
  1 Thes. 2:2.
23*a* 2 Cor. 11:23.

TG Cruelty.
25*a* Ps. 119:62.
  b TG Singing.
26*a* Acts 5:19 (15–20);
  Alma 14:27 (27–28);
  3 Ne. 28:19 (19–20);
  4 Ne. 1:30.

saying, Do thyself no harm: for we are all here.

29 Then he called for a light, and sprang in, and came trembling, and fell down before Paul and Silas,

30 And brought them out, and said, Sirs, what must I do to be saved?

31 And they said, ^aBelieve on the Lord Jesus Christ, and thou shalt be saved, and thy house.

32 And they spake unto him the word of the Lord, and to all that were in his house.

33 And he took them the same hour of the night, and washed *their* stripes; and was baptized, he and all his, straightway.

34 And when he had brought them into his house, he set meat before them, and rejoiced, believing in God with all his house.

35 And when it was day, the magistrates sent the serjeants, saying, Let those men go.

36 And the keeper of the prison told this saying to Paul, The magistrates have sent to let you go: now therefore depart, and go in peace.

37 But Paul said unto them, They have beaten us openly uncondemned, being ^aRomans, and have cast *us* into prison; and now do they thrust us out ^bprivily? nay verily; but let them come themselves and fetch us out.

38 And the serjeants told these words unto the magistrates: and they feared, when they heard that they were Romans.

39 And they came and besought them, and brought *them* out, and desired *them* to depart out of the city.

40 And they went out of the prison, and entered into *the house of* ^aLydia: and when they had seen the brethren, they comforted them, and departed.

CHAPTER 17

Paul and Silas preach and are persecuted in Thessalonica and in Berea—Paul, in Athens, preaches from Mars' Hill about the unknown god—He says, We are the offspring of God.

Now when they had passed through Amphipolis and Apollonia, they came to ^aThessalonica, where was a synagogue of the Jews:

2 And Paul, as his manner was, went in unto them, and three sabbath days ^areasoned with them out of the ^bscriptures,

3 Opening and alleging, that Christ must needs have suffered, and risen again from the dead; and that this Jesus, whom I preach unto you, is Christ.

4 And some of them believed, and consorted with Paul and Silas; and of the devout ^aGreeks a great multitude, and of the chief ^bwomen not a few.

5 ¶ But the ^aJews which believed not, moved with envy, took unto them certain ^blewd fellows of the baser sort, and gathered a company, and set all the city on an ^cuproar, and ^dassaulted the house of Jason, and sought to bring them out to the people.

6 And when they found them not, they drew Jason and certain brethren unto the rulers of the city, crying, These that have turned the world upside down are come hither also;

7 Whom Jason hath received: and these all do contrary to the decrees of Cæsar, saying that there is another king, *one* Jesus.

8 And they troubled the people and the rulers of the city, when they heard these things.

9 And when they had taken security of Jason, and of the other, they let them go.

31*a* Mosiah 4:10 (9–10);
    Hel. 14:13.
    TG Baptism,
    Qualifications for.
37*a* Acts 22:25.
  b OR secretly.

40*a* Acts 16:14 (14–15).
17 1*a* 1 Thes. 1:1.
  2*a* Acts 18:19; 1 Thes. 2:2.
    TG Missionary Work.
  b Alma 14:1.
  4*a* John 12:20.

  b Acts 13:50.
5*a* 2 Cor. 11:26.
  b GR wicked, evil.
  c TG Rioting and
    Reveling.
  d 1 Thes. 1:6; 2:14.

10 ¶ And the brethren immediately sent away Paul and Silas by night unto Berea: who coming *thither* went into the synagogue of the Jews.

11 These were more noble than those in Thessalonica, in that they received the word with all readiness of mind, and ªsearched the scriptures daily, whether those things were so.

12 Therefore many of them believed; also of honourable women which were Greeks, and of men, not a few.

13 But when the Jews of Thessalonica had knowledge that the word of God was preached of Paul at Berea, they came thither also, and stirred up the people.

14 And then immediately the brethren sent away Paul to go as it were to the sea: but Silas and ªTimotheus abode there still.

15 And they that conducted Paul brought him unto ªAthens: and receiving a commandment unto Silas and Timotheus for to come to him with all speed, they departed.

16 ¶ Now while Paul waited for them at Athens, his spirit was stirred in him, when he saw the city ªwholly given to ᵇidolatry.

17 Therefore ªdisputed he in the ᵇsynagogue with the Jews, and with the devout persons, and in the market daily with them that met with him.

18 Then certain philosophers of the Epicureans, and of the Stoicks, encountered him. And some said, What will this babbler say? other some, He seemeth to be a setter forth of strange gods: because he preached unto them Jesus, and the resurrection.

19 And they took him, and brought him unto ªAreopagus, saying, May we know what this new doctrine, whereof thou speakest, *is*?

20 For thou bringest certain strange things to our ears: we would know therefore what these things mean.

21 (For all the Athenians and strangers which were there ªspent their time in nothing else, but either to tell, or to hear some new thing.)

22 ¶ Then Paul stood in the midst of Mars' hill, and said, Ye men of Athens, I perceive that in all things ye are ªtoo superstitious.

23 For as I passed by, and beheld your ªdevotions, I found an altar with this inscription, TO THE ᵇUNKNOWN GOD. Whom therefore ye ᶜignorantly worship, him ᵈdeclare I unto you.

24 God that ªmade the world and all things therein, seeing that he is Lord of heaven and earth, ᵇdwelleth not in temples made with hands;

25 Neither is ªworshipped with men's hands, as though he needed any thing, seeing he giveth to all life, and ᵇbreath, and all things;

26 And hath ªmade of ᵇone ᶜblood ᵈall ᵉnations of men for to dwell on all the face of the earth, and hath ᶠdetermined the ᵍtimes before ʰappointed, and the ⁱbounds of their habitation;

27 That they should ªseek the

11a TG Scriptures, Study of.
14a Acts 16:1 (1–4).
15a 1 Thes. 3:1.
16a GR full of idols; i.e., grossly idolatrous.
  b TG Idolatry.
17a TG Disputations.
  b Acts 18:4 (4, 19); 19:8.
19a GR Hill of Ares (Mars); probably meaning the civil council which met there. Acts 17:34.
21a TG Waste.
22a GR most religious; i.e.,

careful in divine things.
23a GR sacred, venerated objects.
  b D&C 93:19. TG God, Knowledge about.
  c TG Ignorance.
  d TG Preaching.
24a TG Creation.
  b Acts 7:48.
25a TG Worship.
  b TG Breath of Life.
26a Job 31:15; Mal. 2:10.
  b Acts 10:34 (34–35); 15:9.

c D&C 38:25 (24–27).
  d TG Gentiles.
  e TG Nations.
  f TG God, Foreknowledge of; God, Omniscience of.
  g Eccl. 3:2; Alma 40:10. TG Time.
  h TG Foreordination.
  i Deut. 32:8 (8–9); Job 14:5. TG Order; Separation.
27a TG God, Access to.

Lord, *b*if haply they might *c*feel after him, and find him, though he be not far from every one of us:

28 For in him we *a*live, and move, and have our being; as certain also of your own poets have said, For we are also his *b*offspring.

29 Forasmuch then as we are the *a*offspring of God, we ought not to think that the Godhead is like unto *b*gold, or silver, or stone, graven by art and man's *c*device.

30 And the times of this *a*ignorance God *b*winked at; but now *c*commandeth all men every where to *d*repent:

31 Because he hath appointed a day, in the which he will *a*judge the world in righteousness by *that* man whom he hath *b*ordained; *whereof* he hath given assurance unto all *men*, in that he hath *c*raised him from the dead.

32 ¶ And when they heard of the *a*resurrection of the dead, some *b*mocked: and others said, We will hear thee again of this *matter*.

33 So Paul departed from among them.

34 Howbeit certain men clave unto him, and believed: among the which *was* Dionysius the *a*Areopagite, and a woman named Damaris, and others with them.

CHAPTER 18

Being rejected by the Jews, Paul turns to the Gentiles—He preaches, minis- *ters, and travels—Apollos also preaches with power.*

AFTER these things Paul departed from Athens, and came to Corinth;

2 And found a certain Jew named *a*Aquila, born in Pontus, lately come from Italy, with his wife Priscilla; (because that Claudius had commanded all Jews to depart from Rome:) and came unto them.

3 And because he was of the same craft, he abode with them, and *a*wrought: for by their occupation they were *b*tentmakers.

4 And he reasoned in the *a*synagogue every *b*sabbath, and persuaded the Jews and the Greeks.

5 And when Silas and *a*Timotheus were come from Macedonia, Paul was pressed in the spirit, and *b*testified to the Jews *that* Jesus *was* *c*Christ.

6 And when they opposed themselves, and blasphemed, he *a*shook *his* raiment, and said unto them, Your *b*blood *be* upon your own heads; I *am* clean: from henceforth I will go unto the Gentiles.

7 ¶ And he departed thence, and entered into a certain *man's* house, named Justus, *one* that worshipped God, whose house joined hard to the synagogue.

8 And *a*Crispus, the chief ruler of the synagogue, believed on the Lord with all his house; and many of the Corinthians hearing *b*believed, and were baptized.

27b JST Acts 17:27 . . . if they
       are willing to find him,
       for he *is* not far from
       every one of us;
    c D&C 101:8.
28a Deut. 30:20;
       D&C 45:1.
    b TG Man, Antemortal
       Existence of.
29a TG Man, a Spirit Child
       of Heavenly Father;
       Man, Physical Creation
       of; Man, Potential
       to Become like
       Heavenly Father;
       Sons and Daughters
       of God;
       Spirit Creation.

    b TG Idolatry.
    c Jer. 44:8.
30a Acts 14:16 (16–17);
       1 Pet. 1:14 (1–16);
       2 Ne. 9:25 (25–27);
       D&C 76:72.
    b OR overlooked,
       disregarded.
       Moro. 8:22 (9–26).
    c D&C 18:9.
    d TG Repent.
31a TG Jesus Christ, Judge;
       Judgment, the Last.
    b TG Jesus Christ,
       Authority of.
    c Acts 10:40.
32a Alma 12:15 (12–18).
    b TG Mocking.

34a Acts 17:19 (19, 22).
18 2a 1 Cor. 16:19.
 3a Acts 20:34;
       1 Thes. 2:9.
    b TG Skill.
 4a Acts 17:17; 19:8.
    b TG Sabbath.
 5a 1 Thes. 1:1.
    b Alma 7:26 (16, 26).
    c TG Jesus Christ,
       Messiah.
 6a Matt. 10:14;
       Acts 13:51 (44–51);
       D&C 24:15; 60:15.
    b Ezek. 33:4 (3–5).
 8a 1 Cor. 1:14.
    b TG Baptism,
       Qualifications for.

9 Then spake the Lord to Paul in the night by a ªvision, Be not afraid, but speak, and hold not thy peace:

10 For I am with thee, and no man shall set on thee to hurt thee: for I have much ªpeople in this city.

11 And he continued *there* a year and six months, teaching the word of God among them.

12 ¶ And when Gallio was the deputy of Achaia, the Jews made insurrection with one accord against Paul, and brought him to the judgment seat,

13 Saying, This *fellow* persuadeth men to ªworship God contrary to the law.

14 And when Paul was now about to open *his* mouth, Gallio said unto the Jews, If it were a matter of wrong or ªwicked ᵇlewdness, O *ye* Jews, reason would that I should bear with you:

15 But if it be a ªquestion of words and names, and *of* your law, look ye *to it*; for I will be no judge of such *matters*.

16 And he drave them from the judgment seat.

17 Then all the Greeks took Sosthenes, the chief ruler of the synagogue, and beat *him* before the judgment seat. And Gallio cared for none of those things.

18 ¶ And Paul *after this* tarried *there* yet a good while, and then took his leave of the brethren, and sailed thence into Syria, and with him Priscilla and Aquila; having shorn *his* head in Cenchrea: for he had a ªvow.

19 And he came to Ephesus, and left them there: but he himself entered into the synagogue, and ªreasoned with the Jews.

20 When they desired *him* to tarry longer time with them, he consented not;

21 But bade them farewell, saying,

I must by all means keep this feast that cometh in Jerusalem: but I will return again unto you, if God will. And he sailed from Ephesus.

22 And when he had landed at Cæsarea, and gone up, and saluted the church, he went down to Antioch.

23 And after he had spent some time *there,* he departed, and went over *all* the country of Galatia and Phrygia in order, strengthening all the disciples.

24 ¶ And a certain Jew named ªApollos, born at Alexandria, an eloquent man, *and* ᵇmighty in the scriptures, came to Ephesus.

25 This man was ªinstructed in the way of the Lord; and being ᵇfervent in the spirit, he spake and taught ᶜdiligently the things of the Lord, knowing only the baptism of ᵈJohn.

26 And he began to speak boldly in the synagogue: whom when Aquila and Priscilla had heard, they took him unto *them,* and expounded unto him the way of God more perfectly.

27 And when he was disposed to pass into Achaia, the brethren ªwrote, exhorting the disciples to receive him: who, when he was come, helped them much which had believed through grace:

28 For he mightily convinced the Jews, *and that* publickly, ªshewing by the scriptures that ᵇJesus was Christ.

CHAPTER 19

Paul confers the gift of the Holy Ghost by the laying on of hands—He preaches and works many miracles—The sons of Sceva fail to cast out devils by exorcism—The worshippers of Diana (Artemis) raise a tumult against Paul.

AND it came to pass, that, while Apollos was at Corinth, Paul having

---

9a ᴛɢ Jesus Christ,
    Appearances,
    Postmortal;
    Vision.
10a D&C 111:2 (2–11).
13a Alma 30:7 (7–11).
14a Acts 25:5.

    b ɢʀ crime.
15a Acts 23:29.
18a ᴛɢ Vow.
19a Acts 17:2.
24a 1 Cor. 16:12.
    b D&C 100:11.
25a ᴛɢ Education.

    b ᴛɢ Zeal.
    c ɢʀ accurately, precisely,
       diligently.
    d Acts 19:3 (3–6).
27a D&C 42:11.
28a ᴛɢ Scriptures, Study of.
    b ᴏʀ Jesus is the Christ.

passed through the upper ^acoasts came to Ephesus: and finding certain disciples,

2 He said unto them, Have ye received the Holy Ghost since ye believed? And they said unto him, We have not so much as heard whether there be any Holy Ghost.

3 And he said unto them, Unto what then were ye baptized? And they said, Unto ^aJohn's baptism.

4 Then said Paul, John verily baptized with the baptism of ^arepentance, saying unto the people, that they should believe on him which should come after him, that is, on Christ Jesus.

5 When they heard *this*, they were ^abaptized in the name of the Lord Jesus.

6 And when Paul had laid *his* hands upon them, the Holy Ghost came on them; and they spake with ^atongues, and prophesied.

7 And all the men were about twelve.

8 And he went into the ^asynagogue, and spake boldly for the space of three months, ^bdisputing and persuading the things concerning the kingdom of God.

9 But when divers were hardened, and believed not, but spake evil of that way before the multitude, he departed from them, and separated the disciples, disputing daily in the school of one Tyrannus.

10 And this continued by the space of two years; so that all they which dwelt in Asia heard the word of the Lord Jesus, both Jews and Greeks.

11 And God wrought special ^amiracles by the hands of Paul:

12 So that from his body were brought unto the sick ^ahandkerchiefs or aprons, and the diseases departed from them, and the evil spirits went out of them.

13 ¶ Then certain of the vagabond Jews, ^aexorcists, took upon them to call over them which had evil spirits the ^bname of the Lord Jesus, saying, We ^cadjure you by Jesus whom Paul preacheth.

14 And there were seven sons of *one* Sceva, a Jew, *and* chief of the priests, which did so.

15 And the ^aevil spirit answered and said, Jesus I know, and Paul I know; but who are ye?

16 And the man in whom the evil spirit was leaped on them, and overcame them, and prevailed against them, so that they fled out of that house naked and wounded.

17 And this was known to all the Jews and Greeks also dwelling at Ephesus; and fear fell on them all, and the name of the Lord Jesus was magnified.

18 And many that believed came, and ^aconfessed, and shewed their deeds.

19 Many of them also which used curious ^aarts brought their books together, and burned them before all *men:* and they counted the price of them, and found *it* fifty thousand *pieces* of silver.

20 So mightily grew the word of God and prevailed.

21 ¶ After these things were ended, Paul purposed in the ^aspirit, when he had passed through Macedonia and Achaia, to go to Jerusalem, saying, After I have been there, I must also see ^bRome.

22 So he sent into Macedonia two of them that ministered unto him, Timotheus and Erastus; but he himself stayed in Asia for a season.

---

19 1 *a* OR parts, region.
  3 *a* TG Matt. 3:11; Acts 18:25.
  4 *a* TG Baptism,
    Qualifications for.
  5 *a* TG Baptism, Essential.
  6 *a* TG Holy Ghost, Mission
    of; Language.
  8 *a* Acts 17:17; 18:4 (4, 19).
    b TG Disputations.

11 *a* TG Priesthood,
    Authority;
    Priesthood, Power of.
12 *a* 2 Kgs. 4:29;
    Luke 8:44 (43–48);
    Acts 5:15.
13 *a* Mark 9:38 (38–49);
    Luke 11:19.
    TG Sorcery.

  b TG Profanity.
  c TG Unrighteous
    Dominion.
15 *a* TG Spirits, Evil or
    Unclean.
18 *a* TG Confession.
19 *a* TG Sorcery.
21 *a* Acts 20:22.
  b Acts 23:11.

23 And the same time there arose no small stir about that way.

24 For a certain *man* named Demetrius, a silversmith, which made silver shrines for ᵃDiana, brought no small gain unto the craftsmen;

25 Whom he called together with the workmen of like occupation, and said, Sirs, ye know that by this craft we have our wealth.

26 Moreover ye see and hear, that not alone at Ephesus, but almost throughout all Asia, this Paul hath persuaded and turned away much people, saying that they be no gods, which are made with hands:

27 So that not only this our ᵃcraft is in danger to be set at nought; but also that the temple of the great goddess Diana should be despised, and her magnificence should be destroyed, whom all Asia and the world worshippeth.

28 And when they heard *these sayings,* they were full of wrath, and cried out, saying, Great *is* Diana of the Ephesians.

29 And the whole city was filled with confusion: and having caught Gaius and ᵃAristarchus, men of Macedonia, Paul's companions in travel, they rushed with one accord into the theatre.

30 And when Paul would have entered in unto the people, the disciples suffered him not.

31 And certain of the chief of Asia, which were his friends, sent unto him, desiring *him* that he would not adventure himself into the theatre.

32 Some therefore cried one thing, and some another: for the assembly was confused; and the more part knew not wherefore they were come together.

33 And they drew Alexander out of the multitude, the Jews putting him forward. And ᵃAlexander beckoned with the hand, and would have made his defence unto the people.

34 But when they knew that he was a Jew, all with one voice about the space of two hours cried out, Great *is* Diana of the Ephesians.

35 And when the townclerk had ᵃappeased the people, he said, Ye men of Ephesus, what man is there that knoweth not how that the city of the Ephesians is a ᵇworshipper of the great goddess Diana, and of the *image* which fell down from ᶜJupiter?

36 Seeing then that these things cannot be spoken against, ye ought to be quiet, and to do nothing ᵃrashly.

37 For ye have brought hither these men, which are neither robbers of churches, nor yet blasphemers of your goddess.

38 Wherefore if Demetrius, and the craftsmen which are with him, have a matter against any man, ᵃthe law is open, and there are deputies: let them implead one another.

39 But if ye inquire any thing concerning other matters, it shall be determined in a lawful assembly.

40 For we are in danger to be called in question for this day's ᵃuproar, there being no cause whereby we may give an account of this concourse.

41 And when he had thus spoken, he dismissed the assembly.

CHAPTER 20

Paul raises Eutychus from death—Paul is free from the blood of all men—He predicts apostasy from within the Church—He reveals a teaching from Jesus, It is more blessed to give than to receive.

AND after the ᵃuproar was ceased, Paul called unto *him* the disciples, and ᵇembraced *them,* and departed for to go into Macedonia.

24ᵃ GR Artemis.
27ᵃ Alma 11:24 (23–24).
29ᵃ Acts 20:4; 27:2; Col. 4:10.
33ᵃ 1 Tim. 1:20.
35ᵃ Acts 5:38 (34–42).
  ᵇ GR temple keeper, guardian.
  ᶜ GR Zeus.
36ᵃ TG Rashness.
38ᵃ GR court days are conducted.
40ᵃ TG Rioting and Reveling.
20 1ᵃ TG Rioting and Reveling.
  ᵇ OR greeted, bade farewell, expressed good wishes.

2 And when he had gone over those parts, and had given them much exhortation, he came into Greece,

3 And *there* abode three months. And when the Jews laid wait for him, as he was about to sail into Syria, he purposed to return through Macedonia.

4 And there accompanied him into Asia Sopater of Berea; and of the Thessalonians, *a*Aristarchus and Secundus; and Gaius of Derbe, and *b*Timotheus; and of Asia, *c*Tychicus and *d*Trophimus.

5 These going before tarried for us at Troas.

6 And we sailed away from Philippi after the days of *a*unleavened bread, and came unto them to Troas in five days; where we abode seven days.

7 And upon the *a*first *b*day of the week, when the disciples came *c*together to *d*break *e*bread, Paul preached unto them, ready to depart on the morrow; and continued his speech until midnight.

8 And there were many lights in the upper chamber, where they were gathered together.

9 And there sat in a window a certain young man named Eutychus, being fallen into a deep sleep: and as Paul was long preaching, he sunk down with sleep, and fell down from the third loft, and was taken up dead.

10 And Paul went down, and fell on him, and *a*embracing *him* said, Trouble not yourselves; for his life is in him.

11 When he therefore was come up again, and had broken bread, and eaten, and talked a long while, even till break of day, so he departed.

12 And they brought the young man *a*alive, and were not a little comforted.

13 ¶ And we went before to ship, and sailed unto Assos, there intending to take in Paul: for so had he appointed, minding himself to *a*go afoot.

14 And when he met with us at Assos, we took him in, and came to Mitylene.

15 And we sailed thence, and came the next *day* over against Chios; and the next *day* we arrived at Samos, and tarried at Trogyllium; and the next *day* we came to Miletus.

16 For Paul had determined to sail by Ephesus, because he would not spend the time in Asia: for he *a*hasted, if it were possible for him, to be at Jerusalem the day of *b*Pentecost.

17 ¶ And from Miletus he sent to Ephesus, and called the *a*elders of the church.

18 And when they were come to him, he said unto them, Ye know, from the first day that I came into Asia, after what manner I have been with you at all seasons,

19 *a*Serving the Lord with all *b*humility of mind, and with many *c*tears, and *d*temptations, which befell me by the lying in wait of the Jews:

20 *And* how I kept back nothing that was profitable *unto you*, but have shewed you, and have taught you publickly, and from house to house,

21 Testifying both to the Jews, and also to the Greeks, repentance toward God, *a*and faith toward our Lord *b*Jesus Christ.

22 And now, behold, I go bound in the *a*spirit unto Jerusalem, not knowing the things that shall befall me there:

4a Acts 19:29; 27:2; Col. 4:10.
  b Acts 16:1.
  c Eph. 6:21.
  d Acts 21:29.
6a Ex. 12:15 (14–15).
7a TG Sabbath.
  b TG Jesus Christ, Types of, in Memory.
  c TG Assembly for Worship; Meetings.
  d D&C 20:75. TG Sacrament.
  e TG Bread.
10a 1 Kgs. 17:21.
12a TG Death, Power over.
13a GR travel by land, on foot.
16a TG Haste.
  b Acts 2:1.
17a D&C 67:1.
19a TG D&C 4:2 (2, 6).
  b TG Humility.
  c 2 Ne. 33:3.
  d TG Test.
21a JST Acts 20:21 . . . and faith *on the name of* our Lord Jesus Christ.
  b D&C 68:25.
22a Acts 19:21; 1 Ne. 4:6.

23 Save that the Holy Ghost witnesseth in every city, saying that bonds and ^aafflictions ^babide me.

24 But none of these things ^amove me, neither count I my ^blife dear unto myself, so that I might finish my course with joy, and the ministry, which I have received of the Lord Jesus, to testify the ^cgospel of the ^dgrace of God.

25 And now, behold, I know that ye all, among whom I have gone preaching the kingdom of God, shall see my face no more.

26 Wherefore I take you to record this day, that I *am* pure from the ^ablood of all *men.*

27 For I have not shunned to declare unto you all the ^acounsel of God.

28 ¶ Take heed therefore unto yourselves, and to all the ^aflock, over the which the Holy Ghost hath made you ^boverseers, to feed the ^cchurch of God, which he hath purchased with his own ^dblood.

29 For I know this, that after my departing shall ^agrievous wolves enter in among you, not sparing the flock.

30 Also of your own selves shall men arise, speaking ^aperverse things, to ^bdraw away disciples after them.

31 Therefore watch, and remember, that by the space of three years I ceased not to ^awarn every one night and day with tears.

32 And now, brethren, I commend you to God, and to the word of his grace, which is able to build you up, and to give you an ^ainheritance among all them which are sanctified.

33 I have ^acoveted no man's silver, or ^bgold, or apparel.

34 Yea, ye yourselves know, that these ^ahands have ^bministered unto my necessities, and to them that were with me.

35 I have shewed you all things, how that so labouring ye ought to support the weak, and to remember the words of the Lord Jesus, how he said, It is more blessed to ^agive than to receive.

36 ¶ And when he had thus spoken, he kneeled down, and prayed with them all.

37 And they all wept sore, and fell on Paul's neck, and kissed him,

38 ^aSorrowing most of all for the words which he spake, that they should see his face no more. And they accompanied him unto the ship.

CHAPTER 21

Paul journeys to Jerusalem—He is persecuted, arrested, and bound.

AND it came to pass, that after we were gotten from them, and had launched, we came with a straight course unto Coos, and the *day* following unto Rhodes, and from thence unto Patara:

2 And finding a ship sailing over unto Phenicia, we went aboard, and set forth.

3 Now when we had discovered Cyprus, we left it on the left hand, and sailed into Syria, and landed at Tyre: for there the ship was to unlade her burden.

4 And finding disciples, we tarried there seven days: who said to Paul through the ^aSpirit, that he should not go up to Jerusalem.

5 And when we had accomplished those days, we departed and went

---

23a 1 Thes. 3:3.
  b GR wait for me.
24a Dan. 3:16;
    Matt. 10:19.
  b Acts 21:13.
    TG Martyrdom.
  c TG Gospel.
  d TG Grace.
26a Jacob 1:19.
27a D&C 100:5 (5–8).
    TG Counsel.
28a TG Church.

  b OR bishops.
    TG Bishop.
  c TG Church.
  d Heb. 9:12;
    1 Jn. 1:7.
29a TG Apostasy of the
    Early Christian Church.
30a TG False Doctrine.
  b Rom. 16:17 (17–19).
    TG Apostasy of
    Individuals.
31a Hel. 10:4.

    TG Warn.
32a TG Inheritance.
33a TG Covet.
  b Mosiah 2:12 (12–18).
34a Acts 18:3;
    1 Cor. 9:18 (4–18);
    1 Thes. 2:9.
  b TG Labor.
35a TG Almsgiving;
    Generosity.
38a TG Mourning.
21 4a D&C 38:33.

our way; and they all brought us on our way, with wives and children, till *we were* out of the city: and we kneeled down on the shore, and prayed.

6 And when we had taken our leave one of another, we took ship; and they returned home again.

7 And when we had finished *our* course from Tyre, we came to Ptolemais, and saluted the brethren, and abode with them one day.

8 And the next *day* we that were of Paul's company departed, and came unto ªCæsarea: and we entered into the house of ᵇPhilip the ᶜevangelist, which was *one* of the seven; and abode with him.

9 And the same man had four daughters, virgins, which did ªprophesy.

10 And as we tarried *there* many days, there came down from Judæa a certain prophet, named Agabus.

11 And when he was come unto us, he took Paul's girdle, and bound his own hands and feet, and said, Thus saith the ªHoly Ghost, So shall the Jews at Jerusalem bind the man that owneth this girdle, and shall deliver *him* into the hands of the Gentiles.

12 And when we heard these things, both we, and they of that place, besought him not to go up to Jerusalem.

13 Then Paul answered, What mean ye to weep and to break mine heart? for I am ready not to be bound only, but also to ªdie at Jerusalem for the name of the Lord Jesus.

14 And when he would not be persuaded, we ceased, saying, The ªwill of the Lord be done.

15 And after those days we ªtook up our carriages, and went up to Jerusalem.

16 There went with us also *certain* of the disciples of Cæsarea, and brought with them one Mnason of Cyprus, an ªold disciple, with whom we should lodge.

17 And when we were come to Jerusalem, the brethren received us gladly.

18 And the *day* following Paul went in with us unto ªJames; and all the elders were present.

19 And when he had saluted them, he declared particularly what things God had wrought among the ªGentiles by his ministry.

20 And when they heard *it,* they glorified the Lord, and said unto him, Thou seest, brother, how many thousands of Jews there are which believe; and they are all ªzealous of the law:

21 And they are informed of thee, that thou teachest all the Jews which are among the Gentiles to forsake Moses, saying that they ought not to ªcircumcise *their* children, neither to walk after the ᵇcustoms.

22 What is it therefore? the multitude must needs come together: for they will hear that thou art come.

23 Do therefore this that we say to thee: We have four men which have a ªvow on them;

24 Them take, and purify thyself with them, and ªbe at charges with them, that they may ᵇshave *their* heads: and all may know that those things, whereof they were informed concerning thee, are nothing; but *that* thou thyself also walkest orderly, and keepest the law.

25 As touching the Gentiles which believe, we have written *and* concluded that they observe no such thing, save only that they keep themselves from *things* offered to

8a Acts 8:40.
  b Acts 6:5;
    Eph. 4:11.
  c 2 Tim. 4:5.
9a Judg. 4:4 (4–5);
    Acts 2:17.
11a Acts 2:18; 11:28 (27–28).
13a Acts 20:24;

D&C 103:28 (27–28).
14a Matt. 26:42.
15a GR made preparation, packed baggage.
16a TG Old Age.
18a Gal. 1:19.
19a Acts 11:18; Alma 26:31 (11–36).

20a TG Zeal.
21a TG Circumcision.
  b Acts 6:14.
23a TG Vow.
24a GR pay expenses for them.
  b Lev. 14:8; Num. 6:18 (2–18).

^aidols, and from blood, and from strangled, and from ^bfornication.

26 Then Paul took the men, and the next day purifying himself with them entered into the temple, to signify the ^aaccomplishment of the days of ^bpurification, until that an ^coffering should be offered for every one of them.

27 And when the ^aseven days were almost ended, the Jews which were of Asia, when they saw him in the temple, stirred up all the people, and laid hands on him,

28 Crying out, Men of Israel, help: This is the man, that teacheth all *men* every where against the people, and the law, and this place: and further brought Greeks also into the ^atemple, and hath ^bpolluted this holy place.

29 (For they had seen before with him in the city ^aTrophimus an Ephesian, whom they supposed that Paul had brought into the temple.)

30 And all the city was moved, and the people ran together: and they took Paul, and drew him out of the temple: and forthwith the doors were shut.

31 And as they went about to ^akill him, tidings came unto the chief captain of the band, that all Jerusalem was in an ^buproar.

32 Who immediately took soldiers and centurions, and ran down unto them: and when they saw the chief ^acaptain and the soldiers, they left beating of Paul.

33 Then the chief ^acaptain came near, and took him, and commanded *him* to be bound with two chains; and demanded who he was, and what he had done.

34 And some cried one thing, some another, among the multitude: and when he could not know the certainty for the tumult, he com-manded him to be carried into the ^acastle.

35 And when he came upon the stairs, so it was, that he was borne of the soldiers for the violence of the people.

36 For the multitude of the people followed after, crying, Away with him.

37 And as Paul was to be led into the castle, he said unto the chief captain, May I speak unto thee? Who said, Canst thou speak Greek?

38 Art not thou that Egyptian, which before these days madest an uproar, and leddest out into the wilderness four thousand men that were murderers?

39 But Paul said, I am a man *which am* a Jew of ^aTarsus, *a city* in Cilicia, a citizen of no mean city: and, I beseech thee, suffer me to speak unto the people.

40 And when he had given him licence, Paul stood on the stairs, and ^abeckoned with the hand unto the people. And when there was made a great ^bsilence, he spake unto *them* in the Hebrew tongue, saying,

CHAPTER 22

Paul recounts the story of his conversion and also tells of seeing Jesus in a vision—He is accorded some privileges as a Roman citizen.

MEN, brethren, and fathers, hear ye my defence *which I make* now unto you.

2 (And when they heard that he spake in the Hebrew tongue to them, they kept the more silence: and he saith,)

3 I am verily a man *which am* a ^aJew, born in Tarsus, *a city* in Cilicia, yet brought up in this city at the ^bfeet of ^cGamaliel, *and* taught according to the perfect manner of the

25*a* Acts 15:20 (19–20).
   b TG Fornication.
26*a* Num. 6:13.
   b TG Purification.
   c Num. 6:11 (9–12).
27*a* Num. 6:9.
28*a* Acts 24:6.

   b TG Pollution.
29*a* Acts 20:4.
31*a* Acts 26:21;
    2 Cor. 11:26.
   b TG Rioting and Reveling.
32*a* Acts 23:27.
33*a* Acts 24:7.

34*a* Acts 22:24.
39*a* Acts 23:34.
40*a* Acts 12:17.
   b TG Silence.
22 3*a* Rom. 11:1.
   b Deut. 33:3.
   c Acts 5:34.

ᵈlaw of the fathers, and was ᵉzealous toward God, as ye all are this day.

4 And I ᵃpersecuted this way unto the death, binding and delivering into prisons both men and women.

5 As also the high priest doth bear me witness, and all the estate of the elders: from whom also I received ᵃletters unto the brethren, and went to Damascus, to bring them which were there bound unto Jerusalem, for to be punished.

6 And it came to pass, that, as I made my journey, and was come nigh unto Damascus about noon, suddenly there shone from heaven a great ᵃlight round about me.

7 And I fell unto the ground, and heard a voice saying unto me, ᵃSaul, Saul, why persecutest thou me?

8 And I answered, Who art thou, Lord? And he said unto me, I am ᵃJesus of Nazareth, whom thou persecutest.

9 And they that were with me saw indeed the light, and were afraid; but they heard not the ᵃvoice of him that spake to me.

10 And I said, What shall I do, Lord? And the Lord said unto me, Arise, and go into Damascus; and there it shall be told thee of all things which are appointed for thee to do.

11 And when I could not see for the glory of that light, being led by the hand of them that were with me, I came into Damascus.

12 And one ᵃAnanias, a devout man according to the law, having a good ᵇreport of all the Jews which dwelt there,

13 Came unto me, and stood, and said unto me, Brother Saul, receive thy ᵃsight. And the same hour I looked up upon him.

14 And he said, The God of our fathers hath chosen thee, that thou shouldest know his ᵃwill, and see that Just One, and shouldest hear the voice of his mouth.

15 For thou shalt be his ᵃwitness unto all men of what thou hast seen and heard.

16 And now why tarriest thou? arise, and be ᵃbaptized, and ᵇwash away thy sins, calling on the name of the Lord.

17 And it came to pass, that, when I was come again to Jerusalem, even while I prayed in the temple, I was in a ᵃtrance;

18 And ᵃsaw him saying unto me, Make haste, and get thee quickly out of Jerusalem: for they will not receive thy testimony concerning me.

19 And I said, Lord, they know that I ᵃimprisoned and beat in every synagogue them that believed on thee:

20 And when the blood of thy ᵃmartyr Stephen was shed, I also was standing by, and ᵇconsenting unto his death, and kept the ᶜraiment of them that slew him.

21 And he said unto me, Depart: for I will send thee far hence unto the ᵃGentiles.

22 And they gave him ᵃaudience unto this word, and *then* lifted up their voices, and said, Away with such a *fellow* from the earth: for it is not fit that he should live.

23 And as they cried out, and cast off *their* clothes, and threw dust into the air,

24 The chief captain commanded him to be brought into the ᵃcastle, and bade that he should be examined by ᵇscourging; that he might know wherefore they cried so against him.

3d Acts 26:5.
  e TG Zeal.
4a Acts 8:3; 26:10;
      1 Tim. 1:13.
5a Acts 9:2.
6a TG Vision.
7a Acts 9:4 (1–9);
      26:14 (9–17).
8a Acts 23:9.
9a Acts 9:7.
12a Acts 9:10.

b 1 Tim. 3:7.
13a TG Sight.
14a TG God, Will of.
15a Luke 24:48 (45–49);
      Acts 9:15; 13:31 (29–33);
      26:16.
16a TG Baptism; Baptism,
      Essential; Conversion.
  b TG Wash.
17a Acts 10:10 (9–18);
      11:5 (1–18).

18a TG Jesus Christ, Appearances, Postmortal.
19a Acts 8:3 (3–4).
20a TG Martyrdom.
  b Luke 11:48 (47–49).
  c Acts 7:58.
21a Acts 26:17 (17–18);
      Rom. 11:13.
22a 2 Ne. 27:32.
24a Acts 21:34.
  b TG Cruelty.

25 And as they bound him with thongs, Paul said unto the centurion that stood by, Is it lawful for you to scourge a man that is a ^aRoman, and uncondemned?

26 When the centurion heard *that*, he went and told the chief captain, saying, Take heed what thou doest: for this man is a Roman.

27 Then the chief captain came, and said unto him, Tell me, art thou a Roman? He said, Yea.

28 And the ^achief captain answered, With a great sum obtained I this freedom. And Paul said, But I was *free* born.

29 ^aThen straightway they departed from him which should have examined him: and the chief captain also was afraid, after he knew that he was a Roman, and because he had bound him.

30 On the morrow, because he would have known the certainty wherefore he was ^aaccused of the Jews, he loosed him from *his* bands, and commanded the chief priests and all their council to appear, and brought Paul down, and set him before them.

CHAPTER 23

Paul is smitten at Ananias's order—The Lord again appears to Paul—Forty Jews plot his death—He is delivered over to Felix.

AND Paul, earnestly beholding the council, said, Men *and* brethren, I have lived in all good ^aconscience before God until this day.

2 And the high priest ^aAnanias commanded them that stood by him to ^bsmite him on the mouth.

3 Then said Paul unto him, God shall smite thee, *thou* ^awhited wall:

for sittest thou to judge me after the law, and commandest me to be smitten contrary to the law?

4 And they that stood by said, ^aRevilest thou God's high priest?

5 Then said Paul, I ^awist not, brethren, that he was the high priest: for it is written, Thou shalt not speak evil of the ^bruler of thy people.

6 But when Paul perceived that the one part were Sadducees, and the other Pharisees, he cried out in the council, Men *and* brethren, I am a ^aPharisee, the son of a Pharisee: of the ^bhope and ^cresurrection of the dead I am called in question.

7 And when he had so said, there arose a dissension between the Pharisees and the Sadducees: and the multitude was divided.

8 For the ^aSadducees say that there is no ^bresurrection, neither angel, nor spirit: but the Pharisees confess both.

9 And there arose a great cry: and the ^ascribes *that were* of the Pharisees' part arose, and strove, saying, We find no evil in this man: but if a spirit or an ^bangel hath spoken to him, let us not ^cfight against God.

10 And when there arose a great dissension, the chief captain, fearing lest Paul should have been pulled in pieces of them, commanded the soldiers to go down, and to take him by force from among them, and to bring *him* into the castle.

11 And the night following the ^aLord ^bstood by him, and said, Be of good ^ccheer, Paul: for as thou hast testified of me in Jerusalem, so must thou bear witness also at ^dRome.

12 And when it was day, certain of the Jews banded together, and

---

25a Acts 16:37; 23:27.
28a Acts 23:26.
29a JST Acts 22:29–30
   (Appendix).
30a Acts 23:28.
23 1a TG Conscience.
  2a Acts 24:1.
   b John 18:22 (20–23).
  3a Ps. 5:9 (9–10);
   Matt. 23:27;

   Luke 11:44.
  4a TG Reviling.
  5a OR knew.
   b TG Citizenship.
  6a Acts 26:5;
   Philip. 3:5.
   b Acts 28:20.
   c Acts 24:21.
  8a Matt. 22:23.
   b Acts 4:2.

  9a TG Scribe.
   b Acts 22:8 (6–10).
   c Acts 5:39 (34–40).
 11a TG Vision.
   b TG Jesus Christ,
   Appearances,
   Postmortal.
   c Hel. 10:4 (2–5);
   D&C 121:7 (1–7).
   d Acts 19:21.

bound themselves under a *a*curse, saying that they would neither eat nor drink till they had *b*killed Paul.

13 And they were more than forty which had made this *a*conspiracy.

14 And they came to the chief priests and elders, and said, We have bound ourselves under a great curse, that we will eat nothing until we have slain Paul.

15 Now therefore ye with the council signify to the chief captain that he bring him down unto you to morrow, as though ye would inquire something more perfectly concerning him: and we, *a*or ever he come near, are ready to kill him.

16 And when Paul's sister's son heard of their lying in wait, he went and entered into the castle, and told Paul.

17 Then Paul called one of the centurions unto *him,* and said, Bring this young man unto the chief captain: for he hath a certain thing to tell him.

18 So he took him, and brought *him* to the chief captain, and said, Paul the prisoner called me unto *him,* and prayed me to bring this young man unto thee, who hath something to say unto thee.

19 Then the chief captain took him by the hand, and went *with him* aside privately, and asked *him,* What is that thou hast to tell me?

20 And he said, The Jews have agreed to desire thee that thou wouldest bring down Paul to morrow into the council, as though they would inquire somewhat of him more perfectly.

21 But do not thou yield unto them: for there lie in wait for him of them more than forty men, which have bound themselves with an *a*oath, that they will neither eat nor drink till they have killed him: and now are they ready, looking for a promise from thee.

22 So the chief captain *then* let the young man depart, and charged *him, See thou* tell no man that thou hast shewed these things to me.

23 And he called unto *him* two centurions, saying, Make ready two hundred soldiers to go to Cæsarea, and horsemen threescore and ten, and spearmen two hundred, at the third hour of the night;

24 And provide *them* beasts, that they may set Paul on, and bring *him* safe unto Felix the governor.

25 And he wrote a letter after this manner:

26 Claudius *a*Lysias unto the most excellent governor Felix *sendeth* greeting.

27 This man was taken of the Jews, and *a*should have been killed of them: then came I with an *b*army, and rescued him, having understood that he was a *c*Roman.

28 And when I would have known the cause wherefore they *a*accused him, I brought him forth into their council:

29 Whom I perceived to be accused of *a*questions of their law, but to have nothing laid to his charge worthy of *b*death or of bonds.

30 And when it was told me how that the Jews laid wait for the man, I sent *a*straightway to thee, and gave commandment to his accusers also to say before thee what *they had* against him. Farewell.

31 Then the soldiers, as it was commanded them, took Paul, and brought *him* by night to Antipatris.

32 On the morrow they left the horsemen to go with him, and returned to the castle:

33 Who, when they came to Cæsarea, and delivered the epistle to the governor, presented Paul also before him.

34 And when the governor had read *the letter,* he asked of what

---

12*a* TG Curse.
  b Acts 25:3 (2–3);
     Alma 49:27 (26–27); 51:9.
13*a* TG Conspiracy.
15*a* OR before he gets here.
21*a* TG Vow.
26*a* Acts 22:28; 24:22.
27*a* JST Acts 23:27 . . .
     would . . .
  b Acts 21:32.
  c Acts 22:25.
28*a* Acts 22:30.
29*a* Acts 18:15 (12–17).
  b Acts 25:25.
30*a* GR immediately.

province he was. And when he understood that *he was* of ªCilicia;

35 I will hear thee, said he, when thine accusers are also come. And he commanded him to be kept in Herod's ªjudgment hall.

CHAPTER 24

Paul is accused of sedition—He answers in defense of his life and doctrine—He teaches Felix of righteousness, temperance, and the judgment to come.

AND after five days ªAnanias the high priest descended with the elders, and *with* a certain orator *named* Tertullus, who informed the governor against Paul.

2 And when he was called forth, Tertullus began to accuse *him,* saying, Seeing that by thee we enjoy great quietness, and that very worthy deeds are done unto this nation by thy providence,

3 We accept *it* always, and in all places, most noble Felix, with all thankfulness.

4 Notwithstanding, that I be not further tedious unto thee, I pray thee that thou wouldest hear us of thy clemency a few words.

5 For we have found this man *a* pestilent *fellow,* and a mover of sedition among all the Jews throughout the world, and a ringleader of the sect of the Nazarenes:

6 Who also hath gone about to profane the ªtemple: whom we took, and would have judged according to our law.

7 But the chief ªcaptain Lysias came *upon us,* and with great violence took *him* away out of our hands,

8 Commanding his accusers to come unto thee: by examining of whom thyself mayest take knowledge of all these things, whereof we accuse him.

9 And the Jews also assented, saying that these things were so.

10 Then Paul, after that the governor had beckoned unto him to speak, answered, Forasmuch as I know that thou hast been of many years a judge unto this nation, I do the more cheerfully answer for myself:

11 Because that thou mayest understand, that there are yet but twelve days since I went up to Jerusalem for to worship.

12 And they neither found me in the temple ªdisputing with any man, neither raising up the people, neither in the synagogues, nor in the city:

13 Neither can they prove the things whereof they now accuse me.

14 But this I confess unto thee, that after the way which they call heresy, so worship I the God of my fathers, believing all things which are written in the law and in the ªprophets:

15 And have hope toward God, which they themselves also allow, that there shall be a ªresurrection of the dead, both of the just and unjust.

16 And herein do I exercise myself, to have always a ªconscience void of offence toward God, and *toward* men.

17 Now after many years I came to bring ªalms to my nation, and offerings.

18 Whereupon certain Jews from Asia found me ªpurified in the temple, neither with multitude, nor with tumult.

19 Who ought to have been here before thee, and object, if they had ought against me.

20 Or else let these same *here* say, if they have found any evil doing in me, while I stood before the council,

21 Except it be for this one voice, that I cried standing among them, Touching the ªresurrection of the

---

34*a* Acts 21:39.
35*a* GR *praetorium*
    (the governor's
    headquarters).
24 1*a* Acts 23:2 (1–5).

6*a* Acts 21:28.
7*a* Acts 21:33.
12*a* TG Disputations.
14*a* Acts 28:23.
15*a* TG Resurrection.

16*a* TG Conscience.
17*a* 1 Cor. 16:1.
    TG Almsgiving.
18*a* TG Purification.
21*a* Acts 23:6 (6–8).

dead I am called in question by you this day.

22 And when Felix heard these things, having more perfect knowledge of *that* way, he deferred them, and said, When ªLysias the chief captain shall come down, I will know the uttermost of your matter.

23 And he commanded a centurion to keep Paul, and to let *him* have liberty, and that he should forbid none of his acquaintance to minister or come unto him.

24 And after certain days, when Felix came with his wife Drusilla, which was a Jewess, he sent for Paul, and heard him concerning the faith in Christ.

25 And as he reasoned of righteousness, ªtemperance, and judgment to come, Felix ᵇtrembled, and answered, Go thy way for this time; when I have a convenient season, I will call for thee.

26 He hoped also that ªmoney should have been given him of Paul, that he might loose him: wherefore he sent for him the oftener, and communed with him.

27 But after two years Porcius Festus came into Felix' room: and Felix, willing to shew the Jews a pleasure, left Paul bound.

CHAPTER 25

Paul, before Festus, appeals unto Cæsar—Agrippa desires to hear Paul.

Now when Festus was come into the province, after three days he ascended from Cæsarea to Jerusalem.

2 Then the high priest and the chief of the Jews informed him against Paul, and besought him,

3 And desired favour against him, that he would send for him to Jerusalem, laying wait in the way to ªkill him.

4 But Festus answered, that Paul should be kept at Cæsarea, and that he himself would depart shortly thither.

5 Let them therefore, said he, which among you are able, go down with *me,* and accuse this man, if there be any ªwickedness in him.

6 And when he had tarried among them more than ten days, he went down unto Cæsarea; and the next day sitting on the judgment seat commanded Paul to be brought.

7 And when he was come, the Jews which came down from Jerusalem stood round about, and laid many and grievous complaints against Paul, which they could not prove.

8 While he answered for himself, Neither against the law of the Jews, neither against the temple, nor yet against Cæsar, have I offended any thing at all.

9 But Festus, willing to do the Jews a pleasure, answered Paul, and said, Wilt thou go up to Jerusalem, and there be judged of these things before me?

10 Then said Paul, I stand at Cæsar's judgment seat, where I ought to be judged: to the Jews have I done no wrong, as thou very well knowest.

11 For if I be an offender, or have committed any thing worthy of death, I refuse not to die: but if there be none of these things whereof these accuse me, no man may deliver me unto them. I appeal unto ªCæsar.

12 Then Festus, when he had conferred with the council, answered, Hast thou appealed unto Cæsar? unto Cæsar shalt thou go.

13 And after certain days king Agrippa and Bernice came unto Cæsarea to salute Festus.

14 And when they had been there many days, Festus declared Paul's cause unto the king, saying, There is a certain man left in bonds by Felix:

15 About whom, when I was at Jerusalem, the chief priests and the elders of the Jews informed *me,* desiring *to have* judgment against him.

22ª Acts 23:26 (17–30).
25ª GR self-control.
  ᵇ GR feared.
26ª TG Bribe;
        Selfishness.
25 3ª Acts 23:12.
5ª Acts 18:14.
  TG Wickedness.
11ª Acts 26:32.

16 To whom I answered, It is not the manner of the Romans to deliver any man to die, before that he which is accused have the accusers face to face, and have licence to answer for himself concerning the crime laid against him.

17 Therefore, when they were come hither, without any delay on the morrow I sat on the judgment seat, and commanded the man to be brought forth.

18 Against whom when the accusers stood up, they brought none accusation of such things as I supposed:

19 But had certain questions against him of their own ªsuperstition, and of one Jesus, which was dead, whom Paul affirmed to be alive.

20 And because I ªdoubted of such manner of questions, I asked *him* whether he would go to Jerusalem, and there be judged of these matters.

21 But when Paul had appealed to be reserved unto the hearing of Augustus, I commanded him to be kept till I might send him to Cæsar.

22 Then Agrippa said unto Festus, I would also hear the man myself. To morrow, said he, thou shalt hear him.

23 And on the morrow, when Agrippa was come, and Bernice, with great pomp, and was entered into the place of hearing, with the chief captains, and principal men of the city, at Festus' commandment Paul was brought forth.

24 And Festus said, King Agrippa, and all men which are here present with us, ye see this man, about whom all the multitude of the Jews have dealt with me, both at Jerusalem, and *also* here, crying that he ought not to live any longer.

25 But when I found that he had committed nothing worthy of ªdeath, and that he himself hath appealed to Augustus, I have determined to send him.

26 Of whom I have no certain thing to write unto my lord. Wherefore I have brought him forth before you, and specially before thee, O king Agrippa, that, after examination had, I might have somewhat to write.

27 For it seemeth to me unreasonable to send a prisoner, and not withal to signify the crimes *laid* against him.

CHAPTER 26

Paul recounts his former persecution of the Saints as a Pharisee—He testifies of the appearance of Jesus on the Damascus road—Paul bears his testimony to King Agrippa.

THEN Agrippa said unto Paul, Thou art permitted to speak for thyself. Then Paul stretched forth the hand, and answered for himself:

2 I think myself happy, king Agrippa, because I shall answer for myself this day before thee touching all the things whereof I am accused of the Jews:

3 Especially *because I know* thee to be expert in all customs and questions which are among the Jews: wherefore I beseech thee to hear me patiently.

4 My manner of life from my youth, which was at the first among mine own nation at Jerusalem, know all the Jews;

5 Which knew me from the beginning, if they would testify, that after the most straitest sect of our religion I lived a ªPharisee.

6 And now I stand and am judged for the hope of the promise made of God unto our fathers:

7 Unto which *promise* our ªtwelve tribes, ᵇinstantly serving *God* day and night, hope to come. For which hope's sake, king Agrippa, I am accused of the Jews.

19a GR religion.
20a GR was perplexed concerning this inquiry

or dispute.
25a Acts 23:29.
26 5a Acts 22:3; 23:6 (6–9).

7a TG Israel, Twelve Tribes of.
b GR earnestly, intently.

8 Why should it be thought a thing incredible with you, that God should ^araise the dead?

9 I verily thought with myself, that I ought to do many things ^acontrary to the ^bname of Jesus of Nazareth.

10 Which thing I also did in Jerusalem: and many of the ^asaints did I shut up in prison, having received authority from the chief priests; and when they were put to ^bdeath, I gave my ^cvoice against *them.*

11 And I punished them oft in every synagogue, and compelled *them* to blaspheme; and being exceedingly mad against them, I persecuted *them* even unto ^astrange cities.

12 Whereupon as I went to Damascus with authority and commission from the chief priests,

13 At midday, O king, I saw in the way a ^alight from heaven, above the brightness of the sun, shining round about me and them which journeyed with me.

14 And when we were all fallen to the earth, I heard a voice speaking unto me, and saying in the Hebrew tongue, ^aSaul, Saul, why persecutest thou me? *it is* hard for thee to kick ^bagainst the pricks.

15 And I said, Who art thou, Lord? And he said, I am Jesus whom thou persecutest.

16 But rise, and stand upon thy feet: for I have ^aappeared unto thee for this purpose, to make thee a minister and a ^bwitness both of these things which thou hast seen, and of those things in the which I will appear unto thee;

17 Delivering thee from the people, and *from* the Gentiles, unto whom now I ^asend thee,

18 To open their eyes, *and* to turn *them* from ^adarkness to ^blight, and *from* the power of Satan unto God, that they may receive forgiveness of sins, and inheritance among them which are sanctified by faith that is in me.

19 Whereupon, O king Agrippa, I was not ^adisobedient unto the heavenly ^bvision:

20 But shewed first unto them of Damascus, and at Jerusalem, and throughout all the coasts of Judæa, and *then* to the Gentiles, that they should repent and turn to God, and do works meet for repentance.

21 For these causes the Jews caught me in the temple, and went about to ^akill *me.*

22 Having therefore obtained help of God, I continue unto this day, witnessing both to small and great, saying none other things than those which the ^aprophets and Moses did say should come:

23 That Christ should ^asuffer, *and* that he should be the first that should ^brise from the dead, and should shew light unto the people, and to the Gentiles.

24 And as he thus spake for himself, Festus said with a loud voice, Paul, thou art beside thyself; much learning doth make thee ^amad.

25 But he said, I am not mad, most noble Festus; but speak forth the words of truth and soberness.

26 For the king knoweth of these things, before whom also I speak freely: for I am persuaded that none of these things are hidden from him; for this thing was not done in a corner.

27 King Agrippa, believest thou the prophets? I know that thou ^abelievest.

8a TG Resurrection.
9a 1 Tim. 1:13.
  b TG Name.
10a Acts 9:1, 13 (13–14), 21;
   22:4 (4–5).
  b TG Martyrdom.
  c GR vote.
11a GR foreign.
13a JS—H 1:16.
14a Acts 9:4 (1–9);
   22:7 (6–16).

  b TG Opposition.
16a TG Jesus Christ,
   Appearances,
   Postmortal.
  b Luke 1:2;
   John 1:14;
   Acts 5:32; 9:15; 22:15;
   D&C 14:8.
   TG Conversion.
17a Acts 22:21.
18a TG Walking in Darkness.

  b TG Light [noun].
19a TG Disobedience.
  b TG Vision.
21a Acts 21:31 (30–31).
22a Acts 28:23.
23a TG Martyrdom.
  b TG Jesus Christ,
   Resurrection.
24a JS—H 1:24 (24–25).
27a Alma 30:42 (41–42).

28 Then Agrippa said unto Paul, Almost thou ªpersuadest me to be a ᵇChristian.

29 And Paul said, I would to God, that not only thou, but also all that hear me this day, were both almost, and altogether such as I am, except these bonds.

30 And when he had thus spoken, the king rose up, and the governor, and Bernice, and they that sat with them:

31 And when they were gone aside, they talked between themselves, saying, This man doeth nothing worthy of ªdeath or of bonds.

32 Then said Agrippa unto Festus, This man might have been set at liberty, if he had not appealed unto ªCæsar.

CHAPTER 27

Paul, in a perilous voyage, travels toward Rome—An angel comforts him—He uses the gift of seership—He is shipwrecked.

AND when it was determined that we should sail into Italy, they delivered Paul and certain other prisoners unto *one* named Julius, a centurion of Augustus' band.

2 And entering into a ship of Adramyttium, we launched, meaning to sail by the coasts of Asia; *one* ªAristarchus, a Macedonian of Thessalonica, being with us.

3 And the next *day* we touched at Sidon. And Julius courteously entreated Paul, and gave *him* liberty to go unto his friends to refresh himself.

4 And when we had launched from thence, we sailed under Cyprus, because the winds were contrary.

5 And when we had sailed over the sea of Cilicia and Pamphylia, we came to Myra, *a city* of Lycia.

6 And there the centurion found a ship of Alexandria sailing into Italy; and he put us therein.

7 And when we had sailed slowly many days, and scarce were come over against Cnidus, the wind not suffering us, we sailed under Crete, over against Salmone;

8 And, hardly passing it, came unto a place which is called The fair havens; nigh whereunto was the city *of* Lasea.

9 Now when much time was spent, and when sailing was now dangerous, because the ªfast was now already past, Paul admonished *them*,

10 And said unto them, Sirs, I perceive that this voyage will be with hurt and much damage, not only of the lading and ship, but also of our lives.

11 Nevertheless the centurion believed the master and the ªowner of the ship, more than those things which were spoken by Paul.

12 And because the haven was not commodious to winter in, the more part advised to depart thence also, if by any means they might attain to Phenice, *and there* to winter; *which is* an haven of Crete, and lieth toward the south west and north west.

13 And when the south wind blew softly, supposing that they had obtained *their* purpose, loosing *thence*, they sailed close by Crete.

14 But not long after there arose against it a tempestuous wind, called Euroclydon.

15 And when the ship was caught, and could not bear up into the wind, we let *her* drive.

16 And running under a certain island which is called Clauda, we had much work to come by the boat:

17 Which when they had taken up, they used helps, undergirding the ship; and, fearing lest they should fall into the quicksands, strake sail, and so were driven.

18 And we being exceedingly tossed with a tempest, the next *day* they lightened the ship;

28a ᴛɢ Missionary Work.
  b Acts 11:26.
31a ᴛɢ Capital Punishment.

32a Acts 25:11.
27 2a Acts 19:29; 20:4;
  Col. 4:10.

9a Lev. 23:27 (27, 29).
  ᴛɢ Fast, Fasting.
11a ɢʀ ship master, captain.

19 And the third *day* we cast out with our own hands the tackling of the ship.

20 And when neither sun nor stars in many days appeared, and no small tempest lay on *us,* all hope that we should be saved was then taken away.

21 But after long abstinence Paul stood forth in the midst of them, and said, Sirs, ye should have hearkened unto me, and not have loosed from Crete, and to have gained this harm and loss.

22 And now I exhort you to be of good cheer: for there shall be no loss of *any man's* ^alife among you, but of the ship.

23 For there stood by me this night the ^aangel of God, whose I am, and whom I serve,

24 Saying, Fear not, Paul; thou must be brought before Cæsar: and, lo, God hath given thee all them that sail with thee.

25 Wherefore, sirs, be of good cheer: for I believe God, that it shall be even as it was told me.

26 Howbeit we must be cast upon a certain island.

27 But when the fourteenth night was come, as we were driven up and down in ^aAdria, about midnight the shipmen deemed that they drew near to some country;

28 And sounded, and found *it* twenty fathoms: and when they had gone a little further, they sounded again, and found *it* fifteen fathoms.

29 Then fearing lest we should have fallen upon rocks, they cast four anchors out of the stern, and wished for the day.

30 And as the shipmen were about to flee out of the ship, when they had let down the boat into the sea, under colour as though they would have cast anchors out of the foreship,

31 Paul said to the centurion and to the soldiers, Except these abide in the ship, ye cannot be saved.

32 Then the soldiers cut off the ropes of the boat, and let her fall off.

33 And while the day was coming on, Paul besought *them* all to take meat, saying, This day is the fourteenth day that ye have tarried and continued ^afasting, having taken nothing.

34 Wherefore I pray you to take *some* meat: for this is for your ^ahealth: for there shall not an hair fall from the head of any of you.

35 And when he had thus spoken, he took bread, and gave thanks to God in presence of them all: and when he had broken *it,* he began to eat.

36 Then were they all of good cheer, and they also took *some* meat.

37 And we were in all in the ship two hundred threescore and sixteen souls.

38 And when they had eaten enough, they lightened the ship, and cast out the wheat into the sea.

39 And when it was day, they knew not the land: but they discovered a certain ^acreek with a shore, into the which they were minded, if it were possible, to thrust in the ship.

40 And when they had ^ataken up the anchors, they committed *themselves* unto the sea, and loosed the rudder bands, and hoised up the mainsail to the wind, and made toward shore.

41 And falling into a place where two seas met, they ran the ship aground; and the forepart stuck fast, and remained unmoveable, but the hinder part was broken with the violence of the waves.

42 And the soldiers' counsel was to kill the prisoners, lest any of them should swim out, and escape.

43 But the centurion, willing to save Paul, kept them from *their* purpose; and commanded that they which could swim should cast *themselves* first *into the sea,* and get to land:

44 And the rest, some on boards,

22 *a* Acts 27:44.
23 *a* TG Angels; Vision.
27 *a* IE the Adriatic Sea.
33 *a* TG Fast, Fasting.
34 *a* TG Health.
39 *a* GR bay.
40 *a* GR cut off anchors
(they left them in the sea).

and some on *broken pieces* of the ship. And so it came to pass, that they escaped all ªsafe to land.

CHAPTER 28

Paul is unharmed by a viper's bite—He heals the sick in Melita—He preaches in Rome, first to the Jews and then to the Gentiles.

AND when they were escaped, then they knew that the island was called Melita.

2 And the ªbarbarous people shewed us no little ᵇkindness: for they kindled a fire, and received us every one, because of the present rain, and because of the cold.

3 And when Paul had gathered a bundle of sticks, and laid *them* on the fire, there came a ªviper out of the heat, and fastened on his hand.

4 And when the barbarians saw the *venomous* beast hang on his hand, they said among themselves, No doubt this man is a murderer, whom, though he hath escaped the sea, yet vengeance suffereth not to live.

5 And he shook off the beast into the fire, and felt no ªharm.

6 Howbeit they looked when he should have swollen, or fallen down dead suddenly: but after they had looked a great while, and saw no harm come to him, they changed their minds, and said that he was a ªgod.

7 In the same quarters were possessions of the chief man of the island, whose name was Publius; who received us, and lodged us three days ªcourteously.

8 And it came to pass, that the father of Publius lay ªsick of a fever and of a ᵇbloody flux: to whom Paul entered in, and prayed, and laid his ᶜhands on him, and healed him.

9 So when this was done, others also, which had diseases in the island, came, and were healed:

10 Who also honoured us with many honours; and when we departed, they laded *us* with such things as were necessary.

11 And after three months we departed in a ship of Alexandria, which had wintered in the isle, whose sign was Castor and Pollux.

12 And landing at Syracuse, we tarried *there* three days.

13 And from thence we ªfetched a compass, and came to Rhegium: and after one day the south wind blew, and we came the next day to Puteoli:

14 Where we found brethren, and were desired to tarry with them seven days: and so we went toward Rome.

15 And from thence, when the brethren heard of us, they came to meet us as far as Appii forum, and The three taverns: whom when Paul saw, he ªthanked God, and took ᵇcourage.

16 And when we came to Rome, the centurion delivered the prisoners to the captain of the guard: but Paul was suffered to dwell by himself with a soldier that kept him.

17 And it came to pass, that after three days Paul called the chief of the Jews together: and when they were come together, he said unto them, Men *and* brethren, though I have committed nothing against the people, or customs of our fathers, yet was I delivered prisoner from Jerusalem into the hands of the Romans.

18 Who, when they had examined me, would have let *me* go, because there was no cause of death in me.

19 But when the Jews spake against *it,* I was constrained to appeal unto Cæsar; not that I had ought to accuse my nation of.

44a Acts 27:22.
28 2a Rom. 1:14.
  b TG Hospitality.
  3a TG Mark 16:18;
    D&C 24:13;
    84:72 (71–72);
    124:99 (98–100).

5a Luke 10:19.
6a Acts 14:11 (8–11).
7a TG Courtesy.
8a TG Sickness.
  b GR dysentery.
  c TG Administrations
    to the Sick;

Hands, Laying on of.
13a GR went around, took a
    circuitous course.
15a TG Thanksgiving.
  b TG Courage.

20 For this cause therefore have I called for you, to see *you,* and to speak with *you:* because that for the ^ahope of Israel I am bound with this chain.

21 And they said unto him, We neither received letters out of Judæa concerning thee, neither any of the brethren that came shewed or spake any harm of thee.

22 But we desire to hear of thee what thou thinkest: for as concerning this sect, we know that every where it is spoken against.

23 And when they had appointed him a day, there came many to him into *his* lodging; to whom he ^aexpounded and testified the kingdom of God, persuading them concerning Jesus, both out of the law of Moses, and *out of* the ^bprophets, from morning till evening.

24 And some believed the things which were spoken, and some ^abelieved not.

25 And when they agreed not among themselves, they departed, after that Paul had spoken one word, Well ^aspake the Holy Ghost by Esaias the prophet unto our fathers,

26 Saying, Go unto this people, and say, Hearing ye shall hear, and shall not understand; and seeing ye shall see, and not ^aperceive:

27 For the ^aheart of this people is waxed gross, and their ears are dull of hearing, and their ^beyes have they closed; lest they should see with *their* eyes, and hear with *their* ears, and understand with *their* heart, and should be converted, and I should heal them.

28 Be it known therefore unto you, that the salvation of God is sent unto the ^aGentiles, and *that* they will hear it.

29 And when he had said these words, the Jews departed, and had great reasoning among themselves.

30 And Paul dwelt two whole years in his own hired house, and received all that came in unto him,

31 Preaching the kingdom of God, and teaching those things which concern the Lord Jesus Christ, with all confidence, no man forbidding him.

THE EPISTLE OF PAUL THE APOSTLE

TO THE

ROMANS

CHAPTER 1

The gospel is the power of God unto salvation through Jesus Christ—The wrath of God rests on those guilty of murder, homosexual practices, fornication, and other sins if the guilty do not repent.

PAUL, a ^aservant of Jesus Christ, called *to be* an ^bapostle, ^cseparated unto the gospel of God,

---

20*a* Acts 23:6.
     TG Hope.
23*a* D&C 68:1.
   b Acts 3:18 (18–21);
      24:14; 26:22;
      Alma 18:36.
24*a* TG Unbelief.

25*a* TG Holy Ghost,
      Mission of.
26*a* Isa. 6:9.
27*a* TG Hardheartedness.
   b TG Spiritual Blindness.
28*a* Acts 13:46.

[ROMANS]
1 1*a* TG Servant.
   b 1 Cor. 4:9 (1–21);
      D&C 18:9.
   c GR set apart.
      TG Setting Apart.

2 (Which he had promised afore by his prophets in the holy scriptures,)

3 Concerning his Son ^aJesus Christ our Lord, which was made of the ^bseed of ^cDavid according to the flesh;

4 And ^adeclared *to be* the ^bSon of God with ^cpower, according to the spirit of holiness, by the resurrection ^dfrom the dead:

5 By whom we have received ^agrace and apostleship, ^bfor ^cobedience to the faith among all nations, for his name:

6 Among whom are ye also the called of Jesus Christ:

7 To all that be in Rome, beloved of God, called *to be* ^asaints: Grace to you and peace from God our Father, and the Lord Jesus Christ.

8 First, I thank my God through Jesus Christ for you all, that your ^afaith is ^bspoken of throughout the whole world.

9 For God is my witness, whom I serve with my spirit in the gospel of his Son, that without ceasing I make mention of you always in my prayers;

10 Making request, if by any means now at length I might have a prosperous journey by the will of God to come unto you.

11 For I long to see you, that I may impart unto you some spiritual ^agift, to the end ye may be established;

12 That is, that I may be ^acomforted together with you by the mutual faith both of you and me.

13 Now I would not have you ignorant, brethren, that oftentimes I purposed to come unto you, (but was ^alet hitherto,) that I might have some ^bfruit among you also, even as among other Gentiles.

14 I am debtor both to the Greeks, and to the ^aBarbarians; both to the wise, and to the unwise.

15 So, as much as in me is, I am ^aready to preach the gospel to you that are at Rome also.

16 For I am not ^aashamed of the ^bgospel of Christ: for it is the ^cpower of God unto ^dsalvation to every one that believeth; to the Jew first, and also to the Greek.

17 For therein is the ^arighteousness of God revealed ^bfrom faith to faith: as it is written, The just shall live by ^cfaith.

18 For the ^awrath of God is revealed from heaven against all ungodliness and unrighteousness of men, ^bwho ^chold the truth in ^dunrighteousness.

19 Because that which may be known of God is manifest ^ain them; for God hath shewed *it* unto them.

20 For the ^ainvisible things of him

3*a* The Greek text omits the name and title at this point.
  b TG Jesus Christ, Birth of.
  c TG Jesus Christ, Davidic Descent of.
4*a* GR appointed, decreed, set forth.
  b D&C 10:57; 11:28; 14:9; 45:52.
  c TG Jesus Christ, Power of.
  d GR from the dead of Jesus Christ our Lord.
5*a* TG Grace.
  b JST Rom. 1:5–6 . . . *through* obedience, *and* faith *in his name, to preach the gospel* among all nations; among whom ye also *are* called of Jesus Christ;
  c TG Obedience.
7*a* TG Saints.

8*a* Rom. 16:19.
  b GR proclaimed.
11*a* D&C 46:11 (8–32).
12*a* TG Sustaining Church Leaders.
13*a* GR hindered, restrained, prevented. Rom. 15:22.
  b D&C 111:2 (2–11).
14*a* Acts 28:2.
15*a* TG Commitment.
16*a* Ps. 119:46; Matt. 10:33 (32–33); 2 Tim. 1:12; 2:12 (10–15); 2 Ne. 31:14 (12–21); D&C 101:5 (1–5). TG Loyalty; Shame.
  b TG Gospel.
  c 1 Cor. 1:18; 1 Pet. 1:5; D&C 68:4.

TG Jesus Christ, Power of.
  d 1 Cor. 15:2. TG Salvation.
17*a* Ps. 4:1; 2 Cor. 5:21. TG God, the Standard of Righteousness.
  b JST Rom. 1:17 . . . *through* faith *on his name; as it is written* . . .
  c TG Faith.
18*a* TG God, Indignation of.
  b JST Rom. 1:18 . . . who *love not* the truth, *but remain* in unrighteousness.
  c IE restrain the truth by unrighteousness.
  d TG Unrighteous Dominion.
19*a* GR among, within.
20*a* Acts 14:17.

from the creation of the world are clearly seen, being understood by the things that are made, *even* his *b*eternal *c*power and Godhead; so that they are without excuse:

21 Because that, when they knew God, they glorified *him* not as God, neither were *a*thankful; but became *b*vain in their imaginations, and their *c*foolish heart was *d*darkened.

22 Professing themselves to be *a*wise, they became fools,

23 And changed the glory of the *a*uncorruptible God into an *b*image made like to *c*corruptible man, and to birds, and fourfooted beasts, and creeping things.

24 Wherefore God also *a*gave them up to *b*uncleanness through the lusts of their own hearts, to dishonour their own bodies between themselves:

25 Who changed the truth of God into a lie, and worshipped and served the creature more than the Creator, who is blessed for ever. Amen.

26 For this cause God *a*gave them up unto *b*vile *c*affections: for even their *d*women did change the natural use into that which is against nature:

27 And likewise also the men, leaving the natural use of the woman, burned in their *a*lust one toward another; men with men working that which is unseemly, and receiving in themselves that recompence of their error which was meet.

28 And even as they did not like to *a*retain God in *their* knowledge, God *b*gave them over to a *c*reprobate mind, to do those things which are not convenient;

29 Being filled with all unrighteousness, fornication, *a*wickedness, covetousness, *b*maliciousness; full of envy, murder, *c*debate, *d*deceit, malignity; whisperers,

30 *a*Backbiters, haters of God, *b*despiteful, *c*proud, *d*boasters, inventors of evil things, *e*disobedient to parents,

31 Without *a*understanding, covenantbreakers, without natural affection, implacable, unmerciful:

32 Who knowing the judgment of God, that they which commit such things are worthy of *a*death, not only do the same, but *b*have *c*pleasure in them that do them.

CHAPTER 2

God will render to every person according to his or her deeds—Both Jews and Gentiles will be judged by gospel laws.

THEREFORE thou art inexcusable, O man, whosoever thou art that judgest: for wherein thou *a*judgest another, thou condemnest thyself; for thou that judgest doest the same things.

2 But we *a*are sure that the *b*judgment of God is according to truth against them which commit such things.

20*b* TG God, Eternal
    Nature of.
  c TG Jesus Christ, Power of.
21*a* TG Ingratitude.
  b GR corrupt in
    their reasonings,
    deliberations.
    2 Kgs. 17:15.
  c Isa. 44:20;
    Hosea 4:12.
  d TG Darkness, Spiritual.
22*a* 2 Ne. 9:28.
    TG Learn.
23*a* GR incorruptible,
    immortal.
  b Ex. 32:4.
  c GR (also) perishable.
24*a* Acts 7:42.

  b TG Uncleanness.
26*a* GR abandoned,
    delivered.
  b GR sufferings, passions
    of dishonor.
    2 Tim. 3:3.
  c Judg. 19:22.
  d TG Woman.
27*a* TG Homosexual
    Behavior;
    Lust.
28*a* GR discern, choose.
  b Ps. 81:12.
  c GR worthless, unable to
    stand test.
29*a* TG Wickedness.
  b TG Malice.
  c GR strife, discord.

  d TG Deceit.
30*a* GR Slanderers.
    TG Backbiting.
  b GR violent, overbearing.
  c TG Pride.
  d TG Boast;
    Haughtiness.
  e TG Disobedience;
    Family, Children,
    Duties of.
31*a* TG Understanding.
32*a* TG Capital Punishment.
  b TG approve of them,
    sympathize with them.
  c Jer. 5:31.
2 1*a* TG Judgment.
  2*a* GR know.
  b TG Judgment, the Last.

3 And thinkest thou this, O man, that ^ajudgest them which do such things, and doest the same, that thou shalt escape the ^bjudgment of God?

4 Or despisest thou the ^ariches of his ^bgoodness and ^cforbearance and longsuffering; not knowing that the goodness of God leadeth thee to repentance?

5 But ^aafter thy ^bhardness and impenitent heart treasurest up unto thyself wrath against the day of wrath and revelation of the righteous judgment of God;

6 Who will ^arender to every man ^baccording to his ^cdeeds:

7 To them who by ^apatient ^bcontinuance in well doing seek for glory and honour and ^cimmortality, eternal life:

8 But unto them that are ^acontentious, and do not ^bobey the truth, but obey unrighteousness, ^cindignation and wrath,

9 ^aTribulation and ^banguish, upon every soul of man that doeth evil, of the Jew first, and also of the ^cGentile;

10 But glory, honour, and ^apeace, to every man that ^bworketh good, to the Jew first, and also to the ^cGentile:

11 For there is no ^arespect of ^bpersons with God.

12 For as many as have sinned without ^alaw shall also perish without law: and as many as have sinned in the law shall be judged by the law;

13 (For not the hearers of the law *are* just before God, but the ^adoers of the law shall be ^bjustified.

14 For when the Gentiles, which have not the law, do by nature the things contained in the law, these, having not the law, are a law unto themselves:

15 ^aWhich shew the work of the ^blaw written in their hearts, their ^cconscience also bearing ^dwitness, and *their* thoughts the mean while accusing or else excusing one another;)

16 In the day when God shall ^ajudge the secrets of men by Jesus Christ according to my ^bgospel.

17 Behold, thou art called a Jew, and restest in the law, and makest thy boast of God,

18 And knowest *his* will, and approvest the things that are more excellent, being instructed out of the law;

19 And art confident that thou thyself art a guide of the blind, a light of them which are in darkness,

20 An instructor of the foolish, a teacher of babes, which hast the ^aform of knowledge and of the truth in the law.

21 Thou therefore which teachest another, ^ateachest thou not thyself? thou that ^bpreachest a man should not ^csteal, dost thou steal?

22 Thou that sayest a man should

3a Ezek. 16:52.
b D&C 10:28.
  TG Judgment, the Last.
4a TG Treasure.
b Mosiah 4:20 (19–20).
c TG Forbear.
5a GR in accordance with.
b TG Hardheartedness;
  Stiffnecked.
6a GR give back,
  recompense, restore.
b TG Accountability.
c Rom. 11:6 (5–6).
  TG Good Works.
7a TG Patience.
b D&C 67:13.
  TG Perseverance.
c TG Immortality.
8a TG Contention.

b TG Disobedience.
c TG God, Indignation of.
9a Ps. 32:10.
b TG Sorrow.
c GR Greek.
10a TG Peace of God.
b TG Work, Value of.
c GR Greek.
11a GR partiality.
  Deut. 10:17;
  Acts 10:34;
  Rom. 10:12 (12–13);
  Hel. 3:28 (27–30).
  TG God, Access to.
b 1 Ne. 17:35 (35–40);
  2 Ne. 26:33 (23–33).
12a Luke 12:48.
  TG Accountability;
  Law of Moses.

13a TG Good Works.
b Acts 13:39 (26–41).
15a GR Who.
b Jer. 31:33 (31–34);
  D&C 84:46 (44–47).
c 2 Ne. 32:5.
  TG Conscience.
d D&C 6:23 (22–23).
16a 1 Cor. 4:5.
  TG Jesus Christ, Judge.
b TG Gospel.
20a GR system, appearance.
  2 Tim. 3:5.
21a TG Hypocrisy.
b 1 Cor. 9:14 (13–14);
  Alma 39:11 (11–12).
c TG Stealing.

not commit ^aadultery, dost thou commit adultery? thou that abhorrest idols, dost thou ^bcommit ^csacrilege?

23 Thou that makest thy boast of the law, through breaking the law dishonourest thou God?

24 For the name of God is ^ablasphemed among the Gentiles through you, as it is written.

25 For ^acircumcision verily profiteth, if thou keep the law: but if thou be a breaker of the law, thy circumcision is made uncircumcision.

26 Therefore if the uncircumcision keep the righteousness of the law, shall not his uncircumcision be counted for circumcision?

27 And shall not uncircumcision which is by nature, if it fulfil the law, judge thee, who by the letter and circumcision dost transgress the law?

28 For he is not a Jew, which is one outwardly; neither *is that* circumcision, which is outward in the flesh:

29 But he *is* a Jew, which is one inwardly; and ^acircumcision *is that* of the heart, in the ^bspirit, *and* not in the letter; whose praise *is* not of men, but of God.

CHAPTER 3

Man is not justified by the law of Moses—He is justified through righteousness, which comes through faith in Christ, made possible through Christ's atoning sacrifice.

^aWHAT ^badvantage then hath the Jew? or what profit *is there* of ^ccircumcision?

2 Much every way: chiefly, because that unto them were committed the ^aoracles of God.

3 For what if some did not believe? shall their ^aunbelief make the faith of God without effect?

4 ^aGod forbid: yea, let God be true, but every man a ^bliar; as it is written, That thou mightest be ^cjustified in thy sayings, and mightest overcome when thou art judged.

5 ^aBut if our unrighteousness ^bcommend the righteousness of God, what shall we say? *Is* God ^cunrighteous who taketh vengeance? (I speak as a man)

6 ^aGod forbid: for then how shall God ^bjudge the world?

7 For if the truth of God hath more abounded ^athrough my lie unto his glory; why yet am I also judged as a sinner?

8 And not *rather,* (as we be slanderously reported, and as some affirm that we say,) Let us do evil, that good may come? whose ^adamnation is just.

9 What then? are we better *than they?* No, in no wise: for we have before proved both Jews and Gentiles, that they are all under sin;

10 As it is written, There is ^anone ^brighteous, no, not one:

11 There is none that understandeth, there is none that seeketh after God.

12 They are all gone out of the ^away, they are together become ^bunprofitable; there is none that doeth ^cgood, no, not one.

13 Their ^athroat *is* an open sepulchre; with their tongues they have

---

22a TG Adulterer.
  b GR rob shrines, temples.
  c TG Sacrilege.
24a TG Blaspheme.
25a Gal. 5:3.
    TG Circumcision.
29a Acts 7:51; 2 Ne. 9:33.
    TG Circumcision.
  b Rom. 7:6.
3 1a JST Rom. 3:1–2 What advantage then hath the Jew *over the Gentile?* or what profit of circumcision, *who is not a Jew from*

the heart? But he who is a Jew from the heart, I say hath much every way . . .
  b GR preeminence.
  c TG Circumcision.
2a Acts 7:38;
    2 Ne. 29:4 (4–6).
3a 1 Ne. 8:28 (26–33).
4a GR May it not be!
  b Alma 30:42 (37–42).
  c Ps. 51:4.
5a JST Rom. 3:5–8 (Appendix).
  b GR recommend.

  c 2 Ne. 26:7;
    Alma 42:1 (1, 13–25).
6a GR May it not be!
  b TG Jesus Christ, Judge.
7a GR in, by, because of.
8a TG Damnation.
10a Ps. 14:2–3; 53:1 (1–3).
  b TG Man, Natural, Not Spiritually Reborn.
12a D&C 82:6.
  b Luke 17:10 (7–10);
    Mosiah 2:21 (20–21).
  c D&C 33:4; 35:12.
13a Ps. 5:9.

used deceit; the *b*poison of asps *is* under their lips:

14 Whose mouth *is* full of cursing and *a*bitterness:

15 Their feet *are* swift to *a*shed blood:

16 Destruction and *a*misery *are* in their ways:

17 And the way of *a*peace have they not known:

18 There is no *a*fear of God before their eyes.

19 Now we know that what things soever the law saith, it saith to them who are under the law: that every *a*mouth may be stopped, and all the world may become *b*guilty before God.

20 Therefore by the *a*deeds of the *b*law there shall no flesh be *c*justified in his sight: for *d*by the law *is* the knowledge of sin.

21 But now the *a*righteousness of God *b*without the law is manifested, being witnessed by the law and the prophets;

22 Even the righteousness of God *which is* by faith of Jesus Christ unto all and upon all them that believe: for there is no difference:

23 For all have *a*sinned, and come short of the glory of God;

24 *a*Being *b*justified freely by his *c*grace through the *d*redemption that is in Christ Jesus:

25 Whom God hath *a*set forth *to be* a *b*propitiation through faith in his *c*blood, to declare his righteousness for the *d*remission of sins that are past, through the *e*forbearance of God;

26 To declare, *I say*, at this time his righteousness: that he might be *a*just, and the justifier of him which believeth in Jesus.

27 Where *is* *a*boasting then? It is excluded. By what law? of works? Nay: but by the law of faith.

28 Therefore we conclude that a man is *a*justified by *b*faith *c*without the deeds of the law.

29 *Is he* the *a*God of the Jews only? *is he* not also of the Gentiles? Yes, of the *b*Gentiles also:

30 Seeing *it is* *a*one God, which shall justify the *b*circumcision by faith, and uncircumcision through faith.

31 Do we then make void the law through faith? *a*God forbid: *b*yea, we establish the law.

CHAPTER 4

Abraham's faith was accounted to him for righteousness—Man is justified by faith, righteous works, and grace.

WHAT shall we say then that Abraham our father, as pertaining to the flesh, hath found?

2 *a*For if Abraham were justified by works, he hath *b*whereof to glory; but not before God.

3 For what saith the scripture?

13*b* Ps. 140:3 (1–13).
14*a* Alma 41:11;
    Morm. 8:31.
15*a* Isa. 59:7 (7–8).
16*a* Mosiah 3:25;
    Morm. 8:38.
17*a* 1 Ne. 20:22 (18–22).
18*a* D&C 10:56 (55–56).
19*a* Ezek. 16:63.
   b TG Guilt.
20*a* 2 Ne. 25:23.
   b TG Law of Moses.
   c 2 Ne. 2:5 (5–8).
   d GR through.
21*a* TG God, the Standard of Righteousness.
   b GR apart from, without intervention of.
23*a* Prov. 20:9;

1 Ne. 10:6.
   TG Man, Natural, Not Spiritually Reborn; Sin.
24*a* JST Rom. 3:24 *Therefore being justified only by his grace . . .*
   b D&C 20:30.
   c TG Grace.
   d TG Jesus Christ, Redeemer.
25*a* GR purposed, designed beforehand.
   b GR mercy seat.
   TG Jesus Christ, Atonement through; Redemption.
   c TG Blood, Symbolism of.
   d TG Remission of Sins.

e TG Forbear.
26*a* TG God, Justice of.
27*a* Alma 26:36 (10–12, 36);
   D&C 3:4; 84:73.
28*a* TG Justification.
   b TG Faith.
   c GR apart from, without intervention of.
29*a* 2 Ne. 30:2 (1–2).
   b TG Gentiles.
30*a* 1 Tim. 2:5;
   D&C 121:28.
   b TG Circumcision.
31*a* TG May it not be!
   b GR but.
4 2*a* JST Rom. 4:2–5 (Appendix).
   b GR ground, reason for boasting.

Abraham [a]believed God, and it was counted unto him for [b]righteousness.

4 Now to him that worketh is the [a]reward not [b]reckoned of grace, but of debt.

5 But to him that worketh not, but believeth on him that justifieth the ungodly, his faith is counted for righteousness.

6 Even as David also describeth the blessedness of the man, unto whom God imputeth righteousness without works,

7 Saying, [a]Blessed are they whose iniquities are forgiven, and whose sins are covered.

8 Blessed is the man to whom the Lord will not impute sin.

9 Cometh this blessedness then upon the circumcision only, or upon the uncircumcision also? for we say that faith was reckoned to Abraham for righteousness.

10 How was it then reckoned? when he was in circumcision, or in uncircumcision? Not in circumcision, but in uncircumcision.

11 And he received the [a]sign of [b]circumcision, a seal of the righteousness of the faith which he had yet being uncircumcised: that he might be the [c]father of all them that believe, though they be not circumcised; that righteousness might be imputed unto them also:

12 And the father of circumcision to them who are not of the circumcision only, but who also [a]walk in the steps of that faith of our father Abraham, which he had being yet uncircumcised.

13 For the promise, that he should be the [a]heir of the world, was not to Abraham, or to his [b]seed, through the law, but through the righteousness of faith.

14 For if they which are of the law be heirs, faith is made void, and the promise made of none effect:

15 Because the law worketh wrath: for where no [a]law is, there is no [b]transgression.

16 [a]Therefore it is of faith, that it might be by [b]grace; to the end the promise might be sure to all the seed; not to that only which is of the law, but to that also which is of the [c]faith of Abraham; who is the [d]father of us all,

17 (As it is written, I have made thee a father of many nations,) before him whom he believed, even God, who [a]quickeneth the dead, and calleth those things which be not as though they were.

18 Who against hope believed in [a]hope, that he might become the father of many [b]nations, according to that which was spoken, So shall thy [c]seed be.

19 And being not weak in faith, he considered not his own body now dead, when he was about an hundred years [a]old, neither yet the deadness of Sara's womb:

20 He [a]staggered not at the promise of God through unbelief; but was strong in faith, giving glory to God;

21 And being fully persuaded that, what he had [a]promised, he was able also to perform.

22 And therefore it was imputed to him for righteousness.

3a See JST Gen. 15:9–12
   (Appendix).
   TG Faith.
 b TG Righteousness.
4a GR wage, hire.
 b GR considered a favor
   but as his due.
7a Ps. 32:1.
11a TG Signs.
 b TG Circumcision.
 c Abr. 2:10.
12a TG Walking with God.
13a TG Birthright.
 b TG Seed of Abraham.

15a Rom. 5:13;
   2 Ne. 9:25;
   Alma 42:17 (12–24).
 b TG Transgress.
16a JST Rom. 4:16 Therefore
   ye are justified of faith
   and works, through
   grace, to the end the
   promise might be sure
   to all the seed; not to
   them only who are of
   the law, but to them
   also who are of the faith
   of Abraham; who is the

father of us all,
 b TG Grace.
 c TG Faith.
 d TG Family, Patriarchal.
17a TG God, Power of;
   Resurrection.
18a TG Hope.
 b TG Nations.
 c TG Seed of Abraham.
19a TG Old Age.
20a GR doubted, hesitated.
21a Gen. 18:14;
   Luke 1:37.
   TG Promise.

23 Now it was not written for his sake alone, that it was imputed to him;

24 But for ^aus also, to whom it shall be imputed, if we believe on him that raised up Jesus our Lord from the dead;

25 Who was delivered for our ^aoffences, and was raised again for our ^bjustification.

CHAPTER 5

Man is justified through the blood of Christ—Adam fell, and Christ atoned that man might be saved.

THEREFORE being ^ajustified by ^bfaith, we have ^cpeace with God through our Lord Jesus Christ:

2 By whom also we have access by ^afaith into this grace wherein we stand, and rejoice in hope of the glory of God.

3 And not only *so,* but we glory in ^atribulations also: knowing that ^btribulation worketh ^cpatience;

4 And patience, experience; and experience, hope:

5 And ^ahope maketh not ashamed; because the ^blove of God is shed abroad in our hearts by the Holy Ghost which is given unto us.

6 For when we were yet without ^astrength, in due time Christ died for the ungodly.

7 For scarcely for a righteous man will one die: yet peradventure for a good man some would even dare to die.

8 But God commendeth his love toward us, in that, while we were yet ^asinners, ^bChrist died for us.

9 Much more then, being now ^ajustified by his ^bblood, we shall be saved from wrath through him.

10 For if, when we were enemies, we were ^areconciled to God by the ^bdeath of his Son, much more, being reconciled, we shall be saved by his life.

11 And not only *so,* but we also joy in God through our Lord Jesus Christ, by whom we have now received the ^aatonement.

12 Wherefore, as by one man ^asin entered into the world, and ^bdeath by sin; and so ^cdeath passed upon all men, for that all have ^dsinned:

13 (For until the law sin was in the world: but ^asin is not imputed when there is no ^blaw.

14 Nevertheless death reigned from Adam to Moses, even over them that had not sinned after the similitude of Adam's ^atransgression, who is the ^bfigure of him that was to come.

15 But not as the offence, so also *is* the free gift. For if through the offence of one many be dead, much more the grace of God, and the gift by grace, *which is* by ^aone man, Jesus Christ, hath abounded unto many.

16 And not as *it was* by one that sinned, *so is* the gift: for the judgment *was* by one to condemnation, but the free gift *is* of many offences unto justification.

17 For if by one man's offence death reigned by one; much more they which receive abundance of ^agrace and of the gift of righteousness shall reign in life by one, Jesus Christ.)

18 Therefore as by the offence of

24a 3 Ne. 20:25 (24–27).
25a Isa. 53:5; Mark 10:45.
   b TG Justification.
5 1a TG Justification.
   b TG Faith.
   c TG Peace of God.
2a Gal. 5:5 (5–6).
3a 2 Cor. 4:17.
   b TG Tribulation.
   c TG Patience.
5a Ps. 119:116.
   TG Hope.
   b TG Love.
6a TG Strength.

8a Mosiah 4:11.
   b TG Salvation, Plan of.
9a TG Jesus Christ, Atonement through.
   b TG Blood, Symbolism of.
10a TG Jesus Christ, Redeemer; Reconciliation.
   b TG Jesus Christ, Death of.
11a GR reconciliation, restoration to favor.
   TG Jesus Christ, Atonement through; Redemption.

12a Gen. 3:6.
   TG Fall of Man; Sin.
   b 1 Cor. 15:21.
   c TG Death.
   d TG Man, Natural, Not Spiritually Reborn.
13a TG Sin.
   b Rom. 4:15; 2 Ne. 9:25; Alma 42:17 (12–24).
14a TG Transgress.
   b GR type, pattern. 1 Cor. 15:45.
15a 2 Cor. 5:14.
17a TG Grace.

one *judgment came* upon all men to condemnation; even so by the *a*righteousness of one *the free gift came* upon all men unto *b*justification of life.

19 For as by one man's *a*disobedience many were made sinners, so by the *b*obedience of one shall many be made righteous.

20 Moreover the law entered, that the offence might abound. But where sin abounded, grace did much more abound:

21 That as sin hath reigned unto death, even so might grace reign through *a*righteousness unto *b*eternal life by Jesus Christ our Lord.

CHAPTER 6

Baptism is in similitude of the death, burial, and resurrection of Christ—The wages of sin is death—Christ brings eternal life.

WHAT shall we say then? Shall we continue in sin, that *a*grace may abound?

2 *a*God forbid. How shall we, that are dead to *b*sin, live any longer therein?

3 Know ye not, that so many of us as were *a*baptized into Jesus Christ were baptized into his death?

4 Therefore we are *a*buried with him by *b*baptism into death: that like as Christ was raised up from the *c*dead by the glory of the Father, even so we also should *d*walk in *e*newness of life.

5 For if we have been planted together in the *a*likeness of his *b*death, we shall be also *in the likeness* of *his* *c*resurrection:

6 Knowing this, that our *a*old man is crucified with *him,* that the *b*body of sin might be *c*destroyed, that henceforth we should not serve *d*sin.

7 For he that is *a*dead is *b*freed from sin.

8 Now if we be *a*dead with Christ, we believe that we shall also live with him:

9 Knowing that Christ being *a*raised from the dead dieth no more; death hath no more dominion over him.

10 For in that he died, he died unto *a*sin *b*once: but in that he liveth, he liveth unto God.

11 Likewise reckon ye also yourselves to be dead indeed unto sin, but *a*alive unto God through Jesus Christ our Lord.

12 Let not sin therefore reign in your *a*mortal body, that ye should obey it in the *b*lusts thereof.

13 Neither *a*yield ye your *b*members as *c*instruments of unrighteousness unto sin: but *d*yield yourselves unto God, as those that are alive from the dead, and your members *as* instruments of *e*righteousness unto God.

14 *a*For sin shall not have *b*dominion over you: for ye are not under the law, but under grace.

15 What then? shall we sin, because

18*a* TG Righteousness.
 b TG Justification.
19*a* TG Disobedience.
 b TG Obedience.
21*a* TG Righteousness.
 b TG Eternal Life.
6 1*a* D&C 20:32 (29–34).
 2*a* GR May it not be!
 b Mosiah 2:41.
 3*a* Mosiah 27:25.
 4*a* TG Baptism, Immersion.
 b TG Baptism.
 c TG Jesus Christ,
     Death of.
 d TG Walking with God.
 e TG Baptism,
     Qualifications for;

Man, New, Spiritually
     Reborn.
5*a* TG Jesus Christ, Types
     of, in Memory.
 b Col. 2:20; 3:3;
     2 Tim. 2:11.
 c TG Resurrection.
6*a* Eph. 4:22 (22–24);
     Col. 3:9.
 b Col. 2:11.
 c GR brought to an end,
     freed.
 d Moro. 10:32 (32–33).
7*a* JST Rom. 6:7 . . . dead *to*
     sin . . .
 b GR acquitted, cleared.
8*a* TG Jesus Christ,

Death of.
9*a* TG Jesus Christ,
     Resurrection.
10*a* Heb. 9:28.
 b Heb. 7:27; 10:10.
11*a* Gal. 2:19.
12*a* TG Mortality.
 b TG Lust.
13*a* 2 Ne. 4:27 (27–28).
 b Col. 3:5.
 c GR weapons.
 d Mosiah 3:19;
     Hel. 3:35.
 e TG Righteousness.
14*a* JST Rom. 6:14 For *in so*
     doing sin . . .
 b 2 Ne. 2:29 (26–29).

we are not under the law, but under ^agrace? ^bGod forbid.

16 Know ye not, that to whom ye yield yourselves ^aservants to obey, his servants ye are to whom ye ^bobey; whether of sin unto death, or of obedience unto righteousness?

17 But God be thanked, that ye were the servants of sin, but ye have ^aobeyed from the heart that form of doctrine which was delivered you.

18 Being then made ^afree from ^bsin, ye became the servants of righteousness.

19 I speak after the manner of men because of the infirmity of your flesh: for as ye have yielded your members servants to uncleanness and to iniquity unto iniquity; even so now yield your members servants to righteousness unto holiness.

20 For when ye were the servants of sin, ye were ^afree from righteousness.

21 What ^afruit had ye then in those things whereof ye are now ashamed? for the end of those things is death.

22 But now being made ^afree from sin, and become servants to God, ye have your ^bfruit unto ^choliness, and the end everlasting life.

23 For the ^awages of ^bsin is ^cdeath; but the ^dgift of God is ^eeternal life through Jesus Christ our Lord.

CHAPTER 7

The law of Moses is fulfilled in Christ—Paul delights in the law of God after the inward man.

Know ye not, brethren, (for I speak to them that know the law,) how that the ^alaw hath dominion over a man as long as he liveth?

2 For the ^awoman which hath an ^bhusband is bound by the law to *her* husband so long as he liveth; but if the husband be dead, she is loosed from the law of *her* husband.

3 So then if, while *her* husband liveth, she be married to another man, she shall be called an adulteress: but if her husband be dead, she is free from that law; so that she is no adulteress, though she be married to another man.

4 Wherefore, my brethren, ye also are become ^adead to the ^blaw by the body of Christ; that ye should be married to another, *even* to him who is raised from the dead, that we should bring forth fruit unto God.

5 ^aFor when we were in the flesh, the ^bmotions of sins, which were by the law, did work in our members to bring forth fruit unto ^cdeath.

6 But now we are ^adelivered from the law, that being ^bdead wherein we were held; that we should serve in newness of ^cspirit, and not *in* the oldness of the letter.

7 What shall we say then? *Is* the law sin? ^aGod forbid. Nay, I had not known sin, but by the ^blaw: for I had not known ^clust, except the law had said, Thou shalt not ^dcovet.

8 But sin, taking occasion by the commandment, wrought in me all manner of concupiscence. For without the ^alaw sin *was* dead.

15*a* TG Grace.
   b GR May it not be!
16*a* John 8:34.
   b Alma 3:27 (26–27);
     34:34 (33–36);
     Hel. 14:31 (29–31).
     TG Obedience.
17*a* TG Commitment.
18*a* Mosiah 5:8 (7–8).
     TG Remission of Sins.
   b TG Bondage, Spiritual;
     Sin.
20*a* GR unrestricted by.
21*a* GR benefit, reward.
22*a* Rom. 8:2 (1–4);
     Rev. 2:17 (17, 26).

   b GR benefit, reward.
   c TG Sanctification.
23*a* TG Wages.
   b TG Sin.
   c TG Death;
     Death, Spiritual, First.
   d TG God, Gifts of.
   e TG Eternal Life.
7 1*a* Mosiah 13:30 (29–32).
  2*a* TG Marriage, Wives.
   b TG Marriage, Marry.
  4*a* Gal. 2:19;
     2 Ne. 25:25 (24–27);
     D&C 74:5 (2–6).
   b Mosiah 13:28 (27–29).
  5*a* JST Rom. 7:5–27

     (Appendix).
   b GR sufferings,
     afflictions.
   c 2 Ne. 2:5 (4–10); 25:23;
     Alma 42:14 (12–16).
  6*a* GR released, freed from.
   b 2 Cor. 5:17.
   c Rom. 2:29 (28–29).
  7*a* GR May it not be!
   b D&C 82:3 (3–4).
     TG Law of Moses.
   c TG Lust.
   d GR lust for, set the heart
     upon.
     TG Covet.
  8*a* Alma 42:17 (14–24).

9 For I was alive without the law once: but when the commandment came, sin revived, and I died.

10 And the commandment, which *was ordained* to life, I found *to be* unto ªdeath.

11 For sin, ªtaking occasion by the commandment, deceived me, and by it slew *me*.

12 Wherefore the law *is* holy, and the commandment holy, and just, and good.

13 Was then that which is good made death unto me? ªGod forbid. But sin, that it might appear sin, working death in me by that which is good; that sin by the commandment might become exceeding sinful.

14 For we know that the ªlaw is spiritual: but I am ᵇcarnal, ᶜsold under sin.

15 ªFor ᵇthat which I do I ᶜallow not: for what ᵈwould, that do I not; but what I hate, that do I.

16 If then I do that which I ªwould not, I consent unto the law that *it is* good.

17 Now then it is no more I that ªdo it, but sin that dwelleth in me.

18 For I know that in me (that is, in my ªflesh,) ᵇdwelleth no good thing: for to will is present with me; but *how* to ᶜperform that which is good I find not.

19 For the ªgood that I ᵇwould I do not: but the evil which I would not, that I do.

20 Now if I do ªthat I would not, it is no more I that do it, but sin that dwelleth in me.

21 I find then a law, that, when I would do good, evil is ªpresent with me.

22 For I ªdelight in the law of God after the inward man:

23 But I see another law in my members, ªwarring against the law of my mind, and bringing me into ᵇcaptivity to the law of sin which is in my members.

24 O ªwretched man that I am! who shall deliver me from the body of this death?

25 I thank God through Jesus Christ our Lord. So then with the mind I myself serve the law of God; but with the flesh the law of sin.

CHAPTER 8

The law of Christ brings life and peace—Those adopted as children of God become joint heirs with Christ—God's elect are foreordained to eternal life—Christ makes intercession for man.

THERE *is* therefore now no condemnation to them which are in Christ Jesus, who ªwalk not after the ᵇflesh, but after the ᶜSpirit.

2 For the law of the Spirit of life in Christ Jesus hath made me ªfree from the law of sin and death.

3 For what the law could not do, in that it was ªweak through the flesh, God sending his own Son in the likeness of sinful ᵇflesh, and for sin, condemned sin in the flesh:

4 That the righteousness of the law might be fulfilled in us, who walk not after the flesh, but after the ªSpirit.

10a 2 Cor. 3:7.
11a GR having taken opportunity.
13a GR May it not be!
14a D&C 29:34.
  b TG Carnal Mind.
  c GR devoted to, a slave to.
15a JST Rom. 7:15–17 (Appendix).
  b GR what I produce, achieve.
  c GR know, understand.
  d GR choose, intend, design.
16a GR choose, intend,

design.
17a GR produce, work.
18a TG Man, Natural, Not Spiritually Reborn.
  b Alma 22:15.
  c 2 Ne. 4:19 (17–20, 26).
19a TG Opposition.
  b GR intend, choose.
20a GR what I do not intend, choose.
21a Heb. 12:1; 2 Ne. 4:18 (17–19).
22a TG Spirituality.
23a Alma 13:28.
  b TG Bondage, Spiritual.

24a 2 Ne. 4:17.
  TG Sorrow.
8 1a TG Walking with God.
  b TG Trust Not in the Arm of Flesh.
  c Alma 13:12 (12, 28); D&C 11:12 (12–13).
2a Rom. 6:22 (11–22); 2 Cor. 3:17; Mosiah 5:2 (2–9). TG Bondage, Spiritual.
3a Heb. 7:18.
  b TG Jesus Christ, Condescension of.
4a Mosiah 3:19.

5 For they that are after the flesh do ^amind the things of the flesh; but they that are after the Spirit the things of the Spirit.

6 For to be ^acarnally minded *is* ^bdeath; but to be ^cspiritually minded *is* life and ^dpeace.

7 Because the ^acarnal mind *is* ^benmity against God: for it is not subject to the law of God, neither indeed can be.

8 So then they that are ^ain the flesh cannot please God.

9 ^aBut ye are not in the flesh, but in the Spirit, if so be that the ^bSpirit of God ^cdwell in you. Now if any man have not the ^dSpirit of Christ, he is none of his.

10 And if ^aChrist *be* in you, ^bthe body *is* dead because of sin; but the Spirit *is* life because of ^crighteousness.

11 But if the Spirit of him that raised up Jesus from the dead dwell in you, he that raised up Christ from the dead shall also ^aquicken your ^bmortal bodies by his Spirit that dwelleth in you.

12 Therefore, brethren, we are debtors, not to the flesh, to live after the flesh.

13 For if ye live after the flesh, ye ^ashall die: but if ye through the Spirit do ^bmortify the deeds of the body, ye shall live.

14 For as many as are ^aled by the ^bSpirit of God, they are the ^csons of God.

15 For ye have not received the spirit of ^abondage again to fear; but ye have received the Spirit of ^badoption, whereby we cry, Abba, Father.

16 The Spirit itself beareth ^awitness with our ^bspirit, that we are the ^cchildren of God:

17 And if children, then heirs; ^aheirs of God, and joint-heirs with Christ; if so be that we ^bsuffer with *him,* that we may be also glorified together.

18 For I reckon that the ^asufferings of this present time *are* not worthy *to be compared* with the ^bglory which shall be revealed ^cin us.

19 For the ^aearnest expectation of the ^bcreature waiteth for the ^cmanifestation of the sons of God.

20 For the creature was made subject to ^avanity, not willingly, but by reason of him who hath subjected *the same* in hope,

21 Because the ^acreature itself also shall be ^bdelivered from the bondage of ^ccorruption into the glorious ^dliberty of the children of God.

22 For we know that the whole creation ^agroaneth and travaileth in pain together until now.

23 And not only *they,* but ourselves also, ^awhich have the ^bfirstfruits of

---

5a GR watch, guard.
6a TG Carnal Mind; Chastity; Man, Natural, Not Spiritually Reborn.
 b TG Death; Death, Spiritual, First.
 c TG Spirituality.
 d TG Peace of God.
7a TG Fall of Man.
 b TG Opposition.
8a JST Rom. 8:8 . . . *after* the flesh . . .
9a JST Rom. 8:9 But ye are not *after* the flesh, but *after* the Spirit . . .
 b D&C 8:2.
 c 1 Jn. 3:24 (19–24).
 d TG Holy Ghost, Loss of.
10a 2 Cor. 13:5.
 b JST Rom. 8:10 . . . *though* the body *shall die* because of sin, *yet* the Spirit is life, because of righteousness.

c TG Righteousness.
11a GR make alive. D&C 84:33.
 TG God, Power of; Resurrection.
 b TG Mortality.
13a GR are at the point of withering, dying.
 b GR put to death, subdue. Col. 3:5.
14a TG Leadership.
 b TG God, Spirit of.
 c TG Sons and Daughters of God.
15a TG Bondage, Spiritual.
 b Isa. 56:3 (3–8).
16a TG Witness.
 b TG Spirit Creation.
 c TG Man, a Spirit Child of Heavenly Father.
17a Luke 12:44 (42–44).
 TG Birthright; Election; Eternal Life; Exaltation;

Man, Potential to Become like Heavenly Father.
 b TG Persecution; Suffering.
18a TG Adversity; Pain; Self-Sacrifice.
 b D&C 58:4; 63:66; 136:31.
 c GR to us.
19a GR eager hope.
 b GR creation, material universe.
 c GR revelation.
20a JST Rom. 8:20 . . . *tribulation* . . .
 TG Vanity.
21a GR creation, material universe.
 b TG Deliver.
 c 1 Cor. 15:42.
 d TG Liberty.
22a TG Earth, Curse of.
23a GR who.
 b Gal. 5:22 (16–26).

the Spirit, even we ourselves groan within ourselves, waiting for the ^cadoption, *to wit,* the redemption of our body.

24 For we are saved by ^ahope: but hope that is ^bseen is not hope: for what a man seeth, why doth he yet hope for?

25 But if we hope for that we see not, *then* do we with patience wait for *it.*

26 Likewise the Spirit also ^ahelpeth our infirmities: for we know not what we should ^bpray for as we ought: but the Spirit itself maketh ^cintercession for us with ^dgroanings which cannot be uttered.

27 And he that ^asearcheth the hearts knoweth what *is* the mind of the Spirit, because he maketh ^bintercession for the saints according to *the will of* God.

28 And we know that all things work together for ^agood to them that love God, to them who are the called according to *his* purpose.

29 ^aFor whom he did ^bforeknow, he also ^cdid predestinate ^d*to be* conformed to the ^eimage of his Son, that he might be the ^ffirstborn among many brethren.

30 Moreover whom he ^adid predestinate, them he also called: and whom he called, them he also justified: and whom he justified, them he also glorified.

31 What shall we then say to these things? If God *be* for us, who *can* ^abe against us?

32 He that spared not his own ^aSon, but ^bdelivered him up for us all, how shall he not with him also freely give us ^call things?

33 Who shall ^alay any thing to the charge of God's elect? *It is* God that justifieth.

34 Who *is* he that condemneth? *It is* Christ that died, yea rather, that is risen again, who is even at the right hand of God, who also maketh ^aintercession for us.

35 Who shall separate us from the ^alove of Christ? *shall* ^btribulation, or distress, or ^cpersecution, or famine, or nakedness, or peril, or sword?

36 As it is written, For thy sake we are ^akilled all the day long; we are accounted as ^bsheep for the slaughter.

37 Nay, in all these things we are ^amore than ^bconquerors through him that loved us.

38 For I am persuaded, that neither death, nor life, nor angels, nor principalities, nor powers, nor things present, nor things to come,

39 Nor height, nor depth, nor any other creature, shall be able to ^aseparate us from the ^blove of God, which is in Christ Jesus our Lord.

CHAPTER 9

Paul explains how the law of election (foreordination) operates—The people of Israel are chosen (foreordained) to receive the adoption, covenants,

23c 2 Cor. 5:2.
24a TG Hope.
  b 2 Cor. 4:18.
26a TG Holy Ghost, Gifts of.
  b James 4:3;
    D&C 46:28 (28–30);
    88:65 (64–65).
  c TG Communication.
  d GR sighings.
27a TG Judgment.
  b TG Holy Ghost, Mission of.
28a Ezra 8:22;
    Alma 36:3;
    D&C 90:24; 100:15.
29a JST Rom. 8:29–30 (Appendix).
  b TG God, Foreknowledge

of; Man, Antemortal Existence of.
  c GR appointed beforehand, foreordained.
    TG Foreordination.
  d GR to have the same form as.
  e 2 Cor. 3:18;
    Col. 3:10.
    TG God, Body of, Corporeal Nature.
  f TG Jesus Christ, Firstborn.
30a GR appointed beforehand, foreordained.
31a JST Rom. 8:31 . . . *prevail* against us?
32a TG Jesus Christ,

Atonement through.
  b Isa. 50:8.
  c D&C 84:38 (33–41).
33a GR accuse God's elect.
34a Isa. 53:12;
    Heb. 7:25.
35a D&C 29:5.
  b TG Tribulation.
  c TG Persecution.
36a Ps. 44:22;
    2 Cor. 4:11.
  b TG Sheep.
37a GR abundantly victorious.
  b 2 Cor. 2:14.
39a Matt. 10:31 (29–31);
    D&C 121:33.
  b 2 Ne. 1:15.

promises, and blessings of the gospel;
yet they are not all Israel who are of
Israel—They must seek their blessings
by faith—The Gentiles also attain to
righteousness and salvation by faith.

I SAY the truth in Christ, I ªlie not,
my ᵇconscience also bearing me
witness in the Holy Ghost,

2 That I have great heaviness and
continual sorrow in my heart.

3 ªFor I could wish that myself
were ᵇaccursed from Christ for my
brethren, my kinsmen according
to the flesh:

4 Who are Israelites; to whom *per-*
taineth the ªadoption, and the glory,
and the ᵇcovenants, and the giving
of the law, and the service *of God,*
and the promises;

5 Whose *are* the fathers, and of
whom as concerning the ªflesh
Christ *came,* who is over all, God
blessed for ever. Amen.

6 Not as though the word of God
ªhath taken none effect. For they
are not all Israel, which are of
ᵇIsrael:

7 ªNeither, because they are the
seed of Abraham, *are they* all children: but, In ᵇIsaac shall thy seed
be called.

8 That is, They which are the children of the flesh, these *are* not the
ªchildren of God: but the children
of the promise are counted for
the seed.

9 For this *is* the word of promise,
At this time will I come, and Sara
shall have a ªson.

10 And not only *this;* but when

ªRebecca also had conceived by one,
even by our father Isaac;

11 (For *the children* being not yet
born, neither having done any good
or evil, that the purpose of God according to ªelection might stand, not
of works, but of him that calleth;)

12 It was said unto her, The ªelder
shall serve the younger.

13 As it is written, Jacob have I
ªloved, but Esau have I hated.

14 What shall we say then? *Is there*
ªunrighteousness with God? ᵇGod
forbid.

15 For he saith to Moses, I will have
mercy on whom I will have mercy,
and I will have ªcompassion on
whom I will have compassion.

16 So then *it is* not of him that will-
eth, nor of him that runneth, but of
God that sheweth ªmercy.

17 For the scripture saith unto
Pharaoh, Even for this same ªpurpose have I raised thee up, that I
might shew my power in thee, and
that my name might be declared
throughout all the earth.

18 Therefore hath he ªmercy on
whom he will *have mercy,* and whom
he will ᵇhardeneth.

19 Thou wilt say then unto me,
Why doth he yet find fault? For
who hath resisted his will?

20 Nay but, O man, who art thou
that ªrepliest against God? Shall the
thing formed say to him that formed
it, Why hast thou ᵇmade me thus?

21 Hath not the ªpotter power over
the clay, of the same lump to make
one vessel unto honour, and another
unto dishonour?

9 1*a* 1 Tim. 2:7.
   b TG Conscience.
  3*a* JST Rom. 9:3 (For *once I*
    could *have wished* that
    myself were accursed
    from Christ,) . . .
   b Ex. 32:32.
  4*a* TG Election;
    Sons and Daughters of
    God.
   b TG Abrahamic
    Covenant.
  5*a* TG Jesus Christ,
    Condescension of.
  6*a* GR has been fruitless,

    ineffectual.
   b 2 Ne. 30:2.
  7*a* JST Rom. 9:7 Neither,
    because they are *all*
    children of Abraham, are
    they *the seed;*
    but, In Isaac . . .
   b TG Seed of Abraham.
  8*a* TG Sons and Daughters
    of God.
  9*a* TG Seed of Abraham.
 10*a* Gen. 22:23.
 11*a* TG Foreordination;
    God, Foreknowledge of.
 12*a* Gen. 25:23.

 13*a* Mal. 1:2 (2–3).
 14*a* Ps. 92:15.
    TG God, Perfection of.
   b GR May it not be!
 15*a* TG Compassion.
 16*a* TG God, Mercy of.
 17*a* Ex. 9:16 (15–17).
 18*a* TG Forgive.
   b GR leaves to
    stubbornness, hardness.
    Deut. 2:30.
 20*a* GR contradictest,
    disputest.
   b Job 9:12.
 21*a* Isa. 45:9; Jer. 18:6.

22 *What* if God, willing to shew *his* wrath, and to make his power known, endured with much long-suffering the vessels of wrath fitted to ª destruction:

23 And that he might make known the ª riches of his ᵇ glory on the vessels of mercy, which he had afore prepared unto glory,

24 Even us, whom he hath called, not of the Jews only, but also of the Gentiles?

25 As he saith also in ª Osee, I will call them my people, which were not my ᵇ people; and her beloved, which was not beloved.

26 And it shall come to pass, *that* in the place where it was said unto them, Ye *are* not my people; there shall they be called the ª children of the living God.

27 ª Esaias also crieth concerning Israel, Though the ᵇ number of the children of ᶜ Israel be as the sand of the sea, a ᵈ remnant shall be saved:

28 For he will finish the work, and cut *it* short in ª righteousness: because a short work will the Lord make upon the earth.

29 And as Esaias said before, Except the Lord of ª Sabaoth had left us a ᵇ seed, we had been as Sodoma, and been made like unto Gomorrha.

30 What shall we say then? That the Gentiles, which followed not after righteousness, have attained to righteousness, even the ª righteousness which is of faith.

31 But ª Israel, which followed after the law of righteousness, hath not attained to the law of righteousness.

32 ª Wherefore? Because *they sought*

it not by faith, but as it were by the works of the law. For they ᵇ stumbled at that stumblingstone;

33 As it is written, Behold, I lay in Sion a ª stumblingstone and ᵇ rock of ᶜ offence: and whosoever believeth on him shall not be ashamed.

CHAPTER 10

Salvation comes through righteousness to those who believe in Christ—Faith comes by hearing the gospel taught by legal administrators sent of God.

BRETHREN, my heart's desire and prayer to God for Israel is, that they might be ª saved.

2 For I bear them record that they have a ª zeal of God, but not according to knowledge.

3 For they being ignorant of God's ª righteousness, and ᵇ going about to establish their own righteousness, have not ᶜ submitted themselves unto the righteousness of God.

4 For Christ *is* the ª end of the law for righteousness to every one that believeth.

5 For Moses describeth the righteousness which is of the law, That the man which doeth those things shall live by them.

6 But the ª righteousness which is of faith speaketh on this wise, Say not in thine heart, Who shall ascend into heaven? (that is, to bring Christ down *from above:*)

7 Or, Who shall descend into the deep? (that is, to bring up Christ again from the dead.)

8 But what saith it? The word is nigh thee, *even* in thy mouth, and in

---

22*a* 1 Pet. 2:8 (4–8).
23*a* TG Treasure.
  b TG Celestial Glory;
    God, Glory of.
25*a* IE Hosea.
  b Hosea 2:23;
    Zech. 13:9.
26*a* GR sons.
  TG Sons and Daughters
  of God.
27*a* IE Isaiah.
  b Isa. 10:22.
  c TG Israel, Blessings of.

  d TG Israel, Remnant of.
28*a* D&C 52:11.
29*a* HEB hosts.
  b GR posterity.
30*a* TG Righteousness.
31*a* TG Apostasy of Israel.
32*a* GR Why?
  b Isa. 8:14 (13–15);
    Matt. 21:44 (43–45);
    Luke 2:34.
33*a* TG Cornerstone;
    Jesus Christ, Prophecies
    about.

  b TG Rock.
  c TG Offense.
10 1*a* TG Reconciliation.
  2*a* TG Zeal.
  3*a* TG God, the Standard
    of Righteousness.
  b GR desiring,
    endeavoring.
  c TG Apostasy of Israel;
    Submissiveness.
  4*a* 2 Ne. 2:7 (7–10).
  6*a* TG Righteousness.

thy heart: that is, the word of faith, which we preach;

9 That if thou shalt confess with thy mouth the Lord Jesus, and shalt believe in thine heart that God hath raised him from the dead, thou shalt be saved.

10 For with the [a]heart man [b]believeth unto righteousness; and with the mouth confession is made unto [c]salvation.

11 For the scripture saith, Whosoever believeth on him shall not be ashamed.

12 For there is no [a]difference between the Jew and the Greek: for the same Lord over all is [b]rich unto all that [c]call upon him.

13 For whosoever shall [a]call upon the name of the Lord shall be saved.

14 How then shall they call on him in whom they have not [a]believed? and how shall they believe in him of whom they have not heard? and how shall they hear without a [b]preacher?

15 And how shall they [a]preach, except they be [b]sent? as it is written, How beautiful are the [c]feet of them that preach the [d]gospel of [e]peace, and bring glad tidings of good things!

16 But they have not all [a]obeyed the gospel. For Esaias saith, Lord, who hath [b]believed our report?

17 So then [a]faith cometh by [b]hearing, and hearing by the word of God.

18 But I say, Have they not heard? Yes verily, their sound went into all the earth, and their [a]words unto the ends of the [b]world.

19 But I say, Did not Israel know? First Moses saith, I will provoke you to [a]jealousy by *them that are* no people, *and* by a foolish nation I will anger you.

20 But [a]Esaias is very bold, and saith, I was found of them that [b]sought me not; I was made manifest unto them that asked not after me.

21 But to Israel he saith, All day long I have stretched forth my hands unto a [a]disobedient and [b]gainsaying people.

CHAPTER 11

Israel was chosen (foreordained) according to the election of grace—But some harden their hearts against it—The Gentiles are adopted into the house of Israel—The gospel goes preferentially to the Gentiles until the fulness of the Gentiles.

I SAY then, Hath God cast away his people? [a]God forbid. For I also am an [b]Israelite, of the seed of Abraham, *of the tribe of Benjamin.*

2 God hath not cast away his [a]people which he [b]foreknew. [c]Wot ye not what the scripture saith of [d]Elias? how he maketh intercession to God against Israel, saying,

3 Lord, they have [a]killed thy prophets, and digged down thine altars; and I am [b]left alone, and they seek my life.

4 But what saith the answer of God unto him? I have [a]reserved to myself seven thousand men, who have not bowed the knee to *the image of* Baal.

10a TG Heart.
  b D&C 46:14 (11–14).
  c TG Salvation.
12a Acts 10:35 (34–35);
     Rom. 2:11;
     Gal. 3:28 (26–29).
  b TG Treasure.
  c TG God, Access to.
13a TG Prayer.
14a TG Apostasy of Israel;
     Hypocrisy.
  b D&C 42:6.
15a TG Missionary Work;
     Preaching.
  b TG Called of God.
  c Nahum 1:15.
  d TG Gospel.

  e TG Peacemakers;
     Peace of God.
16a TG Apostasy of Israel.
  b Isa. 53:1;
     John 12:38.
17a TG Faith.
  b Gal. 3:2;
     2 Ne. 33:1 (1–4);
     Alma 31:5 (5, 8–11);
     D&C 100:8 (7–8).
18a Ps. 19:4.
  b D&C 23:2; 24:10.
19a Deut. 32:21.
     TG Jealous.
20a IE Isaiah.
  b Isa. 65:1.
21a Isa. 65:2.

     TG Apostasy of Israel;
     Disobedience.
  b GR contradicting,
     opposing.
11 1a GR May it not be!
  b Acts 22:3;
     2 Cor. 11:22.
2a TG Israel, Blessings of.
  b TG Foreordination;
     God, Foreknowl-
     edge of.
  c GR Know.
  d IE Elijah.
3a TG Apostasy of Israel;
     Martyrdom.
  b 1 Kgs. 19:14 (10–18).
4a D&C 49:8.

5 Even so then at this present time also there is a remnant according to the ^aelection of grace.

6 And if by ^agrace, then *is it* no more of ^bworks: otherwise grace is no more grace. But if *it be* of works, then is it no more grace: otherwise work is no more work.

7 What then? Israel hath not obtained that which he seeketh for; but the election hath obtained it, and the rest ^awere blinded

8 (According as it is written, God hath given them the spirit of ^aslumber, eyes that they should not see, and ears that they should not ^bhear;) unto this day.

9 And David saith, Let their table be made a ^asnare, and a trap, and a stumblingblock, and a ^brecompence unto them:

10 Let their eyes be darkened, that they may not see, and bow down their back alway.

11 I say then, Have they stumbled that they should fall? ^aGod forbid: but *rather* through their fall salvation *is come* unto the Gentiles, for to provoke them to ^bjealousy.

12 Now if the fall of them *be* the riches of the world, and the ^adiminishing of them the riches of the Gentiles; how much more their fulness?

13 For I speak to you ^aGentiles, inasmuch as I am the apostle of the Gentiles, I ^bmagnify mine office:

14 If by any means I may provoke to emulation *them which are* my flesh, and might save some of them.

15 For if the casting away of them *be* the ^areconciling of the world, what *shall* the receiving *of them be*, but life from the dead?

16 For if the firstfruit *be* holy, the lump *is* also *holy:* and if the ^aroot *be* holy, so *are* the branches.

17 And if some of the branches be broken off, and thou, being a wild olive ^atree, wert grafted in among them, and with them partakest of the root and fatness of the olive tree;

18 ^aBoast not against the branches. But if thou boast, thou bearest not the root, but the root thee.

19 Thou wilt say then, The branches were broken off, that I might be grafted in.

20 Well; because of ^aunbelief they were ^bbroken off, and thou standest by ^cfaith. Be not highminded, but ^dfear:

21 For if God spared not the ^anatural branches, *take heed* lest he also ^bspare not thee.

22 Behold therefore the goodness and severity of God: on them which fell, severity; but toward thee, goodness, if thou continue in *his* goodness: otherwise thou also shalt be cut off.

23 And they also, if they abide not still in unbelief, shall be grafted in: for God is able to graft them in again.

24 For if thou wert cut out of the olive tree which is wild by nature, and wert grafted contrary to nature into a good olive tree: how much more shall these, which be the natural *branches*, be grafted into their own olive tree?

25 For I would not, brethren, that ye should be ignorant of this mystery, lest ye should be wise in your own ^aconceits; that ^bblindness in part is happened to Israel, until the ^cfulness of the ^dGentiles be come in.

5a TG Election.
6a TG Grace.
  b Rom. 2:6 (5–10).
7a GR became callous.
8a GR deep sleep, stupor.
   Isa. 29:10.
  b Matt. 13:14;
   2 Ne. 16:10.
9a Ps. 69:22.
  b GR retribution, requital.
11a GR May it not be!
  b TG Jealous.

12a GR default, failure.
13a Acts 22:21.
  b Jacob 2:2 (2–3);
   D&C 24:3; 66:11.
15a TG Reconciliation.
16a TG Israel, Mission of.
17a TG Vineyard of the Lord.
18a TG Boast.
20a TG Apostasy of Israel;
   Unbelief.
  b Ps. 80:12 (12–16).
   TG Israel, Scattering of.

  c 2 Cor. 1:24.
  d TG Reverence.
21a Jacob 5:3 (1–77);
   6:1 (1–13).
  b TG Apostasy of the
   Early Christian Church.
25a Prov. 26:12.
  b GR callousness.
   Jacob 4:14.
  c TG Restoration of the
   Gospel.
  d TG Gentiles.

26 And so all ^aIsrael shall be saved: as it is written, There shall come out of ^bSion the ^cDeliverer, and shall turn away ungodliness from Jacob:

27 For this *is* my ^acovenant unto them, when I shall take away their sins.

28 As concerning the gospel, *they are* enemies for your sakes: but as touching the election, *they are* beloved for the fathers' sakes.

29 For the gifts and calling of God *are* without repentance.

30 For as ye in times past ^ahave not believed God, yet have now obtained mercy through their ^bunbelief:

31 Even so have these also now not ^abelieved, that through your mercy they also may obtain mercy.

32 For God hath ^aconcluded them all in unbelief, that he might have mercy upon all.

33 O the depth of the ^ariches both of the ^bwisdom and ^cknowledge of God! how ^dunsearchable *are* his judgments, and his ways past ^efinding out!

34 For who hath known the ^amind of the Lord? or who hath been his ^bcounsellor?

35 Or who hath first given to him, and it shall be recompensed unto him again?

36 For of him, and ^athrough him, and to him, *are* all things: to whom *be* glory for ever. Amen.

CHAPTER 12

Paul counsels the Saints to present their bodies as a living sacrifice, to use their own grace-given gifts, and to live as Saints should live.

I BESEECH you therefore, brethren, by the mercies of God, that ye present your ^abodies a living ^bsacrifice, holy, ^cacceptable unto God, *which is* your reasonable ^dservice.

2 And be not conformed to this ^aworld: but be ye ^btransformed by the ^crenewing of your ^dmind, that ye may ^eprove what *is* that good, and acceptable, and perfect, ^fwill of God.

3 For I say, through the grace given unto me, to every man that is among you, not to ^athink *of himself* more highly than he ought to think; but to think ^bsoberly, according as ^cGod hath dealt to every man the measure of faith.

4 For as we have many members in one body, and all members have not the same ^aoffice:

5 So we, *being* many, are ^aone ^bbody in Christ, and every one members one of another.

6 Having then gifts differing according to the ^agrace that is given to us, whether prophecy, *let us prophesy* according to the proportion of ^bfaith;

7 Or ministry, *let us wait* on *our* ministering: or he that teacheth, on teaching;

8 Or he that exhorteth, on

26a TG Israel, Restoration of.
  b TG Zion.
  c Isa. 59:20;
    Alma 11:40 (37–41).
27a Isa. 59:21 (20–21);
    Heb. 10:16 (16–17);
    D&C 49:9 (5–9).
    TG Abrahamic
    Covenant.
30a GR were disbelieving,
    disobedient to.
  b GR disobedience,
    disbelief.
31a GR obeyed.
32a GR closed up together.
33a TG Treasure.
  b TG God, Intelligence of.
  c TG God, Omniscience of.

  d Isa. 40:28.
  e Prov. 25:2.
34a Jacob 4:8 (8–13);
    Mosiah 4:9.
  b 1 Cor. 2:16;
    D&C 22:4.
    TG Counselor.
36a D&C 76:24 (22–24);
    93:10.
12 1a TG Body, Sanctity of.
  b Mosiah 2:34;
    Moro. 10:32 (30–33);
    D&C 93:1.
    TG Self-Sacrifice.
  c Lev. 1:4.
  d TG Service.
2a TG World;
    Worldliness.

  b Eph. 5:8;
    1 Jn. 5:4 (1–5).
    TG Self-Mastery.
  c TG Man, New,
    Spiritually Reborn.
  d TG Mind.
  e GR test, try, prove.
  f TG God, Will of.
3a TG Humility.
  b D&C 18:21; 43:35.
  c 1 Cor. 7:17.
4a GR function, operation.
5a TG Unity.
  b TG Church.
6a TG Grace.
  b TG Faith.

exhortation: he that giveth, *let him do it* with simplicity; he that ruleth, with diligence; he that sheweth mercy, with *a*cheerfulness.

9 *Let* love be *a*without dissimulation. Abhor that which is *b*evil; cleave to that which is good.

10 *Be* kindly *a*affectioned one to another with *b*brotherly *c*love; in honour preferring one another;

11 Not slothful in *a*business; *b*fervent in spirit; serving the Lord;

12 Rejoicing in hope; *a*patient in *b*tribulation; *c*continuing instant in prayer;

13 Distributing to the necessity of saints; given to *a*hospitality.

14 Bless them which *a*persecute you: bless, and *b*curse not.

15 Rejoice with them that do rejoice, and *a*weep with them that weep.

16 *Be* of the same mind one toward another. Mind not high things, but *a*condescend to men of low estate. Be not wise in your own *b*conceits.

17 *a*Recompense to no man *b*evil for evil. Provide things *c*honest in the *d*sight of all men.

18 If it be possible, as much as lieth in you, live *a*peaceably with all men.

19 Dearly beloved, *a*avenge not yourselves, but *rather* give place unto wrath: for it is written, Vengeance *is* mine; I will repay, saith the Lord.

20 Therefore if thine *a*enemy hunger, feed him; if he thirst, give him drink: for in so doing thou shalt heap coals of fire on his head.

21 Be not overcome of evil, but *a*overcome evil with good.

CHAPTER 13

Paul counsels, Be subject unto God's ministers; keep the commandments; love one another; righteousness leads to salvation.

LET every soul *a*be subject unto the higher *b*powers. For there is no *c*power *d*but of God: the *e*powers that be are ordained of God.

2 Whosoever therefore resisteth the power, resisteth the ordinance of God: and they that *a*resist shall receive to themselves *b*damnation.

3 For rulers are not a terror to good works, but to the evil. Wilt thou then not be afraid of the *a*power? do that which is *b*good, and thou shalt have praise of the same:

4 For he is *a*the minister of God to thee for good. But if thou do that which is evil, be afraid; for he beareth not the sword in vain: for he is the minister of God, a revenger to *execute* wrath upon him that doeth evil.

5 Wherefore *ye* must needs be subject, not only for wrath, but also for *a*conscience sake.

6 *a*For for this cause pay ye tribute also: for they are God's ministers, attending continually upon this very thing.

8*a* TG Cheerful.
9*a* GR sincere, unfeigned, real.
  b Ps. 26:4; 2 Ne. 4:31; Alma 13:12; D&C 38:42. TG Evil.
10*a* Philip. 2:2 (1–4).
  b TG Brotherhood and Sisterhood.
  c TG Love.
11*a* GR haste, diligence.
  b TG Zeal.
12*a* D&C 24:8; 31:9.
  b TG Adversity.
  c GR constantly persisting in.
13*a* TG Hospitality.
14*a* TG Enemies;

Persecution.
  b TG Curse.
15*a* TG Compassion.
16*a* GR conforming willingly with the humble. 3 Ne. 12:5.
  b Prov. 26:12. TG Pride.
17*a* TG Forgive; Retribution.
  b TG Evil.
  c TG Honesty.
  d 2 Cor. 8:21.
18*a* Prov. 3:30. TG Peace; Peacemakers.
19*a* TG Forbear; Retribution.
20*a* 2 Kgs. 6:22. TG Enemies.

21*a* Rev. 2:17.
13 1*a* GR be submissive, render obedience. D&C 58:22 (21–22). TG Citizenship; Governments.
  b GR authorities.
  c John 19:11 (10–12).
  d JST Rom. 13:1 . . . *in the church* but of God . . .
  e TG Governments.
2*a* TG Rebellion.
  b TG Damnation.
3*a* GR authority.
  b TG Retribution.
4*a* GR a servant.
5*a* TG Conscience.
6*a* JST Rom. 13:6–7 (Appendix).

7 Render therefore to all their dues: tribute to whom tribute *is due;* custom to whom custom; fear to whom fear; *a*honour to whom honour.

8 *a*Owe no man any thing, but to love one another: for he that *b*loveth another hath fulfilled the law.

9 For this, Thou shalt not commit *a*adultery, Thou shalt not kill, Thou shalt not *b*steal, Thou shalt not bear false witness, Thou shalt not *c*covet; and if *there be* any other commandment, it is briefly comprehended in this saying, namely, Thou shalt love thy *d*neighbour as thyself.

10 *a*Love worketh no ill to his neighbour: therefore love *is* the fulfilling of the *b*law.

11 And that, knowing the time, that now *it is* high *a*time to awake out of *b*sleep: for now *is* our salvation nearer than when we believed.

12 The night is far spent, the *a*day is at hand: let us therefore cast off the works of *b*darkness, and let us put on the *c*armour of *d*light.

13 Let us walk *a*honestly, as in the day; not in *b*rioting and *c*drunkenness, not in *d*chambering and wantonness, not in strife and *e*envying.

14 But *a*put ye on the Lord Jesus Christ, and make not provision for the flesh, to *fulfil* the *b*lusts *thereof.*

CHAPTER 14

Avoid quarreling about opinions and making unrighteous judgment of each

other—*Every knee will bow to Christ—The kingdom of God embraces righteousness, peace, and joy in the Holy Ghost.*

HIM that is *a*weak in the faith receive ye, *but* not to *b*doubtful *c*disputations.

2 For one believeth that he may eat all things: another, who is weak, eateth *a*herbs.

3 Let not him that eateth despise him that eateth not; and let not him which eateth not *a*judge him that eateth: for God hath received him.

4 Who art thou that *a*judgest another man's servant? to his own master he standeth or falleth. Yea, he shall be holden up: for God is able to make him stand.

5 One man esteemeth one *a*day above another: another esteemeth every day *alike.* Let every man be fully persuaded in his own mind.

6 He that regardeth the day, regardeth *it* unto the Lord; and he that regardeth not the day, to the Lord he doth not regard *it.* He that eateth, eateth to the Lord, for he giveth God thanks; and he that eateth not, to the Lord he eateth not, and giveth God thanks.

7 For none of us *a*liveth to himself, and no man dieth to himself.

8 For whether we live, we live unto the Lord; and whether we die, we *a*die unto the Lord: whether we live therefore, or die, we are the Lord's.

9 For to this end Christ both died, and rose, and revived, that he might

---

7a D&C 134:6.
  TG Honor.
8a TG Debt.
  b TG Love.
9a TG Adulterer.
  b TG Stealing.
  c TG Covet.
  d TG Neighbor.
10a Moro. 7:47 (1, 44–47).
  TG Motivations.
  b Matt. 22:40 (36–40);
    Gal. 5:14 (13–14).
11a TG Time.
  b TG Apathy;
    Sleep.
12a John 9:4;
    Alma 34:31 (31–34).
  b 2 Cor. 5:17;

1 Thes. 5:4.
  TG Darkness,
    Spiritual.
  c Isa. 59:17 (16–17);
    2 Cor. 6:7;
    Eph. 6:11 (10–24);
    1 Thes. 5:8;
    D&C 27:15 (15–18).
  d TG Children of Light;
    Light [noun].
13a GR with propriety,
    decently, gracefully.
  TG Honesty.
  b TG Rioting and
    Reveling.
  c TG Drunkenness.
  d GR lewdness,
    whoredoms.

e TG Envy.
14a Gal. 3:27 (24–29).
  b TG Lust.
14 1a Isa. 35:3;
    Rom. 15:1 (1–3);
    1 Cor. 8:9;
    Gal. 6:1;
    D&C 81:5; 84:106.
  b TG Doubt.
  c TG Disputations.
2a GR vegetables.
3a Col. 2:16.
4a D&C 11:12.
5a Gal. 4:10 (9–10).
7a 2 Cor. 5:15 (14–16);
    Gal. 2:20.
8a D&C 42:44 (44–47);
    63:49.

be ^aLord both of the ^bdead and living.

10 But why dost thou ^ajudge thy brother? or why dost thou set at nought thy brother? for we shall all stand before the ^bjudgment seat of Christ.

11 For it is written, *As* I live, saith the Lord, every ^aknee shall bow to me, and every tongue shall ^bconfess to God.

12 So then every one of us shall give account of himself to God.

13 Let us not therefore judge one another any more: but judge this rather, that no man put a ^astumblingblock or an occasion to fall in *his* brother's way.

14 I know, and am persuaded by the Lord Jesus, that *there is* nothing ^aunclean of itself: but to him that ^besteemeth any thing to be unclean, to him *it is* unclean.

15 But if thy brother be grieved with *thy* meat, ^anow walkest thou not ^bcharitably. Destroy not him ^cwith thy meat, for whom Christ died.

16 Let not then your good be evil spoken of:

17 For the kingdom of God is not ^ameat and drink; but ^brighteousness, and ^cpeace, and ^djoy in the Holy Ghost.

18 For he that in these things serveth Christ *is* acceptable to God, and approved of men.

19 Let us therefore follow after the things which make for ^apeace, and

things wherewith one may ^bedify another.

20 ^aFor meat destroy not the ^bwork of God. All things indeed *are* pure; but *it is* evil for that man who eateth with offence.

21 *It is* good neither to eat flesh, nor to drink wine, nor *any thing* whereby thy brother stumbleth, or is ^aoffended, or is made weak.

22 Hast thou faith? have *it* to thyself before God. Happy *is* he that condemneth not himself ^ain that thing which he alloweth.

23 And he that ^adoubteth is damned if he eat, because *he eateth* not of faith: for whatsoever *is* not of ^bfaith is ^csin.

CHAPTER 15

True Saints fellowship one another—Paul recounts his diligence in preaching the gospel—The gifts of the Spirit are poured out upon the Gentiles.

WE then that are strong ought to ^abear the infirmities of the ^bweak, and not to please ourselves.

2 Let every one of us please *his* ^aneighbour for *his* good to ^bedification.

3 For even Christ pleased not himself; but, as it is written, The ^areproaches of them that reproached thee fell on me.

4 For whatsoever things were ^awritten aforetime were ^bwritten for our ^clearning, that we through

---

9*a* TG Jesus Christ, Authority of; Jesus Christ, Power of.
 b Luke 20:38.
  TG Genealogy and Temple Work; Salvation for the Dead.
10*a* TG Judgment.
 b TG Judgment, the Last.
11*a* Isa. 45:23; Philip. 2:10.
 b GR praise, profess openly.
13*a* Lev. 19:14; 1 Cor. 8:9 (9–13); 10:32 (24–33); 2 Cor. 6:3; Alma 39:11.
14*a* GR ceremonially unclean.
  TG Uncleanness.

 b TG Motivations.
15*a* JST Rom. 14:15 . . . *thou walkest not charitably if thou eatest. Therefore destroy not him with thy meat . . .*
 b GR according to love.
 c GR on account of food.
17*a* GR food.
  TG Food.
 b TG Righteousness.
 c TG Contentment; Peace of God.
 d TG Joy.
19*a* TG Peace; Peacemakers.
 b TG Edification.
20*a* GR Because of food.
 b TG God, Works of.
21*a* 1 Cor. 8:13.

22*a* GR by what he tries, approves.
23*a* TG Doubt.
 b TG Faith.
 c TG Sin.
15 1*a* GR remove, endure, bear with. Alma 31:33.
 b Rom. 14:1 (1–3).
 2*a* TG Neighbor.
 b TG Edification.
 3*a* GR revilings, insults. TG Reproach.
 4*a* 1 Cor. 10:11. TG Scriptures, Writing of.
 b 1 Cor. 9:10.
 c TG Scriptures, Value of; Understanding.

^dpatience and comfort of the ^escriptures might have ^fhope.

5 Now the God of patience and ^aconsolation grant you to be ^blikeminded one toward another according to Christ Jesus:

6 That ye may with one mind *and* one mouth glorify God, even the ^aFather of our Lord Jesus Christ.

7 Wherefore receive ye one another, as Christ also received us to the glory of God.

8 Now I say that Jesus Christ was a minister of the ^acircumcision for the truth of God, to ^bconfirm the ^cpromises *made* unto the fathers:

9 And that the Gentiles might glorify God for *his* ^amercy; as it is written, For this cause I will ^bconfess to thee among the ^cGentiles, and sing unto thy name.

10 And again he saith, Rejoice, ye ^aGentiles, with his people.

11 And again, Praise the Lord, all ye Gentiles; and laud him, all ye people.

12 And again, ^aEsaias saith, There shall be a root of ^bJesse, and he that shall rise to reign over the Gentiles; in him shall the Gentiles trust.

13 Now the God of hope fill you with all joy and ^apeace in believing, that ye may abound in ^bhope, through the power of the Holy Ghost.

14 And I myself also am persuaded of you, my brethren, that ye also are full of goodness, filled with all ^aknowledge, able also to ^badmonish one another.

15 Nevertheless, brethren, I have written the more boldly unto you in ^asome sort, as putting you in mind, because of the ^bgrace that is given to me of God,

16 That I should be the ^aminister of Jesus Christ to the Gentiles, ministering the gospel of God, that the ^boffering up of the Gentiles might be acceptable, being ^csanctified by the Holy Ghost.

17 I have therefore whereof I may ^aglory through Jesus Christ in those things which pertain to God.

18 For I will not dare to speak of any of those things which Christ hath not wrought by me, to make the Gentiles obedient, by word and deed,

19 Through mighty ^asigns and wonders, by the power of the ^bSpirit of God; so that from Jerusalem, and round about unto Illyricum, I have fully preached the gospel of Christ.

20 Yea, so have I strived to preach the gospel, not where Christ was named, lest I should build upon another man's ^afoundation:

21 But as it is written, To whom he was not ^aspoken of, they shall see: and they that have not heard shall understand.

22 For which cause also I have been much ^ahindered from coming to you.

23 But now having no more ^aplace in these parts, and having a great desire these many years to come unto you;

24 Whensoever I take my journey into Spain, I will come to you: for I trust to see you in my journey, and to be brought on my way thitherward by you, if first I be somewhat filled with your *company*.

4d TG Patience.
 e TG Scriptures, Study of.
 f TG Hope.
5a GR comfort.
 b 1 Cor. 1:10 (9–16);
   1 Thes. 5:13 (13–15);
   Mosiah 18:21.
6a TG Jesus Christ, Divine
   Sonship.
8a TG Circumcision.
 b GR establish, make
   constant.
 c 2 Cor. 1:20.
9a TG God, Mercy of.

 b GR profess openly,
   praise.
 c Ps. 18:49.
10a Acts 9:15 (1–19);
   3 Ne. 30:2 (1–2).
12a IE Isaiah.
 b TG Jesus Christ, Davidic
   Descent of.
13a TG Peace of God.
 b TG Hope.
14a TG Knowledge.
 b TG Warn.
15a GR part.
 b TG Grace.

16a GR servant at one's own
   expense.
 b GR sacrifice, offering.
 c TG Holy Ghost,
   Gifts of.
17a Alma 26:16 (16, 35).
19a Morm. 9:19 (19–21);
   D&C 63:10 (7–10).
 b TG God, Spirit of.
20a 2 Cor. 10:15;
   D&C 52:33.
21a Isa. 52:15.
22a Rom. 1:13.
23a GR opportunity.

25 But now I go unto Jerusalem to minister unto the saints.

26 For it hath pleased them of Macedonia and Achaia to make a certain ªcontribution for the poor saints which are at Jerusalem.

27 It hath pleased them verily; and their debtors they are. For if the Gentiles have been made partakers of their ªspiritual things, their ᵇduty is also to minister unto them in ᶜcarnal things.

28 When therefore I have performed this, and have sealed to them this ªfruit, I will come by you into Spain.

29 And I am sure that, when I come unto you, I shall come in the ªfulness of the blessing of the gospel of Christ.

30 Now I beseech you, brethren, for the Lord Jesus Christ's sake, and for the love of the Spirit, that ye strive together with me in *your* prayers to God for me;

31 That I may be delivered from them that ªdo not believe in Judæa; and that my service which *I have* for Jerusalem may be accepted of the saints;

32 That I may come unto you with joy by the will of God, and may with you be ªrefreshed.

33 Now the God of peace *be* with you all. Amen.

CHAPTER 16

Paul sends greetings to various Saints— He counsels the Saints to avoid those who cause divisions—The Saints should be wise concerning good and innocent concerning evil.

I COMMEND unto you Phebe our sister, which is a servant of the church which is at Cenchrea:

2 That ye receive her in the Lord, as becometh saints, and that ye assist her in whatsoever business she hath need of you: for she hath been a succourer of many, and of myself also.

3 Greet Priscilla and Aquila my helpers in Christ Jesus:

4 Who have for my life laid down their own necks: unto whom not only I give thanks, but also all the churches of the Gentiles.

5 Likewise *greet* the church that is in their house. Salute my wellbeloved Epænetus, who is the firstfruits of Achaia unto Christ.

6 Greet Mary, who bestowed much labour on us.

7 Salute Andronicus and Junia, my kinsmen, and my fellowprisoners, who are of note among the apostles, who also were in Christ before me.

8 Greet Amplias my beloved in the Lord.

9 Salute Urbane, our helper in Christ, and Stachys my beloved.

10 Salute Apelles approved in Christ. Salute them which are of Aristobulus' ªhousehold.

11 Salute Herodion my kinsman. Greet them that be of the ªhousehold of Narcissus, which are in the Lord.

12 Salute Tryphena and Tryphosa, who labour in the Lord. Salute the beloved Persis, which laboured much in the Lord.

13 Salute Rufus chosen in the Lord, and his mother and mine.

14 Salute Asyncritus, Phlegon, Hermas, Patrobas, Hermes, and the brethren which are with them.

15 Salute Philologus, and Julia, Nereus, and his sister, and Olympas, and all the saints which are with them.

16 Salute one another with an holy ªkiss. The ᵇchurches of Christ salute you.

17 Now I beseech you, brethren, ªmark them which cause ᵇdivisions

---

26a TG Almsgiving; Welfare.
27a 1 Cor. 9:11.
  b TG Duty.
  c GR material, temporal.
28a Philip. 4:17; Titus 3:14.
29a D&C 1:23; 14:10; 35:17; 39:11 (11–18); 42:12; JS—H 1:34.
31a GR refuse belief or obedience.
32a 2 Cor. 7:13.
16 10a JST Rom. 16:10 . . . church.
11a JST Rom. 16:11 . . . church . . .
16a JST Rom. 16:16 . . .
salutation . . .
  b TG Jesus Christ, Head of the Church.
17a GR watch, beware of.
  b Acts 20:30 (28–30); 1 Cor. 1:10 (10–13); 2 Thes. 3:6 (2–6); 2 Ne. 26:21 (20–21).

and ^coffences contrary to the ^ddoctrine which ye have learned; and ^eavoid them.

18 For they that are such serve not our Lord Jesus Christ, but their own belly; and by good words and ^afair speeches deceive the hearts of the ^bsimple.

19 For your ^aobedience is come abroad unto all *men*. I am glad therefore on your behalf: but yet I would have you ^bwise unto that which is good, and ^csimple concerning evil.

20 And the God of ^apeace shall ^bbruise ^cSatan under your feet shortly. The grace of our Lord Jesus Christ *be* with you. Amen.

21 Timotheus my workfellow, and Lucius, and Jason, and Sosipater, my kinsmen, salute you.

22 I Tertius, who wrote *this* epistle, salute you in the Lord.

23 Gaius mine host, and of the whole church, saluteth you. Erastus the chamberlain of the city saluteth you, and Quartus a brother.

24 The ^agrace of our Lord Jesus Christ *be* with you all. Amen.

25 Now to him that is of power to ^astablish you according to my gospel, and the preaching of Jesus Christ, according to the revelation of the ^bmystery, which was kept secret since the world began,

26 But now is made manifest, and by the scriptures of the prophets, according to the commandment of the ^aeverlasting God, made known to all nations for the ^bobedience of faith:

27 To God only wise, *be* glory through Jesus Christ for ever. Amen.

¶ Written to the Romans from Corinthus, *and sent* by Phebe servant of the church at Cenchrea.

THE FIRST EPISTLE OF
PAUL THE APOSTLE TO THE
CORINTHIANS

CHAPTER 1

True Saints are perfectly united in the same mind and in the same judgment—Preach the gospel and save souls—The gospel is preached by the weak and the simple.

PAUL, called *to be* an apostle of Jesus Christ through the will of God, and Sosthenes *our* brother,

2 Unto the church of God which is at Corinth, to them that are ^asanctified in Christ Jesus, called *to be* ^bsaints, with all that in every place

---

17c GR stumbling blocks, scandals.
   d 3 Ne. 11:40 (31–41).
   e 1 Cor. 5:11.
18*a* 2 Pet. 2:3.
   b GR innocent, guileless.
19*a* Rom. 1:8.
   b TG Wisdom.
   c GR blameless, innocent.
20*a* Moro. 7:3 (3–4).
   b GR break the power of,

crush.
   Gen. 3:15.
   TG Jesus Christ, Prophecies about; Redemption.
   c TG Devil.
24*a* Rev. 22:21 (17–21).
25*a* 1 Thes. 3:2.
   b Eph. 3:4; Col. 1:26 (25–26); D&C 6:7 (7–11);

42:65 (61–65); 121:27 (25–27).
26*a* Gen. 21:33.
   b TG Obedience.

[1 CORINTHIANS]

1 2*a* TG Sanctification.
   b TG Mission of Early Saints; Saints.

call upon the name of Jesus Christ our Lord, both theirs and ours:

3 Grace *be* unto you, and ^apeace, from God our Father, and *from* the Lord Jesus Christ.

4 I thank my God always on your behalf, for the grace of God which is given you by Jesus Christ;

5 That in every thing ye are enriched by him, in all utterance, and *in* all knowledge;

6 Even as the ^atestimony of Christ was ^bconfirmed in you:

7 So that ye ^acome behind in no gift; waiting for the ^bcoming of our Lord Jesus Christ:

8 Who shall also ^aconfirm you unto the end, *that ye may be* ^bblameless in the day of our Lord Jesus Christ.

9 God *is* faithful, by whom ye were called unto the ^afellowship of his Son Jesus Christ our Lord.

10 Now I beseech you, brethren, by the name of our Lord Jesus Christ, that ye all speak the same thing, and *that* there be no ^adivisions among you; but *that* ye be perfectly joined together in the same ^bmind and in the same judgment.

11 For it hath been declared unto me ^aof you, my brethren, by them *which are of the house* of Chloe, that there are ^bcontentions among you.

12 Now this I say, that every one of you saith, I am of Paul; and I of Apollos; and I of Cephas; and I of ^aChrist.

13 Is Christ ^adivided? was Paul crucified for you? or were ye baptized in the name of Paul?

14 I thank God that I baptized none of you, ^abut ^bCrispus and Gaius;

15 Lest any should say that I had baptized in mine own name.

16 And I baptized also the household of ^aStephanas: besides, I know not whether I baptized any other.

17 For Christ sent me not to baptize, but to preach the gospel: not with ^awisdom of words, lest the cross of Christ should be made of none effect.

18 For the ^apreaching of the cross is to them that perish foolishness; but unto us which are saved it is the ^bpower of God.

19 For it is written, I will destroy the wisdom of the wise, and will bring to nothing the ^aunderstanding of the ^bprudent.

20 Where *is* the wise? where *is* the ^ascribe? where *is* the ^bdisputer of this ^cworld? hath not God made foolish the ^dwisdom of this ^eworld?

21 For after that in the wisdom of God the world ^aby wisdom knew not God, it pleased God by the foolishness of ^bpreaching to save them that believe.

22 For the Jews require a ^asign, and the Greeks seek after wisdom:

23 But we ^apreach Christ ^bcrucified, unto the Jews a ^cstumblingblock, and unto the Greeks foolishness;

24 But unto them ^awhich are

3a TG Peace of God.
6a TG Testimony.
 b GR established, strengthened.
7a GR come short, miss, need.
 b GR revelation. 1 Thes. 3:13; D&C 45:44 (25–44).
8a GR secure, establish, strengthen.
 b 3 Ne. 27:20; D&C 4:2.
9a TG Fellowshipping.
10a GR factions, schisms. Acts 4:32; Rom. 15:5 (1–7); 16:17 (17–18); Eph. 4:13 (11–14);
3 Ne. 11:28 (28–30). TG Church.
 b 1 Cor. 12:25; 2 Cor. 13:11; D&C 38:27. TG Mind.
11a GR about, concerning.
 b TG Apostasy of the Early Christian Church; Contention.
12a 3 Ne. 27:8 (4–9).
13a 2 Ne. 28:3 (3–5, 12–13).
14a GR except.
 b Acts 18:8.
16a 1 Cor. 16:15.
17a TG Wisdom.
18a 1 Pet. 2:8 (4–8).
 b Rom. 1:16; 1 Cor. 4:20.
19a TG Understanding.
 b TG Prudence.
20a TG Scribe.
 b TG Disputations.
 c GR age.
 d Isa. 44:25; Jer. 8:8 (8–9); D&C 133:58.
 e TG Worldliness.
21a GR by means of, through.
 b TG Gospel.
22a TG Sign Seekers.
23a TG Missionary Work.
 b TG Jesus Christ, Crucifixion of.
 c Jacob 4:15.
24a JST 1 Cor. 1:24 . . . *who believe*, both Jews and Greeks . . .

called, both Jews and Greeks, Christ the [b]power of God, and the [c]wisdom of God.

25 Because the [a]foolishness of God is wiser than men; and the weakness of God is stronger than men.

26 For ye see your calling, brethren, how that not many wise men after the [a]flesh, not many mighty, not many noble, *are* [b]called:

27 But God hath chosen the [a]foolish things of the world to [b]confound the wise; and God hath chosen the [c]weak things of the world to confound the things which are mighty;

28 And base things of the world, and things which are despised, hath God chosen, *yea*, and things which are not, to bring to nought things that are:

29 That no flesh should glory in his presence.

30 But of him are ye in Christ Jesus, who of God is made unto us wisdom, and righteousness, and [a]sanctification, and redemption:

31 That, according as it is written, He that glorieth, let him [a]glory in the Lord.

CHAPTER 2

The gospel is preached by the power of the Spirit—The Spirit reveals all things to the Saints—The unrepentant natural man cannot receive the things of the Spirit of God.

AND I, brethren, when I came to you, came not with excellency of speech or of wisdom, declaring unto you the [a]testimony of God.

2 For I determined not to know any thing among you, [a]save Jesus Christ, and him [b]crucified.

3 And I was with you in [a]weakness, and in fear, and in much trembling.

4 And my [a]speech and my preaching *was* not with [b]enticing words of man's wisdom, but in demonstration of the [c]Spirit and of [d]power:

5 That your faith should not stand in the wisdom of men, but in the [a]power of God.

6 Howbeit we speak wisdom among them that are [a]perfect: yet not the wisdom of this world, nor of the princes of this world, that come to nought:

7 But we speak the [a]wisdom of God in a [b]mystery, *even* the hidden [c]wisdom, which God [d]ordained before the world unto our glory:

8 Which none of the princes of this world knew: for had they known *it*, they would not have [a]crucified the Lord of glory.

9 But as it is written, [a]Eye hath not seen, nor ear heard, neither have entered into the heart of man, the things which God hath [b]prepared for them that love him.

10 But God hath [a]revealed *them* unto us by his [b]Spirit: for the [c]Spirit [d]searcheth all things, yea, the deep things of God.

11 For what man [a]knoweth the things of a man, save the spirit of man which is in him? even so the

24b TG God, Power of.
  c TG Jesus Christ, Relationships with the Father.
25a TG Foolishness.
26a TG Man, Natural, Not Spiritually Reborn.
  b JST 1 Cor. 1:26 ... *chosen* ... John 12:43 (42–43). TG Called of God.
27a James 2:5 (1–9); D&C 1:23 (18–20, 23).
  b GR shame, frustrate. Alma 37:7 (6–7); D&C 133:58 (58–59).
  c Ether 12:27 (23–29); D&C 35:13; 124:1.

30a TG Sanctification.
31a Jer. 9:24 (23–24); 1 Cor. 5:6; Alma 26:16 (16, 35).
2 1a TG Testimony.
  2a GR except.
  b TG Jesus Christ, Crucifixion of.
  3a Gal. 4:13; Ether 12:23 (23–29).
  4a 1 Thes. 1:5.
  b GR persuasive.
  c TG Teaching with the Spirit.
  d 2 Ne. 28:4 (3–5). TG Priesthood, Power of.
  5a 2 Cor. 4:7.
  6a TG Perfection.

7a TG Wisdom.
  b TG Mysteries of Godliness.
  c Col. 2:3.
  d GR foreordained.
8a TG Jesus Christ, Crucifixion of.
9a Isa. 64:4; D&C 76:10.
  b TG Blessing; Reward.
10a Alma 5:46 (45–48). TG Revelation.
  b 1 Thes. 4:8; 1 Jn. 3:24; D&C 42:17.
  c D&C 35:19.
  d GR explores, investigates. D&C 63:59.
11a TG Education.

things of God [b]knoweth no man, [c]but the [d]Spirit of God.

12 Now we have received, not the [a]spirit of the world, but the spirit which is of God; that we might know the things that are freely given to us of God.

13 Which things also we speak, not in the words which man's [a]wisdom teacheth, but which the Holy Ghost [b]teacheth; comparing spiritual things with spiritual.

14 But the [a]natural man [b]receiveth not the things of the [c]Spirit of God: for they are [d]foolishness unto him: neither can he [e]know *them,* because they are [f]spiritually [g]discerned.

15 But he that is spiritual [a]judgeth all things, yet he himself is judged of no man.

16 For who hath known the mind of the Lord, that he may [a]instruct him? But we have the [b]mind of Christ.

CHAPTER 3

Milk comes before meat in the Church— Men's works will be tried by fire—The Saints are the temple of God, and if they are faithful, they will inherit all things.

AND I, brethren, could not speak unto you as unto spiritual, but as unto carnal, *even* as unto babes in Christ.

2 I have fed you with [a]milk, and not with meat: for hitherto ye were not able *to bear it,* neither yet now are ye able.

3 For ye are yet [a]carnal: for whereas *there is* among you [b]envying, and [c]strife, and [d]divisions, are ye not carnal, and walk as men?

4 For while one saith, I am of Paul; and another, I *am* of Apollos; are ye not carnal?

5 Who then is Paul, and who *is* Apollos, but [a]ministers by whom ye believed, even as the Lord gave to every man?

6 I have [a]planted, Apollos watered; but God [b]gave the [c]increase.

7 So then neither is he that planteth any thing, neither he that watereth; but God that giveth the increase.

8 Now he that planteth and he that watereth are one: and every man shall receive his own [a]reward according to his own labour.

9 For we are [a]labourers together with God: ye are God's [b]husbandry, *ye are* God's building.

10 According to the [a]grace of God which is given unto me, as a wise masterbuilder, I have laid the foundation, and another buildeth thereon. But let every man take heed how he buildeth thereupon.

11 For other [a]foundation can no man lay than that is laid, which is Jesus Christ.

12 Now if any man build upon this foundation gold, silver, precious stones, wood, hay, stubble;

13 Every man's work shall be made manifest: for the day shall

---

11b Mark 6:52; John 1:5;
   Jacob 4:8 (8–10, 13);
   Alma 26:21 (21–22).
  c JST 1 Cor. 2:11 . . . *except*
   he has the Spirit of God.
  d TG Holy Ghost, Source
   of Testimony.
12a D&C 50:15.
13a 2 Cor. 1:12.
  b TG Holy Ghost,
   Mission of.
14a 2 Ne. 9:43 (42–43).
   TG Learn; Man, Natural,
   Not Spiritually Reborn.
  b TG Teachable.
  c TG God, Spirit of.
  d Ether 12:25 (23–28, 38).
   TG Foolishness.
  e TG God, Knowledge

about; Knowledge.
  f TG Spirituality.
  g GR examined, tried,
   judged.
   TG Discernment,
   Spiritual.
15a GR examines, tries,
   judges.
16a Rom. 11:34;
   D&C 22:4.
   TG Counsel.
  b 1 Jn. 3:24 (19–24);
   4:12 (7–21);
   Moses 4:6.
3 2a Heb. 5:12 (11–14);
   1 Pet. 2:2 (1–3);
   D&C 19:22; 50:40.
  3a TG Carnal Mind;
   Man, Natural, Not

Spiritually Reborn.
  b TG Envy.
  c TG Strife.
  d TG Apostasy of the
   Early Christian Church.
5a GR servants.
   2 Cor. 3:6.
6a John 4:37 (36–38);
   1 Cor. 9:1.
  b GR caused, gave growth.
  c Mark 4:27 (26–29).
8a TG Reward; Wages.
9a 2 Cor. 6:1.
  b GR cultivated field,
   farm.
10a TG Grace.
11a Matt. 16:18;
   2 Ne. 4:30.
   TG Cornerstone.

declare it, because it shall be revealed by fire; and the [a]fire shall [b]try every man's work of what sort it is.

14 If any man's work abide which he hath built thereupon, he shall receive a reward.

15 If any man's work shall be burned, he shall suffer loss: but he himself [a]shall be saved; yet so as by fire.

16 Know ye not that ye are the [a]temple of God, and *that* the [b]Spirit of God dwelleth [c]in you?

17 If any man [a]defile the temple of God, him shall God destroy; for the temple of God is [b]holy, which *temple* ye are.

18 Let no man deceive himself. If any man among you [a]seemeth to be wise in this world, let him become a [b]fool, that he may be [c]wise.

19 For the [a]wisdom of this [b]world is [c]foolishness with God. For it is written, He taketh the wise in their own [d]craftiness.

20 And again, The Lord [a]knoweth the thoughts of the wise, that they are [b]vain.

21 Therefore let no man [a]glory in men. For all things are yours;

22 Whether [a]Paul, or Apollos, or Cephas, or the world, or life, or death, or things present, or things to come; [b]all are yours;

23 And ye are [a]Christ's; and Christ is God's.

CHAPTER 4

Christ's ministers must be faithful—The Apostles suffer, minister, and keep the faith—The kingdom of God is not in word but in power.

LET a man so account of us, as of the ministers of Christ, and stewards of the [a]mysteries of God.

2 Moreover it is required in [a]stewards, that a man be found [b]faithful.

3 But with me it is a very small thing that I should be judged of you, or of man's judgment: yea, I judge not mine own self.

4 For I know nothing [a]by myself; yet am I not hereby justified: but he that [b]judgeth me is the Lord.

5 Therefore judge nothing before the time, until the Lord come, who both will bring to light the [a]hidden things of darkness, and will make [b]manifest the counsels of the hearts: and then shall every man have praise of God.

6 And these things, brethren, I have in a figure transferred to myself and *to* Apollos for your sakes; that ye might learn in us not to think *of men* above that which is written, that no one of you be [a]puffed up for one against another.

7 For who maketh thee [a]to differ *from another?* and what hast thou that thou didst not [b]receive? now if thou didst receive *it,* why dost thou glory, as if thou hadst not received *it?*

8 Now ye are full, now ye are rich, ye have reigned as kings without us: and I would to God ye did reign, that we also might reign with you.

13a Mal. 3:2 (2–3).
  b GR test, put to proof.
    TG Test.
15a JST 1 Cor. 3:15 . . . *may* . . .
16a TG Body, Sanctity of;
    Life, Sanctity of;
    Temple.
  b TG God, Spirit of.
  c GR in, within, among.
17a GR spoil, corrupt,
    deprave.
    TG Cleanliness;
    Filthiness;
    Holy Ghost, Loss of;
    Pollution; Sacrilege;
    Uncleanness;
    Word of Wisdom.

  b TG Holiness; Sacred.
18a TG Boast.
  b 2 Ne. 9:42 (42–43).
  c TG Learn.
19a TG God, Wisdom of;
    Knowledge; Wisdom.
  b TG World; Worldliness.
  c TG Foolishness.
  d GR cunning, villainy.
20a TG God, Omni-
    science of.
  b GR deceptive, fruitless.
21a 1 Cor. 5:6;
    D&C 76:61 (58–62).
22a D&C 76:99.
  b Luke 12:44.
23a 2 Cor. 10:7.

4 1a TG God, Knowledge
    about;
    Mysteries of Godliness.
2a TG Delegation of
    Responsibility;
    Stewardship.
  b TG Trustworthiness.
4a JST 1 Cor. 4:4 . . . *against*
    myself . . .
  b TG Jesus Christ, Judge.
5a D&C 123:13.
  b Rom. 2:16.
6a GR proud, arrogant.
    D&C 38:24.
7a GR different from,
    superior to.
  b Mosiah 4:19.

9 For I think that God hath set forth us the *a*apostles last, as it were *b*appointed to death: for we are made a spectacle unto the world, and to angels, and to men.

10 We *are* fools for Christ's sake, but ye *are* wise in Christ; we *are* weak, but ye *are* strong; ye *are* honourable, but we *are* despised.

11 Even unto this present hour we both hunger, and thirst, and are naked, and are *a*buffeted, and have no certain dwellingplace;

12 And *a*labour, working with our *b*own *c*hands: being *d*reviled, we bless; being *e*persecuted, we *f*suffer it:

13 Being defamed, we entreat: we are made as the filth of the world, *and are* the offscouring of all things unto this day.

14 I write not these things to *a*shame you, but as my beloved *b*sons I *c*warn *you.*

15 For though ye have ten thousand instructors in Christ, yet *have* ye not many fathers: for in Christ Jesus I have begotten you through the *a*gospel.

16 Wherefore I beseech you, be ye *a*followers of me.

17 For this cause have I sent unto you *a*Timotheus, who is my beloved son, and faithful in the Lord, who shall bring you into remembrance of my ways which be in Christ, as I teach every where in every church.

18 Now some are *a*puffed up, as though I would not come to you.

19 But I will come to you shortly, if the Lord will, and will know, not the speech of them which are puffed up, but the power.

20 For the kingdom of God *is* not in word, but in *a*power.

21 *a*What will ye? shall I come unto you with a rod, or in love, and *in* the spirit of *b*meekness?

CHAPTER 5

The Church cannot fellowship sinners —Christ, our passover, was sacrificed for us.

IT is reported commonly *that there is* *a*fornication among you, and such fornication as is not so much as named among the Gentiles, that one should have his father's wife.

2 And ye are *a*puffed up, and have not rather mourned, that he that hath done this deed might be taken away from among you.

3 For I verily, *a*as absent in body, but present in spirit, have judged already, as though I were present, *concerning* him that hath so done this deed,

4 In the name of our Lord Jesus Christ, when ye are gathered together, *a*and my spirit, with the power of our Lord Jesus Christ,

5 To *a*deliver such an one unto Satan for the *b*destruction of the flesh, that the spirit may be saved in the *c*day of the Lord Jesus.

6 Your *a*glorying *is* not good. Know ye not that a little leaven leaveneth the whole lump?

7 *a*Purge out therefore the old leaven, that ye may be a new lump, as ye are *b*unleavened. For even

9*a* GR last apostles.
    Rom. 1:1;
    1 Ne. 11:34 (33–34).
  b D&C 42:48.
11*a* GR roughly treated,
    afflicted.
12*a* TG Labor.
  b TG Self-Sacrifice.
  c D&C 38:40.
  d TG Malice;
    Reviling.
  e TG Persecution.
  f GR endure patiently.
14*a* TG Shame.
  b 1 Thes. 2:11.

  c TG Warn.
15*a* TG Gospel.
16*a* GR imitators.
    1 Cor. 11:1.
17*a* Acts 16:1;
    1 Tim. 1:2.
18*a* TG Apostasy of the
    Early Christian Church.
20*a* 1 Cor. 1:18 (17–18);
    D&C 18:47; 42:14.
    TG Priesthood, Power of.
21*a* IE Which do you choose?
  b GR gentleness, kindness.
5 1*a* GR sexual immorality.
    TG Sexual Immorality.

2*a* Alma 5:53 (53–56); 6:3.
3*a* GR as it were.
4*a* JST 1 Cor. 5:4 . . . and
    have the Spirit, with . . .
5*a* 1 Tim. 1:20;
    D&C 78:12 (11–12).
  b TG Punish.
  c D&C 2:1; 19:3; 39:21;
    45:12 (12–34);
    Moses 7:65 (59–67).
6*a* GR boasting.
    1 Cor. 1:31;
    3:21 (18–21).
7*a* D&C 43:11.
  b TG Bread, Unleavened.

Christ our ^cpassover is sacrificed for us:

8 Therefore let us keep the ^afeast, not with old ^bleaven, neither with the leaven of malice and wickedness; but with the unleavened *bread* of ^csincerity and truth.

9 I wrote unto you in an ^aepistle not to ^bcompany with ^cfornicators:

10 Yet not altogether with the fornicators of this world, or with the ^acovetous, or ^bextortioners, or with idolaters; for then must ye needs go out of the world.

11 But now I have written unto you not to keep ^acompany, if any man that is called a brother be a fornicator, or covetous, or an idolater, or a railer, or a ^bdrunkard, or an extortioner; with such an one ^cno not to ^deat.

12 For what have I to do to judge them also that are ^awithout? do not ye ^bjudge them that are within?

13 But them that are without God judgeth. Therefore put away from among yourselves that wicked person.

CHAPTER 6

Church members should not fight one another in the courts—The unrighteous will not be saved—True Saints are the temple of the Holy Ghost.

DARE any of you, having a ^amatter against another, go to ^blaw before the unjust, and not before the saints?

2 Do ye not know that the saints shall ^ajudge the ^bworld? and if the world shall be judged by you, are ye unworthy to judge the smallest matters?

3 Know ye not that we shall judge angels? how much more things that pertain to this life?

4 If then ye have judgments of things pertaining to this life, set them to judge who are least esteemed in the church.

5 I speak to your ^ashame. Is it so, that there is not a wise man among you? no, not one that shall be able to judge between his brethren?

6 But brother goeth to law with brother, and that before the unbelievers.

7 Now therefore there is utterly a fault among you, because ye go to law one with another. Why do ye not rather take ^awrong? why do ye not rather ^bsuffer yourselves to be ^cdefrauded?

8 Nay, ye do wrong, and ^adefraud, and that *your* brethren.

9 Know ye not that the ^aunrighteous shall not ^binherit the kingdom of God? Be not deceived: neither ^cfornicators, nor idolaters, nor ^dadulterers, nor ^eeffeminate, nor ^fabusers of themselves with mankind,

10 Nor ^athieves, nor covetous, nor ^bdrunkards, nor ^crevilers, nor ^dextortioners, shall inherit the kingdom of God.

11 And such were some of you: but ye are ^awashed, but ye are ^bsanctified, but ye are justified in the ^cname

---

7c TG Jesus Christ, Types of, in Anticipation; Passover.
8a Ex. 12:14 (14–17).
  b TG Leaven.
  c TG Sincere.
9a TG Scriptures, Lost.
  b 2 Thes. 3:6 (6, 11–15).
  c GR sexually immoral persons, male prostitutes. TG Fornication.
10a TG Covet.
  b GR swindlers, robbers.
11a Rom. 16:17.
  b TG Drunkenness.
  c GR not even.
  d 2 Jn. 1:10.
12a GR outside, foreign, not belonging.

  b 1 Cor. 6:1.
6 1a Ex. 18:16.
  b Matt. 18:17; 1 Cor. 5:12; D&C 64:12 (9–12).
2a See JST Matt. 7:1–2 (Matt. 7:1 note a). Dan. 7:22; Rev. 20:4. TG Judgment, the Last.
  b TG World.
5a TG Shame.
7a TG Retribution.
  b TG Forbear.
  c Luke 6:29 (29–30).
8a TG Fraud; Injustice; Selfishness.
9a 1 Ne. 10:21; Alma 11:37; 40:26; Moses 6:57. TG Worthiness.
  b John 3:5; 1 Cor. 15:50.

  c GR sexually immoral persons, male prostitutes. TG Fornication.
  d TG Adulterer; Sexual Immorality.
  e GR catamites.
  f GR male homosexuals. TG Homosexual Behavior.
10a TG Stealing.
  b TG Drunkenness; Word of Wisdom.
  c TG Reviling.
  d GR robbers.
11a TG Baptism; Wash.
  b TG Sanctification.
  c TG Jesus Christ, Taking the Name of; Name.

of the Lord Jesus, and by the [d]Spirit of our God.

12 [a]All things are lawful unto me, but all things are not [b]expedient: all things are lawful for me, but I will not be brought under the power of any.

13 Meats for the belly, and the belly for meats: but God shall destroy both it and them. Now the body is not for [a]fornication, but for the Lord; and the Lord for the body.

14 And God hath both raised up the Lord, and will also [a]raise up us by his own power.

15 Know ye not that your bodies are the [a]members of Christ? shall I then take the members of Christ, and make them the members of an harlot? God forbid.

16 What? know ye not that he which is joined to an harlot is one body? for two, saith he, shall be [a]one flesh.

17 But he that is joined unto the Lord is [a]one spirit.

18 Flee fornication. Every sin that a man doeth is without the body; but he that committeth fornication sinneth against his own body.

19 What? know ye not that your [a]body is the [b]temple of the Holy Ghost which is in you, which ye have of God, and ye are not your [c]own?

20 For ye are [a]bought with a price: therefore glorify God in your body, and in your spirit, which are God's.

CHAPTER 7

Paul answers special questions about marriage among those called on missions—Paul praises self-discipline.

Now concerning the things whereof ye wrote unto me: [a]It is good for a man not to touch a woman.

2 Nevertheless, [a]to avoid [b]fornication, let every man have his own [c]wife, and let every woman have her own husband.

3 Let the [a]husband render unto the [b]wife due [c]benevolence: and likewise also the wife unto the husband.

4 The wife hath not power of her own body, but the husband: and likewise also the husband hath not power of his own body, but the wife.

5 [a]Defraud ye not one the other, except it be with consent for a time, that ye may give yourselves to fasting and prayer; and come together again, that [b]Satan [c]tempt you not for your incontinency.

6 But I speak this by permission, and not of commandment.

7 For I would that all men were even as I myself. But every man hath his [a]proper [b]gift of God, one after this manner, and another after that.

8 I say therefore to the unmarried and [a]widows, It is good for them if they abide even as I.

9 [a]But if they cannot [b]contain, let them marry: for it is better to marry than to [c]burn.

---

11 d TG God, Spirit of.
12 a JST 1 Cor. 6:12 All these things are not lawful unto me, and all these things are not expedient. All things are not lawful for me, therefore I will not . . .
   b GR beneficial, advantageous.
13 a GR sexual immorality. TG Chastity; Fornication.
14 a TG Resurrection.
15 a Eph. 5:30.
16 a TG Marriage, Marry.
17 a 3 Ne. 19:23 (23, 29).
19 a TG Body, Sanctity of; Chastity.

   b TG Temple.
   c 1 Cor. 7:23.
20 a Ex. 15:16; 1 Pet. 1:18 (17–21); 2 Pet. 2:1.
7 1 a JST 1 Cor. 7:1 . . . saying, It is good . . .
2 a JST 1 Cor. 7:2 . . . I say, to avoid . . .
   b TG Fornication.
   c TG Marriage, Marry; Marriage, Wives.
3 a TG Marriage, Husbands.
   b TG Marriage, Wives.
   c TG Benevolence; Family, Love within; Marriage, Continuing Courtship in.
5 a JST 1 Cor. 7:5 Depart

ye not one from the other . . .
   TG Family, Love within; Fraud.
   b TG Devil.
   c TG Test.
7 a GR own.
   b TG God, Gifts of; Holy Ghost, Gifts of.
8 a TG Widows.
9 a JST 1 Cor. 7:9 But if they cannot abide, let them marry; for it is better to marry than that any should commit sin.
   b GR use self-control.
   c GR burn with lust.

10 And unto the married I command, *yet* not I, but the Lord, Let not the ^awife ^bdepart from *her* husband:

11 But and if she depart, let her remain unmarried, or be ^areconciled to *her* husband: and let not the husband ^bput away *his* wife.

12 But to the rest speak I, not the Lord: If any brother hath a wife that believeth not, and she be pleased to dwell with him, let him not put her away.

13 And the woman which hath an ^ahusband that believeth not, and if he be pleased to dwell with her, let her not leave him.

14 ^aFor the unbelieving ^bhusband is ^csanctified by the wife, and the unbelieving wife is ^dsanctified by the husband: else were your children unclean; but now are they holy.

15 But if the unbelieving depart, let him depart. A brother or a sister is not under bondage in such *cases:* but God hath called us ^ato peace.

16 For what knowest thou, O wife, whether thou shalt ^asave *thy* husband? or how knowest thou, O man, whether thou shalt save *thy* wife?

17 But as ^aGod hath distributed to every man, as the Lord hath called every one, so let him walk. And so ^bordain I in all churches.

18 Is any man called being circumcised? let him not ^abecome uncircumcised. Is any called in uncircumcision? let him not be circumcised.

19 ^aCircumcision is nothing, and uncircumcision is nothing, but the keeping of the commandments of God.

20 Let every man abide in the same calling wherein he was called.

21 Art thou called *being* a servant? care not for it: but if thou mayest be made free, use *it* rather.

22 For he that is called in the Lord, *being* a servant, is the Lord's ^afreeman: likewise also he that is called, *being* free, is Christ's ^bservant.

23 Ye are ^abought with a price; be not ye the ^bservants of men.

24 Brethren, let every man, wherein he is called, therein abide with God.

25 Now concerning virgins I have no commandment of the Lord: yet I give my judgment, as one that hath obtained ^amercy of the Lord to be faithful.

26 I suppose therefore that this is good for the present ^adistress, I *say,* that *it is* good for a man so to be.

27 Art thou bound unto a wife? seek not to be loosed. Art thou loosed from a wife? seek not a wife.

28 But and if thou marry, thou hast not sinned; and if a virgin marry, she hath not sinned. Nevertheless such shall have trouble in the flesh: but I spare you.

29 ^aBut this I say, brethren, the time *is* short: it remaineth, that both they that have wives be as though they had none;

30 And they that weep, as though they wept not; and they that rejoice, as though they rejoiced not; and they that buy, as though they possessed not;

31 And they that use this world, as not abusing *it:* for the ^afashion of this ^bworld passeth away.

10a Matt. 5:32.
   TG Chastity;
   Family, Patriarchal.
 b TG Divorce.
11a TG Peacemakers;
   Reconciliation.
 b TG Divorce.
13a TG Marriage, Husbands.
14a D&C 74.
 b TG Marriage, Interfaith.
 c TG Sanctification.
 d GR cleansed.

15a GR in.
16a TG Family, Love within.
17a Rom. 12:3.
 b GR order, prescribe.
18a GR conceal, obliterate circumcision.
19a TG Circumcision.
22a Mosiah 5:8;
   D&C 88:86.
 b Eph. 6:6;
   Col. 3:24.
23a 1 Cor. 6:19 (19–20).

 b GR slaves.
25a 1 Tim. 1:13.
26a GR trial, affliction.
   JST 1 Cor. 7:26 . . .
   distress, for a man so
   to *remain that he may do
   greater good.*
29a JST 1 Cor. 7:29–33, 38
   (Appendix).
31a James 4:14;
   1 Jn. 2:17.
 b TG Worldliness.

32 But I would have you without ^acarefulness. He that is unmarried careth for the things that belong to the Lord, how he may please the Lord:

33 But he that is married careth for the things that are of the world, how he may please *his* wife.

34 There is difference *also* between a wife and a virgin. The unmarried woman careth for the things of the Lord, that she may be holy both in body and in spirit: but she that is married careth for the things of the world, how she may please *her* husband.

35 And this I speak for your own profit; not that I may cast a snare upon you, but for that which is comely, and that ye may attend upon the Lord without distraction.

36 But if any man think that he behaveth himself uncomely toward his virgin, if she pass the flower of *her* age, and need so require, let him do what he will, he sinneth not: let them marry.

37 Nevertheless he that standeth steadfast in his heart, having no necessity, but hath power over his own will, and hath so decreed in his heart that he will keep his virgin, doeth well.

38 ^aSo then he that giveth *her* in marriage doeth well; but he that giveth *her* not in marriage doeth better.

39 The ^awife is bound by the ^blaw as long as her husband liveth; but if her husband be dead, she is at liberty to be married to whom she will; only in the Lord.

40 But she is happier if she so abide, after my judgment: and I think also that I have the Spirit of God.

CHAPTER 8

There are many gods and many lords— To us there is one God (the Father) and one Lord, who is Christ.

Now ^aas touching things offered unto ^bidols, we know that we all have knowledge. Knowledge puffeth up, but ^ccharity ^dedifieth.

2 And if any man think that he knoweth any thing, he knoweth nothing yet as he ought to ^aknow.

3 But if any man love God, the same is ^aknown of him.

4 As concerning therefore the eating of those things ^athat are offered in sacrifice unto ^bidols, we know that an ^cidol *is* nothing in the world, and that *there is* none other God but one.

5 For though there be that are called gods, whether in heaven or in earth, (as there be gods many, and lords many,)

6 But to us *there is but* one ^aGod, the ^bFather, of whom *are* all things, and we in him; and one ^cLord Jesus Christ, by whom *are* ^dall things, and we by him.

7 Howbeit *there is* not in every man that knowledge: for some with conscience of the idol unto this hour eat *it* as a thing offered unto an idol; and their ^aconscience being weak is defiled.

8 But ^ameat commendeth us not to God: for neither, if we eat, are we the better; neither, if we eat not, are we the worse.

9 But take heed lest by any means this ^aliberty of yours become a

32*a* GR cares.
38*a* JST 1 Cor. 7:38 So then he that giveth *himself* in marriage doeth well; but he that giveth *himself* not in marriage doeth better.
39*a* TG Marriage, Wives.
    b TG Marriage, Temporal.
8 1*a* GR concerning.
    b Acts 15:29.
    c GR love.
       TG Charity.

d GR builds up, strengthens, establishes, repairs.
   TG Edification.
2*a* TG Education; Study.
3*a* John 10:14.
4*a* JST 1 Cor. 8:4 . . . *which are in the world* offered in sacrifice unto idols, we know that an idol is nothing, and . . .
    b Gal. 4:8.

TG Idolatry.
   c 1 Cor. 10:19 (19–20).
6*a* TG Godhead.
    b Dan. 2:47; Eph. 4:6.
    c TG Jesus Christ, Lord.
    d TG Jesus Christ, Power of.
7*a* TG Conscience.
8*a* TG Food.
9*a* TG Liberty; Motivations.

*b*stumblingblock to them that are *c*weak.

10 For if any man see thee which hast knowledge sit at meat in the idol's temple, shall not the conscience of him which is weak be emboldened to eat those things which are offered to idols;

11 And through thy knowledge shall the weak brother perish, for whom Christ died?

12 But when ye sin so against the *a*brethren, and wound their weak conscience, ye sin against Christ.

13 Wherefore, if meat *a*make my brother to *b*offend, I will *c*eat no flesh while the world standeth, lest I make my brother to offend.

CHAPTER 9

Paul rejoices in his Christian liberty—He preaches the gospel to all without charge—He is all things to all men to gain converts.

AM I not an *a*apostle? am I not free? have I not *b*seen Jesus Christ our Lord? are not ye my *c*work in the Lord?

2 If I be not an apostle unto others, yet doubtless I am to you: for the *a*seal of mine apostleship are ye in the Lord.

3 Mine *a*answer to them that do *b*examine me is this,

4 Have we not power to eat and to drink?

5 Have we not power to lead about a sister, a *a*wife, as well as other apostles, and *as* the *b*brethren of the Lord, and Cephas?

6 Or I only and Barnabas, have not we power to forbear working?

7 Who goeth a *a*warfare any time at his own charges? who planteth a *b*vineyard, and *c*eateth not of the fruit thereof? or who feedeth a flock, and eateth not of the milk of the flock?

8 Say I these things as a man? or saith not the law the same also?

9 For it is written in the law of Moses, Thou shalt not *a*muzzle the mouth of the ox that treadeth out the corn. Doth God take care for oxen?

10 Or saith he *it* altogether for our sakes? For our sakes, no doubt, *this* is *a*written: that he that ploweth should plow in hope; and that he that thresheth in hope should be *b*partaker of his hope.

11 If we have sown unto you *a*spiritual things, *is it* a great thing if we shall reap your carnal things?

12 If others be partakers of *this* power over you, *are* not we rather? Nevertheless we have not used this *a*power; but suffer all things, lest we should hinder the gospel of Christ.

13 Do ye not know that they which *a*minister about holy things *b*live *of the things* of the temple? and they which wait at the altar are partakers with the altar?

14 Even so hath the Lord ordained that they which *a*preach the *b*gospel should *c*live of the gospel.

15 But I have used none of these things: neither have I written these things, that it should be so done unto me: for *it were* better for me to die, than that any man should make my glorying void.

16 For though I preach the *a*gospel, I have nothing to glory of: for

9*b* Rom. 14:13;
    1 Cor. 10:32 (24–33).
c Rom. 14:1.
12*a* 1 Jn. 3:14 (10–18).
13*a* GR cause my brother to stumble, falter.
b Rom. 14:21 (20–21).
c TG Abstain.
9 1*a* 2 Cor. 12:11 (11–12);
    Gal. 2:7 (7–8);
    1 Tim. 2:7.
b Acts 9:17 (3, 17);
    2 Cor. 12:1 (1, 7);

Gal. 1:12.
c 1 Cor. 3:6.
2*a* GR certification, proof, token.
    2 Cor. 3:2.
3*a* GR defense.
b GR question, call into account, judge.
5*a* Matt. 8:14.
b Matt. 12:46;
    John 7:3 (3, 5, 10).
7*a* 2 Cor. 10:4.
b Deut. 20:6.

c Prov. 27:18.
9*a* Deut. 25:4.
10*a* Rom. 15:4.
b 2 Tim. 2:6 (5–6).
11*a* Rom. 15:27.
12*a* GR authority.
13*a* Deut. 18:1 (1–2).
b GR eat.
14*a* Rom. 2:21 (21–23);
    Alma 39:11 (11–12).
b TG Gospel.
c Matt. 10:10.
16*a* TG Gospel.

*b*necessity is laid upon me; yea, woe is unto me, if I *c*preach not the gospel!

17 For if I do this thing *a*willingly, I have a *b*reward: but if against my will, a *c*dispensation *of the gospel* is committed unto me.

18 What is my reward then? *Verily* that, when I preach the gospel, I may make the gospel of Christ without *a*charge, that I abuse not my power in the gospel.

19 For though I be free from all *men*, yet have I made myself *a*servant unto all, that I might gain the more.

20 And unto the Jews I became as a Jew, that I might gain the Jews; to them that are under the law, as under the law, that I might gain them that are under the law;

21 To them that are without law, as without law, (being not without law to God, but under the law to Christ,) that I might gain them that are without law.

22 To the weak became I as *a*weak, that I might gain the weak: I am made *b*all things to all *men*, that I might by all means save some.

23 And this I do for the gospel's sake, that I might be partaker thereof with *you*.

24 Know ye not that they which run in a race run all, but one receiveth the prize? So run, that ye may obtain.

25 And every man that striveth for the *a*mastery is *b*temperate in all things. Now they *do it* to obtain a corruptible *c*crown; but we an *d*incorruptible.

26 I therefore so run, not as uncertainly; so fight I, not as one that beateth the air:

27 But I *a*keep under my *b*body, and bring *it* into subjection: lest that by any means, when I have preached to others, I myself should be a castaway.

CHAPTER 10

Christ is the God of Israel and the spiritual Rock that guided them— Ancient Israel rebelled against Christ —Paul contrasts true and false sacraments.

MOREOVER, brethren, I would not that ye should be ignorant, how that all our fathers were under the *a*cloud, and all passed through the *b*sea;

2 And were all *a*baptized unto Moses in the cloud and in the sea;

3 And did all eat the same spiritual *a*meat;

4 And did all drink the same spiritual drink: for they drank of that spiritual Rock that followed them: and that *a*Rock was Christ.

5 But with many of them *a*God was not well *b*pleased: for they were *c*overthrown in the *d*wilderness.

6 Now these things were our *a*examples, to the intent we should not *b*lust after evil things, as they also lusted.

7 Neither be ye idolaters, as *were* some of them; as it is written, The *a*people sat down to eat and drink, and rose up to play.

8 Neither let us commit *a*fornication, as some of them committed,

16*b* TG Duty.
  c TG Missionary Work;
      Preaching.
17*a* TG Initiative.
  b TG Reward.
  c Gal. 2:7.
      TG Dispensations.
18*a* Acts 20:34 (33–34);
      2 Cor. 11:7;
      1 Thes. 2:9;
      Mosiah 2:14 (12, 14–18).
19*a* 2 Cor. 4:5.
      TG Servant.
22*a* 2 Cor. 11:29.
  b 1 Cor. 10:33 (32–33).
25*a* 2 Tim. 2:5.

      TG Self-Mastery.
  b TG Temperance.
  c TG Reward.
  d 1 Pet. 1:4 (1–16).
27*a* GR rigorously discipline.
  b TG Chastity.
10 1*a* Ps. 99:7;
      D&C 103:20 (19–20).
  b TG Israel,
      Deliverance of.
2*a* TG Baptism;
      Baptism, Essential.
3*a* Ex. 16:15.
4*a* 3 Ne. 15:5.
      TG Cornerstone;
      Jesus Christ, Jehovah;

      Jesus Christ, Types of,
      in Anticipation;
      Rock.
5*a* Num. 21:5;
      Ezek. 20:13 (10–26).
  b D&C 68:31.
  c GR strewn, buried.
      Heb. 3:17.
  d Num. 26:65 (64–65);
      Jude 1:5.
6*a* GR types.
  b GR desire, long for.
      TG Lust.
7*a* Ex. 32:6.
8*a* TG Fornication.

and fell in one day three and twenty thousand.

9 Neither let us ^atempt Christ, as some of them also tempted, and were destroyed of serpents.

10 Neither ^amurmur ye, as some of them also murmured, and were ^bdestroyed of the destroyer.

11 Now all these things happened unto them for ^aensamples: ^band they are ^cwritten for our ^dadmonition, upon whom the ends of the world are come.

12 Wherefore let him that thinketh he ^astandeth take heed lest he ^bfall.

13 There hath no temptation ^ataken you but such as is common to man: but God *is* faithful, who will not suffer you to be ^btempted above that ye are able; but will with the ^ctemptation also make a way to ^descape, that ye may be able to ^ebear *it*.

14 Wherefore, my dearly beloved, flee from ^aidolatry.

15 I speak as to wise men; judge ye what I say.

16 The ^acup of ^bblessing which we bless, is it not the ^ccommunion of the blood of Christ? The bread which we break, is it not the communion of the body of Christ?

17 For we *being* many are one bread, *and* one body: for we are all partakers of that one bread.

18 Behold Israel after the flesh: are not they which eat of the sacrifices ^apartakers of the altar?

19 What say I then? that the idol is any thing, or that which is offered in sacrifice to ^aidols is any thing?

20 But *I say*, that the things which the Gentiles sacrifice, they ^asacrifice to devils, and not to God: and I would not that ye should have fellowship with devils.

21 Ye cannot drink the ^acup of the Lord, and the cup of devils: ye cannot be partakers of the Lord's table, and of the table of devils.

22 Do we provoke the Lord to ^ajealousy? are we stronger than he?

23 ^aAll things are lawful for me, but all things are not ^bexpedient: all things are lawful for me, but all things ^cedify not.

24 Let no man seek his ^aown, but every man another's ^bwealth.

25 Whatsoever is sold in the ^ashambles, *that* eat, asking no question for conscience sake:

26 For the ^aearth *is* the Lord's, and the fulness thereof.

27 If any of them that believe not bid you *to a ^afeast*, and ye be disposed to go; whatsoever is set before you, eat, asking no question for conscience sake.

28 But if any man say unto you, This is offered in sacrifice unto idols, eat not for his sake that shewed it, and for conscience sake: for the earth *is* the Lord's, and the fulness thereof:

29 Conscience, I say, not thine own, but of the other: for why is my

9 *a* TG Test.
10 *a* TG Murmuring.
   b Num. 14:37.
11 *a* GR types.
   TG Example.
   b JST 1 Cor. 10:11 . . . and they *were* written for our admonition *also, and for an admonition for those* upon whom the *end* of the world *shall* come.
   c Rom. 15:4.
   d TG Warn.
12 *a* Philip. 4:1 (1–7).
   b Acts 1:25;
   D&C 3:9; 58:15.
13 *a* GR seized upon.

   b Job 4:7 (1, 2, 7); 37:23;
   Ps. 34:17 (17, 19);
   1 Ne. 22:19;
   Alma 14:11.
   TG Test.
   c TG Temptation.
   d D&C 95:1.
   e TG Strength.
14 *a* TG Idolatry.
16 *a* Matt. 26:27 (26–29).
   b TG Blessing.
   c GR aid, fellowship, partnership.
18 *a* GR sharers, partners.
19 *a* 1 Cor. 8:4.
20 *a* Deut. 32:17.
   TG Sacrifice;
   Superstitions.

21 *a* 2 Cor. 6:16 (14–17).
22 *a* TG Jealous.
23 *a* JST 1 Cor. 10:23 All things are *not* lawful for me, *for* all things are not expedient; all things are *not* lawful, *for* all things edify not.
   b GR advantageous, appropriate, beneficial.
   c TG Edification.
24 *a* Philip. 2:21 (17–30).
   b JST 1 Cor. 10:24 . . . *good*.
25 *a* GR market.
26 *a* Ps. 24:1.
   TG God, Works of.
27 *a* Ex. 34:15.

liberty judged of another *man's* ^aconscience?

30 For if I ^aby grace be a partaker, why am I evil spoken of for that for which I give thanks?

31 Whether therefore ye eat, or drink, or whatsoever ye do, ^ado all to the glory of God.

32 Give none ^aoffence, neither to the Jews, nor to the Gentiles, nor to the church of God:

33 Even as I please all *men* in all *things*, not ^aseeking mine own profit, but the ^b*profit* of many, that they may be ^csaved.

CHAPTER 11

Paul speaks of certain customs of hair and grooming—Heresies will arise that test and prove the faithful—The sacramental emblems are partaken in remembrance of the flesh and blood of Christ—Beware of partaking unworthily.

BE ye ^afollowers of me, even as I also *am* of Christ.

2 Now I praise you, brethren, ^athat ye remember me in all things, and keep the ^bordinances, as I delivered *them* to you.

3 But I would have you know, that the head of every man is Christ; and the ^ahead of the ^bwoman *is* the man; and the ^chead of Christ *is* God.

4 Every man praying or prophesying, having *his* head covered, dishonoureth his head.

5 But every woman that prayeth or prophesieth with *her* head uncovered dishonoureth her head: for that is ^aeven all one as if she were shaven.

6 For if the woman be not covered, let her also be shorn: but if it be a ^ashame for a woman to be shorn or shaven, let her be covered.

7 For a man indeed ought not to cover *his* head, forasmuch as he is the image and glory of God: but the woman is the glory of the man.

8 For the man is not of the woman; but the woman of the man.

9 Neither was the man created for the woman; but the woman for the man.

10 For this cause ought the woman to have power on *her* head because of the angels.

11 Nevertheless neither is the ^aman without the woman, neither the ^bwoman without the man, in the Lord.

12 For as the woman *is* of the man, even so *is* the man also by the woman; but all things of God.

13 Judge in yourselves: is it ^acomely that a woman pray unto God uncovered?

14 Doth not even nature itself teach you, that, if a man have long ^ahair, it is a shame unto him?

15 But if a woman have long hair, it is a glory to her: for *her* hair is given her for a covering.

16 But if any man seem to be ^acontentious, we have no such custom, neither the churches of God.

17 Now in this that I declare *unto you* I praise *you* not, that ye come together not for the better, but for the worse.

18 For first of all, when ye come

29*a* TG Conscience.
30*a* GR with gratitude, graciousness.
31*a* Col. 3:17 (17–23).
32*a* Rom. 14:13 (11–21); 1 Cor. 8:9 (7–13). TG Offense.
33*a* 2 Cor. 12:14.
  b GR benefit, advantage.
  c 1 Cor. 9:22 (19–23).
11 1*a* GR imitators. 1 Cor. 4:16; Eph. 5:1 (1–5).

2*a* GR because.
  b GR precepts, doctrines, traditions. TG Ordinance.
3*a* TG Marriage, Husbands.
  b TG Marriage, Wives; Woman.
  c TG Jesus Christ, Relationships with the Father.
5*a* GR one and the same as.
6*a* TG Shame.

11*a* TG Family, Eternal; Marriage, Celestial; Marriage, Continuing Courtship in; Marriage, Husbands.
  b TG Marriage, Wives.
13*a* GR proper, fitting, becoming.
14*a* Ezek. 44:20.
16*a* 1 Cor. 14:33 (33, 40); 3 Ne. 11:22. TG Contention.

together in the ªchurch, I hear that there be ᵇdivisions among you; and I partly believe it.

19 For there must be also ªheresies among you, that they which are approved may be made manifest among you.

20 When ye come together therefore into one place, ªthis is not to eat the Lord's supper.

21 For in eating every one taketh before *other* his own supper: and one is hungry, and another is drunken.

22 What? have ye not houses to eat and to drink in? or despise ye the ªchurch of God, and ᵇshame them that have not? What shall I say to you? shall I praise you in this? I praise *you* not.

23 For I have received of the Lord that which also I delivered unto you, That the Lord Jesus the *same* night in which he was betrayed took ªbread:

24 And when he had given thanks, he brake *it,* and said, Take, eat: this is my body, which is broken for you: this do in ªremembrance of me.

25 After the same manner also *he took* the cup, when he had supped, saying, This cup is the new testament in my blood: this do ye, as oft as ye drink *it,* in remembrance of me.

26 For as often as ye eat this ªbread, and drink this cup, ye do ᵇshew the Lord's ᶜdeath till he come.

27 Wherefore whosoever shall eat this ªbread, and drink *this* cup of the Lord, ᵇunworthily, shall ᶜbe ᵈguilty of the body and blood of the Lord.

28 But let a man ªexamine himself,

and so let him eat of *that* bread, and drink of *that* cup.

29 For he that eateth and drinketh ªunworthily, eateth and drinketh ᵇdamnation to himself, not discerning the Lord's body.

30 For this cause many *are* weak and ªsickly among you, and many sleep.

31 For if we would ªjudge ourselves, we should not be judged.

32 But when we are judged, we are ªchastened of the Lord, that we should not be condemned with the world.

33 Wherefore, my brethren, when ye come together to eat, tarry one for another.

34 And if any man hunger, let him eat at home; that ye come not together unto condemnation. And the rest will I set in order when I come.

CHAPTER 12

The Holy Ghost reveals that Jesus is the Christ—Spiritual gifts are present among the Saints—Apostles, prophets, and miracles are found in the true Church.

Now concerning spiritual *gifts,* brethren, I would not have you ignorant.

2 Ye know that ye were Gentiles, ªcarried away unto these dumb ᵇidols, even as ye were led.

3 Wherefore I give you to understand, that no man speaking by the Spirit of God calleth Jesus accursed: and *that* no man can ªsay that Jesus is the ᵇLord, but by the ᶜHoly Ghost.

4 Now there are diversities of ªgifts, but the same Spirit.

18a TG Assembly for
    Worship; Meetings.
  b GR dissensions, schisms.
    TG Apostasy of the
    Early Christian Church;
    Church.
19a GR sects, factions.
20a JST 1 Cor. 11:20 . . . *is
    it* not to eat the Lord's
    supper?
22a TG Church.
  b TG Shame.
23a 3 Ne. 20:8 (3–9).
24a TG Jesus Christ, Types
    of, in Memory.

26a TG Sacrament.
  b GR proclaim, announce.
  c TG Jesus Christ,
    Death of.
27a TG Bread of Life.
  b 3 Ne. 18:29 (28–32);
    Morm. 9:29.
  c GR offend against.
  d TG Guilt.
28a 2 Cor. 13:5 (5–7).
29a TG Sacrament.
  b GR condemnation,
    judgment.
    TG Damnation.
30a TG Sickness.

31a GR scrutinize, examine.
32a TG Chastening.
12 2a GR led astray.
  b TG Idolatry.
3a TG Revelation;
    Testimony.
  b TG Jesus Christ, Lord.
  c John 6:44 (44, 63–65).
    TG Holy Ghost,
    Mission of; Holy Ghost,
    Source of Testimony;
    Inspiration.
4a TG God, Gifts of;
    Holy Ghost, Gifts of;
    Holy Ghost, Mission of.

5 And there are differences of administrations, but the same Lord.

6 And there are diversities of operations, but it is the same God which worketh all in all.

7 But the manifestation of the ^aSpirit is given to every man to profit withal.

8 For to one is ^agiven by the ^bSpirit the ^cword of ^dwisdom; to another the word of ^eknowledge by the same Spirit;

9 To another ^afaith by the same Spirit; to another the gifts of ^bhealing by the same Spirit;

10 To another the working of ^amiracles; to another ^bprophecy; to another ^cdiscerning of spirits; to another *divers* kinds of tongues; to another the interpretation of ^dtongues:

11 But all these worketh that one and the selfsame Spirit, dividing to every man severally as he will.

12 For as the body is one, and hath many members, and all the members of that one body, being many, are one body: so also *is* Christ.

13 For by one Spirit are we all baptized into one ^abody, whether *we be* Jews or ^bGentiles, whether *we be* ^cbond or free; and have been all made to drink into one Spirit.

14 For the body is not one member, but many.

15 If the foot shall say, Because I am not the hand, I am not of the body; is it therefore not of the body?

16 And if the ear shall say, Because I am not the eye, I am not of the body; is it therefore not of the body?

17 If the whole body *were* an eye, where *were* the hearing? If the whole *were* hearing, where *were* the smelling?

18 But now hath God set the members every one of them in the body, as it hath pleased him.

19 And if they were all one member, where *were* the body?

20 But now *are they* many members, yet but one body.

21 And the eye cannot say unto the hand, I have no need of thee: nor again the ^ahead to the feet, I have no need of you.

22 Nay, much more those members of the body, which seem to be ^amore feeble, are necessary:

23 And those *members* of the body, which we think to be less honourable, upon these we bestow more abundant honour; and our uncomely *parts* have more abundant comeliness.

24 For our comely *parts* have no need: but God hath tempered the body together, having given more abundant honour to that *part* which lacked:

25 That there should be no schism in the body; but *that* the members should have the same ^acare one for another.

26 And whether one member ^asuffer, all the members ^bsuffer with it; or one member be honoured, all the members rejoice with it.

27 Now ye are the body of ^aChrist, and ^bmembers in particular.

28 And God hath set some in the church, first ^aapostles, secondarily ^bprophets, thirdly ^cteachers, after that miracles, then gifts of healings, helps, ^dgovernments, diversities of tongues.

29 *Are* all apostles? *are* all prophets?

7*a* D&C 46:16 (8–18).
  TG God, Spirit of.
8*a* D&C 35:23.
  b D&C 25:7; 35:19.
  c D&C 89:2.
  d TG Wisdom.
  e Moro. 10:10.
  TG Holy Ghost, Gifts of;
  Knowledge.
9*a* TG Faith.
  b TG Heal.
10*a* TG Miracle.
  b TG Prophecy.
  c TG Discernment,
  Spiritual.
  d TG Language.
13*a* TG Church.
  b GR Greeks.
  Col. 3:11.
  c GR slaves.
  D&C 24:11; 43:20.
21*a* D&C 84:109.
  TG Leadership.
22*a* GR weaker.
25*a* 1 Cor. 1:10 (10–15).
26*a* TG Suffering.
  b TG Compassion.
27*a* TG Jesus Christ, Head of
  the Church.
  b TG Church
  Organization.
28*a* TG Apostles.
  b TG Prophets,
  Mission of.
  c TG Teacher.
  d TG Governments.

are all teachers? *are* all workers of
^amiracles?

30 Have all the gifts of healing?
do all speak with tongues? do all
interpret?

31 But ^acovet earnestly the best
^bgifts: and yet shew I unto you a
more ^cexcellent way.

CHAPTER 13

*Paul discusses the high status of char-
ity—Charity, a pure love, excels and
exceeds almost all else.*

THOUGH I speak with the tongues
of men and of angels, and have not
^acharity, I am become *as* sounding
brass, or a tinkling cymbal.

2 And though I have *the gift of*
^aprophecy, and understand all
^bmysteries, and all knowledge; and
though I have all faith, so that I
could remove mountains, and have
not charity, I am nothing.

3 And though I bestow all my goods
to feed *the* ^apoor, and though I give
my body to be burned, and have
not charity, it profiteth me nothing.

4 ^aCharity ^bsuffereth long, *and* is
^ckind; charity ^denvieth not; charity
vaunteth not itself, is not puffed up,

5 Doth not behave itself ^aunseemly,
^bseeketh not her own, is not easily
^cprovoked, thinketh no evil;

6 Rejoiceth not in ^ainiquity, but
rejoiceth in the ^btruth;

7 Beareth all things, believeth all
things, hopeth all things, endureth
all things.

8 Charity never ^afaileth: but
whether *there be* prophecies, they

shall fail; whether *there be* tongues,
they shall cease; whether *there be*
knowledge, it shall vanish away.

9 For we know in part, and we
prophesy in part.

10 But when that which is perfect
is come, then that which is in part
shall be done away.

11 When I was a child, I spake as
a child, I understood as a child, I
thought as a child: but when I became a man, I put away childish
things.

12 For now we see through a ^aglass,
^bdarkly; but then face to face: now I
know in part; but then shall I know
even as also I am known.

13 And now abideth ^afaith, ^bhope,
^ccharity, these three; but the great-
est of these *is* charity.

CHAPTER 14

*People should desire spiritual gifts—
Tongues and prophecy are compared—
Prophecy is the greater gift—Paul says,
You may all prophesy; covet to prophesy.*

^aFOLLOW after charity, and desire
spiritual ^bgifts, but rather that ye
may prophesy.

2 For he that speaketh in ^aan *unknown* tongue speaketh not unto
men, but unto God: for no man
understandeth *him*; howbeit in the
spirit he speaketh mysteries.

3 But he that ^aprophesieth speaketh unto men *to* ^bedification, and
exhortation, and comfort.

4 He that speaketh in an *unknown*
tongue edifieth himself; but he that
prophesieth edifieth the church.

29a TG Miracle.
31a GR seek earnestly, be
   zealous for.
   D&C 46:8 (8–9).
   TG Covet.
 b TG Holy Ghost, Gifts of.
 c Ether 12:11 (11–12, 32).
13 1a GR love.
 2a TG Prophecy.
 b TG Mysteries of
   Godliness.
 3a TG Welfare.
 4a TG Charity;
   Courtesy.
 b TG Forbear;
   Suffering.

 c TG Benevolence.
 d TG Envy.
 5a GR indecently,
   unbecomingly.
 b TG Selfishness.
 c TG Anger;
   Provoking;
   Self-Mastery.
 6a GR injustice,
   unrighteousness.
 b TG Truth.
 8a TG Dependability.
12a 2 Cor. 3:18;
   James 1:23 (22–27).
   TG Veil.
 b GR obscurely,

   enigmatically.
13a TG Faith.
 b TG Hope.
 c TG Love.
14 1a GR Pursue, follow
   eagerly, earnestly.
 b TG Holy Ghost, Gifts of.
 2a JST 1 Cor. 14:2 . . .
   another tongue . . .
   (Note: JST uses
   "another" in place of
   "an unknown" in every
   instance in vv. 4, 13, 14,
   19, 27.)
 3a TG Prophecy.
 b TG Edification.

5 I *a*would that ye all spake with tongues, but rather that ye *b*prophesied: for greater *is* he that prophesieth than he that speaketh with tongues, except he interpret, that the church may receive edifying.

6 Now, brethren, if I come unto you speaking with tongues, what shall I profit you, *a*except I shall speak to you either by *b*revelation, or by knowledge, or by prophesying, or by doctrine?

7 And even things without life giving sound, whether pipe or harp, except they give a distinction in the sounds, how shall it be known what is piped or harped?

8 For if the trumpet give an uncertain sound, who shall prepare himself to the battle?

9 So likewise ye, except ye utter by the tongue words easy to be understood, how shall it be known what is spoken? for ye shall speak into the air.

10 There are, it may be, so many kinds of *a*voices in the world, and none of them *is* without signification.

11 Therefore if I know not the meaning of the voice, I shall be unto him that speaketh a barbarian, and he that speaketh *shall be* a barbarian unto me.

12 Even so ye, *a*forasmuch as ye are zealous of spiritual *b*gifts, seek that ye may excel to the *c*edifying of the church.

13 Wherefore let him that speaketh in an *unknown* tongue pray that he may interpret.

14 For if I pray in an *unknown* tongue, my spirit prayeth, but my *a*understanding is unfruitful.

15 What is it then? I will pray with the spirit, and I will pray with the understanding also: I will sing with the spirit, and I will sing with the understanding also.

16 Else when thou shalt bless with the spirit, how shall he that occupieth the room of the unlearned say Amen at thy giving of thanks, seeing he understandeth not what thou sayest?

17 For thou verily givest thanks well, but the other is not edified.

18 I thank my God, I speak with tongues more than ye all:

19 Yet in the church I had rather *a*speak five words with my understanding, that *by my voice* I might teach others also, than ten thousand words in an *unknown* tongue.

20 Brethren, be not *a*children in *b*understanding: howbeit in *c*malice be ye children, but in *d*understanding be men.

21 In the law it is written, With *men of* other tongues and other lips will I speak unto this people; and yet for all that will they not *a*hear me, saith the Lord.

22 Wherefore *a*tongues are for a *b*sign, not to them that believe, but to them that believe not: but *c*prophesying *serveth* not for them that believe not, but for them which believe.

23 If therefore the whole church come together into one place, and all speak with tongues, and there come in *those that are* unlearned, or *a*unbelievers, will they not say that ye are mad?

24 But if all prophesy, and there come in one that believeth not, or *one* unlearned, he is convinced of all, he is judged of all:

25 And thus are the *a*secrets of his heart made manifest; and so falling down on *his* face he will worship God, and report that God is in you of a truth.

26 How is it then, brethren? when ye come together, every one of you hath a psalm, hath a doctrine, hath a tongue, hath a revelation, hath an

---

5*a* GR wish.
  b TG Prophecy.
6*a* GR unless.
  b TG Revelation.
10*a* TG Revelation.
12*a* GR since.
  b D&C 46:10.
  c TG Edification.

14*a* GR mind.
19*a* TG Language.
20*a* Matt. 18:3 (1–6);
    Eph. 4:14.
  b TG Understanding.
  c GR wickedness,
    depravity.
    TG Malice.

d TG Education.
21*a* GR listen to, heed.
22*a* Acts 2:11.
  b TG Signs.
  c TG Prophecy.
23*a* Acts 2:13 (12–13).
25*a* Heb. 4:12 (12–13).

interpretation. Let all things be done unto ^aedifying.

27 If any man speak in an *unknown* tongue, *let it be* by two, or at the most *by* three, and *that* by course; and let one interpret.

28 But if there be no interpreter, let him keep ^asilence in the church; and let him speak to himself, and to God.

29 Let the prophets speak two or three, and let the other judge.

30 If *any thing* be revealed to another that sitteth by, let the first hold his peace.

31 For ye may all prophesy one by one, that all may learn, and all may be comforted.

32 And the spirits of the prophets are subject to the prophets.

33 For God is not *the* ^aauthor of ^bconfusion, but of ^cpeace, as in all ^dchurches of the ^esaints.

34 Let your ^awomen keep silence in the churches: for it is not permitted unto them to ^bspeak; but *they are commanded* ^cto be under ^dobedience, as also saith the law.

35 And if they will learn any thing, let them ask their husbands at home: for it is a shame for women to ^aspeak in the church.

36 What? came the word of God out from you? or came it unto you only?

37 If any man think himself to be a prophet, or spiritual, let him acknowledge that the things that I write unto you are the commandments of the Lord.

38 But if any man be ignorant, let him be ignorant.

39 Wherefore, brethren, ^acovet to prophesy, and forbid not to speak with tongues.

40 Let all things be done decently and in ^aorder.

CHAPTER 15

Christ died for our sins—He rose from the dead and was seen by many—All men will be resurrected—Paul speaks of baptism for the dead—The three degrees of glory are described—Victory over death comes through Christ.

MOREOVER, brethren, I ^adeclare unto you the ^bgospel which I preached unto you, which also ye have received, and wherein ye stand;

2 By which also ye are ^asaved, if ye ^bkeep in memory what I preached unto you, unless ye have believed in vain.

3 For I delivered unto you first of all that which I also received, how that Christ ^adied for our ^bsins according to the scriptures;

4 And that he was buried, and that he ^arose again the third day according to the scriptures:

5 And that he was ^aseen of ^bCephas, then of the twelve:

6 After that, he was ^aseen of ^babove five hundred brethren at once; of whom the greater part remain unto this present, but some are fallen asleep.

7 After that, he was seen of James; then of all the apostles.

8 And last of all he was ^aseen of me also, as of one born out of due time.

9 For I am the least of the apostles, that am not ^ameet to be called an

26a 2 Cor. 12:19;
   D&C 50:23.
28a TG Silence.
33a 1 Cor. 11:16 (16–19).
   b Eph. 4:5 (3–6), 13;
    D&C 1:30.
   c TG Peace; Peace of God.
   d TG Church.
   e TG Saints.
34a TG Woman.
   b JST 1 Cor. 14:34 ... *rule* ...
   c GR to be submissive.
   d TG Obedience.
35a JST 1 Cor. 14:35 ... *rule* ...

39a IE be eager, zealous.
   TG Covet.
40a TG Order.
15 1a TG Missionary Work.
   b TG Gospel.
2a Rom. 1:16.
   b GR hold fast to, retain.
3a D&C 54:1.
   TG Jesus Christ,
    Death of;
    Jesus Christ, Redeemer.
   b Acts 3:18;
    Alma 5:27.
4a TG Jesus Christ,

   Resurrection.
5a TG Jesus Christ,
    Appearances,
    Postmortal.
   b Luke 24:34 (33–36).
6a TG Jesus Christ,
    Appearances,
    Postmortal.
   b GR more than, over.
8a TG Jesus Christ,
    Appearances,
    Postmortal.
9a GR adequate, sufficient,
    competent.

apostle, because I [b]persecuted the church of God.

10 But by the [a]grace of God I am what I am: and his grace which *was* bestowed upon me was not in vain; but I [b]laboured more abundantly than they all: yet not I, but the grace of God which was with me.

11 Therefore whether *it were* I or they, so we preach, and so ye believed.

12 Now if Christ be preached that he rose from the dead, how say some among you that there is no resurrection of the dead?

13 But if there be no resurrection of the dead, then is Christ not risen:

14 And if Christ be not risen, then *is* our preaching vain, and your faith *is* also vain.

15 Yea, and we are found false witnesses of God; because we have [a]testified of God that he raised up Christ: whom he raised not up, if so be that the dead rise not.

16 For if the dead rise not, then is not Christ raised:

17 And if Christ be not raised, your faith *is* [a]vain; ye are yet in your sins.

18 Then they also which are fallen asleep in Christ are [a]perished.

19 If in this [a]life only we have [b]hope in Christ, we are of all men most miserable.

20 But now is [a]Christ [b]risen from the dead, *and* become the [c]firstfruits of them that slept.

21 For since by man *came* [a]death, by man *came* also the [b]resurrection of the dead.

22 For as in [a]Adam all [b]die, even so in [c]Christ shall all be made [d]alive.

23 But every man in his own [a]order: Christ the [b]firstfruits; afterward they that are Christ's at his [c]coming.

24 Then *cometh* the end, when he shall have delivered up the kingdom to God, even the Father; when he shall have [a]put down all [b]rule and all [c]authority and [d]power.

25 For he must [a]reign, till he hath put all [b]enemies under his [c]feet.

26 The last [a]enemy *that* shall be [b]destroyed *is* [c]death.

27 For he hath put all things under his feet. But when he saith all things are put under *him, it is* [a]manifest that he is excepted, which did put all things under him.

28 And when all things shall be [a]subdued unto him, then shall the Son also himself be [b]subject unto him that put all things under him, that God may be all in all.

29 Else what shall they do which are [a]baptized [b]for the dead, if the dead [c]rise not at all? why are they then baptized for the [d]dead?

30 And why stand we in [a]jeopardy every hour?

9b Acts 8:3.
10a TG Grace.
  b 2 Cor. 11:23.
15a Acts 4:33.
17a GR useless, empty, ineffective.
18a GR lost, destroyed.
19a TG Salvation for the Dead.
  b TG Hope.
20a 1 Pet. 1:3.
  b Eph. 1:20.
  c GR firstling.
21a Rom. 5:12.
  TG Death.
  b TG Resurrection.
22a TG Adam; Fall of Man.
  b Ps. 82:7.
  c TG Salvation, Plan of.
  d TG Immortality; Jesus Christ, Atonement

through;
Jesus Christ, Mission of;
Jesus Christ,
Resurrection;
Salvation.
23a GR rank.
  TG Order.
  b GR firstling.
  TG Resurrection.
  c TG Jesus Christ, Second Coming.
24a GR brought to an end, abolished.
  b Isa. 60:12;
  Dan. 2:44; 7:9.
  c TG Authority.
  d TG Jesus Christ, Power of.
25a TG Jesus Christ, Millennial Reign.
  b D&C 88:106.

c Heb. 2:8.
26a TG Enemies.
  b TG Death, Power over.
  c 2 Tim. 1:10;
  Rev. 20:14 (11–15).
27a GR clear, plain, evident.
28a Philip. 3:21;
  D&C 76:106.
  b TG Jesus Christ, Relationships with the Father.
29a TG Baptism, Essential; Baptism for the Dead; Genealogy and Temple Work.
  b GR in behalf of, for the sake of.
  c TG Immortality.
  d TG Salvation for the Dead.
30a GR danger, peril.

31 ^aI protest by your rejoicing which I have in Christ Jesus our Lord, I die daily.

32 If after the manner of men I have fought with beasts at Ephesus, what advantageth it me, if the dead rise not? let us ^aeat and drink; for ^bto morrow we die.

33 Be not deceived: evil ^acommunications corrupt good manners.

34 Awake to righteousness, and sin not; for some have not the knowledge of God: I speak *this* to your ^ashame.

35 But some *man* will say, How are the dead raised up? and with what body do they come?

36 *Thou* fool, that which thou sowest is not quickened, except it ^adie:

37 And that which thou sowest, thou sowest not that body that shall be, but bare grain, ^ait may chance of wheat, or of some other *grain:*

38 But God giveth it a body as it hath pleased him, and to every seed his own body.

39 All flesh *is* not the same flesh: but *there is* one *kind of* flesh of men, another flesh of beasts, another of fishes, *and* another of birds.

40 ^a*There are* also celestial bodies, and bodies terrestrial: but the glory of the ^bcelestial *is* one, and the glory of the ^cterrestrial *is* another.

41 *There is* one glory of the ^asun, and another glory of the moon, and another glory of the ^bstars: for *one* star ^cdiffereth from *another* star in ^dglory.

42 So also *is* the resurrection of the dead. It is sown in ^acorruption; it is raised in incorruption:

43 It is sown in dishonour; it is raised in ^aglory: it is sown in weakness; it is raised in power:

44 It is sown a ^anatural body; it is raised a ^bspiritual body. There is a natural body, and there is a spiritual body.

45 And so it is written, The ^afirst man ^bAdam was made a living soul; the last ^cAdam *was made* a ^dquickening spirit.

46 Howbeit that *was* not ^afirst which is spiritual, but that which is natural; and afterward that which is spiritual.

47 The first man *is* of the earth, earthy: the second man *is* the Lord from heaven.

48 As *is* the earthy, such *are* they also that are earthy: and as *is* the heavenly, such *are* they also that are heavenly.

49 And as we have borne the image of the earthy, we shall also bear the image of the heavenly.

50 Now this I say, brethren, that ^aflesh and ^bblood cannot ^cinherit the kingdom of God; neither doth ^dcorruption inherit incorruption.

51 Behold, I shew you a mystery; We shall not all ^asleep, but we shall all be ^bchanged,

52 In a moment, in the ^atwinkling of an eye, at the last trump: for the ^btrumpet shall sound, and the ^cdead shall be raised incorruptible, and we shall be ^dchanged.

31a JST 1 Cor. 15:31 I protest *unto you the resurrection of the dead; and this is my* rejoicing which I have in Christ Jesus our Lord *daily, though I die.*
32a Isa. 22:13;
    Luke 12:19;
    2 Ne. 28:7.
   b TG Procrastination.
33a GR conversations, associations.
34a TG Shame.
36a John 12:24 (24–29).
37a IE whether it be.
40a JST 1 Cor. 15:40 Also celestial bodies, and bodies terrestrial, *and*

bodies telestial; but the glory of the celestial, one; and the terrestrial, another; *and the telestial, another.*
   b TG Celestial Glory.
   c TG Terrestrial Glory.
41a TG Astronomy.
   b TG Telestial Glory.
   c D&C 76:98.
   d TG Glory.
42a Rom. 8:21;
    Mosiah 16:10.
43a Col. 3:4.
44a D&C 29:43.
   b Alma 11:45;
    D&C 88:27.
45a D&C 84:16.

   b TG Adam.
   c Rom. 5:14.
   d John 5:21.
46a D&C 29:32;
    128:14 (13–14).
50a TG Flesh and Blood.
   b Lev. 17:14 (11, 14).
   c John 3:5;
    1 Cor. 6:9.
   d Alma 41:4.
51a GR die, sleep in death.
    1 Thes. 4:17.
   b Philip. 3:21;
    D&C 43:32.
52a D&C 63:51 (50–51).
   b D&C 29:26.
   c TG Death.
   d D&C 101:31.

53 For this ^acorruptible must put on incorruption, and this ^bmortal *must* put on immortality.

54 So when this corruptible shall have put on incorruption, and this mortal shall have put on ^aimmortality, then shall be brought to pass the saying that is written, ^bDeath is swallowed up in victory.

55 O ^adeath, where *is* thy sting? O ^bgrave, where *is* thy victory?

56 The sting of ^adeath *is* sin; and the ^bstrength of sin *is* the law.

57 But ^athanks *be* to God, which giveth us the ^bvictory through our Lord Jesus Christ.

58 Therefore, my beloved brethren, be ye ^asteadfast, unmoveable, always abounding in the work of the Lord, forasmuch as ye know that your labour is not in vain in the Lord.

CHAPTER 16

Paul counsels, Stand fast in the faith; let all things be done with charity.

Now concerning the ^acollection for the saints, as I have ^bgiven order to the churches of Galatia, even so do ye.

2 Upon the ^afirst *day* of the week let every one of you lay by him in store, as *God* hath ^bprospered him, that there be no gatherings when I come.

3 And when I come, whomsoever ye shall approve by *your* letters, them will I send to bring your ^aliberality unto Jerusalem.

4 And if it be ^ameet that I go also, they shall go with me.

5 Now I will come unto you, when I shall pass through Macedonia: for I do pass through Macedonia.

6 And it may be that I will abide, yea, and winter with you, that ye may bring me on my journey whithersoever I go.

7 For I will not see you now ^aby the way; but I ^btrust to ^ctarry a while with you, if the Lord permit.

8 But I will tarry at Ephesus until Pentecost.

9 For a great ^adoor and ^beffectual is opened unto me, and *there are* many adversaries.

10 Now if ^aTimotheus come, see that he may be with you without fear: for he worketh the work of the Lord, as I also *do*.

11 Let no man therefore ^adespise him: but conduct him forth in peace, that he may come unto me: for I look for him with the brethren.

12 As touching *our* brother ^aApollos, I greatly desired him to come unto you with the brethren: but his will was not at all to come at this time; but he will come when he shall have convenient time.

13 ^aWatch ye, ^bstand fast in the ^cfaith, ^dquit you like ^emen, be strong.

14 Let all your things be done with ^acharity.

15 I beseech you, brethren, (ye know the house of ^aStephanas, that it is the firstfruits of Achaia, and *that* they have ^baddicted themselves to the ministry of the saints,)

16 That ye submit yourselves unto such, and to every one that helpeth with *us,* and laboureth.

17 I am glad of the coming of Stephanas and Fortunatus and Achaicus: for that which was ^alacking on your part they have supplied.

18 For they have refreshed my

53a Alma 41:4.
  b TG Mortality.
54a TG Immortality.
  b Isa. 25:8.
55a Mosiah 16:8 (7–8).
  b GR Hades, hell.
56a D&C 42:45–46.
  b GR power.
57a TG Thanksgiving.
  b 1 Jn. 5:4 (4–5).
58a TG Perseverance;
    Steadfastness.
16 1a Acts 24:17 (17, 26).

 b GR directed, arranged.
2a TG Sabbath.
  b Deut. 16:10.
3a GR gift.
  TG Generosity.
4a GR suitable,
    worthwhile.
7a GR in passing.
  b GR hope.
  c 2 Cor. 1:15 (15–16).
9a Col. 4:3.
  b GR energetic, efficient.
10a 2 Cor. 1:19;

 1 Thes. 3:2.
11a 1 Tim. 4:12.
12a Acts 18:24.
13a TG Watch.
  b Philip. 4:1 (1–7).
  c D&C 9:14.
  d GR behave like men.
  e 1 Sam. 4:9;
    Isa. 46:8.
14a TG Charity.
15a 1 Cor. 1:16.
  b GR devoted, appointed.
17a 2 Cor. 11:9.

spirit and yours: therefore acknowledge ye them that are such.

19 The churches of Asia salute you. [a]Aquila and Priscilla salute you much in the Lord, with the church that is in their house.

20 All the brethren greet you. Greet ye one another with an holy [a]kiss.

21 The salutation of *me* Paul with mine own hand.

22 If any man love not the Lord Jesus Christ, let him be Anathema [a]Maran-atha.

23 The grace of our Lord Jesus Christ *be* with you.

24 My love *be* with you all in Christ Jesus. Amen.

¶ The first *epistle* to the Corinthians was written from Philippi by Stephanas, and Fortunatus, and Achaicus, and Timotheus.

THE SECOND EPISTLE OF
PAUL THE APOSTLE TO THE
CORINTHIANS

CHAPTER 1

God comforts and cares for His Saints—The Saints are sealed and given assurance by the Spirit in their hearts.

PAUL, an [a]apostle of Jesus Christ by the will of God, and Timothy *our* brother, unto the church of God which is at Corinth, with all the saints which are in all Achaia:

2 Grace *be* to you and peace from God our Father, and *from* the Lord Jesus Christ.

3 Blessed *be* God, even the Father of our Lord Jesus Christ, the Father of [a]mercies, and the God of all [b]comfort;

4 Who comforteth us in all our [a]tribulation, that we may be able to comfort them which are in any trouble, by the [b]comfort wherewith we ourselves are comforted of God.

5 For as the [a]sufferings of Christ abound in us, so our consolation also aboundeth by Christ.

6 And whether we be afflicted, *it is* for your consolation and salvation, which is [a]effectual in the [b]enduring of the same sufferings which we also suffer: or whether we be comforted, *it is* for your consolation and salvation.

7 And our hope of you *is* steadfast, knowing, that as ye are partakers of the [a]sufferings, so *shall ye be* also of the consolation.

8 For we would not, brethren, have you ignorant of our trouble which came to us in Asia, that we were pressed out of measure, above strength, insomuch that we [a]despaired even of life:

19a Acts 18:2.
20a JST 1 Cor. 16:20 . . .
    salutation.
22a Aramaic, meaning "The Lord will come!" or "Come, O Lord!"

[2 CORINTHIANS]
1 1a D&C 21:1.
  3a TG God, Mercy of.
   b TG Comfort.
  4a TG Tribulation.
   b Philip. 3:10;
     2 Thes. 2:16.

5a Col. 1:24.
   TG Suffering.
6a GR active, operative.
   b D&C 63:20; 101:35.
7a TG Persecution;
   Suffering.
8a TG Despair.

9 But we had the sentence of death in ourselves, that we should not trust in ourselves, but in God which ^araiseth the dead:

10 Who ^adelivered us from so great a death, and doth deliver: in whom we trust that he will yet deliver *us*;

11 Ye also helping together by ^aprayer for us, that for the gift *bestowed* upon us by the means of many persons thanks may be given by many on our behalf.

12 For our rejoicing is this, the ^atestimony of our conscience, that in ^bsimplicity and godly sincerity, not with fleshly ^cwisdom, but by the grace of God, we have had our conversation in the world, and more abundantly to you-ward.

13 For we ^awrite none other things unto you, than what ye read or acknowledge; and I trust ye shall acknowledge even to the end;

14 As also ye have acknowledged us in part, that we are your rejoicing, even as ye also *are* ours in the ^aday of the Lord Jesus.

15 And in this confidence I was minded to ^acome unto you before, that ye might have a second benefit;

16 And to pass by you into Macedonia, and to come again out of Macedonia unto you, and of you to be brought on my way toward Judæa.

17 When I therefore was thus minded, did I use ^alightness? or the things that I purpose, do I purpose according to the flesh, that with me there should be yea yea, and nay nay?

18 But *as* God *is* true, our word toward you was not yea and nay.

19 For the ^aSon of God, Jesus Christ, who was preached among you by us, *even* by me and ^bSilvanus and ^cTimotheus, was not yea and nay, but in him was yea.

20 For all the ^apromises of God in him *are* yea, and in him Amen, unto the glory of God by us.

21 Now he which stablisheth us with you in Christ, and hath ^aanointed us, *is* God;

22 Who hath also ^asealed us, and given the earnest of the Spirit in our hearts.

23 Moreover I call God for a record upon my soul, that to spare you I came not as yet unto Corinth.

24 Not for that we have dominion over your faith, but are helpers of your joy: for by ^afaith ye stand.

CHAPTER 2

Saints should love and forgive one another—They always triumph in Christ.

BUT I determined this with myself, that I would not come again to you in heaviness.

2 For if I make you sorry, who is he then that maketh me glad, but the same which is made sorry by me?

3 And I wrote this same unto you, lest, when I came, I should have sorrow from them of whom I ought to rejoice; having ^aconfidence in you all, that my joy is *the joy* of you all.

4 For out of much affliction and anguish of heart I wrote unto you with many tears; not that ye should be grieved, but that ye might know the love which I have more abundantly unto you.

5 But if any have caused grief, he hath not grieved me, but in part: that I may not overcharge you all.

6 Sufficient to such a man *is* this punishment, which *was inflicted* of many.

7 So that contrariwise ye *ought* rather to ^aforgive *him*, and comfort *him*, lest perhaps such a one should

9a TG Resurrection.
10a TG Deliver.
11a Philip. 1:19;
   Philem. 1:22.
12a TG Testimony.
  b GR plainness, singleness of heart.
  c 1 Cor. 2:13.

13a TG Scriptures, Writing of.
14a D&C 1:9 (8–10).
15a 1 Cor. 16:7 (5–7).
17a GR light-mindedness, levity.
19a Luke 1:35.
  b Acts 15:34 (32–34);
   1 Thes. 1:1; 1 Pet. 5:12.

  c 1 Cor. 16:10 (10–11);
   1 Thes. 3:2.
20a Rom. 15:8.
21a TG Anointing.
22a TG Sealing.
24a Rom. 11:20.
2 3a 2 Cor. 8:22.
  7a TG Forgive.

be swallowed up with overmuch sorrow.

8 Wherefore I beseech you that ye would confirm *your* love toward him.

9 For to this end also did I *a*write, that I might know the proof of you, whether ye be *b*obedient in all things.

10 To whom ye forgive any thing, I *forgive* also: for if I forgave any thing, to whom I forgave *it*, for your sakes *forgave I it* in the *a*person of Christ;

11 Lest *a*Satan should get an advantage of us: for we are not ignorant of his devices.

12 Furthermore, when I came to Troas to *preach* Christ's gospel, and a *a*door was opened unto me of the Lord,

13 I had no rest in my spirit, because I found not Titus my brother: but taking my leave of them, I went from thence into Macedonia.

14 Now thanks *be* unto God, which always causeth us to *a*triumph in Christ, and maketh manifest the savour of his knowledge by us in every place.

15 For we are unto God a sweet savour of Christ, in them that are saved, and in them that perish:

16 To the one *we are* the savour of death unto death; and to the other the savour of life unto life. And who *is* *a*sufficient for these things?

17 For we are not as many, which *a*corrupt the *b*word of God: but as of *c*sincerity, but as of God, in the sight of God speak we in Christ.

CHAPTER 3

The gospel surpasses the law of Moses —Where the Spirit of the Lord is, there is liberty.

Do we begin again to commend our-

selves? or need we, as some *others*, epistles of commendation to you, or *letters* of commendation from you?

2 Ye are our *a*epistle written in our hearts, known and read of all men:

3 *Forasmuch as ye are* manifestly declared to be the epistle of Christ ministered by us, *a*written not with ink, but with the Spirit of the living God; not in *b*tables of stone, but in *c*fleshy tables of the *d*heart.

4 And such trust have we through Christ to God-ward:

5 Not that we are sufficient of ourselves to think any thing as of ourselves; but our *a*sufficiency *is* of God;

6 Who also hath made us able *a*ministers of the new testament; not of the letter, but of the spirit: for the letter killeth, but the *b*spirit giveth life.

7 But if the ministration of *a*death, written *and* engraven in stones, was glorious, so that the children of Israel could not steadfastly behold the face of Moses for the *b*glory of his countenance; which *glory* was to be done away:

8 How shall not the ministration of the spirit be rather glorious?

9 For if the ministration of condemnation *be* glory, much more doth the ministration of righteousness exceed in glory.

10 For even that which was made glorious had no glory in this respect, by reason of the glory that excelleth.

11 For if that which is done away *was* glorious, much more that which remaineth *is* glorious.

12 Seeing then that we have such hope, we use great *a*plainness of speech:

13 And not as Moses, *which* put a veil over his face, that the children

9a TG Scriptures, Writing of.
  b 2 Cor. 7:15.
10a GR presence.
11a 2 Pet. 2:20 (20–22).
12a Acts 14:27;
   1 Cor. 16:9.
14a Rom. 8:37.
16a 2 Cor. 3:5 (5–6).
17a 2 Cor. 4:2.
   TG Apostasy of the

Early Christian Church.
  b TG Scriptures,
   Preservation of.
  c TG Sincere.
3 2a 1 Cor. 9:2.
 3a Deut. 9:10 (10–11).
  b Ex. 24:12; 31:18; 34:1;
   Deut. 4:13;
   Prov. 3:3.
  c Ezek. 11:19 (19–20).

d Jer. 31:33;
   Heb. 8:10.
5a 2 Cor. 2:16;
   Alma 26:12.
6a 1 Cor. 3:5.
  b John 6:63.
7a Rom. 7:10.
  b TG Transfiguration.
12a GR boldness, frankness.

of Israel could not steadfastly look to the end of that which is abolished:

14 But their *a*minds were *b*blinded: for until this day remaineth the same veil untaken away in the *c*reading of the old testament; which *d*veil is done away in Christ.

15 But even unto this day, when Moses is read, the veil is upon their *a*heart.

16 Nevertheless when it shall turn to the Lord, the veil shall be taken away.

17 Now the Lord is *a*that Spirit: and where the *b*Spirit of the Lord *is*, there *is* *c*liberty.

18 But we all, with open face beholding as in a *a*glass the *b*glory of the Lord, are changed into the same *c*image from *d*glory to glory, *even* as by the Spirit of the Lord.

CHAPTER 4

Gospel light shines on the Saints—Mortal trials are nothing as contrasted with eternal glory.

THEREFORE seeing we have this ministry, as we have received *a*mercy, we faint not;

2 But have *a*renounced the hidden things of *b*dishonesty, not walking in craftiness, nor handling the word of God *c*deceitfully; but by manifestation of the *d*truth commending ourselves to every man's *e*conscience in the sight of God.

3 But if our gospel be hid, it is hid to them that are lost:

4 In whom the *a*god of this *b*world hath *c*blinded the *d*minds of them which *e*believe not, lest the *f*light of the glorious gospel of Christ, who is the *g*image of *h*God, should shine unto them.

5 For we *a*preach not ourselves, but Christ Jesus the Lord; and ourselves your *b*servants for Jesus' sake.

6 For God, who *a*commanded the light to shine out of darkness, hath *b*shined in our hearts, to *give* the *c*light of the knowledge of the *d*glory of God in the face of Jesus Christ.

7 But we have this treasure in earthen vessels, that the excellency of the *a*power may be of God, and not of us.

8 *We are* *a*troubled on every side, yet not distressed; *we are* perplexed, but not in *b*despair;

9 *a*Persecuted, but not forsaken; cast down, but not *b*destroyed;

10 Always bearing about in the body the dying of the Lord Jesus, that the life also of Jesus might be made manifest in our body.

11 For we which live are alway delivered unto *a*death for Jesus' sake, that the life also of Jesus might be made manifest in our *b*mortal flesh.

12 So then death worketh in us, but life in you.

13 We having the same spirit of

14a TG Mind.
  b TG Spiritual Blindness.
  c Acts 15:21.
  d TG Jesus Christ, Types of, in Anticipation; Veil.
15a TG Hardheartedness.
17a GR the Spirit.
  b Alma 61:15.
    TG God, Spirit of.
  c Rom. 8:2.
    TG Governments; Liberty.
18a 1 Cor. 13:12.
  b TG Celestial Glory.
  c Rom. 8:29.
  d TG Man, Potential to Become like Heavenly Father.
4 1a Alma 12:34.
2a TG Priesthood, Qualifying for.

  b GR shame, disgrace.
    TG Honesty.
  c 2 Cor. 2:17; 1 Thes. 2:3 (3, 5).
  d D&C 19:37; 75:4.
  e TG Conscience.
4a Eph. 6:12.
    TG Devil.
  b TG Worldliness.
  c Alma 19:6; Moro. 7:12; D&C 93:39 (38–39).
    TG Spiritual Blindness.
  d TG Mind.
  e TG Unbelief.
  f TG Light [noun].
  g TG God, Body of, Corporeal Nature.
  h TG Godhead.
5a Gal. 1:11 (11–12).
    TG Missionary Work.

  b 1 Cor. 9:19; Alma 26:3.
6a Ps. 33:9; Moses 2:5 (4–5).
  b D&C 45:9.
  c TG Intelligence; Light of Christ.
  d TG God, Glory of; Jesus Christ, Relationships with the Father.
7a 1 Cor. 2:5; D&C 19:3; 88:13 (7–13).
8a 2 Cor. 7:5.
    TG Adversity.
  b TG Despair.
9a 2 Cor. 11:23 (23–27); D&C 101:35.
  b Ps. 129:2.
11a Rom. 8:36.
    TG Martyrdom.
  b TG Mortality.

faith, according as it is written, I ᵃbelieved, and therefore have I spoken; we also believe, and therefore ᵇspeak;

14 Knowing that he which raised up the Lord Jesus shall raise up us also by Jesus, and shall present *us* with you.

15 For all things *are* for your sakes, that the abundant grace might through the ᵃthanksgiving of many redound to the glory of God.

16 For which cause we faint not; but though our outward man perish, yet the ᵃinward *man* is renewed day by day.

17 For our light ᵃaffliction, which is but for a moment, worketh for us a far more exceeding *and* ᵇeternal ᶜweight of glory;

18 While we look not at the things which are ᵃseen, but at the things which are not seen: for the things which are seen *are* temporal; but the things which are not ᵇseen *are* ᶜeternal.

CHAPTER 5

Saints walk by faith and seek tabernacles of immortal glory—The gospel reconciles man to God—God's ministers carry the word of reconciliation to the world.

FOR we know that if our earthly house of *this* tabernacle were dissolved, we have a building of God, an house not made with hands, eternal in the heavens.

2 For in this we groan, earnestly desiring to be ᵃclothed upon with our house which is from heaven:

3 If so be that being clothed we shall not be found naked.

4 For we that are in *this* tabernacle

do ᵃgroan, being burdened: not for that we would be unclothed, but clothed upon, that ᵇmortality might be swallowed up of life.

5 Now he that hath wrought us for the selfsame thing *is* God, who also hath given unto us the earnest of the Spirit.

6 Therefore *we are* always ᵃconfident, knowing that, whilst we are at home in the body, we are absent from the Lord:

7 (For we walk by ᵃfaith, not by ᵇsight:)

8 We are confident, *I say,* and willing rather to be absent from the body, and to be present with the Lord.

9 Wherefore we ᵃlabour, that, whether present or absent, we may be accepted of him.

10 For we must all appear before the ᵃjudgment seat of Christ; that every one may receive the things *done* in *his* body, ᵇaccording to that he hath ᶜdone, whether *it be* good or bad.

11 Knowing therefore the terror of the Lord, we persuade men; but we are made manifest unto God; and I trust also are made manifest in your ᵃconsciences.

12 For we commend not ourselves again unto you, but give you occasion to glory on our behalf, that ye may have somewhat to *answer* them which glory in appearance, and not in heart.

13 ᵃFor whether we be beside ourselves, *it is* to God: or whether we be sober, *it is* for your cause.

14 For the love of Christ constraineth us; because we thus judge, that if ᵃone ᵇdied for all, then were all dead:

15 And *that* he died for all, that

13a D&C 14:8.
   b D&C 18:21.
15a TG Thanksgiving.
16a 2 Ne. 4:20;
   Mosiah 24:15.
17a Rom. 5:3.
   TG Persecution;
   Suffering.
   b TG Eternal Life.
   c D&C 63:66.
18a Rom. 8:24.

   b Ether 12:6.
   c TG Eternity.
5 2a Rom. 8:23.
 4a TG Mourning.
   b TG Mortality.
 6a GR of good courage, of
      good cheer.
 7a TG Faith.
   b TG Sight.
 9a Moro. 9:6.
10a TG Jesus Christ, Judge.

   b TG Accountability.
   c TG Good Works.
11a TG Conscience.
13a JST 2 Cor. 5:13 For *we
      bear record that we are
      not beside ourselves; for
      whether we glory, it is to
      God, or whether we be
      sober, it is for your sakes.*
14a Rom. 5:15.
   b D&C 19:16.

they which live should not henceforth *a*live unto themselves, but unto him which died for them, and rose again.

16 *a*Wherefore henceforth know we no man after the flesh: yea, though we have known Christ after the flesh, yet now henceforth know we *him* no more.

17 Therefore if any man *be* *a*in Christ, he is a *b*new creature: *c*old things are *d*passed away; behold, all things are become *e*new.

18 And all things *are* of God, who hath *a*reconciled us to himself by Jesus Christ, and hath given to us the ministry of reconciliation;

19 To wit, that God was in Christ, *a*reconciling the world unto himself, not imputing their trespasses unto them; and hath committed unto us the word of reconciliation.

20 Now then we are *a*ambassadors for Christ, as though God did beseech *you* by us: we pray *you* in Christ's stead, be ye reconciled to God.

21 For he hath made him *to be* *a*sin for us, who knew no *b*sin; that we might be made the *c*righteousness of God in him.

CHAPTER 6

Now is the day of salvation—God's ministers must walk uprightly and bear all things—Saints should not be unequally yoked with unbelievers.

WE then, *as* *a*workers together *with* *b*him, beseech *you* also that ye receive not the *c*grace of God in vain.

2 (For he saith, I have heard thee in a *a*time accepted, and in the *b*day of *c*salvation have I succoured thee: behold, now *is* the accepted time; behold, now *is* the day of salvation.)

3 Giving no *a*offence in any thing, that the ministry be not blamed:

4 But in all *things* approving ourselves as the *a*ministers of God, in much *b*patience, in *c*afflictions, in necessities, in distresses,

5 In stripes, in imprisonments, in *a*tumults, in labours, in watchings, in fastings;

6 By *a*pureness, by knowledge, by *b*longsuffering, by *c*kindness, by the Holy Ghost, by *d*love unfeigned,

7 By the word of truth, by the power of God, by the *a*armour of *b*righteousness on the right hand and on the left,

8 By honour and dishonour, by evil report and good report: as deceivers, and *yet* true;

9 As unknown, and *yet* well known; as dying, and, behold, we live; as chastened, and not killed;

10 As *a*sorrowful, yet alway rejoicing; as *b*poor, yet making many *c*rich; as having nothing, and *yet* possessing all things.

11 O *ye* Corinthians, our mouth is open unto you, our heart is *a*enlarged.

12 Ye are not straitened in us, but ye are straitened in your own *a*bowels.

13 Now for a recompence in the same, (I speak as unto *my* children,) be ye also enlarged.

15*a* Rom. 14:7 (7–9).
16*a* JST 2 Cor. 5:16
    Wherefore, henceforth
    live we no more after
    the flesh; yea, though we
    once lived after the flesh,
    yet since we have known
    Christ, now henceforth
    live we no more after
    the flesh.
17*a* 1 Jn. 2:5 (2–5).
  b TG Man, New,
    Spiritually Reborn.
  c Rom. 7:6; 13:12 (12–14);
    Heb. 8:13.
  d D&C 29:24; 63:49.
  e Rev. 21:5.

18*a* TG Reconciliation.
19*a* TG Reconciliation.
20*a* Luke 14:23.
21*a* Isa. 53:6.
  b 1 Jn. 3:3.
  c Rom. 1:17.
6 1*a* 1 Cor. 3:9.
  b JST 2 Cor. 6:1 . . .
    Christ . . .
  c TG Grace.
2*a* Isa. 49:8.
  b Alma 34:32 (31–34).
  c TG Salvation.
3*a* Rom. 14:13.
    TG Offense.
4*a* 2 Cor. 11:23.
    TG Priesthood, Magnify-

ing Callings within.
  b TG Patience.
  c D&C 127:2 (2–3).
5*a* TG Rioting and Reveling.
6*a* TG Purity.
  b TG Forbear.
  c TG Kindness.
  d D&C 121:41 (41–42).
7*a* Rom. 13:12.
  b TG Righteousness.
10*a* TG Mourning.
  b 2 Cor. 8:9.
  c TG Treasure.
11*a* Ps. 119:32 (25–32).
12*a* D&C 121:45.

14 Be ye not unequally ^ayoked together with unbelievers: for what ^bfellowship hath righteousness with ^cunrighteousness? and what communion hath ^dlight with darkness?

15 And what concord hath Christ with Belial? or what part hath he that believeth with an infidel?

16 And what ^aagreement hath the temple of God with idols? for ye are the ^btemple of the living God; as God hath said, I will ^cdwell in them, and walk in *them*; and I will be their God, and they shall be my people.

17 Wherefore ^acome out from among them, and be ye ^bseparate, saith the Lord, and touch not the ^cunclean *thing*; and I will receive you,

18 And will be a ^aFather unto you, and ye shall be my ^bsons and daughters, saith the Lord ^cAlmighty.

CHAPTER 7

Godly sorrow for sin leads to repentance—The sorrow of the world leads to death.

HAVING therefore these promises, dearly beloved, let us ^acleanse ourselves from all ^bfilthiness of the flesh and spirit, perfecting ^choliness in the fear of God.

2 Receive us; we have ^awronged no man, we have corrupted no man, we have ^bdefrauded no man.

3 I speak not *this* to condemn *you:* for I have said before, that ye are in our hearts to die and live with *you.*

4 Great *is* my boldness of speech toward you, great *is* my glorying of you: I am filled with ^acomfort, I am exceeding ^bjoyful in all our ^ctribulation.

5 For, when we were come into Macedonia, our flesh had no rest, but we were ^atroubled on every side; without *were* fightings, within *were* ^bfears.

6 Nevertheless God, that comforteth those that are cast down, comforted us by the coming of Titus;

7 And not by his coming only, but by the consolation wherewith he was ^acomforted in you, when he told us your earnest desire, your mourning, your fervent mind toward me; so that I rejoiced the more.

8 For though I made you sorry with a letter, I do not repent, though I did repent: for I perceive that the same epistle hath made you sorry, though *it were* but for a season.

9 Now I rejoice, not that ye were made sorry, but that ye sorrowed to repentance: for ye were made ^asorry after a godly manner, that ye might receive damage by us in nothing.

10 For ^agodly ^bsorrow worketh ^crepentance to ^dsalvation not to be repented of: but the ^esorrow of the world worketh death.

11 For behold this selfsame thing, that ye sorrowed after a godly sort, what carefulness it wrought in you, yea, *what* clearing of yourselves, yea, *what* indignation, yea, *what* fear, yea, *what* vehement desire, yea, *what* zeal, yea, *what* revenge! In all *things* ye have approved yourselves to be clear in this matter.

14a TG Marriage, Interfaith; Marriage, Temporal.
  b TG Fellowshipping.
  c 2 Kgs. 3:13; Ezek. 14:3.
  d TG Light [noun].
16a 1 Cor. 10:21 (19–22).
  b TG Body, Sanctity of; Temple.
  c Lev. 26:12. TG God, Presence of.
17a D&C 25:10; 53:2; 84:50 (49–53).
  b TG Separation.
  c Isa. 52:11. TG Uncleanness.

18a Jer. 31:9 (1, 9).
  b TG Sons and Daughters of God.
  c TG God, Power of.
7 1a TG Chastity; Cleanliness; Purification.
  b GR pollution, stain, defilement. TG Filthiness.
  c TG Holiness.
2a 1 Thes. 2:3 (3–10).
  b TG Fraud.
4a TG Comfort.
  b TG Joy.
  c 3 Ne. 12:12 (11–12).

5a 2 Cor. 4:8.
  b D&C 10:55.
7a TG Comfort.
9a TG Poor in Spirit.
10a TG Godliness.
  b Eccl. 7:3; Isa. 22:12; Joel 2:17; James 4:9 (8–10); Alma 36:17 (5–28); 42:29. TG Mourning; Sorrow.
  c TG Repent.
  d TG Salvation.
  e Morm. 2:13.

12 Wherefore, though I wrote unto you, *I did it* not for his cause that had done the wrong, nor for his cause that suffered wrong, but that our care for you in the sight of God might appear unto you.

13 Therefore we were comforted in your comfort: yea, and exceedingly the more joyed we for the joy of Titus, because his spirit was *a*refreshed by you all.

14 For if I have *a*boasted any thing to him of you, I am not ashamed; but as we spake all things to you in truth, even so our *b*boasting, which *I made* before Titus, is found a truth.

15 And his *a*inward affection is more abundant toward you, whilst he remembereth the *b*obedience of you all, how with fear and trembling ye received him.

16 I rejoice therefore that I have confidence in you in all *things.*

CHAPTER 8

True Saints impart of their substance to the poor—Christ, out of His poverty, brought eternal riches.

MOREOVER, brethren, *a*we do you to wit of the grace of God bestowed on the churches of Macedonia;

2 How that in a great *a*trial of *b*affliction the abundance of their joy and their deep *c*poverty abounded unto the riches of their *d*liberality.

3 For to *their* power, I bear record, yea, and beyond *their* power *they were* willing of themselves;

4 Praying us with much entreaty that we would receive the gift, and *take upon us* the *a*fellowship of the ministering to the saints.

5 And *this they did,* not as we hoped, but first *a*gave their own selves to the Lord, and unto us by the will of God.

6 Insomuch that we desired Titus, that as he had begun, so he would also finish in you the same grace also.

7 Therefore, as ye abound in every *thing, in* faith, and utterance, and knowledge, and *in* all *a*diligence, and *in* your love to us, *see* that ye abound in this grace also.

8 I speak *a*not by commandment, but by occasion of the forwardness of others, and to prove the *b*sincerity of your love.

9 For ye know the *a*grace of our Lord Jesus Christ, that, though he was *b*rich, yet for your sakes he became *c*poor, that ye through his *d*poverty might be rich.

10 And herein I give *my* advice: for this is expedient for you, who have begun before, not only to do, but also to be forward a year ago.

11 Now therefore perform the doing *of it;* that as *there was* a readiness to will, so *there may be* a performance also out of that which ye have.

12 For if there be first a *a*willing *b*mind, *it is* accepted according to that a man hath, *and* not according to that he hath not.

13 For *I mean* not that other men be eased, and ye burdened:

14 But by an equality, *that* now at this time your abundance *may be a supply* for their want, that their *a*abundance also may be *a supply* for your want: that there may be *b*equality:

15 As it is written, He that *had* *a*gathered much had nothing over; and he that *had gathered* little had no lack.

16 But thanks *be* to God, which put the same earnest care into the heart of Titus for you.

13a Rom. 15:32.
14a 2 Cor. 9:2.
 b TG Boast.
15a GR heart, tender affections, compassion.
 b 2 Cor. 2:9; 10:6.
 TG Obedience.
8 1a GR we make known (or declare) to you the grace.

2a TG Probation; Test.
 b TG Affliction.
 c Mark 12:44 (43–44).
 d GR sincerity, purity of mind.
 TG Generosity.
4a D&C 88:133.
5a TG Self-Sacrifice.
7a TG Diligence.
8a D&C 63:22.

 b TG Sincere.
9a TG Grace.
 b TG Treasure.
 c Philip. 2:7 (5–8).
 d 2 Cor. 6:10.
12a Ex. 25:2 (1–7).
 b D&C 64:34.
14a Alma 1:30 (29–30).
 b TG Consecration.
15a Ex. 16:18.

17 For indeed he accepted the exhortation; but being more forward, of his own accord he went unto you.

18 And we have sent with him the brother, whose praise *is* in the gospel throughout all the churches;

19 And not *that* only, but who was also chosen of the churches to travel with us with this grace, which is administered by us to the glory of the same Lord, and *declaration of* your ready mind:

20 Avoiding this, that no man should blame us in this abundance which is administered by us:

21 Providing for ªhonest things, not only in the sight of the Lord, but also in the ᵇsight of men.

22 And we have sent with them our brother, whom we have oftentimes proved diligent in many things, but now much more diligent, upon the great ªconfidence which *I have* in you.

23 Whether *any do inquire* of Titus, *he is* my partner and fellowhelper concerning you: or our brethren *be inquired of, they are* the messengers of the churches, *and* the glory of Christ.

24 Wherefore shew ye to them, and before the churches, the proof of your love, and of our boasting on your behalf.

CHAPTER 9

God loves and rewards a cheerful giver—Thanks be to God for His unspeakable gift.

FOR as touching the ministering to the saints, it is superfluous for me to write to you:

2 For I know the forwardness of your mind, for which I ªboast of you to them of Macedonia, that Achaia was ready a year ago; and your zeal hath ᵇprovoked very many.

3 Yet have I sent the brethren, lest our boasting of you should be in vain in this behalf; that, as I said, ye may be ready:

4 Lest haply if they of Macedonia come with me, and find you unprepared, we (that we say not, ye) should be ashamed in this same confident boasting.

5 Therefore I thought it necessary to exhort the brethren, that they would go before unto you, and make up beforehand your ªbounty, whereof ye had notice before, that the same might be ready, as *a matter of* bounty, and not as *of* covetousness.

6 But this I *say,* He which soweth sparingly shall ªreap also sparingly; and he which ᵇsoweth bountifully shall reap also bountifully.

7 Every man according as he ªpurposeth in his heart, *so let him give;* not ᵇgrudgingly, or of necessity: for God loveth a ᶜcheerful ᵈgiver.

8 And God *is* able to make all ªgrace abound toward you; that ye, always having all sufficiency in all *things,* may abound to every good work:

9 (As it is written, He hath dispersed abroad; he hath given to the poor: his righteousness remaineth for ever.

10 Now he that ministereth seed to the sower both minister bread for *your* food, and multiply your seed sown, and increase the fruits of your ªrighteousness;)

11 Being enriched in every thing to all bountifulness, which causeth through us ªthanksgiving to God.

12 For the ªadministration of this service not only supplieth the want of the saints, but is abundant also by many thanksgivings unto God;

13 Whiles by the experiment of this ministration they glorify God for your professed subjection unto the gospel of Christ, and for *your* liberal distribution unto them, and unto all *men;*

21a TG Honesty.
  b Rom. 12:17.
22a 2 Cor. 2:3.
9 2a 2 Cor. 7:14.
  b TG Provoking.
  5a GR gift, blessing, benevolence.

6a TG Harvest.
  b TG Accountability.
7a D&C 6:33 (33–34).
  b TG Hypocrisy.
  c TG Cheerful.
  d TG Generosity.
8a Philip. 4:18 (15–23);

Jacob 2:19 (17–19).
  TG Grace.
10a TG Righteousness.
11a TG Thanksgiving.
12a Heb. 13:16.

14 And by their prayer for you, which long after you for the exceeding grace of God in you.

15 ᵃThanks be unto God for his unspeakable ᵇgift.

CHAPTER 10

Bring every thought into obedience— Paul glories in the Lord.

NOW I Paul myself beseech you by the ᵃmeekness and gentleness of Christ, who in presence *am* base among you, but being absent am bold toward you:

2 But I beseech *you,* that I may not be bold when I am present with that confidence, wherewith I think to be bold against some, which think of us as if we walked according to the flesh.

3 For though we walk in the flesh, we do not ᵃwar after the flesh:

4 (For the ᵃweapons of our ᵇwarfare *are* not carnal, but mighty through God to the pulling down of strong holds;)

5 Casting down imaginations, and every high thing that exalteth itself against the knowledge of God, and bringing into captivity every ᵃthought to the ᵇobedience of Christ;

6 And having in a readiness to revenge all ᵃdisobedience, when your ᵇobedience is fulfilled.

7 Do ye look on things after the outward ᵃappearance? If any man trust to himself that he is Christ's, let him of himself think this again, that, as he *is* Christ's, even so *are* we ᵇChrist's.

8 For though I should boast somewhat more of our ᵃauthority, which the Lord hath given us for ᵇedification, and not for your destruction, I should not be ashamed:

9 That I may not seem as if I would terrify you by letters.

10 For *his* letters, say they, *are* weighty and powerful; but *his* ᵃbodily presence *is* weak, and *his* speech ᵇcontemptible.

11 Let such an one think this, that, such as we are in word by letters when we are absent, such *will we be* also in deed when we are present.

12 For we dare not make ourselves of the number, or compare ourselves with some that commend themselves: but they measuring themselves by themselves, and comparing themselves among themselves, are not wise.

13 But we will not ᵃboast of things without *our* measure, but according to the measure of the rule which God hath distributed to us, a measure to reach even unto you.

14 For we stretch not ourselves beyond *our measure,* as though we reached not unto you: for we are come as far as to you also in *preaching* the gospel of Christ:

15 Not boasting of things without *our* measure, *that is,* of other men's ᵃlabours; but having hope, when your faith is increased, that we shall be enlarged by you according to our rule abundantly,

16 To preach the gospel in the *regions* beyond you, *and* not to boast in another man's line of things made ready to our hand.

17 But he that glorieth, let him ᵃglory in the Lord.

18 For not he that ᵃcommendeth himself is approved, but whom the Lord commendeth.

CHAPTER 11

Maintain the simplicity that is in Christ—Satan sends forth false apostles—Paul glories in his sufferings for Christ.

15*a* TG Thanksgiving.
  b James 1:17.
10 1*a* D&C 19:23; 25:5 (5, 14).
  3*a* TG War.
  4*a* Eph. 6:11 (10–24).
  b 1 Cor. 9:7.
  5*a* TG Motivations.
  b TG Obedience.

6*a* TG Disobedience.
  b 2 Cor. 7:15.
  7*a* 1 Sam. 16:7.
  b 1 Cor. 3:23.
  8*a* 2 Cor. 13:10.
  TG Called of God.
  b TG Edification.
  10*a* Gal. 4:13.

b 2 Cor. 11:6.
13*a* TG Boast.
15*a* Rom. 15:20.
17*a* Jer. 9:24 (23–24);
  Alma 26:16 (11–16).
18*a* Luke 18:14.
  TG Boast.

WOULD to God ye could bear with me a little in *my* folly: and indeed bear with me.

2 For I am *a*jealous over you with godly jealousy: for I have *b*espoused you to one husband, that I may present *you as* a chaste virgin to Christ.

3 But I fear, lest by any means, as the *a*serpent *b*beguiled Eve through his *c*subtilty, so your minds should be *d*corrupted from the *e*simplicity that is in Christ.

4 For if he that cometh preacheth another *a*Jesus, whom we have not preached, or *if* ye receive another spirit, which ye have not received, or another *b*gospel, which ye have not accepted, ye might well bear with *him*.

5 For I suppose I was not a whit behind the very chiefest apostles.

6 But though *I be* *a*rude in speech, yet not in knowledge; but we have been throughly made manifest among you in all things.

7 Have I committed an offence in abasing myself that ye might be exalted, because I have preached to you the gospel of God *a*freely?

8 I *a*robbed other churches, taking *b*wages *of them*, to do you service.

9 And when I was present with you, and wanted, I was *a*chargeable to no man: for that which was *b*lacking to me the brethren which came from Macedonia *c*supplied: and in all *things* I have kept myself from being burdensome unto you, and *so* will I keep *myself*.

10 As the truth of Christ is in me, no man shall stop me of this boasting in the regions of Achaia.

11 Wherefore? because I love you not? God knoweth.

12 But what I do, that I will do, that I may cut off occasion from them which desire occasion; that wherein they *a*glory, they may be found even as we.

13 For such *are* *a*false apostles, deceitful workers, transforming themselves into the apostles of Christ.

14 And no marvel; for *a*Satan himself is transformed into an *b*angel of light.

15 Therefore *it is* no great thing if his ministers also be transformed as the ministers of righteousness; whose *a*end shall be according to their works.

16 I say again, Let no man think me a fool; if otherwise, yet as a fool *a*receive me, that I may *b*boast myself a little.

17 That which I speak, I speak *it* not after the Lord, but as it were foolishly, in this confidence of boasting.

18 Seeing that many glory after the flesh, I will glory also.

19 For ye suffer fools gladly, seeing ye *yourselves* are wise.

20 For ye suffer, if a man bring you into *a*bondage, if a man devour *you*, if a man take *of you*, if a man exalt himself, if a man smite you on the face.

21 I speak as concerning *a*reproach, as though we had been weak. Howbeit whereinsoever any is bold, (I speak foolishly,) I am bold also.

22 Are they *a*Hebrews? so *am* I. Are they *b*Israelites? so *am* I. Are they the seed of Abraham? so *am* I.

23 Are they *a*ministers of Christ?

11 2*a* TG Jealous.
  b D&C 20:77.
 3*a* TG Devil.
  b TG Fall of Man;
    Temptation.
  c Gen. 3:1.
  d Heb. 13:9.
  e Jacob 4:14.
 4*a* Gal. 1:6.
  b TG Gospel.
 6*a* 2 Cor. 10:10.
 7*a* 1 Cor. 9:18.
 8*a* GR despoiled other

churches, having taken provisions for you.
  b TG Wages.
 9*a* 2 Cor. 12:13 (13, 16);
    1 Thes. 2:9.
  b 1 Cor. 16:17.
  c Philip. 4:10.
 12*a* GR boast; so in chapters 11–12.
 13*a* TG False Priesthoods;
    False Prophets.
 14*a* 2 Ne. 9:9;
    D&C 129:8.

  TG Devil.
  b TG Angels.
 15*a* Philip. 3:19.
 16*a* GR listen to, bear with,
    follow.
  b TG Boast.
 20*a* TG Bondage, Physical.
 21*a* TG Reproach.
 22*a* Philip. 3:5.
  b Rom. 11:1.
 23*a* 2 Cor. 6:4 (4–10).

(I speak as a fool) [b]I *am* more; in [c]labours more abundant, in [d]stripes above measure, in [e]prisons more frequent, in deaths oft.

24 Of the Jews five times received I [a]forty *stripes* save one.

25 Thrice was I [a]beaten with rods, once was I stoned, thrice I suffered shipwreck, a night and a day I have been in the deep;

26 *In* journeyings often, *in* perils of waters, *in* perils of robbers, *in* perils by *mine own* [a]countrymen, *in* perils by the [b]heathen, *in* [c]perils in the city, *in* perils in the wilderness, *in* perils in the sea, *in* perils among false brethren;

27 In [a]weariness and [b]painfulness, in watchings often, in hunger and thirst, in fastings often, in cold and nakedness.

28 Beside those things that are without, that which cometh upon me daily, the care of all the churches.

29 Who is weak, and I am not [a]weak? who is offended, and I [b]burn not?

30 If I must needs glory, I will glory of the things which concern mine infirmities.

31 The God and Father of our Lord Jesus Christ, which is blessed for evermore, knoweth that I lie not.

32 In Damascus the governor under Aretas the king kept the city of the Damascenes with a garrison, desirous to [a]apprehend me:

33 And through a window in a basket was I let down by the wall, and escaped his hands.

CHAPTER 12

Paul is caught up to the third heaven—The Lord gives men weaknesses that they may triumph over them—Paul manifests the signs of an Apostle.

It is not expedient for me doubtless to [a]glory. I will come to [b]visions and [c]revelations of the Lord.

2 [a]I knew a man in Christ above fourteen years ago, (whether in the [b]body, I cannot tell; or whether out of the body, I cannot tell: God knoweth;) such an one caught up to the [c]third [d]heaven.

3 And I knew such a man, (whether in the body, or out of the body, I cannot tell: God knoweth;)

4 How that he was caught up into [a]paradise, and heard [b]unspeakable words, which it is [c]not [d]lawful for a man to utter.

5 Of such an one will I glory: yet of myself I will not [a]glory, but in mine infirmities.

6 For though I would desire to glory, I shall not be a fool; for I will say the truth: but *now* I forbear, lest any man should think of me above that which he seeth me *to be*, or *that* he heareth of me.

7 And lest I should be [a]exalted above measure through the abundance of the revelations, there was given to me a [b]thorn in the flesh, the messenger of Satan to buffet me, lest I should be exalted above measure.

8 For this thing I besought the Lord thrice, that it might depart from me.

9 And he said unto me, My [a]grace is sufficient for thee: for my [b]strength

---

23b JST 2 Cor. 11:23 . . . *so am I; in labors . . .*
  c 1 Cor. 15:10.
  d Acts 16:23;
    James 5:10 (10–11);
    Alma 26:29 (29–31).
  e 2 Cor. 4:9.
24a Deut. 25:3.
25a Acts 16:22.
    TG Persecution.
26a Acts 14:5; 17:5.
  b TG Heathen.
  c Acts 21:31.

27a GR toil, trouble.
  b TG Pain.
29a 1 Cor. 9:22.
  b JST 2 Cor. 11:29 . . .
    anger not?
32a Acts 9:23 (23–25).
12 1a TG Boast.
  b 1 Cor. 9:1.
  c TG Revelation.
2a GR I know a man in Christ who fourteen years ago.
  b D&C 137:1.

  c TG Celestial Glory.
  d TG Heaven.
4a TG Paradise.
  b GR ineffable.
  c 3 Ne. 17:17;
    19:34 (32–34).
  d GR possible, permitted.
5a TG Boast.
7a D&C 3:4.
  b TG Pain.
9a TG Grace.
  b TG Strength.

is made perfect in ᶜweakness. Most gladly therefore will I rather glory in my infirmities, that the power of Christ may ᵈrest upon me.

10 Therefore I take pleasure in ᵃinfirmities, in reproaches, in necessities, in ᵇpersecutions, in distresses for Christ's sake: for when I am ᶜweak, then am I ᵈstrong.

11 I am become a fool in glorying; ye have compelled me: for I ought to have been commended of you: for in nothing am I behind the very ᵃchiefest apostles, though I be nothing.

12 Truly the ᵃsigns of an apostle were wrought among you in all patience, in signs, and wonders, and mighty deeds.

13 For what is it wherein ye were inferior to other churches, except it be that I myself was not ᵃburdensome to you? forgive me this wrong.

14 Behold, the third time I am ready to come to you; and I will not be burdensome to you: for I ᵃseek not yours, but you: for the children ought not to lay up for the parents, but the parents for the children.

15 And I will very gladly spend and be spent for you; though the more abundantly I love you, the less I be loved.

16 But be it so, I did not burden you: nevertheless, being crafty, I caught you with guile.

17 Did I make a gain of you by any of them whom I sent unto you?

18 I desired Titus, and with him I sent a brother. Did Titus make a gain of you? walked we not in the same spirit? walked we not in the same steps?

19 Again, think ye that we excuse ourselves unto you? we speak before God in Christ: but we do all things, dearly beloved, for your ᵃedifying.

20 For I fear, lest, when I come, I shall not find you such as I would, and that I shall be found unto you such as ye would not: lest there be debates, envyings, wraths, ᵃstrifes, ᵇbackbitings, whisperings, swellings, ᶜtumults:

21 And lest, when I come again, my God will humble me among you, and that I shall bewail many which have sinned already, and have not repented of the uncleanness and fornication and lasciviousness which they have committed.

CHAPTER 13

Saints should test themselves as to righteousness—Be perfect and of one mind; live in peace.

THIS is the third time I am coming to you. In the mouth of two or three ᵃwitnesses shall every word be established.

2 I told you before, and foretell you, as if I were present, the second time; and being absent now I write to them which heretofore have sinned, and to all other, that, if I come again, I will not spare:

3 Since ye seek a proof of Christ speaking in me, which to you-ward is not weak, but is mighty in you.

4 For though he was ᵃcrucified through weakness, yet he liveth by the power of God. For we also are weak in him, but we shall live with him by the power of God toward you.

5 ᵃExamine yourselves, whether ye be in the faith; prove your own selves. Know ye not your own selves, how that ᵇJesus ᶜChrist is in you, except ye be reprobates?

6 But I trust that ye shall know that we are not reprobates.

7 Now I pray to God that ye do no evil; not that we should appear approved, but that ye should do that

---

9c 2 Cor. 13:9;
    Ether 12:27 (26–28).
  d D&C 39:12.
10a TG Adversity.
  b TG Persecution.
  c TG Humility.
  d Joel 3:10; D&C 50:16.
11a 1 Cor. 9:1.
12a TG Signs.

13a 2 Cor. 11:9 (8–9).
14a 1 Cor. 10:33.
19a 1 Cor. 14:26.
    TG Edification.
20a TG Strife.
  b TG Backbiting.
  c TG Rioting and
    Reveling.
13 1a Deut. 19:15;

D&C 6:28.
    TG Book of Mormon;
    Witness.
4a TG Jesus Christ,
    Crucifixion of.
5a 1 Cor. 11:28 (27–31).
  b 1 Jn. 3:24 (19–24);
    4:12 (7–21).
  c Rom. 8:10.

which is *honest, though we be as reprobates.

8 For we can do nothing against the truth, but for the truth.

9 For we are glad, when we are *weak, and ye are strong: and this also we wish, *even* your perfection.

10 Therefore I write these things being absent, lest being present I should use sharpness, according to the *power which the Lord hath given me to edification, and not to destruction.

11 Finally, brethren, farewell. Be *perfect, be of good comfort, be of *one *mind, live in *peace; and the God of *love and peace shall be with you.

12 Greet one another with an holy *kiss.

13 All the saints salute you.

14 The grace of the Lord Jesus Christ, and the love of God, and the communion of the Holy Ghost, *be* with you all. Amen.

¶ The second *epistle* to the Corinthians was written from Philippi, *a city* of Macedonia, by Titus and Lucas.

THE EPISTLE OF PAUL THE APOSTLE

TO THE

GALATIANS

CHAPTER 1

Preachers of false gospels are accursed— Paul received the gospel by revelation— He believed, was taught, and preached to the Gentiles.

PAUL, an *apostle, (not of men, neither by man, but by Jesus Christ, and God the Father, who raised him from the dead;)

2 And all the brethren which are with me, unto the churches of Galatia:

3 Grace *be* to you and peace from God the Father, and *from* our Lord Jesus Christ,

4 Who *gave himself for our sins, that he might *deliver us from this present evil world, according to the *will of God and our Father:

5 To whom *be* glory for ever and ever. Amen.

6 I marvel that ye are so soon *removed from him that called you into the grace of Christ unto another *gospel:

7 Which is not another; but there be some that *trouble you, and would *pervert the *gospel of Christ.

8 But though we, or an *angel from heaven, preach any *other *gospel unto you than that which we have preached unto you, let him be *accursed.

9 As we said before, so say I now again, If any *man* preach any other

---

7*a* TG Honesty.
9*a* 2 Cor. 12:9.
10*a* 2 Cor. 10:8.
11*a* TG Perfection.
  b TG Unity.
  c 1 Cor. 1:10 (10–13).
  d TG Peace.
  e TG God, Love of.
12*a* JST 2 Cor. 13:12 . . .
  salutation.

[GALATIANS]

1 1*a* TG Apostles;
  Priesthood, Authority.
4*a* TG Jesus Christ,
  Redeemer.
  b TG Redemption.
  c TG God, Will of.
6*a* TG Apostasy of
  Individuals;
  Apostasy of the Early

Christian Church.
  b 2 Cor. 11:4.
7*a* GR agitate, raise doubts,
  perplex.
  b Gal. 5:10.
  c TG Gospel.
8*a* TG Angels.
  b 1 Tim. 1:3.
  c TG Gospel.
  d Gal. 5:12.

^agospel unto you than that ye have received, let him be ^baccursed.

10 For do I now ^apersuade men, or God? or do I seek to ^bplease men? for if I yet ^cpleased men, I should not be the servant of Christ.

11 But I ^acertify you, brethren, that the gospel which was ^bpreached of me is not after man.

12 For I neither received it ^aof man, neither was I taught *it,* but ^bby the ^crevelation of Jesus Christ.

13 For ye have heard of my ^aconversation in time past in the Jews' religion, how that beyond measure I ^bpersecuted the church of God, and ^cwasted it:

14 And ^aprofited in the Jews' religion above many ^bmy equals in mine own nation, being more exceedingly ^czealous of the ^dtraditions of my fathers.

15 But when it pleased God, who separated me from my mother's womb, and called *me* by his ^agrace,

16 To reveal his Son in me, that I might preach him among the ^aheathen; immediately I conferred not with ^bflesh and blood:

17 Neither went I up to Jerusalem to them which were apostles before me; but I went into Arabia, and returned again unto Damascus.

18 Then after three years I went up to ^aJerusalem to see Peter, and abode with him fifteen days.

19 But other of the ^aapostles saw I none, save ^bJames the Lord's ^cbrother.

20 Now the things which I ^awrite unto you, behold, before God, I lie not.

21 Afterwards I came into the regions of Syria and Cilicia;

22 And was unknown by face unto the churches of Judæa which were in Christ:

23 But they had heard only, That he which persecuted us in times past now preacheth the faith which once he destroyed.

24 And they glorified God in me.

CHAPTER 2

Paul goes to Jerusalem—He contends for the true gospel—Salvation comes through Christ.

THEN fourteen years after I went up again to ^aJerusalem with ^bBarnabas, and took Titus with *me* also.

2 And I went up by ^arevelation, and ^bcommunicated unto them that gospel which I preach among the Gentiles, but privately to them which were of reputation, lest by any means I should run, or had run, in vain.

3 But neither Titus, who was with me, being a Greek, was compelled to be ^acircumcised:

4 ^aAnd that because of false brethren unawares brought in, who came in privily to spy out our ^bliberty which we have in Christ Jesus, that they might bring us into ^cbondage:

5 To whom we gave place by subjection, no, not for an hour; that the truth of the gospel might continue with you.

6 But of these who seemed to be somewhat, (whatsoever they were, it maketh no matter to me: God accepteth no man's person:) for they

---

9a TG False Doctrine.
  b 2 Ne. 28:15.
10a GR appease, aspire to the favor of.
    JST Gal. 1:10 . . . *please* . . .
  b TG Peer Influence.
  c TG Courage.
11a GR declare, make known to.
  b 2 Cor. 4:5.
12a GR from a man.
  b GR through a revelation.
  c 1 Cor. 9:1;
    D&C 84:1.
    TG Testimony.
13a GR conduct.

  b Acts 9:21 (10–22).
  c GR was ravaging, destroying.
14a GR was advancing.
  b GR men of my age.
  c TG Zeal.
  d TG Traditions of Men.
15a TG Grace.
16a GR nations, Gentiles.
    TG Heathen.
  b TG Flesh and Blood.
18a Acts 9:26.
19a TG Apostles.
  b Acts 21:18.
  c TG Jesus Christ, Family of.

20a TG Scriptures, Writing of.
2 1a Acts 15:2.
  b Acts 4:36 (36–37).
2a Alma 8:16;
    Hel. 13:3.
  b GR reported.
3a TG Circumcision.
4a JST Gal. 2:4
    Notwithstanding, there were some brought in by false brethren unawares, who . . .
  b TG Liberty.
  c TG Bondage, Spiritual.

who seemed *to be somewhat* in conference added nothing to me:

7 But contrariwise, when they saw that the [a]gospel of the uncircumcision was committed unto me, as *the gospel* of the [b]circumcision *was* unto [c]Peter;

8 (For he that wrought effectually in Peter to the apostleship of the circumcision, the same was mighty in me toward the Gentiles:)

9 And when James, [a]Cephas, and John, who seemed to be pillars, perceived the [b]grace that was given unto me, they gave to me and Barnabas the right hands of [c]fellowship; that we *should go* unto the [d]heathen, and they unto the circumcision.

10 Only *they would* that we should remember the poor; the same which I also was forward to do.

11 But when Peter was come to Antioch, I withstood him to the face, because he was to be blamed.

12 For before that certain came from James, he did eat with the Gentiles: but when they were come, he withdrew and separated himself, fearing them which were of the circumcision.

13 And the other Jews dissembled likewise with him; insomuch that Barnabas also was carried away with their [a]dissimulation.

14 But when I saw that they walked not uprightly according to the truth of the gospel, I said unto Peter before *them* all, If thou, being a Jew, livest after the manner of Gentiles, and not as do the Jews, why compellest thou the Gentiles to live as do the Jews?

15 We *who are* Jews by nature, and not sinners of the Gentiles,

16 Knowing that a man is not [a]justified by the works of the [b]law, but by the faith of Jesus Christ, even we have believed in Jesus Christ, that we might be justified by the [c]faith of Christ, and not by the [d]works of the [e]law: for by the works of the law shall no flesh be [f]justified.

17 But if, while we seek to be justified by Christ, we ourselves also are found sinners, *is* therefore Christ the minister of sin? God forbid.

18 For if I build again the things which I destroyed, I make myself a transgressor.

19 For I through the law am [a]dead to the law, that I might [b]live unto God.

20 I am crucified with Christ: nevertheless I live; yet not I, but [a]Christ [b]liveth in me: and the life which I now live in the flesh I live by the [c]faith of the Son of God, who loved me, and gave himself for me.

21 I do not frustrate the [a]grace of God: for if righteousness *come* by the [b]law, then Christ is dead in vain.

CHAPTER 3

God gave the gospel to Abraham—The Mosaic law was added because of transgressions—The law was a schoolmaster until Christ—The Saints are children of God by faith—All who are of the faith and baptized into Christ become Abraham's seed.

O FOOLISH Galatians, who hath [a]bewitched you, that ye should not obey the truth, before whose eyes Jesus Christ hath been evidently set forth, crucified among you?

2 This only would I learn of you, Received ye the Spirit by the works of the [a]law, or by the [b]hearing of faith?

3 Are ye so foolish? having begun

7a 1 Cor. 9:17.
 b TG Circumcision.
 c 1 Cor. 9:1.
9a John 1:42.
 b TG Grace.
 c TG Fellowshipping.
 d GR nations, Gentiles.
13a GR hypocrisy.
16a TG Justification.
 b D&C 22:2.

c Moro. 7:33 (7–33).
d Mosiah 13:28 (27–32).
e 2 Ne. 2:5 (5–8).
f GR vindicated,
   approved, guiltless.
19a Rom. 7:4 (1–7).
 b Rom. 6:11 (9–11).
20a John 17:22 (20–23).
 b Rom. 14:7 (7–9).
 c TG Faith.

21a TG Grace.
 b Mosiah 13:28 (27–31).
3 1a Jacob 7:18 (16–18).
   TG Apostasy of the
   Early Christian Church.
2a 2 Ne. 2:5;
   Mosiah 13:28 (27–28).
 b Rom. 10:17.

in the Spirit, are ye now made perfect by the flesh?

4 Have ye suffered so many things in vain? if *it be* yet in vain.

5 He therefore that *a*ministereth to you the Spirit, and worketh miracles among you, *doeth he it* by the works of the law, or by the hearing of faith?

6 Even as Abraham believed God, and it was accounted to him for *a*righteousness.

7 Know ye therefore that they which are of faith, the same are the *a*children of Abraham.

8 And the scripture, foreseeing that God would justify the *a*heathen through faith, preached before the *b*gospel unto Abraham, *saying*, In thee shall all *c*nations be *d*blessed.

9 So then they which be of faith are *a*blessed with faithful Abraham.

10 For as many as are of the works of the law are under the curse: for it is written, *a*Cursed *is* every one that continueth not in all things which are written in the book of the law to do them.

11 But that no man is justified by the law in the sight of God, *it is* evident: for, The just shall live by *a*faith.

12 And the law is not of faith: but, The man that doeth them shall live in them.

13 Christ hath *a*redeemed us from the *b*curse of the *c*law, being made a curse for us: for it is written, *d*Cursed *is* every one that hangeth on a tree:

14 That the *a*blessing of Abraham might come on the Gentiles through *b*Jesus Christ; that we might receive the *c*promise of the Spirit through faith.

15 Brethren, I speak after the manner of men; Though *it be* but a man's covenant, yet *if it be* confirmed, no man disannulleth, or addeth thereto.

16 Now to *a*Abraham and his seed were the *b*promises made. He saith not, And to seeds, as of many; but as of one, And to thy seed, which is Christ.

17 And this I say, *that* the covenant, that was confirmed before of God in Christ, the law, which was *a*four hundred and thirty years after, cannot disannul, that it should make the promise of none effect.

18 For if the *a*inheritance *be* of the law, *it is* no more of promise: but God gave *it* to Abraham by promise.

19 *a*Wherefore then *serveth* the law? It was *b*added because of transgressions, till the seed should come to whom the promise was made; *and it was* ordained by angels in the hand of a mediator.

20 Now a mediator is not *a mediator* of one, but God is one.

21 *Is* the law then against the promises of God? God forbid: for if there had been a law given which could have given life, verily righteousness should have been by the law.

22 But the scripture hath concluded all under *a*sin, that the promise by faith of Jesus Christ might be given to them that believe.

23 But before faith came, we were kept under the law, shut up unto the faith which should afterwards be revealed.

24 Wherefore the *a*law was our *b*schoolmaster *to bring us* unto Christ,

---

5a GR grants, furnishes.
6a TG Righteousness.
7a TG Abrahamic
Covenant.
8a TG Heathen.
  b TG Gospel.
  c TG Israel, Mission of.
  d TG Mission of
Latter-day Saints.
9a TG Israel, Blessings of.
10a TG Curse.
11a TG Faith.
13a Gal. 4:5.

  b TG Bondage, Spiritual;
Curse.
  c Alma 42:22 (1–28).
  d Deut. 21:23.
14a TG Blessing;
Israel, Mission of.
  b Acts 8:35 (29–35).
  c TG Promise.
16a Ps. 132:11;
Luke 1:55 (54–55).
  b D&C 107:40.
17a TG Israel, Bondage of,
in Egypt.

18a TG Inheritance.
19a JST Gal. 3:19–20
(Appendix).
  b 1 Tim. 1:9.
22a D&C 49:8.
24a TG Law of Moses.
  b GR pedagogue, director,
supervisor of children.
JST Gal. 3:24 . . .
schoolmaster *until*
Christ . . .
TG Jesus Christ, Types
of, in Anticipation.

that we might be ^cjustified by faith.

25 But after that faith is come, we are no longer under a schoolmaster.

26 For ye are all the ^achildren of God by ^bfaith in Christ Jesus.

27 For as many of you as have been ^abaptized into Christ have put on Christ.

28 There is neither Jew nor ^aGreek, there is neither bond nor free, there is neither male nor female: for ye are all ^bone in Christ Jesus.

29 And if ye *be* Christ's, then are ye ^aAbraham's ^bseed, and ^cheirs according to the promise.

CHAPTER 4

The Saints are children of God by adoption—Paul calls the Galatians back to Christ—He compares the two covenants.

NOW I say, *That* the heir, as long as he is a child, differeth nothing from a servant, though he be lord of all;

2 But is under tutors and governors until the time appointed of the father.

3 Even so we, when we were children, were in ^abondage under the elements of the world:

4 But when the fulness of the time was come, God ^asent forth his ^bSon, ^cmade of a ^dwoman, made under the law,

5 To ^aredeem them that were under the law, that we might receive the ^badoption of sons.

6 And because ye are sons, God hath sent forth the Spirit of his Son into your hearts, crying, Abba, Father.

7 Wherefore thou art no more a ^aservant, but a ^bson; and if a son, then an ^cheir of God through Christ.

8 Howbeit then, when ye knew not God, ye ^adid ^bservice unto them which by nature are no ^cgods.

9 But now, after that ye have known God, or rather are known of God, how turn ye again to the weak and beggarly elements, whereunto ye desire again to be in ^abondage?

10 Ye observe ^adays, and months, and times, and years.

11 I am afraid ^aof you, lest I have bestowed upon you labour in vain.

12 Brethren, I beseech you, be as I *am;* for I *am* as ye *are:* ye have not injured me at all.

13 Ye know how through ^ainfirmity of the ^bflesh I preached the gospel unto you at the first.

14 And my ^atemptation which was in my flesh ye despised not, nor rejected; but received me as an angel of God, *even* as Christ Jesus.

15 Where is then the blessedness ye spake of? for I bear you record, that, if *it had been* possible, ye would have plucked out your own eyes, and have given them to me.

16 Am I therefore become your enemy, because I tell you the ^atruth?

17 They zealously affect you, *but* not well; yea, they would exclude you, that ye might affect them.

18 But *it is* good to be ^azealously affected always in *a* good *thing,* and not only when I am present with you.

24c See JST Rom. 4:16 (Rom. 4:16 note *a*). Moro. 10:32 (32–33).
26a TG Sons and Daughters of God.
  b TG Baptism, Qualifications for.
27a Rom. 13:14; 2 Ne. 31:13 (12–13); Mosiah 5:8 (2–14). TG Baptism.
28a TG Gentiles.
  b Rom. 10:12 (12–13). TG Unity.
29a TG Conversion.
  b TG Seed of Abraham.

  c Gal. 4:28.
4 3a TG Bondage, Spiritual.
  4a John 8:42; 16:28 (27–28, 30); 17:8. TG Jesus Christ, Condescension of.
  b TG Jesus Christ, Birth of.
  c GR born.
  d TG Woman.
  5a Gal. 3:13.
  b TG Election.
  7a GR slave.
  b TG Sons and Daughters of God.
  c TG Eternal Life; Man, Potential to

Become like Heavenly Father.
  8a GR were slaves, were in bondage.
  b 1 Cor. 8:4.
  c Jer. 44:3.
  9a D&C 84:51 (50–51).
10a Rom. 14:5 (5–6).
11a GR concerning.
13a GR weakness, feebleness. 1 Cor. 2:3 (2–4).
  b 2 Cor. 10:10.
14a GR trial, test.
16a Hel. 13:26. TG Truth.
18a TG Zeal.

19 My little children, of whom I travail in birth again until Christ be formed in you,

20 I desire to be present with you now, and to change my voice; for I ªstand in doubt of you.

21 Tell me, ye that desire to be under the law, do ye not hear the law?

22 For it is written, that Abraham had two sons, the one by a ªbondmaid, the other by a freewoman.

23 But he *who was* of the bondwoman was born after the flesh; but he of the freewoman *was* by promise.

24 Which things are an allegory: for these are the two covenants; the one from the mount Sinai, which gendereth to ªbondage, which is ᵇAgar.

25 For this Agar is mount Sinai in Arabia, and answereth to Jerusalem which now is, and is in bondage with her children.

26 But ªJerusalem which is above is free, which is the mother of us all.

27 For it is written, ªRejoice, *thou* ᵇbarren that bearest not; break forth and cry, thou that travailest not: for the desolate hath many more children than she which hath an husband.

28 Now we, brethren, as Isaac was, are the ªchildren of promise.

29 But as then he that was born after the ªflesh ᵇpersecuted him *that was born* after the Spirit, even so *it is* now.

30 Nevertheless what saith the scripture? ªCast out the bondwoman and her son: for the son of the bondwoman shall not be heir with the son of the freewoman.

31 So then, brethren, we are not children of the bondwoman, but of the free.

CHAPTER 5

Stand fast in gospel liberty—Seek faith, love, Christ, and the Spirit—The works of the flesh and the fruits of the Spirit are named.

ªSTAND fast therefore in the ᵇliberty wherewith Christ hath made us ᶜfree, and be not ᵈentangled again with the yoke of ᵉbondage.

2 Behold, I Paul say unto you, that if ye be circumcised, Christ shall profit you nothing.

3 For I testify again to every man that is ªcircumcised, that he is a debtor to do the whole law.

4 Christ is become of no effect unto you, whosoever of you are justified by the ªlaw; ye are fallen from ᵇgrace.

5 For we through the Spirit wait for the hope of righteousness by ªfaith.

6 For in Jesus Christ neither ªcircumcision ᵇavaileth any thing, nor uncircumcision; but ᶜfaith which worketh by ᵈlove.

7 Ye did run well; who did hinder you that ye should not ªobey the truth?

8 This persuasion *cometh* not of him that calleth you.

9 A little leaven leaveneth the whole lump.

10 I have ªconfidence in you through the Lord, that ye ᵇwill be none otherwise minded: but he that ᶜtroubleth you shall bear his judgment, whosoever he be.

20a GR am perplexed about.
22a Gen. 16:2 (1–3);
    D&C 132:30 (30–34), 65;
    Abr. 2:9 (9–11).
24a TG Law of Moses.
  b Gen. 16:1.
26a TG Jerusalem, New.
27a Gen. 21:6.
  b TG Barren.
28a Gal. 3:29.
    TG Mission of
    Early Saints;
    Seed of Abraham.
29a TG Man, Natural, Not

Spiritually Reborn.
  b Gen. 21:9.
30a Gen. 21:10.
5 1a Philip. 4:1 (1–7).
  b TG Liberty.
  c 2 Ne. 2:26 (26–27);
    Mosiah 5:8;
    Alma 61:9 (9, 21).
  d D&C 88:86.
  e TG Bondage, Spiritual;
    Law of Moses.
3a Rom. 2:25.
4a TG Law of Moses.
  b TG Grace.

5a Rom. 5:2 (1–5);
    1 Pet. 1:21 (21–22).
6a TG Circumcision.
  b GR has any power,
    validity, service.
  c TG Faith.
  d TG Love.
7a TG Disobedience.
10a TG Dependability.
  b GR will take no other
    view, will not have a
    different opinion.
  c Gal. 1:7.

11 And I, brethren, if I yet preach circumcision, why do I yet suffer persecution? then is the ^aoffence of the cross ceased.

12 I would they were even ^acut off which ^btrouble you.

13 For, brethren, ye have been called unto ^aliberty; only *use* not liberty for an occasion to the flesh, but by love ^bserve one another.

14 For all the ^alaw is fulfilled in one word, *even* in this; Thou shalt ^blove thy neighbour as thyself.

15 But if ye bite and devour one another, take heed that ye be not consumed one of another.

16 *This* I say then, ^aWalk in the ^bSpirit, and ye shall not fulfil the ^clust of the flesh.

17 For the flesh lusteth against the ^aSpirit, and the Spirit against the flesh: and these are contrary the one to the other: so that ye cannot do the things that ye would.

18 But if ye be ^aled of the Spirit, ye are not under the ^blaw.

19 Now the works of the ^aflesh are manifest, which are *these*; Adultery, ^bfornication, ^cuncleanness, lasciviousness,

20 Idolatry, witchcraft, hatred, variance, emulations, wrath, ^astrife, seditions, heresies,

21 ^aEnvyings, murders, ^bdrunkenness, ^crevellings, and such like: of the which I tell you before, as I have also told *you* in time past, that they which do such things shall not inherit the kingdom of God.

22 But the ^afruit of the ^bSpirit is ^clove, ^djoy, ^epeace, ^flongsuffering, ^ggentleness, goodness, ^hfaith,

23 ^aMeekness, ^btemperance: against such there is no law.

24 And they that are Christ's have crucified the flesh with the ^aaffections and lusts.

25 If we live in the Spirit, let us also walk in the Spirit.

26 Let us not be desirous of vain glory, ^aprovoking one another, envying one another.

CHAPTER 6

Bear one another's burdens—As you sow, so shall you reap—Be not weary in well-doing.

BRETHREN, if a man be ^aovertaken in a ^bfault, ye which are spiritual, ^crestore such an one in the spirit of meekness; ^dconsidering thyself, lest thou also be tempted.

2 Bear ye one another's ^aburdens, and so fulfil the law of Christ.

3 For if a man think himself to be something, when he is nothing, he deceiveth himself.

4 But let every man ^aprove his own ^bwork, and then shall he have rejoicing in himself alone, and not in another.

5 For every man shall ^abear his own burden.

11*a* GR stumbling block, cause of misery.
12*a* TG Excommunication.
  b Gal. 1:8 (8–9).
13*a* TG Abundant Life; Liberty.
  b TG Self-Sacrifice.
14*a* Rom. 13:10 (8–10); 1 Tim. 1:5. TG God, Law of.
  b TG Love.
16*a* TG Walking with God.
  b TG Guidance, Divine.
  c TG Chastity; Lust.
17*a* TG Holy Ghost, Loss of.
18*a* D&C 20:45; 28:4; 42:13.
  b Acts 15:5 (1–11); Mosiah 13:29 (29–31).

19*a* Mosiah 16:3 (3–5); D&C 67:12 (10–12).
  b TG Fornication.
  c TG Uncleanness.
20*a* TG Strife.
21*a* TG Envy.
  b TG Drunkenness; Word of Wisdom.
  c TG Rioting and Reveling.
22*a* Rom. 8:23. TG Holy Ghost, Mission of.
  b TG Inspiration; Spirituality.
  c Col. 3:12.
  d TG Joy.
  e TG Contentment; Peace of God.
  f TG Forbear.

  g TG Benevolence; Kindness.
  h TG Faith.
23*a* TG Meek.
  b GR self-control. TG Temperance.
24*a* GR sufferings, afflictions, passions.
26*a* TG Provoking.
6 1*a* Rom. 14:1; D&C 20:80.
  b GR transgression, trespass.
  c Heb. 12:13.
  d GR watching.
2*a* TG Compassion.
4*a* TG Test.
  b TG Good Works.
5*a* Prov. 9:12.

6 Let him that is taught in the word ªcommunicate unto him that teacheth in all good things.

7 Be not ªdeceived; God is not ᵇmocked: for whatsoever a man ᶜsoweth, that shall he also ᵈreap.

8 For he that soweth to his flesh shall of the flesh reap corruption; but he that soweth to the Spirit shall of the Spirit reap life everlasting.

9 And let us not be ªweary in well doing: for in due season we shall ᵇreap, if we faint not.

10 As we have therefore opportunity, let us do ªgood unto all *men*, especially unto them who are of the household of faith.

11 Ye see how large a letter I have written unto you with mine own hand.

12 As many as desire to make a fair shew in the flesh, they constrain you to be circumcised; only lest they should suffer ªpersecution for the cross of Christ.

13 For neither they themselves who are circumcised keep the law; but desire to have you circumcised, that they may glory in your flesh.

14 But God forbid that I should glory, save in the cross of our Lord Jesus Christ, by whom the world is crucified unto me, and I unto the world.

15 For in Christ Jesus neither ªcircumcision availeth any thing, nor uncircumcision, but a new creature.

16 And as many as walk according to this rule, ªpeace *be* on them, and mercy, and upon the Israel of God.

17 From henceforth let no man trouble me: for I bear in my body the marks of the Lord Jesus.

18 Brethren, the grace of our Lord Jesus Christ *be* with your spirit. Amen.

¶ Unto the Galatians written from Rome.

THE EPISTLE OF PAUL THE APOSTLE
TO THE
EPHESIANS

CHAPTER 1

The Saints are foreordained to receive the gospel—The gospel is to be restored in the latter days—The Saints are sealed by the Holy Spirit of Promise—They know God and Christ by revelation.

PAUL, an apostle of Jesus Christ by the will of God, to the ªsaints which are at Ephesus, and to the faithful in Christ Jesus:

2 Grace *be* to you, and peace, from God our Father, and *from* the Lord Jesus Christ.

3 Blessed *be* the God and Father of our Lord Jesus Christ, who hath blessed us with all ªspiritual blessings in heavenly *places* in Christ:

4 According as he hath ªchosen us in him ᵇbefore the foundation of the world, that we should be ᶜholy and without blame before him in love:

6a TG Communication.
7a TG Deceit.
  b TG Mocking.
  c Ezek. 32:27.
    TG Accountability;
    Agency; Good Works.
  d Ps. 7:16.
    TG Harvest.

9a Luke 8:14 (14–15);
    2 Thes. 3:13; D&C 64:33.
    TG Steadfastness.
  b TG Abundant Life.
10a Prov. 3:27.
12a TG Persecution.
15a TG Circumcision.
16a Ps. 125:5.

[EPHESIANS]

1 1a TG Saints.
  3a TG Spirituality.
  4a TG Election;
    Foreordination.
  b TG Man, Antemortal
    Existence of.
  c TG Holiness.

5 Having ^apredestinated us unto the ^badoption of children by Jesus Christ to himself, according to the good pleasure of his will,

6 To the praise of the glory of his grace, wherein he hath made us accepted in the beloved.

7 In whom we have ^aredemption through his blood, the ^bforgiveness of sins, according to the ^criches of his ^dgrace;

8 Wherein he hath abounded toward us in all ^awisdom and ^bprudence;

9 Having made known unto us the ^amystery of his ^bwill, according to his good pleasure which he hath purposed in himself:

10 That in the ^adispensation of the fulness of times he might ^bgather together in one ^call things in Christ, both which are in heaven, and which are on earth; *even* in him:

11 In whom also we have obtained an inheritance, being ^apredestinated according to the purpose of him who worketh all things after the counsel of his own will:

12 That we should be to the praise of his glory, who ^afirst trusted in Christ.

13 In whom ye also *trusted*, after that ye heard the word of truth, the ^agospel of your salvation: in whom also after that ye believed, ye were ^bsealed with that holy Spirit of ^cpromise,

14 Which is the earnest of our inheritance until the redemption of the purchased possession, unto the praise of his glory.

15 Wherefore I also, after I heard of your ^afaith in the Lord Jesus, and love unto all the saints,

16 Cease not to give thanks for you, making mention of you in my prayers;

17 That the God of our Lord Jesus Christ, the Father of glory, may give unto you the spirit of ^awisdom and ^brevelation in the knowledge of him:

18 The eyes of your ^aunderstanding being ^benlightened; that ye may know what is the hope of his calling, and what the ^criches of the glory of his ^dinheritance in the saints,

19 And what *is* the exceeding greatness of his ^apower to us-ward who believe, according to the working of his mighty power,

20 Which he wrought in Christ, when he ^araised him from the dead, and set *him* at his own right hand in the ^bheavenly *places,*

21 Far above all principality, and power, and might, and dominion, and every ^aname that is named, not only in this world, but also in that which is to come:

22 And hath put ^aall *things* under his ^bfeet, and gave him *to be* the ^chead over all *things* to the ^dchurch,

23 Which is his body, the fulness of him that filleth all in all.

CHAPTER 2

We are saved by grace through faith—The blood of Christ saves Jew and Gentile alike—The Church is built upon the foundation of apostles and prophets.

---

5 *a* GR foreordained.
  Eph. 1:11.
  TG Foreordination.
  b TG Sons and Daughters
  of God.
7 *a* TG Jesus Christ,
  Atonement through;
  Jesus Christ, Redeemer;
  Redemption.
  b TG Forgive.
  c TG Treasure.
  d TG Grace.
8 *a* TG God, Omniscience of.
  b TG Prudence.
9 *a* Eph. 3:4; D&C 107:19.
  b TG God, Will of.

10 *a* TG Dispensations;
  Last Days; Restoration
  of the Gospel.
  b TG Israel, Gathering of.
  c TG Jesus Christ, Power of.
11 *a* Eph. 1:5.
12 *a* GR trusted, hoped
  beforehand.
13 *a* D&C 93:51.
  TG Gospel.
  b TG Sealing.
  c TG Promise.
15 *a* Col. 1:4 (4–5).
17 *a* TG Wisdom.
  b TG Revelation.
18 *a* TG Understanding.

b D&C 6:15; 11:13.
  TG Education.
c TG Treasure.
d TG Inheritance.
19 *a* Col. 2:12.
20 *a* Acts 2:32;
  1 Cor. 15:20 (14–20).
  b Heb. 7:26.
21 *a* Heb. 1:4.
  TG Name.
22 *a* TG Jesus Christ, Power of.
  b Heb. 2:8.
  c TG Jesus Christ,
  Head of the Church;
  Jesus Christ, Messiah.
  d TG Church.

AND you *hath he quickened,* who were [a]dead in trespasses and sins;

2 Wherein in time past ye walked according to the course of this [a]world, according to the prince of the power of the air, the spirit that now worketh in the children of [b]disobedience:

3 Among whom also we all had our conversation in times past in the [a]lusts of our flesh, fulfilling the desires of the flesh and of the mind; and were by [b]nature the children of wrath, even as others.

4 But God, who is rich in [a]mercy, for his great love wherewith he loved us,

5 Even when we were dead in sins, hath [a]quickened us together with Christ, (by grace ye are saved;)

6 And hath raised *us* up together, and made *us* sit together in heavenly *places* in Christ Jesus:

7 That in the ages to come he might shew the exceeding [a]riches of his grace in *his* kindness toward us through Christ Jesus.

8 For by [a]grace are ye [b]saved through [c]faith; and that not of yourselves: *it is* the [d]gift of God:

9 Not of works, lest any man should [a]boast.

10 For we are his [a]workmanship, created in Christ Jesus unto good [b]works, which God hath before ordained that we should [c]walk in them.

11 Wherefore remember, that ye *being* in time past Gentiles in the flesh, who are called [a]Uncircumcision by that which is called the Circumcision in the flesh made by hands;

12 That at that time ye were without Christ, being aliens from the commonwealth of Israel, and [a]strangers from the [b]covenants of promise, having no [c]hope, and [d]without God in the world:

13 But now in Christ Jesus ye who sometimes were far off are made nigh by the blood of Christ.

14 For he is our [a]peace, who hath made both one, and hath broken down the middle [b]wall of partition *between us;*

15 Having [a]abolished in his flesh the enmity, *even* the law of commandments *contained* in [b]ordinances; for to make in himself of twain one [c]new man, *so* making peace;

16 And that he might [a]reconcile both unto God in one body by the cross, having slain the enmity thereby:

17 And came and preached peace to you which were afar off, and to them that were nigh.

18 For through him we both have access by one Spirit unto the Father.

19 Now therefore ye are no more [a]strangers and foreigners, but [b]fellowcitizens with the [c]saints, and of the [d]household of God;

20 And are built upon the foundation of the [a]apostles and [b]prophets, Jesus Christ himself being the chief [c]corner *stone;*

21 In whom all the building fitly framed together groweth unto an holy temple in the Lord:

22 In whom ye also are builded together for an habitation of God through the Spirit.

2 1*a* Col. 1:21; Rev. 3:1.
  2*a* TG Worldliness.
    b D&C 121:17.
      TG Disobedience.
  3*a* TG Lust.
    b TG Man, Natural, Not Spiritually Reborn.
  4*a* TG God, Mercy of.
  5*a* TG Resurrection.
  7*a* TG Treasure.
  8*a* Alma 22:14 (13–14); 42:14 (10–25); D&C 20:30 (29–34).
      TG Grace.
    b TG Salvation; Salvation, Plan of.

    c TG Faith.
    d TG God, Gifts of.
  9*a* TG Boast.
 10*a* Ps. 100:3; Isa. 60:21; D&C 29:25.
    b TG Good Works.
    c TG Walking with God.
 11*a* TG Circumcision.
 12*a* TG Stranger.
    b TG Covenants.
    c 1 Thes. 4:13.
    d 1 Thes. 4:5; Mosiah 27:31; Alma 41:11.
 14*a* TG Peace; Peace of God.
    b TG Veil.

 15*a* Col. 2:14.
    b TG Ordinance.
    c TG Man, New, Spiritually Reborn.
 16*a* TG Jesus Christ, Atonement through.
 19*a* TG Gentiles; Stranger.
    b TG Citizenship; Fellowshipping.
    c TG Saints.
    d TG Sons and Daughters of God.
 20*a* TG Apostles; Church Organization.
    b TG Prophets, Mission of.
    c TG Cornerstone.

CHAPTER 3

The Gentiles are fellow heirs with Israel—The love of Christ surpasses all understanding.

FOR this cause I Paul, the prisoner of Jesus Christ for you Gentiles,

2 If ye have heard of the ªdispensation of the grace of God which is given me to you-ward:

3 How that by revelation he made ªknown unto me the mystery; (as I ᵇwrote afore in few words,

4 Whereby, when ye read, ye may understand my knowledge in the ªmystery of Christ)

5 Which in other ages was not made known unto the sons of men, as it is now ªrevealed unto his holy apostles and ᵇprophets by the Spirit;

6 That the ªGentiles should be fellowheirs, and of the same body, and partakers of his promise in Christ by the gospel:

7 Whereof I was made a minister, according to the gift of the grace of God given unto me by the effectual working of his power.

8 Unto me, who am less than the least of all saints, is this ªgrace given, that I should preach among the Gentiles the unsearchable ᵇriches of Christ;

9 And to make all *men* see what is the fellowship of the ªmystery, which from the beginning of the world hath been hid in God, who ᵇcreated all things by ᶜJesus Christ:

10 To the intent that now unto the principalities and powers in heavenly *places* might be known by the church the manifold wisdom of God,

11 According to the eternal ªpurpose which he purposed in Christ Jesus our Lord:

12 In whom we have boldness and access with confidence by the faith of him.

13 Wherefore I desire that ye faint not at my tribulations for you, which is your glory.

14 For this cause I bow my knees unto the ªFather of our Lord Jesus Christ,

15 Of whom the whole ªfamily in heaven and earth is named,

16 That he would grant you, according to the ªriches of his glory, to be ᵇstrengthened with might by his Spirit in the inner man;

17 That Christ may dwell in your hearts by faith; that ye, being ªrooted and ᵇgrounded in love,

18 May be able to comprehend with all saints what *is* the breadth, and length, and depth, and height;

19 And to know the ªlove of Christ, which passeth knowledge, that ye might be filled with all the fulness of God.

20 Now unto him that is able to do exceeding abundantly above all that we ask or think, according to the power that worketh in us,

21 Unto him *be* glory in the church by Christ Jesus throughout all ages, ªworld without end. Amen.

CHAPTER 4

There is one Lord, one faith, and one baptism—Apostles and prophets are essential to the Church—The Saints are exhorted to live righteously—They are sealed unto the day of redemption.

I THEREFORE, the prisoner of the Lord, beseech you that ye walk ªworthy of the ᵇvocation wherewith ye are called,

2 With all lowliness and meekness, with longsuffering, ªforbearing one another in love;

---

3 2ª TG Dispensations.
3ª Col. 1:27 (26–27).
　b TG Scriptures, Lost.
4ª Rom. 16:25;
　　Eph. 1:9 (9–11).
5ª TG Revelation.
　b TG Prophets, Mission of.
6ª TG Gentiles.
8ª TG Grace.
　b TG Treasure.

9ª TG Mysteries of
　　Godliness.
　b TG Creation;
　　God, Creator;
　　Jesus Christ, Creator.
　c TG Jesus Christ,
　　Jehovah.
11ª TG Earth, Purpose of.
14ª TG Godhead.
15ª TG Family.

16ª TG Treasure.
　b Col. 1:11.
　　TG Strength.
17ª Col. 2:7.
　b Col. 1:23.
19ª TG God, Love of.
21ª D&C 76:112.
4 1ª TG Worthiness.
　b GR calling.
2ª TG Forbear.

3 Endeavouring to keep the ^aunity of the Spirit in the bond of peace.

4 *There is* one ^abody, and one Spirit, even as ye are called in one hope of your calling;

5 One Lord, one ^afaith, one ^bbaptism,

6 One God and ^aFather of all, who *is* above all, and through all, and in you all.

7 But unto every one of us is given ^agrace according to the measure of the gift of Christ.

8 Wherefore he saith, When he ^aascended up on high, he led captivity captive, and gave gifts unto men.

9 (Now that he ascended, what is it but that he also descended first into the lower parts of the earth?

10 He that descended is the same also that ^aascended up far above all heavens, that he might fill all things.)

11 And he ^agave some, ^bapostles; and some, ^cprophets; and some, ^devangelists; and some, ^epastors and ^fteachers;

12 For the ^aperfecting of the saints, for the work of the ministry, for the ^bedifying of the body of Christ:

13 Till we all come in the ^aunity of the faith, and of the ^bknowledge of the Son of God, unto a ^cperfect man, unto the measure of the stature of the fulness of Christ:

14 That we *henceforth* be no more ^achildren, tossed to and fro, and carried about with every wind of ^bdoctrine, by the sleight of men, *and* cunning craftiness, whereby they lie in wait to deceive;

15 But speaking the ^atruth in love, may grow up into him in all things, which is the ^bhead, *even* Christ:

16 From whom the whole body fitly joined together and compacted by that which every joint supplieth, according to the effectual working in the measure of every part, maketh increase of the body unto the edifying of itself in love.

17 This I say therefore, and testify in the Lord, that ye henceforth walk not as other ^aGentiles walk, in the ^bvanity of their ^cmind,

18 Having the ^aunderstanding darkened, being alienated from the life of God through the ^bignorance that is in them, because of the ^cblindness of their ^dheart:

19 Who being ^apast ^bfeeling have given themselves over unto lasciviousness, to work all uncleanness with greediness.

20 But ye have not so learned Christ;

21 If so be that ye have heard him, and have been taught by him, as the truth is in Jesus:

22 That ye ^aput off concerning the former conversation the ^bold man, which is corrupt according to the deceitful ^clusts;

23 And be renewed in the spirit of your mind;

3*a* TG Unity.
4*a* TG Church.
5*a* 1 Cor. 14:33; Eph. 4:13; D&C 1:30.
　　 TG Gospel.
　b TG Baptism, Essential; Baptism, Immersion.
6*a* Mal. 2:10; 1 Cor. 8:6.
　　 TG God the Father, Elohim.
7*a* TG Grace.
8*a* Ps. 68:18; Acts 1:9; D&C 88:6.
10*a* TG Jesus Christ, Ascension of.
11*a* TG Authority.
　b TG Apostles; Church Organization; Priesthood, History of.

c TG Prophets, Mission of.
d Acts 21:8; 2 Tim. 4:5.
　 TG Patriarch.
e TG Bishop.
f TG Teacher.
12*a* TG Priesthood, Magnifying Callings within.
　b TG Edification.
13*a* 1 Cor. 1:10; 14:33; Eph. 4:5 (3–6); 3 Ne. 11:28 (28–30); D&C 1:30; 38:27.
　b TG Learn.
　c TG God, Perfection of; Man, Potential to Become like Heavenly Father; Perfection.
14*a* 1 Cor. 14:20.

b Heb. 13:9.
15*a* TG Reproof.
　b Col. 2:19.
　　 TG Jesus Christ, Head of the Church.
17*a* 1 Thes. 4:5.
　b TG Vanity.
　c TG Mind.
18*a* D&C 10:2.
　　 TG Understanding.
　b TG Ignorance.
　c GR hardness.
　　 TG Spiritual Blindness.
　d TG Hardheartedness.
19*a* 1 Ne. 17:45.
　b TG Conscience.
22*a* Col. 3:8.
　b Rom. 6:6 (1–7).
　c TG Lust.

24 And that ye put on the ªnew man, which after God is created in ᵇrighteousness and true holiness.

25 Wherefore putting away ªlying, speak every man ᵇtruth with his neighbour: for we are members one of another.

26 ªBe ye angry, and sin not: let not the sun go down upon your ᵇwrath:

27 Neither give place to the ªdevil.

28 Let him that stole ªsteal no more: but rather let him ᵇlabour, working with *his* hands the thing which is good, that he may have to ᶜgive to him that needeth.

29 Let no corrupt ªcommunication proceed out of your mouth, but that which is good to the use of edifying, that it may minister grace unto the hearers.

30 And ªgrieve not the holy ᵇSpirit of God, whereby ye are ᶜsealed unto the day of redemption.

31 Let all bitterness, and wrath, and ªanger, and clamour, and ᵇevil ᶜspeaking, be put away from you, with all ᵈmalice:

32 And be ye ªkind one to another, tenderhearted, ᵇforgiving one another, even as God for Christ's sake hath forgiven you.

CHAPTER 5

The Saints are exhorted to avoid uncleanness and walk uprightly—Husbands and wives should love each other.

BE ye therefore ªfollowers of God, as dear children;

2 And ªwalk in love, as Christ also hath loved us, and hath given himself for us an ᵇoffering and a ᶜsacrifice to God for a sweetsmelling ᵈsavour.

3 But ªfornication, and all uncleanness, or covetousness, let it not be once named among you, as becometh ᵇsaints;

4 Neither ªfilthiness, nor ᵇfoolish ᶜtalking, nor jesting, which are not convenient: but rather giving of thanks.

5 For this ye know, that no ªwhoremonger, nor ᵇunclean person, nor covetous man, who is an idolater, hath any ᶜinheritance in the kingdom of Christ and of God.

6 Let no man ªdeceive you with vain words: for because of these things cometh the ᵇwrath of God upon the children of ᶜdisobedience.

7 Be not ye therefore partakers with them.

8 For ye were sometimes darkness, but now *are* ye light in the Lord: walk as ªchildren of ᵇlight:

9 (For the fruit of the Spirit *is* in all ªgoodness and righteousness and truth;)

10 Proving what is acceptable unto the Lord.

11 And have no ªfellowship with the unfruitful works of ᵇdarkness, but rather ᶜreprove *them.*

24a TG Man, New,
    Spiritually Reborn;
    Mission of Early Saints.
  b TG Righteousness.
25a TG Lying.
  b TG Honesty; Truth.
26a JST Eph. 4:26 *Can ye be
    angry, and not sin?* . . .
  b TG Anger.
27a Mosiah 2:32 (32–33);
    3 Ne. 11:29.
28a TG Stealing.
  b TG Labor;
    Work, Value of.
  c Prov. 21:26.
29a TG Communication;
    Gossip; Profanity.
30a Gen. 6:6.
  b TG God, Spirit of.
  c TG Sealing.

31a TG Anger.
  b TG Backbiting.
  c TG Slander.
  d TG Malice.
32a TG Benevolence;
    Courtesy; Family, Love
    within; Kindness.
  b TG Forgive.
5 1a GR imitators.
    1 Cor. 11:1;
    Philip. 3:17 (13–21).
    TG God, the Standard of
    Righteousness;
    Jesus Christ, Exemplar.
  2a TG Walking with God.
  b Heb. 8:3.
  c TG Self-Sacrifice.
  d Gen. 8:21;
    Lev. 1:9.
  3a TG Chastity;

Fornication;
    Sexual Immorality.
  b TG Saints.
4a TG Filthiness.
  b TG Levity.
  c Eccl. 5:2; Matt. 12:36.
5a TG Chastity; Whore.
  b TG Uncleanness.
  c TG Inheritance;
    Worthiness.
6a TG Deceit.
  b TG God, Indignation of.
  c TG Disobedience.
8a TG Children of Light.
  b Rom. 12:2.
9a TG Good Works.
11a Gen. 49:6; Ps. 1:1 (1–2);
    Prov. 1:10 (10–19).
  b TG Darkness, Spiritual.
  c TG Reproof.

12 For it is a ªshame even to speak of those things which are done of them in secret.

13 But all things that are reproved are made manifest by the light: for whatsoever doth make manifest is light.

14 Wherefore he saith, Awake thou that sleepest, and arise from the dead, and Christ shall give thee ªlight.

15 See then that ye walk circumspectly, not as fools, but as wise,

16 Redeeming the time, because the days are evil:

17 Wherefore be ye not ªunwise, but understanding what the will of the Lord is.

18 And be not ªdrunk with wine, wherein is ᵇexcess; but be filled with the Spirit;

19 Speaking to yourselves in psalms and ªhymns and spiritual songs, singing and making ᵇmelody in your heart to the Lord;

20 Giving ªthanks always for all things unto God and the Father in the name of our Lord Jesus Christ;

21 ªSubmitting yourselves one to another in the fear of God.

22 ªWives, ᵇsubmit yourselves unto your own husbands, as unto the Lord.

23 For the ªhusband is the head of the wife, even as Christ is the ᵇhead of the ᶜchurch: and he is the saviour of the body.

24 Therefore as the church is subject unto Christ, so let the wives be to their own husbands in every thing.

25 ªHusbands, ᵇlove your ᶜwives, even as Christ also loved the church, and gave himself for it;

26 That he might ªsanctify and ᵇcleanse it with the washing of water by the word,

27 That he might present it to himself a glorious church, not having spot, or wrinkle, or any such thing; but that it should be holy and without blemish.

28 So ought men to love their wives as their own bodies. He that loveth his ªwife loveth himself.

29 For no man ever yet ªhated his own ᵇflesh; but nourisheth and cherisheth it, even as the Lord the church:

30 For we are ªmembers of his body, of his flesh, and of his bones.

31 For this cause shall a man leave his father and mother, and shall be joined unto his wife, and they two shall be ªone flesh.

32 This is a great ªmystery: but I speak concerning Christ and the church.

33 Nevertheless let every one of you in particular so love his wife even as himself; and the ªwife see that she ᵇreverence her husband.

CHAPTER 6

Children should honor their parents—Servants and masters are judged by the same law—Saints should put on the whole armor of God.

ªCHILDREN, ᵇobey your parents in the Lord: for this is right.

2 ªHonour thy father and mother; (which is the first commandment with promise;)

3 That it may be well with thee, and thou mayest live long on the earth.

12a TG Shame.
14a TG Jesus Christ, Light of the World; Light [noun].
17a TG Wisdom.
18a TG Drunkenness; Word of Wisdom.
  b TG Temperance.
19a TG Singing.
  b 2 Kgs. 3:15.
20a TG Thanksgiving.
21a TG Reconciliation.
22a TG Marriage, Continuing Courtship in.
  b Esth. 1:20 (20–22).

TG Submissiveness.
23a TG Marriage, Husbands.
  b TG Jesus Christ, Head of the Church.
  c TG Church.
25a TG Family, Patriarchal.
  b TG Family, Love within; Love.
  c TG Marriage, Continuing Courtship in.
26a TG Sanctification.
  b TG Purification.
28a TG Marriage, Wives.
29a TG Hate.
  b TG Body, Sanctity of.

30a 1 Cor. 6:15.
31a TG Marriage, Celestial; Unity.
32a TG Mysteries of Godliness.
33a TG Marriage, Wives.
  b TG Courtesy; Respect.
6 1a TG Children.
  b TG Counsel; Family, Children, Duties of; Respect.
2a TG Honoring Father and Mother.

4 And, ye *fathers, *provoke not your *children to wrath: but bring them up in the nurture and admonition of the Lord.

5 *Servants, be obedient to them that are *your *masters according to the flesh, with fear and trembling, in singleness of your heart, as unto Christ;

6 Not with eyeservice, as menpleasers; but as the *servants of Christ, doing the *will of God from the heart;

7 With good will doing *service, as to the Lord, and not to men:

8 Knowing that whatsoever good thing any man doeth, the same shall he *receive of the Lord, whether *he be* bond or free.

9 And, ye *masters, do the same things unto them, forbearing threatening: knowing that your *Master also is in heaven; neither is there *respect of persons with him.

10 Finally, my brethren, be *strong in the Lord, and in the power of his might.

11 Put on the whole *armour of God, that ye may be able to stand against the wiles of the devil.

12 For we *wrestle not *against *flesh and blood, but against principalities, against powers, against the *rulers of the *darkness of this world, against spiritual *wickedness in high *places.

13 Wherefore take unto you the whole armour of God, that ye may be able to withstand in the evil day, and having done all, to stand.

14 Stand therefore, having your loins *girt about with *truth, and having on the *breastplate of *righteousness;

15 And your feet shod with the preparation of the gospel of *peace;

16 Above all, taking the shield of *faith, wherewith ye shall be able to quench all the fiery *darts of the wicked.

17 And take the helmet of *salvation, and the sword of the Spirit, which is the word of God:

18 *Praying always with all prayer and supplication in the Spirit, and watching thereunto with all *perseverance and supplication for all saints;

19 And for me, that utterance may be given unto me, that I may open my mouth boldly, to make known the *mystery of the gospel,

20 For which I am an ambassador in bonds: that therein I may speak *boldly, as I ought to speak.

21 But that ye also may know my affairs, *and* how I do, *Tychicus, a beloved brother and faithful minister in the Lord, shall make known to you all things:

22 Whom I have sent unto you for the same purpose, that ye might know our affairs, and *that* he might comfort your hearts.

23 Peace *be* to the brethren, and love with faith, from God the Father and the Lord Jesus Christ.

24 Grace *be* with all them that love our Lord Jesus Christ in *sincerity. Amen.

¶ Written from Rome unto the Ephesians by Tychicus.

4a TG Family, Love within; Family, Patriarchal; Marriage, Fatherhood.
  b TG Provoking.
  c TG Family, Children, Responsibilities toward.
5a Titus 2:9.
  b 1 Pet. 2:18 (13–25).
6a 1 Cor. 7:22 (21–24).
  b TG God, Will of.
7a TG Service.
8a Col. 3:24.
9a Mal. 3:5; Col. 4:1.
  b TG Leadership.
  c Moro. 8:12; D&C 38:16.

10a TG Strength.
11a Ps. 91:4; Rom. 13:12; 2 Cor. 10:4 (3–6); 1 Thes. 5:8; D&C 27:15 (15–18). TG Chastity; Protection, Divine; Watch.
12a JS—H 1:15 (15–17).
  b TG Opposition.
  c TG Flesh and Blood.
  d 2 Cor. 4:4.
  e TG Darkness, Spiritual; Secret Combinations.
  f TG Governments; Wickedness.

14a Isa. 11:5.
  b TG Truth.
  c Isa. 59:17; 61:10.
  d TG Righteousness.
15a TG Peace of God.
16a TG Faith.
  b 1 Ne. 15:24; D&C 3:8.
17a TG Salvation.
18a TG Prayer.
  b TG Perseverance.
19a TG Mysteries of Godliness.
20a D&C 60:2 (2–3).
21a Acts 20:4.
24a TG Sincere.

THE EPISTLE OF PAUL THE APOSTLE

TO THE

PHILIPPIANS

CHAPTER 1

All that happened to Paul furthered the gospel cause—Our conduct should be worthy of the gospel.

PAUL and Timotheus, the [a]servants of Jesus Christ, to all the saints in Christ Jesus which are at Philippi, with the [b]bishops and [c]deacons:

2 Grace *be* unto you, and peace, from God our Father, and *from* the Lord Jesus Christ.

3 I thank my God upon every remembrance of you,

4 Always in every prayer of mine for you all making request with joy,

5 For your fellowship in the gospel from the first day until now;

6 Being confident of this very thing, that he which hath begun a good work in you will [a]perform *it* until the day of Jesus Christ:

7 Even as it is [a]meet for me to think this of you all, because I have you in my heart; inasmuch as both in my bonds, and in the defence and [b]confirmation of the gospel, ye all are partakers of my [c]grace.

8 For God is my [a]record, how greatly I long after you all in the [b]bowels of Jesus Christ.

9 And this I pray, that your [a]love may abound yet more and more in knowledge and *in* all judgment;

10 That ye may [a]approve things that are excellent; that ye may be [b]sincere and without offence till the day of Christ;

11 Being filled with the fruits of [a]righteousness, which are by Jesus Christ, unto the glory and praise of God.

12 But I would ye should understand, brethren, that the things *which happened* unto me have [a]fallen out rather unto the furtherance of the gospel;

13 So that my bonds in Christ are manifest in all the [a]palace, and in all other *places;*

14 And many of the brethren in the Lord, waxing confident by my bonds, are much more bold to speak the word without [a]fear.

15 Some indeed preach Christ even of envy and [a]strife; and some also of good will:

16 The one preach Christ of contention, not sincerely, supposing to add affliction to my bonds:

17 But the other of love, knowing that I am set for the defence of the gospel.

18 What then? notwithstanding, every way, whether in pretence, or in truth, Christ is preached; and I therein do rejoice, yea, and will rejoice.

19 For I know that this shall turn to my salvation through your [a]prayer, and the supply of the [b]Spirit of Jesus Christ,

20 According to my earnest

---

1 1a TG Servant.
  b TG Bishop; Church Organization.
  c TG Deacon.
6a GR complete, accomplish.
7a GR just, right.
  b GR establishment, strengthening.

c TG Grace.
8a GR witness.
  b GR affections, compassions.
9a Moses 7:18.
10a GR prove, put to the test.
  b GR pure, spotless.
11a TG Righteousness.
12a GR come.

13a Philip. 4:22.
14a Luke 1:74 (68–75); 1 Jn. 4:18 (15–18); D&C 68:6 (5–6).
15a TG Strife.
19a 2 Cor. 1:11; Philem. 1:22.
  b TG God, Spirit of.

expectation and *my* ^ahope, that in nothing I shall be ashamed, but *that* with all boldness, as always, *so* now also Christ shall be ^bmagnified in my body, whether *it be* by life, or by death.

21 For to me to live *is* Christ, and to die *is* gain.

22 But if I live in the flesh, this *is* the fruit of my labour: yet what I shall choose I ^awot not.

23 For I am ^ain a strait betwixt two, having a desire to depart, and to be with Christ; which is far better:

24 Nevertheless to ^aabide in the flesh *is* more needful for you.

25 And having this confidence, I know that I shall abide and continue with you all for your furtherance and joy of faith;

26 That your rejoicing may be more abundant in Jesus Christ for me by my coming to you again.

27 Only let your conversation be as it becometh the gospel of Christ: that whether I come and see you, or else be absent, I may hear of your affairs, that ye ^astand fast in one spirit, with ^bone ^cmind ^dstriving together for the faith of the gospel;

28 And in nothing terrified by your adversaries: ^awhich is to them an evident token of perdition, but to you of salvation, and that of God.

29 For unto you it is given in the behalf of Christ, not only to believe on him, but also to ^asuffer for his sake;

30 Having the same conflict which ye saw in me, and now hear *to be* in me.

CHAPTER 2

Saints should be of one mind and one spirit—Every knee will bow to Christ—Saints must work out their salvation—Paul faces martyrdom with joy.

IF *there be* therefore any consolation in Christ, if any comfort of love, if any fellowship of the Spirit, if any ^abowels and mercies,

2 Fulfil ye my joy, that ye be likeminded, having the same ^alove, *being* of ^bone ^caccord, of one mind.

3 *Let* nothing *be done* through ^astrife or vainglory; but in lowliness of mind let each ^besteem other better than themselves.

4 Look not every man on his own things, but every man also on the things of others.

5 Let this mind be in you, which was also in Christ Jesus:

6 Who, being in the ^aform of God, thought it not robbery to be ^bequal with God:

7 But made himself of no reputation, and took upon him the form of a ^aservant, and was made in the likeness of men:

8 And being found in ^afashion as a man, he ^bhumbled himself, and became ^cobedient unto ^ddeath, even the ^edeath of the cross.

9 Wherefore God also hath highly ^aexalted him, and given him a ^bname which is above every name:

10 That at the ^aname of Jesus every ^bknee should bow, of *things* in heaven, and *things* in earth, and *things* under the earth;

20 *a* Ps. 119:116.
  b Ps. 34:3 (1–3).
22 *a* GR know.
23 *a* GR hard-pressed to choose.
24 *a* 3 Ne. 28:9 (1–12); D&C 7:5 (1–8).
27 *a* Philip. 4:1 (1–7).
  b TG Unity.
  c TG Mind.
  d Jude 1:3.
28 *a* JST Philip. 1:28 . . . *who reject the gospel, which bringeth on them destruction; but you who receive the gospel,* salvation; and that of God.

29 *a* TG Suffering.
2 1 *a* GR tender affections of the heart and compassion.
2 *a* TG Benevolence.
  b TG Unity.
  c Rom. 12:10 (10–18); Moses 7:18 (18–21).
3 *a* TG Strife.
  b TG Humility; Love; Respect.
6 *a* TG God, Body of, Corporeal Nature; Man, Physical Creation of.
  b TG Jesus Christ, Relationships with the Father.

7 *a* Isa. 53:4 (3–7); 2 Cor. 8:9 (8–15); Heb. 2:9.
8 *a* GR outward appearance.
  b TG Humility; Meek.
  c Isa. 50:5.
  d TG Jesus Christ, Death of.
  e TG Jesus Christ, Atonement through.
9 *a* TG Exaltation.
  b Mal. 1:11; Heb. 1:4. TG Name.
10 *a* Mosiah 27:31; D&C 76:110 (106–11); 88:104 (103–4).
  b Isa. 45:23; Rom. 14:11.

11 And *that* every tongue should confess that Jesus Christ is ᵃLord, to the glory of God the Father.

12 Wherefore, my beloved, as ye have always obeyed, not as in my presence only, but now much more in my absence, ᵃwork out your own ᵇsalvation with fear and trembling.

13 For it is God which worketh in you both to will and to do of *his* good pleasure.

14 Do all things without murmurings and ᵃdisputings:

15 That ye may be blameless and harmless, the ᵃsons of God, without rebuke, in the midst of a crooked and perverse ᵇnation, among whom ye ᶜshine as lights in the world;

16 Holding forth the word of life; that I may rejoice in the day of Christ, that I have not run in vain, neither laboured in vain.

17 Yea, and if I be ᵃoffered upon the sacrifice and service of your faith, I joy, and rejoice with you all.

18 For the same cause also do ye joy, and rejoice with me.

19 But I trust in the Lord Jesus to send Timotheus shortly unto you, that I also may be of good comfort, when I know your state.

20 For I have no man likeminded, who will naturally care for your state.

21 For all ᵃseek their ᵇown, not the things which are Jesus Christ's.

22 But ye know the ᵃproof of him, that, as a son with the father, he hath served with me in the gospel.

23 Him therefore I hope to send presently, so soon as I shall see how it will go with me.

24 But I trust in the Lord that I also myself shall come shortly.

25 Yet I supposed it necessary to send to you ᵃEpaphroditus, my brother, and companion in labour, and fellowsoldier, but your messenger, and he that ministered to my wants.

26 For he longed after you all, and was full of heaviness, because that ye had heard that he had been sick.

27 For indeed he was sick nigh unto death: but God had mercy on him; and not on him only, but on me also, lest I should have sorrow upon sorrow.

28 I sent him therefore the more carefully, that, when ye see him again, ye may rejoice, and that I may be the less sorrowful.

29 Receive him therefore in the Lord with all ᵃgladness; and ᵇhold such in ᶜreputation:

30 Because for the work of Christ he was nigh unto death, not regarding his life, to supply your ᵃlack of service toward me.

CHAPTER 3

Paul sacrifices all things for Christ— True ministers set examples of righteousness.

FINALLY, my brethren, rejoice in the Lord. To write the same things to you, to me indeed *is* not grievous, but for you *it is* safe.

2 Beware of dogs, beware of evil workers, beware of the concision.

3 For we are the ᵃcircumcision, which ᵇworship God in the spirit, and rejoice in Christ Jesus, and have no confidence in the ᶜflesh.

4 Though I might also have confidence in the flesh. If any other man thinketh that he hath whereof he might trust in the flesh, I more:

5 Circumcised the eighth day, of the stock of Israel, *of* the tribe of Benjamin, an ᵃHebrew of the Hebrews; as touching the law, a ᵇPharisee;

6 Concerning zeal, persecuting the

11a ᴛɢ Jesus Christ, Messiah.
12a Alma 34:37; Morm. 9:27.
     ᴛɢ Good Works.
   b ᴛɢ Salvation.
14a ᴛɢ Disputations.
15a ᴛɢ Sons and Daughters of God.

   b ɢʀ generation.
   c ᴛɢ Mission of Early Saints.
17a 1 Thes. 2:8; D&C 98:13.
21a ᴛɢ Apathy.
   b 1 Cor. 10:24.
22a ɢʀ trial.
25a Philip. 4:18.
29a ᴛɢ Cheerful.

   b 1 Thes. 5:13.
   c ɢʀ honor.
30a Philip. 4:10.
3 3a ᴛɢ Circumcision.
   b ᴛɢ Worship.
   c ᴛɢ Trust Not in the Arm of Flesh.
5a 2 Cor. 11:22.
   b Acts 23:6.

church; touching the righteousness which is in the law, blameless.

7 But what things were gain to me, those I counted loss for Christ.

8 Yea doubtless, and I count all things *but* loss for the excellency of the knowledge of Christ Jesus my Lord: for whom I have ªsuffered the ᵇloss of all things, and do count them *but* ᶜdung, that I may win Christ,

9 And be found in him, not having mine own righteousness, which is of the law, but that which is through the faith of Christ, the ªrighteousness which is of God by faith:

10 That I may know him, and the power of his resurrection, and the ªfellowship of his sufferings, being made conformable unto his death;

11 If by any means I might attain unto the resurrection of the ªdead.

12 Not as though I had already attained, either were already ªperfect: but I ᵇfollow after, if that I may apprehend that for which also I am apprehended of Christ Jesus.

13 Brethren, I count not myself to have apprehended: but *this* one thing I *do*, forgetting those things which are behind, and reaching forth unto those things which are before,

14 I ªpress toward the mark for the ᵇprize of the high calling of God in Christ Jesus.

15 Let us therefore, as many as be ªperfect, be thus minded: and if in any thing ye be otherwise minded, God shall reveal even this unto you.

16 Nevertheless, whereto we have already attained, let us walk by the same rule, let us mind the same thing.

17 Brethren, be ªfollowers together of me, and mark them which walk so as ye have us for an ᵇensample.

18 (For many walk, of whom I have told you often, and now tell you even weeping, *that they are* the enemies of the cross of Christ:

19 Whose ªend *is* destruction, whose God *is their* belly, ᵇand *whose* glory *is* in their ᶜshame, who mind earthly things.)

20 For our conversation is in heaven; from whence also we look for the ªSaviour, the Lord Jesus Christ:

21 Who shall ªchange our ᵇvile body, ᶜthat it may be fashioned like unto his glorious ᵈbody, according to the working whereby he is able even to ᵉsubdue all things unto himself.

CHAPTER 4

Stand fast in the Lord—We believe in being honest, true, and chaste.

THEREFORE, my brethren dearly beloved and longed for, my joy and crown, so ªstand fast in the Lord, *my* dearly beloved.

2 I beseech Euodias, and beseech Syntyche, that they be of the same mind in the Lord.

3 And I entreat thee also, true ªyokefellow, help those women which laboured with me in the gospel, with Clement also, and *with* other my fellowlabourers, whose names *are* in the ᵇbook of life.

4 Rejoice in the Lord alway: *and* again I say, Rejoice.

5 Let your ªmoderation be known unto all men. The Lord *is* at hand.

8a TG Self-Sacrifice; Suffering.
b Omni 1:26; Mosiah 2:34.
c GR refuse.
9a TG Righteousness.
10a 2 Cor. 1:4; 2 Thes. 2:16.
11a JST Philip. 3:11 . . . *just.*
12a TG Perfection.
b GR press forward.
14a TG Steadfastness.
b TG Objectives.
15a Moro. 10:32 (32–33).
17a Matt. 16:24 (24–26);

Eph. 5:1; 1 Thes. 1:6.
b TG Example.
19a 2 Cor. 11:15.
b JST Philip. 3:19 . . . and *who* glory in their shame . . .
c TG Shame.
20a TG Jesus Christ, Savior.
21a 1 Cor. 15:51. TG Jesus Christ, Resurrection.
b GR humble, of low estate.
c TG Resurrection.

d TG God, Body of, Corporeal Nature.
e 1 Cor. 15:28; D&C 19:2; 76:106.
4 1a 1 Cor. 10:12; 16:13 (13–14); Gal. 5:1; Philip. 1:27; D&C 87:8.
3a GR associate.
b TG Book of Life.
5a GR gentleness. TG Modesty; Temperance.

6 *a*Be *b*careful for nothing; but in every thing by *c*prayer and supplication with *d*thanksgiving let your requests be made known unto God.

7 And the *a*peace of God, which passeth all *b*understanding, shall *c*keep your hearts and minds through Christ Jesus.

8 Finally, brethren, whatsoever things are *a*true, whatsoever things are *b*honest, whatsoever things are *c*just, whatsoever things are *d*pure, whatsoever things are *e*lovely, *f*whatsoever things are of good report; if there be any *g*virtue, and if there be any praise, *h*think on these things.

9 Those things, which ye have both learned, and *a*received, and heard, and seen in me, do: and the God of peace shall be with you.

10 But I rejoiced in the Lord greatly, that now at the last your *a*care of me hath flourished again; wherein ye were also careful, but ye *b*lacked opportunity.

11 Not that I speak in respect of want: for I have learned, in whatsoever state I am, therewith to be *a*content.

12 I know both how to be *a*abased, and I know how to abound: every where and in all things I am instructed both to be full and to be hungry, both to abound and to suffer need.

13 I can do all things through *a*Christ which *b*strengtheneth me.

14 Notwithstanding ye have well done, that ye did *a*communicate with my affliction.

15 Now ye Philippians know also, that in the beginning of the gospel, when I departed from Macedonia, no church communicated with me as concerning giving and receiving, but ye only.

16 For even in Thessalonica ye sent once and again unto my necessity.

17 Not because I desire a gift: but I desire *a*fruit that may abound to your account.

18 But I have all, and *a*abound: I am full, having received of *b*Epaphroditus the things which were sent from you, an odour of a sweet smell, a sacrifice acceptable, well-pleasing to God.

19 But my God shall supply all your *a*need according to his *b*riches in glory by Christ Jesus.

20 Now unto God and our Father be glory for ever and ever. Amen.

21 Salute every saint in Christ Jesus. The brethren which are with me greet you.

22 All the saints salute you, chiefly they that are of *a*Cæsar's household.

23 The grace of our Lord Jesus Christ be with you all. Amen.

¶ It was written to the Philippians from Rome by Epaphroditus.

6*a* GR Don't be unduly concerned about anything.
b JST Philip. 4:6 . . . afflicted . . .
  Ps. 55:22;
  Prov. 16:3;
  Matt. 6:25.
c TG Prayer.
d TG Thanksgiving.
7*a* TG Peace of God.
b TG Understanding.
c GR guard.
8*a* TG Truth.

b TG Honesty.
c TG Righteousness.
d TG Purity.
e TG Beauty.
f A of F 1:13.
g TG Chastity; Virtue.
h TG Motivations; Study.
9*a* 1 Thes. 4:1.
10*a* 2 Cor. 11:9.
b Philip. 2:30 (25, 30).
11*a* TG Contentment.
12*a* GR humble.

TG Self-Sacrifice.
13*a* John 15:5 (4–5).
b 1 Tim. 1:12; Alma 26:12 (11–13).
14*a* GR participate.
17*a* Rom. 15:28 (25–28); Titus 3:14.
18*a* 2 Cor. 9:8.
b Philip. 2:25 (25–30).
19*a* Ps. 23:1.
b TG Treasure.
22*a* Philip. 1:13.

THE EPISTLE OF PAUL THE APOSTLE

TO THE

COLOSSIANS

CHAPTER 1

Redemption comes through Christ—He created all things, is in the image of God, and is the Firstborn of the Father.

PAUL, an apostle of Jesus Christ by the will of God, and Timotheus *our* brother,

2 To the saints and faithful brethren in Christ which are at Colosse: Grace *be* unto you, and peace, from God our Father and the Lord Jesus Christ.

3 We give thanks to God and the Father of our Lord Jesus Christ, praying always for you,

4 Since we heard of your ªfaith in Christ Jesus, and of the ᵇlove *which ye have* to all the saints,

5 For the ªhope which is laid up for you in heaven, whereof ye heard before in the word of the truth of the ᵇgospel;

6 Which is come unto you, ªas *it is* in all the world; and bringeth forth ᵇfruit, as *it doth* also in you, since the day ye heard *of it*, and knew the ᶜgrace of God in truth:

7 As ye also learned of ªEpaphras our dear fellowservant, who is for you a faithful minister of Christ;

8 Who also declared unto us your love in the Spirit.

9 For this cause we also, since the day we heard *it*, do not cease to pray for you, and to desire that ye might be filled with the ªknowledge of his ᵇwill in all wisdom and spiritual ᶜunderstanding;

10 That ye might ªwalk ᵇworthy of the Lord unto all ᶜpleasing, being fruitful in every good work, and increasing in the ᵈknowledge of God;

11 ªStrengthened with all might, according to his ᵇglorious ᶜpower, unto all patience and longsuffering with ᵈjoyfulness;

12 Giving ªthanks unto the Father, which hath ᵇmade us meet to be partakers of the ᶜinheritance of the saints in light:

13 Who hath delivered us from the power of ªdarkness, and hath translated *us* into the ᵇkingdom of his dear ᶜSon:

14 In whom we have ªredemption through his blood, *even* the ᵇforgiveness of sins:

15 Who is the ªimage of the invisible ᵇGod, the ᶜfirstborn of ᵈevery creature:

---

1 4a Eph. 1:15 (12–15);
   1 Thes. 5:8.
  b Heb. 6:10.
 5a 1 Pet. 1:4.
  b TG Gospel.
 6a JST Col. 1:6 . . . as in
   all *generations of* the
   world . . .
  b Alma 32:42 (28–42);
   3 Ne. 14:16;
   D&C 52:34 (18, 34).
  c TG Grace.
 7a Col. 4:12 (12–13);
   Philem. 1:23.
 9a TG Knowledge.
  b TG God, Will of.

  c TG Understanding.
10a TG Walking with God.
  b TG Worthiness.
  c 1 Thes. 4:1.
  d TG Education.
11a Eph. 3:16.
  b TG Glory.
  c TG Jesus Christ,
   Power of.
  d Acts 5:41 (40–41).
   TG Joy.
12a Col. 3:17.
  b GR qualified us.
  c 2 Ne. 9:18;
   D&C 45:58 (57–58);
   84:38 (33–38).

13a D&C 21:6; 38:11.
  b TG Kingdom of God, in
   Heaven.
  c TG Jesus Christ, Divine
   Sonship.
14a TG Jesus Christ,
   Atonement through;
   Redemption.
  b TG Remission of Sins.
15a TG God, Body of,
   Corporeal Nature.
  b TG Godhead.
  c TG Firstborn;
   Jesus Christ, Firstborn.
  d GR all creation.

16 For by him were all *a*things *b*created, that are in heaven, and that are in earth, visible and invisible, whether *they be* thrones, or dominions, or *c*principalities, or powers: all things were *d*created by him, and for him:

17 And he is before all things, and by him all things *a*consist.

18 And he is the *a*head of the body, the church: who is the beginning, the *b*firstborn from the dead; that in all *things* he might have the preeminence.

19 For it pleased *the Father* that in him should all *a*fulness dwell;

20 And, having made peace through the blood of his cross, by him to *a*reconcile all things unto himself; by him, *I say*, whether *they be* things in earth, or things in heaven.

21 And you, that were *a*sometime *b*alienated and enemies in *your* mind by wicked works, yet now hath he reconciled

22 In the body of his flesh through *a*death, to present you holy and *b*unblameable and unreproveable in his sight:

23 If ye *a*continue in the faith *b*grounded and settled, and *be* not *c*moved away from the *d*hope of the gospel, which ye have heard, *and* which was preached to every creature which is under heaven; whereof I Paul am made a minister;

24 Who now rejoice in my sufferings for you, and fill up that which is behind of the *a*afflictions of Christ in my flesh for his body's sake, which is the church:

25 Whereof I am made a minister, according to the *a*dispensation of God which is given to me for you, to fulfil the word of God;

26 *Even* the *a*mystery which hath been hid from ages and from generations, but now is made *b*manifest to his saints:

27 To whom God would make *a*known what *is* the *b*riches of the glory of this mystery among the Gentiles; which is Christ in you, the hope of glory:

28 Whom we *a*preach, *b*warning every man, and teaching every man in all wisdom; that we may present every man perfect in Christ Jesus:

29 Whereunto I also labour, striving according to his working, which worketh in me mightily.

CHAPTER 2

The fulness of the Godhead dwells in Christ—Beware of being deceived by the traditions of men—The handwriting against us was nailed to the cross of Christ.

FOR I would that ye knew what great *a*conflict I have for you, and *for* them at *b*Laodicea, and *for* as many as have not seen my face in the flesh;

2 That their hearts might be comforted, being knit together in love, and unto all riches of the full assurance of *a*understanding, to the acknowledgement of the mystery of God, *b*and of the Father, and of Christ;

3 In whom are hid all the *a*treasures of *b*wisdom and *c*knowledge.

16a Heb. 2:10 (9–10).
  b TG Creation.
  c Col. 2:10;
    1 Pet. 3:22.
  d TG Jesus Christ, Creator.
17a D&C 88:13 (5–13).
18a TG Jesus Christ, Head of
    the Church.
  b TG Jesus Christ,
    Firstborn; Jesus Christ,
    Resurrection.
19a TG Jesus Christ,
    Relationships with
    the Father.
20a TG Reconciliation.
21a GR formerly.

  b Eph. 2:1.
22a TG Jesus Christ, Death of.
  b Mosiah 3:21;
    D&C 4:2.
23a TG Perseverance.
  b GR established and
    steadfast.
    Eph. 3:17 (17–19).
  c John 15:6.
  d TG Hope.
24a 2 Cor. 1:5.
25a TG Dispensations.
26a Rom. 16:25 (25–26).
    TG Mysteries of
    Godliness.
  b 2 Tim. 1:10.

27a Eph. 3:3.
  b TG Treasure.
28a TG Preaching.
  b TG Warn.
2 1a GR anguish.
  b Col. 4:15 (12–16);
    Rev. 1:11.
2a TG Understanding.
  b JST Col. 2:2 . . . *and of
    Christ, who is of God,
    even the Father;*
3a TG Treasure.
  b 1 Cor. 2:7 (6–7).
    TG God, Intelligence of;
    God, Omniscience of.
  c TG Knowledge.

4 And this I say, lest any man should beguile you with enticing words.

5 For though I be absent in the flesh, yet am I with you in the spirit, joying and beholding your *a*order, and the steadfastness of your faith in Christ.

6 As ye have therefore received Christ Jesus the Lord, so *a*walk ye in him:

7 *a*Rooted and built up in him, and stablished in the faith, as ye have been taught, abounding therein with *b*thanksgiving.

8 Beware lest any man *a*spoil you through *b*philosophy and vain *c*deceit, after the *d*tradition of men, after the rudiments of the *e*world, and not after Christ.

9 For in him dwelleth all the *a*fulness of the Godhead bodily.

10 And ye are *a*complete in him, which is the head of all *b*principality and power:

11 In whom also ye are circumcised with the *a*circumcision made without hands, in putting off the *b*body of the sins of the flesh by the circumcision of Christ:

12 *a*Buried with him in *b*baptism, wherein also ye are *c*risen with *him* through the faith of the *d*operation of God, who hath raised him from the dead.

13 And you, being dead in your sins and the uncircumcision of your flesh, hath he *a*quickened together with him, having forgiven you all trespasses;

14 *a*Blotting out the handwriting of ordinances that was against us, which was contrary to us, and took it out of the way, nailing it to his cross;

15 *And* having spoiled principalities and powers, he made a shew of them openly, triumphing over them in it.

16 Let no man therefore *a*judge you in *b*meat, or in drink, or in respect of an holyday, or of the new moon, or of the *c*sabbath *days:*

17 Which are a *a*shadow of things to come; but the body *is* of Christ.

18 Let no man *a*beguile you of your reward in a voluntary *b*humility and worshipping of angels, intruding into those things which he hath not seen, vainly puffed up by his fleshly mind,

19 And not holding the *a*Head, from which all the body by joints and bands having nourishment ministered, and knit together, increaseth with the increase of God.

20 Wherefore if ye be *a*dead with Christ from the rudiments of the world, why, as though living in the world, are ye subject to *b*ordinances,

21 *a*(Touch not; taste not; handle not;

22 Which all are to perish with the using;) after the *a*commandments and *b*doctrines of men?

23 Which things have indeed a shew of wisdom in will worship, and humility, and neglecting of the body; not in any honour to the satisfying of the flesh.

5*a* TG Order.
6*a* TG Walking with God.
7*a* Eph. 3:17.
  b TG Thanksgiving.
8*a* Heb. 13:9.
  b D&C 123:12.
     TG Learn.
  c TG Deceit; Education; Fraud.
  d TG Traditions of Men.
  e TG Worldliness.
9*a* TG Jesus Christ, Relationships with the Father.
10*a* John 1:16.
   b Col. 1:16; 1 Pet. 3:22.

11*a* TG Circumcision.
   b Rom. 6:6.
12*a* TG Jesus Christ, Types of, in Memory.
   b TG Baptism; Baptism, Immersion.
   c Col. 3:1.
   d Eph. 1:19 (19–20).
13*a* GR caused to become alive.
     TG Resurrection.
14*a* Eph. 2:15.
16*a* Rom. 14:3 (1–3).
   b TG Word of Wisdom.
   c TG Sabbath.
17*a* TG Jesus Christ, Types of, in Anticipation.

18*a* Matt. 24:4 (4–5); Mosiah 26:6; D&C 123:12.
   b TG Humility.
19*a* Eph. 4:15 (15–16).
20*a* Rom. 6:5 (2–5); Col. 3:3.
   b TG Ordinance.
21*a* JST Col. 2:21–22 (Appendix).
22*a* Titus 1:14; D&C 46:7; JS—H 1:19.
     TG Apostasy of the Early Christian Church.
   b Matt. 15:9; 2 Ne. 28:9.

CHAPTER 3

Some lives are hidden with God in Christ—The Saints are told to be holy and to serve the Lord Jesus Christ.

IF ye then be ᵃrisen with Christ, seek those things which are above, where Christ sitteth on the right hand of God.

2 Set your ᵃaffection on ᵇthings ᶜabove, not on things on the ᵈearth.

3 For ye are ᵃdead, and your life is hid with Christ in God.

4 When Christ, *who is* our ᵃlife, shall ᵇappear, then shall ye also appear with him in ᶜglory.

5 ᵃMortify therefore your ᵇmembers which are upon the earth; fornication, uncleanness, ᶜinordinate affection, evil concupiscence, and ᵈcovetousness, which is ᵉidolatry:

6 For which things' sake the ᵃwrath of God cometh on the children of ᵇdisobedience:

7 In the which ye also walked ᵃsome time, when ye lived in them.

8 But now ye also ᵃput off all these; ᵇanger, wrath, ᶜmalice, ᵈblasphemy, filthy ᵉcommunication out of your mouth.

9 ᵃLie not one to another, seeing that ye have put off the ᵇold man with his deeds;

10 And have put on the ᵃnew *man*, which is renewed in knowledge after the ᵇimage of him that ᶜcreated him:

11 Where there is neither ᵃGreek nor Jew, ᵇcircumcision nor uncircumcision, Barbarian, Scythian, bond *nor* free: but Christ *is* all, and in all.

12 Put on therefore, as the ᵃelect of God, holy and beloved, ᵇbowels of ᶜmercies, ᵈkindness, ᵉhumbleness of mind, ᶠmeekness, longsuffering;

13 ᵃForbearing one another, and ᵇforgiving one another, if any man have a quarrel against any: even as Christ forgave you, so also *do* ye.

14 And above all these things *put on* ᵃcharity, which is the bond of perfectness.

15 And let the ᵃpeace of God rule in your hearts, to the which also ye are called in one body; and be ye ᵇthankful.

16 Let the ᵃword of Christ dwell in you richly in all ᵇwisdom; ᶜteaching and admonishing one another in psalms and ᵈhymns and spiritual songs, singing with grace in your hearts to the Lord.

17 And whatsoever ye do in word or deed, ᵃdo all in the name of the Lord Jesus, giving ᵇthanks to God and the Father by him.

18 ᵃWives, submit yourselves unto your own husbands, as it is fit in the Lord.

19 ᵃHusbands, ᵇlove *your* wives, and be not bitter against them.

20 ᵃChildren, ᵇobey *your* parents in

---

3 1a Col. 2:12.
2a GR mind.
  b Matt. 6:33.
  c Prov. 15:24.
  d TG Worldliness.
3a Rom. 6:5 (2–5);
  Col. 2:20.
4a Ether 4:12.
  b 1 Jn. 3:2.
  c 1 Cor. 15:43 (42–44).
5a Rom. 8:13.
  b Rom. 6:13.
  c TG Sexual Immorality.
  d TG Covet.
  e TG Idolatry.
6a TG God, Indignation of.
  b TG Disobedience.
7a GR formerly.
8a Eph. 4:22 (22–24).
  b TG Anger.
  c TG Malice.

  d TG Blaspheme.
  e TG Profanity.
9a TG Honesty;
  Lying.
  b Rom. 6:6;
  Mosiah 3:19.
10a TG Man, New,
  Spiritually Reborn.
  b Rom. 8:29.
  c TG Jesus Christ, Creator;
  Man, Physical
  Creation of.
11a 1 Cor. 12:13.
  b TG Circumcision.
12a TG Election.
  b Gal. 5:22.
  c TG Mercy.
  d TG Benevolence.
  e TG Humility.
  f TG Meek.
13a TG Forbear.

  b Mosiah 26:31 (30–31).
14a TG Charity.
15a TG Peace of God.
  b TG Thanksgiving.
16a 2 Ne. 32:3.
  b TG God, Intelligence of.
  c TG Teaching.
  d TG Singing.
17a 1 Cor. 10:31.
  b Col. 1:12.
  TG Prayer.
18a TG Marriage, Wives.
19a TG Marriage, Husbands.
  b TG Marriage, Continuing Courtship in.
20a TG Children;
  Family, Love within.
  b TG Family, Children,
  Duties of;
  Honoring Father and
  Mother.

all things: for this is well pleasing unto the Lord.

21 ^aFathers, ^bprovoke not your children *to* ^canger, lest they be discouraged.

22 ^aServants, obey in all things *your* masters according to the flesh; not with eyeservice, as menpleasers; but in ^bsingleness of heart, ^cfearing God:

23 And whatsoever ye do, do *it* ^aheartily, as to the Lord, and not unto men;

24 Knowing that of the Lord ye shall ^areceive the ^breward of the ^cinheritance: for ye ^dserve the Lord Christ.

25 But he that doeth ^awrong shall receive for the wrong which he hath done: and there is no ^brespect of persons.

CHAPTER 4

The Saints are told to be wise in all things—Luke and others greet the Colossians.

^aMASTERS, give unto *your* servants that which is just and equal; knowing that ye also have a ^bMaster in ^cheaven.

2 Continue in prayer, and watch in the same with thanksgiving;

3 Withal praying also for us, that God would open unto us a ^adoor of utterance, to speak the mystery of Christ, for which I am also in bonds:

4 That I may make it manifest, as I ought to speak.

5 ^aWalk in ^bwisdom toward them that are without, redeeming the time.

6 Let your ^aspeech *be* alway with grace, seasoned with ^bsalt, that ye may know how ye ought to answer every man.

7 All my state shall Tychicus declare unto you, *who is* a beloved brother, and a faithful minister and fellowservant in the Lord:

8 Whom I have sent unto you for the same purpose, that he might know your estate, and comfort your hearts;

9 With ^aOnesimus, a faithful and beloved brother, who is *one* of you. They shall make known unto you all things which *are done* here.

10 ^aAristarchus my fellowprisoner saluteth you, and ^bMarcus, ^csister's son to Barnabas, (touching whom ye received commandments: if he come unto you, receive him;)

11 And Jesus, which is called Justus, who are of the ^acircumcision. These only *are my* fellowworkers unto the kingdom of God, which have been a comfort unto me.

12 ^aEpaphras, who is *one* of you, a servant of Christ, saluteth you, always labouring fervently for you in prayers, that ye may stand perfect and complete in all the will of God.

13 For I bear him record, that he hath a great ^azeal for you, and them *that are* in Laodicea, and them in Hierapolis.

14 Luke, the beloved physician, and ^aDemas, greet you.

15 Salute the brethren which are in ^aLaodicea, and Nymphas, and the church which is in his house.

16 And when this epistle is read among you, cause that it be read also in the church of the Laodiceans; and

21a TG Family, Children, Responsibilities toward.
  b TG Provoking.
  c TG Anger.
22a 1 Tim. 6:1 (1–2);
    Titus 2:9 (9–10);
    1 Pet. 2:18.
  b TG Sincere.
  c TG Reverence.
23a TG Commitment;
    Industry; Laziness.
24a Eph. 6:8.
  b TG Reward.

  c TG Inheritance.
  d 1 Cor. 7:22.
25a TG Injustice.
  b D&C 1:35; 38:16.
4 1a Mal. 3:5;
    Eph. 6:9.
  b Matt. 23:8.
  c TG Heaven.
3a 1 Cor. 16:9.
5a TG Walking with God.
  b TG Wisdom.
6a TG Communication.
  b TG Salt.

9a Philem. 1:10.
10a Acts 19:29; 20:4; 27:2.
  b Acts 15:37 (37–39);
    2 Tim. 4:11.
  c GR cousin, kinsman.
11a TG Circumcision.
12a Col. 1:7 (7–8);
    Philem. 1:23.
13a TG Zeal.
14a 2 Tim. 4:10;
    Philem. 1:24.
15a Col. 2:1;
    Rev. 1:11.

that ye likewise read the *epistle* from Laodicea.

17 And say to *Archippus, Take heed to the ministry which thou hast received in the Lord, that thou fulfil it.

18 The salutation by the *hand of me Paul. Remember my *bonds. Grace *be* with you. Amen.

¶ Written from Rome to the Colossians by Tychicus and Onesimus.

THE FIRST EPISTLE OF
PAUL THE APOSTLE TO THE
THESSALONIANS

CHAPTER 1

The gospel comes both in word and in power.

PAUL, and *Silvanus, and *Timotheus, *unto the *church of the *Thessalonians *which is* in God the Father and *in* the Lord Jesus Christ: Grace *be* unto you, and peace, from God our Father, and the Lord Jesus Christ.

2 We give *thanks to God always for you all, making mention of you in our prayers;

3 Remembering without ceasing your work of *faith, and *labour of love, and *patience of hope in our Lord Jesus Christ, in the sight of God and our Father;

4 Knowing, brethren *beloved, your *election of God.

5 For our *gospel *came not unto you in *word only, but also in *power, and in the *Holy Ghost, and in much assurance; as ye know what *manner of men we were among you for your sake.

6 And ye became *followers of us, and of the Lord, having received the word in much *affliction, with *joy of the Holy Ghost:

7 So that ye were *ensamples to all that believe in Macedonia and Achaia.

8 For from you sounded out the word of the Lord not only in Macedonia and Achaia, but also in every *place your faith to God-ward is spread abroad; so that we need not to speak any thing.

9 For they themselves shew of us what manner of entering in we had

---

16*a* TG Scriptures, Lost.
17*a* Philem. 1:2.
18*a* 2 Thes. 3:17.
 b Heb. 13:3.

[1 THESSALONIANS]
1 1*a* Acts 15:34 (32–34);
 2 Cor. 1:19;
 1 Pet. 5:12.
 b Acts 16:1 (1–2);
 18:5 (1, 5);
 1 Thes. 3:2 (2, 6).
 c JST 1 Thes. 1:1 . . .
 servants of God the Father and the Lord Jesus Christ,

unto the church of the Thessalonians; grace unto you . . .
 d TG Jesus Christ, Head of the Church.
 e Acts 17:1 (1, 11).
2*a* D&C 46:32.
3*a* 1 Thes. 5:8;
 James 2:17.
 b Heb. 6:10.
 c TG Patience.
4*a* GR beloved of God, your election.
 b TG Election.
5*a* TG Gospel.

 b 1 Thes. 2:1.
 c 1 Cor. 2:4.
 d TG Holy Ghost, Gifts of.
 e TG Holy Ghost, Source of Testimony.
 f 1 Thes. 2:10;
 2 Thes. 3:7.
6*a* GR imitators.
 Philip. 3:17.
 b Acts 17:5 (5–10).
 TG Affliction.
 c Acts 5:41.
7*a* TG Example.
8*a* 2 Thes. 1:4.

unto you, and how ye turned to God from *a*idols to serve the *b*living and true God;

10 And to wait for his Son from *a*heaven, whom he raised from the dead, *even* Jesus, which *b*delivered us from the *c*wrath to come.

CHAPTER 2

True ministers preach in a godly manner—Converts are the glory and joy of missionaries.

For yourselves, brethren, know our *a*entrance in unto you, that it was not in vain:

2 But even after that we had suffered before, and were shamefully *a*entreated, as ye know, at Philippi, we were bold in our God to *b*speak unto you the gospel of God with much contention.

3 For our exhortation *was* not of *a*deceit, nor of uncleanness, nor in *b*guile:

4 But as we were *a*allowed of God to be *b*put in *c*trust with the gospel, even so we *d*speak; not as *e*pleasing men, but God, which *f*trieth our hearts.

5 For neither at any time used we *a*flattering words, as ye know, nor a cloak of *b*covetousness; God *is* witness:

6 Nor of men sought we *a*glory, neither of you, nor *yet* of others, when we might have been burdensome, as the apostles of Christ.

7 But we were gentle among you, even as a nurse cherisheth her children:

8 So being affectionately desirous of you, we were willing to have imparted unto you, not the gospel of God only, but also our own *a*souls, because ye were dear unto us.

9 For ye remember, brethren, our labour and *a*travail: for *b*labouring night and day, because we would not be *c*chargeable unto any of you, we preached unto you the gospel of God.

10 Ye *are* *a*witnesses, and God *also*, how holily and justly and unblameably we behaved ourselves among you that believe:

11 As ye know how we exhorted and comforted and charged every one of you, as a father *doth* his *a*children,

12 That ye would *a*walk *b*worthy of God, who hath called you unto his kingdom and glory.

13 For this cause also *a*thank we God without ceasing, because, when ye received the word of God which ye heard of us, ye received *it* *as* the word of men, but as it is in truth, the word of God, which effectually worketh also in you that believe.

14 For ye, brethren, became *a*followers of the churches of God which in Judæa are in Christ Jesus: for ye also have *b*suffered like things of your own countrymen, even as they *have* of the Jews:

15 Who both *a*killed the Lord Jesus, and their own prophets, and have persecuted us; and they please not God, and are contrary to all men:

16 *a*Forbidding us to speak to the Gentiles that they might be saved,

---

9*a* TG Idolatry.
　b D&C 20:19.
10*a* Acts 1:11 (9–11).
　b TG Deliver.
　c 1 Thes. 5:9.
2 1*a* 1 Thes. 1:5.
　2*a* Acts 16:22 (19–24).
　b Acts 17:2 (2–3).
　3*a* 2 Cor. 4:2; 7:2.
　b TG Guile.
　4*a* GR approved, found worthy, chosen. 2 Tim. 1:11.
　b GR entrusted.
　c D&C 12:8; 124:113.

　d Titus 2:1; 1 Pet. 4:11.
　e TG Peer Influence.
　f GR examines, proves by trial. TG Test.
　5*a* TG Flatter.
　b TG Covet.
　6*a* John 5:44 (41–44); D&C 76:61.
　8*a* Philip. 2:17.
　9*a* GR toil.
　b Acts 18:3; 20:34. TG Work, Value of.
　c GR burdensome.

　1 Cor. 9:18 (4–18); 2 Cor. 11:9.
10*a* 1 Thes. 1:5.
11*a* 1 Cor. 4:14.
12*a* TG Walking with God.
　b 1 Pet. 1:15 (15–16).
13*a* TG Thanksgiving.
14*a* TG imitators.
　b Acts 17:5 (5–7); 2 Thes. 1:4 (4–5).
15*a* TG Martyrdom; Prophets, Rejection of.
16*a* Luke 11:52; Acts 13:45 (45, 50).

to fill up their sins *b*alway: for the wrath is come upon them to the uttermost.

17 But we, brethren, being taken from you for a short time in presence, not in heart, endeavoured the more abundantly to see your *a*face with great desire.

18 Wherefore we would have come unto you, even I Paul, once and again; but Satan hindered us.

19 For what *is* our hope, or joy, or crown of rejoicing? *Are* not even ye in the presence of our Lord Jesus Christ at his *a*coming?

20 For ye are our glory and joy.

CHAPTER 3

The Saints are told to perfect that which is lacking in their faith.

WHEREFORE when we could no longer forbear, we thought it good to be left at *a*Athens alone;

2 And sent *a*Timotheus, our brother, and minister of God, and our fellow-labourer in the gospel of Christ, to *b*establish you, and to comfort you concerning your faith:

3 That no man should be *a*moved by these *b*afflictions: for yourselves know that we are *c*appointed thereunto.

4 For verily, when we were with you, we told you before that we should suffer tribulation; even as it came to pass, and ye know.

5 For this cause, when I could no longer forbear, I sent to know your faith, lest by some means the *a*tempter have *b*tempted you, and our labour be in vain.

6 But now when Timotheus came from you unto us, and brought us

good tidings of your faith and charity, and that ye have good remembrance of us always, desiring greatly to see us, as we also *to see* you:

7 Therefore, brethren, we were *a*comforted over you in all our *b*affliction and distress by your faith:

8 For now we live, if ye stand fast in the Lord.

9 For what thanks can we render to God again for you, for all the *a*joy wherewith we joy for your sakes before our God;

10 Night and day praying exceedingly that we might see your *a*face, and might *b*perfect that which is lacking in your faith?

11 Now God himself and our Father, and our Lord Jesus Christ, direct our way unto you.

12 And the Lord make you to increase and *a*abound in *b*love one toward another, and toward all *men*, even as we *do* toward you:

13 To the end he may stablish your hearts unblameable in holiness before God, even our Father, at the *a*coming of our Lord Jesus Christ with all his *b*saints.

CHAPTER 4

The Saints are told to be holy, sanctify themselves, and love one another—The Lord will come, and the dead will rise.

FURTHERMORE then we beseech you, brethren, and exhort *you* by the Lord Jesus, that as ye have *a*received of us how ye ought to *b*walk and to *c*please God, *so* ye would *d*abound more and more.

2 For ye know what commandments *a*we gave you by the Lord Jesus.

16*b* GR always.
17*a* 1 Thes. 3:10.
19*a* 1 Thes. 3:13;
  Rev. 1:7; 22:12;
  D&C 88:97.
3 1*a* Acts 17:15.
2*a* Acts 16:1 (1–2);
  1 Cor. 16:10 (10–11);
  2 Cor. 1:19;
  1 Thes. 1:1.
  b Rom. 16:25.
3*a* GR disturbed, perturbed.

b Acts 20:23;
  JS—H 1:24 (23–24).
c Acts 9:15 (15–16).
5*a* D&C 29:39 (39–40, 47);
  Moses 4:4 (3–4).
  b GR put to trial, test.
7*a* TG Sustaining Church
  Leaders.
  b TG Affliction.
9*a* Alma 26:11 (11–13);
  D&C 18:16 (14–16).
10*a* 1 Thes. 2:17.

b TG Perfection.
12*a* 1 Thes. 4:1.
  b D&C 121:45.
13*a* 1 Cor. 1:7 (7–8);
  1 Thes. 2:19;
  Rev. 1:7; 22:12.
  b TG Saints.
4 1*a* Philip. 4:9.
  b TG Walking with God.
  c Col. 1:10.
  d 1 Thes. 3:12.
2*a* D&C 1:38.

3 For this is the will of God, *even* your ^asanctification, that ye should ^babstain from ^cfornication:

4 That every one of you should know how to possess his ^avessel in ^bsanctification and honour;

5 Not in the ^alust of concupiscence, even as the ^bGentiles which ^cknow not God:

6 That no *man* ^ago beyond and defraud his brother in ^b*any* matter: because that the Lord *is* the ^cavenger of all such, as we also have forewarned you and testified.

7 For God hath not called us unto ^auncleanness, but unto holiness.

8 He therefore that ^adespiseth, ^bdespiseth not man, but God, who hath also given unto us his ^choly Spirit.

9 But as touching ^abrotherly love ye need not that I write unto you: for ye yourselves are ^btaught of God to ^clove one another.

10 And indeed ye do it toward all the brethren which are in all Macedonia: but we beseech you, brethren, that ye increase more and more;

11 And that ye ^astudy to be quiet, and to do your own business, and to ^bwork with your own ^chands, as we commanded you;

12 That ye may walk ^ahonestly toward them that are without, and *that* ye may have lack of nothing.

13 But I would not have you to be ignorant, brethren, concerning them which are asleep, that ye ^asorrow not, even as others which have no ^bhope.

14 For if we believe that Jesus died and rose again, even so them also which ^asleep in Jesus will God bring with him.

15 For this we say unto you by the word of the Lord, ^athat ^bwe which are alive *and* remain unto the coming of the Lord shall not ^cprevent them which are asleep.

16 For the Lord himself shall ^adescend from heaven with ^ba shout, with the voice of the ^carchangel, and with the ^dtrump of God: and the dead in Christ shall ^erise first:

17 ^aThen we which are alive *and* remain shall be ^bcaught up together with them in the clouds, to meet the ^cLord in the ^dair: and so shall we ^eever be with the ^fLord.

18 Wherefore comfort one another with these words.

CHAPTER 5

The Saints will know the season of the Second Coming of Christ—Live the way Saints should live—Rejoice evermore—Do not despise prophesyings.

<hr>

3*a* Heb. 12:14.
  b TG Abstain.
  c GR immorality.
    TG Chastity;
    Fornication; Sexual
    Immorality; Whore.
4*a* TG Body, Sanctity of.
  b TG Sanctification.
5*a* GR passion of lust.
    TG Lust;
    Marriage, Husbands.
  b Eph. 4:17 (17, 19).
  c Eph. 2:12 (11–12).
6*a* GR take advantage of, wrong.
  b GR the matter.
  c 2 Thes. 1:8.
7*a* TG Uncleanness.
8*a* GR rejects, sets aside, violates.
  b Luke 10:16.
  c 1 Cor. 2:10; 1 Jn. 3:24.
9*a* TG Brotherhood and Sisterhood.

  b John 6:45;
    1 Jn. 2:27 (20, 27).
  c TG Love.
11*a* GR strive, endeavor earnestly.
  b TG Industry; Labor; Skill; Work, Value of.
  c Prov. 31:13.
12*a* TG Dependability; Honesty.
13*a* TG Despair; Mourning; Sorrow.
  b Eph. 2:12.
14*a* Zech. 14:5.
15*a* JST 1 Thes. 4:15 . . . that *they who* are alive *at* the coming of the Lord, shall not prevent them *who remain unto the coming of the Lord, who* are asleep.
  b 2 Thes. 2:2 (1–3).
  c GR precede, make progress over.

16*a* TG Jesus Christ, Second Coming.
  b GR a cry of command, a cheer.
  c TG Adam.
  d Matt. 24:31.
  e TG Resurrection.
17*a* JST 1 Thes. 4:17 Then *they who* are alive, shall be caught up together *into* the clouds *with them who remain,* to meet the Lord in the air; and so shall we be ever with the Lord.
  b 1 Cor. 15:51; D&C 88:96 (96–97); 101:31; 109:75.
  c Jude 1:14 (14–16).
  d Moro. 10:34.
  e TG Immortality.
  f John 14:3; Rev. 22:4 (3–5).

BUT of the times and the seasons, brethren, ye have no need that I write unto you.

2 For yourselves know perfectly that the ᵃday of the Lord so cometh as a ᵇthief in the night.

3 For when they shall say, Peace and ᵃsafety; then sudden destruction cometh upon them, as travail upon a woman with child; and they shall not ᵇescape.

4 But ye, brethren, are not in ᵃdarkness, that that ᵇday should overtake you as a thief.

5 Ye are all the ᵃchildren of light, and the children of the day: we are not of the night, nor of darkness.

6 Therefore let us not ᵃsleep, as *do* others; but let us ᵇwatch and be ᶜsober.

7 For they that sleep sleep in the night; and they that be drunken are drunken in the night.

8 But let us, who are of the day, be ᵃsober, putting on the ᵇbreastplate of ᶜfaith and love; and for an helmet, the ᵈhope of salvation.

9 For God hath not appointed us to ᵃwrath, but to obtain ᵇsalvation by our Lord Jesus Christ,

10 Who died for us, that, whether we wake or sleep, we should ᵃlive together with him.

11 Wherefore ᵃcomfort yourselves together, and ᵇedify one another, even as also ye do.

12 And we beseech you, brethren, to know them which ᵃlabour among you, and are over you in the Lord, and admonish you;

13 And to ᵃesteem them very highly in love for their work's sake. *And* be at ᵇpeace among yourselves.

14 Now we exhort you, brethren, ᵃwarn them that are ᵇunruly, ᶜcomfort the ᵈfeebleminded, ᵉsupport the ᶠweak, be patient toward all *men*.

15 See that none ᵃrender ᵇevil for evil unto any ᶜman; but ever follow that which is good, both among yourselves, and to all *men*.

16 ᵃRejoice evermore.

17 ᵃPray without ceasing.

18 In every thing give ᵃthanks: for this is the will of God in Christ Jesus concerning you.

19 ᵃQuench not the ᵇSpirit.

20 Despise not prophesyings.

21 ᵃProve all things; hold fast that which is good.

22 ᵃAbstain from all ᵇappearance of ᶜevil.

23 And the very God of peace ᵃsanctify you wholly; and I *pray God* your whole spirit and soul and body be preserved blameless unto the coming of our Lord Jesus Christ.

---

5 2a TG Day of the Lord;
   Millennium, Preparing
   a People for.
  b D&C 106:4.
 3a TG Refuge.
  b D&C 1:2.
 4a Rom. 13:12 (12–13).
  b Luke 17:24; 21:34.
 5a GR sons.
   TG Children of Light.
 6a TG Sleep.
  b TG Watch.
  c GR sober, vigilant,
   circumspect.
   TG Abstain.
 8a TG Levity.
  b Rom. 13:12;
   Eph. 6:11 (11–18).
  c Col. 1:4 (4–5);
   1 Thes. 1:3.
  d TG Hope.

 9a 1 Thes. 1:10;
   1 Pet. 2:8 (6–8).
  b TG Salvation.
10a TG Immortality.
11a GR exhort, console,
   encourage.
  b TG Edification.
12a TG Leadership.
13a Philip. 2:29.
   TG Respect.
  b Mark 9:50;
   Rom. 15:5 (1–7);
   D&C 20:54 (53–55).
14a TG Warn.
  b 2 Thes. 3:11.
  c GR encourage, console.
  d GR faint-hearted,
   despondent.
  e GR care for.
  f GR infirm, doubting,
   timid.

15a TG Retribution.
  b TG Forbear.
  c TG Enemies.
16a TG Joy.
17a TG Prayer.
18a TG Communication;
   Thanksgiving.
19a GR Extinguish, Hinder,
   Suppress.
  b TG Holy Ghost, Gifts of;
   Holy Ghost, Loss of.
21a GR Examine, Put to
   the test.
   1 Jn. 4:1 (1–6).
   TG Study;
   Test.
22a TG Abstain.
  b GR kinds.
   TG Apparel.
  c TG Evil.
23a TG Sanctification.

24 Faithful *is* he that calleth you, who also will do *it*.

25 Brethren, pray for us.

26 Greet all the brethren with an holy ᵃkiss.

27 I charge you by the Lord that this epistle be read unto all the holy brethren.

28 The grace of our Lord Jesus Christ *be* with you. Amen.

¶ The first *epistle* unto the Thessalonians was written from Athens.*

THE SECOND EPISTLE OF
PAUL THE APOSTLE TO THE

THESSALONIANS

CHAPTER 1

At His Second Coming, the Lord Jesus will take vengeance upon the ungodly.

PAUL, and Silvanus, and Timotheus, ᵃunto the ᵇchurch of the Thessalonians in God our Father and the Lord Jesus Christ:

2 Grace unto you, and peace, from God our Father and the Lord Jesus Christ.

3 We are bound to thank God always for you, brethren, as it is meet, because that your faith groweth exceedingly, and the charity of every one of you all toward each other aboundeth;

4 So that we ourselves glory in you in the ᵃchurches of God for your ᵇpatience and faith in all your ᶜpersecutions and tribulations that ye endure:

5 *Which is* a manifest token of the righteous judgment of God, that ye may be counted worthy of the kingdom of God, for which ye also ᵃsuffer:

6 Seeing *it is* a righteous thing with God to recompense tribulation to them that trouble you;

7 And to you who are troubled ᵃrest with us, when the ᵇLord Jesus shall be ᶜrevealed from heaven with his mighty ᵈangels,

8 In flaming ᵃfire taking ᵇvengeance on them that know not God, and that ᶜobey not the ᵈgospel of our Lord Jesus Christ:

9 Who shall be ᵃpunished with ᵇeverlasting ᶜdestruction from the presence of the Lord, and from the glory of his power;

10 When he shall come to be ᵃglorified in his ᵇsaints, and to be admired in all them that believe (because our testimony among you was believed) in that day.

11 Wherefore also we pray always

26a JST 1 Thes. 5:26 . . .
    salutation.

* More recent scholarship concludes that 1 and 2 Thes. were most likely written from Corinth.

[2 THESSALONIANS]

1 1a JST 2 Thes. 1:1 . . . *the servants of God the Father and our Lord Jesus Christ,*

unto the church of the Thessalonians;
  b TG Jesus Christ, Head of the Church.
4a 1 Thes. 1:8.
  b GR endurance. D&C 58:2.
  c 1 Thes. 2:14.
5a TG Suffering.
7a TG Rest.
  b TG Day of the Lord.
  c TG Jesus Christ, Second

Coming.
  d D&C 76:21.
8a TG World, End of.
  b 1 Thes. 4:6.
  c TG Disobedience.
  d TG Gospel.
9a TG Punish.
  b TG Eternity.
  c TG Damnation; Sons of Perdition.
10a Isa. 66:5.
  b TG Saints.

for you, that our God would count you *a*worthy of *this* calling, and fulfil all the good pleasure of *his* goodness, and the work of faith with power:

12 That the name of our Lord Jesus Christ may be glorified in you, and ye in him, according to the *a*grace of our God and the Lord Jesus Christ.

CHAPTER 2

Apostasy is to precede the Second Coming—The gospel prepares men for eternal glory.

Now we beseech you, brethren, *a*by the coming of our Lord Jesus Christ, and *by* our gathering together unto him,

2 That ye be not soon shaken in mind, *a*or be troubled, neither by spirit, nor by word, nor by *b*letter as from us, as that the *c*day of Christ is at hand.

3 Let no man deceive you by any means: *a*for *that day shall not come*, except there come a *b*falling away first, and that *c*man of *d*sin be revealed, the son of perdition;

4 Who *a*opposeth and exalteth himself above all that is called God, or that is worshipped; so that he as God sitteth in the temple of God, shewing himself that he is God.

5 Remember ye not, that, when I was yet with you, I told you these things?

6 And now ye know *a*what withholdeth that he might be *b*revealed in his time.

7 *a*For the *b*mystery of *c*iniquity doth already work: only *d*he who now letteth *will let*, until he be taken out of the way.

8 And then shall that *a*Wicked be revealed, whom the Lord shall consume with the spirit of his mouth, and shall destroy with the brightness of his *b*coming:

9 *Even him*, whose coming is after the working of Satan with all *a*power and *b*signs and lying wonders,

10 And with all deceivableness of unrighteousness in them that perish; because they received not the love of the truth, that they might be saved.

11 And for this cause God shall send them strong delusion, that they should believe a lie:

12 That they all might be *a*damned who *b*believed not the truth, but had pleasure in unrighteousness.

13 But we are bound to give thanks alway to God for you, brethren beloved of the Lord, because God hath from the beginning *a*chosen you to salvation through *b*sanctification of the Spirit and belief of the truth:

14 Whereunto he called you by our *a*gospel, to the obtaining of the glory of our Lord Jesus Christ.

15 Therefore, brethren, stand fast, and hold the traditions which ye have been taught, whether by word, or our epistle.

16 Now our Lord Jesus Christ himself, and God, even our Father, which hath *a*loved us, and hath

---

11*a* TG Worthiness.
12*a* TG Grace.
2 1*a* GR concerning.
 2*a* JST 2 Thes. 2:2 . . . or be troubled *by letter, except ye receive it from us*; neither by spirit, nor by word, as that the day of Christ is at hand.
  b 1 Thes. 4:15 (13–17).
  c Luke 19:11.
 3*a* JST 2 Thes. 2:3 . . . for there *shall* come a falling away first . . .
  b GR apostasy, defection. TG Apostasy of the

Early Christian Church.
  c TG Antichrist; Devil.
  d TG Sin.
 4*a* TG Opposition.
 6*a* GR the one who possesses, holds in firm grasp, restrains.
  b GR disclosed, discovered, manifested.
 7*a* JST 2 Thes. 2:7–9 (Appendix).
  b TG Conspiracy; Secret Combinations.
  c GR lawlessness.
  d GR he who now

possesses, holds in firm grasp, restrains.
 8*a* GR Lawless one.
  b TG Jesus Christ, Second Coming.
 9*a* TG False Priesthoods.
  b TG Signs.
12*a* GR brought to account, trial. TG Damnation.
  b TG Unbelief.
13*a* TG Election; Foreordination.
  b TG Sanctification.
14*a* TG Gospel.
16*a* 1 Jn. 4:10.

given *us* everlasting ᵇconsolation and good hope through ᶜgrace,

17 Comfort your hearts, and stablish you in every good word and work.

CHAPTER 3

Pray for the triumph of the gospel cause—Paul preaches the gospel of work—Be not weary in well-doing.

FINALLY, brethren, pray for us, that the word of the Lord ᵃmay have *free* course, and be glorified, even as *it is* with you:

2 And that we may be delivered from ᵃunreasonable and wicked men: for all *men* have not faith.

3 But the Lord is faithful, who shall stablish you, and keep *you* from ᵃevil.

4 And we have ᵃconfidence in the Lord touching you, that ye both do and will do the things which we command you.

5 And the Lord ᵃdirect your hearts into the ᵇlove of God, and into the patient waiting for Christ.

6 Now we command you, brethren, in the name of our Lord Jesus Christ, that ye ᵃwithdraw yourselves from every brother that walketh ᵇdisorderly, and not after the tradition which he received of us.

7 For yourselves know how ye ought to ᵃfollow us: for we ᵇbehaved not ourselves disorderly among you;

8 Neither did we eat any man's bread ᵃfor nought; but wrought with ᵇlabour and travail night and day, that we might not be chargeable to any of you:

9 Not because we have not ᵃpower, but to make ourselves an ᵇensample unto you to follow us.

10 For even when we were with you, this we commanded you, that if any would not ᵃwork, neither should he eat.

11 For we hear that there are some which walk among you ᵃdisorderly, working not at all, but are busybodies.

12 Now them that are such we command and exhort by our Lord Jesus Christ, that with quietness they work, and eat their own ᵃbread.

13 But ye, brethren, be not ᵃweary in well doing.

14 And if any man obey not our word by this epistle, note that man, and have no company with him, that he may be ashamed.

15 Yet count *him* not as an ᵃenemy, but ᵇadmonish *him* as a ᶜbrother.

16 Now the Lord of peace himself give you peace always by all means. The Lord *be* with you all.

17 The salutation of Paul with mine own ᵃhand, which is the token in every epistle: so I write.

18 The grace of our Lord Jesus Christ *be* with you all. Amen.

¶ The second *epistle* to the Thessalonians was written from Athens.*

16b 2 Cor. 1:4;
    Philip. 3:10.
  c TG Grace.
3 1*a* GR may progress freely, rapidly.
  2*a* GR unsuitable, absurd, improper.
  3*a* GR the evil one, the devil.
  4*a* TG Dependability.
  5*a* TG Guidance, Divine.
  b Deut. 11:13.
  6*a* 1 Cor. 5:9 (1–13);
    Alma 1:24 (21–24);

5:57 (56–57).
  TG Excommunication.
  b Rom. 16:17 (17–19).
7*a* GR imitate.
  b 1 Thes. 1:5.
8*a* GR undeservedly, gratuitously.
  b TG Work, Value of.
9*a* GR authority.
  b TG Example.
10*a* TG Idleness;
    Industry;
    Labor;
    Laziness.

11*a* 1 Thes. 5:14.
12*a* TG Bread.
13*a* Gal. 6:9.
15*a* TG Enemies.
  b TG Warn.
  c TG Brotherhood and Sisterhood.
17*a* Col. 4:18.

* More recent scholarship concludes that 1 and 2 Thes. were most likely written from Corinth.

THE FIRST EPISTLE OF PAUL THE APOSTLE TO

TIMOTHY

CHAPTER 1

Counsel is given to teach true doctrine only—Christ came to save repentant sinners.

PAUL, an apostle of Jesus Christ by the commandment of God our Saviour, and Lord Jesus Christ, *which is* our hope;

2 Unto ᵃTimothy, ᵇ*my* ᶜown son in the faith: Grace, mercy, *and* peace, from God our Father and Jesus Christ our Lord.

3 As I besought thee to abide still at Ephesus, when I went into Macedonia, that thou mightest charge some that they ᵃteach no ᵇother doctrine,

4 Neither give heed to ᵃfables and endless genealogies, which ᵇminister ᶜquestions, rather than godly ᵈedifying which is in faith: *so do.*

5 Now the end of the ᵃcommandment is ᵇcharity out of a ᶜpure heart, and *of* a good conscience, and *of* faith unfeigned:

6 From which some having ᵃswerved have ᵇturned aside unto ᶜvain jangling;

7 Desiring to be teachers of the law; understanding neither what they say, nor whereof they ᵃaffirm.

8 But we know that the law *is* good, if a man use it lawfully;

9 Knowing this, that the ᵃlaw is not made for a ᵇrighteous man, but for the ᶜlawless and ᵈdisobedient, for the ungodly and for sinners, for unholy and profane, for murderers of fathers and murderers of mothers, for manslayers,

10 For ᵃwhoremongers, for ᵇthem that ᶜdefile themselves with mankind, for ᵈmenstealers, for liars, for perjured persons, and if there be any other thing that is contrary to sound ᵉdoctrine;

11 According to the glorious gospel of the blessed God, which was committed to my ᵃtrust.

12 And I thank Christ Jesus our Lord, who hath ᵃenabled me, for that he counted me faithful, putting me into the ministry;

13 Who was before a ᵃblasphemer, and a ᵇpersecutor, and ᶜinjurious: but I obtained ᵈmercy, because I did *it* ᵉignorantly in unbelief.

14 And the ᵃgrace of our Lord was exceeding abundant with faith and love which is in Christ Jesus.

15 This *is* a faithful ᵃsaying, and worthy of all acceptation, that Christ

---

1 2*a* Acts 16:1 (1–4);
   1 Cor. 4:17.
   b GR a true son
   according to.
   c GR lawful, true.
3*a* 1 Tim. 6:3 (3–5);
   3 Ne. 11:40.
   b Gal. 1:8 (6–8).
4*a* Titus 1:14;
   2 Pet. 1:16.
   b GR offer, present.
   c 1 Tim. 6:4.
   d TG Edification.
5*a* Gal. 5:14.

   b TG Charity.
   c 2 Tim. 2:22.
6*a* GR missed the mark.
   b TG Apostasy of the
   Early Christian Church.
   c GR vain, idle, fruitless
   discussion.
7*a* GR strongly assert.
9*a* TG Law of Moses.
   b TG Godliness.
   c Gal. 3:19.
   d TG Disobedience.
10*a* TG Whore.
   b GR homosexuals.

   c TG Homosexual
   Behavior.
   d GR kidnappers.
   e 2 Tim. 4:3.
11*a* TG Trustworthiness.
12*a* Philip. 4:13.
13*a* Acts 26:9.
   b Acts 8:3; 22:4.
   c GR violent.
   d 1 Cor. 7:25.
   e John 9:39 (39–41).
   TG Ignorance.
14*a* TG Grace.
15*a* 1 Tim. 3:1.

Jesus came into the world to ^bsave ^csinners; of whom I am chief.

16 Howbeit for this cause I obtained ^amercy, that in me first Jesus Christ might shew forth all ^blongsuffering, for a ^cpattern to them which should hereafter believe on him to life everlasting.

17 Now unto the ^aKing eternal, ^bimmortal, invisible, the only wise God, *be* honour and glory for ever and ever. Amen.

18 This charge I commit unto thee, son Timothy, according to the ^aprophecies which went before on thee, that thou by them mightest war a good warfare;

19 ^aHolding faith, and a good conscience; which some having put away concerning faith have made ^bshipwreck:

20 Of whom is ^aHymenæus and ^bAlexander; whom I have ^cdelivered unto Satan, that they may learn not to blaspheme.

CHAPTER 2

We should pray for all people—Christ is our Mediator—Women should dress modestly—Women are blessed in childbearing and are admonished to continue in faith, charity, and holiness.

I EXHORT therefore, that, first of all, supplications, prayers, intercessions, *and* giving of thanks, be made for all men;

2 For ^akings, and *for* all that are in authority; that we may lead a quiet and ^bpeaceable ^clife in all godliness and ^dhonesty.

3 For this *is* good and acceptable in the sight of God our Saviour;

4 ^aWho ^bwill have ^call men to be ^dsaved, and to come unto the knowledge of the truth.

5 For *there is* ^aone God, and one ^bmediator between God and men, the man Christ Jesus;

6 Who ^agave himself a ^bransom for all, to be ^ctestified in due time.

7 Whereunto I am ^aordained a ^bpreacher, and an ^capostle, (I speak the truth in Christ, *and* ^dlie not;) a teacher of the ^eGentiles in faith and ^fverity.

8 I ^awill therefore that men ^bpray every where, lifting up holy ^chands, without wrath and ^ddoubting.

9 In like manner also, that ^awomen adorn themselves in ^bmodest ^capparel, with ^dshamefacedness and sobriety; not with ^ebroided hair, or gold, or pearls, or costly array;

10 But (which becometh women professing ^agodliness) with good works.

11 Let the woman learn in ^asilence with all subjection.

12 But I suffer not a woman to

15*b* Matt. 9:13 (12–13).
   TG Jesus Christ,
   Atonement through.
   c Luke 5:32;
   John 9:39 (39–41).
16*a* TG God, Mercy of.
   b TG Forbear.
   c TG Example.
17*a* 1 Tim. 6:15 (15–16).
   b TG God, Eternal
   Nature of;
   Immortality.
18*a* 1 Tim. 4:14 (14–16);
   2 Tim. 1:6.
19*a* 1 Ne. 15:24; D&C 6:13.
   b TG Apostasy of Individuals; Apostasy of the
   Early Christian Church.
20*a* 2 Tim. 2:17.
   b Acts 19:33 (33–34).
   c 1 Cor. 5:5;
   D&C 78:12;
   104:10 (9–10); 132:26.

2 2*a* TG Governments;
   Kings, Earthly.
   b TG Peace;
   Peacemakers.
   c TG Citizenship.
   d GR dignity, gravity.
   TG Honesty.
4*a* JST 1 Tim. 2:4
   (Appendix).
   b GR desires.
   c D&C 6:11.
   d Ezek. 18:23 (23–24).
5*a* Rom. 3:30 (28–31);
   D&C 121:28.
   b Heb. 12:24.
   TG Jesus Christ,
   Authority of.
6*a* TG Self-Sacrifice.
   b Job 33:24.
   TG Jesus Christ,
   Atonement through;
   Jesus Christ, Redeemer.
   c Heb. 9:16 (16–17);

   D&C 135:5.
7*a* TG Called of God.
   b TG Preaching.
   c 1 Cor. 9:1.
   TG Apostles.
   d Rom. 9:1.
   e Acts 9:15.
   f GR truth.
8*a* GR desire.
   b D&C 19:28; 20:47; 23:6.
   c Ps. 24:4.
   d GR dispute, contention, doubt.
   TG Doubt.
9*a* TG Marriage, Wives;
   Woman.
   b TG Chastity;
   Modesty.
   c TG Apparel.
   d GR modesty, reverence.
   e GR plaited, braided.
10*a* TG Godliness.
11*a* TG Silence.

ᵃteach, nor to ᵇusurp authority over the man, but to be in ᶜsilence.

13 For Adam was first ᵃformed, then Eve.

14 And Adam was not deceived, but the woman being ᵃdeceived was in the ᵇtransgression.

15 Notwithstanding ᵃshe shall be saved in ᵇchildbearing, if they continue in faith and charity and ᶜholiness with ᵈsobriety.

CHAPTER 3

Qualifications are given for bishops and deacons—Great is the mystery of godliness.

THIS *is* a true ᵃsaying, If a man desire the office of a ᵇbishop, he desireth a good work.

2 A bishop then must be ᵃblameless, the husband of one wife, vigilant, ᵇsober, of good behaviour, given to ᶜhospitality, apt to ᵈteach;

3 Not given to ᵃwine, no ᵇstriker, not greedy of ᶜfilthy lucre; but patient, not a brawler, not covetous;

4 One that ᵃruleth well his own ᵇhouse, having his ᶜchildren in subjection with all gravity;

5 (For if a man know not how to ᵃrule his own house, how shall he take care of the church of God?)

6 Not a ᵃnovice, lest being lifted up with ᵇpride he fall into the ᶜcondemnation of the devil.

7 Moreover he must have a good ᵃreport of them which are ᵇwithout; lest he fall into reproach and the ᶜsnare of the devil.

8 Likewise *must* the ᵃdeacons *be* ᵇgrave, not ᶜdoubletongued, not given to much wine, not greedy of filthy lucre;

9 Holding the mystery of the faith in a pure ᵃconscience.

10 And let these also first be ᵃproved; then let them use the office of a deacon, being *found* blameless.

11 ᵃEven so *must their* ᵇwives *be* ᶜgrave, not ᵈslanderers, ᵉsober, ᶠfaithful in all things.

12 Let the deacons be the husbands of one wife, ruling their children and their own houses well.

13 For they that have used the office of a deacon well ᵃpurchase to themselves a good degree, and great boldness in the faith which is in Christ Jesus.

14 These things write I unto thee, hoping to come unto thee shortly:

15 ᵃBut if I tarry long, that thou mayest know how thou oughtest to behave thyself in the house of God, which is the ᵇchurch of the living

---

12a TG Teaching.
  b GR exercise dominion, be autocratic, domineer.
  c GR quietness, tranquillity.
13a TG Man, Physical Creation of.
14a TG Fall of Man.
  b TG Transgress.
15a JST 1 Tim. 2:15 . . . *they* . . .
  b TG Birth Control; Marriage, Motherhood.
  c TG Holiness.
  d GR modesty.
3 1a 1 Tim. 1:15.
  b TG Bishop.
 2a TG Priesthood, Qualifying for.
  b GR temperate, circumspect. TG Levity.
  c TG Hospitality.

d 2 Tim. 2:24.
3a TG Drunkenness; Word of Wisdom.
  b GR bully, violent person.
  c TG Filthiness.
4a TG Marriage, Husbands.
  b TG Marriage, Fatherhood.
  c TG Family, Children, Responsibilities toward; Family, Patriarchal.
5a Esth. 1:22; D&C 93:43 (41–43, 50). TG Family, Love within.
6a GR recent convert.
  b TG Pride.
  c 2 Pet. 2:4.
7a Acts 6:3; 22:12.
  b GR outside the faith.
  c TG Bondage, Spiritual.
8a TG Deacon.
  b GR honorable, dignified. TG Levity.

c GR deceitful.
9a TG Conscience.
10a 1 Tim. 5:22. TG Test.
11a GR Women in like manner.
  b TG Marriage, Wives.
  c GR honorable, dignified.
  d TG Slander.
  e GR temperate, vigilant, circumspect.
  f TG Trustworthiness.
13a GR earn, acquire for themselves good standing rank.
15a JST 1 Tim. 3:15–16 (Appendix). Note the change, emphasizing that the "pillar and ground of the truth" is Jesus Christ.
  b TG Church.

God, the pillar and ^cground of the ^dtruth.

16 And without controversy great is the ^amystery of godliness: ^bGod was ^cmanifest in the ^dflesh, ^ejustified in the Spirit, seen of angels, preached unto the Gentiles, believed on in the world, ^freceived up into glory.

CHAPTER 4

Paul describes the latter-day apostasy—Christ is the Savior of all men, especially of those who believe.

Now the Spirit speaketh expressly, that in the ^alatter times some shall ^bdepart from the faith, giving heed to ^cseducing spirits, and ^ddoctrines of devils;

2 Speaking ^alies in ^bhypocrisy; having their ^cconscience seared with a hot iron;

3 ^aForbidding to ^bmarry, *and commanding* to ^cabstain from ^dmeats, which God hath ^ecreated to be received with ^fthanksgiving of them which believe and know the truth.

4 For every ^acreature of God *is* ^bgood, and nothing to be refused, if it be received with ^cthanksgiving:

5 For it is sanctified by the word of God and prayer.

6 If thou put the brethren in re-membrance of these things, thou shalt be a good minister of Jesus Christ, nourished up in the words of faith and of good doctrine, ^awhereunto thou hast attained.

7 But refuse profane and old wives' fables, and exercise thyself *rather* unto godliness.

8 For bodily exercise profiteth ^alittle: but ^bgodliness is profitable unto all things, having promise of the life that now is, and of that which is to come.

9 This *is* a faithful saying and worthy of all acceptation.

10 For therefore we both ^alabour and suffer ^breproach, because we ^ctrust in the living God, who is the ^dSaviour of all men, specially of those that ^ebelieve.

11 These things command and teach.

12 Let no man ^adespise thy youth; but be thou an ^bexample of the believers, in word, in ^cconversation, in charity, in spirit, in faith, in ^dpurity.

13 Till I come, give attendance to ^areading, to exhortation, to doctrine.

14 ^aNeglect not the ^bgift that is in thee, which was given thee by ^cprophecy, with the ^dlaying on of the ^ehands of the ^fpresbytery.

15 ^aMeditate upon these things;

15c GR foundation.
  d TG Truth.
16a D&C 19:10.
    TG Mysteries of Godliness.
  b Ps. 1:3 (2–3);
    John 10:33 (30–33);
    Mosiah 3:5; 15:1 (1–5).
    TG Jesus Christ, Jehovah.
  c TG God, Manifestations of.
  d TG Jesus Christ, Condescension of.
  e GR approved by the.
  f TG Jesus Christ, Ascension of.
4 1a TG Last Days.
  b TG Holy Ghost, Loss of.
  c GR deceitful.
    TG Apostasy of the Early Christian Church;
    Spirits, Evil or Unclean.
  d TG False Doctrine.
2a TG Lying.

  b TG Hypocrisy.
  c TG Conscience;
    Spiritual Blindness.
3a Matt. 8:14;
    D&C 49:15.
    TG Marriage, Temporal.
  b TG Marriage, Marry.
  c TG Abstain.
  d TG Food;
    Word of Wisdom.
  e D&C 49:19.
  f D&C 89:11 (11–13).
4a GR creation.
  b Gen. 1:31.
  c TG Thanksgiving.
6a GR which thou hast followed closely.
8a GR a little while.
  b Luke 12:31.
    TG Godliness.
10a TG Labor.
  b TG Reproach.
  c TG Trust in God.
  d TG Jesus Christ, Atonement through;

    Jesus Christ, Savior.
  e TG Faith.
12a 1 Cor. 16:11 (10–11).
  b TG Example;
    Priesthood,
    Qualifying for.
  c GR conduct, behavior.
  d TG Chastity;
    Purity;
    Virtue.
13a TG Study.
14a TG Priesthood,
    Magnifying Callings within.
  b TG God, Gifts of;
    Stewardship;
    Talents.
  c 1 Tim. 1:18.
    TG Prophecy.
  d TG Priesthood,
    Authority;
    Priesthood, Ordination.
  e TG Hands, Laying on of.
  f GR elders.
15a TG Meditation.

give thyself wholly to them; that thy [b]profiting may [c]appear to all.

16 Take heed unto thyself, and unto the doctrine; continue in them: for in doing this thou shalt both [a]save thyself, and them that hear thee.

CHAPTER 5

Saints are to care for their worthy poor—Policies concerning elders are given.

[a]REBUKE not an elder, but [b]entreat *him* as a father; *and* the younger men as brethren;

2 The elder women as mothers; the younger as [a]sisters, with all purity.

3 Honour [a]widows that are widows indeed.

4 But if any widow have [a]children or [b]nephews, let them learn first to shew [c]piety at home, and to requite their parents: for that is good and acceptable before God.

5 Now she that is a widow indeed, and [a]desolate, trusteth in God, and continueth in supplications and prayers night and day.

6 But she that liveth [a]in [b]pleasure is dead while she liveth.

7 And these things [a]give in charge, that they may be blameless.

8 But if any [a]provide not for his own, and specially for those of his own house, he hath denied the faith, and is worse than an infidel.

9 Let not a widow be taken into the number under threescore years [a]old, having been the wife of one man,

10 Well reported of for good works; if she have brought up children, if she have [a]lodged strangers, if she have [b]washed the saints' [c]feet, if she have relieved the afflicted, if she have diligently followed every good work.

11 But the younger widows refuse: for when they have begun to wax wanton against Christ, they will marry;

12 Having [a]damnation, because they have cast off their first faith.

13 And withal they learn *to be* [a]idle, wandering about from house to house; and not only idle, but tattlers also and [b]busybodies, speaking things which they ought not.

14 I [a]will therefore that the younger [b]women marry, bear [c]children, guide the [d]house, give none occasion to the adversary to speak reproachfully.

15 For some are already turned aside after Satan.

16 If any man or woman that believeth have widows, let them [a]relieve them, and let not the church be [b]charged; that it may relieve them that are widows indeed.

17 Let the [a]elders that rule well be counted worthy of double honour, especially they who labour in the word and doctrine.

18 For the scripture saith, Thou shalt not [a]muzzle the ox that treadeth out the corn. And, The [b]labourer *is* worthy of his [c]reward.

19 Against an elder receive not an accusation, but before two or three [a]witnesses.

20 Them that sin [a]rebuke before all, that others also may fear.

15b GR progress, advancement.
   c GR be manifest in all.
16a James 5:20 (19–20); D&C 101:39 (39–40).
5 1a TG Chastening.
   b TG Respect.
2a TG Brotherhood and Sisterhood.
3a TG Widows.
4a TG Children.
   b GR grandchildren, descendants.
   c TG Family, Love within; Respect.
5a GR left alone.

6a GR wantonly.
   b TG Pleasure.
7a GR instruct, command.
8a TG Family, Children, Responsibilities toward; Family, Managing Finances in; Marriage, Husbands.
9a TG Old Age.
10a Acts 16:15 (14–15).
   b TG Wash.
   c JST 1 Tim. 5:10 . . . *clothes* . . .
12a GR judgment, condemnation. TG Damnation.
13a TG Idleness.

   b TG Gossip.
14a GR desire.
   b TG Marriage, Wives; Woman.
   c TG Children.
   d Titus 2:5 (4–5).
16a TG Welfare.
   b GR burdened down, troubled.
17a TG Elder, Melchizedek Priesthood.
18a Deut. 25:4.
   b TG Labor.
   c GR wage. TG Wages.
19a Deut. 19:15.
20a TG Chastening.

21 I charge *thee* before God, and the Lord Jesus Christ, and the elect ^aangels, that thou observe these things ^bwithout preferring one before another, doing nothing by partiality.

22 ^aLay ^bhands suddenly on no ^cman, neither be ^dpartaker of other men's sins: keep thyself ^epure.

23 Drink no longer water, but use a little wine for thy stomach's sake and thine often infirmities.

24 Some men's sins are open beforehand, going before to judgment; and some *men* they ^afollow after.

25 Likewise also the good works *of some* are manifest beforehand; and they that are otherwise cannot be hid.

CHAPTER 6

The love of money is the root of all evil—Fight the good fight of faith—Do not trust in worldly riches.

LET as many ^aservants as are under the ^byoke count their own masters worthy of all honour, that the name of God and *his* doctrine be not blasphemed.

2 And they that have believing masters, let them not despise *them,* because they are ^abrethren; but rather do *them* ^bservice, because they are faithful and beloved, partakers of the benefit. These things teach and exhort.

3 If any man ^ateach otherwise, and consent not to ^bwholesome words,

even the words of our Lord Jesus Christ, and to the doctrine which is according to godliness;

4 He is ^aproud, knowing nothing, but ^bdoting about ^cquestions and ^dstrifes of words, whereof cometh ^eenvy, strife, railings, ^fevil surmisings,

5 Perverse ^adisputings of men of corrupt minds, and destitute of the truth, supposing that ^bgain is godliness: from such withdraw thyself.

6 But ^agodliness with ^bcontentment is great gain.

7 For we brought ^anothing into *this* world, *and it is* certain we can carry nothing out.

8 And having ^afood and raiment let us be therewith ^bcontent.

9 But ^athey that will be ^brich fall into ^ctemptation and a snare, and *into* many foolish and hurtful ^dlusts, which drown men in destruction and ^eperdition.

10 For the ^alove of ^bmoney is the root of all evil: which while some ^ccoveted after, they have ^derred from the faith, and pierced themselves through with many ^esorrows.

11 But thou, O man of God, flee these things; and follow after ^arighteousness, godliness, faith, love, patience, meekness.

12 Fight the good fight of faith, lay hold on ^aeternal life, whereunto thou art also called, and hast ^bprofessed a good profession before many witnesses.

13 I give thee charge in the sight of God, who ^aquickeneth all things,

21 *a* TG Angels.
  b GR apart from prejudice.
22 *a* TG Setting Apart.
  b TG Hands, Laying on of.
  c 1 Tim. 3:10.
  d 2 Jn. 1:11.
  e James 1:27 (22–27).
24 *a* GR appear later.
6 1 *a* GR slaves.
    Col. 3:22;
    Titus 2:9 (9–10);
    1 Pet. 2:18.
  b TG Bondage, Physical.
2 *a* 1 Jn. 3:14 (10–18).
  b TG Service.
3 *a* 1 Tim. 1:3; D&C 10:68.
  b Titus 2:8.
4 *a* TG Pride.

  b GR obsessed with
    questions.
  c 1 Tim. 1:4.
  d TG Strife.
  e TG Envy.
  f GR wicked suspicions.
5 *a* TG Disputations.
  b Titus 1:11.
6 *a* TG Godliness.
  b TG Contentment.
7 *a* Job 1:21.
8 *a* TG Food.
  b TG Contentment.
9 *a* GR those desiring to
    be rich.
  b TG Treasure.
  c TG Temptation.
  d TG Lust.

  e TG Death, Spiritual,
    Second.
10 *a* Ps. 119:36;
    James 5:3 (1–6).
  b TG Selfishness.
  c TG Covet.
  d GR wandered,
    apostatized.
  e TG Sorrow.
11 *a* TG Priesthood,
    Magnifying Callings
    within; Righteousness.
12 *a* TG Eternal Life.
  b Heb. 10:23.
13 *a* GR brings to life.
    D&C 33:16; 88:17.
    TG God, Power of;
    Resurrection.

and *before* Christ Jesus, who before [b]Pontius Pilate [c]witnessed a good confession;

14 That thou keep *this* commandment without spot, unrebukeable, until the appearing of our Lord Jesus Christ:

15 [a]Which in his times he shall shew, *who is* the blessed and only [b]Potentate, the [c]King of kings, and Lord of lords;

16 Who only hath [a]immortality, dwelling in the [b]light which no man can approach unto; whom no man hath [c]seen, nor can see: to whom *be* honour and power everlasting. Amen.

17 Charge them that are [a]rich in this world, that they be not highminded, nor trust in uncertain [b]riches, but in the living God, who giveth us richly all things to enjoy;

18 That they do good, that they be rich in good works, ready to [a]distribute, willing to [b]communicate;

19 [a]Laying up in [b]store for themselves a good foundation [c]against the time to come, that they may lay hold on [d]eternal life.

20 O Timothy, keep that which is committed to thy [a]trust, avoiding profane *and* vain babblings, and [b]oppositions of science falsely so called:

21 Which some professing have erred concerning the faith. Grace *be* with thee. Amen.

¶ The first to Timothy was written from Laodicea, which is the chiefest city of Phrygia Pacatiana.

THE SECOND EPISTLE OF
PAUL THE APOSTLE TO
TIMOTHY

CHAPTER 1

Christ brings immortality and eternal life through the gospel—Be strong in the faith.

PAUL, an apostle of Jesus Christ by the will of God, according to the [a]promise of life which is in Christ Jesus,

2 To Timothy, *my* dearly beloved son: Grace, mercy, *and* peace, from God the Father and Christ Jesus our Lord.

3 I thank God, whom I serve from *my* forefathers with pure [a]conscience, that without ceasing I have remembrance of thee in my prayers night and day;

4 Greatly desiring to see thee, being mindful of thy tears, that I may be filled with joy;

5 When I call to remembrance the

13b John 18:37 (29–40).
  c GR testified.
    TG God, the Standard of Righteousness.
15a JST 1 Tim. 6:15–16 (Appendix).
  b D&C 41:4.
  c Zech. 14:16; 1 Tim. 1:17; Rev. 17:14.
16a TG Immortality.
  b D&C 88:12 (6–13);

130:7 (6–9).
  c TG God, Privilege of Seeing.
17a Hel. 4:12 (11–13);
    3 Ne. 6:12 (10–16).
  b James 1:11 (8–16).
18a TG Generosity.
  b TG Communication.
19a D&C 14:3.
  b D&C 4:4.
  c GR for the future.

d D&C 11:3.
20a TG Trustworthiness.
  b GR disputations of what is falsely called knowledge.
    2 Ne. 26:20;
    D&C 1:19.

[2 TIMOTHY]

1 1a Titus 1:2.
3a TG Conscience.

unfeigned faith that is in thee, which dwelt first in thy grandmother Lois, and thy mother ^aEunice; and I am persuaded that in thee also.

6 Wherefore I put thee in remembrance that thou ^astir up the ^bgift of God, which is in thee by the putting on of my ^chands.

7 For God hath not given us the spirit of ^afear; but of ^bpower, and of ^clove, and of a sound mind.

8 Be not thou therefore ^aashamed of the ^btestimony of our Lord, nor of me his prisoner: but be thou partaker of the afflictions of the gospel according to the power of God;

9 Who hath saved us, and called *us* with an holy ^acalling, not according to our works, but according to his own purpose and ^bgrace, which was given us in Christ Jesus before the world began,

10 But is now made ^amanifest by the appearing of our Saviour Jesus Christ, who hath abolished ^bdeath, and hath brought ^clife and ^dimmortality to light through the gospel:

11 Whereunto I am ^aappointed a preacher, and an ^bapostle, and a teacher of the Gentiles.

12 For the which cause I also suffer these things: nevertheless I am not ^aashamed: for I know whom I have believed, and am persuaded that he is able to keep that which I have committed unto him against that day.

13 Hold fast the ^aform of ^bsound words, which thou hast heard of me, in faith and love which is in Christ Jesus.

14 That good thing which was committed unto thee keep by the Holy Ghost which ^adwelleth in us.

15 This thou knowest, that all they which are in Asia be ^aturned away from me; of whom are Phygellus and Hermogenes.

16 The Lord give mercy unto the house of Onesiphorus; for he oft ^arefreshed me, and was not ashamed of my chain:

17 But, when he was in Rome, he sought me out very diligently, and found *me*.

18 The Lord grant unto him that he may find ^amercy of the Lord in that day: and in how many things he ministered unto me at Ephesus, thou knowest very well.

CHAPTER 2

Christ gives eternal glory to the elect— Shun contention and seek godliness.

THOU therefore, my son, be strong in the grace that is in Christ Jesus.

2 And the things that thou hast heard of me among many witnesses, the same commit thou to faithful men, who shall be able to ^ateach others also.

3 Thou therefore endure ^ahardness, as a good soldier of Jesus Christ.

4 No man that warreth entangleth himself with the affairs of *this* life; that he may please him who hath chosen him to be a soldier.

5 And if a man also ^astrive for ^bmasteries, *yet* is he not ^ccrowned, except he strive lawfully.

6 The husbandman that laboureth

5*a* Acts 16:1.
6*a* GR rekindle, revive.
  TG Priesthood,
  Magnifying Callings
  within.
  b 1 Tim. 1:18;
  D&C 8:4.
  TG Holy Ghost, Gifts of.
  c TG Hands, Laying on of.
7*a* TG Courage;
  Fearful.
  b Acts 1:8.
  c TG Love.
8*a* TG Shame.
  b TG Testimony.
9*a* TG Foreordination.
  b TG Grace.
10*a* Col. 1:26.
  b 1 Cor. 15:26;
  Heb. 2:14;
  Rev. 20:13 (11–15).
  TG Jesus Christ,
  Atonement through;
  Jesus Christ, Death of.
  c 1 Jn. 5:11 (10–21).
  d TG Immortality.
11*a* 1 Thes. 2:4.
  b TG Apostles.
12*a* Rom. 1:16.
13*a* GR sketch, model,
  example.
  b GR uncorrupted.
14*a* D&C 130:22.
15*a* TG Apostasy of the
  Early Christian Church.
16*a* TG Hospitality.
18*a* TG God, Mercy of.
2 2*a* D&C 38:23.
  TG Teaching.
3*a* GR afflictions,
  vexations.
5*a* GR compete in a contest.
  b 1 Cor. 9:25.
  c TG Reward.

must be first *partaker of the fruits.

7 Consider what I say; and the Lord give thee understanding in all things.

8 Remember that Jesus Christ of the seed of David was *raised from the dead according to my *gospel:

9 Wherein I suffer trouble, as an evil doer, *even* unto bonds; but the word of God is not bound.

10 Therefore I endure all things for the elect's sakes, that they may also obtain the salvation which is in Christ Jesus with eternal glory.

11 *It is* a faithful saying: For if we be *dead with *him,* we shall also live with *him:*

12 If we *suffer, we shall also *reign with *him:* if we *deny *him,* he also will deny us:

13 If we *believe not, *yet* he abideth faithful: he cannot *deny himself.

14 Of these things put *them* in remembrance, charging *them* before the Lord that they *strive not about words to no profit, *but* to the subverting of the hearers.

15 *Study to shew thyself approved unto God, a workman that needeth not to be ashamed, *rightly dividing the word of truth.

16 But shun profane *and *vain babblings: for they will increase unto more *ungodliness.

17 And their *word will eat as doth a canker: of whom is *Hymenæus and Philetus;

18 Who concerning the truth have *erred, saying that the resurrection is past already; and overthrow the faith of some.

19 Nevertheless the foundation of God standeth sure, having this seal, The Lord knoweth them that are his. And, Let every one that nameth the name of Christ depart from iniquity.

20 But in a great house there are not only vessels of gold and of silver, but also of wood and of *earth; and some to honour, and some to dishonour.

21 If a man therefore purge himself from these, he shall be a *vessel unto honour, *sanctified, and *meet for the master's use, *and* prepared unto every good work.

22 Flee also youthful *lusts: but follow *righteousness, faith, charity, *peace, with them that call on the Lord out of a *pure heart.

23 But *foolish and unlearned *questions avoid, knowing that they do gender *strifes.

24 And the servant of the Lord must not *strive; but be gentle unto all *men,* apt to *teach, patient,

25 In *meekness *instructing those that oppose themselves; if God *peradventure will give them repentance to the acknowledging of the truth;

26 And *that* they may recover themselves out of the snare of the devil, who are taken *captive by him at his will.

6a 1 Cor. 9:10.
8a TG Jesus Christ,
   Resurrection.
 b TG Gospel.
11a Rom. 6:5 (5, 8).
12a GR endure, remain
   constant.
   TG Persecution;
   Suffering.
 b TG Millennium,
   Preparing a People for.
 c Matt. 10:33 (32–33);
   Rom. 1:16 (15–18);
   2 Ne. 31:14 (12–21);
   D&C 101:5 (1–5).
13a GR are unfaithful.
 b D&C 39:16.
   TG God, Perfection of.

14a GR dispute not about
   words, or trivialities.
15a TG Scriptures, Study of.
 b GR setting forth without
   perversion, distortion.
16a GR vain disputation.
 b TG Godliness.
17a GR teaching will spread
   like gangrene.
 b 1 Tim. 1:20.
18a TG Apostasy of the
   Early Christian Church.
20a GR clay, earthenware.
21a TG Body, Sanctity of.
 b Isa. 52:11.
 c GR useful, profitable.
22a GR impure, violent
   desires.

   TG Chastity;
   Lust.
 b TG Priesthood,
   Magnifying Callings
   within.
 c TG Peace.
 d 1 Tim. 1:5.
23a Titus 3:9.
 b D&C 19:31 (29–31).
 c TG Strife.
24a 3 Ne. 11:29 (29–30);
   D&C 18:20; 136:23.
 b 1 Tim. 3:2.
25a TG Meek.
 b D&C 20:53.
 c GR perchance.
26a Moses 7:26.
   TG Bondage, Spiritual.

CHAPTER 3

Paul describes the apostasy and perilous times of the last days—The scriptures guide man to salvation.

THIS know also, that in the ªlast days perilous ᵇtimes shall come.

2 For men shall be lovers of their own selves, ªcovetous, boasters, ᵇproud, blasphemers, ᶜdisobedient to parents, ᵈunthankful, unholy,

3 Without ªnatural ᵇaffection, ᶜtrucebreakers, ᵈfalse accusers, ᵉincontinent, fierce, despisers of those that are good,

4 ªTraitors, ᵇheady, ᶜhighminded, lovers of ᵈpleasures more than lovers of God;

5 Having a ªform of godliness, but ᵇdenying the power thereof: from such turn away.

6 For of this sort are they which creep into houses, and lead captive silly ªwomen laden with sins, led away with divers ᵇlusts,

7 Ever ªlearning, and never able to come to the ᵇknowledge of the ᶜtruth.

8 Now as Jannes and Jambres withstood Moses, so do these also ªresist the truth: men of ᵇcorrupt minds, reprobate concerning the faith.

9 But they shall proceed no fur-ther: for their ªfolly shall be manifest unto all *men,* as theirs also was.

10 But thou hast ªfully known my doctrine, manner of life, purpose, faith, longsuffering, charity, patience,

11 Persecutions, afflictions, which came unto me at Antioch, at Iconium, at Lystra; what ªpersecutions I endured: but out of *them* all the Lord delivered me.

12 Yea, and all that will live ªgodly in Christ Jesus shall ᵇsuffer ᶜpersecution.

13 But evil men and ªseducers shall wax worse and worse, deceiving, and being deceived.

14 But ªcontinue thou in the things which thou hast learned and hast been assured of, knowing of whom thou hast learned *them;*

15 And that from a ªchild thou hast known the holy ᵇscriptures, which are able to make thee ᶜwise unto ᵈsalvation through faith which is in Christ Jesus.

16 ªAll ᵇscripture *is* given by ᶜinspiration of God, and is ᵈprofitable for ᵉdoctrine, for ᶠreproof, for correction, for ᵍinstruction in ʰrighteousness:

17 That the man of God may be ªperfect, throughly furnished unto all ᵇgood works.

---

3 1a Morm. 1:17 (13–17);
   8:28 (26–33).
   TG Last Days.
  b 2 Tim. 4:3.
 2a TG Covet.
  b TG Pride.
  c TG Contention;
   Disobedience;
   Family, Children,
   Duties of.
  d TG Ingratitude.
 3a Rom. 1:26 (26–28).
  b TG Sexual Immorality.
  c TG Honesty.
  d GR slanderers.
  e GR without self-control.
 4a TG Rebellion.
  b GR rash, reckless.
  c GR puffed up, conceited.
  d TG Pleasure.
 5a Rom. 2:20;
   2 Ne. 28:5;
   JS—H 1:19.
  b TG Apostasy of the

Early Christian Church.
 6a TG Woman.
  b TG Lust.
 7a TG Learn.
  b TG Ignorance;
   Knowledge.
  c TG Truth.
 8a TG Opposition.
  b Ps. 14:1;
   D&C 10:21 (20–23);
   112:23 (23–24).
 9a D&C 35:7; 45:49; 63:15.
10a GR followed closely,
   conformed to.
11a Acts 15:26.
12a TG Godliness.
  b Ps. 34:19.
   TG Suffering.
  c TG Cruelty;
   Persecution.
13a GR diviners, imposters,
   cheats.
14a D&C 66:12.
15a Deut. 4:9 (6–9).

  b TG Scriptures, Study of.
  c TG Understanding.
  d TG Salvation.
16a JST 2 Tim. 3:16 *And*
   all scripture given by
   inspiration of God, is
   profitable . . .
  b TG Book of Mormon;
   Scriptures, Writing of;
   Scriptures to Come
   Forth.
  c TG Inspiration.
  d GR beneficial or useful
   for instruction.
  e TG Scriptures, Value of.
  f TG Chastening;
   Reproof.
  g TG Education.
  h TG Righteousness.
17a GR suited, ready,
   complete.
   TG Perfection.
  b TG Good Works.

CHAPTER 4

Paul gives a solemn charge to preach the gospel in a day of apostasy—Paul and all Saints are assured of exaltation.

I CHARGE *thee* therefore before God, and the Lord Jesus Christ, who shall [a]judge the quick and the dead at his appearing and his kingdom;

2 [a]Preach the word; [b]be [c]instant in season, out of season; [d]reprove, rebuke, exhort with all longsuffering and doctrine.

3 For the time will come when they will not [a]endure sound [b]doctrine; but after their own [c]lusts shall they heap to themselves [d]teachers, having itching ears;

4 And they shall turn away *their* ears from the [a]truth, and shall be turned unto [b]fables.

5 But [a]watch thou in all things, endure afflictions, do the work of an [b]evangelist, [c]make full proof of thy ministry.

6 For I am now ready to be offered, and the time of my departure is at hand.

7 I have fought a good [a]fight, I have [b]finished *my* course, I have kept the faith:

8 Henceforth there is laid up for me a [a]crown of [b]righteousness, which the Lord, the righteous [c]judge, shall give me at that day: and not to me only, but unto all them also that love his appearing.

9 Do thy diligence to come shortly unto me:

10 For [a]Demas hath [b]forsaken me, having loved this present [c]world, and is departed unto Thessalonica; Crescens to Galatia, Titus unto Dalmatia.

11 Only [a]Luke is with me. Take [b]Mark, and bring him with thee: for he is profitable to me for the ministry.

12 And Tychicus have I sent to Ephesus.

13 The cloak that I left at Troas with Carpus, when thou comest, bring *with thee*, and the [a]books, *but* especially the parchments.

14 Alexander the coppersmith did me much evil: the Lord reward him according to his [a]works:

15 Of whom be thou ware also; for he hath greatly [a]withstood our words.

16 At my first [a]answer no man stood with me, but all *men* forsook me: *I pray God* that it may not be laid to their [b]charge.

17 Notwithstanding the [a]Lord stood with me, and strengthened me; that by me the preaching might be fully known, and *that* all the Gentiles might hear: and I was delivered out of the mouth of the lion.

18 And the Lord shall deliver me from every evil work, and will [a]preserve *me* unto his heavenly kingdom: to whom *be* glory for ever and ever. Amen.

19 Salute Prisca and Aquila, and the household of Onesiphorus.

20 Erastus abode at Corinth: but Trophimus have I left at Miletum sick.

---

4 1*a* TG Jesus Christ, Judge.
  2*a* TG Missionary Work; Preaching.
   b JST 2 Tim. 4:2 . . . be instant in season, *those who are* out of season . . .
   c GR urgent, earnest.
   d TG Chastening; Reproof.
  3*a* 2 Tim. 3:1; Hel. 13:28 (26–30).
   b 1 Tim. 1:10.
   c TG Lust.
   d TG False Prophets; Teacher.
  4*a* TG Truth.

   b TG Apostasy of the Early Christian Church.
  5*a* TG Watch.
   b Acts 21:8; Eph. 4:11 (11–14).
   c GR fulfill your ministry.
  7*a* TG Contentment.
   b TG Dedication.
  8*a* TG Exaltation; Reward.
   b TG God, the Standard of Righteousness.
   c TG Jesus Christ, Judge.
 10*a* Col. 4:14; Philem. 1:24.
   b TG Apostasy of

     Individuals.
   c TG Worldliness.
 11*a* Acts 1:1.
   b Acts 15:37 (37–39); Col. 4:10.
 13*a* Luke 1:1 (1–4); 1 Ne. 13:26 (24–26).
 14*a* D&C 64:11.
 15*a* GR opposed, resisted.
 16*a* GR defense.
   b Acts 7:60 (59–60); 3 Ne. 12:44.
 17*a* John 14:18.
 18*a* GR save, rescue.

21 Do thy diligence to come before winter. Eubulus greeteth thee, and Pudens, and Linus, and Claudia, and all the brethren.

22 The [a]Lord Jesus Christ *be* with thy spirit. Grace *be* with you. Amen.

¶ The second *epistle* unto Timotheus, ordained the first bishop of the church of the Ephesians, was written from Rome, when Paul was brought before Nero the second time.

THE EPISTLE OF PAUL TO

TITUS

CHAPTER 1

Eternal life was promised before the world began—The qualifications of bishops are given—Unto the pure, all things are pure.

PAUL, a [a]servant of God, and an [b]apostle of Jesus Christ, according to the faith of God's [c]elect, and the acknowledging of the truth which is after godliness;

2 In [a]hope of [b]eternal life, which God, that cannot [c]lie, [d]promised before the world began;

3 But hath in due times manifested his word through preaching, which is committed unto me according to the commandment of God our Saviour;

4 To Titus, [a]*mine* own son after the common faith: Grace, mercy, *and* peace, from God the Father and the Lord Jesus Christ our Saviour.

5 For this cause left I thee in Crete, that thou shouldest set in [a]order the things that are wanting, and [b]ordain [c]elders in every city, as I had [d]appointed thee:

6 If any be blameless, the husband of one wife, having faithful children not accused of [a]riot or unruly.

7 For a [a]bishop must be blameless, as the [b]steward of God; not [c]selfwilled, not soon [d]angry, not given to wine, no striker, not given to filthy lucre;

8 But a lover of [a]hospitality, a lover of [b]good men, sober, just, holy, [c]temperate;

9 Holding fast the faithful word as he hath been taught, that he may be able by sound doctrine both to exhort and to [a]convince the [b]gainsayers.

10 For there are many unruly and [a]vain talkers and [b]deceivers, specially they of the [c]circumcision:

11 Whose mouths must be stopped, who subvert whole houses, teaching

---

22a TG Jesus Christ, Lord.

[TITUS]

1 1a TG Servant.
  b TG Apostles.
  c TG Election.
2a TG Hope.
  b TG Salvation, Plan of.
  c TG God, Perfection of; Lying.
  d 2 Tim. 1:1; Abr. 3:26.
4a GR a true son according to.
5a TG Order.

b TG Priesthood, Authority; Priesthood, Ordination.
c TG Church Organization; Elder, Melchizedek Priesthood.
d GR directed, ordered.
6a GR debauchery or insubordination.
7a TG Bishop; Leadership.
  b TG Delegation of Responsibility; Stewardship.
  c GR obstinate, arrogant.

d TG Anger.
8a TG Hospitality.
  b GR what is good.
  c GR self-controlled. TG Temperance.
9a D&C 11:21.
  b GR those who deny, contradict.
10a GR idle speakers, disputers.
  b TG Apostasy of the Early Christian Church.
  c TG Circumcision.

things which they ought not, for filthy ^alucre's sake.

12 One of themselves, *even* a prophet of their own, said, The Cretians *are* alway liars, evil beasts, ^aslow bellies.

13 This witness is true. Wherefore ^arebuke them sharply, that they may be sound in the faith;

14 Not giving heed to Jewish ^afables, and ^bcommandments of men, ^cthat turn from the truth.

15 ^aUnto the pure all things *are* ^bpure: but unto them that are ^cdefiled and unbelieving *is* nothing pure; but even their ^dmind and ^econscience is ^fdefiled.

16 They ^aprofess that they ^bknow God; but in ^cworks they ^ddeny *him*, being abominable, and ^edisobedient, and unto every good work ^freprobate.

CHAPTER 2

Saints should live righteously, deny ungodliness, and seek the Lord.

BUT ^aspeak thou the things which become sound ^bdoctrine:

2 That the ^aaged men be ^bsober, grave, ^ctemperate, sound in faith, in charity, in patience.

3 The aged women likewise, that *they be* in behaviour as becometh holiness, not ^afalse ^baccusers, not given to much wine, teachers of good things;

4 That they may teach the young ^awomen to be sober, to ^blove their husbands, to love their children,

5 *To be* discreet, ^achaste, ^bkeepers at ^chome, good, obedient to their own husbands, that the word of God be not blasphemed.

6 Young men likewise exhort to be sober minded.

7 In all things shewing thyself a pattern of good works: in doctrine *shewing* uncorruptness, ^agravity, ^bsincerity,

8 ^aSound speech, that cannot be ^bcondemned; that he that is ^cof the contrary part may be ashamed, having no evil thing to say of you.

9 *Exhort* ^aservants to be obedient unto their own masters, *and* to please *them* well in all *things*; not ^banswering again;

10 Not ^apurloining, but shewing all good fidelity; that they may ^badorn the doctrine of God our Saviour in all things.

11 For the ^agrace of God ^bthat bringeth salvation hath appeared to all men,

12 Teaching us that, denying ^aungodliness and ^bworldly ^clusts, we should live ^dsoberly, ^erighteously, and godly, in this present world;

11a 1 Tim. 6:5;
  Mosiah 29:40;
  Alma 11:24.
12a GR lazy gluttons.
13a D&C 84:117 (87, 117).
14a 1 Tim. 1:4.
  b Matt. 15:9; Col. 2:22;
    D&C 3:6 (6–7);
    45:29; 46:7;
    JS—H 1:19.
  c GR who reject,
    repudiate the truth.
15a JST Titus 1:15 Unto the
    pure, *let* all things be
    pure . . .
  b TG Purity.
  c TG Pollution.
  d Luke 11:39 (39–41).
    TG Mind.
  e TG Conscience.
  f Mark 7:15; 2 Ne. 19:17;
    D&C 93:35.
16a Matt. 7:21 (21–23).
    TG False Prophets;

    Hypocrisy.
  b Hosea 8:2.
    TG Ignorance.
  c Matt. 15:8 (7–9).
  d TG Apostasy of the
    Early Christian Church.
  e TG Disobedience.
  f GR unfit, worthless.
2 1a 1 Thes. 2:4; 1 Pet. 4:11.
    TG Teaching.
  b D&C 88:77 (77–78).
2a TG Old Age.
  b GR circumspect.
  c TG Temperance.
3a GR slanderers, traitors,
    devils.
  b TG Gossip.
4a TG Marriage, Wives.
  b TG Family, Love within.
5a TG Chastity; Modesty.
  b GR housekeepers,
    guards.
  c 1 Tim. 5:14.
7a GR dignity,

    respectfulness.
  b TG Sincere.
8a 1 Tim. 6:3.
  b 1 Pet. 2:12 (11–12).
  c GR an opponent, enemy.
9a Eph. 6:5; Col. 3:22;
    1 Tim. 6:1 (1–2);
    1 Pet. 2:18.
  b GR arguing against,
    opposing, contradicting.
10a GR misappropriating,
    robbing.
    TG Stealing.
  b GR honor, put in order.
11a TG Grace.
  b JST Titus 2:11 . . . *which*
    bringeth salvation *to all
    men*, hath appeared;
12a TG Godliness.
  b TG Worldliness.
  c TG Lust.
  d TG Levity.
  e TG Abundant Life;
    Righteousness.

13 Looking for that blessed hope, and the ^aglorious appearing of the great God and our Saviour Jesus Christ;

14 Who gave ^ahimself for us, that he might ^bredeem us from all iniquity, and ^cpurify unto himself a ^dpeculiar people, ^ezealous of good works.

15 These things speak, and exhort, and ^arebuke with all ^bauthority. Let no man ^cdespise thee.

CHAPTER 3

Saints must live righteously after baptism.

PUT them in mind to be ^asubject to ^bprincipalities and powers, to obey magistrates, to be ready to every good work,

2 To ^aspeak evil of no man, to be ^bno brawlers, *but* gentle, shewing all ^cmeekness unto all men.

3 For we ourselves also were ^asometimes foolish, ^bdisobedient, deceived, serving divers ^clusts and pleasures, living in ^dmalice and envy, hateful, *and* hating one another.

4 But after that the kindness and love of God our Saviour toward man appeared,

5 Not by works of ^arighteousness which we have done, but according to his ^bmercy he saved us, by the ^cwashing of regeneration, and ^drenewing of the Holy Ghost;

6 Which he shed on us abundantly through Jesus Christ our Saviour;

7 That being ^ajustified by his grace, we should be made ^bheirs according to the hope of eternal life.

8 *This is* a faithful saying, and these things I will that thou affirm constantly, that they which have believed in God might be careful to maintain good ^aworks. These things are good and profitable unto men.

9 But avoid ^afoolish questions, and genealogies, and ^bcontentions, and strivings about the law; for they are unprofitable and vain.

10 A man that is an ^aheretick after the first and second ^badmonition reject;

11 Knowing that he that is such is ^asubverted, and sinneth, being condemned of himself.

12 When I shall send Artemas unto thee, or Tychicus, be diligent to come unto me to Nicopolis: for I have determined there to winter.

13 Bring Zenas the lawyer and Apollos on their journey diligently, that nothing be wanting unto them.

14 And let ^aours also learn to maintain ^bgood works for necessary uses, that they be not unfruitful.

15 All that are with me salute thee. Greet them that love us in the faith. Grace *be* with you all. Amen.

¶ It was written to Titus, ordained the first bishop of the church of the Cretians, from Nicopolis of Macedonia.

13*a* TG Glory.
14*a* TG Self-Sacrifice.
  b TG Jesus Christ,
    Atonement through;
    Jesus Christ, Redeemer;
    Redemption.
  c TG Purification;
    Purity.
  d TG Peculiar People.
  e TG Zeal.
15*a* TG Chastening.
  b TG Authority.
  c GR disregard.

3 1*a* TG Citizenship.
  b TG Governments.
2*a* TG Slander.
  b GR not quarrelsome.
  c D&C 38:41.
3*a* GR once, formerly.
  b TG Disobedience.
  c TG Lust.
  d TG Malice.
5*a* TG Righteousness.
  b TG God, Mercy of.
  c TG Baptism, Essential.
  d TG Holy Ghost, Gifts of.

7*a* TG Justification.
  b D&C 70:8.
8*a* TG Good Works.
9*a* 2 Tim. 2:23 (23–26).
  b TG Contention.
10*a* TG Apostasy of
    Individuals.
  b Matt. 18:17.
11*a* GR perverted, changed.
14*a* GR our people.
  b Rom. 15:28 (25–28);
    Philip. 4:17.

PHILEMON

The gospel changes a servant into a brother.

PAUL, a prisoner of Jesus Christ, and Timothy *our* brother, unto Philemon our dearly beloved, and fellowlabourer,

2 And to *our* beloved Apphia, and ^aArchippus our fellowsoldier, and to the church in thy house:

3 Grace to you, and peace, from God our Father and the Lord Jesus Christ.

4 I thank my God, making mention of thee always in my prayers,

5 Hearing of thy love and faith, which thou hast toward the Lord Jesus, and toward all saints;

6 That the ^acommunication of thy faith may become ^beffectual by the acknowledging of every good thing which is in you in Christ Jesus.

7 For we have great joy and consolation in thy love, because the ^abowels of the saints are refreshed by thee, brother.

8 Wherefore, though I might be much bold in Christ to enjoin thee that which is convenient,

9 Yet for love's sake I rather beseech *thee,* being such an one as Paul the aged, and now also a prisoner of Jesus Christ.

10 I beseech thee for my son ^aOnesimus, whom I have begotten in my bonds:

11 Which in time past was to thee unprofitable, but now profitable to thee and to me:

12 Whom I have sent again: thou therefore receive him, that is, mine own bowels:

13 Whom I would have retained with me, that in thy stead he might have ministered unto me in the bonds of the gospel:

14 But without thy ^amind would I do nothing; that thy benefit should not be as it were of necessity, but willingly.

15 For perhaps he therefore departed for a season, that thou shouldest receive him for ever;

16 Not now as a servant, but above a servant, a ^abrother beloved, specially to me, but how much more unto thee, both in the flesh, and in the Lord?

17 If thou count me therefore a partner, receive him as myself.

18 If he hath wronged thee, or oweth *thee* ^aought, put that on mine account;

19 I Paul have written *it* with mine own hand, I will repay *it:* albeit I do not say to thee how thou owest unto me even thine own self besides.

20 Yea, brother, let me have joy of thee in the Lord: refresh my bowels in the Lord.

21 Having confidence in thy obedience I wrote unto thee, knowing that thou wilt also do more than I say.

22 But withal prepare me also a lodging: for I trust that through your ^aprayers I shall be given unto you.

23 There salute thee ^aEpaphras, my fellowprisoner in Christ Jesus;

24 Marcus, Aristarchus, ^aDemas, Lucas, my fellowlabourers.

25 The grace of our Lord Jesus Christ *be* with your spirit. Amen.

¶ Written from Rome to Philemon, by Onesimus a servant.

---

1 2*a* Col. 4:17.
  6*a* GR participation, fellowship.
  b GR active.
  7*a* GR affections, compassion.
  10*a* Col. 4:9.

14*a* GR assent, suggestion.
  TG Mind.
16*a* TG Brotherhood and Sisterhood.
18*a* GR something, anything.
22*a* 2 Cor. 1:11;
  Philip. 1:19.

23*a* Col. 1:7 (7–8);
  4:12 (12–13).
24*a* Col. 4:14;
  2 Tim. 4:10.

THE EPISTLE OF PAUL THE APOSTLE
TO THE
HEBREWS

CHAPTER 1

The Son is in the express image of the person of the Father—Christ is the Only Begotten Son and thus above the angels.

GOD, who ᵃat sundry times and in divers manners spake in time past unto the ᵇfathers by the ᶜprophets,

2 Hath in these last days spoken unto us by *his* ᵃSon, whom he hath ᵇappointed ᶜheir of all things, by whom also he ᵈmade the ᵉworlds;

3 Who being the brightness of *his* ᵃglory, and the express image of his ᵇperson, and upholding all things by the word of his ᶜpower, when he had by himself ᵈpurged our sins, sat down on the ᵉright hand of the ᶠMajesty on high;

4 Being made so much better than the angels, as he hath by inheritance obtained a more excellent ᵃname than they.

5 For unto which of the angels said he at any time, Thou art my ᵃSon, this day have I begotten thee? And again, I will be to him a ᵇFather, and he shall be to me a Son?

6 And again, when he bringeth in the ᵃfirstbegotten into the world, he saith, ᵇAnd let all the angels of God ᶜworship him.

7 And of the angels he saith, Who maketh his angels spirits, and his ministers a flame of fire.

8 But unto the Son *he saith*, Thy ᵃthrone, O God, *is* for ᵇever and ever: a sceptre of righteousness *is* the sceptre of thy kingdom.

9 Thou hast loved ᵃrighteousness, and hated iniquity; therefore God, *even* thy God, hath anointed thee with the oil of gladness above thy fellows.

10 And, Thou, Lord, in the beginning hast laid the ᵃfoundation of the earth; and the heavens are the works of thine ᵇhands:

11 They shall perish; but thou remainest; and they all shall ᵃwax old as doth a garment;

12 And as a vesture shalt thou fold

---

1 1a GR in many locations and various ways.
  b TG Family, Patriarchal.
  c TG Prophets, Mission of.
2a TG Godhead; Jesus Christ, Divine Sonship; Jesus Christ, Jehovah.
  b TG Jesus Christ, Authority of.
  c Matt. 21:38 (33–46). TG Jesus Christ, Relationships with the Father.
  d TG Jesus Christ, Creator.
  e TG Astronomy; Creation; God, Creator.

3a John 1:14. TG Celestial Glory.
  b TG God, Body of, Corporeal Nature.
  c TG God, Power of.
  d GR made purification, expiation for.
  e Acts 7:55 (55–56); D&C 76:23.
  f Heb. 12:2.
4a Eph. 1:21 (20–21); Philip. 2:9 (9–10). TG Name.
5a Heb. 5:5. TG Jesus Christ, Divine Sonship.
  b 2 Sam. 7:14; 1 Chr. 17:13.
6a TG Jesus Christ,

Firstborn.
  b JST Heb. 1:6–7 . . . And let all the angels of God worship him, *who maketh his ministers as a flame of fire. And of the angels he saith, Angels are ministering spirits.*
  c TG Worship.
8a TG Kingdom of God, in Heaven.
  b D&C 88:104.
9a TG Righteousness.
10a TG Jesus Christ, Creator.
  b D&C 67:2.
11a GR grow old, become worn.

them up, and they shall be changed: but thou art the same, and thy years shall not fail.

13 But to which of the angels said he at any time, Sit on my [a]right hand, until I make thine enemies thy footstool?

14 Are they not all [a]ministering [b]spirits, sent forth [c]to minister for them who shall be heirs of salvation?

CHAPTER 2

Jesus came to suffer death and save men—He came to make reconciliation for the sins of the people.

THEREFORE we ought to give the more [a]earnest [b]heed to the things which we have heard, lest at any time we should let *them* slip.

2 For if the word spoken by angels was steadfast, and every transgression and [a]disobedience received a [b]just recompence of reward;

3 How shall we [a]escape, if we neglect so great salvation; which at the first began to be spoken by the Lord, and was confirmed unto us by them that heard *him;*

4 God also bearing *them* witness, both with [a]signs and [b]wonders, and with divers miracles, and gifts of the Holy Ghost, according to his own [c]will?

5 For unto the angels hath he not put in subjection the world to come, whereof we speak.

6 But one in a certain place testified, saying, What is [a]man, that thou art mindful of him? or the son of man, that thou visitest him?

7 Thou madest him a little lower than the [a]angels; thou crownedst him with glory and honour, and didst set him over the works of thy hands:

8 Thou hast put all things in subjection under his [a]feet. For in that he put all in subjection under him, he left nothing *that is* not put under him. But now we see not yet all things put under him.

9 But we see Jesus, who was made a little [a]lower than the [b]angels [c]for the suffering of [d]death, [e]crowned with glory and honour; that he by the [f]grace of God should taste [g]death for every man.

10 For [a]it became him, for whom *are* all things, and by whom *are* all [b]things, in bringing many sons unto glory, to make the [c]captain of their salvation [d]perfect through sufferings.

11 For both he that sanctifieth and they who are [a]sanctified *are* all of [b]one: for which cause he is not ashamed to call them [c]brethren,

12 Saying, I will declare thy [a]name unto my brethren, in the midst of the church will I sing praise unto thee.

13 And again, I will put my [a]trust in him. And again, Behold I and the children which God hath given me.

14 [a]Forasmuch then as the children are partakers of [b]flesh and blood, he also himself likewise took part of the same; that through death he might [c]destroy him that had the power of [d]death, that is, the [e]devil;

15 And deliver them who through

13a Ps. 110:1.
14a D&C 7:6.
  TG Angels.
  b Zech. 6:5 (4–8).
  c GR for service.
2 1a TG Zeal.
  b D&C 21:4.
  2a TG Disobedience.
  b TG God, Justice of.
  3a Heb. 10:29; 12:25.
  4a Acts 5:12 (12–23).
    TG Holy Ghost, Gifts of;
    Symbolism.
  b TG Miracle.
  c TG God, Will of.
  6a Ps. 8:4 (4–6).

7a HEB gods;
  GR angels.
8a Matt. 28:18;
  1 Cor. 15:25;
  Eph. 1:22.
9a TG Jesus Christ,
    Condescension of.
  b Philip. 2:7 (7–9).
  c GR through.
  d TG Jesus Christ, Death of.
  e Acts 2:33.
  f TG Grace.
  g TG Jesus Christ,
    Atonement through.
10a GR it was fitting, suitable, proper for Him.

b Col. 1:16 (13–19).
c TG Jesus Christ, Messiah.
d TG Perfection.
11a TG Sanctification.
  b TG Unity.
  c TG Brotherhood and
    Sisterhood.
12a Ps. 22:22.
13a Ps. 18:2.
14a GR Since.
  b TG Flesh and Blood.
  c Gen. 3:15.
  d 2 Tim. 1:10.
    TG Redemption.
  e TG Devil.

fear of death were all their lifetime subject to ^abondage.

16 For verily he took not on *him the nature of* ^aangels; but he took on *him* the ^bseed of Abraham.

17 Wherefore in all things it behoved him to be made like unto *his* brethren, that he might be a merciful and faithful high priest in things *pertaining* to God, to make ^areconciliation for the sins of the people.

18 For in that he himself hath suffered being ^atempted, he is able to ^bsuccour them that are tempted.

CHAPTER 3

Christ is the Apostle and High Priest of our profession—Jesus, being the Son, is more than a servant—Now is the time and the day of our salvation.

WHEREFORE, holy brethren, partakers of the heavenly calling, ^aconsider the ^bApostle and ^cHigh Priest of our profession, Christ Jesus;

2 Who was faithful to him that appointed him, as also Moses *was faithful* in all his house.

3 For this *man* was counted worthy of more glory than Moses, inasmuch as he who hath builded the house hath more honour than the house.

4 For every house is builded by some *man*; but he that built all things *is* God.

5 And Moses verily *was* faithful in all his house, as a ^aservant, for a testimony of those things which were to be spoken after;

6 But Christ as a son over his own

^ahouse; whose ^bhouse are we, if we hold fast the confidence and the rejoicing of the hope firm unto the end.

7 Wherefore (as the ^aHoly Ghost saith, ^bTo day if ye will hear his voice,

8 ^aHarden not your hearts, as in the ^bprovocation, in the day of temptation in the wilderness:

9 When your fathers tempted me, ^aproved me, and saw my works forty years.

10 Wherefore I was grieved with that ^ageneration, and said, They do alway err in *their* heart; and they have not known my ways.

11 So I sware in my wrath, They shall not ^aenter into my ^brest.)

12 Take heed, brethren, lest there be in any of you an evil ^aheart of ^bunbelief, in ^cdeparting from the living God.

13 But ^aexhort one another daily, while it is called ^bTo day; lest any of you be hardened through the deceitfulness of sin.

14 For we are made partakers of Christ, if we hold the beginning of our confidence ^asteadfast unto the end;

15 While it is said, To day if ye will hear his voice, ^aharden not your hearts, as in the ^bprovocation.

16 For some, when they had heard, did provoke: howbeit not all that came out of Egypt by Moses.

17 But with whom was he grieved forty years? *was it* not with them that had sinned, whose ^acarcases fell in the wilderness?

15*a* TG Bondage, Spiritual;
  Law of Moses.
16*a* TG Angels.
  b TG Seed of Abraham.
17*a* TG Jesus Christ, Redeemer; Reconciliation.
18*a* GR tried, subjected to trial.
  TG Jesus Christ, Temptation of; Test.
  b Alma 7:12;
  D&C 62:1.
3 1*a* TG Meditation.
  b TG Jesus Christ, Messenger of the Covenant.
  c TG High Priest, Melchizedek Priesthood.

5*a* TG Servant.
6*a* TG Church.
  b 1 Pet. 2:5 (4–8).
7*a* Heb. 10:15.
  b Ps. 95:7 (7–11).
8*a* TG Hardheartedness.
  b Num. 14:23 (2–23);
  Jacob 1:7 (7–8);
  Alma 12:36.
9*a* TG Test.
10*a* Prov. 30:12 (11–14).
11*a* Ps. 95:11.
  b D&C 84:24.
  TG God, Presence of;
  God, Privilege of
  Seeing; Rest.
12*a* Gen. 6:5;

Matt. 15:19;
  Hel. 12:4.
  b TG Stiffnecked.
  c GR apostatizing,
  withdrawing from.
  TG Apostasy of
  Individuals.
13*a* Alma 34:39;
  D&C 38:23.
  TG Chastening.
  b D&C 45:6.
14*a* TG Perseverance;
  Steadfastness.
15*a* TG Contrite Heart.
  b TG Provoking.
17*a* Num. 14:29 (29, 37);
  1 Cor. 10:5 (2–7).

18 And to whom sware he that they should not enter into his rest, but to them that believed not?

19 So we see that they could not enter in because of ᵃunbelief.

CHAPTER 4

The gospel was offered to ancient Israel—Saints enter into the rest of the Lord—Though tempted in all points, Jesus was without sin.

LET us therefore fear, lest, a promise being left *us* of entering into his ᵃrest, any of you should seem to come short of it.

2 For unto us was the ᵃgospel preached, as well as unto them: but the word preached did not profit them, not being mixed with ᵇfaith in them that heard *it.*

3 ᵃFor we which have believed do enter into rest, as he said, As I have sworn in my wrath, if they shall enter into my ᵇrest: although the works were finished from the foundation of the world.

4 For he spake in a certain place of the ᵃseventh *day* on this wise, And God did rest the seventh day from all his works.

5 ᵃAnd in this *place* again, If they shall enter into my rest.

6 Seeing therefore it remaineth that some must enter therein, and ᵃthey to whom it was first preached entered not in because of ᵇunbelief:

7 Again, he ᵃlimiteth a certain day, saying in David, To day, after so long a time; as it is said, To day if ye will ᵇhear his voice, ᶜharden not your hearts.

8 For if ᵃJesus had given them rest, then would he not afterward have spoken of another day.

9 There remaineth therefore a rest to the people of God.

10 For he that is entered into his rest, he also hath ceased from his own works, as God *did* from his.

11 Let us ᵃlabour therefore to enter into that rest, lest any man fall after the same example of ᵇunbelief.

12 For the ᵃword of God *is* ᵇquick, and powerful, and sharper than any twoedged ᶜsword, ᵈpiercing even to the dividing asunder of ᵉsoul and spirit, and of the joints and marrow, and *is* a ᶠdiscerner of the ᵍthoughts and ʰintents of the heart.

13 Neither is there any creature that is not manifest in his sight: but all things *are* naked and opened unto the ᵃeyes of him with whom we have to do.

14 Seeing then that we have a great high priest, that is passed into the ᵃheavens, Jesus the Son of God, let us hold fast *our* profession.

15 For we have not an high priest ᵃwhich cannot be touched with the feeling of our infirmities; but was in all points ᵇtempted like as *we are,* *yet* without ᶜsin.

16 Let us therefore come boldly unto the throne of ᵃgrace, that we may obtain mercy, and find grace to help in time of need.

19a TG Unbelief.
4 1a TG God, Glory of; Rest.
  2a TG Gospel.
    b TG Faith.
  3a JST Heb. 4:3 (Appendix).
    b D&C 19:9.
  4a TG Sabbath.
  5a JST Heb. 4:5 And in this place again, If they *harden not their hearts they* shall enter into my rest.
  6a GR those who formerly were taught the gospel.
    b GR disobedience, unbelief, obstinacy.
  7a GR appoints, decrees, constitutes.

  b Ps. 95:7.
  c TG Hardheartedness.
  8a Ex. 17:9;
     Acts 7:45.
 11a GR hasten, be eager.
    b GR obstinacy, disobedience.
     TG Unbelief.
 12a Alma 31:5;
     D&C 6:2; 11:2; 12:2;
     14:2; 33:1.
    b GR living.
    c Isa. 49:2;
     Rev. 2:12 (12–17).
    d Hosea 6:5;
     D&C 85:6.
    e JST Heb. 4:12 . . . *body* . . .
    f 1 Cor. 14:25 (24–25).

     TG God, Omniscience of.
    g D&C 6:16.
    h TG Motivations.
 13a Prov. 5:21.
 14a Heb. 9:24.
 15a GR unable to sympathize with our frailties, imperfections.
    b TG Jesus Christ, Exemplar;
     Jesus Christ, Temptation of;
     Temptation; Test.
    c John 8:46;
     Heb. 7:26;
     D&C 45:4.
     TG Sin.
 16a TG Grace.

CHAPTER 5

For a man to hold the priesthood, he must be called of God as was Aaron—Christ was a priest forever after the order of Melchizedek—Jesus Christ is the Author of eternal salvation.

FOR every high priest taken from among men is [a]ordained for men in things *pertaining* to God, that he may offer both gifts and [b]sacrifices for sins:

2 Who can have [a]compassion on the ignorant, and on them that are [b]out of the way; for that he himself also is compassed with infirmity.

3 And by reason hereof he ought, as for the people, so also for himself, to offer for [a]sins.

4 And no man taketh this [a]honour unto himself, but he that is [b]called of God, as *was* [c]Aaron.

5 So also Christ glorified not himself to be made an high priest; but he that said unto him, Thou art my [a]Son, to day have I begotten thee.

6 As he saith also in another *place*, Thou *art* a [a]priest [b]for ever after the order of [c]Melchisedec.

7 Who in the days of his flesh, when he had offered up [a]prayers and supplications with [b]strong crying and tears unto him that was able to save him from death, and was heard [c]in that he feared;

8 Though he were a Son, yet [a]learned he [b]obedience by the things which he [c]suffered;

9 And being made [a]perfect, he became the [b]author of eternal [c]salvation unto all them that obey him;

10 [a]Called of God an [b]high priest after the order of Melchisedec.

11 Of whom we have many things to say, and [a]hard to be [b]uttered, seeing ye are dull of [c]hearing.

12 For when for the time ye ought to be teachers, ye have need that one teach you again which *be* the first principles of the oracles of God; and are become such as have need of [a]milk, and not of strong meat.

13 For every one that useth [a]milk *is* unskilful in the word of righteousness: for he is a babe.

14 But strong meat belongeth to them that are of full age, *even* those who by reason of use have their senses exercised to discern both good and evil.

CHAPTER 6

Let us go on to perfection—The sons of perdition crucify Christ anew—God swears with an oath that the faithful will be saved.

THEREFORE [a]leaving the principles of the doctrine of Christ, let us go on unto [b]perfection; not laying again

---

5 1a TG Priesthood; Priesthood, Ordination.
 b TG Sacrifice.
 2a TG Compassion.
 b GR straying, wandering.
 3a Lev. 4:3.
 4a TG Leadership.
 b TG Called of God; Priesthood, Authority; Priesthood, Qualifying for.
 c Ex. 28:1. TG Priesthood, Aaronic.
 5a Heb. 1:5.
 6a TG Priesthood, Melchizedek.
 b D&C 124:130.
 c TG Priesthood, History of.
 7a Matt. 26:39 (39, 42, 44).
 b GR mighty, powerful supplication.

 c GR because of his piety, reverence.
 8a TG Jesus Christ, Exemplar.
 b TG Agency; Obedience.
 c TG Jesus Christ, Temptation of; Pain; Suffering.
 9a TG God, Perfection of; Perfection.
 b TG Jesus Christ, Authority of.
 c TG Gospel; Jesus Christ, Atonement through; Jesus Christ, Mission of; Salvation; Salvation, Plan of.
 10a TG Jesus Christ, Authority of.

 b TG High Priest, Melchizedek Priesthood; Jesus Christ, Types of, in Anticipation.
 11a GR difficult to be explained.
 b John 16:12 (12–13).
 c Ezek. 33:31 (30–33); Matt. 11:15; 2 Ne. 9:31; D&C 1:14.
 12a 1 Cor. 3:2 (2–3); D&C 19:22 (21–22); 50:40.
 13a 1 Pet. 2:2 (1–3).
 6 1a GR having left behind the beginning of the doctrine. JST Heb. 6:1 . . . *not* leaving . . .
 b TG Perfection.

the foundation of ^{c}repentance from dead works, and of faith toward God,

2 Of the ^{a}doctrine of ^{b}baptisms, and of ^{c}laying on of ^{d}hands, and of resurrection of the dead, and of eternal judgment.

3 ^{a}And this will we do, if God permit.

4 For *it is* impossible for those who were once ^{a}enlightened, and have tasted of the heavenly gift, and were made partakers of the Holy Ghost,

5 And have ^{a}tasted the good word of God, and the powers of the ^{b}world to come,

6 If they shall ^{a}fall away, to renew them again unto repentance; seeing they ^{b}crucify to themselves the Son of God afresh, and put *him* to an open ^{c}shame.

7 For the earth which drinketh in the rain that cometh oft upon it, and bringeth forth herbs ^{a}meet for them by whom it is ^{b}dressed, receiveth blessing from God:

8 But that which beareth thorns and briers *is* rejected, and *is* nigh unto ^{a}cursing; whose end *is* to be burned.

9 But, beloved, we are persuaded better things of you, and things that accompany salvation, though we thus speak.

10 For God *is* not ^{a}unrighteous to forget your work and ^{b}labour of ^{c}love, which ye have shewed toward his ^{d}name, in that ye have ministered to the saints, and do minister.

11 And we desire that every one of you do shew the same ^{a}diligence

to the full assurance of hope unto the end:

12 That ye be not ^{a}slothful, but followers of them who through ^{b}faith and ^{c}patience inherit the ^{d}promises.

13 For when God made promise to Abraham, because he could ^{a}swear by no greater, he ^{b}sware by himself,

14 Saying, Surely blessing I will ^{a}bless thee, and multiplying I will multiply thee.

15 And so, after he had patiently ^{a}endured, he obtained the promise.

16 For men verily swear by the greater: and an ^{a}oath for confirmation *is* to them an end of all ^{b}strife.

17 Wherein God, willing more abundantly to shew unto the heirs of promise the immutability of his ^{a}counsel, ^{b}confirmed *it* by an ^{c}oath:

18 That by two immutable things, in which *it was* impossible for God to ^{a}lie, we might have a strong consolation, who have fled for ^{b}refuge to lay hold upon the ^{c}hope set before us:

19 Which *hope* we have as an ^{a}anchor of the soul, both sure and steadfast, and which entereth into that within the ^{b}veil;

20 Whither the forerunner is for us entered, *even* Jesus, made an ^{a}high priest for ever after the order of Melchisedec.

CHAPTER 7

The Melchizedek Priesthood brings exaltation and administers the gospel—It is received with an oath and covenant

---

1c TG Repent.
2a D&C 68:25.
  b TG Baptism, Essential.
  c D&C 107:67.
  d TG Hands, Laying on of.
3a JST Heb. 6:3–10
  (Appendix).
4a 2 Pet. 2:20.
5a 1 Pet. 2:3 (1–3).
  b TG World.
6a TG Apostasy of
  Individuals;
  Holy Ghost, Loss of; Sin.
  b TG Holy Ghost,
  Unpardonable Sin
  against; Jesus Christ,
  Crucifixion of.

  c TG Shame.
7a GR suitable, fit, proper.
  b GR cultivated, tilled.
8a D&C 104:3.
10a TG God, Perfection of.
  b 1 Thes. 1:3.
  c Col. 1:4.
  d TG Name.
11a TG Dependability;
  Diligence.
12a TG Idleness; Laziness.
  b Heb. 10:22 (22–24).
  c TG Patience.
  d TG Promise.
13a GR promise, confirm by
  an oath.
  b Jer. 44:26;

  Amos 6:8.
14a TG Abrahamic
  Covenant.
15a TG Perseverance.
16a TG Oath.
  b TG Strife.
17a GR design, purpose.
  TG Counselor.
  b TG Vow.
  c TG Covenants.
18a TG God, Perfection of.
  b TG Refuge.
  c TG Hope.
19a Ether 12:4.
  b TG Veil.
20a TG High Priest,
  Melchizedek Priesthood.

—The superiority of the Melchizedek Priesthood over the Aaronic Priesthood is explained—Salvation comes through the intercession of Christ.

FOR this Melchisedec, king of Salem, ^apriest of the most high God, who met Abraham returning from the slaughter of the kings, and blessed him;

2 To whom also Abraham gave a ^atenth part of all; first being by interpretation King of ^brighteousness, and after that also King of ^cSalem, which is, King of peace;

3 ^aWithout father, without mother, without descent, having neither ^bbeginning of days, nor end of life; but made like unto the Son of God; abideth a ^cpriest continually.

4 Now consider how great this man *was*, unto whom even the ^apatriarch Abraham gave the tenth of the spoils.

5 And verily they that are of the sons of ^aLevi, who receive the ^boffice of the priesthood, have a commandment to take tithes of the people according to the law, that is, of their brethren, though they come out of the loins of Abraham:

6 But he whose descent is not counted from them received tithes of Abraham, and blessed him that had the promises.

7 And without all contradiction the less is blessed of the better.

8 And here men that die receive tithes; but there he *receiveth them*, of whom it is witnessed that he liveth.

9 And as I may so say, Levi also, who receiveth tithes, payed tithes in Abraham.

10 For he was yet in the loins of his father, when Melchisedec met him.

11 If therefore ^aperfection were by the ^bLevitical priesthood, (for under it the people received the law,) what further need *was there* that another priest should rise after the order of Melchisedec, and not be called after the order of Aaron?

12 For the ^apriesthood being changed, there is made of necessity a change also of the law.

13 For he of whom these things are spoken pertaineth to another tribe, of which no man gave attendance at the altar.

14 For *it is* evident that our Lord sprang out of ^aJuda; of which tribe Moses spake nothing concerning priesthood.

15 And it is yet far more evident: for that after the similitude of Melchisedec there ariseth another priest,

16 Who is made, not after the law of a ^acarnal commandment, but after the power of an endless life.

17 For he testifieth, Thou *art* a priest for ever after the order of ^aMelchisedec.

18 For there is verily a disannulling of the commandment going before for the ^aweakness and unprofitableness thereof.

19 ^aFor the law made nothing ^bperfect, but the bringing in of a ^cbetter hope *did*; by the which we draw nigh unto God.

20 And inasmuch as not without an ^aoath *he was made priest:*

21 (For those ^apriests were made without an oath; but this with an ^boath by him that said unto him, The Lord sware and will not repent,

7 1 *a* TG Priesthood,
　　　　Melchizedek.
　2 *a* TG Tithing.
　　b TG Righteousness.
　　c TG Jerusalem.
　3 *a* JST Heb. 7:3 (Appendix).
　　b D&C 84:17.
　　c TG Jesus Christ,
　　　　Authority of.
　4 *a* TG Family, Patriarchal;
　　　　Patriarch.
　5 *a* TG Priest, Aaronic

　　　　Priesthood.
　　　　BD Priests.
　　b TG Priesthood, Aaronic.
11 *a* Heb. 8:7.
　　　　TG Perfection.
　　b TG Priesthood, Aaronic.
12 *a* TG Priesthood,
　　　　History of.
14 *a* Isa. 11:1; Micah 5:2.
　　　　TG Israel, Judah,
　　　　People of.
16 *a* Heb. 9:10.

17 *a* Ps. 110:4.
18 *a* Rom. 8:3.
19 *a* JST Heb. 7:19–21
　　　　(Appendix).
　　b Heb. 9:9.
　　c Heb. 12:24.
20 *a* TG Oath;
　　　　Priesthood, Oath and
　　　　Covenant.
21 *a* TG Priesthood, Aaronic.
　　b TG Priesthood, Oath and
　　　　Covenant.

Thou *art* a priest for ever after the order of Melchisedec:)

22 By so much was Jesus made a surety of a better ªtestament.

23 And they truly were many priests, because they were not suffered to continue by reason of death:

24 But this *man*, because he continueth ever, hath an unchangeable ªpriesthood.

25 Wherefore he is able also to save them ªto the uttermost that ᵇcome unto God by him, seeing he ever liveth to make ᶜintercession for them.

26 ªFor such an ᵇhigh priest became us, *who is* holy, harmless, undefiled, ᶜseparate from ᵈsinners, and made ᵉhigher than the ᶠheavens;

27 Who needeth not ªdaily, as those high priests, to offer up ᵇsacrifice, first for his own sins, and then for the people's: for this he did ᶜonce, when he ᵈoffered up himself.

28 For the law maketh men high priests which have infirmity; but the word of the ªoath, which was since the law, *maketh* the ᵇSon, who is ᶜconsecrated for evermore.

CHAPTER 8

Christ offered Himself as a sacrifice for sin—God promised to make a new covenant with Israel.

Now of the things which we have spoken *this is* the sum: We have such an ªhigh priest, who is set on the right hand of the throne of the Majesty in the heavens;

2 A minister of the sanctuary, and of the ªtrue ᵇtabernacle, which the Lord pitched, and not man.

3 For every high priest is ordained to offer gifts and sacrifices: wherefore *it is* of necessity that this man have somewhat also to ªoffer.

4 ªFor if he were on earth, he should not be a priest, seeing that there are ᵇpriests that offer gifts according to the law:

5 Who serve unto the example and ªshadow of heavenly things, as Moses was admonished of God when he was about to make the ᵇtabernacle: for, See, saith he, *that* thou make all things according to the ᶜpattern shewed to thee in the mount.

6 But now hath he obtained a more excellent ministry, by how much also he is the ªmediator of a better ᵇcovenant, which was established upon better ᶜpromises.

7 For if that first *covenant* had been ªfaultless, then should no place have been sought for the second.

8 For finding fault with them, he saith, Behold, the days come, saith the Lord, when I will make a new covenant with the house of Israel and with the house of ªJudah:

9 Not according to the ªcovenant that I made with their fathers in the day when I took them by the hand to lead them out of the land

---

22a Heb. 8:6.
24a TG Jesus Christ, Authority of; Priesthood.
25a GR perfectly.
  b Isa. 55:3; Heb. 11:6.
  c Isa. 59:16; Rom. 8:34.
26a JST Heb. 7:25–26 (Appendix).
  b TG High Priest, Melchizedek Priesthood.
  c Lev. 3:6. TG Separation.
  d Heb. 4:15; D&C 45:4.
  e TG Priesthood, Magnifying Callings within.
  f Eph. 1:20.
27a Heb. 10:11.
  b TG Sacrifice.
  c Rom. 6:10; Heb. 10:10.

d TG Jesus Christ, Atonement through; Jesus Christ, Redeemer.
28a TG Oath.
  b TG Jesus Christ, Divine Sonship.
  c GR perfected.
8 1a TG High Priest, Melchizedek Priesthood; Jesus Christ, Authority of.
2a Heb. 9:24.
  b Ex. 40:2; Heb. 9:11 (11–24).
3a Eph. 5:2.
4a JST Heb. 8:4 *Therefore while he was on the* earth, *he offered for a sacrifice his own life for the sins of the people. Now every priest under the law, must needs*

offer gifts, *or sacrifices*, according to the law.
  b TG Priest, Aaronic Priesthood. BD Priests.
5a TG Jesus Christ, Types of, in Anticipation.
  b Ex. 35:11.
  c Acts 7:44.
6a TG Jesus Christ, Atonement through; Jesus Christ, Authority of.
  b Heb. 7:22. TG Covenants; Priesthood, Melchizedek.
  c TG Promise.
7a Heb. 7:11 (11–16).
8a TG Israel, Judah, People of.
9a TG Law of Moses.

of Egypt; because they continued not in my covenant, and I regarded them not, saith the Lord.

10 For this *is* the covenant that I will make with the house of Israel after those days, saith the Lord; I will put my *a*laws into their *b*mind, and write them in their *c*hearts: and I will be to them a God, and they shall be to me a people:

11 And they shall not teach every man his neighbour, and every man his brother, saying, Know the Lord: for all shall know me, from the least to the greatest.

12 For I will be merciful to their *a*unrighteousness, and their sins and their iniquities will I *b*remember no more.

13 In that he saith, A *a*new *covenant,* he hath made the first old. Now that which decayeth and waxeth *b*old *is* ready to *c*vanish away.

CHAPTER 9

The Mosaic ordinances prefigured Christ's ministry—Christ is the Mediator of the new covenant.

THEN verily the first *a*covenant had also *b*ordinances of divine *c*service, and a worldly sanctuary.

2 For there was a *a*tabernacle made; the first, wherein *was* the *b*candlestick, and the *c*table, and the *d*shewbread; which is called the sanctuary.

3 And after the second *a*veil, the tabernacle which is called the *b*Holiest of all;

4 Which had the golden censer, and the *a*ark of the covenant overlaid round about with gold, wherein *was* the golden *b*pot that had manna, and *c*Aaron's rod that budded, and the *d*tables of the covenant;

5 And over it the *a*cherubims of glory shadowing the *b*mercyseat; of which we cannot now speak particularly.

6 Now when these things were thus *a*ordained, the *b*priests went always into the first tabernacle, accomplishing the service *of God.*

7 But into the second *went* the *a*high priest alone *b*once every year, not without blood, which he offered for himself, and *for* the errors of the people:

8 The Holy Ghost this signifying, that the way into the holiest of all was not yet made manifest, while as the first tabernacle was yet standing:

9 Which *was* a *a*figure for the time then present, in which were offered both gifts and sacrifices, that could not make him that did the service *b*perfect, as pertaining to the conscience;

10 *Which stood* only in meats and drinks, and divers *a*washings, and *b*carnal *c*ordinances, *d*imposed *on them* until the time of reformation.

11 But Christ being come an *a*high priest of good things to come, by a greater and more perfect *b*tabernacle, not made with hands, that is to say, not of this building;

12 Neither by the blood of goats and calves, but by his own *a*blood he

---

10a TG God, Law of.
  b TG Mind.
  c Jer. 31:33; 2 Cor. 3:3.
12a D&C 38:14.
  b TG Forgive.
13a Heb. 9:15;
    3 Ne. 12:47 (46–47);
    15:3 (2–10);
    Ether 13:9.
    TG New and Everlasting Covenant.
  b 2 Cor. 5:17.
  c 3 Ne. 12:46 (19, 46).
9 1a TG Law of Moses.
  b TG Ordinance.
  c TG Service.
  2a Ex. 26:1 (1–37); 39:33.

  b Ex. 25:31 (31–39); 26:35.
  c Ex. 25:23 (23–29);
    Lev. 24:6.
  d Ex. 25:30.
3a TG Jesus Christ, Types of, in Anticipation; Veil.
  b GR Holy of holies.
4a TG Ark of the Covenant.
  b Ex. 16:33 (33–34).
  c Num. 17:10.
  d Ex. 25:16 (16, 20, 40).
5a TG Cherubim.
  b Ex. 25:17.
6a GR prepared, built.
  b TG Priest, Aaronic Priesthood.
    BD Priests.

7a Heb. 9:25; 10:3.
  b Ex. 30:10.
9a GR similitude, type, parable.
    TG Jesus Christ, Types of, in Anticipation.
  b Heb. 7:19.
10a TG Wash.
  b Heb. 7:16.
  c TG Ordinance.
  d Mosiah 13:29 (27–32).
11a TG High Priest, Melchizedek Priesthood.
  b Mark 14:58;
    Heb. 8:2.
12a Acts 20:28;
    Heb. 10:10.

entered in once into the ᵇholy place, having obtained eternal ᶜredemption *for us.*

13 For if the ᵃblood of bulls and of goats, and the ashes of an heifer sprinkling the unclean, sanctifieth to the ᵇpurifying of the flesh:

14 How much more shall the ᵃblood of Christ, who through the eternal Spirit offered himself ᵇwithout ᶜspot to God, ᵈpurge your ᵉconscience from dead works to serve the living God?

15 And for this cause he is the ᵃmediator of the ᵇnew ᶜtestament, that by means of ᵈdeath, for the redemption of the ᵉtransgressions *that were* under the first ᶠtestament, they which are called might receive the ᵍpromise of eternal ʰinheritance.

16 For where a ᵃtestament *is,* there must also of necessity be the ᵇdeath of the ᶜtestator.

17 For a ᵃtestament *is* of force after men are dead: ᵇotherwise it is of no strength at all while the testator liveth.

18 Whereupon neither the first *testament* was dedicated without blood.

19 For when Moses had ᵃspoken every precept to all the people according to the law, he took the ᵇblood of calves and of goats, with water, and scarlet wool, and hyssop, and ᶜsprinkled both the book, and all the people,

20 Saying, This *is* the blood of the testament which God hath enjoined unto you.

21 Moreover he sprinkled with blood both the tabernacle, and all the vessels of the ministry.

22 And almost all things are by the law purged with blood; and without ᵃshedding of blood is no ᵇremission.

23 *It was* therefore necessary that the ᵃpatterns of things in the heavens should be purified with these; but the heavenly things themselves with better sacrifices than these.

24 For Christ is not entered into the holy places made with hands, *which are* the figures of the ᵃtrue; but into ᵇheaven itself, now to appear in the ᶜpresence of God for us:

25 Nor yet that he should offer himself often, as the ᵃhigh priest entereth into the holy place every year with blood of others;

26 For then must he often have suffered since the foundation of the world: but now once ᵃin the ᵇend of the world hath he appeared to put away sin by the ᶜsacrifice of himself.

27 And as it is appointed unto men once to die, but after this the judgment:

28 So Christ was once ᵃoffered to ᵇbear the ᶜsins of many; and unto them that look for him shall he ᵈappear the second time without sin unto salvation.

12b Lev. 16:2 (2–4); Heb. 10:19.
  c D&C 138:23 (18–23). TG Jesus Christ, Redeemer; Redemption.
13a Lev. 4:5.
  b TG Purification.
14a TG Blood, Symbolism of.
  b GR blameless.
  c Lev. 1:3; 22:20.
  d TG Purification.
  e TG Conscience.
15a TG Jesus Christ, Authority of; Jesus Christ, Mission of.
  b Heb. 8:13.
  c JST Heb. 9:15 . . . *covenant* . . . (Note: JST uses "covenant" in place of "testament" in every instance in vv. 15–18, 20.)
  d TG Jesus Christ, Death of.

  e TG Transgress.
  f JST Heb. 9:15 . . . *covenant* . . .
  g Heb. 10:36.
  h D&C 137:7 (7–10). TG Inheritance.
16a JST Heb. 9:16 . . . *covenant* . . .
  b Ex. 24:8 (3–8); Matt. 26:28 (26–28). TG Martyrdom.
  c JST Heb. 9:16 . . . *victim.* (Note: JST uses "victim" in place of "testator" also in v. 17.) 1 Tim. 2:5–6; D&C 135:5.
17a TG Witness.
  b GR since.
19a Ex. 24:7.
  b Ex. 24:6.
  c Ex. 24:8.

22a TG Blood, Symbolism of.
  b TG Remission of Sins.
23a TG Symbolism.
24a Heb. 8:2.
  b Heb. 4:14.
  c TG Jesus Christ, Atonement through.
25a Heb. 9:7.
26a JST Heb. 9:26 . . . in the *meridian* of *time* hath he . . .
  b GR consummation of the ages.
  c TG Self-Sacrifice.
28a TG Jesus Christ, Atonement through; Jesus Christ, Redeemer; Remission of Sins.
  b D&C 76:41.
  c Rom. 6:10.
  d 2 Pet. 3:12; Rev. 1:7.

CHAPTER 10

We are sanctified by the shedding of the blood of Christ—The superiority of His sacrifice is explained—Those who fall from grace through willful sin are damned—The just will live by faith.

FOR the ^alaw having a ^bshadow of good things to come, *and* not the very image of the things, can never with those sacrifices which they offered ^cyear by year continually make the comers thereunto perfect.

2 For then would they not have ceased to be offered? because that the worshippers once ^apurged should have had no more ^bconscience of sins.

3 But in those ^a*sacrifices there is* a ^bremembrance again *made* of sins every year.

4 For *it is* not possible that the blood of bulls and of goats should take away sins.

5 Wherefore when he cometh into the world, he saith, Sacrifice and offering thou wouldest not, but a body hast thou prepared me:

6 In burnt offerings and ^asacrifices for sin thou hast had no pleasure.

7 Then said I, Lo, I come (in the volume of the book it is written of me,) to do thy will, O God.

8 Above when he said, Sacrifice and offering and burnt offerings and *offering* for sin thou wouldest not, neither hadst pleasure *therein;* which are offered by the law;

9 Then said he, Lo, I come to do thy will, O God. He taketh away the first, that he may establish the second.

10 By the which will we are ^asanctified through the ^boffering ^cof the ^dbody of Jesus Christ ^eonce *for all.*

11 And every priest standeth ^adaily ministering and offering oftentimes the same sacrifices, which can never take away ^bsins:

12 But this man, after he had offered one ^asacrifice for sins for ever, sat down on the right hand of God;

13 ^aFrom henceforth expecting till his enemies be made his footstool.

14 For by one offering he hath perfected for ever them that are sanctified.

15 *Whereof* the ^aHoly Ghost also is a ^bwitness to us: for after that he had said before,

16 This *is* the ^acovenant that I will make with them after those days, saith the Lord, I will put my laws into their hearts, and in their ^bminds will I write them;

17 And their sins and iniquities will I remember no more.

18 Now where ^aremission of these *is, there is* no more offering for sin.

19 Having therefore, brethren, ^aboldness to enter into the ^bholiest by the blood of Jesus,

20 By a new and living way, which he hath consecrated for us, through the ^aveil, that is to say, his flesh;

21 And *having* an ^ahigh priest over the house of God;

22 Let us ^adraw ^bnear with a true heart in full assurance of ^cfaith, having our hearts ^dsprinkled from an evil ^econscience, and our bodies washed with pure water.

10 1*a* Mosiah 3:15 (14–15); 13:28 (28–32).
   b TG Jesus Christ, Types of, in Anticipation; Symbolism.
   c JST Heb. 10:1 . . . *continually* year by year make . . .
  2*a* TG Remission of Sins.
   b TG Peace of God.
  3*a* TG Sacrifice.
   b Lev. 16:21; Heb. 9:7.
  6*a* 1 Sam. 15:22; Micah 6:7.
 10*a* TG Sanctification.
   b TG Jesus Christ, Types

of, in Anticipation.
   c JST Heb. 10:10 . . . *once* of the body of Jesus Christ.
   d John 6:51; Heb. 9:12.
   e Rom. 6:10.
 11*a* Heb. 7:27.
   b Lev. 4:20 (20, 26).
 12*a* TG Sacrifice; Self-Sacrifice.
 13*a* JST Heb. 10:13 From henceforth *to reign until* his enemies . . .
 15*a* Heb. 3:7.
   b TG Holy Ghost, Mission of; Witness.
 16*a* Isa. 59:21 (20–21);

Rom. 11:27; D&C 49:9 (5–9).
   b Jer. 31:31–33.
 18*a* TG Remission of Sins.
 19*a* GR license, authority.
   b Lev. 16:2 (2–4); Heb. 9:12.
 20*a* TG Veil.
 21*a* TG High Priest, Melchizedek Priesthood.
 22*a* TG God, Presence of.
   b TG God, Access to.
   c Heb. 6:12 (10–12); 1 Pet. 1:5 (3–8).
   d GR purified.
   e TG Conscience.

23 Let us hold fast the ^aprofession of *our* ^bfaith without wavering; (for he *is* faithful that promised;)

24 And let us ^aconsider one another to ^bprovoke unto love and to good works:

25 Not forsaking the ^aassembling of ourselves together, as the manner of some *is*; but exhorting *one another*: and so much the more, as ye see the day approaching.

26 For if we ^asin ^bwilfully after that we have received the knowledge of the truth, there remaineth no more sacrifice for sins,

27 But a certain fearful looking for of judgment and fiery ^aindignation, which shall devour the adversaries.

28 He that ^adespised Moses' law died without mercy under two or three witnesses:

29 Of how much sorer ^apunishment, suppose ye, shall he be thought worthy, who hath trodden under foot the Son of God, and hath counted the blood of the covenant, wherewith he was sanctified, an unholy thing, and hath done ^bdespite unto the Spirit of grace?

30 For we know him that hath said, ^aVengeance *belongeth* unto me, I will ^brecompense, saith the Lord. And again, The Lord shall ^cjudge his people.

31 *It is* a fearful thing to fall into the hands of the living God.

32 But call to remembrance the former days, in which, after ye were illuminated, ye endured a great ^afight of afflictions;

33 Partly, whilst ye were made a gazingstock both by reproaches and afflictions; and partly, whilst ye became companions of them that were so used.

34 For ye had compassion of me in my bonds, and took ^ajoyfully the spoiling of your goods, knowing in yourselves that ye have in heaven a better and an enduring ^bsubstance.

35 Cast not away therefore your confidence, which hath great recompence of reward.

36 For ye have need of ^apatience, that, after ye have done the ^bwill of God, ye might receive the ^cpromise.

37 For yet a little while, and he that shall come will come, and will not tarry.

38 Now the just shall live by faith: but if *any man* ^adraw back, my soul shall have no pleasure in him.

39 But we are not of them who ^adraw back unto ^bperdition; but of them that believe to the saving of the soul.

CHAPTER 11

By faith we understand the word and work of God—The faith of the ancients was centered in Christ—By faith, men subdued kingdoms, wrought righteousness, and worked miracles.

Now ^afaith is the ^bsubstance of things ^choped for, the ^devidence of things not seen.

2 For by it the elders ^aobtained a good ^breport.

3 Through faith we understand that the worlds were ^aframed by the ^bword of God, so that things which

23a 1 Tim. 6:12 (12–13).
  b GR hope.
24a GR understand.
  b TG Provoking.
25a TG Assembly for
     Worship;
     Meetings.
26a TG Apostasy of
     Individuals;
     Sin.
  b TG Holy Ghost, Unpardonable Sin against.
27a TG God, Indignation of.
28a GR rejected, violated.
29a Heb. 2:3.
  b GR insult.

30a TG Retribution.
  b TG God, Justice of.
  c TG Jesus Christ, Judge.
32a Heb. 12:4.
34a TG Joy.
  b Matt. 6:20.
36a TG Patience.
  b TG God, Will of.
  c Heb. 9:15;
     1 Pet. 1:9 (1–16).
38a TG Apostasy of
     Individuals.
39a 2 Pet. 2:21 (20–21).
  b GR ruin, destruction.
     TG Death, Spiritual,
     Second;

     Sons of Perdition.
11 1a TG Faith.
    b GR assurance, basis,
       foundation.
       JST Heb. 11:1 . . .
       assurance of things
       hoped for . . .
    c TG Hope.
    d GR proof.
  2a GR received witness,
     testimony.
    b Heb. 11:39.
  3a TG Creation.
    b TG Jesus Christ,
       Creator.

are seen were not made of things which do appear.

4 By faith ^aAbel offered unto God a more excellent ^bsacrifice than Cain, by which he obtained witness that he was righteous, God testifying of his gifts: and by it he being dead yet speaketh.

5 By faith ^aEnoch was ^btranslated that he should not see death; and was not found, because God had translated him: for before his translation he had this ^ctestimony, that he pleased God.

6 But without ^afaith *it is* impossible to please *him:* for he that ^bcometh to God must believe that he is, and *that* he is a ^crewarder of them that ^ddiligently ^eseek him.

7 By faith ^aNoah, being ^bwarned of God of things not seen as yet, ^cmoved with fear, prepared an ark to the saving of his house; by the which he condemned the world, and became heir of the ^drighteousness which is by faith.

8 By faith ^aAbraham, when he was called to go out into a place which he should after receive for an ^binheritance, ^cobeyed; and he went out, not ^dknowing whither he went.

9 By faith he ^asojourned in the ^bland of ^cpromise, as *in* a strange country, dwelling in ^dtabernacles with Isaac and Jacob, the heirs with him of the same promise:

10 For he looked for a ^acity which hath foundations, whose builder and maker *is* God.

11 Through faith also Sara herself received strength to conceive seed, and was delivered of a child when she was past age, because she judged him faithful who had promised.

12 Therefore sprang there even of one, and him as good as dead, *so many* as the stars of the sky in ^amultitude, and as the sand which is by the sea shore innumerable.

13 These all died in faith, not having received the ^apromises, but having seen them afar off, and were persuaded of *them,* and embraced *them,* and confessed that they were ^bstrangers and pilgrims on the earth.

14 For they that say such things declare plainly that they seek a ^acountry.

15 And truly, if they had been mindful of that *country* from whence they came out, they might have had opportunity to have returned.

16 But now they desire a better ^acountry, that is, an heavenly: wherefore God is not ashamed to be called their God: for he hath prepared for them a city.

17 By ^afaith Abraham, when he was ^btried, ^coffered up Isaac: and he that had received the ^dpromises offered up his only begotten *son,*

18 Of whom it was said, That in ^aIsaac shall thy ^bseed be called:

19 ^aAccounting that God *was* able to raise *him* up, even from the dead; from whence also he received him in a figure.

20 By faith Isaac ^ablessed Jacob and Esau concerning things to come.

21 By faith ^aJacob, when he was

4a Gen. 4:4.
  b TG Sacrifice.
5a Jude 1:14 (14–16).
  b TG Translated Beings; Zion.
  c TG Testimony.
6a TG Faith.
  b Heb. 7:25.
  c TG Reward.
  d TG Diligence.
  e Ps. 34:4 (4, 6, 10); Lam. 3:25; Alma 37:37 (36–37).
7a Gen. 6:22; 8:1; 1 Pet. 3:20 (20–21); 2 Pet. 2:5.

  b TG Warn.
  c GR being cautious, reverent.
  d TG Righteousness.
8a Gen. 12:1.
  b TG Lands of Inheritance.
  c TG Obedience.
  d 2 Chr. 20:12; 1 Ne. 4:6.
9a Gen. 26:3.
  b TG Israel, Land of; Promised Lands.
  c D&C 38:18.
  d Gen. 25:27.
10a D&C 76:66.
12a TG Seed of Abraham.

13a Matt. 13:17; 1 Pet. 1:10 (10–11).
  b TG Stranger.
14a GR homeland, native place.
16a D&C 45:12 (12–14).
17a James 2:21 (21–23).
  b TG Test.
  c TG Sacrifice.
  d TG Promise.
18a TG Seed of Abraham.
  b TG Abrahamic Covenant.
19a GR Considering.
20a Gen. 27:27.
21a Gen. 48:2 (1–2, 5, 16).

a dying, blessed both the sons of Joseph; and worshipped, *leaning* upon the top of his staff.

22 By faith *a*Joseph, when he died, made mention of the departing of the children of Israel; and gave commandment concerning his bones.

23 By faith *a*Moses, when he was born, was hid three months of his parents, because they saw *he was* a *b*proper child; and they were not afraid of the king's commandment.

24 By faith Moses, when he was come to years, refused to be called the *a*son of Pharaoh's daughter;

25 Choosing rather to *a*suffer affliction with the *b*people of God, than to enjoy the pleasures of sin for a season;

26 Esteeming the *a*reproach of Christ greater *b*riches than the treasures in Egypt: for he had respect unto the recompence of the reward.

27 By faith he forsook Egypt, not fearing the wrath of the king: for he endured, as seeing him who is invisible.

28 Through faith he kept the *a*passover, and the sprinkling of *b*blood, lest he that destroyed the firstborn should touch them.

29 By faith they passed through the *a*Red sea as by dry *land:* which the Egyptians assaying to do were drowned.

30 By faith the *a*walls of Jericho fell down, after they were compassed about seven days.

31 By *a*faith the harlot *b*Rahab perished not with *c*them that believed not, when she had received the spies with peace.

32 And what shall I more say? for the time would fail me to tell of Gedeon, and of *a*Barak, and of Samson, and of *b*Jephthae; of David also, and Samuel, and of the prophets:

33 Who through faith subdued kingdoms, wrought righteousness, obtained *a*promises, stopped the mouths of *b*lions,

34 Quenched the violence of *a*fire, escaped the edge of the sword, out of weakness were made *b*strong, waxed valiant in fight, turned to flight the armies of the aliens.

35 Women received their dead raised to life again: and others were tortured, not accepting *a*deliverance; that they might obtain *b*a better resurrection:

36 And others had trial of *a*cruel *b*mockings and scourgings, yea, moreover of bonds and imprisonment:

37 They were *a*stoned, they were sawn asunder, were tempted, were slain with the sword: they wandered about in sheepskins and goatskins; being destitute, afflicted, tormented;

38 (Of whom the world was not worthy:) they wandered in deserts, and *in* mountains, and *in* dens and caves of the earth.

39 And these all, having obtained a *a*good *b*report through faith, received not the promise:

40 *a*God having *b*provided some better thing for us, that they without us should not be made *c*perfect.

22*a* TG Israel, Joseph,
     People of.
23*a* Ex. 2:2.
   b GR handsome.
24*a* Ex. 2:10.
25*a* TG Suffering.
   b Ex. 2:11 (11–15);
     Acts 7:23 (22–36).
26*a* TG Reproach.
   b TG Treasure.
28*a* Ex. 12:28 (21–28).
   b Ex. 12:22 (21–22).
29*a* TG Israel, Deliverance of.
30*a* Josh. 6:20.
31*a* James 2:25.

   b Josh. 2:1.
   c GR those who
     were unbelieving,
     disobedient.
32*a* Judg. 4:6 (1–24).
   b Judg. 11:6.
33*a* TG Promise.
   b Dan. 6:22.
34*a* Dan. 3:27.
   b Joel 3:10;
     Ether 12:27.
35*a* TG Deliver.
   b JST Heb. 11:35 . . . *the*
     first resurrection;
36*a* TG Cruelty.

   b TG Mocking;
     Persecution.
37*a* TG Martyrdom;
     Prophets, Rejection of.
39*a* GR testimony, witness.
   b Heb. 11:2.
40*a* JST Heb. 11:40 God
     having provided some
     better *things for them*
     through their sufferings,
     for without sufferings
     they could not be made
     perfect.
   b GR provided beforehand.
   c TG Perfection.

CHAPTER 12

Whom the Lord loves He chastens—God is the Father of spirits—To see God, follow peace and holiness—Exalted Saints belong to the Church of the Firstborn.

WHEREFORE seeing we also are compassed about with so great a cloud of witnesses, let us lay aside every weight, and the ᵃsin which doth so easily ᵇbeset *us,* and let us run with ᶜpatience the race that is set before us,

2 Looking unto Jesus the ᵃauthor and ᵇfinisher of *our* faith; who for the joy that was set before him ᶜendured the cross, despising the ᵈshame, and is set down at the right hand of the ᵉthrone of God.

3 For consider him that endured such ᵃcontradiction of sinners against himself, lest ye be wearied and faint in your minds.

4 Ye have not yet resisted unto blood, ᵃstriving against sin.

5 And ye have forgotten the exhortation which speaketh unto you as unto children, My son, despise not thou the chastening of the Lord, nor faint when thou art rebuked of him:

6 For whom the Lord loveth he ᵃchasteneth, and scourgeth every son whom he receiveth.

7 If ye ᵃendure ᵇchastening, God dealeth with you as with ᶜsons; for what son is he whom the father chasteneth not?

8 But if ye be without chastisement, whereof all are partakers, then are ye bastards, and not sons.

9 Furthermore we have had ᵃfathers of our flesh which ᵇcorrected *us,* and we gave *them* ᶜreverence: shall we not much rather be in ᵈsubjection unto the ᵉFather of ᶠspirits, and live?

10 For they verily for a few days chastened *us* after their own pleasure; but he for *our* profit, that *we* might be partakers of his ᵃholiness.

11 Now no chastening for the present seemeth to be joyous, but grievous: nevertheless afterward it yieldeth the ᵃpeaceable fruit of righteousness unto them which are ᵇexercised thereby.

12 Wherefore lift up the hands which hang down, and the ᵃfeeble knees;

13 And make straight paths for your feet, lest that which is lame be turned out of the way; but let it rather be ᵃhealed.

14 Follow ᵃpeace with all *men,* and ᵇholiness, without which no man shall ᶜsee the Lord:

15 Looking diligently lest any man ᵃfail of the ᵇgrace of God; lest any root of bitterness springing up trouble *you,* and thereby many be defiled;

16 Lest there *be* any fornicator, or profane person, as Esau, who for one morsel of meat sold his ᵃbirthright.

17 For ye know how that afterward, when he would have inherited the blessing, he was rejected: for he found no place of repentance, though he sought it carefully with ᵃtears.

---

12 1 *a* TG Sin.
  b Rom. 7:21 (15–25); 2 Ne. 4:18 (17–19).
  c TG Patience; Perseverance.
2 *a* TG Jesus Christ, Authority of; Jesus Christ, Messiah.
  b GR one who completes, perfects.
  c 1 Pet. 1:11.
  d TG Shame.
  e Heb. 1:3.
3 *a* GR rebellion, opposition.
4 *a* Heb. 10:32 (32–34).
6 *a* TG Chastening; Persecution.

7 *a* TG Steadfastness.
  b GR correction, instruction.
  TG Teachable.
  c TG Sons and Daughters of God.
9 *a* TG Marriage, Fatherhood.
  b TG Family, Love within.
  c TG Reverence.
  d TG Agency; Submissiveness.
  e TG God the Father, Elohim; Man, Potential to Become like Heavenly Father.
  f TG Man, Antemortal Existence of; Man, a

Spirit Child of Heavenly Father; Spirit Body; Spirit Creation.
10 *a* TG Holiness.
11 *a* TG Peace.
  b GR trained, disciplined.
12 *a* Isa. 35:3.
13 *a* Gal. 6:1.
14 *a* TG Peace of God.
  b 1 Thes. 4:3.
  c TG God, Privilege of Seeing.
15 *a* GR want, fall short of, lack.
  b TG Grace.
16 *a* TG Birthright.
17 *a* Gen. 27:38 (34–38).

18 For ye are not come unto the ^amount that might be touched, and that burned with fire, nor unto blackness, and darkness, and tempest,

19 And the sound of a trumpet, and the voice of words; which ^avoice they that heard entreated that the word should not be spoken to them any more:

20 (For they could not endure that which was commanded, And if so much as a beast touch the mountain, it shall be stoned, or thrust through with a dart:

21 And so terrible was the sight, *that* Moses said, I exceedingly fear and quake:)

22 But ye are come unto mount ^aSion, and unto the city of the living God, the heavenly Jerusalem, and to an innumerable company of ^bangels,

23 To the general assembly and church of the ^afirstborn, which are ^bwritten in heaven, and to God the ^cJudge of all, and to the ^dspirits of ^ejust men made perfect,

24 And to Jesus the ^amediator of the ^bnew ^ccovenant, and to the ^dblood of sprinkling, that speaketh ^ebetter things than *that of* Abel.

25 See that ye refuse not him that speaketh. For if they ^aescaped not who refused him that spake on earth, much more *shall not* we *escape*, if we turn away from him that *speaketh* from heaven:

26 Whose voice then shook the earth: but now he hath promised, saying, Yet once more I ^ashake not the earth only, but also heaven.

27 And this *word*, Yet once more, sig-nifieth the removing of those things that are shaken, as of things that are made, that those things which cannot be shaken may remain.

28 Wherefore we receiving a kingdom which cannot be moved, let us have grace, whereby we may serve God acceptably with ^areverence and godly ^bfear:

29 For our God *is* a consuming fire.

CHAPTER 13

Marriage is honorable—Christ is the same everlastingly—Paul explains how the Saints are to offer acceptable sacrifices.

LET ^abrotherly ^blove continue.

2 Be not forgetful to ^aentertain ^bstrangers: for thereby some have entertained ^cangels ^dunawares.

3 Remember them that are in ^abonds, as bound with them; *and* them which ^bsuffer adversity, as being yourselves also in the body.

4 ^aMarriage *is* honourable in all, and the bed undefiled: but ^bwhoremongers and ^cadulterers God will ^djudge.

5 *Let your* conversation *be* without ^acovetousness; *and be* ^bcontent with such things as ye have: for he hath said, I will never leave thee, nor ^cforsake thee.

6 So that we may boldly say, The Lord *is* my helper, and I will not fear what man shall do unto me.

7 Remember them which have the rule over you, who have spoken unto you the word of God: whose faith follow, considering the end of *their* conversation.

18*a* Ex. 19:12 (12, 16, 18).
19*a* Ex. 20:19.
22*a* TG Zion.
　b TG Angels.
23*a* TG Firstborn;
　　Jesus Christ, Firstborn.
　b Luke 10:20;
　　D&C 128:6 (6–7).
　c TG Jesus Christ, Judge;
　　Judgment.
　d TG Spirits,
　　Disembodied.
　e Ezek. 18:5 (5–9);
　　D&C 76:69 (66–69).
24*a* 1 Tim. 2:5.

　b TG New and
　　Everlasting Covenant.
　c TG Covenants.
　d Lev. 1:5;
　　1 Pet. 1:2.
　e Heb. 7:19.
25*a* Heb. 2:3.
26*a* TG Last Days.
28*a* TG Reverence.
　b Eccl. 3:14;
　　Mosiah 4:1.
13 1*a* TG Brotherhood and
　　Sisterhood.
　b TG Benevolence; Love.
2*a* TG Hospitality.

　b TG Stranger.
　c TG Angels; Translated
　　Beings.
　d Luke 24:16 (13–16, 28).
3*a* Matt. 25:36;
　　Col. 4:18.
　b TG Compassion.
4*a* TG Marriage, Marry;
　　Marriage, Temporal.
　b TG Whore.
　c TG Adulterer.
　d TG Jesus Christ, Judge.
5*a* TG Covet.
　b TG Contentment.
　c Josh. 1:5; 1 Kgs. 6:13.

8 Jesus Christ the ^asame yesterday, and to day, and for ever.

9 Be not ^acarried about with divers and strange ^bdoctrines. For *it is* a good thing that the heart be established with grace; not with meats, which have not profited them that have been occupied therein.

10 We have an altar, whereof they have no right to eat which serve the tabernacle.

11 For the bodies of those beasts, whose blood is brought into the sanctuary by the high priest for sin, are burned without the camp.

12 Wherefore Jesus also, that he might ^asanctify the people with his own ^bblood, ^csuffered ^dwithout the gate.

13 Let us go forth therefore unto him without the camp, bearing his ^areproach.

14 For here have we no continuing city, but we seek one to come.

15 By him therefore let us offer the ^asacrifice of praise to God continually, that is, the ^bfruit of *our* lips giving thanks to his name.

16 But to do good and to ^acommunicate forget not: for with such ^bsacrifices God is well pleased.

17 ^aObey them that have the rule over you, and ^bsubmit yourselves: for they watch for your souls, as they that must give account, that they may do it with joy, and not with grief: for that *is* unprofitable for you.

18 Pray for us: for we trust we have a good ^aconscience, in all things willing to live ^bhonestly.

19 But I beseech *you* the rather to do this, that I may be restored to you the sooner.

20 Now the God of peace, that brought again from the dead our Lord Jesus, that great ^ashepherd of the sheep, through the blood of the ^beverlasting ^ccovenant,

21 Make you perfect in every good ^awork to do his ^bwill, working in you that which is wellpleasing in his sight, through Jesus Christ; to whom *be* glory for ever and ever. Amen.

22 And I beseech you, brethren, suffer the word of exhortation: for I have written a letter unto you in few words.

23 Know ye that *our* brother Timothy is set at liberty; with whom, if he come shortly, I will see you.

24 Salute all them that have the rule over you, and all the saints. They of Italy salute you.

25 Grace *be* with you all. Amen.

¶ Written to the Hebrews from Italy by Timothy.

8*a* TG God, Eternal
　　Nature of.
9*a* 2 Cor. 11:3;
　　Col. 2:8.
　b Eph. 4:14.
12*a* TG Sanctification.
　b TG Blood, Symbolism of.
　c John 19:17 (17–18).
　d GR outside of.
　　Lev. 4:12.

13*a* TG Reproach.
15*a* Ps. 119:108.
　b Isa. 57:19.
16*a* TG Communication.
　b 2 Cor. 9:12 (7–12).
17*a* TG Sustaining Church
　　Leaders.
　b TG Submissiveness.
18*a* TG Conscience.
　b TG Honesty.

20*a* TG Jesus Christ, Good
　　Shepherd;
　　Shepherd.
　b TG New and Everlasting
　　Covenant.
　c TG Covenants.
21*a* TG Good Works.
　b TG God, Will of.

JAMES

CHAPTER 1

If any of you lack wisdom, let him ask of God—Resist temptation—Be doers of the word—James explains how to recognize pure religion.

JAMES, a [a]servant of God and of the Lord Jesus Christ, to the twelve tribes which are [b]scattered abroad, greeting.

2 My brethren, count it all joy when ye fall into [a]divers [b]temptations;

3 Knowing *this,* that the [a]trying of your faith worketh [b]patience.

4 But let patience have *her* perfect work, that ye may be [a]perfect and entire, wanting nothing.

5 [a]If any of you lack [b]wisdom, let him ask of God, that [c]giveth to all *men* liberally, and [d]upbraideth not; and it shall be given him.

6 But let him [a]ask in [b]faith, nothing [c]wavering. For he that wavereth is like a wave of the sea driven with the wind and tossed.

7 For let not that man think that he shall receive any thing of the Lord.

8 A [a]double minded man *is* unstable in all his ways.

9 Let the brother of [a]low degree rejoice in that he is exalted:

10 But the rich, in that he is made low: because as the flower of the [a]grass he shall pass away.

11 For the sun is no sooner risen with a burning heat, but it withereth the grass, and the flower thereof falleth, and the [a]grace of the fashion of it perisheth: so also shall the [b]rich man fade away in his ways.

12 [a]Blessed *is* the man that [b]endureth temptation: for when he is [c]tried, he shall receive the [d]crown of life, which the Lord hath promised to them that love him.

13 Let no man say when he is tempted, I am tempted of God: for God cannot be [a]tempted with [b]evil, neither tempteth he any man:

14 But every man is [a]tempted, when he is drawn away of his own [b]lust, and enticed.

15 Then when lust hath conceived, it bringeth forth [a]sin: and sin, when it is finished, bringeth forth death.

16 Do not err, my beloved brethren.

17 Every [a]good [b]gift and every perfect [c]gift is from above, and [d]cometh down from the [e]Father of lights, with whom is no [f]variableness, neither shadow of turning.

---

1 1a TG Servant.
  b TG Israel, Twelve Tribes of.
2a JST James 1:2 . . . *many afflictions;*
  b TG Temptation.
3a GR approval by trial.
  TG Opposition; Test.
  b TG Patience.
4a TG Perfection.
5a D&C 42:68; JS—H 1:11.
  b TG Guidance, Divine; Learn; Wisdom.
  c TG Benevolence; Revelation.
  d GR reproaches, censures.

6a TG Prayer.
  b TG Faith.
  c GR doubting, hesitating. TG Doubt.
8a 1 Kgs. 18:21; Ps. 12:2; Hosea 10:2. TG Integrity.
9a Matt. 23:12.
10a Isa. 40:6–8.
11a GR beauty of its appearance.
  b 1 Tim. 6:17 (17–19).
12a 1 Pet. 3:14. TG Blessing.
  b JST James 1:12 . . . *resisteth* temptation . . . TG Steadfastness.
  c TG Test.

  d TG Exaltation; Reward.
13a TG God, Perfection of.
  b TG Evil.
14a TG Temptation.
  b TG Chastity; Lust; Motivations; Sensuality.
15a TG Sin.
17a Ps. 85:12.
  b Moro. 7:12 (12–13).
  c John 3:27; 2 Cor. 9:15. TG God, Gifts of.
  d D&C 67:9.
  e D&C 67:4, 9.
  f TG God, Perfection of.

18 Of his own will begat he us with the word of truth, that we should be a kind of firstfruits of his creatures.

19 Wherefore, my beloved brethren, let every man be swift to hear, slow to ªspeak, ᵇslow to ᶜwrath:

20 For the wrath of man worketh not the righteousness of God.

21 Wherefore lay apart all ªfilthiness and ᵇsuperfluity of naughtiness, and receive with ᶜmeekness the ᵈengrafted word, which is able to save your souls.

22 But be ye ªdoers of the word, and not hearers only, deceiving your own selves.

23 For if any be a ªhearer of the word, and not a doer, he is like unto a man beholding his natural face in a ᵇglass:

24 For he beholdeth himself, and goeth his way, and straightway forgetteth what manner of man he was.

25 But whoso looketh into the perfect ªlaw of ᵇliberty, and continueth *therein*, he being not a forgetful hearer, but a doer of the work, this man shall be blessed in his deed.

26 If any man among you seem to be religious, and bridleth not his ªtongue, but deceiveth his own heart, this man's religion *is* ᵇvain.

27 Pure ªreligion and undefiled before God and the Father is this, To ᵇvisit the ᶜfatherless and ᵈwidows in their ᵉaffliction, *and* to keep himself ᶠunspotted from ᵍthe ʰworld.

CHAPTER 2

God has chosen the poor of this world who are rich in faith—Salvation is gained by keeping the whole law—Faith without works is dead.

MY brethren, ªhave not the faith of our ᵇLord Jesus Christ, *the Lord* of glory, with respect of persons.

2 For if there come unto your assembly a man with a gold ring, in goodly apparel, and there come in also a ªpoor man in ᵇvile raiment;

3 And ye have respect to him that weareth the ªgay clothing, and say unto him, Sit thou here in a good place; and say to the poor, Stand thou there, or sit here under my footstool:

4 ªAre ye not then partial in yourselves, and are become judges of evil thoughts?

5 Hearken, my beloved brethren, Hath not God chosen the ªpoor of this world rich in faith, and heirs of the kingdom which he hath promised to them that love him?

6 But ye have despised the poor. Do not rich men ªoppress you, and draw you before the judgment seats?

7 Do not they blaspheme that worthy ªname by the which ye are called?

8 If ye fulfil the royal law according to the scripture, Thou shalt ªlove thy ᵇneighbour as thyself, ye do well:

19a Prov. 17:27.
 b TG Patience.
 c TG Anger.
21a TG Filthiness.
 b GR overabundance of malice, trouble, evil.
 c TG Meek.
 d GR implanted, ingrafted.
22a TG Commitment; Duty; Good Works; Hypocrisy.
23a Luke 6:49 (47–49).
 b 1 Cor. 13:12.
25a TG God, Law of.
 b TG Liberty.
26a TG Gossip; Profanity.
 b GR useless, deceptive, erroneous.
27a TG Charity.
 b D&C 44:6.
   TG Benevolence;

Good Works; Welfare.
 c Deut. 26:13; Job 22:9; 31:21 (21–22); Ps. 10:14; 146:9 (1–10); 3 Ne. 24:5; D&C 136:8 (7–9).
 d TG Widows.
 e TG Affliction.
 f 1 Tim. 5:22; 1 Jn. 5:18; D&C 59:9. TG Chastity.
 g JST James 1:27 . . . *the vices of* the world.
 h TG Worldliness.
2 1a GR not with partiality, have the faith of our Lord.
   JST James 2:1 . . . *ye cannot* have the faith of

our Lord Jesus Christ, the Lord of glory, *and yet have respect to* persons.
 b TG Jesus Christ, Lord.
2a TG Poor.
 b GR dirty.
3a GR splendid.
4a JST James 2:4 Are ye not then in yourselves *partial judges,* and become evil *in your* thoughts?
5a Prov. 15:16; Matt. 5:3; Luke 6:20; 1 Cor. 1:27 (27–28). TG Poor.
6a TG Oppression.
7a TG Name.
8a TG Love.
 b TG Neighbor.

9 But if ye have ^arespect to persons, ye commit sin, and are convinced of the law as transgressors.

10 For whosoever shall keep the ^awhole law, and yet ^boffend in one *point*, he is ^cguilty of all.

11 For he that said, Do not commit ^aadultery, said also, Do not kill. Now if thou commit no adultery, yet if thou kill, thou art become a transgressor of the law.

12 So speak ye, and so do, as they that shall be judged by the law of ^aliberty.

13 For he shall have ^ajudgment without ^bmercy, that hath shewed no mercy; and mercy rejoiceth against judgment.

14 ^aWhat *doth it* profit, my brethren, though a man say he hath ^bfaith, and have not works? can faith save him?

15 If a ^abrother or sister be naked, and destitute of daily ^bfood,

16 And one of you say unto them, Depart in peace, be *ye* warmed and filled; notwithstanding ye ^agive them not those things which are needful to the body; what *doth it* profit?

17 Even so ^afaith, if it hath not ^bworks, is dead, being alone.

18 Yea, a man may say, Thou hast faith, and I have works: shew me thy faith without thy works, and I will shew thee my ^afaith by my ^bworks.

19 Thou believest that there is one God; thou doest well: the ^adevils also ^bbelieve, and tremble.

20 But wilt thou know, O vain man, that ^afaith without ^bworks is dead?

21 Was not Abraham our father ^ajustified by works, when he had ^boffered Isaac his son upon the altar?

22 Seest thou how faith wrought with his works, and by ^aworks was faith made ^bperfect?

23 And the scripture was fulfilled which saith, Abraham ^abelieved God, and it was imputed unto him for ^brighteousness: and he was called the ^cFriend of God.

24 Ye see then how that by ^aworks a man is ^bjustified, and not by faith only.

25 Likewise also was not ^aRahab the harlot ^bjustified by works, when she had received the messengers, and had sent *them* out another way?

26 For as the body without the ^aspirit is ^bdead, so faith without ^cworks is dead also.

CHAPTER 3

By governing the tongue, we gain perfection—Heavenly wisdom is pure, peaceable, and full of mercy.

My brethren, ^abe not many ^bmasters, knowing that we shall ^creceive the greater condemnation.

2 For in many things we ^aoffend all. If any man ^boffend not in ^cword, the

---

9a Deut. 1:17; Prov. 28:21.
10a D&C 50:28 (28–29).
  b GR stumble, err.
    TG Offense; Sin.
  c TG Guilt.
11a TG Adulterer.
12a TG Liberty.
13a Ps. 109:7.
  b TG Mercy.
14a JST James 2:14–21 (Appendix).
  b D&C 20:69.
15a TG Brotherhood and Sisterhood.
  b TG Food.
16a Luke 3:11 (8–14); D&C 104:18.
17a 1 Thes. 1:3.
  b TG Obedience.
18a TG Faith.

b Matt. 7:20 (15–20); D&C 20:37.
19a JST James 2:19 . . . devils also believe, and tremble; *thou hast made thyself like unto them, not being justified.* Acts 16:17.
  b Luke 8:28 (27–28).
20a TG Faith.
  b Prov. 24:12.
21a Heb. 11:17.
  b Gen. 22:9 (9–12).
22a TG Good Works.
  b TG Perfection.
23a Gen. 22:12.
    TG Faith.
  b TG Righteousness.
  c Isa. 41:8.
    TG Friendship.

24a 2 Ne. 25:23.
    TG Commitment.
  b TG Justification.
25a Josh. 2:1.
  b Heb. 11:31.
26a TG Spirit Body; Spirits, Disembodied.
  b TG Death.
  c TG Good Works.
3 1a JST James 3:1 . . . *strive not for the mastery, knowing that in so doing we shall receive the greater condemnation.*
  b GR (also) teachers.
  c D&C 82:3.
2a GR stumble, err.
  b TG Offense.
  c Ps. 39:1; Prov. 21:23.

same *is* a ^dperfect man, *and* able also to bridle the whole body.

3 Behold, we put bits in the horses' mouths, that they may obey us; and we turn about their whole body.

4 Behold also the ships, which though *they be* so great, and *are* driven of fierce winds, yet are they turned about with a very small helm, whithersoever the ^agovernor listeth.

5 Even so the tongue is a little member, and ^aboasteth great things. Behold, how great a ^bmatter a little fire kindleth!

6 And the ^atongue *is* a fire, a world of iniquity: so is the tongue among our members, that it defileth the whole body, and setteth on fire the course of nature; and it is set on fire of hell.

7 For every kind of beasts, and of birds, and of serpents, and of things in the sea, is tamed, and hath been tamed of mankind:

8 But the ^atongue can no man tame; *it is* an ^bunruly evil, full of deadly poison.

9 Therewith bless we God, even the Father; and therewith ^acurse we men, which are made after the ^bsimilitude of God.

10 Out of the same ^amouth proceedeth blessing and cursing. My brethren, these things ought not so to be.

11 Doth a ^afountain send forth at the same place sweet *water* and bitter?

12 Can the fig tree, my brethren, bear olive berries? either a vine,

figs? so *can* no fountain both yield salt water and fresh.

13 Who *is* a wise man and endued with knowledge among you? let him shew out of a good ^aconversation his works with ^bmeekness of wisdom.

14 But if ye have bitter envying and ^astrife in your hearts, ^bglory not, and lie not against the truth.

15 This wisdom descendeth not from above, but *is* earthly, sensual, devilish.

16 For where ^aenvying and ^bstrife *is*, there *is* confusion and every evil work.

17 But the ^awisdom that is from above is first pure, then peaceable, gentle, *and* ^beasy to be entreated, full of ^cmercy and good fruits, without partiality, and without ^dhypocrisy.

18 And the fruit of ^arighteousness is sown in ^bpeace of them that make ^cpeace.

CHAPTER 4

Wars are born of lusts—The friends of the world are the enemies of God—Sin is failure to walk in the light we have received.

FROM whence *come* ^awars and ^bfightings among you? *come they* not hence, *even* of your ^clusts that war in your members?

2 Ye lust, and have not: ye kill, and desire to have, and cannot obtain: ye fight and war, yet ye have not, because ye ask not.

3 Ye ^aask, and receive not, because ye ^bask ^camiss, that ye may ^dconsume *it* upon your ^elusts.

4 Ye ^aadulterers and adulteresses,

2*d* TG Perfection.
4*a* GR helmsman, pilot.
5*a* TG Boast; Rashness.
  b GR forest.
6*a* Prov. 16:27;
    Mark 7:20 (19–23);
    Alma 12:14; D&C 88:121.
8*a* TG Gossip; Profanity.
  b GR untameable,
    uncontrollable.
9*a* TG Curse.
  b TG God, Body of,
    Corporeal Nature.
10*a* Matt. 12:34; Luke 6:45.
    TG Hypocrisy.
11*a* GR spring, well.

Moro. 7:11 (6–11).
13*a* Prov. 12:13 (13–19).
  b TG Meek.
14*a* TG Strife.
  b GR do not assume
    superiority over.
16*a* TG Envy.
  b TG Contention.
17*a* TG God, Intelligence of;
    Wisdom.
  b GR pliant, easily
    persuaded.
  c TG God, Mercy of.
  d D&C 121:42.
18*a* TG Righteousness.
  b TG Peace; Peace of God.

  c TG Peacemakers.
4 1*a* TG War.
  b TG Apostasy of the
    Early Christian Church.
  c GR pleasures,
    gratifications, passions.
3*a* TG Prayer.
  b Hel. 10:5 (4–6).
  c GR wickedly, wrongly.
    Rom. 8:26 (26–27);
    D&C 46:30 (28–30);
    88:65 (64–65).
  d GR waste, expend.
    D&C 46:9.
  e TG Lust.
4*a* TG Whore.

know ye not that the friendship of the *b*world is *c*enmity with God? whosoever therefore will be a friend of the world is the *d*enemy of God.

5 Do ye think that the scripture saith in vain, The spirit that dwelleth in us lusteth to *a*envy?

6 But he giveth more *a*grace. Wherefore he saith, God resisteth the *b*proud, but giveth grace unto the *c*humble.

7 *a*Submit yourselves therefore to God. *b*Resist the *c*devil, and he will flee from you.

8 *a*Draw *b*nigh to God, and he will draw nigh to you. *c*Cleanse *your* hands, *ye* sinners; and *d*purify *your* hearts, *ye* double minded.

9 *a*Be afflicted, and mourn, and *b*weep: let your laughter be turned to *c*mourning, and *your* joy to heaviness.

10 *a*Humble yourselves in the sight of the Lord, and he shall lift you up.

11 *a*Speak not evil one of another, brethren. He that speaketh evil of *his* brother, and judgeth his brother, speaketh evil of the *b*law, and judgeth the law: but if thou judge the law, thou art not a doer of the law, but a judge.

12 There is one lawgiver, who is able to save and to destroy: who art thou that *a*judgest another?

13 Go to now, ye that say, To day or to *a*morrow we will go into such a city, and continue there a year, and buy and sell, and get gain:

14 Whereas ye know not what *shall* be on the morrow. For what *is* your life? It is even a *a*vapour, that appeareth for a little time, and then vanisheth away.

15 For that ye *ought* to say, If the Lord will, we shall live, and do this, or that.

16 But now ye rejoice in your *a*boastings: all such rejoicing is evil.

17 Therefore to him that *a*knoweth to do good, and *b*doeth *it* not, to him it is *c*sin.

CHAPTER 5

Misery awaits the wanton rich—Await the Lord's coming with patience—The elders are to anoint and heal the sick.

Go to now, ye rich men, *a*weep and howl for your miseries that shall come upon *you*.

2 Your *a*riches are corrupted, and your garments are motheaten.

3 Your *a*gold and silver is *b*cankered; and the *c*rust of them shall be a witness against you, and shall eat your flesh as it were fire. Ye have heaped treasure together for the last days.

4 Behold, the *a*hire of the *b*labourers who have reaped down your fields, which is of you kept back by fraud, crieth: and the cries of them which have reaped are entered into the ears of the Lord of sabaoth.

5 Ye have lived *a*in pleasure on the earth, and been wanton; ye have nourished your hearts, as in a day of slaughter.

4*b* TG World; Worldliness.
c TG Opposition.
d TG Enemies.
5*a* TG Envy.
6*a* TG Grace.
b TG Pride.
c TG Poor in Spirit.
7*a* TG Reconciliation; Submissiveness.
b TG Abstain; Self-Mastery.
c TG Devil.
8*a* TG God, Presence of.
b Ps. 69:18; D&C 88:63.
c TG Repent.

d TG Purification; Purity.
9*a* GR Endure hardship, Suffer harassment.
b Isa. 22:12; Joel 2:17; 2 Cor. 7:10.
c TG Mourning.
10*a* TG Contrite Heart; Humility.
11*a* TG Gossip.
b TG Citizenship.
12*a* Morm. 8:20 (19–20).
13*a* Prov. 27:1.
14*a* 1 Cor. 7:31 (29–31); Jacob 7:26.
16*a* TG Boast.

17*a* Luke 12:47; 2 Ne. 9:25 (25–27).
b TG Disobedience; Good Works; Obedience.
c TG Sin.
5 1*a* TG Mourning.
2*a* TG Treasure.
3*a* 1 Tim. 6:10 (10, 17); Jacob 2:17 (17–19).
b GR rusted, tarnished. D&C 56:16.
c GR venom, poison.
4*a* TG Wages.
b Jer. 22:13.
5*a* GR luxuriously, delicately.

6 Ye have condemned *and* killed the just; *and* he doth not resist you.

7 Be patient therefore, brethren, unto the coming of the Lord. Behold, the husbandman waiteth for the precious fruit of the earth, and hath long patience for it, until he receive the early and latter rain.

8 Be ye also ªpatient; ᵇstablish your hearts: for the ᶜcoming of the Lord draweth nigh.

9 ªGrudge not one against another, brethren, lest ye be condemned: behold, the judge standeth before the door.

10 Take, my brethren, the prophets, who have spoken in the name of the Lord, for an ªexample of ᵇsuffering affliction, and of patience.

11 Behold, we count them ªhappy which ᵇendure. Ye have heard of the patience of ᶜJob, and have seen the end of the Lord; that the Lord is very ᵈpitiful, and of tender ᵉmercy.

12 But above all things, my brethren, ªswear not, neither by heaven, neither by the earth, neither by any other ᵇoath: but let your yea be yea; and *your* nay, nay; lest ye fall into condemnation.

13 Is any among you ªafflicted? let him pray. Is any merry? let him sing psalms.

14 Is any ªsick among you? let him call for the ᵇelders of the church; and let them ᶜpray over him, ᵈanointing him with oil in the name of the Lord:

15 And the ªprayer of ᵇfaith shall save the sick, and the Lord shall raise him up; and if he have committed sins, they shall be ᶜforgiven him.

16 ªConfess *your* faults one to another, and ᵇpray one for another, that ye may be healed. ᶜThe effectual ᵈfervent ᵉprayer of a righteous man availeth much.

17 Elias was a man subject to like ªpassions as we are, and he prayed earnestly that it might not rain: and it ᵇrained not on the earth by the space of three years and six months.

18 And he prayed again, and the heaven gave rain, and the earth brought forth her fruit.

19 Brethren, if any of you do err from the truth, and one convert him;

20 Let him know, that he which ªconverteth the sinner from the error of his way shall ᵇsave a soul from death, and shall ᶜhide a multitude of sins.

8a TG Patience.
  b 2 Ne. 31:20 (17–21).
  c D&C 106:4.
9a TG Backbiting;
    Malice.
10a TG Example.
  b 2 Cor. 11:23 (23–33);
    Mosiah 17:13 (10–20);
    Alma 14:26 (20–27);
    JS—H 1:22.
    TG Suffering.
11a TG Happiness.
  b TG Perseverance;
    Steadfastness.
  c Job 1:1.
  d TG Compassion.
  e TG God, Mercy of;
    Kindness.
12a TG Swearing.
  b TG Oath.
13a TG Affliction.
14a TG Sickness.
  b TG Elder, Melchizedek
    Priesthood;
    Heal.
  c TG Prayer.
  d Ex. 31:11.
    TG Administrations to
    the Sick;
    Anointing.
15a D&C 104:80.
  b Matt. 15:28 (25–28).
    TG Faith.
  c Mark 2:5 (3–9).
    TG Forgive.
16a TG Confession.
  b TG Benevolence.
  c Ex. 33:17.
  d Jer. 29:13;
    1 Ne. 1:5 (5–8);
    2 Ne. 4:24 (23–25);
    Moro. 7:9.
  e TG Prayer.
17a Acts 14:15 (11–15).
  b TG Drought.
20a D&C 6:11.
    TG Conversion.
  b 1 Tim. 4:16.
  c See JST 1 Pet. 4:8 (1 Pet.
    4:8 note *a*).

THE FIRST EPISTLE GENERAL OF

PETER

CHAPTER 1

The trial of our faith precedes salvation—Christ was foreordained to be the Redeemer.

PETER, an apostle of Jesus Christ, to the [a]strangers scattered throughout Pontus, Galatia, Cappadocia, Asia, and Bithynia,

2 [a]Elect according to the [b]foreknowledge of God the Father, through [c]sanctification of the Spirit, unto [d]obedience and [e]sprinkling of the [f]blood of Jesus Christ: Grace unto you, and peace, be multiplied.

3 Blessed *be* the God and Father of our Lord Jesus Christ, which according to his abundant [a]mercy hath [b]begotten us again unto a [c]lively [d]hope by the resurrection of [e]Jesus Christ from the dead,

4 To an [a]inheritance incorruptible, and undefiled, and that fadeth not away, reserved in heaven for you,

5 Who are kept by the [a]power of God through [b]faith unto salvation [c]ready to be revealed in the last time.

6 Wherein ye greatly rejoice, though now for a [a]season, if need be, ye are in heaviness through manifold [b]temptations:

7 That the [a]trial of your faith, being much more precious than of gold that perisheth, though it be tried with fire, might be found unto praise and honour and glory at the [b]appearing of Jesus Christ:

8 Whom having not seen, ye love; in whom, though now ye see *him* not, yet [a]believing, ye rejoice with joy unspeakable and full of glory:

9 Receiving the [a]end of your [b]faith, *even* the [c]salvation of *your* souls.

10 Of which [a]salvation the [b]prophets have inquired and searched diligently, who prophesied of the grace *that should come* unto you:

11 Searching what, or what manner of time the Spirit of Christ which was in them did signify, when it [a]testified beforehand the [b]sufferings of Christ, and the [c]glory that should follow.

12 Unto whom it was revealed, that not unto themselves, but unto us they did minister the things, which are now reported unto you by them that have [a]preached the gospel unto you with the Holy Ghost sent down from heaven; which things the [b]angels desire to look into.

13 Wherefore gird up the loins of your mind, be [a]sober, and hope [b]to

---

1 1a TG Stranger.
　2a John 6:44 (44, 63–65).
　　TG Election.
　　b TG Foreordination;
　　　God, Foreknowledge of.
　　c TG Sanctification.
　　d TG Obedience.
　　e Isa. 52:15.
　　f Ex. 24:8 (5–8);
　　　Heb. 12:24.
　3a TG God, Mercy of.
　　b TG Holy Ghost,
　　　Baptism of;
　　　Man, New, Spiritually
　　　Reborn.
　　c GR living.
　　d TG Hope.
　　e 1 Cor. 15:20.

4a Matt. 6:20;
　1 Cor. 9:25 (24–25);
　Col. 1:5.
5a Rom. 1:16.
　b Heb. 10:22 (22–24);
　　1 Pet. 1:21 (21–22).
　c GR prepared.
6a TG Probation.
　b GR trials, afflictions.
　　TG Temptation.
7a TG Opposition;
　　Test.
　b GR revelation.
8a John 20:29.
9a GR goal, purpose,
　consummation.
　JST 1 Pet. 1:9 . . . *object* of
　your faith . . .

　b D&C 76:51 (51–70).
　c Heb. 10:36.
10a TG Salvation.
　b Matt. 13:17;
　　Luke 24:27 (26–27);
　　Heb. 11:13;
　　2 Pet. 3:2.
11a Jacob 4:4; 7:11 (11–12);
　　Mosiah 13:33 (33–35);
　　D&C 20:26.
　b Heb. 12:2.
　c D&C 58:3 (3–4).
12a TG Holy Ghost,
　　Mission of.
　b TG Angels.
13a TG Levity.
　b GR perfectly, completely.

the end for the ^cgrace that is to be brought unto you at the revelation of Jesus Christ;

14 As obedient children, not fashioning yourselves according to the former ^alusts in your ^bignorance:

15 But as he which hath called you is holy, so be ye ^aholy in all manner of ^bconversation;

16 Because it is written, Be ye holy; for I am ^aholy.

17 And if ye call on the Father, who without respect of persons judgeth according to every man's ^awork, pass the time of your sojourning here in ^bfear:

18 Forasmuch as ye know that ye were not ^aredeemed with corruptible things, *as* silver and gold, from your ^bvain conversation *received* by ^ctradition from your fathers;

19 But with the precious ^ablood of Christ, as of a ^blamb without ^cblemish and without spot:

20 ^aWho verily was ^bforeordained before the foundation of the world, but was manifest in these last times for you,

21 Who by him do believe in God, that raised him up from the dead, and gave him ^aglory; that your ^bfaith and ^chope might be in God.

22 Seeing ye have ^apurified your ^bsouls in obeying the truth through the Spirit unto unfeigned ^clove of the brethren, *see that ye* ^dlove one another with a pure heart fervently:

23 Being ^aborn again, not of corruptible seed, but of incorruptible, by the word of God, which liveth and ^babideth for ever.

24 For all ^aflesh *is* as grass, and all the glory of man as the flower of grass. The grass withereth, and the flower thereof falleth away:

25 But the ^aword of the Lord endureth for ever. And this is the word which by the gospel is preached unto you.

CHAPTER 2

Converts are newborn babes in Christ—He is the chief cornerstone—Saints hold a royal priesthood and are a peculiar people—Saints are in subjection to the laws of man.

WHEREFORE laying aside all ^amalice, and all ^bguile, and hypocrisies, and envies, and all evil ^cspeakings,

2 As ^anewborn babes, desire the ^bsincere ^cmilk of the word, that ye may grow thereby:

3 If so be ye have ^atasted that the Lord *is* gracious.

4 To whom coming, *as unto* a living stone, disallowed indeed of men, but ^achosen of God, *and* precious,

5 Ye also, as ^alively stones, are built up a ^bspiritual ^chouse, an holy priesthood, to offer up ^dspiritual ^esacrifices, acceptable to God by Jesus Christ.

6 Wherefore also it is contained in

13c TG Grace.
14a TG Lust.
  b Acts 17:30 (29–31).
15a 1 Thes. 2:12.
  b 2 Pet. 3:11;
    D&C 136:24 (23–24).
16a 1 Jn. 3:3.
17a TG Good Works.
  b TG Reverence.
18a 1 Cor. 6:20.
    TG Jesus Christ,
    Redeemer.
  b GR erroneous, fruitless
    conduct.
  c TG Traditions of Men.
19a TG Jesus Christ,
    Atonement through.
  b TG Jesus Christ, Lamb of
    God; Jesus Christ, Types
    of, in Anticipation;
    Passover.

  c Lev. 1:3; 3:6; 22:20;
    Deut. 15:21.
20a GR Having been
    foreknown before the
    foundation.
  b TG Foreordination; Jesus
    Christ, Authority of;
    Jesus Christ, Foreor-
    dained; Salvation, Plan of.
21a Acts 3:13 (13–15).
  b Gal. 5:5 (5–6);
    1 Pet. 1:5 (3–8).
  c TG Hope.
22a TG Purification; Purity.
  b TG Soul.
  c Moro. 8:26 (25–26).
  d TG Love.
23a TG Holy Ghost,
    Baptism of.
  b TG Steadfastness.
24a TG Mortality.

25a Ps. 119:89.
2 1a TG Malice.
  b TG Guile.
  c TG Backbiting; Slander.
2a TG Man, New, Spiritually
    Reborn.
  b GR pure, genuine.
  c 1 Cor. 3:2 (2–3);
    Heb. 5:13 (13–14);
    Mosiah 3:19.
3a GR experienced.
    Heb. 6:5 (4–6);
    Alma 36:26 (24–26).
4a D&C 50:44.
5a GR living.
  b TG Spirituality.
  c Heb. 3:6.
  d TG Priesthood, Magnify-
    ing Callings within.
  e TG Jesus Christ, Types of,
    in Memory; Sacrifice.

the scripture, Behold, I lay in Sion a chief ᵃcorner ᵇstone, elect, precious: and he that ᶜbelieveth on him shall not be ᵈconfounded.

7 Unto you therefore which believe *he is* precious: but unto them which be ᵃdisobedient, the stone which the builders ᵇdisallowed, the same is made the head of the corner,

8 And a ᵃstone of ᵇstumbling, and a ᶜrock of ᵈoffence, *even to them* which ᵉstumble at the word, being disobedient: whereunto also they were ᶠappointed.

9 But ye *are* a ᵃchosen generation, a ᵇroyal ᶜpriesthood, an ᵈholy ᵉnation, a ᶠpeculiar people; that ye should shew forth the praises of him who hath called you out of ᵍdarkness into his marvellous ʰlight:

10 Which in time past *were* not a people, but *are* now the people of God: which had not obtained mercy, but now have obtained mercy.

11 Dearly beloved, I beseech *you* as ᵃstrangers and ᵇpilgrims, ᶜabstain from fleshly ᵈlusts, which ᵉwar against the soul;

12 Having your conversation ᵃhonest among the Gentiles: that, whereas they speak against you as evildoers, they may by *your* good ᵇworks, which they shall behold, glorify God in the day of visitation.

13 ᵃSubmit yourselves to every ᵇordinance of man for the Lord's sake: whether it be to the king, as ᶜsupreme;

14 Or unto governors, as unto them that are sent by him for the punishment of evildoers, and for the praise of them that do well.

15 For so is the will of God, that with well doing ye may put to ᵃsilence the ᵇignorance of foolish men:

16 As free, and not using *your* ᵃliberty for a cloak of ᵇmaliciousness, but as the ᶜservants of God.

17 ᵃHonour all *men*. Love the ᵇbrotherhood. ᶜFear God. Honour the ᵈking.

18 ᵃServants, *be* subject to *your* ᵇmasters with all fear; not only to the good and gentle, but also to the ᶜfroward.

19 For this *is* ᵃthankworthy, if a man for conscience toward God endure ᵇgrief, suffering wrongfully.

20 For what glory *is it*, if, when ye be buffeted for your faults, ye shall take it ᵃpatiently? but if, when ye do well, and ᵇsuffer *for it*, ye take it ᶜpatiently, this *is* ᵈacceptable with God.

6a TG Cornerstone.
  b Isa. 28:16.
  c 3 Ne. 11:39 (37–40).
  d GR ashamed, disappointed.
7a TG Disobedience.
  b Matt. 21:42 (42–46); Luke 9:22.
8a 1 Cor. 1:18 (18–24).
  b Isa. 28:16; 2 Ne. 18:14 (13–15).
  c TG Rock.
  d TG Offense.
  e Matt. 21:44 (33–46).
  f Rom. 9:22 (9–23); 1 Thes. 5:9.
9a TG Election.
  b TG Mission of Early Saints; Mission of Latter-day Saints.
  c TG Priesthood; Priesthood, Melchizedek.
  d Ex. 19:6. TG Israel, Blessings of.
  e TG Nations.

f GR purchased, preserved; note that in Ex. 19:5 the Hebrew word is *segullah*, meaning "special possession or property." TG Israel, Mission of; Modesty; Peculiar People.
  g TG Walking in Darkness.
  h TG Light [noun].
11a TG Stranger.
  b GR resident aliens, sojourners.
  c TG Abstain.
  d TG Lust.
  e TG War.
12a TG Children of Light; Honesty.
  b Matt. 5:16 (14–16); Titus 2:8.
13a TG Citizenship; Submissiveness.
  b TG Governments.
  c GR superior.

15a TG Silence.
  b TG Ignorance.
16a TG Liberty.
  b TG Malice.
  c TG Servant.
17a TG Respect.
  b TG Brotherhood and Sisterhood.
  c Prov. 24:21.
  d TG Citizenship; Kings, Earthly.
18a Col. 3:22; 1 Tim. 6:1 (1–2); Titus 2:9 (9–10).
  b Eph. 6:5 (5–8).
  c GR crooked, wicked.
19a GR pleasing, gracious.
  b TG Tribulation.
20a D&C 122:7 (7–8).
  b TG Forbear; Suffering.
  c Alma 12:24. TG Patience.
  d GR pleasing, gracious.

21 For even hereunto were ye called: because Christ also ^asuffered for us, leaving us an ^bexample, that ye should follow his steps:

22 Who did no ^asin, neither was ^bguile found in his mouth:

23 Who, when he was ^areviled, reviled not again; when he suffered, he threatened not; but ^bcommitted *himself* to him that judgeth righteously:

24 Who his own self ^abare our ^bsins in his own body on the tree, that we, being dead to sins, should live unto righteousness: by whose ^cstripes ye were healed.

25 For ye were as ^asheep going astray; but are now returned unto the ^bShepherd and ^cBishop of your souls.

CHAPTER 3

Husbands and wives should honor each other—Saints should live by gospel standards—Christ preached to the spirits in prison.

LIKEWISE, ye ^awives, *be* in subjection to your own husbands; that, if any ^bobey not the word, they also may without the word be won by the ^cconversation of the wives;

2 While they behold your ^achaste ^bconversation *coupled* with fear.

3 Whose adorning let it not be that outward ^aadorning of plaiting the hair, and of wearing of gold, or of putting on of apparel;

4 But *let it be* the hidden man of the heart, in that which is not corruptible, *even the* ^aornament of a ^bmeek and quiet spirit, which is in the sight of God of great price.

5 For after this manner in the old time the holy ^awomen also, who ^btrusted in God, adorned themselves, being ^cin subjection unto their own husbands:

6 Even as Sara obeyed Abraham, calling him lord: whose ^adaughters ye are, as long as ye do well, and are not afraid with any ^bamazement.

7 Likewise, ye ^ahusbands, dwell with *them* according to ^bknowledge, giving ^chonour unto the ^dwife, as unto the weaker vessel, and as being ^eheirs together of the grace of life; that your ^fprayers be not hindered.

8 Finally, *be* ye all of ^aone mind, having ^bcompassion one of another, love as ^cbrethren, *be* ^dpitiful, *be* ^ecourteous:

9 Not ^arendering ^bevil for evil, or railing for railing: but contrariwise blessing; knowing that ye are thereunto called, that ye should inherit a ^cblessing.

10 For he that will love life, and see good days, let him ^arefrain his ^btongue from evil, and his lips that they speak no ^cguile:

21a TG Jesus Christ,
   Atonement through;
   Redemption;
   Self-Sacrifice.
 b TG Example;
   Jesus Christ, Exemplar.
22a Isa. 53:9.
   TG Sin.
 b TG Guile; Sincere.
23a Isa. 53:3 (3–6).
   TG Jesus Christ, Trials of;
   Retribution;
   Reviling.
 b TG Commitment.
24a TG Accountability;
   Self-Sacrifice.
 b TG Jesus Christ,
   Atonement through;
   Jesus Christ, Redeemer.
 c Isa. 53:5.
25a TG Sheep.
 b TG Jesus Christ, Good
   Shepherd; Shepherd.

c TG Bishop.
3 1a TG Family, Love within;
   Marriage, Wives.
 b TG Disobedience.
 c JST 1 Pet. 3:1 . . .
   conduct . . .
2a TG Chastity.
 b JST 1 Pet. 3:2 . . .
   conduct . . .
3a TG Apparel;
   Modesty.
4a TG Beauty.
 b GR gentle, mild,
   forgiving.
5a TG Woman.
 b TG Trust in God.
 c GR obedient,
   submissive to.
6a TG Seed of Abraham.
 b GR dismay,
   consternation.
7a TG Family;
   Marriage, Husbands.

b D&C 121:42.
 c TG Marriage, Continuing
   Courtship in.
 d TG Marriage, Wives;
   Woman.
 e TG Marriage, Celestial.
 f TG Prayer.
8a TG Unity.
 b TG Compassion;
   Kindness;
   Welfare.
 c TG Brotherhood and
   Sisterhood.
 d GR tenderhearted,
   compassionate.
 e TG Courtesy.
9a TG Retribution.
 b TG Forbear.
 c TG Blessing.
10a TG Self-Mastery.
 b TG Gossip;
   Slander.
 c TG Guile.

11 Let him ^aeschew evil, and do good; let him seek ^bpeace, and ^censue it.

12 For the ^aeyes of the Lord *are* over the ^brighteous, and his ears *are open* unto their ^cprayers: but the face of the Lord *is* against them that do ^devil.

13 And who *is* he that will harm you, if ye be ^afollowers of that which is good?

14 But and if ye ^asuffer for ^brighteousness' sake, ^chappy *are ye:* and be not afraid of their terror, neither be troubled;

15 But ^asanctify the Lord God in your hearts: and *be* ready always to *give* ^ban answer to every man that asketh you a reason of the ^chope that is in you with ^dmeekness and ^efear:

16 Having a good ^aconscience; that, whereas they speak evil of you, as of evildoers, they may be ashamed that falsely accuse your good ^bconversation in Christ.

17 For *it is* better, if the will of God be so, that ye ^asuffer for well doing, than for evil doing.

18 For Christ also hath once ^asuffered for sins, the just for the ^bunjust, that he might bring us to God, being put to ^cdeath in the flesh, but quickened by the ^dSpirit:

19 By which also he went and ^apreached unto the ^bspirits in ^cprison;

20 ^aWhich sometime were ^bdisobedient, when once the ^clongsuffering of God waited in the days of ^dNoah, while the ark was a preparing, wherein few, that is, eight souls were ^esaved by ^fwater.

21 The like figure whereunto *even* ^abaptism doth also now save us (not the putting away of the filth of the flesh, but the answer of a good conscience toward God,) by the resurrection of Jesus Christ:

22 Who is gone into ^aheaven, and is on the right hand of God; ^bangels and ^cauthorities and powers being made subject unto him.

CHAPTER 4

Peter explains why the gospel is preached to the dead—Saints should speak as the oracles of God—The righteous will be tried and tested in all things.

FORASMUCH then as Christ hath suffered for us in the flesh, arm yourselves likewise with the same ^amind: ^bfor he that hath suffered in the flesh hath ceased from ^csin;

2 That he no longer should live the rest of *his* time in the flesh to

11 *a* GR turn away from, avoid.
   b TG Peacemakers; Peace of God.
   c GR pursue, follow eagerly.
12 *a* Ps. 33:18. TG Abundant Life; Reward.
   b TG Righteousness.
   c TG Prayer.
   d TG Evil.
13 *a* TG Commitment.
14 *a* Luke 6:22; James 1:12 (8–16). TG Suffering.
   b TG Righteousness.
   c TG Happiness.
15 *a* GR reverence as holy.
   b GR a defense.
   c TG Hope.
   d TG Meek.
   e GR reverence, awe.
16 *a* TG Conscience.
   b JST 1 Pet. 3:16 . . .

conduct . . .
17 *a* TG Self-Sacrifice.
18 *a* TG Jesus Christ, Atonement through; Jesus Christ, Redeemer; Pain; Redemption.
   b TG Injustice.
   c TG Death; Jesus Christ, Death of.
   d TG God, Spirit of.
19 *a* TG Genealogy and Temple Work; Preaching.
   b TG Salvation for the Dead; Spirit Body; Spirits, Disembodied; Spirits in Prison.
   c Luke 1:79 (77–79); D&C 138:8 (5–10, 18). TG Hell.
20 *a* JST 1 Pet. 3:20 *Some of whom* were disobedient *in the days of Noah, while* the long-suffering of God waited, while the

ark was preparing . . .
   b TG Disobedience.
   c TG Forbear.
   d Gen. 7:1. TG Earth, Cleansing of.
   e Gen. 8:1; Heb. 11:7; 2 Pet. 2:5.
   f TG Flood.
21 *a* TG Baptism; Baptism, Essential.
22 *a* John 7:34.
   b TG Angels.
   c Col. 1:16; 2:10. TG Authority.
4 1 *a* GR intent, idea, thought.
   b JST 1 Pet. 4:2 For *you who have* suffered in the flesh *should cease* from sin, that *you* no longer *the rest of your time in the flesh,* should live to the lusts of men, but to the will of God.
   c TG Sin.

the [a]lusts of men, but to the will of God.

3 For the time past of *our* life may suffice us to have wrought the will of the Gentiles, when we walked in lasciviousness, lusts, [a]excess of wine, [b]revellings, banquetings, and [c]abominable [d]idolatries:

4 Wherein they think it strange that ye run not with *them* to the same excess of riot, speaking evil of *you:*

5 Who shall give account to him that is ready to [a]judge the [b]quick and the dead.

6 [a]For for this cause was the [b]gospel [c]preached also to them that are [d]dead, that they might be [e]judged according to men in the flesh, but live according to God in the spirit.

7 [a]But the end of all things is at hand: be ye therefore sober, and [b]watch unto prayer.

8 And above all things have fervent charity among yourselves: [a]for [b]charity shall cover the multitude of sins.

9 Use [a]hospitality one to another without [b]grudging.

10 As every man hath received the gift, *even so* [a]minister the same one to another, as good [b]stewards of the manifold grace of God.

11 If any man [a]speak, *let him speak* as the [b]oracles of God; if any man minister, *let him do it* as of the ability which God giveth: that God in all things may be glorified through Jesus Christ, to whom be praise and dominion for ever and ever. Amen.

12 Beloved, think it not strange concerning the fiery [a]trial which is to try you, as though some strange thing happened unto you:

13 But [a]rejoice, inasmuch as ye are [b]partakers of Christ's [c]sufferings; that, when his glory shall be [d]revealed, ye may be glad also with exceeding joy.

14 If ye be [a]reproached for the name of Christ, [b]happy *are ye;* for the spirit of glory and of God resteth upon you: on their part he is evil spoken of, but on your part he is glorified.

15 But let none of you suffer as a murderer, or *as* a thief, or *as* an evildoer, or as a busybody in other men's matters.

16 Yet if *any man suffer* as a [a]Christian, let him not be ashamed; but let him glorify God on this behalf.

17 For the time *is come* that [a]judgment must begin at the house of God: and if *it* first *begin* at us, what shall the end *be* of them that [b]obey not the gospel of God?

18 And if the [a]righteous scarcely be saved, where shall the [b]ungodly and the sinner appear?

19 Wherefore let them that suffer according to the [a]will of God commit the [b]keeping of their souls *to him* in well doing, as unto a faithful Creator.

2*a* TG Lust.
3*a* TG Temperance.
  b TG Rioting and Reveling.
  c TG Devil, Church of.
  d TG Idolatry.
5*a* TG Jesus Christ, Judge.
  b OR living.
6*a* JST 1 Pet. 4:6 *Because of this, is* the gospel preached to them *who* are dead, that they might be judged according to men in the flesh, but live *in the spirit* according to *the will of* God.
  b TG Gospel.
  c TG Genealogy and Temple Work.

  d TG Hell; Salvation, Plan of; Salvation for the Dead; Spirits, Disembodied; Spirits in Prison.
  e D&C 88:99; 138:10, 34.
7*a* JST 1 Pet. 4:7 *But to you, the end of all things is at hand . . .*
  b TG Watch.
8*a* JST 1 Pet. 4:8 *. . . for charity preventeth a multitude of sins.*
  b TG Charity.
9*a* TG Hospitality.
  b TG Motivations.
10*a* TG Priesthood, Magnifying Callings within.
  b TG Stewardship.

11*a* 1 Thes. 2:4; Titus 2:1.
  b TG Authority; Teaching with the Spirit.
12*a* TG Test.
13*a* Acts 5:41.
  b TG Persecution.
  c TG Suffering.
  d D&C 66:2.
14*a* TG Reproach.
  b TG Happiness.
16*a* Acts 11:26 (19–26).
17*a* TG Judgment.
  b D&C 18:46. TG Disobedience.
18*a* TG Righteousness.
  b TG Godliness.
19*a* TG God, Will of.
  b TG Refuge.

CHAPTER 5

The elders are to feed the flock of God—Humility and godly graces lead to perfection.

THE [a]elders which are among you I exhort, who am also an elder, and a witness of the sufferings of Christ, and also a [b]partaker of the glory that shall be revealed:

2 [a]Feed the [b]flock of God which is among you, taking the [c]oversight *thereof*, not by constraint, but [d]willingly; not for [e]filthy [f]lucre, but of a ready mind;

3 Neither as being [a]lords over *God's* heritage, but being [b]ensamples to the flock.

4 And when the chief [a]Shepherd shall appear, ye shall receive a [b]crown of [c]glory that fadeth not away.

5 Likewise, ye younger, [a]submit yourselves unto the elder. Yea, all *of you* be subject one to another, and be clothed with [b]humility: for God [c]resisteth the [d]proud, and giveth grace to the [e]humble.

6 [a]Humble yourselves therefore under the mighty hand of God, that he may exalt you in due time:

7 Casting all your care upon him; for he careth for you.

8 Be [a]sober, be [b]vigilant; because your adversary the [c]devil, as a roaring lion, walketh about, seeking whom he may devour:

9 Whom resist [a]steadfast in the faith, knowing that the same afflictions are [b]accomplished in your brethren that are in the world.

10 But the God of all [a]grace, who hath called us unto his eternal glory by Christ Jesus, after that ye have suffered a while, make you [b]perfect, stablish, strengthen, settle *you.*

11 To him *be* glory and dominion for ever and ever. Amen.

12 By [a]Silvanus, a faithful brother unto you, as I suppose, I have written briefly, exhorting, and testifying that this is the true grace of God wherein ye stand.

13 The *church that is* at [a]Babylon, elected together with *you,* saluteth you; and *so doth* Marcus my son.

14 Greet ye one another with a kiss of charity. Peace *be* with you all that are in Christ Jesus. Amen.

---

5 1a TG Elder, Melchizedek Priesthood; Leadership.
  b D&C 66:2; 93:22.
2a GR Tend, Superintend. John 21:16 (15–16).
  b TG Church.
  c GR overseeing, guarding, watching.
  d TG Initiative.
  e TG Filthiness.
  f TG Priestcraft.
3a D&C 121:41 (41–42).
  b TG Example.

4a TG Jesus Christ, Good Shepherd; Shepherd.
  b Luke 12:44. TG Exaltation.
  c D&C 66:12.
5a TG Respect; Submissiveness.
  b TG Humility.
  c GR opposes, is adverse to.
  d TG Pride.
  e TG Poor in Spirit.
6a TG Contrite Heart.
8a TG Levity.

  b TG Watch.
  c TG Devil.
9a TG Perseverance; Steadfastness.
  b GR laid upon, endured by.
10a TG Grace.
  b TG Worthiness.
12a Acts 15:34 (32–34); 2 Cor. 1:19; 1 Thes. 1:1.
13a TG Babylon.

THE SECOND EPISTLE GENERAL OF
PETER

CHAPTER 1

Peter urges the Saints to make their calling and election sure—Prophecy comes by the power of the Holy Ghost.

SIMON Peter, a *a*servant and an *b*apostle of Jesus Christ, to them that have obtained *c*like precious faith with us through the *d*righteousness *e*of God and our Saviour Jesus Christ:

2 Grace and peace be multiplied unto you through the *a*knowledge of God, and of Jesus our Lord,

3 According as his divine power hath given unto us *a*all things that *pertain* unto *b*life and *c*godliness, through the knowledge of him that hath called us *d*to glory and *e*virtue:

4 Whereby are given unto us exceeding great and precious *a*promises: that by these ye might be *b*partakers of the *c*divine *d*nature, having *e*escaped the *f*corruption that is in the world through *g*lust.

5 And beside this, giving all *a*diligence, add to your faith *b*virtue; and to virtue *c*knowledge;

6 And to knowledge *a*temperance; and to temperance *b*patience; and to patience *c*godliness;

7 And to godliness *a*brotherly *b*kindness; and to brotherly kindness *c*charity.

8 For if these things be in you, and *a*abound, they make *you that ye shall* neither *be* *b*barren nor *c*unfruitful in the knowledge of our Lord Jesus Christ.

9 But he that lacketh these things is blind, and cannot see afar off, and hath forgotten that he was purged from his old sins.

10 Wherefore the rather, brethren, give diligence to make your calling and *a*election sure: for if ye do these things, ye shall never *b*fall:

11 For so an entrance shall be ministered unto you abundantly into the *a*everlasting *b*kingdom of our Lord and Saviour Jesus Christ.

12 Wherefore I will not be negligent to put you always in remembrance of these things, though ye know *them*, and be established in the present truth.

13 Yea, I think it *a*meet, as long as I am in this *b*tabernacle, to stir you up by putting *you* in remembrance;

14 Knowing that shortly I must put off *this* my tabernacle, even as our Lord Jesus Christ hath *a*shewed me.

15 Moreover I will endeavour that ye may be able after my decease to

1 1a TG Servant.
  b D&C 107:23.
  c GR equally precious.
  d TG God, the Standard of Righteousness.
  e GR of our God and Savior.
2a D&C 76:7 (5–10).
3a D&C 76:55 (53–60).
  b D&C 45:8.
  c TG Godliness.
  d GR through, by.
  e TG Virtue.
4a TG Promise.
  b D&C 93:28 (27–28).
  c TG Earth, Purpose of.
  d 1 Sam. 10:6.
  e 2 Pet. 2:18.

f TG Man, Natural, Not Spiritually Reborn.
g TG Lust.
5a TG Diligence.
  b TG Chastity; Good Works; Virtue.
  c TG Knowledge; Learn; Study.
6a GR self-control. TG Temperance.
  b TG Patience.
  c GR reverence, piety, godliness.
7a TG Brotherhood and Sisterhood.
  b TG Benevolence;

Kindness.
  c TG Charity.
8a TG Abundant Life.
  b GR idle, unprofitable, injurious. TG Barren.
  c D&C 107:31 (30–31).
10a TG Election.
  b D&C 50:44.
11a TG Immortality.
  b TG Kingdom of God, on Earth.
13a GR right, just, righteous.
  b D&C 93:4, 35.
14a John 21:19 (18–19).

have these things always in remembrance.

16 For we have not followed cunningly devised ªfables, when we made known unto you the power and coming of our Lord Jesus Christ, but were ᵇeyewitnesses of his majesty.

17 For he received from God the Father honour and glory, when there came such a voice to him from the excellent glory, This is my ªbeloved Son, in whom I am well pleased.

18 And this ªvoice which came from heaven we heard, when we were with him in the holy ᵇmount.

19 ªWe have also a more ᵇsure word of ᶜprophecy; whereunto ye do well that ye take heed, as unto a light that shineth in a dark place, until the day dawn, and the day ᵈstar arise in your hearts:

20 Knowing this first, that ªno ᵇprophecy of the ᶜscripture is of any private ᵈinterpretation.

21 For the ªprophecy came not in old time by the will of man: but holy men of God ᵇspake *as they were* ᶜmoved by the ᵈHoly Ghost.

CHAPTER 2

False teachers among the Saints are damned—Lustful Saints will perish in their own corruption.

BUT there were ªfalse prophets also among the people, even as there shall be ᵇfalse ᶜteachers among you, who privily shall bring in damnable heresies, even denying the Lord that ᵈbought them, and bring upon themselves swift destruction.

2 And many shall follow their pernicious ways; by reason of whom the way of ªtruth shall be evil spoken of.

3 And through covetousness shall they with ªfeigned words make merchandise of you: whose ᵇjudgment now of a long time lingereth not, and their ᶜdamnation slumbereth not.

4 For if God spared not the ªangels that sinned, but cast *them* down to ᵇhell, and delivered *them* into chains of darkness, to be reserved unto ᶜjudgment;

5 And spared not the old world, but saved ªNoah the eighth *person*, a preacher of ᵇrighteousness, bringing in the ᶜflood upon the world of the ungodly;

6 And turning the cities of ªSodom and Gomorrha into ashes condemned *them* with an overthrow, making *them* an ᵇensample unto those that after should live ungodly;

7 And delivered just ªLot, ᵇvexed with the ᶜfilthy conversation of the wicked:

8 (For that righteous man dwelling among them, in seeing and hearing,

---

16a 1 Tim. 1:4.
  b Matt. 17:2 (1–9);
    John 1:14.
    TG Witness.
17a TG Witness of the
    Father.
18a TG Revelation;
    Witness of the Father.
  b Luke 9:28 (28–36).
19a JST 2 Pet. 1:19 We have
    therefore a more sure
    knowledge of the word
    of prophecy, *to which*
    word of prophecy ye
    do well that ye take
    heed . . .
  b D&C 68:12; 88:3 (3–4);
    132:19, 49.
  c D&C 131:5.
  d Rev. 2:28; 22:16 (6–16).
20a JST 2 Pet. 1:20 . . .
    no prophecy of the

scriptures *is given* of any
    private *will of man.*
  b TG Prophecy.
  c TG Scriptures, Study of.
  d Gen. 40:8.
21a TG Prophecy;
    Scriptures, Value of;
    Scriptures, Writing of.
  b TG Holy Ghost,
    Mission of.
  c TG Inspiration.
  d TG Holy Ghost, Gifts of.
2 1a TG Apostasy of the
    Early Christian Church;
    False Prophets.
  b TG False Doctrine;
    False Priesthoods.
  c TG Teacher.
  d 1 Cor. 6:20.
2a TG Truth.
3a Rom. 16:18.
  b Deut. 32:35.

  c TG Damnation.
4a TG Angels;
    Death, Spiritual, First;
    Spirits, Evil or Unclean.
  b 1 Tim. 3:6.
    TG Hell.
  c TG Judgment, the Last.
5a Gen. 8:1;
    Heb. 11:7;
    1 Pet. 3:20 (20–21).
  b TG Righteousness.
  c TG Earth, Cleansing of;
    Flood.
6a Gen. 19:24;
    Jude 1:7 (4–7).
  b GR token, example.
7a Gen. 19:15 (12–22).
  b GR oppressed by the
    outrageous behavior
    of the lawless.
  c TG Filthiness.

ªvexed *his* righteous soul from day to day with *their* unlawful deeds;)

9 The Lord knoweth how to ªdeliver the ᵇgodly out of ᶜtemptations, and to ᵈreserve the unjust unto the day of ᵉjudgment to be punished.

10 But chiefly them that ªwalk after the flesh in the ᵇlust of ᶜuncleanness, and despise ᵈgovernment. ᵉPresumptuous *are they,* selfwilled, they are not afraid to speak evil of dignities.

11 Whereas angels, which are greater in power and might, bring not railing accusation against them before the Lord.

12 But these, as ªnatural brute beasts, made to be taken and destroyed, speak evil of the things that they understand not; and shall utterly ᵇperish in their own corruption;

13 And shall receive the ªreward of unrighteousness, *as* they that count it ᵇpleasure to ᶜriot in the day time. Spots *they are* and blemishes, sporting themselves with their own deceivings while they feast with you;

14 Having eyes full of adultery, and that cannot cease from sin; beguiling unstable souls: an heart they have exercised with covetous practices; cursed children:

15 Which have ªforsaken the right ᵇway, and are gone ᶜastray, following the way of ᵈBalaam *the son* of Bosor, who loved the ᵉwages of unrighteousness;

16 But was rebuked for his iniquity: the dumb ªass speaking with man's voice forbad the madness of the prophet.

17 These are ªwells without water, clouds that are carried with a tempest; to whom the ᵇmist of ᶜdarkness is reserved for ever.

18 For when they ªspeak great swelling *words* of ᵇvanity, they ᶜallure through the ᵈlusts of the flesh, *through much* wantonness, those that were clean ᵉescaped from them who live in error.

19 While they promise them ªliberty, they themselves are the ᵇservants of ᶜcorruption: for of whom a man is overcome, of the same is he brought in ᵈbondage.

20 For if after they have ªescaped the ᵇpollutions of the world through the knowledge of the Lord and Saviour Jesus Christ, they are ᶜagain ᵈentangled therein, and ᵉovercome, the latter end is ᶠworse with them than the beginning.

21 For it had been better for them not to have ªknown the way of ᵇrighteousness, than, after they have known *it,* to ᶜturn from the holy commandment delivered unto them.

22 But it is happened unto them according to the true proverb, The dog *is* turned to his own ªvomit again; and the sow that was ᵇwashed to her wallowing in the mire.

8a GR oppressed, afflicted.
9a TG Deliver.
  b TG Godliness.
  c TG Temptation.
  d D&C 38:5 (5–6).
  e Alma 11:44 (41–44);
    12:15 (14–18).
10a TG Walking in Darkness.
  b TG Lust;
    Sexual Immorality.
  c TG Uncleanness.
  d GR constituted authority.
    TG Governments.
  e TG Boast.
12a Mosiah 3:19.
  b Morm. 4:5.
13a TG Reward.
  b TG Pleasure.
  c TG Rioting and Reveling.
15a TG Apostasy of
    Individuals.

 b Hag. 1:7.
 c Prov. 21:16;
   Isa. 53:6.
 d Num. 22:5;
   Deut. 23:4;
   Rev. 2:14 (12–17).
 e TG Selfishness;
   Wages.
16a Num. 22:30.
17a Jude 1:12 (7–21).
 b 1 Ne. 76:23 (23–24); 12:17.
 c D&C 95:12;
   133:72 (71–74).
18a Ps. 73:8;
   Jude 1:16.
 b TG Vanity.
 c GR entice, entrap.
 d Jude 1:11 (7–21).
 e 2 Pet. 1:4.
19a TG Liberty.
 b GR slaves.

   Jude 1:4.
 c TG Sin.
 d TG Bondage, Spiritual.
20a Heb. 6:4 (4–6);
   1 Ne. 8:28 (24–28).
 b TG Pollution.
 c Ps. 85:8;
   D&C 42:26.
 d 2 Cor. 2:11;
   D&C 20:5.
 e D&C 76:35 (34–35).
 f Alma 24:30.
21a TG God, Knowledge
   about.
 b TG Righteousness.
 c Heb. 10:39.
22a Prov. 26:11.
   TG Apostasy of Individuals; Apostasy of the
   Early Christian Church.
 b TG Wash.

CHAPTER 3

Some in the latter days will doubt the Second Coming—The elements will melt at the coming of the Lord.

THIS second epistle, beloved, I now *a*write unto you; in *both* which I stir up your pure minds by way of *b*remembrance:

2 That ye may be mindful of the words which were spoken before by the holy *a*prophets, and of the commandment of us the apostles of the Lord and Saviour:

3 *a*Knowing this first, that there shall come in the *b*last days scoffers, walking after their own *c*lusts,

4 And saying, *a*Where is the *b*promise of his *c*coming? for since the fathers fell asleep, all things continue as *they were* from the beginning of the creation.

5 For this they willingly are *a*ignorant of, that by the *b*word of God the heavens were of old, and the *c*earth standing out of the water and in the water:

6 Whereby the world that then was, being *a*overflowed with *b*water, perished:

7 But the heavens and the earth, which are now, by the same word are kept in store, reserved unto *a*fire against the day of judgment and *b*perdition of ungodly men.

8 But, beloved, be not ignorant of this one thing, that one day *is* with the Lord as a thousand *a*years, and a thousand years as one day.

9 The Lord is not slack concerning his promise, as some men count slackness; but is *a*longsuffering to us-ward, not willing that any should *b*perish, but that all should come to *c*repentance.

10 But the *a*day of the Lord will *b*come as a thief in the night; in the which the heavens shall *c*pass away with a great noise, and the *d*elements shall melt with fervent heat, the *e*earth also and the works that are therein shall be burned up.

11 *Seeing* then *that* all these things shall be dissolved, what *a*manner *of persons* ought ye to be in *all* holy *b*conversation and godliness,

12 *a*Looking for and *b*hasting unto the *c*coming of the *d*day of God, wherein the heavens being on fire shall be dissolved, and the elements shall melt with fervent heat?

13 Nevertheless we, according to his promise, look for new *a*heavens and a *b*new *c*earth, wherein dwelleth *d*righteousness.

14 Wherefore, beloved, seeing that ye look for such things, be *a*diligent that ye may be found of him in peace, without *b*spot, and blameless.

15 And *a*account *that* the *b*longsuffering of our Lord *is* salvation; even as our beloved brother Paul also according to the wisdom given unto him hath written unto you;

16 As also in all *his* epistles, speaking in them of these things; in which are some things hard to be understood, which they that are unlearned

---

3 1*a* TG Scriptures, Writing of.
  b Alma 5:6 (3–13).
2*a* 1 Pet. 1:10.
  TG Prophets, Mission of.
3*a* JST 2 Pet. 3:3–13 (Appendix).
  b TG Last Days.
  c TG Lust; Selfishness.
4*a* D&C 45:26.
  b Matt. 16:3 (1–5).
  c Isa. 5:19 (18–19).
5*a* TG Ignorance.
  b TG Jesus Christ, Creator.
  c TG Creation.
6*a* TG Flood.
  b Gen. 7:19.

7*a* TG Earth, Cleansing of.
  b TG Death, Spiritual, Second;
  Sons of Perdition.
8*a* Alma 40:8;
  Abr. 3:4 (4–9).
  TG Time.
9*a* TG Forbear.
  b Ezek. 18:23 (23–24).
  c TG Repent.
10*a* TG Day of the Lord.
  b TG Jesus Christ, Second Coming.
  c Ps. 102:26 (25–26);
  Isa. 51:6.
  d TG World, End of.
  e TG Earth, Destiny of.
11*a* 3 Ne. 27:27.

  b 1 Pet. 1:15.
12*a* D&C 35:15; 49:23.
  b TG Haste.
  c Heb. 9:28;
  Rev. 1:7;
  D&C 39:23.
  d D&C 45:30.
13*a* TG Heaven.
  b TG Earth, Renewal of;
  Millennium.
  c Ether 13:9.
  d TG Righteousness.
14*a* D&C 88:63; 101:38.
  TG Dedication;
  Diligence.
  b D&C 38:31.
15*a* GR count, regard.
  b TG Forbear.

and unstable *wrest, as *they do* also the other *b*scriptures, unto their own destruction.

17 Ye therefore, beloved, *seeing ye know *these things* before, beware lest ye also, being *b*led *c*away with the error of the wicked, fall from your own *d*steadfastness.

18 But grow in *grace, and *in* the knowledge of our Lord and Saviour Jesus Christ. To him *be* glory both now and for ever. Amen.

THE FIRST EPISTLE GENERAL OF
JOHN

CHAPTER 1

The Saints gain fellowship with God by obedience—We must confess our sins to gain forgiveness.

*a*THAT which was from the *b*beginning, which we have heard, which we have seen with our eyes, which we have looked upon, and our hands have handled, of the *c*Word of life;

2 (For the life was manifested, and we have seen *it,* and bear witness, and *a*shew unto you that *b*eternal life, which was with the Father, and was manifested unto us;)

3 That which we have *a*seen and heard declare we unto you, that ye also may have fellowship with us: and truly our *b*fellowship *is* with the *c*Father, and with his Son Jesus Christ.

4 And these things *a*write we unto you, that your joy may be full.

5 This then is the message which we have heard of him, and declare unto you, that God is *a*light, and in him is no *b*darkness at all.

6 If we say that we have fellowship with him, and *a*walk in *b*darkness, we lie, and do not the truth:

7 But if we *a*walk in the light, as he is in the light, we have fellowship one with another, and the *b*blood of Jesus Christ his Son *c*cleanseth us from all sin.

8 If we say that we have *a*no *b*sin, we *c*deceive ourselves, and the truth is not in us.

9 If we *a*confess our sins, he is

16*a* GR twist, distort.
　　1 Ne. 13:29 (24–29);
　　Alma 13:20;
　　D&C 10:63.
　b TG Scriptures,
　　Preservation of.
17*a* JST 2 Pet. 3:17 . . . seeing
　　ye know before *the*
　　things which are coming,
　　beware lest . . .
　b 2 Ne. 28:14 (3–14).
　c TG Apostasy of the
　　Early Christian Church.
　d TG Steadfastness.
18*a* TG Grace.

[1 JOHN]

1 1*a* JST 1 Jn. 1:1 *Brethren, this*

is the testimony which we
give of that which was
from the beginning . . .
　b John 1:2 (1–4, 14).
　c TG Jesus Christ,
　　Messenger of the
　　Covenant.
2*a* GR declare, announce,
　　bring tidings.
　b John 17:3;
　　1 Jn. 5:20.
3*a* TG Witness.
　b TG Fellowshipping.
　c Moses 6:68.
4*a* TG Scriptures, Writing of.
5*a* John 8:12.
　　TG God, Perfection of;
　　Light [noun].

　b TG Darkness, Spiritual;
　　Walking in Darkness.
6*a* TG Walking in Darkness.
　b 2 Ne. 15:20.
7*a* TG Walking with God.
　b Acts 20:28;
　　Rev. 7:14;
　　D&C 29:17.
　　TG Blood, Symbolism of.
　c Rev. 12:11 (10–12);
　　D&C 50:28.
　　TG Jesus Christ,
　　Atonement through.
8*a* Prov. 30:20.
　b TG Sin.
　c TG Lying.
9*a* TG Confession;
　　Repent.

faithful and *b*just to *c*forgive us *our* sins, and to *d*cleanse us from all unrighteousness.

10 If we say that we have *a*not sinned, we make him a liar, and his word is not in us.

CHAPTER 2

Christ is our Advocate with the Father— We know God by obedience—Love not the world—Anti-Christs will come in the last days.

My little children, these things write I unto you, that ye sin not. *a*And if any man sin, we have an *b*advocate with the Father, Jesus Christ the righteous:

2 And he is the *a*propitiation for our sins: and not for ours only, but also for *the sins of* the whole *b*world.

3 And hereby we do know that we know him, if we *a*keep his commandments.

4 He that saith, I know him, and keepeth not his *a*commandments, is a *b*liar, and the truth is not in him.

5 But whoso *a*keepeth his word, in him verily is the love of God perfected: hereby know we that we are *b*in him.

6 He that saith he *a*abideth in him ought himself also so to *b*walk, even as he walked.

7 *a*Brethren, I write no new com-

mandment unto you, but an old commandment which ye had from the beginning. The old commandment is the word which ye have heard from the beginning.

8 Again, a new commandment I write unto you, *a*which thing is true in him and in you: because the *b*darkness is *c*past, and the true *d*light now shineth.

9 He that saith he is in the light, and hateth his brother, is in darkness even until now.

10 He that *a*loveth his *b*brother abideth in the light, and there is none occasion of stumbling in him.

11 But he that hateth his brother is in darkness, and *a*walketh in darkness, and knoweth not whither he goeth, because that darkness hath blinded his eyes.

12 I *a*write unto you, little *b*children, because your sins are forgiven you *c*for his *d*name's sake.

13 I write unto you, fathers, because ye have known him *that is* from the beginning. I write unto you, young men, because ye have overcome the wicked one. I write unto you, little children, because ye have known the Father.

14 I have written unto you, fathers, because ye have known him *that is* from the beginning. I have written unto you, young men, because ye

---

9b TG God, Justice of; Justice.
c TG Forgive.
d TG Purification; Purity.
10a Prov. 28:13.
2 1a JST 1 Jn. 2:1 . . . *But if any man sin and repent, we have an advocate* . . .
b GR intercessor, helper, comforter.
TG Jesus Christ, Authority of; Jesus Christ, Relationships with the Father; Salvation, Plan of.
2a TG Jesus Christ, Atonement through; Jesus Christ, Redeemer; Jesus Christ, Savior; Redemption; Remission of Sins.

b Alma 11:41 (40–41); D&C 21:9; 76:41 (41–43).
3a 1 Jn. 3:22 (22–24); 5:3 (2–3).
4a 1 Jn. 3:6.
b TG Lying.
5a TG Obedience.
b 2 Cor. 5:17.
6a John 15:4.
b Matt. 11:29; 2 Ne. 31:12 (12–13); Moro. 7:4 (3–4); D&C 19:23.
7a JST 1 Jn. 2:7 Brethren, I write *a* new commandment unto you, but *it is the same* commandment which ye had from the beginning . . .
8a JST 1 Jn. 2:8 . . . which thing *was of old ordained of God; and* is true in

him, and in you . . .
b TG Darkness, Spiritual.
c GR passing away.
d 2 Ne. 3:5; D&C 50:24.
10a D&C 95:12.
TG Family, Love within; Love.
b TG Brotherhood and Sisterhood.
11a TG Walking in Darkness.
12a TG Scriptures, Writing of.
b Mosiah 5:7; Moses 6:52.
c GR because of, through His name.
d 1 Sam. 12:22; Ps. 23:3; Acts 4:12; 1 Ne. 20:9.

are strong, and the word of God abideth in you, and ye have overcome the wicked one.

15 Love not the [a]world, neither the things *that are* in the [b]world. If any man love the world, the [c]love of the Father is not in him.

16 For all that *is* in the world, the [a]lust of the flesh, and the lust of the eyes, and the [b]pride of life, is not of the Father, but is of the [c]world.

17 And the [a]world [b]passeth away, and the lust thereof: but he that doeth the [c]will of God [d]abideth for ever.

18 Little children, it is the last time: and as ye have heard that [a]antichrist shall come, even now are there many [b]antichrists; whereby we know that it is the last time.

19 They went out from us, but they were not of us; for if they had been of us, they would *no doubt* have continued with us: but *they went out*, that they might be made manifest that they were not all of us.

20 But ye have an [a]unction from the [b]Holy One, and ye know all things.

21 I have not written unto you because ye know not the truth, but because ye know it, and that no lie is of the truth.

22 Who is a [a]liar but he that denieth that Jesus is the Christ? He is [b]antichrist, that denieth the Father and the Son.

23 Whosoever denieth the Son, the same hath not the Father: [*but*] he that [a]acknowledgeth the Son hath the Father also.

24 Let that therefore abide in you, which ye have heard from the beginning. If that which ye have heard from the [a]beginning shall remain in you, ye also shall continue in the Son, and in the Father.

25 And this is the [a]promise that he hath promised us, *even* [b]eternal life.

26 These *things* have I written unto you concerning them that [a]seduce you.

27 But the anointing which ye have received of him abideth in you, and ye need not that any man [a]teach you: but as the same [b]anointing [c]teacheth you of all things, and is truth, and is no lie, and even as it hath taught you, ye shall abide in him.

28 And now, little children, abide in him; that, when he shall appear, we may have confidence, and not be ashamed before him at his coming.

29 If ye know that he is righteous, ye know that every one that doeth [a]righteousness is [b]born of him.

CHAPTER 3

The sons of God will become like Christ—Love for others is required to gain eternal life—Obedience ensures us an answer to our prayers.

BEHOLD, what manner of [a]love the Father hath bestowed upon us, that we should be called the [b]sons of God: therefore the [c]world knoweth us not, because it knew him not.

2 Beloved, now are we the [a]sons of God, and it doth not yet appear what we shall be: but we know that, when he shall [b]appear, we shall be

15a TG World.
  b TG Worldliness.
  c D&C 95:12.
16a TG Chastity;
    Lust;
    Sensuality.
  b GR haughtiness,
    ostentation.
    TG Pride.
  c Mark 7:21 (21–22).
17a 1 Cor. 7:31 (29–31).
  b TG World, End of.
  c TG God, Will of.
  d Ps. 125:1;
    3 Ne. 14:21.
18a TG Antichrist;

False Prophets.
  b TG Apostasy of the
    Early Christian Church.
20a GR anointing.
  b TG Holiness.
22a Alma 5:39 (38–40).
  b TG Antichrist.
23a John 14:7.
24a 2 Jn. 1:6.
25a D&C 88:4.
    TG Promise.
  b John 17:3 (2–3);
    2 Ne. 31:20.
26a GR deceive, lead astray,
    cause to wander.
27a D&C 43:15.

  b TG Anointing.
  c John 6:45;
    1 Thes. 4:9.
29a TG Righteousness.
  b TG Man, New,
    Spiritually Reborn.
3 1a TG God, Love of.
  b GR children, people.
    Isa. 56:5.
  c TG World.
  2a GR children, people.
    TG Sons and Daughters
    of God.
  b Col. 3:4.
    TG God, Body of,
    Corporeal Nature.

^clike him; for we shall ^dsee him as he is.

3 And every man that hath this ^ahope in him ^bpurifieth himself, even as he is ^cpure.

4 Whosoever committeth sin ^atransgresseth also the law: for ^bsin is the transgression of the law.

5 And ye know that he was manifested to take away our ^asins; and in him is no sin.

6 Whosoever abideth in him ^asinneth not: ^bwhosoever sinneth hath not seen him, neither ^cknown him.

7 Little children, let no man deceive you: he that doeth righteousness is righteous, even as he is righteous.

8 He that ^acommitteth ^bsin is of the devil; for the devil ^csinneth from the beginning. For this purpose the Son of God was manifested, that he might destroy the works of the ^ddevil.

9 Whosoever is ^aborn of God ^bdoth not commit sin; for his seed remaineth in him: and he cannot sin, because he is born of God.

10 In this the children of God are ^amanifest, and the ^bchildren of the devil: whosoever doeth not ^crighteousness is not of God, neither he that loveth not his brother.

11 For this is the ^amessage that ye heard from the beginning, that we should love one another.

12 Not as ^aCain, *who* was of that wicked one, and slew his brother. And wherefore slew he him? Because his own works were evil, and his brother's righteous.

13 Marvel not, my brethren, if the world hate you.

14 We know that we have passed from death unto ^alife, because we love the ^bbrethren. He that ^cloveth not *his* brother abideth in ^ddeath.

15 Whosoever ^ahateth his brother is a murderer: and ye know that no ^bmurderer hath eternal life abiding in him.

16 Hereby perceive we the ^alove *of* ^bGod, because he laid down his life for us: and we ought to lay down *our* lives for the brethren.

17 But whoso hath this world's good, and seeth his ^abrother have ^bneed, and ^cshutteth up his bowels *of* ^dcompassion from him, how dwelleth the love of God in him?

18 My little children, let us not love in word, ^aneither in tongue; but in ^bdeed and in truth.

19 And hereby we know that we are of the truth, and shall assure our hearts before him.

2*c* Alma 5:19 (14, 19);
   Moro. 7:48 (47–48).
   TG Eternal Life; Man,
   Potential to Become
   like Heavenly Father;
   Resurrection.
d Job 19:26 (25–27).
   TG God, Privilege of
   Seeing.
3*a* TG Hope; Motivations.
b TG Chastity; Purification;
   Purity.
c 2 Cor. 5:21;
   1 Pet. 1:16 (15–19);
   2 Ne. 31:5 (5–7).
4*a* TG Transgress.
b TG Sin.
5*a* TG Forgive;
   Jesus Christ, Atonement
   through;
   Jesus Christ, Redeemer.
6*a* TG Sin.
b JST 1 Jn. 3:6 . . .
   whosoever *continueth in*
   sin hath not seen . . .

c 1 Jn. 2:4.
8*a* JST 1 Jn. 3:8 . . .
   continueth in sin . . .
b TG Sin.
c Gen. 3:1.
d TG Devil.
9*a* TG Man, New,
   Spiritually Reborn.
b JST 1 Jn. 3:9 . . . doth not
   continue in sin; for *the*
   Spirit of God remaineth
   in him; and he cannot
   continue in sin, because
   he is born of God,
   having received that holy
   Spirit of promise.
10*a* GR conspicuous,
   apparent.
b John 8:44;
   Acts 13:10.
c Matt. 7:20.
11*a* GR precept, doctrine.
12*a* Jude 1:11 (7–13).
14*a* John 5:24;
b 1 Cor. 8:12;

1 Tim. 6:2;
   D&C 45:5; 108:7.
   TG Brotherhood and
   Sisterhood.
c TG Love.
d TG Death, Spiritual,
   First.
15*a* Ps. 109:5 (3–5).
   TG Hate.
b TG Life, Sanctity of;
   Murder.
16*a* John 10:15 (14–15);
   15:13;
   1 Ne. 11:22 (22, 25).
b JST 1 Jn. 3:16 . . . *Christ* . . .
17*a* 1 Jn. 4:20 (20–21).
b Luke 3:11.
c GR is hardhearted,
   void of compassion.
   TG Hardheartedness.
d Mosiah 4:22 (22–25).
   TG Compassion.
18*a* JST 1 Jn. 3:18 . . . neither
   in tongue *only* . . .
b TG Good Works.

20 For if our heart condemn us, God is greater than our heart, and ^aknoweth all things.

21 Beloved, if our heart condemn us not, *then* have we ^aconfidence toward God.

22 And whatsoever we ^aask, we receive of him, because we ^bkeep his ^ccommandments, and do those things that are pleasing in his sight.

23 And this is his ^acommandment, That we should ^bbelieve on the ^cname of his Son Jesus Christ, and ^dlove one another, as he gave us commandment.

24 And he that keepeth his commandments ^adwelleth in him, and he in him. And hereby we know that he ^babideth in us, by the ^cSpirit which he hath given us.

CHAPTER 4

Try the spirits—God is love and dwells in those who love Him.

BELOVED, believe not every ^aspirit, but ^btry the ^cspirits whether they are of God: because many ^dfalse prophets are gone out into the world.

2 Hereby ^aknow ye the ^bSpirit of God: Every spirit that confesseth that Jesus Christ is come in the ^cflesh is of God:

3 And every spirit that confesseth not that Jesus Christ is come in the flesh is ^anot of God: and this is that *spirit* of ^bantichrist, whereof ye have heard that it should come; and even now already is it in the world.

4 Ye are of God, little children, and have overcome them: because greater is he that is in you, than he that is in the world.

5 They are of the ^aworld: therefore speak they of the world, and the world heareth them.

6 We are of God: he that knoweth God ^aheareth us; he that is not of God heareth not us. Hereby ^bknow we the ^cspirit of truth, and the spirit of ^derror.

7 Beloved, let us ^alove one another: for ^blove is of God; and every one that loveth is ^cborn of God, and knoweth God.

8 He that loveth not ^aknoweth not God; for God is love.

9 In this was manifested the love of God toward us, because that God sent his only begotten Son into the world, that we might ^alive through him.

10 Herein is love, not that we loved God, but that he ^aloved us, and ^bsent his Son *to be* the ^cpropitiation for our sins.

11 Beloved, if God so loved us, we ought also to love one another.

12 ^aNo man hath ^bseen God at any time. If we love one another, ^cGod

---

20*a* TG God, Intelligence of.
21*a* Alma 5:27.
22*a* TG Prayer.
   b 1 Jn. 2:3.
   c TG Good Works.
23*a* TG Commandments of God.
   b TG Faith.
   c 2 Ne. 25:20;
     Mosiah 3:17;
     D&C 11:30; 20:29.
     TG Jesus Christ, Taking the Name of.
   d TG Family, Love within.
24*a* John 6:56;
     Rom. 8:9;
     1 Cor. 2:16;
     2 Cor. 13:5;
     1 Jn. 4:13 (7–21).
   b John 14:23.
   c 1 Cor. 2:10; 1 Thes. 4:8.
4 1*a* Moro. 7:12 (12–17).
   b GR test, prove by trial,

discern.
    1 Thes. 5:21;
    D&C 11:12 (12–14);
    50:31 (1–3, 31–35);
    129:9 (1–9).
   c TG Spirits, Evil or Unclean.
   d TG Apostasy of the Early Christian Church; False Prophets.
 2*a* TG Discernment, Spiritual.
   b TG God, Spirit of.
   c TG Flesh and Blood.
 3*a* D&C 50:32.
   b TG Antichrist.
 5*a* TG Worldliness.
 6*a* John 8:47; 13:20;
    D&C 1:38 (14, 37–38);
    29:7; 84:36 (35–39).
   b TG Discernment, Spiritual.
   c TG Holy Ghost,

Mission of.
   d GR deception, wandering, sin.
 7*a* TG Love.
   b TG God, Love of.
   c TG Man, New, Spiritually Reborn.
 8*a* John 17:3.
 9*a* John 3:16.
10*a* 2 Thes. 2:16.
   b TG Jesus Christ, Authority of.
   c TG Jesus Christ, Atonement through; Jesus Christ, Redeemer.
12*a* JST 1 Jn. 4:12 No man hath seen God at any time, *except them who believe* . . .
   b D&C 93:1; 110:2 (1–3); Abr. 3:11 (11–12); JS—H 1:17 (16–17).
   c 2 Cor. 13:5.

ᵈdwelleth in us, and his love is perfected in us.

13 Hereby know we that we ᵃdwell in him, and he in us, because he hath given us of his Spirit.

14 And we have seen and do ᵃtestify that the Father ᵇsent the Son *to be* the ᶜSaviour of the ᵈworld.

15 Whosoever shall ᵃconfess that Jesus is the Son of God, God dwelleth in him, and he in God.

16 And we have known and believed the love that God hath to us. God is love; and he that ᵃdwelleth in love dwelleth in God, and God in him.

17 Herein is our love made perfect, that we may have boldness in the day of judgment: because as he ᵃis, so are we in this world.

18 There is no ᵃfear in ᵇlove; but perfect ᶜlove casteth out fear: because fear hath ᵈtorment. He that feareth is not made perfect in love.

19 We ᵃlove him, because he first loved us.

20 If a man say, I love God, and ᵃhateth his ᵇbrother, he is a ᶜliar: for he that loveth not his ᵈbrother whom he hath seen, how can he love God whom he hath not ᵉseen?

21 And this commandment have we from him, That he who ᵃloveth God love his brother also.

CHAPTER 5

Saints are born of God through belief in Christ—Water, blood, and the Spirit testify of Christ—Belief in Christ is required in order to gain eternal life.

WHOSOEVER believeth that Jesus is the Christ is born of God: and every one that loveth him that begat loveth him also that is begotten of him.

2 By this we know that we ᵃlove the ᵇchildren of God, when we love God, and keep his commandments.

3 For this is the ᵃlove of God, that we ᵇkeep his commandments: and his commandments are not ᶜgrievous.

4 For whatsoever is ᵃborn of God ᵇovercometh the world: and this is the ᶜvictory that overcometh the world, *even* our faith.

5 Who is he that ᵃovercometh the world, but he that believeth that Jesus is the Son of God?

6 This is he that ᵃcame by water and blood, *even* Jesus Christ; not by water only, but by water and blood. And it is the ᵇSpirit that beareth ᶜwitness, because the Spirit is truth.

7 For there are three that bear record in heaven, the ᵃFather, the Word, and the Holy Ghost: and these three are ᵇone.

8 And there are three that bear witness in earth, the ᵃSpirit, and the water, and the ᵇblood: and these three agree in one.

9 If we receive the ᵃwitness of men, the ᵇwitness of God is greater: for this is the ᶜwitness of God which he hath testified of his Son.

12*d* 1 Cor. 2:16.	19*a* TG Love.	Matt. 11:30.
13*a* 1 Jn. 3:24.	20*a* TG Family, Love within;	4*a* Rom. 12:2 (1–2).
14*a* TG Witness.	Hate.	*b* Rev. 3:21;
b TG Jesus Christ,	*b* TG Brotherhood and	D&C 64:2.
Authority of.	Sisterhood.	*c* 1 Cor. 15:57.
c TG Jesus Christ, Savior.	*c* TG Lying.	5*a* Rev. 2:7 (1–7).
d D&C 66:1.	*d* 1 Jn. 3:17 (10–18).	6*a* TG Jesus Christ,
15*a* TG Testimony.	*e* TG God, Privilege of	Condescension of.
16*a* D&C 42:45.	Seeing.	*b* D&C 1:39.
17*a* TG Jesus Christ,	21*a* TG Fellowshipping;	*c* TG Holy Ghost,
Exemplar.	Love.	Mission of.
18*a* Philip. 1:14 (12–17);	5 2*a* TG Family, Love within.	7*a* TG Godhead.
D&C 50:41 (41, 42).	*b* TG Sons and Daughters	*b* TG Unity.
TG Courage;	of God.	8*a* Moses 6:59 (59–60).
Fearful.	3*a* TG God, the Standard of	*b* TG Blood, Symbolism of.
b TG Family, Love within.	Righteousness.	9*a* D&C 6:23 (22–24).
c TG Love.	*b* 1 Jn. 2:3.	*b* TG Witness.
d GR correction,	*c* GR burdensome,	*c* TG Witness of the Father.
punishment.	oppressive.	

10 He that ^abelieveth on the Son of God hath the ^bwitness in himself: he that believeth not God hath made him a liar; because he believeth not the ^crecord that God gave of his Son.

11 And this is the record, that God hath given to us ^aeternal life, and this ^blife is in his Son.

12 He that hath the Son hath life; *and* he that hath not the Son of God hath not life.

13 These things have I ^awritten unto you that believe on the name of the Son of God; that ye may know that ye have eternal ^blife, and that ye may believe on the name of the Son of God.

14 And this is the confidence that we have in him, that, if we ask any thing according to his ^awill, he ^bheareth us:

15 And if we know that he hear us, whatsoever we ^aask, we know that we have the petitions that we ^bdesired of him.

16 If any man see his brother sin a sin *which is* not unto death, he shall ask, and he shall give him life for them that sin not unto death. There is a sin unto death: I do not say that he shall pray for it.

17 All unrighteousness is ^asin: and there is a ^bsin not unto death.

18 We know that whosoever is ^aborn of God ^bsinneth not; but he that is begotten of God ^ckeepeth himself, and that ^dwicked one toucheth him not.

19 *And* we know that we are of ^aGod, and the whole ^bworld lieth in ^cwickedness.

20 And we know that the Son of God is come, and hath given us an understanding, that we may know him that is true, and we are in him that is true, *even* in his Son Jesus Christ. This is the true God, and ^aeternal life.

21 Little children, keep yourselves from idols. Amen.

THE SECOND EPISTLE OF

JOHN

John rejoices because the children of the elect lady are true and faithful.

THE elder unto the elect lady and her children, whom I love in the truth; and not I only, but also all they that have known the truth;

2 For the truth's sake, which dwelleth in us, and shall be with us for ever.

3 Grace be with you, mercy, *and* peace, from God the Father, and from the Lord Jesus Christ, the Son of the Father, in truth and love.

4 I rejoiced greatly that I found of

10a TG Faith.
  b TG Testimony.
  c GR testimony, witness.
11a TG Eternal Life.
  b John 1:4;
    2 Tim. 1:10.
13a John 20:31.
    TG Record Keeping.
  b 2 Ne. 31:20.
14a TG God, Will of.

  b Ps. 4:1 (1, 3).
15a TG Prayer.
  b Ps. 145:19.
17a TG Sin.
  b D&C 64:7.
18a TG Man, New,
    Spiritually Reborn.
  b JST 1 Jn. 5:18 . . .
    continueth not in sin;
    but he that is begotten

    of God *and* keepeth
    himself, that wicked
    one *overcometh* him not.
  c GR guards, shields.
  d James 1:27 (22–27).
19a TG Called of God.
  b D&C 84:49 (49–53).
  c TG Wickedness.
20a 1 Jn. 1:2.

thy children walking in truth, as we have received a commandment from the Father.

5 And now I beseech thee, lady, not as though I wrote a new commandment unto thee, but that which we had from the beginning, that we love one another.

6 And this is ^alove, that we ^bwalk after his commandments. This is the commandment, That, as ye have heard from the ^cbeginning, ye should walk in it.

7 For many ^adeceivers are entered into the world, who confess not that Jesus Christ is come in the flesh. This is a deceiver and an ^bantichrist.

8 Look to yourselves, that we lose not those things which we have ^awrought, but that we receive a full reward.

9 Whosoever transgresseth, and abideth not in the doctrine of Christ, hath not God. He that abideth in the doctrine of Christ, he hath both the Father and the Son.

10 If there come any unto you, and bring not this doctrine, receive him not into *your* ^ahouse, neither bid him God speed:

11 For he that biddeth him God speed is ^apartaker of his evil deeds.

12 Having many things to write unto you, I would not ^a*write* with paper and ink: but I trust to come unto you, and speak face to face, that our joy may be full.

13 The children of thy elect sister greet thee. Amen.

THE THIRD EPISTLE OF

JOHN

John commends Gaius for his help to those who love the truth.

THE elder unto the wellbeloved Gaius, whom I love in the truth.

2 Beloved, I wish above all things that thou mayest prosper and be in health, even as thy soul prospereth.

3 For I rejoiced greatly, when the brethren came and testified of the truth that is in thee, even as thou walkest in the truth.

4 I have no greater ^ajoy than to hear that my ^bchildren ^cwalk in truth.

5 Beloved, thou doest faithfully whatsoever thou doest to the ^abrethren, and to ^bstrangers;

6 Which have borne witness of thy charity before the church: whom if thou bring forward on their journey after a godly sort, thou shalt do well:

7 Because that for his name's sake they went forth, taking nothing of the Gentiles.

8 We therefore ought to receive such, that we might be fellowhelpers to the truth.

9 I wrote unto the church: but Diotrephes, who loveth to have the

1 6*a* TG Family, Love within.
  b TG Walking with God.
  c 1 Jn. 2:24.
7*a* TG Deceit.
  b TG Antichrist.
8*a* GR performed,

acquired.
10*a* 1 Cor. 5:11.
11*a* 1 Tim. 5:22.
12*a* TG Scriptures,
    Writing of.

[3 JOHN]
1 4*a* TG Joy.
  b 1 Jn. 5:21.
  c TG Walking with God.
5*a* D&C 84:88 (88–92).
  b TG Stranger.

[a]preeminence among them, [b]receiveth us not.

10 Wherefore, if I come, I will remember his deeds which he doeth, [a]prating against us with malicious words: and not content therewith, neither doth he himself receive the brethren, and forbiddeth them that would, and casteth *them* out of the church.

11 Beloved, follow not that which is evil, but that which is good. He that doeth [a]good is of God: but he that doeth evil hath not seen God.

12 Demetrius hath good report of all *men,* and of the truth itself: yea, and we *also* bear record; and ye know that our [a]record is true.

13 I had many things to write, but I will not with ink and pen [a]write unto thee:

14 But I trust I shall shortly see thee, and we shall speak face to face. Peace *be* to thee. *Our* friends salute thee. Greet the friends by name.

THE GENERAL EPISTLE OF
JUDE

Contend for the faith—Some angels kept not their first estate—Michael disputed about the body of Moses—Enoch prophesied of the Second Coming—Mockers will come in the last days.

[a]JUDE, the [b]servant of Jesus Christ, and brother of James, to them that are sanctified by God the Father, and preserved in Jesus Christ, *and* called:

2 Mercy unto you, and peace, and love, be multiplied.

3 Beloved, when I gave all diligence to [a]write unto you of the common [b]salvation, it was needful for me to write unto you, and exhort *you* that ye should [c]earnestly [d]contend for the faith which was once delivered unto the saints.

4 For there are certain [a]men crept in unawares, who were before of old ordained to this condemnation, [b]ungodly men, turning the grace of our God into [c]lasciviousness, and [d]denying the only Lord God, and our Lord Jesus Christ.

5 I will therefore put you in remembrance, though ye once knew this, how that the Lord, having [a]saved the people out of the land of Egypt, afterward [b]destroyed them that [c]believed not.

6 And the [a]angels which kept not

9a TG Unrighteous
   Dominion.
  b TG Apostasy of the
   Early Christian Church.
10a Num. 16:3.
11a Moro. 7:12.
12a GR witness, testimony.
13a TG Scriptures, Writing of.

[JUDE]
1 1a JST Jude 1:1 Jude, the
   servant *of God, called*
   of Jesus Christ, and

brother of James; to
them *who* are sanctified
of the Father; and pre-
served in Jesus Christ;
  b TG Servant.
3a TG Scriptures, Lost.
  b 2 Ne. 2:4; 26:33;
   A of F 1:3.
  c TG Zeal.
  d Philip. 1:27;
   D&C 112:5.
4a 2 Pet. 2:19;
   D&C 29:45;

JS—H 1:19.
  b TG Godliness.
  c GR licentiousness.
  d TG Apostasy of the
   Early Christian Church.
5a 1 Cor. 10:5 (5, 9).
  b Deut. 1:35.
  c TG Unbelief.
6a TG Angels;
   Death, Spiritual, First;
   Devil;
   Sons of Perdition;
   Spirits, Evil or Unclean.

their *b*first *c*estate, but left their own habitation, he hath reserved in everlasting chains under darkness unto the *d*judgment of the great day.

7 Even as *a*Sodom and Gomorrha, and the cities about them in like manner, giving themselves over to *b*fornication, and going after *c*strange flesh, are set forth for an *d*example, suffering the *e*vengeance of eternal fire.

8 Likewise also these *a*filthy dreamers *b*defile the flesh, despise dominion, and speak evil of dignities.

9 Yet *a*Michael the *b*archangel, when contending with the devil he disputed about the body of *c*Moses, durst not bring against him a railing accusation, but said, The Lord rebuke thee.

10 But these speak evil of those things which they know not: but what they know naturally, as brute beasts, in those things they corrupt themselves.

11 Woe unto them! for they have gone in the way of *a*Cain, and ran greedily after the error of *b*Balaam for reward, and *c*perished in the gainsaying of Core.

12 These are spots in your feasts of charity, when they feast with you, feeding themselves without fear: *a*clouds *they are* without water, carried about of winds; trees whose fruit withereth, without fruit, twice dead, plucked up by the roots;

13 Raging waves of the sea, foaming out their own shame; wandering *a*stars, to whom is reserved the blackness of darkness for ever.

14 And *a*Enoch also, the seventh from Adam, prophesied of these, saying, Behold, the Lord *b*cometh with ten thousands of his *c*saints,

15 To *a*execute *b*judgment upon all, and to convince all that are ungodly among them of all their ungodly deeds which they have ungodly committed, and of all their hard *c*speeches which ungodly sinners have spoken against him.

16 These are *a*murmurers, complainers, walking after their own *b*lusts; and their mouth *c*speaketh great swelling *words,* having men's persons in admiration because of *d*advantage.

17 But, beloved, remember ye the words which were spoken before of the apostles of our Lord Jesus Christ;

18 How that they told you there should be *a*mockers in the *b*last time, who should *c*walk after their own ungodly lusts.

19 These be they who *a*separate themselves, sensual, having not the *b*Spirit.

20 But ye, beloved, *a*building up yourselves on your most holy faith, praying in the Holy Ghost,

21 Keep yourselves in the love of God, looking for the mercy of our Lord Jesus Christ unto eternal life.

22 And of some have *a*compassion, making a difference:

23 And others save with fear,

6*b* TG Man, Antemortal Existence of.
  c Abr. 3:26 (24–28).
  d TG Judgment, the Last.
7*a* Gen. 19:24; 2 Pet. 2:6 (1–9).
  b TG Fornication.
  c TG Homosexual Behavior.
  d TG Example.
  e D&C 76:105. TG Punish.
8*a* The Greek text omits "filthy."
  b TG Pollution.
9*a* TG Adam.
  b TG Angels.
  c TG Translated Beings.

11*a* Gen. 4:5 (1–15); 1 Jn. 3:12.
  b 2 Pet. 2:18.
  c JST Jude 1:11 . . . *shall perish . . .* Num. 16.
12*a* 2 Pet. 2:17.
13*a* TG Astronomy.
14*a* Gen. 5:23; Heb. 11:5 (5–6). Moses 6:27 (27–65). TG Scriptures, Lost.
  b 1 Thes. 4:17 (13–18); Moses 7:65 (62–66). TG Jesus Christ, Second Coming.
  c TG Saints.
15*a* TG Jesus Christ,

Authority of.
  b TG Accountability; Jesus Christ, Judge.
  c Ps. 139:20 (17–24).
16*a* TG Murmuring.
  b TG Lust.
  c 2 Pet. 2:18 (10–19).
  d GR profit, gain.
18*a* TG Apostasy of Individuals; Mocking.
  b TG Last Days.
  c TG Walking in Darkness.
19*a* Deut. 13:13; Judg. 20:13.
  b TG Holy Ghost, Loss of.
20*a* D&C 21:2.
22*a* TG Compassion.

pulling *them* out of the [a]fire; hating even the [b]garment spotted by the flesh.

24 Now unto him that is able to keep you from falling, and to present *you* [a]faultless before the presence of his glory with exceeding joy,

25 To the only wise God our Saviour, *be* glory and majesty, dominion and power, both now and ever. Amen.

THE REVELATION
OF ST JOHN THE DIVINE

CHAPTER 1

Christ chooses some as kings and priests unto God—Christ will come again—John sees the risen Lord.

[a]THE [b]Revelation of Jesus Christ, which God gave unto him, to shew unto his [c]servants things which must [d]shortly come to pass; and he sent and signified *it* by his [e]angel unto his servant John:

2 Who bare record of the word of God, and of the testimony of Jesus Christ, and of all things that he saw.

3 [a]Blessed *is* he that [b]readeth, and they that hear the words of this prophecy, and keep those things which are written therein: for the [c]time *is* at hand.

4 JOHN to the [a]seven churches which are in Asia: Grace *be* unto you, and peace, from him which [b]is, and which was, and which is to come; and from the seven [c]Spirits which are before his throne;

5 And from Jesus Christ, *who is* the faithful witness, *and* the [a]first begotten of the dead, and the prince of the kings of the earth. Unto him that loved us, and [b]washed us from our sins in his own [c]blood,

6 And hath made us [a]kings and [b]priests unto God and his Father; to him *be* [c]glory and [d]dominion for ever and ever. Amen.

7 Behold, he [a]cometh with clouds; and every eye shall [b]see him, and they *also* which pierced him: and all [c]kindreds of the earth shall [d]wail because of him. Even so, Amen.

8 I am [a]Alpha and Omega, the [b]beginning and the ending, saith the Lord, which is, and which was, and which is to come, the [c]Almighty.

9 I John, who also am your brother, and companion in tribulation, and

---

23a Amos 4:11; Mal. 4:1.
  b D&C 36:6.
24a Rev. 14:4 (2–5).

[REVELATION]

1 1a JST Rev. 1:1–8 (Appendix).
  b 1 Ne. 14:21 (18–27).
  TG Revelation.
  c TG Servant.
  d Rev. 22:6 (6–16); D&C 88:79.
  e Rev. 19:10 (6–10).
3a Rev. 22:7 (7, 18–19).
  b TG Scriptures, Study of.

  c D&C 34:7.
4a D&C 77:5.
  b TG Jesus Christ, Jehovah.
  c Rev. 3:1; 4:5.
5a TG Jesus Christ, Resurrection.
  b TG Jesus Christ, Redeemer.
  c TG Blood, Symbolism of.
6a TG Priesthood, Authority; Salvation, Plan of.
  b D&C 76:56 (50–60).
  TG Priest, Aaronic

  Priesthood.
  BD Priests.
  c TG Celestial Glory.
  d GR might, power.
7a 1 Thes. 2:19; 3:13; Heb. 9:28; 2 Pet. 3:12; Rev. 22:12.
  b TG Jesus Christ, Second Coming.
  c D&C 45:53 (49, 53).
  d Matt. 24:30.
8a D&C 35:1.
  b D&C 38:1.
  c Mosiah 3:5.
  TG God, Power of.

in the kingdom and ªpatience of Jesus Christ, was in the isle that is called Patmos, for the word of God, and for the testimony of Jesus Christ.

10 I was in the Spirit on the ªLord's ᵇday, and heard behind me a great ᶜvoice, as of a trumpet,

11 Saying, I am Alpha and Omega, the ªfirst and the last: and, What thou seest, ᵇwrite in a book, and send *it* unto the seven churches which are in Asia; unto Ephesus, and unto Smyrna, and unto Pergamos, and unto ᶜThyatira, and unto Sardis, and unto Philadelphia, and unto ᵈLaodicea.

12 And I turned to see the voice that spake with me. And being turned, I saw seven golden ªcandlesticks;

13 And in the midst of the seven candlesticks *one* like unto the ªSon of man, ᵇclothed with a garment down to the foot, and girt about the paps with a golden girdle.

14 His head and *his* hairs *were* white like wool, as white as snow; and his ªeyes *were* as a flame of ᵇfire;

15 And his feet like unto fine brass, as if they burned in a furnace; and his ªvoice as the sound of many waters.

16 And he had in his right hand seven stars: and out of his mouth went a sharp twoedged ªsword: and his ᵇcountenance *was* as the ᶜsun shineth in his strength.

17 And when I ªsaw him, I fell at his feet as dead. And he laid his right hand upon me, saying unto me, Fear not; I am the first and the last:

18 I *am* he that ªliveth, and was ᵇdead; and, behold, I am alive for ᶜevermore, Amen; and have the ᵈkeys of ᵉhell and of death.

19 ªWrite the things which thou hast seen, and the things which are, and the things which shall be hereafter;

20 The mystery of the seven stars which thou sawest in my right hand, and the seven golden candlesticks. The seven ªstars are the ᵇangels of the seven churches: and the seven ᶜcandlesticks which thou sawest are the seven churches.

CHAPTER 2

He who overcomes will gain eternal life, avoid the second death, inherit the celestial kingdom, and rule many kingdoms.

UNTO the ªangel of the church of Ephesus ᵇwrite; These things saith he that holdeth the seven stars in his right hand, who walketh in the midst of the seven golden candlesticks;

2 I ªknow thy works, and thy labour, and thy patience, and how thou canst not bear them which are evil: and thou hast tried them which say they are ᵇapostles, and are not, and hast found them liars:

9ª ᴛɢ Patience.
10ª ᴛɢ Sabbath.
  b ᴛɢ Jesus Christ, Types of, in Memory.
  c D&C 29:4.
11ª ᴛɢ Jesus Christ, Firstborn.
  b ᴛɢ Scriptures, Writing of.
  c Rev. 2:18.
  d Col. 2:1; 4:15 (12–16).
12ª Ex. 25:31.
13ª ᴛɢ Jesus Christ, Son of Man.
  b Dan. 10:5.
14ª Rev. 2:18; D&C 110:3.
  b ᴛɢ Jesus Christ, Glory of.

15ª Ezek. 1:24; 43:2; D&C 110:3; 133:22.
16ª Rev. 2:12 (12–17).
  b D&C 110:3.
  c JS—H 1:16 (16–17).
17ª ᴛɢ God, Privilege of Seeing; Jesus Christ, Appearances, Postmortal.
18ª ᴛɢ Jesus Christ, Resurrection; Resurrection.
  b ᴛɢ Jesus Christ, Death of.
  c ᴛɢ Immortality.
  d ᴛɢ Jesus Christ, Authority of.
  e ᴛɢ Hell.
19ª ᴛɢ Record Keeping.

20ª Rev. 3:1.
  b ᴊsᴛ Rev. 1:20 . . . *servants* . . . Rev. 2:18.
  c Ex. 37:17; Zech. 4:2 (1–14); Rev. 2:5.
2 1ª ᴊsᴛ Rev. 2:1 . . . *servant* . . . (Note: ᴊsᴛ uses "servant" in place of "angel" in vv. 1, 8, 12, and 18.)
  b ᴛɢ Scriptures, Writing of.
2ª ᴛɢ God, Omniscience of.
  b D&C 64:39 (38–39). ᴛɢ Apostasy of the Early Christian Church.

3 And hast borne, and hast patience, and for my name's sake hast laboured, and hast not fainted.

4 Nevertheless I have *somewhat* against thee, because thou hast left thy first [a]love.

5 Remember therefore from whence thou art fallen, and repent, and do the first works; or else I will come unto thee quickly, and will remove thy [a]candlestick out of his place, except thou [b]repent.

6 But this thou hast, that thou hatest the deeds of the [a]Nicolaitans, which I also hate.

7 He that hath an ear, let him hear what the [a]Spirit saith unto the churches; To him that [b]overcometh will I give to eat of the [c]tree of life, which is in the midst of the [d]paradise of God.

8 And unto the angel of the church in Smyrna write; These things saith the first and the last, which was dead, and is alive;

9 I know thy works, and tribulation, and poverty, (but thou art rich) and I *know* the [a]blasphemy of them which say they are Jews, and are not, but *are* the synagogue of Satan.

10 Fear none of those things which thou shalt [a]suffer: behold, the devil shall cast *some* of you into prison, that ye may be [b]tried; and ye shall have tribulation ten days: be thou faithful unto [c]death, and I will [d]give thee a [e]crown of life.

11 He that hath an ear, let him hear what the Spirit saith unto the churches; He that overcometh shall not be hurt of the second [a]death.

12 And to the angel of the church in Pergamos write; These things saith he which hath the sharp [a]sword with two edges;

13 I know thy works, and where thou dwellest, *even* where Satan's seat *is:* and thou holdest fast my name, and hast not denied my faith, even in those days wherein Antipas *was* my faithful [a]martyr, who was slain among you, where Satan dwelleth.

14 But I have a few things against thee, because thou hast there them that hold the doctrine of [a]Balaam, who taught Balac to cast a stumblingblock before the children of Israel, to eat things sacrificed unto idols, and to commit [b]fornication.

15 So hast thou also them that hold the doctrine of the Nicolaitans, which thing I hate.

16 Repent; or else I will come unto thee quickly, and will fight against them with the sword of my mouth.

17 He that hath an ear, let him hear what the Spirit saith unto the churches; To him that [a]overcometh will I give to eat of the hidden [b]manna, and will give him a [c]white [d]stone, and in the stone a new [e]name written, which no man knoweth saving he that receiveth *it.*

18 And unto the [a]angel of the church in [b]Thyatira write; These things saith the Son of God, who hath his [c]eyes like unto a flame of fire, and his feet *are* like fine brass;

19 I know thy works, and charity, and [a]service, and faith, and thy patience, and thy works; and the last *to be* more than the first.

4a D&C 4:2 (1–7).
5a Rev. 1:20.
  TG Apostasy of the Early
  Christian Church.
 b TG Repent.
6a TG Secret Combinations.
7a TG Holy Ghost, Gifts of.
 b 1 Jn. 5:5 (1–5);
  Rev. 2:26; 21:7.
 c Gen. 2:9;
  Rev. 22:2 (1–16);
  1 Ne. 8:10 (10–12).
 d TG Paradise.
9a TG Blaspheme.
10a TG Suffering.

 b TG Test.
 c D&C 6:13; 31:13.
  TG Martyrdom.
 d TG God, Gifts of.
 e D&C 20:14.
  TG Reward.
11a TG Death, Spiritual,
  Second.
12a Heb. 4:12;
  Rev. 1:16.
13a TG Martyrdom.
14a 2 Pet. 2:15 (10–22).
 b TG Sexual Immorality.
17a Rom. 6:22 (11–22);
  12:21 (4–21).

 b TG Bread of Life;
  Jesus Christ, Types of, in
  Anticipation.
 c D&C 130:11 (10–11).
 d TG Urim and Thummim.
 e Isa. 62:2; 65:15;
  Rev. 19:12 (12–16).
  TG Name.
18a Rev. 1:20.
 b Rev. 1:11.
 c Rev. 1:14;
  D&C 110:3 (2–3).
19a TG Service.

20 Notwithstanding I have a few things against thee, because thou sufferest that woman Jezebel, which calleth herself a prophetess, to teach and to seduce my servants to commit fornication, and to eat things sacrificed unto idols.

21 And I gave her space to repent of her fornication; and she repented not.

22 Behold, I will cast her ^ainto a bed, and them that commit ^badultery with her into great tribulation, except they repent of their deeds.

23 And I will kill her children with death; and all the churches shall know that I am he which ^asearcheth the ^breins and hearts: and I will give unto every one of you according to your works.

24 But unto you I say, and unto the rest in Thyatira, as many as have not this doctrine, and which have not known the depths of Satan, as they speak; I will put upon you none other burden.

25 But that which ye have *already* ^ahold fast till I come.

26 ^aAnd he that ^bovercometh, and keepeth my works unto the end, to him will I give ^cpower over the nations:

27 And he shall rule them with a ^arod of iron; as the ^bvessels of a potter shall they be broken to shivers: even as I received of my Father.

28 And I will give him the morning ^astar.

29 He that hath an ear, let him hear what the Spirit saith unto the churches.

CHAPTER 3

He who overcomes will retain his name in the book of life, reach godhood, and be with Jesus as He is with the Father.

^aAND unto the ^bangel of the church in Sardis write; These things saith he that hath the seven ^cSpirits of God, and the seven ^dstars; I ^eknow thy works, that thou hast a name that thou livest, and art ^fdead.

2 ^aBe watchful, and strengthen the things which remain, that are ready to die: for I have not found thy works perfect before God.

3 Remember therefore how thou hast received and heard, and hold fast, and repent. If therefore thou shalt not ^awatch, I will come on thee as a ^bthief, and thou shalt not know what hour I will come upon thee.

4 Thou hast a few names even in Sardis which have not ^adefiled their garments; and they shall ^bwalk with me in ^cwhite: for they are ^dworthy.

5 He that ^aovercometh, the same shall be clothed in ^bwhite ^craiment; and I will not ^dblot out his name out of the ^ebook of life, but I will ^fconfess his name before my Father, and before his angels.

6 He that hath an ear, let him hear what the Spirit saith unto the churches.

7 And to the angel of the church

22a JST Rev. 2:22 . . . into
   hell, and them . . .
   b TG Adulterer.
23a TG God, Omniscience of.
   b GR (from Hebrew)
   desires and thoughts.
25a 2 Ne. 31:20.
26a JST Rev. 2:26–27
   (Appendix).
   1 Ne. 11:25.
   b Rev. 2:7; 3:5.
   c Ps. 49:14;
   Mal. 4:3 (2–3).
27a Ps. 2:9;
   1 Ne. 11:25.
   b Ps. 31:12;
   D&C 76:33 (31–33).
28a 2 Pet. 1:19;

Rev. 22:16 (6–16).
3 1a JST Rev. 3:1 And unto
   the *servant* of the
   church in Sardis, write;
   These things saith he
   who hath the seven
   stars, which are the
   seven *servants of God;* I
   know thy . . .
   b Rev. 1:20.
   c Rev. 1:4.
   d Rev. 1:20 (16, 20).
   e GR clothing.
   f Eph. 2:1.
2a JST Rev. 3:2 Be watchful
   therefore, and strengthen
   those who remain, *who*
   are ready to die . . .

3a D&C 39:23.
   TG Watch.
   b Luke 21:35;
   Rev. 16:15.
4a TG Sacrilege.
   b TG Walking with God.
   c Rev. 6:11.
   d TG Worthiness.
5a Rev. 2:26;
   D&C 76:60.
   TG Salvation.
   b TG Remission of Sins.
   c GR clothing.
   d TG Book of Life.
   e TG Record Keeping.
   f GR acknowledge,
   praise.

in Philadelphia write; These things saith he that is holy, he that is true, he that hath the ^akey of David, he that openeth, and no man shutteth; and shutteth, and no man openeth;

8 I know thy works: behold, I have set before thee an open door, and no man can shut it: for thou hast a little strength, and hast kept my word, and hast not denied my name.

9 Behold, I will make them of the synagogue of Satan, which say they are Jews, and are not, but do lie; behold, I will make them to come and ^aworship before thy feet, and to know that I have loved thee.

10 Because thou hast kept the word of my patience, I also will ^akeep thee from the hour of ^btemptation, which shall come upon all the world, to try them that dwell upon the earth.

11 Behold, I come ^aquickly: hold that fast which thou hast, that no man take thy crown.

12 Him that overcometh will I make a pillar in the temple of my God, and he shall go no more out: and I will write upon him the ^aname of my God, and the name of the city of my God, *which is* ^bnew Jerusalem, which cometh down out of heaven from my God: and *I will write upon him* my new name.

13 He that hath an ear, let him hear what the Spirit saith unto the churches.

14 And unto the angel of the church of the Laodiceans write; These things saith the Amen, the ^afaithful and true witness, the ^bbeginning of the ^ccreation of God;

15 I know thy ^aworks, that thou art

neither cold nor hot: I would thou wert cold or hot.

16 So then because thou art ^alukewarm, and neither cold nor hot, I will ^bspue thee out of my mouth.

17 Because thou sayest, I am ^arich, and increased with goods, and have need of nothing; and knowest not that thou art wretched, and miserable, and poor, and blind, and naked:

18 I ^acounsel thee to buy of me ^bgold tried in the fire, that thou mayest be rich; and white raiment, that thou mayest be clothed, and *that* the shame of thy nakedness do not appear; and anoint thine eyes with eyesalve, that thou mayest see.

19 As many as I love, I rebuke and ^achasten: be zealous therefore, and repent.

20 Behold, I stand at the door, and knock: if any man hear my voice, and ^aopen the door, I will ^bcome in to him, and will sup with him, and he with me.

21 To him that ^aovercometh will I grant to ^bsit with me in my ^cthrone, even as I also overcame, and am set down with my Father in his throne.

22 He that hath an ear, let him hear what the Spirit saith unto the churches.

CHAPTER 4

John sees the celestial earth, the throne of God, and all created things worshipping the Lord.

AFTER this I looked, and, behold, a door *was* opened in heaven: and the first voice which I heard *was* as it were of a trumpet talking with me; which said, Come up hither, and I

7a TG Priesthood, Keys of; Sealing.
9a Isa. 49:23; 60:14.
　　TG Worship.
10a TG Refuge.
　 b TG Temptation; Test.
11a D&C 87:8.
12a Rev. 14:1; 22:4 (1–5).
　 b TG Jerusalem, New; Zion.
14a Jer. 42:5.

　 b TG Jesus Christ, Firstborn.
　 c TG Creation.
15a Isa. 66:18.
16a TG Apathy; Apostasy of the Early Christian Church.
　 b GR vomit.
17a TG Treasure.
18a TG Counsel.
　 b Matt. 13:46 (44–46); D&C 6:7.

19a GR instruct, admonish.
　　TG Chastening.
20a D&C 88:63.
　 b John 14:23 (23–25).
21a 1 Jn. 5:4 (4–5).
　 b D&C 6:30.
　 c Matt. 25:21.
　　TG Exaltation; Man, Potential to Become like Heavenly Father; Salvation, Plan of.

will ^ashew thee things which must be hereafter.

2 And immediately I was in the spirit: and, behold, a throne was set in heaven, and *one* sat on the throne.

3 And he that sat was to look upon like a jasper and a sardine stone: and *there was* a ^arainbow round about the throne, in sight like unto an emerald.

4 ^aAnd round about the throne *were* four and twenty ^bseats: and upon the seats I saw four and twenty ^celders sitting, clothed in white raiment; and they had on their heads crowns of gold.

5 And out of the throne proceeded lightnings and thunderings and voices: and *there were* seven lamps of fire burning before the throne, which are the ^aseven ^bSpirits of God.

6 And before the throne *there was* a ^asea of glass like unto crystal: ^band in the midst of the throne, and round about the throne, *were* four ^cbeasts full of eyes before and behind.

7 And the first beast *was* like a lion, and the second beast like a calf, and the third beast had a face as a man, and the fourth beast *was* like a flying eagle.

8 And the four beasts had each of them six wings about *him;* and *they were* full of eyes within: and they rest not day and night, saying, Holy, holy, holy, ^aLord God ^bAlmighty, which was, and is, and is to come.

9 And when those beasts give glory and honour and thanks to him that sat on the throne, who liveth for ever and ever,

10 The four and twenty elders fall down before him that sat on the throne, and worship him that liveth for ever and ever, and cast their crowns before the throne, saying,

11 Thou art worthy, O Lord, to receive glory and honour and power: for thou hast ^acreated all things, and ^bfor thy pleasure they are and were created.

CHAPTER 5

John sees the book sealed with seven seals, and he sees those people redeemed out of every nation—He hears every creature praising God and the Lamb.

AND I saw in the right hand of him that sat on the throne a book ^awritten within and on the backside, ^bsealed with seven ^cseals.

2 And I saw a strong angel proclaiming with a loud voice, Who is ^aworthy to open the book, and to loose the seals thereof?

3 And no man in heaven, nor in earth, neither under the earth, was able to open the book, neither to look thereon.

4 And I wept much, because no man was found worthy to open and to read the book, neither to look thereon.

5 And one of the elders saith unto me, Weep not: behold, the ^aLion of the tribe of ^bJuda, the ^cRoot of David, hath prevailed to open the book, and to loose the seven seals thereof.

6 And I beheld, and, lo, in the midst of the throne and of the four beasts, and in the midst of the elders, stood a ^aLamb as it had been slain, ^bhaving

---

4 1*a* TG Revelation.
  3*a* Ezek. 1:28.
  4*a* JST Rev. 4:4 And *in the midst of* the throne . . .
    b GR thrones.
    c D&C 77:5.
  5*a* JST Rev. 4:5 . . . seven *servants* . . .
    b Ezek. 1:13; Rev. 1:4.
  6*a* Ezek. 1:22; D&C 77:1.
    TG Earth, Destiny of.
    b JST Rev. 4:6 . . . and in the midst of the throne *were*

the four and twenty elders; and round about . . .
    c D&C 77:2.
    TG Cherubim; Symbolism.
  8*a* Isa. 6:3 (2–3); Ezek. 1:28 (9–11, 28).
    b TG God, Power of.
  11*a* TG Jesus Christ, Creator.
    b GR through, on account of Thy will.
5 1*a* Ezek. 2:9 (9–10).
    b D&C 77:6.
    c TG Seal.

2*a* TG Worthiness.
5*a* Gen. 49:9.
  b TG Israel, Judah, People of.
  c Isa. 11:10; Rev. 22:16 (6–16).
6*a* TG Jesus Christ, Types of, in Anticipation.
  b JST Rev. 5:6 . . . having *twelve* horns and *twelve* eyes, which are the *twelve servants* of God, sent forth into all the earth.

seven horns and seven eyes, which are the seven Spirits of God sent forth into all the earth.

7 And he came and took the book out of the right hand of him that sat upon the throne.

8 And when he had taken the book, the four beasts and four *and* twenty elders fell down before the Lamb, having every one of them harps, and golden vials full of *a*odours, which are the *b*prayers of saints.

9 And they *a*sung a new song, saying, Thou art worthy to take the book, and to open the seals thereof: for thou wast slain, and hast *b*redeemed us to God by thy blood out of every *c*kindred, and tongue, and people, and nation;

10 And hast made us unto our God kings and *a*priests: and we shall reign on the earth.

11 And I beheld, and I heard the voice of many angels round about the throne and the beasts and the elders: and the number of them was ten thousand times ten thousand, and *a*thousands of thousands;

12 Saying with a loud voice, Worthy is the *a*Lamb that was slain to receive *b*power, and riches, and *c*wisdom, and strength, and honour, and glory, and blessing.

13 And every *a*creature which is in heaven, and on the earth, and under the earth, and such as are in the sea, and all that are in them, heard I saying, Blessing, and honour, and glory, and *b*power, *be* unto him that sitteth upon the throne, and unto the Lamb for ever and ever.

14 And the four beasts said, Amen. And the four *and* twenty elders fell down and worshipped him that liveth for ever and ever.

CHAPTER 6

Christ opens the six seals, and John sees the events therein—In the fifth seal, he sees the Christian martyrs; and in the sixth, he sees the signs of the times.

*a*AND I saw when the Lamb opened one of the *b*seals, and I heard, as it were the noise of thunder, one of the four *c*beasts saying, Come and see.

2 And I saw, and behold a white horse: and he that sat on him had a bow; and a crown was given unto him: and he went forth conquering, and to conquer.

3 And when he had opened the *a*second seal, I heard the second beast say, Come and see.

4 And there went out another horse *that was* red: and *power* was given to him that sat thereon to take *a*peace from the earth, and that they should kill one another: and there was given unto him a great sword.

5 And when he had opened the third seal, I heard the third beast say, Come and see. And I beheld, and lo a black horse; and he that sat on him had a pair of balances in his hand.

6 And I heard a voice in the midst of the four beasts say, A measure of wheat for a penny, and three measures of barley for a penny; and *see* thou hurt not the oil and the wine.

7 And when he had opened the fourth seal, I heard the voice of the fourth beast say, Come and see.

8 And I looked, and behold a pale horse: and his name that sat on him was Death, and Hell followed with him. And power was given unto them over the fourth part of the earth, to kill with *a*sword, and with hunger, and with death, and with the beasts of the earth.

8a GR incense.
 b 1 Chr. 23:13;
   Ps. 141:2;
   Rev. 8:4 (3–4).
 9a TG Singing.
 b TG Jesus Christ,
   Redeemer; Redemption.
 c Rev. 7:9.
10a TG Priest, Aaronic
   Priesthood.

BD Priests.
11a Dan. 7:10.
12a TG Jesus Christ, Lamb of
   God.
 b TG Jesus Christ,
   Authority of.
 c TG God, Wisdom of.
13a D&C 88:104.
 b TG Jesus Christ, Power of.
6 1a JST Rev. 6:1 And I saw

when the Lamb opened
one of the seals, *one
of the four beasts,* and I
heard . . .
 b TG Seal.
 c TG Cherubim.
3a D&C 77:7;
   Moses 8:28 (22, 28–29).
4a D&C 1:35.
8a Ezek. 5:17; 14:21; 33:27.

9 And when he had opened the fifth seal, I saw under the ^aaltar the souls of them that were ^bslain for the word of God, and for the testimony which they held:

10 And they cried with a loud voice, saying, How long, O Lord, holy and true, dost thou not judge and ^aavenge our blood on them that dwell on the earth?

11 And ^awhite ^brobes were given unto every one of them; and it was said unto them, that they should ^crest yet for a little season, until their fellowservants also and their brethren, that should be killed as they *were*, should be fulfilled.

12 And I beheld when he had opened the ^asixth seal, and, lo, there was a great ^bearthquake; and the ^csun became ^dblack as sackcloth of hair, and the moon became as ^eblood;

13 And the stars of heaven fell unto the earth, even as a fig tree casteth her ^auntimely figs, when she is shaken of a mighty wind.

14 ^aAnd the heaven departed as a ^bscroll when it is rolled together; and every ^cmountain and island were moved out of their places.

15 And the ^akings of the earth, and the great men, and the rich men, and the chief captains, and the mighty men, and every bondman, and every free man, hid themselves in the ^bdens and in the rocks of the mountains;

16 And said to the ^amountains and rocks, Fall on us, and hide us from the face of him that sitteth on the throne, and from the wrath of the Lamb:

17 For the great ^aday of his wrath is come; and who shall be able to ^bstand?

CHAPTER 7

John also sees in the sixth seal the Restoration of the gospel, the sealing of the 144,000, and the hosts of the exalted from all nations.

AND after these things I saw four ^aangels standing on the four corners of the earth, holding the four ^bwinds of the earth, that the wind should not blow on the earth, nor on the sea, nor on any tree.

2 And I saw another angel ^aascending from the east, having the ^bseal of the living God: and he cried with a loud voice to the four angels, to whom it was given to hurt the earth and the sea,

3 Saying, ^aHurt not the earth, neither the sea, nor the trees, till we have ^bsealed the ^cservants of our God in their foreheads.

4 And I heard the number of them which were sealed: *and there were* sealed an ^ahundred *and* forty *and* four thousand of all the ^btribes of the children of ^cIsrael.

5 Of the tribe of ^aJuda *were* sealed twelve thousand. Of the tribe of ^bReuben *were* sealed twelve thousand. Of the tribe of Gad *were* sealed twelve thousand.

6 Of the tribe of Aser *were* sealed twelve thousand. Of the tribe of

9a D&C 135:7.
  b TG Martyrdom;
    Persecution.
10a Deut. 32:43.
11a Rev. 3:4.
  b TG Apparel.
  c TG Paradise.
12a D&C 77:10.
    TG Last Days.
  b Rev. 16:18.
  c TG World, End of.
  d Matt. 24:29; D&C 45:42.
  e Joel 2:31; D&C 88:87.
13a IE figs that ripen late,
    hanging on the tree
    even into the winter.
14a JST Rev. 6:14 And the

heavens *opened* as a
scroll *is opened* when it
is rolled together;
and every mountain,
and island, *was* moved
out of *its place*.
  b Isa. 34:4;
    D&C 88:95.
  c Rev. 16:20 (17–21).
15a TG Kings, Earthly.
  b Isa. 2:19.
16a Hosea 10:8;
    Luke 23:30 (27–31).
17a TG Day of the Lord;
    Jesus Christ, Second
    Coming.
  b Ps. 76:7.

7 1a D&C 77:8.
  b Ezek. 37:9; Dan. 11:4.
2a D&C 77:9.
  b TG Seal.
3a Rev. 9:4.
  b Rev. 22:4 (1–5).
  c TG High Priest,
    Melchizedek Priesthood;
    Servant.
4a D&C 77:11.
  b TG Israel, Twelve
    Tribes of.
  c D&C 77:9.
    TG Israel, Blessings of.
5a TG Israel, Judah,
    People of.
  b Ezek. 48:31 (6–7, 31).

Nepthalim *were* sealed twelve thousand. Of the tribe of Manasses *were* sealed twelve thousand.

7 Of the tribe of Simeon *were* sealed twelve thousand. Of the tribe of Levi *were* sealed twelve thousand. Of the tribe of Issachar *were* sealed twelve thousand.

8 Of the tribe of Zabulon *were* sealed twelve thousand. Of the tribe of [a]Joseph *were* sealed twelve thousand. Of the tribe of Benjamin *were* sealed twelve thousand.

9 After this I beheld, and, lo, a great multitude, which no man could number, of all nations, and [a]kindreds, and people, and tongues, stood before the throne, and before the Lamb, clothed with white robes, and [b]palms in their hands;

10 And cried with a loud voice, saying, Salvation to our God which sitteth upon the throne, and unto the Lamb.

11 And all the angels stood round about the throne, and *about* the elders and the four [a]beasts, and fell before the throne on their faces, and worshipped God,

12 Saying, Amen: Blessing, and glory, and wisdom, and thanksgiving, and honour, and power, and might, *be* unto our God for ever and ever. Amen.

13 And one of the elders answered, saying unto me, What are these which are arrayed in white robes? and whence came they?

14 And I said unto him, Sir, thou knowest. And he said to me, These are they which came [a]out of great [b]tribulation, and have [c]washed their robes, and made them [d]white in the [e]blood of the [f]Lamb.

15 Therefore are they before the throne of God, and serve him day and night in his [a]temple: and he that [b]sitteth on the throne shall [c]dwell among them.

16 They shall hunger no more, neither [a]thirst any more; neither shall the [b]sun light on them, nor any heat.

17 For the Lamb which is in the midst of the throne shall feed them, and shall lead them unto living fountains of [a]waters: and God shall wipe away all [b]tears from their eyes.

CHAPTER 8

John sees fire and desolation poured out during the seventh seal and preceding the Second Coming.

AND when he had [a]opened the [b]seventh seal, there was [c]silence in heaven about the space of half an hour.

2 And I saw the seven angels which stood before God; and to them were given seven [a]trumpets.

3 And another angel came and stood at the altar, having a golden censer; and there was given unto him much [a]incense, that he should offer *it* with the prayers of all saints upon the golden altar which was before the throne.

4 And the smoke of the incense, *which came* with the [a]prayers of the saints, ascended up before God out of the angel's hand.

5 And the angel took the censer, and filled it with fire of the altar, and [a]cast *it* into the earth: and there were [b]voices, and thunderings, and lightnings, and an earthquake.

6 And the seven angels which had the seven [a]trumpets prepared themselves to sound.

7 The first angel sounded, and there followed hail and [a]fire mingled with

---

8*a* TG Israel, Joseph,
    People of.
9*a* Rev. 5:9.
  b Ezek. 41:18 (18–19).
11*a* TG Cherubim.
14*a* TG Peace of God.
  b TG Tribulation.
  c 3 Ne. 27:19.
    TG Purity; Wash.
  d TG Remission of Sins.
  e 1 Jn. 1:7.

f TG Jesus Christ, Lamb
    of God.
15*a* TG Temple.
  b Ps. 47:8;
    D&C 88:13.
  c TG God, Presence of.
16*a* Isa. 49:10.
  b Ps. 121:6.
17*a* TG Living Water.
  b Rev. 21:4.
8 1*a* D&C 77:13.

b TG Jesus Christ, Second
    Coming; Sabbath.
  c TG Silence.
2*a* D&C 77:12.
3*a* Lev. 16:13 (12–13);
    Num. 16:40 (36–40).
4*a* Rev. 5:8.
5*a* Ezek. 10:2.
  b D&C 88:90.
6*a* D&C 77:12.
7*a* Ex. 9:24 (22–25).

blood, and they were cast upon the earth: and the third part of trees was burnt up, and all green grass was burnt up.

8 And the second angel sounded, and as it were a great mountain burning with fire was cast into the sea: and the third part of the sea became ^ablood;

9 And the third part of the creatures which were in the sea, and had life, died; and the third part of the ships were destroyed.

10 And the third angel sounded, and there ^afell a great star from heaven, burning as it were a lamp, and it fell upon the third part of the rivers, and upon the fountains of waters;

11 And the name of the star is called Wormwood: and the third part of the waters became wormwood; and many men died of the waters, because they were made bitter.

12 And the fourth angel sounded, and the third part of the sun was smitten, and the third part of the moon, and the third part of the stars; so as the third part of them was darkened, and the day shone not for a third part of it, and the night likewise.

13 And I beheld, and heard an ^aangel flying through the midst of heaven, saying with a loud voice, ^bWoe, woe, woe, to the inhabiters of the earth by reason of the other voices of the trumpet of the three angels, which are yet to sound!

CHAPTER 9

John also sees the wars and plagues poured out during the seventh seal and before the Lord comes.

AND the fifth angel sounded, and I saw a star fall from heaven unto the earth: ^aand to him was given the key of the ^bbottomless ^cpit.

2 And he opened the bottomless pit; and there arose a smoke out of the pit, as the smoke of a great furnace; and the sun and the air were darkened by reason of the smoke of the pit.

3 And there came out of the smoke locusts upon the earth: and unto them was given power, as the scorpions of the earth have power.

4 And it was commanded them that they should not hurt the grass of the earth, neither any green thing, neither any tree; but only those ^amen which have not the ^bseal of God in their foreheads.

5 And to them it was given that they should not kill them, but that they should be tormented five months: and their torment *was* as the torment of a scorpion, when he striketh a man.

6 And in those days shall men seek ^adeath, and shall not find it; and shall desire to die, and death shall flee from them.

7 And the shapes of the locusts *were* like unto horses prepared unto battle; and on their heads *were* as it were crowns like gold, and their faces *were* as the faces of men.

8 And they had hair as the hair of women, and their teeth were as *the* ^ateeth of lions.

9 And they had breastplates, as it were breastplates of iron; and the sound of their wings *was* as the ^asound of chariots of many horses running to battle.

10 And they had tails like unto scorpions, and there were stings in their tails: and their power *was* to hurt men five months.

11 And they had a king over them, *which is* the angel of the bottomless pit, whose name in the Hebrew tongue *is* Abaddon, but in the Greek tongue hath *his* name Apollyon.

12 One woe is past; *and,* behold, there come two woes more hereafter.

13 And the sixth angel sounded,

8a TG Blood, Symbolism of.
10a Isa. 14:12.
13a D&C 88:92.
  b Hel. 7:22; D&C 5:5.
9 1a JST Rev. 9:1 . . . and to *the*

angel was given the key of the bottomless pit.
  b GR pit of the abyss.
  c Rev. 20:1.
4a Rev. 7:3.

b TG Seal.
6a Job 3:21;
  Jer. 8:3.
8a Joel 1:6.
9a Joel 2:5.

and I heard a voice from the four horns of the golden altar which is before God,

14 Saying to the sixth angel which had the trumpet, Loose the four angels which are bound *a*in the great river Euphrates.

15 And the four angels were loosed, which were prepared for an hour, and a day, and a month, and a year, for to slay the third part of men.

16 And the *a*number of the army of the horsemen *were* two hundred thousand thousand: and I heard the number of them.

17 And thus I saw the horses in the vision, and them that sat on them, having breastplates of fire, and of jacinth, and brimstone: and the heads of the horses *were* as the heads of lions; and out of their mouths issued fire and smoke and brimstone.

18 By these three was the third part of men killed, by the fire, and by the smoke, and by the brimstone, which issued out of their mouths.

19 For their power is in their mouth, and in their tails: for their tails *were* like unto serpents, and had heads, and with them they do hurt.

20 And the rest of the men which were not killed by these plagues yet repented not of the works of their hands, that they should not worship devils, and idols of gold, and silver, and brass, and stone, and of wood: which neither can see, nor hear, nor walk:

21 Neither repented they of their *a*murders, nor of their *b*sorceries, nor of their fornication, nor of their thefts.

CHAPTER 10

John seals up many things relative to the last days—He is commissioned to participate in the restoration of all things.

AND I saw another mighty angel come down from heaven, clothed with a cloud: and a rainbow *was* upon his head, and his face *was* as it were the sun, and his feet as pillars of fire:

2 And he had in his hand a little *a*book open: and he set his right foot upon the sea, and *his* left *foot* on the earth,

3 And cried with a loud voice, as *when* a lion roareth: and when he had cried, seven thunders uttered their voices.

4 And when the seven thunders had uttered their voices, I was about to write: and I heard a voice from heaven saying unto me, Seal up those things which the seven thunders uttered, and write them not.

5 And the angel which I saw *a*stand upon the sea and upon the earth lifted up his hand to heaven,

6 And *a*sware by him that liveth for ever and ever, who created heaven, and the things that therein are, and the earth, and the things that therein are, and the sea, and the things which are therein, that there should be *b*time no longer:

7 But in the days of the voice of the seventh angel, when he shall begin to sound, the *a*mystery of God should be finished, as he hath declared to his servants the prophets.

8 And the voice which I heard from heaven spake unto me again, and said, Go *and* take the little book which is open in the hand of the angel which standeth upon the sea and upon the earth.

9 And I went unto the angel, and said unto him, Give me the little book. And he said unto me, Take *it,* and eat it up; and it shall make thy belly bitter, but it shall be in thy mouth sweet as honey.

10 And I took the little book out of the angel's hand, and *a*ate it up; and it was in my mouth sweet as honey: and as soon as I had eaten it, my belly was bitter.

14a JST Rev. 9:14 . . . in the
    bottomless pit.
16a Joel 1:6.
21a TG Murder.
   b TG Sorcery.

10 2a Ezek. 2:9 (9–10).
   5a D&C 88:110.
   6a Dan. 12:7.
    b TG Time.
   7a TG Mysteries of

Godliness.
10a Jer. 15:16;
    Ezek. 2:8; 3:3 (1–3);
    D&C 77:14.

11 And he said unto me, Thou must prophesy [a]again before many peoples, and nations, and tongues, and kings.

CHAPTER 11

In the last days, two prophets will be slain in Jerusalem—After 3½ days, they will be resurrected—Christ will reign over all the earth.

AND there was given me a [a]reed like unto a rod: [b]and the angel stood, saying, Rise, and [c]measure the temple of God, and the [d]altar, and them that worship therein.

2 But the court which is without the temple leave out, and measure it not; for it is given unto the Gentiles: and the [a]holy city shall they tread under foot forty *and* two months.

3 And I will give [a]*power* unto my two [b]witnesses, and they shall prophesy a thousand two hundred *and* threescore days, clothed in sackcloth.

4 These are the two olive trees, and the two candlesticks standing before the God of the earth.

5 And if any man will hurt them, fire proceedeth out of their mouth, and devoureth their enemies: and if any man will hurt them, he must in this manner be killed.

6 These have power to shut heaven, that it rain not in the days of their prophecy: and have power over waters to [a]turn them to blood, and to smite the earth with all [b]plagues, as often as they will.

7 And when they shall have finished their testimony, the beast that ascendeth out of the bottomless pit shall make war against them, and shall [a]overcome them, and [b]kill them.

8 And their dead bodies *shall lie* in the street of the great city, which spiritually is called Sodom and Egypt, where also our Lord was [a]crucified.

9 And they of the people and kindreds and tongues and nations shall see their dead bodies three days and an half, and shall not suffer their dead bodies to be put in graves.

10 And they that dwell upon the earth shall rejoice over them, and make merry, and shall send gifts one to another; because these two prophets tormented them that dwelt on the earth.

11 And after three days and an half the Spirit of life from God entered into them, and they stood upon their feet; and great fear fell upon them which saw them.

12 And they heard a great voice from heaven saying unto them, Come up hither. And they ascended up to heaven in a cloud; and their enemies beheld them.

13 And the same hour was there a great [a]earthquake, and the tenth part of the city fell, and in the earthquake were slain of men seven thousand: and the remnant were affrighted, and gave glory to the God of heaven.

14 The second woe is past; *and*, behold, the third woe cometh quickly.

15 And the seventh angel sounded; and there were great voices in heaven, saying, The [a]kingdoms of this world are become *the* [b]*kingdoms* of our Lord, and of his [c]Christ; and he shall [d]reign for ever and ever.

16 And the four and twenty elders, which sat before God on their seats, fell upon their faces, and worshipped God,

---

11a John 21:22 (20–25).
11 1a Ezek. 45:1.
   b The Greek text omits "and the angel stood."
   c Ezek. 40:3.
   d Ex. 30:1; Ezek. 41:22.
   2a Neh. 11:1.
   3a The Greek text omits "power."
   b Isa. 51:19 (19–20);

Zech. 4:14 (11–14); 2 Ne. 8:19 (18–20); D&C 77:15. TG Last Days; Witness.
6a Ex. 7:17 (17–21).
   b TG Plague.
7a TG Apostasy of the Early Christian Church.
   b TG Martyrdom.

8a TG Jesus Christ, Crucifixion of.
13a Rev. 16:18 (18–19); D&C 88:89 (87–90).
15a TG Kings, Earthly.
   b TG Kingdom of God, on Earth.
   c Dan. 7:13 (9–14).
   d TG Jesus Christ, Millennial Reign.

17 Saying, We give thee thanks, O Lord God [a]Almighty, which art, and wast, and art to come; because thou hast taken to thee thy great power, and hast reigned.

18 And the nations were angry, and thy wrath is come, and the time of the dead, that they should be [a]judged, and that thou shouldest give reward unto thy servants the prophets, and to the saints, and them that fear thy name, small and great; and shouldest destroy them which [b]destroy the earth.

19 And the temple of God was opened in heaven, and there was seen in his temple the [a]ark of his testament: and there were lightnings, and voices, and thunderings, and an earthquake, and great [b]hail.

CHAPTER 12

John sees the imminent apostasy of the Church—He also sees the War in Heaven in the beginning when Satan was cast out—He sees the continuation of that war on earth.

[a]AND there appeared a great wonder in heaven; a [b]woman clothed with the sun, and the moon under her feet, and upon her head a crown of twelve stars:

2 And she being with [a]child cried, travailing in birth, and pained to be delivered.

3 And there appeared another wonder in heaven; and behold a great red dragon, having seven heads and ten horns, and seven crowns upon his heads.

4 And his tail drew the [a]third part of the stars of heaven, and did cast them to the earth: and the dragon stood before the woman which was ready to be delivered, for to devour her child as soon as it was born.

5 And she brought forth a man child, who was to rule all nations with a [a]rod of iron: and her child was caught up unto God, and *to* his throne.

6 And the [a]woman fled into the wilderness, where she hath a place prepared of God, that they should feed her there a thousand two hundred *and* threescore days.

7 And there was [a]war in heaven: [b]Michael and his [c]angels fought against the dragon; and the [d]dragon fought and his angels,

8 And prevailed not; neither was their place found any more in [a]heaven.

9 And the great dragon was [a]cast out, that old serpent, called the [b]Devil, and Satan, which deceiveth the whole world: he was cast out into the earth, and his angels were cast out with him.

10 And I heard a loud [a]voice saying in heaven, Now is come salvation, and [b]strength, and the kingdom of our God, and the [c]power of his Christ: for the [d]accuser of our brethren is cast down, which accused them before our God day and night.

11 And they [a]overcame him by the blood of the Lamb, and by the word of their [b]testimony; and they loved not their lives unto the [c]death.

12 Therefore rejoice, *ye* heavens, and ye that dwell in them. Woe to the inhabiters of the earth and of the sea! for the devil is come down unto you, having great wrath, because he

---

17a TG God, Power of.
18a Dan. 7:10;
        D&C 29:13.
    b GR corrupt, waste,
        pervert.
19a TG Ark of the Covenant.
    b Ezek. 13:13;
        Rev. 16:21;
        D&C 29:16.
12 1a JST Rev. 12:1–17
        (Appendix). Note the
        changed sequence of
        verses in the JST.
    b D&C 5:14.

2a Isa. 66:7 (7–9).
4a D&C 29:36 (36–38).
        TG Sons of Perdition.
5a 1 Ne. 11:25.
6a Amos 8:11 (11–12);
        D&C 33:5; 86:3.
7a TG Council in Heaven;
        Rebellion;
        War.
    b TG Adam; Man, Antemortal Existence of.
    c TG Angels.
    d TG Devil.
8a TG Death, Spiritual,

        First.
9a 2 Ne. 9:9 (8–9).
    b TG Devil.
10a TG God, Manifestations of.
    b TG Strength.
    c TG Jesus Christ,
        Authority of.
    d Isa. 29:20;
        D&C 88:124.
11a John 16:33;
        1 Jn. 1:7.
    b TG Testimony.
    c TG Martyrdom.

knoweth that he hath but a short time.

13 And when the dragon saw that he was cast unto the earth, he *persecuted the woman which brought forth the man *child*.

14 And to the woman were given two wings of a great eagle, that she might fly into the wilderness, into her place, where she is nourished for a time, and times, and half a time, from the face of the serpent.

15 And the serpent cast out of his mouth water as a flood after the woman, that he might cause her to be carried away of the flood.

16 And the earth helped the woman, and the earth opened her mouth, and swallowed up the flood which the dragon cast out of his mouth.

17 And the *dragon was wroth with the woman, and went to make *war with the remnant of her seed, which keep the commandments of God, and have the testimony of Jesus Christ.

CHAPTER 13

John sees fierce-looking beasts that represent degenerate earthly kingdoms controlled by Satan—The devil works miracles and deceives men.

*AND I stood upon the sand of the sea, and saw a beast rise up out of the *sea, having seven heads and ten horns, and upon his horns ten crowns, and upon his heads the name of blasphemy.

2 And the beast which I saw was like unto a leopard, and his feet were as *the feet* of a bear, and his mouth as the mouth of a lion: and the dragon gave him his *power, and his seat, and great authority.

3 And I saw one of his heads as it were wounded to death; and his deadly wound was healed: and all the world wondered after the beast.

4 And they worshipped the dragon which gave power unto the *beast: and they *worshipped the beast, saying, Who *is* like unto the beast? who is able to make war with him?

5 And there was given unto him a *mouth speaking great things and *blasphemies; and power was given unto him to continue forty *and* two months.

6 And he opened his mouth in blasphemy against God, to blaspheme his *name, and his tabernacle, and them that dwell in heaven.

7 And it was given unto him to make war with the saints, and to overcome them: and *power was given him over all kindreds, and tongues, and nations.

8 And all that dwell upon the earth shall worship him, whose names are not written in the *book of life of the *Lamb slain from the *foundation of the world.

9 If any man have an ear, let him hear.

10 He that leadeth into captivity shall go into captivity: he that *killeth with the sword must be killed with the sword. Here is the *patience and the faith of the *saints.

11 And I beheld another beast coming up out of the earth; and he had two horns like a lamb, and he spake as a dragon.

12 And he exerciseth all the power of the first beast before him, and causeth the earth and them which dwell therein to worship the first beast, whose deadly wound was healed.

13 And he doeth great wonders, so that he maketh fire come down from

---

13a Dan. 7:25; 12:7;
    D&C 10:32; 132:57.
17a TG Devil, Church of.
  b Dan. 7:21.
13 1a JST Rev. 13:1 And I
    saw another sign, in the
    likeness of the kingdoms
    of the earth; a beast rise
    up out of the sea, and
    he stood upon the sand

    of the sea, having seven
    heads . . .
  b Dan. 7:3 (3–7).
2a Luke 4:6.
4a TG Babylon.
  b TG Worship.
5a Dan. 7:8.
  b TG Blaspheme;
    False Doctrine.
6a TG Name.

7a TG False Priesthoods.
8a TG Book of Life.
  b TG Jesus Christ, Lamb
    of God.
  c TG Foreordination.
10a TG Blood, Shedding of;
    Retribution.
  b TG Patience.
  c TG Saints.

heaven on the earth in the sight of men,

14 And ^adeceiveth them that dwell on the earth by *the means of* those ^bmiracles which he had power to do in the sight of the beast; saying to them that dwell on the earth, that they should make an image to the beast, which had the wound by a sword, and did live.

15 And he had power to give life unto the image of the beast, that the image of the beast should both speak, and cause that as many as would not worship the image of the beast should be killed.

16 And he causeth all, both small and great, rich and poor, free and bond, to receive a mark in their right hand, or in their foreheads:

17 And that no man might buy or sell, save he that had the mark, or the name of the beast, or the number of his name.

18 Here is ^awisdom. Let him that hath understanding count the number of the beast: for it is the number of a man; and his number *is* Six hundred threescore *and* six.

CHAPTER 14

The Lamb will stand upon Mount Zion—The gospel will be restored in the last days by angelic ministry—The Son of Man will harvest the earth.

AND I looked, and, lo, a ^aLamb stood on the mount ^bSion, and with him an hundred forty *and* four thousand, having his Father's ^cname written in their foreheads.

2 And I heard a voice from heaven, as the voice of many waters, and as the voice of a great thunder: and I heard the voice of harpers harping with their harps:

3 And they sung as it were a new ^asong before the throne, and before the four beasts, and the elders: and no man could learn that song but the hundred *and* forty *and* four thousand, which were redeemed from the earth.

4 These are they which were not defiled with ^awomen; for they are virgins. These are they which follow the Lamb whithersoever he goeth. These were ^bredeemed from among men, *being* the firstfruits unto God and to the Lamb.

5 And in their mouth was found no ^aguile: for they are without fault before the throne of God.

6 And I saw another ^aangel fly in the midst of heaven, having the ^beverlasting ^cgospel to ^dpreach unto them that dwell on the earth, and to every ^enation, and kindred, and tongue, and people,

7 Saying with a loud voice, ^aFear God, and give glory to him; for the hour of his ^bjudgment is come: and ^cworship ^dhim that made ^eheaven, and earth, and the sea, and the fountains of waters.

8 And there followed another angel, saying, ^aBabylon is ^bfallen, is fallen, that great ^ccity, because she made all nations drink of the wine of the wrath of her ^dfornication.

9 And the third angel followed them, saying with a loud voice, If any man worship the beast and his image, and receive *his* mark in his forehead, or in his hand,

10 The same shall drink of the wine

14*a* Matt. 24:24;
 Rev. 19:20;
 2 Ne. 28:21 (6–21);
 D&C 52:14.
 b TG Miracle.
18*a* D&C 10:34 (34–35);
 57:9.
14 1*a* D&C 133:18.
 b TG Zion.
 c Rev. 3:12; 22:4 (1–5).
 TG Name.
 3*a* TG Singing.
 4*a* TG Woman.

 b GR purchased,
 ransomed, redeemed.
 Jude 1:24;
 D&C 43:29; 77:5.
5*a* TG Guile.
6*a* D&C 133:36.
 TG Angels.
 b D&C 79:1.
 c D&C 27:16.
 TG Book of Mormon;
 Gospel;
 Restoration of the
 Gospel.

 d TG Missionary Work.
 e TG Nations.
7*a* D&C 88:104.
 TG Reverence.
 b TG Judgment, the Last.
 c TG Worship.
 d TG God, Creator.
 e Neh. 9:6.
8*a* Isa. 21:9.
 TG Babylon.
 b D&C 88:105.
 c Rev. 17:18.
 d D&C 88:94.

of the wrath of God, which is ^apoured out without mixture into the cup of his ^bindignation; and he shall be tormented with fire and brimstone in the presence of the holy angels, and in the presence of the Lamb:

11 And the smoke of their torment ascendeth up for ever and ever: and they have no rest day nor night, who worship the beast and his image, and whosoever receiveth the mark of his name.

12 Here is the ^apatience of the saints: here *are* they that keep the commandments of God, and the faith of Jesus.

13 And I heard a voice from heaven saying unto me, Write, ^aBlessed *are* the ^bdead which ^cdie in the Lord from henceforth: Yea, saith the Spirit, that they may ^drest from their labours; and their works do follow them.

14 And I looked, and behold a white cloud, and upon the cloud *one* sat like unto the ^aSon of man, having on his head a golden crown, and in his hand a sharp sickle.

15 And another angel came out of the temple, crying with a loud voice to him that sat on the cloud, ^aThrust in thy sickle, and ^breap: for the time is come for thee to reap; for the ^charvest of the earth is ^dripe.

16 And he that sat on the cloud thrust in his sickle on the earth; and the earth was reaped.

17 And another angel came out of the temple which is in heaven, he also having a sharp sickle.

18 And another angel came out from the altar, which had power over fire; and cried with a loud cry to him that had the sharp sickle, saying, Thrust in thy sharp sickle, and

gather the clusters of the ^avine of the earth; for her grapes are fully ripe.

19 And the angel thrust in his sickle into the earth, and gathered the vine of the earth, and cast *it* into the great ^awinepress of the wrath of God.

20 And the winepress was trodden without the city, and blood came out of the winepress, even unto the horse bridles, by the space of a thousand *and* six hundred furlongs.

CHAPTER 15

Exalted Saints praise God in celestial glory forever.

AND I saw another sign in heaven, great and marvellous, seven angels having the seven last ^aplagues; for in them is filled up the wrath of God.

2 And I saw as it were a ^asea of ^bglass mingled with fire: and them that had gotten the victory over the beast, and over his image, and over his mark, *and* over the number of his name, stand on the sea of glass, having the harps of God.

3 And they ^asing the song of Moses the servant of God, and the song of the Lamb, saying, ^bGreat and marvellous *are* thy works, Lord God Almighty; ^cjust and true *are* thy ways, thou King of ^dsaints.

4 Who shall not fear thee, O Lord, and glorify thy ^aname? for *thou* only *art* holy: for all nations shall come and worship before thee; for thy judgments are made manifest.

5 And after that I looked, and, behold, the temple of the tabernacle of the ^atestimony in heaven was opened:

6 And the seven angels came out of the temple, having the seven ^aplagues, clothed in pure and white

---

10a D&C 115:6.
  b TG God, Indignation of.
12a TG Patience.
13a 1 Ne. 22:22 (22–23);
    D&C 88:26 (25–29);
    Moses 7:63 (1–66).
  b TG Death;
    Spirits, Disembodied.
  c D&C 42:44; 59:2.
  d TG Paradise; Rest.
14a TG Jesus Christ, Son of

Man.
15a D&C 31:5.
  b D&C 12:4.
  c TG Harvest.
  d D&C 18:6.
18a TG Vineyard of the
    Lord.
19a Isa. 63:3 (3–4);
    Joel 3:13;
    Rev. 19:15;
    D&C 88:106.

15 1a TG Plague.
  2a D&C 130:7 (1–11).
    b TG Earth, Destiny of.
  3a TG Singing.
    b D&C 76:114.
    c TG God, Justice of;
      Justice.
    d TG Saints.
  4a Ps. 99:3.
  5a TG Testimony.
  6a TG Last Days.

linen, and having their breasts girded with golden girdles.

7 And one of the four beasts gave unto the seven angels seven golden vials full of the wrath of God, who liveth for ever and ever.

8 And the temple was filled with smoke from the glory of God, and from his power; and no man was able to enter into the temple, till the seven plagues of the seven angels were fulfilled.

CHAPTER 16

God pours out plagues upon the wicked— The nations assemble for Armageddon—Christ comes, islands flee, and mountains cease.

AND I heard a great voice out of the temple saying to the seven angels, Go your ways, and pour out the vials of the wrath of God upon the earth.

2 And the first went, and poured out his vial upon the earth; and there fell a *a*noisome and grievous sore upon the men which had the mark of the beast, and *upon* them which worshipped his image.

3 And the second angel poured out his vial upon the sea; and it became as the blood of a dead *man:* and every living soul died in the sea.

4 And the third angel poured out his vial upon the rivers and fountains of waters; and they became blood.

5 And I heard the angel of the waters say, Thou art righteous, O Lord, which art, and wast, and shalt be, because thou hast *a*judged thus.

6 For they have *a*shed the *b*blood of saints and prophets, and thou hast given them blood to drink; for they are *c*worthy.

7 And I heard another out of the altar say, Even so, Lord God Almighty, true and righteous *are* thy judgments.

8 And the fourth angel poured out his vial upon the sun; and power was given unto him to scorch men with fire.

9 And men were scorched with great heat, and *a*blasphemed the name of God, which hath power over these plagues: and they repented not to give him glory.

10 And the fifth angel poured out his vial upon the seat of the beast; and his kingdom was full of *a*darkness; and they gnawed their tongues for pain,

11 And blasphemed the God of heaven because of their *a*pains and their sores, and repented not of their deeds.

12 And the sixth angel poured out his vial upon the great river Euphrates; and the water thereof was dried up, that the way of the kings of the east might be prepared.

13 And I saw three unclean spirits like frogs *come* out of the mouth of the dragon, and out of the mouth of the beast, and out of the mouth of the *a*false prophet.

14 For they are the *a*spirits of *b*devils, working *c*miracles, *which* go forth unto the kings of the earth and of the whole world, to gather them to the *d*battle of that great day of God Almighty.

15 Behold, I come as a *a*thief. Blessed *is* he that *b*watcheth, and keepeth his garments, lest he walk naked, and they see his shame.

16 And he gathered them together into a place called in the Hebrew tongue *a*Armageddon.

17 And the seventh angel poured out his vial into the air; and there came a great voice out of the temple of heaven, from the throne, saying, It is done.

---

16 2*a* GR bad, evil.
  5*a* TG Jesus Christ, Judge.
  6*a* TG Prophets,
      Rejection of.
    b TG Martyrdom.
    c GR deserving.
  9*a* TG Blaspheme.
  10*a* TG Darkness, Spiritual.

11*a* TG Pain.
13*a* TG Antichrist;
      False Prophets.
14*a* D&C 50:1.
    b Matt. 24:24;
      2 Ne. 9:9 (8–12).
    c TG Miracle.
    d Rev. 17:14.

15*a* Luke 21:35; Rev. 3:3.
    b D&C 49:7 (5–9);
      106:5 (4–5).
      TG Watch.
16*a* Ezek. 38:16 (15–16);
      Joel 3:14 (9–14);
      Zech. 14:2 (2–5);
      Luke 21:20 (20–24).

18 And there were voices, and thunders, and lightnings; and there was a great ªearthquake, such as was not since men were upon the earth, so mighty an earthquake, *and* so great.

19 And the great city was divided into three parts, and the cities of the nations fell: and great ªBabylon came in remembrance before God, to give unto her the cup of the wine of the fierceness of his ᵇwrath.

20 And every island fled away, and the ªmountains were not found.

21 And there fell upon men a great ªhail out of heaven, *every stone* about the weight of a talent: and men blasphemed God because of the plague of the hail; for the plague thereof was exceeding great.

CHAPTER 17

John is shown that Babylon the great, the mother of harlots and abominations, has become established throughout the earth.

AND there came one of the seven angels which had the seven vials, and talked with me, saying unto me, Come hither; I will shew unto thee the ªjudgment of the great ᵇwhore that sitteth upon many ᶜwaters:

2 With whom the kings of the earth have committed fornication, and the ªinhabitants of the earth have been made drunk with the wine of her ᵇfornication.

3 So he carried me away in the spirit into the wilderness: and I saw a woman sit upon a scarlet coloured beast, full of ªnames of blasphemy, having seven heads and ten horns.

4 And the woman was arrayed in purple and scarlet colour, and decked with gold and precious stones and pearls, having a golden cup in her hand ªfull of abominations and ᵇfilthiness of her fornication:

5 And upon her forehead *was a* name written, ªMYSTERY, ᵇBABYLON THE GREAT, THE ᶜMOTHER OF HARLOTS AND ABOMINATIONS OF THE EARTH.

6 And I saw the woman drunken with the ªblood of the saints, and with the blood of the ᵇmartyrs of Jesus: and when I saw her, I wondered with great ᶜadmiration.

7 And the angel said unto me, Wherefore didst thou marvel? I will tell thee the mystery of the woman, and of the beast that carrieth her, which hath the seven heads and ten horns.

8 The beast that thou sawest was, and is not; and shall ascend out of the bottomless pit, and go into ªperdition: and they that dwell on the earth shall wonder, whose names were not written in the ᵇbook of life from the foundation of the world, when they behold the beast that was, and is not, and yet is.

9 And here *is* the ªmind which hath wisdom. The seven heads are seven mountains, on which the woman sitteth.

10 And there are seven ªkings: five are fallen, and one is, *and* the other is not yet come; and when he cometh, he must continue a short space.

11 And the beast that was, and is not, even he is the eighth, and is of the seven, and goeth into perdition.

12 And the ten ªhorns which thou

18a Dan. 12:1;
     Rev. 6:12; 11:13 (13–14).
19a TG Babylon.
   b TG God, Indignation of.
20a Isa. 64:1;
     Rev. 6:14 (12–17);
     D&C 133:22 (1–42).
21a Ex. 9:18 (13–35);
     Josh. 10:11;
     Ezek. 13:13; 38:22;
     Rev. 11:19;
     Mosiah 12:6;

     D&C 29:16.
17 1a Rev. 18:3 (3–9); 19:2.
   b TG Devil, Church of.
   c Jer. 51:13.
2a Isa. 24:6.
   b 1 Ne. 14:13 (9–13).
3a TG Name.
4a D&C 10:21.
   b TG Filthiness.
5a TG Secret
     Combinations.
   b TG Babylon.

   c D&C 88:94.
6a Rev. 18:24 (22–24).
   b TG Martyrdom.
   c GR astonishment,
     wonder.
8a TG Death, Spiritual,
     Second;
     Hell.
   b Ps. 139:16.
9a TG Mind.
10a TG Kings, Earthly.
12a Dan. 7:24.

sawest are ten kings, which have received no kingdom as yet; but receive power as kings one hour with the beast.

13 These have one mind, and shall give their power and strength unto the beast.

14 These shall make ªwar with the Lamb, and the Lamb shall overcome them: for he is ᵇLord of lords, and ᶜKing of kings: and they that are with him *are* called, and chosen, and faithful.

15 And he saith unto me, The waters which thou sawest, where the whore sitteth, are peoples, and multitudes, and nations, and tongues.

16 And the ten horns which thou sawest upon the beast, these shall hate the ªwhore, and shall make her desolate and naked, and shall eat her flesh, and ᵇburn her with fire.

17 For God hath put in their hearts to fulfil his will, and to agree, and ªgive their kingdom unto the beast, until the ᵇwords of God shall be fulfilled.

18 And the woman which thou sawest is that great ªcity, which reigneth over the kings of the earth.

CHAPTER 18

The Saints are called out of Babylon lest they partake of her sins—She falls and is lamented by her supporters.

AND after these things I saw another angel come down from heaven, having great power; and the earth was ªlightened with his glory.

2 And he cried mightily with a strong voice, saying, ªBabylon the great is fallen, is fallen, and is become the habitation of devils, and the ᵇhold of every foul spirit, and a ᶜcage of every unclean and hateful bird.

3 For all nations have drunk of the wine of the wrath of her ªfornication, and the kings of the earth have committed ᵇfornication with her, and the merchants of the earth are waxed rich through the ᶜabundance of her delicacies.

4 And I heard another voice from heaven, saying, ªCome ᵇout of her, my people, that ye be not partakers of her ᶜsins, and that ye receive not of her plagues.

5 For her ªsins have reached unto heaven, and God hath remembered her iniquities.

6 ªReward her even as she rewarded you, and double unto her double according to her works: in the cup which she hath filled fill to her double.

7 How much she hath glorified herself, and lived ªdeliciously, so much torment and sorrow give her: for she saith in her heart, I sit a queen, and am no widow, and shall see no sorrow.

8 Therefore shall her ªplagues come in one day, death, and mourning, and famine; and she shall be utterly ᵇburned with fire: for strong *is* the Lord God who ᶜjudgeth her.

9 And the kings of the earth, who have committed fornication and lived deliciously with her, shall ªbewail her, and lament for her, when they shall see the ᵇsmoke of her burning,

10 Standing afar off for the fear of her torment, saying, Alas, alas, that great city Babylon, that mighty city! for in one hour is thy judgment come.

14a Rev. 16:14.
  b Deut. 10:17;
    Rev. 19:16 (11–16).
    TG Jesus Christ, Lord;
    Jesus Christ, Power of.
  c Dan. 2:47; 1 Tim. 6:15.
16a 1 Ne. 22:13 (13–14).
  b Rev. 18:8 (6–18).
17a Dan. 8:24.
  b D&C 1:37.
18a Rev. 14:8.

18 1a Ezek. 43:2.
  2a TG Babylon.
  b GR ward, prison.
  c GR ward, prison.
  3a Rev. 17:1 (1–2);
    D&C 35:11.
  b Isa. 23:17.
  c GR power of her
    wantonness.
  4a Zech. 2:7.
  b Gen. 19:14.

  c Isa. 52:11.
  5a Jer. 51:9 (8–9).
  6a D&C 1:9.
    TG Retribution.
  7a GR wantonly, riotously.
  8a TG Plague.
  b Rev. 17:16;
    D&C 64:24; 86:7.
  c TG Jesus Christ, Judge.
  9a Jer. 51:8.
  b Gen. 19:28.

11 And the merchants of the earth shall weep and mourn over her; for no man buyeth their merchandise any more:

12 The merchandise of gold, and silver, and precious stones, and of pearls, and fine linen, and purple, and silk, and scarlet, and all thyine wood, and all manner vessels of ivory, and all manner vessels of most precious wood, and of brass, and iron, and marble,

13 And cinnamon, and odours, and ointments, and frankincense, and wine, and oil, and fine flour, and wheat, and beasts, and sheep, and horses, and chariots, and ^aslaves, and souls of men.

14 And the fruits that thy soul ^alusted after are departed from thee, and all things which were dainty and goodly are departed from thee, and thou shalt find them no more at all.

15 The merchants of these things, which were made rich by her, shall stand afar off for the fear of her torment, weeping and wailing,

16 And saying, Alas, alas, that great city, that was clothed in fine linen, and purple, and scarlet, and decked with gold, and precious stones, and pearls!

17 For in one hour so great riches is come to nought. And every shipmaster, and all the company in ships, and sailors, and as many as trade by sea, stood afar off,

18 And cried when they saw the smoke of her burning, saying, What city is like unto this great city!

19 And they cast ^adust on their heads, and cried, weeping and wailing, saying, Alas, alas, that great city, wherein were made rich all that had ships in the sea by reason of her costliness! for in one hour is she made desolate.

20 Rejoice over her, thou heaven, and ye holy apostles and prophets; for God hath avenged you on her.

21 And a mighty angel took up a stone like a great millstone, and cast it into the sea, saying, Thus with violence shall that great city ^aBabylon be thrown down, and shall be found no more at all.

22 And the voice of harpers, and musicians, and of pipers, and trumpeters, shall be heard no more at all in thee; and no craftsman, of whatsoever craft he be, shall be found any more in thee; and the sound of a millstone shall be heard no more at all in thee;

23 And the light of a candle shall shine no more at all in thee; and the ^avoice of the bridegroom and of the bride shall be heard no more at all in thee: for thy merchants were the great men of the earth; for by thy ^bsorceries were all nations deceived.

24 And in her was found the ^ablood of prophets, and of saints, and of all that were slain upon the earth.

CHAPTER 19

The marriage supper of the Lamb is made ready—The testimony of Jesus is the spirit of prophecy—Christ is King of Kings and Lord of Lords.

AND after these things I heard a great voice of much people in heaven, saying, Alleluia; Salvation, and glory, and honour, and power, unto the Lord our God:

2 For true and righteous are his ^ajudgments: for he hath ^bjudged the great ^cwhore, which did corrupt the earth with her fornication, and hath avenged the blood of his servants at her hand.

3 And again they said, Alleluia. And her ^asmoke rose up for ever and ever.

4 And the four and twenty elders and the four ^abeasts fell down and worshipped God that sat on the throne, saying, Amen; Alleluia.

13a TG Slavery.
14a TG Lust.
19a Ezek. 27:30.
21a TG Babylon;
 Devil, Church of.

23a Jer. 7:34.
 b TG Sorcery.
24a Rev. 17:6 (1–18);
 2 Ne. 27:4 (3–4); 28:10;
 Morm. 8:27 (27, 40–41).

19 2a TG Jesus Christ, Judge.
 b Rev. 17:1 (1–2).
 c D&C 29:21.
3a Gen. 19:28.
4a TG Cherubim.

5 And a voice came out of the throne, saying, Praise our God, all ye his servants, and ye that fear him, both small and great.

6 And I heard as it were the voice of a great multitude, and as the voice of many waters, and as the voice of mighty thunderings, saying, Alleluia: for the Lord *a*God *b*omnipotent reigneth.

7 Let us be glad and rejoice, and give honour to him: for the *a*marriage of the *b*Lamb is come, and his wife hath made herself ready.

8 And to her was granted that she should be arrayed in fine linen, clean and white: for the fine *a*linen is the *b*righteousness of saints.

9 And he saith unto me, Write, Blessed *are* they which are called unto the *a*marriage *b*supper of the *c*Lamb. And he saith unto me, These are the true sayings of God.

10 And I *a*fell at his feet to *b*worship him. And he said unto me, See *thou do it* not: I am thy *c*fellowservant, and of thy brethren that have the testimony of Jesus: worship God: for the *d*testimony of Jesus is the spirit of *e*prophecy.

11 And I saw heaven opened, and behold a white horse; and he that sat upon him *was* called Faithful and True, and in righteousness he doth *a*judge and make *b*war.

12 His *a*eyes *were* as a flame of fire, and on his head *were* many crowns;

and he had a *b*name written, that no man knew, but he himself.

13 And he *was* *a*clothed with a vesture dipped in blood: and his *b*name is called The *c*Word of God.

14 And the armies *which were* in heaven followed him upon white horses, *a*clothed in fine linen, white and clean.

15 *a*And out of his mouth goeth a sharp sword, that with it he should smite the nations: and he shall *b*rule them with a rod of iron: and he treadeth the *c*winepress of the fierceness and wrath of Almighty God.

16 And he hath on *his* vesture and on his thigh a name written, *a*KING OF KINGS, AND *b*LORD OF LORDS.

17 And I saw an angel standing in the sun; and he cried with a loud voice, saying to all the fowls that fly in the midst of heaven, Come and gather yourselves together unto the supper of the great God;

18 That ye may eat the flesh of kings, and the flesh of captains, and the flesh of mighty men, and the flesh of horses, and of them that sit on them, and the flesh of all *a*men, *both* free and bond, both small and great.

19 And I saw the beast, and the kings of the earth, and their armies, gathered together to make war against him that sat on the horse, and against his army.

6a Dan. 2:47.
 b TG Jesus Christ, Power of.
7a Isa. 54:5;
 Matt. 22:2 (2–14);
 Luke 5:34;
 Rev. 21:2.
 b TG Jesus Christ, Lamb of God.
8a Matt. 22:11 (11–14);
 1 Ne. 12:10 (10–11).
 b Alma 5:27.
9a D&C 58:11.
 b Luke 14:15; 22:30.
 c TG Jesus Christ, Lamb of God.
10a Rev. 22:8.
 b TG Worship.
 c Acts 10:26;
 Rev. 1:1 (1–6).

 d TG Testimony.
 e TG Prophecy.
11a TG Jesus Christ, Judge.
 b TG War.
12a TG God, Manifestations of.
 b Rev. 2:17 (12–17).
13a Isa. 63:2 (2–3);
 D&C 133:48 (48–51).
 b TG Name.
 c Moses 1:32 (32–33).
 TG Jesus Christ, Messenger of the Covenant.
14a TG Clothing.
15a JST Rev. 19:15 And out of his mouth *proceedeth the word of God, and with it he will* smite the nations; and he *will*

rule them with *the word of his mouth;* and he treadeth the winepress *in the fierceness and wrath of Almighty God.* Isa. 11:4.
 b TG Jesus Christ, Authority of.
 c Isa. 63:3 (3–4);
 Rev. 14:19 (17–20);
 D&C 88:106.
16a TG Jesus Christ, Second Coming.
 b Deut. 10:17;
 Rev. 17:14.
18a JST Rev. 19:18 . . . *who fight against the Lamb, both bond and free, both small and great.*

20 And the beast was taken, and with him the ^afalse prophet that wrought ^bmiracles before him, with which he ^cdeceived them that had received the mark of the beast, and them that worshipped his image. These both were cast alive into a ^dlake of ^efire burning with brimstone.

21 And the remnant were slain ^awith the sword of him that sat upon the horse, which *sword* proceeded out of his mouth: and all the fowls were filled with their flesh.

CHAPTER 20

Satan is bound during the Millennium—The Saints will then live and reign with Christ—The dead stand before God and are judged out of the books according to their works.

AND I saw an ^aangel come down from heaven, having the key of the bottomless ^bpit and a great chain in his hand.

2 And he laid hold on the dragon, that old ^aserpent, which is the ^bDevil, and Satan, and ^cbound him a thousand years,

3 And cast him into the bottomless pit, and shut him up, and set a seal upon him, that he should deceive the ^anations no more, till the thousand years should be fulfilled: and after that he must be ^bloosed a little season.

4 And I saw thrones, and they sat upon them, and ^ajudgment was given unto them: and *I saw* the souls of them that were beheaded for the witness of Jesus, and for the word of

God, and which had not worshipped the beast, neither his image, neither had received *his* mark upon their foreheads, or in their hands; and they lived and ^breigned with Christ a ^cthousand years.

5 But the rest of the ^adead lived not again until the thousand years were finished. This *is* the first resurrection.

6 ^aBlessed and holy *is* he that hath part in the ^bfirst ^cresurrection: on such the ^dsecond death hath no power, but they shall be ^epriests of God and of Christ, and shall reign with him a thousand years.

7 And when the ^athousand years are expired, ^bSatan shall be loosed out of his prison,

8 And shall go out to deceive the nations which are in the four quarters of the earth, ^aGog and Magog, to gather them together to battle: the number of whom *is* as the sand of the sea.

9 And they went up on the breadth of the earth, and compassed the camp of the saints about, and the beloved city: and fire came down from God out of heaven, and devoured them.

10 And the ^adevil that deceived them was ^bcast into the lake of ^cfire and brimstone, where the beast and the false prophet *are*, and shall be tormented day and night for ever and ever.

11 And I saw a great white throne, and him that sat on it, from whose face the ^aearth and the heaven fled

20a TG Antichrist;
   False Prophets.
 b TG Miracle.
 c Rev. 13:14 (11–18).
 d Matt. 8:12; 13:42;
   D&C 112:24.
   TG Hell.
 e Dan. 7:11.
21a JST Rev. 19:21 . . . with
   the *word* of him that sat
   upon the horse, which
   word proceeded out of
   his mouth . . .
20 1a TG Angels.
 b Rev. 9:1;
   D&C 76:48.
 2a Isa. 27:1.

 b TG Devil.
 c D&C 84:100.
 3a TG Nations.
 b D&C 43:31.
 4a Dan. 7:22; 1 Cor. 6:2;
   3 Ne. 27:3;
   D&C 20:13 (5–15);
   75:21 (21–22).
 b TG Jesus Christ,
   Millennial Reign.
 c TG Millennium.
 5a D&C 43:18; 88:101.
   TG Spirits, Disembodied.
 6a JST Rev. 20:6 Blessed
   and holy *are they who
   have* part in the first
   resurrection . . .

 b D&C 63:18.
 c TG Resurrection.
 d TG Death, Spiritual,
   Second.
 e TG Priest, Aaronic
   Priesthood; Priest,
   Melchizedek Priesthood.
   BD Priests.
 7a TG Jesus Christ,
   Millennial Reign.
 b TG Devil.
 8a Gen. 10:2 (2–3);
   Ezek. 38:2.
10a D&C 28:11.
 b D&C 19:3.
 c Dan. 7:11; D&C 76:36.
11a D&C 29:24 (24–25).

away; and there was found no *b*place for them.

12 And I saw the *a*dead, small and great, *b*stand before God; and the *c*books were opened: and another book was opened, which is *the* *d*book of life: and the dead were *e*judged out of those things which were written in the books, according to their *f*works.

13 And the sea gave up the dead which were in it; and *a*death and *b*hell delivered up the dead which were in them: and they were judged every man according to their works.

14 And *a*death and *b*hell were cast into the lake of fire. This is the *c*second death.

15 And whosoever was not found written in the book of life was cast into the lake of fire.

CHAPTER 21

Those who overcome will be sons of God—The earth attains its celestial glory.

AND I saw a *a*new *b*heaven and a new *c*earth: for the first heaven and the first *d*earth were passed away; and there was no more sea.

2 And I John saw the holy city, *a*new *b*Jerusalem, coming down from God out of heaven, prepared as a *c*bride adorned for her husband.

3 And I heard a great voice out of heaven saying, Behold, the taberna-cle of God *is* with men, and he will *a*dwell with them, and they shall be his people, and *b*God himself shall be with them, *and be* their God.

4 And God shall wipe away all tears from their eyes; and there shall be no more *a*death, neither *b*sorrow, nor crying, neither shall there be any more *c*pain: for the former things are passed away.

5 And he that sat upon the throne said, Behold, I make all things *a*new. And he said unto me, *b*Write: for these *c*words are true and faithful.

6 And he said unto me, It is done. *a*I am *b*Alpha and Omega, the beginning and the end. I will give unto him that is athirst of the fountain of the *c*water of life freely.

7 He that *a*overcometh shall *b*inherit *c*all things; and I will be his God, and he shall be my *d*son.

8 But the fearful, and *a*unbelieving, and the abominable, and *b*murderers, and *c*whoremongers, and *d*sorcerers, and idolaters, and all *e*liars, shall have their part in the lake which burneth with fire and brimstone: which is the *f*second *g*death.

9 And there came unto me one of the seven angels which had the seven vials full of the seven last *a*plagues, and talked with me, saying, Come hither, I will shew thee the bride, the Lamb's wife.

10 And he carried me away in the spirit to a great and high *a*mountain, and shewed me that great city, the

---

11*b* Dan. 2:35 (31–36).
12*a* Alma 11:44 (43–44).
  TG Death.
  b TG Resurrection.
  c Dan. 7:10.
  d TG Book of Life.
  e D&C 137:9.
    TG Accountability;
    Judgment, the Last.
  f TG Good Works.
13*a* 2 Tim. 1:10.
  b TG Hell;
    Spirits in Prison.
14*a* 1 Cor. 15:26 (26, 54).
  b TG Damnation.
  c TG Death, Spiritual,
    Second.
21 1*a* TG Celestial Glory.
  b TG Heaven.

  c TG Earth, Destiny of;
    Earth, Renewal of.
  d TG World, End of.
2*a* TG Zion.
  b TG Jerusalem, New.
  c Matt. 22:2 (2–14);
    Luke 5:34;
    Rev. 19:7 (7–9).
3*a* TG God, Presence of.
  b Ezek. 48:35.
4*a* Rev. 7:17.
  b TG Mourning; Sorrow.
  c TG Pain.
5*a* 2 Cor. 5:17;
    D&C 130:5–9.
  b TG Scriptures, Writing of.
  c D&C 1:37.
6*a* TG Jesus Christ, Jehovah.
  b D&C 45:7.

  c TG Living Water.
7*a* Rev. 2:7;
    D&C 76:60 (58–60).
  b TG Exaltation.
  c Ps. 84:11.
    TG Eternal Life.
  d TG Sons and Daughters
    of God.
8*a* TG Stiffnecked.
  b TG Murder.
  c TG Adulterer; Chastity.
  d TG Sorcery.
  e TG Lying.
  f TG Hell.
  g TG Death, Spiritual,
    Second.
9*a* TG Plague.
10*a* Ezek. 40:2;
    Moses 1:1.

holy ^bJerusalem, descending out of heaven from God,

11 Having the ^aglory of God: and her light *was* like unto a stone most precious, even like a jasper stone, clear as crystal;

12 And had a wall great and high, *and* had twelve ^agates, and at the gates twelve angels, and names written thereon, which are *the names* of the twelve tribes of the children of Israel:

13 On the east three gates; on the north three gates; on the south three gates; and on the west three gates.

14 And the wall of the city had twelve foundations, and in them the names of the twelve apostles of the Lamb.

15 And he that talked with me had a golden reed to measure the city, and the gates thereof, and the wall thereof.

16 And the city lieth foursquare, and the ^alength is as large as the breadth: and he measured the city with the reed, twelve thousand ^bfurlongs. The length and the breadth and the height of it are equal.

17 And he measured the wall thereof, an hundred *and* forty *and* four cubits, *according to* the measure of a man, that is, of the angel.

18 And the building of the wall of it was *of* jasper: and the city *was* pure gold, like unto clear glass.

19 And the foundations of the wall of the city *were* garnished with all manner of precious stones. The first foundation *was* jasper; the second, sapphire; the third, a chalcedony; the fourth, an emerald;

20 The fifth, sardonyx; the sixth, sardius; the seventh, chrysolite; the eighth, beryl; the ninth, a topaz; the tenth, a chrysoprasus; the eleventh, a jacinth; the twelfth, an amethyst.

21 And the twelve gates *were* twelve pearls; every several gate was of one pearl: and the street of the city *was* pure ^agold, as it were transparent ^bglass.

22 And I saw no temple therein: for the Lord God ^aAlmighty and the Lamb are the ^btemple of it.

23 And the city had no need of the ^asun, neither of the moon, to shine in it: for the glory of God did lighten it, and the ^bLamb *is* the ^clight thereof.

24 And the nations of them which are saved shall ^awalk in the light of it: and the ^bkings of the ^cearth do bring their glory and honour into it.

25 And the ^agates of it shall not be shut at all by day: for there shall be no night there.

26 And they shall bring the glory and honour of the nations into it.

27 And there shall in no wise enter into it any thing that ^adefileth, neither *whatsoever* worketh abomination, or *maketh* a lie: but they which are written in the Lamb's ^bbook of life.

CHAPTER 22

The Saints will reign in celestial splendor—Christ will come, and men will be judged—Blessed are they who keep His commandments.

AND he shewed me a pure river of ^awater of life, clear as crystal, proceeding out of the throne of God and of the Lamb.

2 In the midst of the street of it, and on either side of the river, *was there* the ^atree of ^blife, which bare twelve *manner of* fruits, *and* yielded her fruit every month: and the ^cleaves of the tree *were* for the healing of the nations.

10b Moses 7:63 (21, 62–64).
11a Ezek. 43:2 (1–6).
12a Ezek. 48:31.
16a Ezek. 40:5.
  b GR stadia. A stadium was about 607 English feet, or 185.2 meters.
21a D&C 137:4 (2–4).
  b TG Earth, Destiny of.
22a TG God, Power of.

  b TG Temple.
23a Isa. 60:19;
     Rev. 22:5.
  b TG Jesus Christ, Lamb of God.
  c TG Jesus Christ, Light of the World.
24a TG Walking with God.
  b TG Kings, Earthly.
  c Isa. 49:22; 60:5.

25a Isa. 60:11.
27a D&C 76:112 (81–112).
  b TG Book of Life.
22 1a Ezek. 47:1; Joel 3:18;
     Zech. 14:8.
  2a Gen. 2:9;
     Rev. 2:7 (1–7);
     1 Ne. 8:10 (1–11).
  b TG Immortality.
  c Ezek. 47:12.

3 And there shall be no more ^acurse: but the ^bthrone of God and of the ^cLamb shall be in it; and his servants shall serve him:

4 And they shall ^asee his ^bface; and his ^cname *shall be* in their foreheads.

5 And there shall be no night there; and they need no candle, neither light of the ^asun; for the Lord God giveth them ^blight: and they shall ^creign ^dfor ever and ever.

6 And he said unto me, These sayings *are* faithful and ^atrue: and the Lord God of the holy prophets sent his angel to shew unto his servants the things which must ^bshortly be done.

7 Behold, I ^acome quickly: ^bblessed *is* he that keepeth the ^csayings of the prophecy of this book.

8 And I John saw these things, and heard *them.* And when I had heard and seen, I ^afell down to worship before the feet of the angel which shewed me these things.

9 Then saith he unto me, See *thou do it* not: for I am thy fellowservant, and of thy brethren the prophets, and of them which keep the sayings of this book: worship God.

10 And he saith unto me, Seal not the sayings of the prophecy of this book: for the time is at hand.

11 He that is ^aunjust, let him be ^bunjust still: and he which is ^cfilthy, let him be filthy still: and he that is righteous, let him be righteous still:

and he that is holy, let him be holy still.

12 And, behold, I ^acome quickly; and my ^breward *is* with me, to give every man according as his ^cwork shall be.

13 I am Alpha and Omega, the beginning and the end, the ^afirst and the last.

14 Blessed *are* they that ^ado his ^bcommandments, that they may have right to the tree of life, and may enter in through the gates into the city.

15 For without *are* dogs, and ^asorcerers, and ^bwhoremongers, and ^cmurderers, and idolaters, and whosoever loveth and maketh a ^dlie.

16 I Jesus have sent mine ^aangel to testify unto you these things in the churches. I am the ^broot and the offspring of David, *and* the bright and morning ^cstar.

17 And the Spirit and the bride say, ^aCome. And let him that heareth say, Come. And let him that is athirst come. And whosoever will, let him take the ^bwater of life freely.

18 For I testify unto every man that heareth the words of the prophecy of this book, If any man shall ^aadd unto these things, God shall add unto him the ^bplagues that are written in this book:

19 And if any man shall take away from the words of the book of this prophecy, God shall take away his

---

3a TG Curse;
  Earth, Curse of.
 b Jer. 3:17;
  Joel 3:21 (18–21);
  Zech. 2:10 (10–12).
 c TG Jesus Christ, Lamb
  of God.
4a TG God, Privilege of
  Seeing.
 b John 14:3;
  1 Thes. 4:17;
  D&C 38:8 (7–8).
  TG God, Body of,
  Corporeal Nature.
 c Rev. 3:12 (7–13);
  7:3 (2–8); 14:1 (1–5).
5a Isa. 60:19;
  Rev. 21:23.
 b TG Earth, Destiny of.
 c Matt. 25:34.
  TG Eternal Life;

Kingdom of God,
  on Earth.
 d D&C 132:20.
6a D&C 68:34.
 b Rev. 1:1 (1–6);
  D&C 88:79.
7a D&C 51:20.
 b Rev. 1:3 (1–6).
 c D&C 58:2.
8a Rev. 19:10.
11a Alma 41:13 (10–15).
 b Dan. 12:10.
 c TG Filthiness.
12a 1 Thes. 2:19; 3:13;
  Rev. 1:7.
 b TG Reward.
 c Alma 41:13.
13a TG God, Eternal
  Nature of.
14a TG Obedience.
 b TG Good Works.

15a TG Sorcery;
  Telestial Glory.
 b TG Adulterer;
  Whore.
 c TG Murder.
 d TG Lying.
16a TG Angels.
 b Isa. 53:2;
  Rev. 5:5 (1–14).
 c 2 Pet. 1:19;
  Rev. 2:28.
17a Moro. 10:32 (30–33).
 b TG Living Water.
18a Deut. 4:2 (2–3);
  3 Ne. 11:40 (39–40);
  D&C 20:35 (35–36).
  TG Scriptures,
  Preservation of.
 b TG Plague.

part out of the *a*book of life, and out of the holy city, and *from* the things which are written in this book.

20 He which testifieth these things saith, Surely I *a*come quickly. Amen. Even so, come, Lord Jesus.

21 The *a*grace of our *b*Lord Jesus Christ *be* with you all. Amen.

19a TG Book of Life.
20a D&C 33:18; 35:27.

21a Rom. 16:24 (20–24).
  b TG Jesus Christ, Lord.

THE END

APPENDIX

JOSEPH SMITH TRANSLATION

SELECTIONS FROM THE JOSEPH SMITH TRANSLATION OF THE BIBLE

Following are selected portions of the Joseph Smith Translation of the King James Version of the Bible (JST). The Lord inspired the Prophet Joseph Smith to restore truths to the King James Bible text that had become lost or changed since the original words were written. These restored truths clarified doctrine and improved scriptural understanding.

Because the Lord revealed to Joseph certain truths that the original authors had once recorded, the Joseph Smith Translation is unlike any other Bible translation in the world. In this sense, the word *translation* is used in a broader and different way than usual, for Joseph's translation was more revelation than literal translation from one language into another.

Joseph Smith's translation of the King James Bible has connections with or is mentioned in several sections of the Doctrine and Covenants (see sections 37, 45, 73, 76, 77, 86, 91, and 132). Also, the book of Moses and Joseph Smith—Matthew are excerpts from the Joseph Smith Translation.

For more information about the Joseph Smith Translation, see "Joseph Smith Translation (JST)" in the Bible Dictionary.

The following illustration shows a sample selection from the Joseph Smith Translation:

This reference in bold type is the passage in Joseph Smith's translation of the King James Bible. Because his translation restored words to the Bible text, the verse numbers may differ from the edition you are using.

JST, Matthew 4:1, 5–6, 8–9. Compare Matthew 4:1, 5–6, 8–9; similar changes were made in Luke 4:2, 5–11

This cross-reference indicates the passage in your Bible you should compare to Joseph Smith's translation.

Jesus is led by the Spirit, not by Satan.

This statement explains what doctrine Joseph Smith clarified with his translation.

This is the text as Joseph Smith translated it. (Italics have been added to show differences from the King James Version wording.)

1 Then *Jesus was* led up of the Spirit, into the wilderness, to be *with God.*

5 Then *Jesus was taken* up into the holy city, and *the Spirit* setteth him on *the* pinnacle of the temple.

6 *Then the devil came unto him and said,* If thou be the Son of God, cast thyself down, for it is written, He shall give his angels charge concerning thee, and in their hands they shall bear thee up, lest at any time thou dash thy foot against a stone.

8 *And* again, *Jesus was in the Spirit, and it* taketh him up into an exceeding high mountain, and showeth him all the kingdoms of the world and the glory of them.

9 And *the devil came unto him again, and said,* All these things will I give *unto* thee, if thou wilt fall down and worship me.

JST, Genesis 1:1–8:18. Compare Genesis 1:1–6:13

This text of the Bible was restored by Joseph Smith and is published in the Pearl of Great Price as Selections from the Book of Moses.

JST, Genesis 9:4–6. Compare Genesis 8:20–22

After the Flood, Noah asks the Lord not to curse the earth again.

4 And Noah builded an altar unto the Lord, and took of every clean beast, and of every clean fowl, and offered burnt offerings on the altar; *and gave thanks unto the Lord, and rejoiced in his heart.*
5 *And the Lord spake unto Noah, and he blessed him.* And *Noah* smelled a sweet savor, and *he* said in his heart;
6 *I will call on the name of the Lord, that he* will not again curse the ground any more for man's sake, for the imagination of man's heart is evil from his youth; *and that he* will *not* again smite any more every thing living, as *he* hath done, while the earth remaineth;

JST, Genesis 9:10–15. Compare Genesis 9:4–9

Man is accountable for shedding the blood of animals and of men. God establishes with Noah and his sons the same covenant He made with Enoch.

10 But, *the blood of all* flesh *which I have given you for meat, shall be shed upon the ground, which taketh life thereof, and the blood ye shall not eat.*
11 And surely, *blood shall not be shed, only for meat, to save your lives; and the blood* of every beast will I require *at your hands.*
12 *And* whoso sheddeth man's blood, by man shall his blood be shed; *for man shall not shed the blood of man.*
13 For *a commandment I give,* that every man's brother *shall preserve* the life of man, for in *mine own* image *have I* made man.
14 *And a commandment I give*

unto you, Be ye fruitful and multiply; bring forth abundantly on the earth, and multiply therein.
15 And God spake unto Noah, and to his sons with him, saying, And I, behold, I *will* establish my covenant with you, *which I made unto your father Enoch, concerning your seed after you.*

JST, Genesis 9:21–25. Compare Genesis 9:16–17

God sets the rainbow in heaven as a reminder of His covenant to Enoch and to Noah. In the last days the general assembly of the Church of the Firstborn will join the righteous on earth.

21 And the bow shall be in the cloud; and I will look upon it, that I may remember the everlasting covenant, *which I made unto thy father Enoch; that, when men should keep all my commandments, Zion should again come on the earth, the city of Enoch which I have caught up unto myself.*
22 *And this is mine everlasting covenant, that when thy posterity shall embrace the truth, and look upward, then shall Zion look downward, and all the heavens shall shake with gladness, and the earth shall tremble with joy;*
23 *And the general assembly of the church of the firstborn shall come down out of heaven, and possess the earth, and shall have place until the end come. And this is mine everlasting covenant, which I made with thy father Enoch.*
24 *And the bow shall be in the cloud, and I will establish my covenant unto thee, which I have made* between *me* and *thee, for every living creature of all flesh that shall be upon the earth.*
25 And God said unto Noah, This is the token of the covenant which I have established between me and *thee; for all flesh that shall be upon the earth.*

JST, Genesis 14:25–40. Compare Genesis 14:18–20

Melchizedek blesses Abram. Melchizedek's great ministry and the powers and blessings of the Melchizedek Priesthood are described.

25 And Melchizedek lifted up his voice and blessed Abram.

26 Now Melchizedek was a man of faith, who wrought righteousness; and when a child he feared God, and stopped the mouths of lions, and quenched the violence of fire.

27 And thus, having been approved of God, he was ordained an high priest after the order of the covenant which God made with Enoch,

28 It being after the order of the Son of God; which order came, not by man, nor the will of man; neither by father nor mother; neither by beginning of days nor end of years; but of God;

29 And it was delivered unto men by the calling of his own voice, according to his own will, unto as many as believed on his name.

30 For God having sworn unto Enoch and unto his seed with an oath by himself; that every one being ordained after this order and calling should have power, by faith, to break mountains, to divide the seas, to dry up waters, to turn them out of their course;

31 To put at defiance the armies of nations, to divide the earth, to break every band, to stand in the presence of God; to do all things according to his will, according to his command, subdue principalities and powers; and this by the will of the Son of God which was from before the foundation of the world.

32 And men having this faith, coming up unto this order of God, were translated and taken up into heaven.

33 And now, Melchizedek was a priest of this order; therefore he obtained peace in Salem, and was called the Prince of peace.

34 And his people wrought righteousness, and obtained heaven, and sought for the city of Enoch which God had before taken, separating it from the earth, having reserved it unto the latter days, or the end of the world;

35 And hath said, and sworn with an oath, that the heavens and the earth should come together; and the sons of God should be tried so as by fire.

36 And this Melchizedek, having thus established righteousness, was called the king of heaven by his people, or, in other words, the King of peace.

37 And he lifted up his voice, and he blessed Abram, being the high priest, and the keeper of the storehouse of God;

38 Him whom God had appointed to receive tithes for the poor.

39 Wherefore, Abram paid unto him tithes of all that he had, of all the riches which he possessed, which God had given him more than that which he had need.

40 And it came to pass, that God blessed Abram, and gave unto him riches, and honor, and lands for an everlasting possession; according to the covenant which he had made, and according to the blessing wherewith Melchizedek had blessed him.

JST, Genesis 15:9–12. Compare Genesis 15:1–6

Abraham learns of the Resurrection and sees a vision of Jesus' mortal ministry.

9 And Abram said, Lord God, how wilt thou give me this land for an everlasting inheritance?

10 And the Lord said, Though thou wast dead, yet am I not able to give it thee?

11 And if thou shalt die, yet thou shalt possess it, for the day cometh, that the Son of Man shall live; but how can he live if he be not dead? he must first be quickened.

12 And it came to pass, that Abram looked forth and saw the days of the Son of Man, and was glad, and his soul found rest, and he believed in the Lord; and the Lord counted it unto him for righteousness.

JST, Genesis 17:3–12. Compare Genesis 17:3–12

The people fail to obey the gospel ordinances, including baptism. God explains to Abraham the covenant of circumcision and the age of accountability of children.

3 And *it came to pass, that* Abram fell on his face, *and called upon the name of the Lord.*

4 And God talked with him, saying, *My people have gone astray from my precepts, and have not kept mine ordinances, which I gave unto their fathers;*

5 *And they have not observed mine anointing, and the burial, or baptism wherewith I commanded them;*

6 *But have turned from the commandment, and taken unto themselves the washing of children, and the blood of sprinkling;*

7 *And have said that the blood of the righteous Abel was shed for sins; and have not known wherein they are accountable before me.*

8 But as for *thee*, behold, *I will* make my covenant with thee, and thou shalt be a father of many nations.

9 *And this covenant I make, that thy children may be known among all nations.* Neither shall thy name any more be called Abram, but thy name shall be called Abraham; for, a father of many nations have I made thee.

10 And I will make thee exceedingly fruitful, and I will make nations of thee, and kings shall come of thee, *and of thy seed.*

11 And I will establish *a covenant of circumcision with thee, and it shall be* my covenant between me and thee, and thy seed after thee, in their generations; *that thou mayest know forever that children are not accountable before me until they are eight years old.*

12 *And thou shalt observe to keep all my covenants wherein I covenanted with thy fathers; and thou shalt keep the commandments which I have given thee with mine own* mouth, *and I will be a God unto thee and thy seed after thee.*

JST, Genesis 17:23–24. Compare Genesis 17:17–18

Abraham rejoices at the prophecy of Isaac's birth and prays for Ishmael.

23 Then Abraham fell on his face and *rejoiced*, and said in his heart, *There* shall a child be born unto him that is an hundred years old, and Sarah that is ninety years old shall bear.

24 And Abraham said unto God, Oh that Ishmael might live *uprightly* before thee!

JST, Genesis 19:9–15. Compare Genesis 19:8–10

Lot resists the wickedness of Sodom, and angels protect him.

9 And they said *unto him*, Stand back. *And they were angry with him.*

10 *And they said among themselves*, This one *man* came in to sojourn *among us*, and he will needs *now make himself to be* a judge; now we will deal worse with *him* than with them.

11 *Wherefore they said unto the man*, We will have the men, and thy daughters also; and we will do with *them as seemeth us good.*

12 *Now this was after the wickedness of Sodom.*

13 And Lot said, Behold now, I have two daughters which have not known man; let me, I pray you, *plead with my brethren that I may not* bring them out unto you; and ye *shall not* do unto them as seemeth good in your eyes;

14 *For God will not justify his servant in this thing; wherefore, let me plead with my brethren, this once only, that unto these men ye do nothing, that they may have peace in my house; for therefore came* they under the shadow of my roof.

15 *And they were angry with Lot* and came near to break the door, but the *angels of God, which were holy men*, put forth their hand and

pulled Lot into the house unto them, and shut the door.

JST, Genesis 21:31–32. Compare Genesis 21:32–34

Abraham worships the everlasting God.

31 Then Abimelech, and Phicol, the chief captain of his hosts, rose up, *and they planted a grove in Beersheba, and called there on the name of the Lord;* and they returned unto the land of the Philistines.

32 And Abraham *worshiped the everlasting God, and* sojourned in the land of the Philistines many days.

JST, Genesis 48:5–11. Compare Genesis 48:5–6

Ephraim and Manasseh become tribes of Israel. Just as ancient Joseph saved his family temporally, his descendants will save Israel spiritually in the latter days.

5 And now, of thy two sons, Ephraim and Manasseh, which were born unto thee in the land of Egypt, before I came unto thee into Egypt; *behold, they are mine, and the God of my fathers shall bless them; even as Reuben and Simeon* they *shall be blessed, for they are* mine; *wherefore they shall be called after my name. (Therefore they were called Israel.)*

6 And thy issue which thou begettest after them, shall be thine, and shall be called after the name of their brethren in their inheritance, *in the tribes; therefore they were called the tribes of Manasseh and of Ephraim.*

7 And Jacob said unto Joseph, When the God of my fathers appeared unto me in Luz, in the land of Canaan; he sware unto me, that he would give unto me, and unto my seed, the land for an everlasting possession.

8 *Therefore, O my son,* he hath blessed me in raising thee up to be a servant unto me, in saving my house from death;

9 *In delivering my people, thy breth-ren, from famine which was sore in the land; wherefore the God of thy* fathers shall bless thee, and the fruit of thy loins, that they shall be blessed above thy brethren, and above thy father's house;

10 For thou hast prevailed, and thy father's house hath bowed down unto thee, even as it was shown unto thee, before thou wast sold into Egypt by the hands of thy brethren; wherefore thy brethren shall bow down unto thee, from generation to generation, unto the fruit of thy loins forever;

11 For thou shalt be a light unto my people, to deliver them in the days of their captivity, from bondage; and to bring salvation unto them, when they are altogether bowed down under sin.

JST, Genesis 50:24–38. Compare Genesis 50:24–26; 2 Nephi 3:4–22

Joseph in Egypt prophesies of Moses freeing Israel from Egyptian bondage; of a branch of Joseph's descendants being led to a faraway land, where they will be remembered in the covenants of the Lord; of God calling a latter-day prophet named Joseph to join the records of Judah and of Joseph; and of Aaron serving as a spokesman for Moses.

24 And Joseph said unto his brethren, I die, *and go unto my fathers; and I go down to my grave with joy. The God of my father Jacob be with you, to deliver you out of af-fliction in the days of your bondage; for the Lord hath visited me, and I have obtained a promise of the Lord, that out of the fruit of my loins, the Lord God will raise up a righteous branch out of my loins; and unto thee, whom my father Jacob hath named Israel, a prophet; (not the Messiah who is called Shilo;) and this prophet shall deliver my peo-ple out of Egypt in the days of thy bondage.*

25 *And it shall come to pass that they shall be scattered again; and a branch shall be broken off, and shall be carried into a far country; nev-ertheless they shall be remembered in the covenants of the Lord, when the Messiah cometh; for he shall be*

made manifest unto them in the latter days, in the Spirit of power; and shall bring them out of darkness into light; out of hidden darkness, and out of captivity unto freedom.

26 A seer shall the Lord my God raise up, who shall be a choice seer unto the fruit of my loins.

27 Thus saith the Lord God of my fathers unto me, A choice seer will I raise up out of the fruit of thy loins, and he shall be esteemed highly among the fruit of thy loins; and unto him will I give commandment that he shall do a work for the fruit of thy loins, his brethren.

28 And he shall bring them to the knowledge of the covenants which I have made with thy fathers; and he shall do whatsoever work I shall command him.

29 And I will make him great in mine eyes, for he shall do my work; and he shall be great like unto him whom I have said I would raise up unto you, to deliver my people, O house of Israel, out of the land of Egypt; for a seer will I raise up to deliver my people out of the land of Egypt; and he shall be called Moses. And by this name he shall know that he is of thy house; for he shall be nursed by the king's daughter, and shall be called her son.

30 And again, a seer will I raise up out of the fruit of thy loins, and unto him will I give power to bring forth my word unto the seed of thy loins; and not to the bringing forth of my word only, saith the Lord, but to the convincing them of my word, which shall have already gone forth among them in the last days;

31 Wherefore the fruit of thy loins shall write, and the fruit of the loins of Judah shall write; and that which shall be written by the fruit of thy loins, and also that which shall be written by the fruit of the loins of Judah, shall grow together unto the confounding of false doctrines, and laying down of contentions, and establishing peace among the fruit of thy loins, and bringing them to a knowledge of their fathers in the latter days; and also to the knowledge of my covenants, saith the Lord.

32 And out of weakness shall he be made strong, in that day when my work shall go forth among all my people, which shall restore them, who are of the house of Israel, in the last days.

33 And that seer will I bless, and they that seek to destroy him shall be confounded; for this promise I give unto you; for I will remember you from generation to generation; and his name shall be called Joseph, and it shall be after the name of his father; and he shall be like unto you; for the thing which the Lord shall bring forth by his hand shall bring my people unto salvation.

34 And the Lord sware unto Joseph that he would preserve his seed forever, saying, I will raise up Moses, and a rod shall be in his hand, and he shall gather together my people, and he shall lead them as a flock, and he shall smite the waters of the Red Sea with his rod.

35 And he shall have judgment, and shall write the word of the Lord. And he shall not speak many words, for I will write unto him my law by the finger of mine own hand. And I will make a spokesman for him, and his name shall be called Aaron.

36 And it shall be done unto thee in the last days also, even as I have sworn. Therefore, Joseph said unto his brethren, God will surely visit you, and bring you out of this land, unto the land which he sware unto Abraham, and unto Isaac, and to Jacob.

37 And Joseph confirmed many other things unto his brethren, and took an oath of the children of Israel, saying unto them, God will surely visit you, and ye shall carry up my bones from hence.

38 So Joseph died when he was an hundred and ten years old; and they embalmed him, and they put him in a coffin in Egypt; and he was kept from burial by the children of Israel, that he might be carried up and laid in the sepulchre with his

father. And thus they remembered the oath which they sware unto him.

JST, Exodus 4:21. Compare
  Exodus 4:21; 7:3, 13; 9:12;
  10:1, 20, 27; 11:10; 14:4, 8, 17;
  Deuteronomy 2:30

The Lord is not responsible for Pharaoh's hardness of heart. See also JST, Exodus 7:3, 13; 9:12; 10:1, 20, 27; 11:10; 14:4, 8, 17; each reference, when correctly translated, shows that Pharaoh hardened his own heart.

21 And the Lord said unto Moses, When thou goest to return into Egypt, see that thou do all those wonders before Pharaoh, which I have put in thine hand, *and I will prosper thee;* but *Pharaoh* will harden his heart, *and he will* not let the people go.

JST, Exodus 4:24–27. Compare
  Exodus 4:24–27

When the Lord threatens to kill Moses for not circumcising his son, Zipporah saves his life by performing the ordinance herself. Moses confesses his sin.

24 And it came to pass, *that the Lord appeared unto him as he was in the way, by the inn. The Lord was angry with Moses, and his hand was about to fall upon him,* to kill him; *for he had not circumcised his son.*
25 Then Zipporah took a sharp stone and *circumcised* her son, and cast *the stone* at his feet, and said, Surely *thou art* a bloody husband unto me.
26 *And the Lord spared Moses and* let him go, *because Zipporah, his wife, circumcised the child.* And she said, Thou art a bloody husband. *And Moses was ashamed, and hid his face from the Lord, and said, I have sinned before the Lord.*
27 And the Lord said unto Aaron, Go into the wilderness to meet Moses, and he went and met him, in the mount of God; *in the mount where God appeared unto him;* and Aaron kissed him.

JST, Exodus 18:1. Compare
  Exodus 18:1

Jethro is a high priest.

1 When Jethro, the *high priest* of Midian, Moses' father-in-law, heard of all that God had done for Moses, and for Israel his people, and that the Lord had brought Israel out of Egypt;

JST, Exodus 22:18. Compare
  Exodus 22:18

Murderers shall not live.

18 Thou shalt not suffer a *murderer* to live.

JST, Exodus 32:14. Compare
  Exodus 32:14

The Lord will spare the Israelites who will repent.

14 And the Lord *said unto Moses, If they will repent* of the evil which *they have done, I will spare them, and turn away my fierce wrath; but, behold, thou shalt execute judgment upon all that will not repent of this evil this day. Therefore, see thou do this thing that I have commanded thee, or I will execute all that which I had* thought to do unto *my* people.

JST, Exodus 33:20, 23. Compare
  Exodus 33:20, 23

No sinful man can see God's face and live.

20 And he said *unto Moses,* Thou canst not see my face *at this time, lest mine anger be kindled against thee also, and I destroy thee, and thy people;* for there shall no man *among them* see me *at this time,* and live, *for they are exceeding sinful. And no sinful man hath at any time, neither shall there be any sinful man at any time, that shall see my face and live.*
23 And I will take away mine hand, and thou shalt see my back parts, but my face shall not be seen, *as at other times; for I am angry with my people Israel.*

JST, Exodus 34:1–2, 14. Compare Exodus 34:1–2, 14; D&C 84:21–26

God again writes the law on tablets of stone prepared by Moses but takes the Melchizedek Priesthood and its ordinances away from the children of Israel. He gives them the law of carnal commandments instead.

1 And the Lord said unto Moses, Hew thee two *other* tables of stone, like unto the first, *and I will write upon them also,* the words *of the law, according as they were written at the* first *on the* tables which thou brakest; *but it shall not be according to the first, for I will take away the priesthood out of their midst; therefore my holy order, and the ordinances thereof, shall not go before them; for my presence shall not go up in their midst, lest I destroy them.*
2 *But I will give unto them the law as at the first, but it shall be after the law of a carnal commandment; for I have sworn in my wrath, that they shall not enter into my presence, into my rest, in the days of their pilgrimage. Therefore do as I have commanded thee,* and be ready in the morning, and come up in the morning unto mount Sinai, and present thyself there to me, in the top of the mount.

Jehovah is one name by which the Old Testament people know the Lord Jesus Christ.

14 For thou shalt worship no other god; for the Lord, whose name is *Jehovah,* is a jealous God.

JST, Deuteronomy 10:2. Compare Deuteronomy 10:2

On the first set of tablets God reveals the everlasting covenant of the holy priesthood.

2 And I will write on the tables the words that were *on the* first tables, which thou brakest, *save the words of the everlasting covenant of the holy priesthood,* and thou shalt put them in the ark.

JST, 1 Samuel 16:14–16, 23. Compare 1 Samuel 16:14–16, 23; similar changes were made to 1 Samuel 18:10 and 19:9

The evil spirit that comes upon Saul is not from the Lord.

14 But the Spirit of the Lord departed from Saul, and an evil spirit *which was not of* the Lord troubled him.
15 And Saul's servants said unto him, Behold now, an evil spirit *which is not of* God troubleth thee.
16 Let our lord now command thy servants, which are before thee, to seek out a man, who is a cunning player on a harp; and it shall come to pass, when the evil spirit, *which is not of* God, is upon thee, that he shall play with his hand, and thou shalt be well.
23 And it came to pass, when the evil spirit, *which was not of* God, was upon Saul, that David took a harp, and played with his hand; so Saul was refreshed, and was well, and the evil spirit departed from him.

JST, 2 Samuel 12:13. Compare 2 Samuel 12:13

David's grievous sin is not put away by God.

13 And David said unto Nathan, I have sinned against the Lord. And Nathan said unto David, The Lord also hath *not* put away thy sin *that* thou shalt not die.

JST, 1 Chronicles 21:15. Compare 1 Chronicles 21:15

God stops an angel from destroying Jerusalem.

15 And God sent an angel unto Jerusalem to destroy it. *And the angel stretched forth his hand unto Jerusalem to destroy it; and God said to the angel, Stay now thine hand, it is enough; for* as he was destroying, the Lord beheld Israel, *that* he repented him of the evil; *therefore the Lord stayed* the angel that destroyed, *as he stood*

by the threshing floor of Ornan, the Jebusite.

JST, 2 Chronicles 18:22. Compare 2 Chronicles 18:22

The Lord does not put a lying spirit into the mouths of prophets.

22 Now therefore, behold, the Lord hath *found* a lying spirit in the mouth of these thy prophets, and the Lord hath spoken evil against thee.

JST, Psalm 11:1–5. Compare Psalm 11:1–5

In the last days the righteous will flee to the mountain of the Lord. When the Lord comes, He will destroy the wicked and redeem the righteous.

1 *In that day thou shalt come, O Lord; and* I will put my trust *in thee. Thou shalt say unto thy people, for mine ear hath heard thy voice; thou shalt say unto every* soul, Flee unto *my* mountain; *and the righteous shall flee like* a bird *that is let go from the snare of the fowler.*

2 For the wicked bend their bow; lo, they make ready their arrow upon the string, that they may privily shoot at the upright in heart, *to destroy their foundation.*

3 *But* the foundations *of the wicked shall* be destroyed, *and* what can *they* do?

4 *For* the Lord, *when he shall come into* his holy temple, *sitting upon God's* throne in heaven, his eyes *shall pierce the wicked.*

5 Behold his eyelids *shall* try the children of men, *and he shall redeem the righteous, and they shall be tried.* The Lord *loveth the* righteous, but the wicked, and him that loveth violence, his soul hateth.

JST, Psalm 14:1–7. Compare Psalm 14:1–7

The Psalmist sees the loss of truth in the last days and looks forward to the establishment of Zion.

1 The fool hath said in his heart, *There is no man that hath seen God.*

Because he showeth himself not unto us, therefore there is no God. *Behold,* they are corrupt; they have done abominable works, *and none of them* doeth good.

2 *For* the Lord looked down from heaven upon the children of men, *and by his voice said unto his servant, Seek ye among the children of men,* to see if there *are* any that *do* understand God. *And he opened his mouth unto the Lord, and said, Behold, all these who say they are thine.*

3 *The Lord answered, and said,* They are all gone aside, they are together become filthy, *thou canst behold* none *of them* that *are doing* good, no, not one.

4 *All they have for their teachers are* workers of iniquity, *and there is* no knowledge *in them. They are they* who eat up my people. They eat bread and call not upon the Lord.

5 They *are* in great fear, for God dwells in the generation of the righteous. *He is the counsel of the poor, because they are ashamed of the wicked, and flee unto the Lord, for their refuge.*

6 *They are ashamed of* the counsel of the poor because the Lord is his refuge.

7 Oh that *Zion were established out of heaven,* the salvation of Israel. *O Lord, when wilt thou establish Zion?* When the Lord bringeth back the captivity of his people, Jacob shall rejoice, Israel shall be glad.

JST, Psalm 24:7–10. Compare Psalm 24:7–10

The King of Glory will redeem His people at His coming.

7 Lift up your heads, O ye *generations of Jacob;* and be ye lifted up; *and* the Lord strong and mighty; the Lord mighty in battle, who is the king of glory, *shall establish you forever.*

8 *And he will roll away the heavens; and will come down to redeem*

his people; to make you an everlasting name; to establish you upon his everlasting rock.

9 Lift up your heads, O ye *generations of Jacob*; lift up *your heads*, ye everlasting *generations*, and the *Lord of hosts, the king of kings*;

10 *Even* the king of glory shall come *unto you; and shall redeem his people, and shall establish them in righteousness.* Selah.

JST, Psalm 109:4. Compare Psalm 109:4

We are to pray for our adversaries.

4 *And, notwithstanding* my love, they are my adversaries; *yet* I *will continue in* prayer *for them.*

JST, Isaiah 29:1–8. Compare Isaiah 29:1–8

The messages formerly preached in Jerusalem by ancient prophets will in the latter days be preached from the Book of Mormon, which came forth "out of the ground."

1 Woe to Ariel, to Ariel, the city where David dwelt! add ye year to year; let them kill sacrifices.

2 Yet I will distress Ariel, and there shall be heaviness and sorrow; *for thus hath the Lord said unto me,* It shall be unto Ariel;

3 *That* I *the Lord* will camp against *her* round about, and will lay siege against *her* with a mount, and I will raise forts against *her*.

4 And *she shall* be brought down, and *shall* speak out of the ground, and *her* speech shall be low out of the dust; and *her* voice shall be as of one that hath a familiar spirit, out of the ground, and *her* speech shall whisper out of the dust.

5 Moreover the multitude of *her* strangers shall be like small dust, and the multitude of the terrible ones shall be as chaff that passeth away; yea, it shall be at an instant suddenly.

6 *For they shall* be visited of the Lord of hosts with thunder, and with earthquake, and great noise, with storm and tempest, and the flame of devouring fire.

7 And the multitude of all the nations that fight against Ariel, even all that fight against her and her munition, and that distress her, shall be as a dream of a night vision.

8 *Yea,* it shall *be unto them even* as *unto* a hungry man *who* dreameth, and behold, he eateth, but he awaketh and his soul is empty; or *like unto* a thirsty man *who* dreameth, and behold, he drinketh, but he awaketh, and behold, he is faint, and his soul hath appetite. *Yea, even* so shall the multitude of all the nations be that fight against mount Zion.

JST, Isaiah 42:19–23. Compare Isaiah 42:19–22

The Lord sends His servant to teach those who have chosen not to see or hear the truth; those who listen and obey will be made perfect.

19 *For I will send my servant unto you who are blind; yea, a messenger to open the eyes of the blind, and unstop the ears of the deaf;*

20 *And they shall be made perfect notwithstanding their blindness, if they will hearken unto the messenger,* the Lord's servant.

21 *Thou art a people,* seeing many things, but thou observest not; opening the ears *to hear, but thou* hearest not.

22 The Lord is *not* well pleased *with such a people, but* for his righteousness' sake he will magnify the law and make it honorable.

23 *Thou art* a people robbed and spoiled; *thine enemies,* all of them, *have* snared *thee* in holes, and they *have hid thee* in prison houses; they *have taken thee* for a prey, and none delivereth; for a spoil, and none saith, Restore.

JST, Jeremiah 26:13. Compare Jeremiah 26:13

The Lord does not repent; men repent.

13 Therefore now, amend your

ways and your doings, and obey the voice of the Lord your God, *and repent*, and the Lord will *turn away* the evil that he hath pronounced against you.

JST, Amos 7:3. Compare Amos 7:3

The Lord does not repent; men repent.

3 And the Lord *said, concerning Jacob, Jacob shall repent* for this, *therefore I will not utterly destroy him*, saith the Lord.

JST, Matthew 3:4–6. Compare Matthew 2:4–6

The prophets foretold that Bethlehem would be the place of the Messiah's birth.

4 And when he had gathered all the chief priests, and scribes of the people together, he demanded of them, *saying, Where is the place that is written of by the prophets, in which* Christ should be born? *For he greatly feared, yet he believed not the prophets.*
5 And they said unto him, *It is written by the prophets, that he should be born* in Bethlehem of Judea, for thus *have they said,*
6 *The word of the Lord came unto us, saying,* And thou Bethlehem, *which lieth* in the land of Judea, *in thee shall be born a prince, which* art not the least among the princes of Judea; for out of thee shall come *the Messiah,* who shall *save* my people Israel.

JST, Matthew 3:24–26. Compare Matthew 2:23

Jesus grows up and waits on the Lord before beginning His ministry.

24 *And it came to pass that Jesus grew up with his brethren, and waxed strong, and waited upon the Lord for the time of his ministry to come.*
25 *And he served under his father, and he spake not as other men, neither could he be taught; for he needed not that any man should teach him.*
26 *And after many years, the hour of his ministry drew nigh.*

JST, Matthew 3:34–36. Compare Matthew 3:8–9

Those who rejected the message of John the Baptist rejected Christ. God can make covenant people of those not of Israel.

34 *Why is it that ye receive not the preaching of him whom God hath sent? If ye receive not this in your hearts, ye receive not me; and if ye receive not me, ye receive not him of whom I am sent to bear record; and for your sins ye have no cloak.*
35 *Repent, therefore, and* bring forth fruits meet for repentance;
36 And think not to say within yourselves, *We are the children of Abraham, and we only have power to bring seed unto our father Abraham;* for I say unto you that God is able of these stones to raise up children *into* Abraham.

JST, Matthew 3:38–40. Compare Matthew 3:11–12

John the Baptist testifies that Jesus has power to baptize with the Holy Ghost and fire.

38 I indeed baptize you with water, *upon your* repentance; *and when he of whom I bear record cometh, who is* mightier than I, whose shoes I am not worthy to bear, *(or whose place I am not able to fill,) as I said, I indeed baptize you before he cometh, that when he cometh he may* baptize you with the Holy Ghost and fire.
39 *And it is he of whom I shall bear record, whose fan shall be in his* hand, and he will thoroughly purge his floor, and gather his wheat into the garner; but *in the fullness of his own time* will burn up the chaff with unquenchable fire.
40 *Thus came John, preaching and baptizing in the river of Jordan; bearing record, that he who was coming after him had power to baptize with the Holy Ghost and fire.*

JST, Matthew 3:43–46. Compare
  Matthew 3:15–17

John baptizes Jesus by immersion, sees the
Holy Ghost descending like a dove, and
hears the Father's voice.

43 And Jesus, answering, said
unto him, Suffer *me to be baptized
of thee,* for thus it becometh us to
fulfill all righteousness. Then he
suffered him.
44 *And John went down into the
water and baptized him.*
45 And Jesus when he was baptized, went up straightway out of
the water; *and John saw,* and lo,
the heavens were opened unto
him, and he saw the Spirit of God
descending like a dove and lighting upon *Jesus.*
46 And lo, *he heard* a voice from
heaven, saying, This is my beloved
Son, in whom I am well pleased.
Hear ye him.

JST, Matthew 4:1, 5–6, 8–9.
  Compare Matthew 4:1, 5–6, 8–9;
  similar changes were made in
  Luke 4:2, 5–11

Jesus is led by the Spirit, not by Satan.

1 Then *Jesus was* led up of the
Spirit, into the wilderness, to be
with God.
5 Then *Jesus was taken* up into
the holy city, and *the Spirit* setteth
him on *the* pinnacle of the temple.
6 *Then the devil came unto him
and said,* If thou be the Son of
God, cast thyself down, for it is
written, He shall give his angels
charge concerning thee, and in
their hands they shall bear thee
up, lest at any time thou dash thy
foot against a stone.
8 *And* again, *Jesus was in the
Spirit, and it* taketh him up into
an exceeding high mountain, and
showeth him all the kingdoms of
the world and the glory of them.
9 And *the devil came unto him
again, and said,* All these things
will I give *unto* thee, if thou wilt
fall down and worship me.

JST, Matthew 4:11. Compare
  Matthew 4:11

Jesus sends angels to minister to John the
Baptist.

11 *And now Jesus knew that John
was cast into prison, and he sent angels,* and, behold, *they* came and
ministered unto him.

JST, Matthew 4:18. Compare
  Matthew 4:19

Old Testament prophets speak of Jesus.

18 And he *said* unto them, *I am
he of whom it is written by the prophets;* follow me, and I will make
you fishers of men.

JST, Matthew 4:22. Compare
  Matthew 4:23

Jesus heals people among those who
believe on His name.

22 And Jesus went about all Galilee teaching in their synagogues,
and preaching the gospel of the
kingdom; and healing all manner of sickness, and all manner of
diseases among the people *which
believed on his name.*

JST, Matthew 5:21. Compare
  Matthew 5:19

Whoso keeps the commandments and
teaches others to do the same will
be saved.

21 Whosoever, therefore, shall
break one of these least commandments, and shall teach men
so *to do, he shall in no wise be saved
in the kingdom of heaven;* but whosoever shall do and teach *these
commandments of the law until it be
fulfilled,* the same shall be called
great, *and shall be saved* in the
kingdom of heaven.

JST, Matthew 6:14. Compare
  Matthew 6:13; similar changes
  were made in Luke 11:4

The Lord does not lead us into temptation.

14 And *suffer* us not *to be led*
into temptation, but deliver us
from evil.

JST, Matthew 6:22. Compare
Matthew 6:22

If our eyes are single to the glory of God, our whole bodies will be filled with light.

22 The light of the body is the eye; if therefore thine eye be single *to the glory of God*, thy whole body shall be full of light.

JST, Matthew 6:25–27. Compare
Matthew 6:25; 10:10

Jesus warns His disciples of the difficulty of their work but promises that He will prepare the way and that Heavenly Father will provide for them.

25 *And, again, I say unto you, Go ye into the world, and care not for the world; for the world will hate you, and will persecute you, and will turn you out of their synagogues.*

26 *Nevertheless, ye shall go forth from house to house, teaching the people; and I will go before you.*

27 *And your heavenly Father will provide for you, whatsoever things ye need for food, what ye shall eat; and for raiment, what ye shall wear or put on.*

JST, Matthew 6:38. Compare
Matthew 6:33

We should seek first to build the kingdom of God.

38 *Wherefore, seek not the things of this world* but seek ye first *to build up* the kingdom of God, and *to establish* his righteousness, and all these things shall be added unto you.

JST, Matthew 7:1–2. Compare
Matthew 7:1–2

Judge not unrighteously.

1 *Now these are the words which Jesus taught his disciples that they should say unto the people.*

2 Judge not *unrighteously*, that ye be not judged; *but judge righteous judgment.*

JST, Matthew 7:4–8. Compare
Matthew 7:3–5

Jesus teaches His disciples to confront scribes, Pharisees, priests, and Levites because of their hypocrisy.

4 *And again, ye shall say unto them, Why is it that thou* beholdest the mote that is in thy brother's eye, but considerest not the beam that is in thine own eye?

5 Or how wilt thou say to thy brother, Let me pull out the mote out of thine eye; *and canst not behold a* beam in thine own eye?

6 *And Jesus said unto his disciples, Beholdest thou the scribes, and the Pharisees, and the priests, and the Levites? They teach in their synagogues, but do not observe the law, nor the commandments; and all have gone out of the way, and are under sin.*

7 Go thou and say unto them, Why *teach ye men the law and the commandments, when ye yourselves are the children of corruption?*

8 *Say unto them, Ye hypocrites,* first cast out the beam out of thine own eye; and then shalt thou see clearly to cast out the mote out of thy brother's eye.

JST, Matthew 7:9–11. Compare
Matthew 7:6

Jesus teaches His disciples to preach repentance and not to share the mysteries of the kingdom with the world.

9 *Go ye into the world, saying unto all, Repent, for the kingdom of heaven has come nigh unto you.*

10 *And the mysteries of the kingdom ye shall keep within yourselves; for it is not meet to give that which is holy unto the dogs; neither cast ye your pearls unto swine, lest they trample them under their feet.*

11 *For the world cannot receive that which ye, yourselves, are not able to bear; wherefore ye shall not give your pearls unto them, lest they* turn again and rend you.

JST, Matthew 7:12–17. Compare Matthew 7:7–8

Jesus teaches His disciples that the Father gives revelation to all who ask.

12 *Say unto them, Ask of God*; ask, and it shall be given you; seek, and ye shall find; knock, and it shall be opened unto you.

13 For everyone that asketh, receiveth; and he that seeketh, findeth; and unto him that knocketh, it shall be opened.

14 *And then said his disciples unto him, They will say unto us, We ourselves are righteous, and need not that any man should teach us. God, we know, heard Moses and some of the prophets; but us he will not hear.*

15 *And they will say, We have the law for our salvation, and that is sufficient for us.*

16 *Then Jesus answered, and said unto his disciples, Thus shall ye say unto them,*

17 *What man among you, having a son, and he shall be standing out, and shall say, Father, open thy house that I may come in and sup with thee, will not say, Come in, my son; for mine is thine, and thine is mine?*

JST, Matthew 9:18–21. Compare Matthew 9:16–17

Jesus rejects the baptism of the Pharisees; it has no value because they do not accept Him. He proclaims that He is the one who gave the law of Moses.

18 *Then said the Pharisees unto him, Why will ye not receive us with our baptism, seeing we keep the whole law?*

19 *But Jesus said unto them, Ye keep not the law. If ye had kept the law, ye would have received me, for I am he who gave the law.*

20 *I receive not you with your baptism, because it profiteth you nothing.*

21 *For when that which is new is come, the old is ready to be put away.*

JST, Matthew 11:13–15. Compare Matthew 11:10–11, 13–14

John the Baptist is the Elias who would come to prepare the way for the Savior.

13 *But the days will come, when the violent shall have no power*; for all the prophets and the law prophesied *that it should be thus until John.*

14 *Yea, as many as have prophesied have foretold of these days.*

15 And if ye will receive it, *verily, he was the Elias, who* was for to come *and prepare all things.*

JST, Matthew 12:37–38. Compare Matthew 12:43–44; see also JST, Luke 12:9–12

Whosoever speaks against the Holy Ghost will not be forgiven.

37 *Then came some of the scribes and said unto him, Master, it is written that, Every sin shall be forgiven; but ye say, Whosoever speaketh against the Holy Ghost shall not be forgiven. And they asked him, saying, How can these things be?*

38 *And he said unto them, When the unclean spirit is gone out of a man, he walketh through dry places, seeking rest and findeth none; but when a man speaketh against the Holy Ghost, then he saith, I will return into my house from whence I came out; and when he is come, he findeth him empty, swept and garnished; for the good spirit leaveth him unto himself.*

JST, Matthew 13:39–44. Compare Matthew 13:39–42; see also D&C 86:1–7

Before the end of the world (the destruction of the wicked), messengers sent of heaven will gather the righteous from among the wicked.

39 The harvest is the end of the world, *or the destruction of the wicked.*

40 The reapers are the angels, *or the messengers sent of heaven.*

41 As, therefore, the tares are gathered and burned in the fire, so shall it be in the end of this world, *or the destruction of the wicked.*

42 *For in that day, before* the Son

of man shall *come, he* shall send forth his angels *and messengers of heaven.*

43 And they shall gather out of his kingdom all things that offend, and them which do iniquity, and shall cast them *out among the wicked; and* there shall be wailing and gnashing of teeth.

44 *For the world shall be burned with fire.*

JST, Matthew 16:25–29. Compare Matthew 16:24–26

Jesus explains what it means "to take up one's cross": to deny all ungodliness and every worldly lust and to keep His commandments.

25 Then said Jesus unto his disciples, If any man will come after me, let him deny himself, and take up his cross and follow me.

26 *And now for a man to take up his cross, is to deny himself all ungodliness, and every worldly lust, and keep my commandments.*

27 *Break not my commandments for to save your lives; for whosoever will save his life in this world,* shall lose it *in the world to come.*

28 And whosoever will lose his life *in this world,* for my sake, shall find it *in the world to come.*

29 *Therefore, forsake the world, and save your souls; for what is a* man profited, if he shall gain the whole world, and lose his own soul? Or what shall a man give in exchange for his soul?

JST, Matthew 17:10–14. Compare Matthew 17:11–13

Jesus teaches of two Eliases—one to prepare and another to restore.

10 And Jesus answered and said unto them, Elias truly shall first come, and restore all things, *as the prophets have written.*

11 *And again* I say unto you that Elias has come already, *concerning whom it is written, Behold, I will send my messenger, and he shall prepare the way before me;* and they knew

him not, and have done unto him, whatsoever they listed.

12 Likewise shall also the Son of man suffer of them.

13 *But I say unto you, Who is Elias? Behold, this is Elias, whom I send to prepare the way before me.*

14 Then the disciples understood that he spake unto them of John the Baptist, *and also of another who should come and restore all things, as it is written by the prophets.*

JST, Matthew 18:11. Compare Matthew 18:11; see also Moroni 8

Little children have no need of repentance.

11 For the Son of man is come to save that which was lost, *and to call sinners to repentance; but these little ones have no need of repentance, and I will save them.*

JST, Matthew 19:13. Compare Matthew 19:13

Little children will be saved.

13 Then were there brought unto him little children, that he should put his hands on them and pray. And the disciples rebuked them, *saying, There is no need, for Jesus hath said, Such shall be saved.*

JST, Matthew 21:33. Compare Matthew 21:32–33

Man must repent before he can believe in Christ.

33 For *he that believed not John concerning me, cannot believe me, except he first repent.*

JST, Matthew 21:47–56. Compare Matthew 21:45–46

Jesus declares that He is the chief cornerstone. The gospel is offered to the Jews and then to the Gentiles. The wicked will be destroyed when Jesus returns.

47 And when the chief priests and Pharisees had heard his parables, they perceived that he spake of them.

48 *And they said among themselves, Shall this man think that he*

alone can spoil this great kingdom? And they were angry with him.

49 But when they sought to lay hands on him, they feared the multitude, because they *learned that the multitude* took him for a prophet.

50 *And now his disciples came to him, and Jesus said unto them, Marvel ye at the words of the parable which I spake unto them?*

51 *Verily, I say unto you, I am the stone, and those wicked ones reject me.*

52 *I am the head of the corner. These Jews shall fall upon me, and shall be broken.*

53 *And the kingdom of God shall be taken from them, and shall be given forth to a nation bringing forth the fruits thereof; (meaning the Gentiles.)*

54 *Wherefore, on whomsoever this stone shall fall, it shall grind him to powder.*

55 *And when the Lord therefore of the vineyard cometh, he will destroy those miserable, wicked men, and will let again his vineyard unto other husbandmen, even in the last days, who shall render him the fruits in their seasons.*

56 *And then understood they the parable which he spake unto them, that the Gentiles should be destroyed also, when the Lord should descend out of heaven to reign in his vineyard, which is the earth and the inhabitants thereof.*

JST, Matthew 23:6. Compare Matthew 23:9

He who is in heaven is our creator.

6 And call no *one* your *creator* upon the earth, or *your heavenly* Father; for one is your *creator and heavenly* Father, *even he who* is in heaven.

JST, Matthew 26:22, 24–25. Compare Matthew 26:26–28; JST, Mark 14:20–25

Jesus first breaks the sacramental bread then blesses it. The sacrament is in remembrance of Jesus' body and blood.

22 And as they were eating, Jesus took bread and *brake* it, and *blessed* it, and gave to *his* disciples, and said, Take, eat; this is *in remembrance of* my body *which I give a ransom for you.*

24 For this is *in remembrance of* my blood of the new testament, which is shed for *as* many *as shall believe on my name,* for the remission of *their* sins.

25 *And I give unto you a commandment, that ye shall observe to do the things which ye have seen me do, and bear record of me even unto the end.*

JST, Matthew 27:3–6. Compare Matthew 27:3–5; Acts 1:18

Judas's death is described.

3 Then Judas, *who* had betrayed him, when he saw that he was condemned, repented himself, and brought again the thirty pieces of silver to the chief priests and elders,

4 Saying, I have sinned in that I have betrayed the innocent blood.

5 And they said *unto him,* What is that to us? See thou to *it; thy sins be upon thee.*

6 And he cast down the pieces of silver in the temple, and departed, and went, and hanged himself *on a tree. And straightway he fell down, and his bowels gushed out, and he died.*

JST, Mark 2:26–27. Compare Mark 2:27–28

The Son of Man is Lord of the Sabbath because He made the Sabbath day.

26 *Wherefore the Sabbath was given unto man for a day of rest; and also that man should glorify God, and not that man should not eat;*

27 *For the Son of man made the Sabbath day,* therefore the Son of man is Lord also of the Sabbath.

JST, Mark 3:21–25. Compare Mark 3:28–30

Jesus will forgive all sinners who repent except those who blaspheme against the Holy Ghost.

21 *And then came certain men unto him, accusing him, saying, Why do ye receive sinners, seeing thou makest thyself the Son of God.*

22 *But he answered them and said,* Verily I say unto you, All sins *which men have committed, when they repent,* shall be forgiven *them; for I came to preach repentance* unto the sons of men.

23 And blasphemies, wherewith soever they shall blaspheme, *shall be forgiven them that come unto me, and do the works which they see me do.*

24 *But there is a sin which shall not be forgiven.* He that shall blaspheme against the Holy Ghost, hath never forgiveness; but is in danger of *being cut down out of the world. And they shall inherit* eternal damnation.

25 *And this he said unto them* because they said, He hath an unclean spirit.

JST, Mark 7:10–12. Compare Mark 7:10

Jesus condemns those who reject the prophets and do not obey the law of Moses.

10 *Full well is it written of you, by the prophets whom ye have rejected.*

11 *They testified these things of a truth, and their blood shall be upon you.*

12 *Ye have kept not the ordinances of God; for Moses said, Honor thy father and thy mother; and whoso curseth father or mother, let him die the death of the transgressor, as it is written in your law; but ye keep not the law.*

JST, Mark 8:37–38. Compare Mark 8:35

Whoever is willing to die for Jesus' sake will receive salvation.

37 For whosoever will save his life, shall lose it; *or whosoever will save his life, shall be willing to lay it down for my sake; and if he is not willing to lay it down for my sake, he shall lose it.*

38 But whosoever shall *be willing* to lose his life for my sake, and the gospel, the same shall save it.

JST, Mark 8:42–43. Compare Mark 8:38

People who are ashamed of Christ have no part in the first resurrection, but those willing to die for Christ will come with Him in His glory.

42 *And they shall not have part in that resurrection when he cometh.*

43 *For verily I say unto you, That he shall come; and he that layeth down his life for my sake and the gospel's, shall come with him, and shall be clothed with his glory in the cloud, on the right hand of the Son of man.*

JST, Mark 9:3. Compare Mark 9:4

John the Baptist is on the Mount of Transfiguration.

3 And there appeared unto them Elias with Moses, *or in other words, John the Baptist and Moses;* and they were talking with Jesus.

JST, Mark 9:40–48. Compare Mark 9:43–48

Jesus compares cutting off an offending hand or foot to discontinuing associations that may lead one astray.

40 *Therefore,* if thy hand offend thee, cut it off; *or if thy brother offend thee and confess not and forsake not, he shall be cut off.* It is better for thee to enter into life maimed, than having two hands, to go into hell.

41 *For it is better for thee to enter into life without thy brother, than for thee and thy brother to be cast into hell;* into the fire that never shall be quenched, where their worm dieth not, and the fire is not quenched.

42 And *again,* if thy foot offend thee, cut it off; *for he that is thy standard, by whom thou walkest, if he become a transgressor, he shall be cut off.*

43 It is better for thee, to enter halt into life, than having two feet to be cast into hell; into the fire that never shall be quenched.

44 *Therefore, let every man stand or fall, by himself, and not for another; or not trusting another.*

45 *Seek unto my Father, and it shall be done in that very moment what ye shall ask, if ye ask in faith, believing that ye shall receive.*

46 And if thine eye *which seeth for thee, him that is appointed to watch over thee to show thee light, become a transgressor and* offend thee, pluck *him* out.

47 It is better for thee to enter into the kingdom of God, with one eye, than having two eyes to be cast into hell fire.

48 *For it is better that thyself should be saved, than to be cast into hell with thy brother,* where their worm dieth not, and where the fire is not quenched.

JST, Mark 12:32. Compare Mark 12:27

God is not a God of the dead, because He raises the dead from their graves.

32 He is not *therefore* the God of the dead, but the God of the living; *for he raiseth them up out of their graves.* Ye therefore do greatly err.

JST, Mark 14:20–26. Compare Mark 14:22–25

Jesus institutes the sacrament in remembrance of His body and blood.

20 And as they did eat, Jesus took bread and blessed it, and brake, and gave to them, and said, Take *it, and* eat.

21 *Behold, this is for you to do in remembrance of my body; for as oft as ye do this ye will remember this hour that I was with you.*

22 And he took the cup, and when he had given thanks, he gave it to them; and they all drank of it.

23 And he said unto them, This is *in remembrance of* my blood which is shed for many, *and the new testament which I give unto you; for of me ye shall bear record unto all the world.*

24 *And as oft as ye do this ordinance, ye will remember me in this hour that I was with you and drank with you of this cup, even the last time in my ministry.*

25 Verily I say unto you, *Of this ye shall bear record; for* I will no more drink of the fruit of the vine *with you,* until that day that I drink it new in the kingdom of God.

26 *And now they were grieved, and wept over him.*

JST, Mark 14:36–38. Compare Mark 14:32–34

At Gethsemane, even the Twelve do not fully grasp Jesus' role as the Messiah.

36 And they came to a place which was named Gethsemane, *which was a garden; and the disciples began to be sore amazed, and to be very heavy, and to complain in their hearts, wondering if this be the Messiah.*

37 *And Jesus knowing their hearts, said* to his disciples, Sit ye here, while I shall pray.

38 And he taketh with him, Peter, and James, and John, *and rebuked them,* and said unto them, My soul is exceeding sorrowful, *even* unto death; tarry ye here and watch.

JST, Mark 16:3–6. Compare Mark 16:4–7; Luke 24:2–4

Two angels greet the women at the tomb of the Savior.

3 *But* when they looked, they saw that the stone was rolled away, (for it was very great,) *and two angels sitting thereon,* clothed in long white *garments;* and they were affrighted.

4 *But the angels said* unto them, Be not affrighted; ye seek Jesus of Nazareth, *who* was crucified; he is risen; he is not here; behold the place where they laid him;

5 *And* go your way, tell his disciples and Peter, that he goeth before you into Galilee; there shall ye see him as he said unto you.

6 And they, entering into the sepulcher, saw the place where they laid Jesus.

JST, Luke 1:8. Compare Luke 1:8
Zacharias, John the Baptist's father, performs priesthood duties.

8 And while he executed the priest's office before God, in the order of his *priesthood,*

JST, Luke 2:46. Compare Luke 2:46
The doctors in the temple listen to Jesus and ask Him questions.

46 And it came to pass, after three days they found him in the temple, sitting in the midst of the doctors, *and they were* hearing *him,* and asking *him* questions.

JST, Luke 3:4–11. Compare Luke 3:4–6
Christ will come as prophesied to bring salvation to Israel and to the Gentiles. In the fulness of times, He will come again to judge the world.

4 As it is written in the book of the *prophet* Esaias; *and these are the words,* saying, The voice of one crying in the wilderness, Prepare ye the way of the Lord, and make his paths straight.
5 *For behold, and lo, he shall come, as it is written in the book of the prophets, to take away the sins of the world, and to bring salvation unto the heathen nations, to gather together those who are lost, who are of the sheepfold of Israel;*
6 *Yea, even the dispersed and afflicted; and also to prepare the way, and make possible the preaching of the gospel unto the Gentiles;*
7 *And to be a light unto all who sit in darkness, unto the uttermost parts of the earth; to bring to pass the resurrection from the dead, and to ascend up on high, to dwell on the right hand of the Father,*
8 *Until the fullness of time, and the law and the testimony shall be sealed, and the keys of the kingdom* shall be delivered up again unto the Father;
9 *To administer justice unto all; to come down in judgment upon all, and to convince all the ungodly of their ungodly deeds, which they have committed; and all this in the day that he shall come;*
10 *For it is a day of power; yea,* every valley shall be filled, and every mountain and hill shall be brought low; the crooked shall be made straight, and the rough ways made smooth;
11 And all flesh shall see the salvation of God.

JST, Luke 3:19–20. Compare Luke 3:10–13
The poor are cared for from the treasury's abundance. Publicans (tax collectors) should take no more than is appointed by law.

19 *For it is well known unto you, Theophilus, that after the manner of the Jews, and according to the custom of their law in receiving money into the treasury, that out of the abundance which was received, was appointed unto the poor, every man his portion;*
20 *And after this manner did the publicans also, wherefore John said unto them, Exact no more than that which is appointed you.*

JST, Luke 6:29–30. Compare Luke 6:29–30
Jesus teaches that it is better to endure persecution than to contend with an enemy.

29 And unto him who smiteth thee on the cheek, offer also the other; *or, in other words, it is better to offer the other, than to revile again.* And him who taketh away thy cloak, forbid not to take thy coat also.
30 *For it is better that thou suffer thine enemy to take these things, than to contend with him. Verily I say unto you, Your heavenly Father who seeth in secret, shall bring that wicked one into judgment.*

JST, Luke 9:24–25. Compare Luke 9:24–25

Gaining worldly wealth is not worth losing one's soul.

24 For whosoever will save his life, *must be willing to* lose it *for my sake; and* whosoever will *be willing to* lose his life for my sake, the same shall save it.

25 For what *doth it profit a man* if he gain the whole world, *and yet he receive him not whom God hath ordained, and he* lose *his own soul, and he* himself be *a* castaway?

JST, Luke 11:53. Compare Luke 11:52

The fulness of the scriptures is the key of knowledge.

53 Woe unto you, lawyers! For ye have taken away the key of knowledge, *the fullness of the scriptures;* ye *enter* not in yourselves *into the kingdom;* and *those who* were entering in, ye hindered.

JST, Luke 12:9–12. Compare Luke 12:9–10; see also JST, Matthew 12:37–38 and D&C 132:26–27

Jesus explains that blasphemy against the Holy Ghost will not be forgiven.

9 But he *who* denieth me before men, shall be denied before the angels of God.

10 *Now his disciples knew that he said this, because they had spoken evil against him before the people; for they were afraid to confess him before men.*

11 *And they reasoned among themselves, saying, He knoweth our hearts, and he speaketh to our condemnation, and we shall not be forgiven. But he answered them, and said unto them,*

12 Whosoever shall speak a word against the Son of man, *and repenteth,* it shall be forgiven him; but unto him *who* blasphemeth against the Holy Ghost, it shall not be forgiven him.

JST, Luke 12:41–57. Compare Luke 12:37–48

Jesus teaches that His servants must always be ready for His coming.

41 *For, behold, he cometh in the first watch of the night, and he shall also come in the second watch, and again he shall come in the third watch.*

42 *And verily I say unto you, He hath already come, as it is written of him; and again when* he shall come in the second watch, or come in the third watch, blessed are those servants *when he cometh, that he* shall find so *doing;*

43 *For the Lord of those servants shall gird himself, and make them to sit down to meat, and will come forth and serve them.*

44 *And now, verily I say these things unto you, that ye may know this, that the coming of the Lord is as a thief in the night.*

45 *And it is like unto a man who is an householder, who, if he watcheth not his goods, the thief cometh in an hour of which he is not aware, and taketh his goods, and divideth them among his fellows.*

46 *And they said among themselves, If the good man of the house had known what hour the thief would come, he would have watched, and not have suffered his house to be broken through and the loss of his goods.*

47 *And he said unto them, Verily I say unto you, be ye therefore ready also; for the Son of man cometh at an hour when ye think not.*

48 *Then Peter said unto him, Lord, speakest thou this parable unto us, or unto all?*

49 *And the Lord said, I speak unto those whom the Lord shall make rulers over his household, to give his children their portion of meat in due season.*

50 *And they said, Who then is that faithful and wise servant?*

51 *And the Lord said unto them, It is that servant who watcheth, to impart his portion of meat in due season.*

52 Blessed *be* that servant whom his *Lord* shall find, when he cometh, so doing.

53 Of a truth I say unto you, that he will make him ruler over all that he hath.

54 *But the evil servant is he who is not found watching. And if that servant is not found watching, he will say in his heart, My Lord delayeth his coming; and shall begin to beat the menservants, and the maidens, and to eat, and drink, and to be drunken.*

55 The *Lord* of that servant will come in a day he looketh not for, and at an hour when he is not aware, and will cut him *down*, and will appoint him his portion with the unbelievers.

56 And that servant who knew his *Lord's* will, and prepared not *for his Lord's coming,* neither did according to his will, shall be beaten with many stripes.

57 But he that knew not *his Lord's will,* and did commit things worthy of stripes, shall be beaten with few. For unto whomsoever much is given, of him shall much be required; and to whom *the Lord* has committed much, of him *will men* ask the more.

JST, Luke 14:35–37. Compare Luke 14:34

Those who know Moses and the prophets believe in Jesus.

35 *Then certain of them came to him, saying, Good Master, we have Moses and the prophets, and whosoever shall live by them, shall he not have life?*

36 *And Jesus answered, saying, Ye know not Moses, neither the prophets; for if ye had known them, ye would have believed on me; for to this intent they were written. For I am sent that ye might have life. Therefore I will liken it unto* salt *which is good;*

37 But if the salt *has* lost *its* savor, wherewith shall it be seasoned?

JST, Luke 16:16–23. Compare Luke 16:16–18

The law and the prophets testify of Jesus. The Pharisees seek to destroy the kingdom. Jesus introduces the parable of the rich man and Lazarus.

16 *And they said unto him, We have the law, and the prophets; but as for this man we will not receive him to be our ruler; for he maketh himself to be a judge over us.*

17 *Then said Jesus unto them,* The law and the prophets *testify of me; yea, and all the prophets who have written, even* until John, *have foretold of these days.*

18 Since that time, the kingdom of God is preached, and every man *who seeketh truth* presseth into it.

19 And it is easier for heaven and earth to pass, than for one tittle of the law to fail.

20 *And why teach ye the law, and deny that which is written; and condemn him whom the Father hath sent to fulfill the law, that ye might all be redeemed?*

21 *O fools! for you have said in your hearts, There is no God. And you pervert the right way; and the kingdom of heaven suffereth violence of you; and you persecute the meek; and in your violence you seek to destroy the kingdom; and ye take the children of the kingdom by force. Woe unto you, ye adulterers!*

22 *And they reviled him again, being angry for the saying, that they were adulterers.*

23 *But he continued, saying,* Whosoever putteth away his wife, and marrieth another, committeth adultery; and whosoever marrieth her who is put away from her husband, committeth adultery. *Verily I say unto you, I will liken you unto the rich man.*

JST, Luke 17:21. Compare Luke 17:20–21

The kingdom of God has already come.

21 Neither shall they say, Lo, here! or, Lo, there! For, behold,

the kingdom of God *has already come unto* you.

JST, Luke 17:36–40. Compare Luke 17:37

Jesus tells the parable of the eagles to explain the gathering of His Saints in the last days.

36 And they answered and said unto him, Where, Lord, *shall they be taken?*

37 And he said unto them, Wheresoever the body is *gathered; or, in other words, whithersoever the saints are gathered,* thither will the eagles be gathered together; *or, thither will the remainder be gathered together.*

38 *This he spake, signifying the gathering of his saints; and of angels descending and gathering the remainder unto them; the one from the bed, the other from the grinding, and the other from the field, whithersoever he listeth.*

39 *For verily there shall be new heavens, and a new earth, wherein dwelleth righteousness.*

40 *And there shall be no unclean thing; for the earth becoming old, even as a garment, having waxed in corruption, wherefore it vanisheth away, and the footstool remaineth sanctified, cleansed from all sin.*

JST, Luke 18:27. Compare Luke 18:27

Trusting in riches prevents a person from entering the kingdom of God.

27 And he said *unto them, It is impossible for them who trust in riches,* to enter into the kingdom of God; *but he who forsaketh the things which are of this world, it is* possible with God, *that he should enter in.*

JST, Luke 21:24–26. Compare Luke 21:25–26

Jesus speaks of some signs of His coming.

24 *Now these things he spake unto them, concerning the destruction of Jerusalem. And then his disciples* asked *him, saying, Master, tell us concerning thy coming?*

25 *And he answered them, and said, In the generation in which the times of the Gentiles shall be fulfilled,* there shall be signs in the sun, and in the moon, and in the stars; and upon the earth distress of nations with perplexity, *like* the sea and the waves roaring. *The earth also shall be troubled, and the waters of the great deep;*

26 Men's hearts failing them for fear, and for looking after those things which are coming on the earth. For the powers of heaven shall be shaken.

JST, Luke 21:32. Compare Luke 21:32

All will be fulfilled when the times of the Gentiles are fulfilled.

32 Verily I say unto you, this generation, *the generation when the times of the Gentiles be fulfilled,* shall not pass away till all be fulfilled.

JST, Luke 23:35. Compare Luke 23:34

Jesus asks forgiveness for the Roman soldiers who are crucifying Him.

35 Then said Jesus, Father, forgive them; for they know not what they do (*Meaning the soldiers who crucified him,*) and they parted his raiment and cast lots.

JST, Luke 24:2–4. Compare Luke 24:2–5

The women see two angels at Jesus' sepulcher.

2 And they found the stone rolled away from the sepulcher, *and two angels standing by it in shining garments.*

3 And they entered *into the sepulcher,* and *not finding* the body of the Lord Jesus, they were much perplexed thereabout;

4 And were *affrighted,* and bowed down their faces to the earth. *But behold the angels said unto them,*

Why seek ye the living among the dead?

JST, John 1:1–34. Compare John 1:1–34

The gospel of Jesus Christ has been preached from the beginning. John the Baptist is the Elias who prepares the way for Christ, and Jesus Christ is the Elias who restores all things and through whom salvation comes.

1 In the beginning was the *gospel preached through the Son. And the gospel was the word,* and the *word* was with *the Son, and the Son was with God,* and the *Son* was *of* God.

2 The same was in the beginning with God.

3 All things were made by him; and without him was not anything made which was made.

4 In him was *the gospel, and the gospel was the life,* and the life was the light of men;

5 And the light shineth *in the world,* and the *world perceiveth* it not.

6 There was a man sent from God, whose name was John.

7 The same came *into the world* for a witness, to bear witness of the *light, to bear record of the gospel through the Son, unto all,* that through him *men* might believe.

8 He was not that *light,* but *came* to bear witness of that *light,*

9 Which was the true *light,* which lighteth every man *who* cometh into the world;

10 *Even the Son of God.* He *who* was in the world, and the world was made by him, and the world knew him not.

11 He came unto his own, and his own received him not.

12 But as many as received him, to them gave he power to become the sons of God; *only* to them who believe on his name.

13 *He was* born, not of blood, nor of the will of the flesh, nor of the will of man, but of God.

14 And the *same word* was made flesh, and dwelt among us, and we beheld his glory, the glory as of the Only Begotten of the Father, full of grace and truth.

15 John *bear* witness of him, and cried, saying, This *is* he of whom I spake; He who cometh after me, is preferred before me; for he was before me.

16 *For in the beginning was the Word, even the Son, who is made flesh, and sent unto us by the will of the Father. And as many as believe on his name shall receive of his fullness. And of his fullness have all we received, even immortality and eternal life, through his* grace.

17 For the law was given *through* Moses, but *life* and truth came *through* Jesus Christ.

18 *For the law was after a carnal commandment, to the administration of death; but the gospel was after the power of an endless life, through Jesus Christ, the Only Begotten Son, who is in the bosom of the Father.*

19 *And* no man hath seen God at any time, *except he hath borne record of the Son; for except it is through him no man can be saved.*

20 And this is the record of John, when the Jews sent priests and Levites from Jerusalem, to ask him; Who art thou?

21 And he confessed, and denied not *that he was Elias;* but confessed, *saying;* I am not the Christ.

22 And they asked him, *saying; How then art thou Elias? And he said, I am not that Elias who was to restore all things. And they asked him, saying,* Art thou that prophet? And he answered, No.

23 Then said they unto him, Who art thou? that we may give an answer to them that sent us. What sayest thou of thyself?

24 He said, I am the voice of one crying in the wilderness, Make straight the way of the Lord, as saith the prophet Esaias.

25 And they who were sent were of the Pharisees.

26 And they asked him, and said unto him; Why baptizest thou then, if thou be not the Christ, nor

Elias *who was to restore all things,* neither that prophet?

27 John answered them, saying; I baptize with water, but there standeth one among you, whom ye know not;

28 He it is *of whom I bear record. He is that prophet, even Elias,* who, coming after me, is preferred before me, whose shoe's latchet I am not worthy to unloose, *or whose place I am not able to fill; for he shall baptize, not only with water, but with fire, and with the Holy Ghost.*

29 The next day John seeth Jesus coming unto him, and said; Behold the Lamb of God, who taketh away the sin of the world!

30 *And John bare record of him unto the people, saying,* This is he of whom I said; After me cometh a man who is preferred before me; for he was before me, and I knew him, *and* that he should be made manifest to Israel; therefore am I come baptizing with water.

31 And John bare record, saying; *When he was baptized of me,* I saw the Spirit descending from heaven like a dove, and it abode upon him.

32 And I knew him; *for he who sent me to baptize with water, the same said unto me;* Upon whom thou shalt see the Spirit descending, and remaining on him, the same is he who baptizeth with the Holy Ghost.

33 And I saw, and bare record that this is the Son of God.

34 *These things were done in Bethabara, beyond Jordan, where John was baptizing.*

JST, John 1:42. Compare John 1:42

Cephas means "seer" or "stone."

42 And he brought him to Jesus. And when Jesus beheld him, he said, Thou art Simon, the son of Jona, thou shalt be called Cephas, which is, by interpretation, *a seer, or a stone. And they were fishermen. And they straightway left all, and followed Jesus.*

JST, John 4:1–4. Compare John 4:1–2

The Pharisees desire to kill Jesus. He performs some baptisms, but His disciples perform more.

1 When therefore the Pharisees had heard that Jesus made and baptized more disciples than John,

2 *They sought more diligently some means that they might put him to death; for many received John as a prophet, but they believed not on Jesus.*

3 *Now the Lord knew this, though he* himself baptized not *so many as his disciples;*

4 *For he suffered them for an example, preferring one another.*

JST, John 4:26. Compare John 4:24

God promises His Spirit to true believers.

26 *For unto such hath* God *promised his* Spirit. And they *who* worship him, must worship in spirit and in truth.

JST, John 6:44. Compare John 6:44

The Father's will is that all receive Jesus. Those who do the will of Jesus will be raised in the resurrection of the just.

44 No man can come unto me, except *he doeth the will of my* Father *who* hath sent me. *And this is the will of him who hath sent me, that ye receive the Son; for the Father beareth record of him; and he who receiveth the testimony, and doeth the will of him who sent me, I will raise up in the resurrection of the just.*

JST, John 13:8–10. Compare John 13:8–10

Jesus washes the feet of the Apostles to fulfill the law of the Jews.

8 Peter saith unto him, Thou *needest not to* wash my feet. Jesus answered him, If I wash thee not, thou hast no part with me.

9 Simon Peter saith unto him, Lord, not my feet only, but also my hands and my head.

10 Jesus saith to him, He that *has* washed *his hands and his head,* needeth not save to wash his feet, but is clean every whit; and ye are clean, but not all. *Now this was the custom of the Jews under their law; wherefore, Jesus did this that the law might be fulfilled.*

JST, John 14:30. Compare John 14:30

The prince of darkness, or Satan, is of this world.

30 Hereafter I will not talk much with you; for the prince *of darkness, who is* of this world, cometh, *but* hath *no power over me, but he* hath power over you.

JST, Acts 9:7. Compare Acts 9:7; 22:9

Those who are with Paul at his conversion see the light, but they do not hear the voice or see the Lord.

7 And *they who were journeying* with him *saw indeed the light, and were afraid; but they heard not the voice of him who spake to him.*

JST, Acts 22:29-30. Compare Acts 22:29-30

The chief captain loosed Paul from his bands.

29 Then straightway they departed from him which should have examined him, and the chief captain also was afraid after he knew that he was a Roman, because he had bound him, *and he loosed him from his bands.*

30 On the morrow, because he would have known the certainty wherefore he was accused of the Jews, *he* commanded the chief priests and all their council to appear, and brought Paul down, and set him before them.

JST, Romans 3:5-8. Compare Romans 3:5-8

Paul teaches that a person cannot do evil to bring about good.

5 But if *we remain in* our unrighteousness *and* commend the righteousness of God, *how dare* we say, God is unrighteous who taketh vengeance? (I speak as a man *who fears God,*)

6 God forbid; for then how shall God judge the world?

7 For if the truth of God hath more abounded through my lie, (*as it is called of the Jews,*) unto his glory; why yet am I also judged as a sinner? and not *received? Because* we *are* slanderously reported;

8 And some affirm that we say, (*whose damnation is just,*) Let us do evil that good may come. *But this is false.*

JST, Romans 4:2-5. Compare Romans 4:2-5

Man can only be saved by the grace of Jesus Christ, not by works related to observance of the law of Moses.

2 For if Abraham were justified by *the law of* works, he hath to glory *in himself;* but not *of* God.

3 For what saith the scripture? Abraham believed God, and it was counted unto him for righteousness.

4 Now to him *who is justified by the law of works,* is the reward reckoned, not of grace, but of debt.

5 But to him that *seeketh not to be justified by the law of works,* but believeth on him who justifieth *not* the ungodly, his faith is counted for righteousness.

JST, Romans 4:16. Compare Romans 4:16

Both faith and works, through grace, are necessary for salvation.

16 Therefore *ye are justified of*

faith *and works, through* grace, to the end the promise might be sure to all the seed; not to *them* only *who are* of the law, but to *them* also *who are* of the faith of Abraham; who is the father of us all,

JST, Romans 7:5–27. Compare Romans 7:5–25

Only Christ has power to permanently change men's souls for good.

5 For when we were in the flesh, the motions of sin, which were *not according to* the law, did work in our members to bring forth fruit unto death.

6 But now we are delivered from the law wherein we were held, *being dead to the law,* that we should serve in newness of spirit, and not in the oldness of the letter.

7 What shall we say then? Is the law sin? God forbid. Nay, I had not known sin, but by the law; for I had not known lust, except the law had said, Thou shalt not covet.

8 But sin, taking occasion by the commandment, wrought in me all manner of concupiscence. For without the law sin was dead.

9 For *once* I was alive without *transgression of* the law, but when the commandment *of Christ* came, sin revived, and I died.

10 And *when I believed not* the commandment *of Christ which came,* which was ordained to life, I found *it condemned me* unto death.

11 For sin, taking occasion, *denied* the commandment, *and* deceived me; and by it *I was slain.*

12 *Nevertheless, I found* the law *to be* holy, and the commandment *to be* holy, and just, and good.

13 Was then that which is good made death unto me? God forbid. But sin, that it might appear sin by that which is good working death in me; that sin, by the commandment, might become exceeding sinful.

14 For we know that the *commandment* is spiritual; but *when I was under the law, I was yet* carnal, sold under sin.

15 *But now I am spiritual;* for that which *I am commanded to do, I do; and that which I am commanded not to allow,* I allow not.

16 For what I *know is not right, I would* not *do;* for that which is sin, I hate.

17 If then I do *not* that which I would not *allow,* I consent unto the law, that it is good; *and I am not condemned.*

18 Now then, it is no more I that do *sin;* but I *seek to subdue that* sin which dwelleth in me.

19 For I know that in me, that is, in my flesh, dwelleth no good thing; for to will is present with me, *but to* perform that which is good I find not, *only in Christ.*

20 For the good that I would *have done when under the law, I find not to be good; therefore,* I do *it* not.

21 But the evil which I would not *do under the law, I find to be good;* that, I do.

22 Now if I do that, *through the assistance of Christ,* I would not *do under the law, I am not under the law; and* it is no more *that I seek to do wrong,* but *to subdue* sin that dwelleth in me.

23 I find then *that under the* law, that when I would do good evil *was* present with me; for I delight in the law of God after the inward man.

24 *And now I see another law, even the commandment of Christ, and it is imprinted in my mind.*

25 *But* my members *are* warring against the law of my mind, and bringing me into captivity to the law of sin which is in my members.

26 *And if I subdue not the sin which is in me, but with the flesh serve the law of sin;* O wretched man that I am! who shall deliver me from the body of this death?

27 I thank God through Jesus Christ our Lord, *then, that so with*

the mind I myself serve the law of God.

JST, Romans 8:8. Compare Romans 8:8

Those who follow after the ways of the flesh cannot please God.

8 So then they that are *after* the flesh cannot please God.

JST, Romans 8:29–30. Compare Romans 8:29–30

Jesus Christ sanctifies the righteous in preparation for their salvation.

29 For *him* whom he did foreknow, he also did predestinate to be conformed to *his own* image, that he might be the firstborn among many brethren.

30 Moreover, *him* whom he did predestinate, *him* he also called; and *him* whom he called, *him* he also *sanctified*; and *him* whom he *sanctified*, *him* he also glorified.

JST, Romans 13:6–7. Compare Romans 13:6–7

Those who honor civil authorities make their honor to God greater and more perfect.

6 For, for this cause pay ye *your consecrations* also *unto them*; for they are God's ministers, attending continually upon this very thing.

7 *But first,* render to all their dues, *according to custom,* tribute to whom tribute, custom to whom custom, *that your consecrations may be done in* fear *of him* to whom fear *belongs, and in* honor *of him* to whom honor *belongs.*

JST, 1 Corinthians 7:1–2, 5, 26, 29–33, 38. Compare 1 Corinthians 7:1–2, 5, 26, 29–38

Paul teaches that marriage is desirable. Those called as missionaries, however, serve God better if they remain single during their ministry.

1 Now concerning the things whereof ye wrote unto me, *saying,* It is good for a man not to touch a woman.

2 Nevertheless, *I say,* to avoid fornication, let every man have his own wife, and let every woman have her own husband.

5 *Depart* ye not one *from* the other, except it be with consent for a time, that ye may give yourselves to fasting and prayer; and come together again, that Satan tempt you not for your incontinency.

26 I suppose therefore that this is good for the present distress, for a man so to *remain that he may do greater good.*

29 But *I speak unto you who are called unto the ministry. For* this I say, brethren, the time *that remaineth* is *but* short, *that ye shall be sent forth unto the ministry. Even* they who have wives, *shall* be as though they had none; *for ye are called and chosen to do the Lord's work.*

30 And *it shall be with them* who weep, as though they wept not; and them who rejoice, as though they rejoiced not, and them who buy, as though they possessed not;

31 And them who use this world, as not *using* it; for the fashion of this world passeth away.

32 But *I would, brethren, that ye magnify your calling.* I would have you without carefulness. For he who is unmarried, careth for the things that belong to the Lord, how he may please the Lord; *therefore he prevaileth.*

33 But he who is married, careth for the things that are of the world, how he may please his wife; *therefore there is a difference, for he is hindered.*

38 So then he that giveth *himself* in marriage doeth well; but he that giveth *himself* not in marriage doeth better.

JST, 1 Corinthians 15:40. Compare 1 Corinthians 15:40

There are three degrees of glory in the Resurrection.

40 Also celestial bodies, and bodies terrestrial, *and bodies telestial;* but the glory of the celestial, one; and the terrestrial, another; *and the telestial, another.*

JST, 2 Corinthians 5:16. Compare 2 Corinthians 5:16

Paul counsels Saints not to live after the manner of the flesh.

16 Wherefore, henceforth *live* we no *more* after the flesh; *yea, though we once lived after the flesh, yet since* we have known Christ, now henceforth *live* we no more *after the flesh.*

JST, Galatians 3:19–20. Compare Galatians 3:19–20

Moses is the mediator of the first covenant, or the law. Jesus Christ is the mediator of the new covenant.

19 Wherefore then, *the law* was added because of transgressions, till the seed should come to whom the promise was made *in the law given to Moses, who* was ordained by *the hand of* angels *to be a mediator of this first covenant, (the law.)*
20 Now *this* mediator *was* not a mediator *of the new covenant; but there is one mediator of the new covenant, who is Christ, as it is written in the law concerning the promises made to Abraham and his seed. Now Christ is the mediator of life; for this is the promise which God made unto Abraham.*

JST, Ephesians 4:26. Compare Ephesians 4:26

Unrighteous anger is sin.

26 *Can ye be* angry, and *not sin?* let not the sun go down upon your wrath;

JST, Colossians 2:21–22. Compare Colossians 2:20–23

The commandments of men might have value in teaching such things as self-discipline, but they neither honor God nor save man.

21 *Which are after the doctrines*

and commandments of men, who teach you to touch not, taste not, handle not; *all those things* which are to perish with the using?
22 Which things have indeed a show of wisdom in will worship, and humility, and neglecting the body *as to the satisfying the flesh,* not in any honor *to God.*

JST, 1 Thessalonians 4:15. Compare 1 Thessalonians 4:15

Those righteous people who are alive at the coming of the Lord will have no advantage over the righteous dead.

15 For this we say unto you by the word of the Lord, that *they who* are alive *at* the coming of the Lord, shall not prevent them *who remain unto the coming of the Lord, who* are asleep.

JST, 2 Thessalonians 2:2–3, 7–9. Compare 2 Thessalonians 2:2–9

Satan will cause a falling away or apostasy before the Lord returns.

2 That ye be not soon shaken in mind, or be troubled *by letter, except ye receive it from us;* neither by spirit, nor by word, as that the day of Christ is at hand.
3 Let no man deceive you by any means; for there *shall* come a falling away first, and that man of sin be revealed, the son of perdition;
7 For the mystery of iniquity doth already work, *and he it is who now worketh, and Christ suffereth him to work,* until *the time is fulfilled that he shall be taken out of* the way.
8 And then shall that wicked *one* be revealed, whom the Lord shall consume with the spirit of his mouth, and shall destroy with the brightness of his coming.
9 *Yea, the Lord, even Jesus, whose* coming is *not until* after *there cometh a falling away,* by the working of Satan with all power, and signs and lying wonders,

JST, 1 Timothy 2:4. Compare
1 Timothy 2:4

Christ is the Only Begotten Son and
Mediator.

4 Who *is willing to* have all men
to be saved, and to come unto the
knowledge of the truth *which is in
Christ Jesus, who is the Only Begotten Son of God, and ordained to be
a Mediator between God and man;
who is one God, and hath power over
all men.*

JST, 1 Timothy 3:15–16. Compare
1 Timothy 3:15–16

The Church is founded on the central
principle that Jesus became mortal, taught
the gospel, and returned to His Father.
Note: The subtle change in the following
verses emphasizes that the "pillar and
ground of the truth" is Jesus Christ.

15 But if I tarry long, that thou
mayest know how thou oughtest
to behave thyself in the house of
God, which is the church of the
living God.
16 The pillar and ground of the
truth *is,* (and without controversy,
great is the mystery of godliness,)
God was manifest in the flesh,
justified in the Spirit, seen of angels, preached unto the Gentiles,
believed on in the world, received
up into glory.

JST, 1 Timothy 6:15–16. Compare
1 Timothy 6:15–16

Those who have the light of immortality
(the gospel) dwelling in them can see Jesus.

15 Which in his times he shall
show, who is the blessed and only
Potentate, the King of kings, and
Lord of lords, *to whom be honor and
power everlasting;*
16 *Whom* no man hath seen, nor
can see, unto whom no man can approach, only he who hath the light
*and the hope of immortality dwell-
ing in him.*

JST, Hebrews 1:6–7. Compare
Hebrews 1:6–7

Angels are ministering spirits.

6 And again, when he bringeth
in the first begotten into the
world, he saith, And let all the angels of God worship him, *who maketh his ministers as a flame of fire.*
7 And of the angels he saith, *Angels are ministering spirits.*

JST, Hebrews 4:3. Compare
Hebrews 4:3

Those who harden their hearts will not be
saved; those who repent will enter into the
Lord's rest.

3 For we who have believed do
enter into rest, as he said, As I
have sworn in my wrath, If they
harden their hearts they shall *not*
enter into my rest; *also, I have
sworn, If they will not harden their
hearts, they shall enter into my rest;*
although the works of God were
prepared, (or finished,) from the
foundation of the world.

JST, Hebrews 6:1–10. Compare
Hebrews 6:1–10

The principles of Christ's doctrine lead to
perfection.

1 Therefore *not* leaving the principles of the doctrine of Christ,
let us go on unto perfection; not
laying again the foundation of repentance from dead works, and of
faith toward God.
2 Of the doctrine of baptisms,
of laying on of hands, and of the
resurrection of the dead, and of
eternal judgment.
3 And *we will go on unto perfection*
if God permit.
4 For *he hath made it* impossible
for those who were once enlight-
ened, and have tasted of the heavenly gift, and were made partakers
of the Holy Ghost,
5 And have tasted the good word
of God, and the powers of the
world to come,
6 If they shall fall away, to *be renewed* again unto repentance; seeing they crucify unto themselves
the Son of God afresh, and put
him to an open shame.
7 For *the day cometh that* the earth

which drinketh in the rain that cometh oft upon it, and bringeth forth herbs meet for them *who dwelleth thereon,* by whom it is dressed, *who now* receiveth blessings from God, *shall be cleansed with fire.*

8 *For* that which beareth thorns and briers is rejected, and is nigh unto cursing; *therefore they who bring not forth good fruits, shall be cast into the fire; for their* end is to be burned.

9 But, beloved, we are persuaded *of* better things of you, and things that accompany salvation, though we thus speak.

10 For God is not unrighteous, *therefore he will not* forget your work and labor of love, which ye have showed toward his name, in that ye have ministered to the saints, and do minister.

JST, Hebrews 7:3. Compare Hebrews 7:3

Melchizedek was a priest after the order of the Son of God. All those who receive this priesthood can become like the Son of God.

3 *For this Melchizedek was ordained a priest after the order of the Son of God, which order was* without father, without mother, without descent, having neither beginning of days, nor end of life. *And all those who are ordained unto this priesthood are* made like unto the Son of God, *abiding* a priest continually.

JST, Hebrews 7:19–21. Compare Hebrews 7:19–21

The law prepared people for Jesus, who is "the surety of a better testament."

19 For the law *was administered without an oath and* made nothing perfect, but *was only* the bringing in of a better hope; by the which we draw nigh unto God.

20 Inasmuch as *this high priest was* not without an oath, *by so much was* Jesus made the surety of a better testament.

21 (For those priests were made without an oath; but this with an oath by him that said unto him, The Lord sware and will not repent, Thou art a priest forever after the order of Melchizedek;)

JST, Hebrews 7:25–26. Compare Hebrews 7:26–27

Jesus offers Himself as a sinless sacrifice for our sins.

25 For such an high priest became us, who is holy, harmless, undefiled, separate from sinners, and made *ruler over* the heavens;

26 *And not* as those high priests *who* offered up sacrifice *daily,* first for *their* own sins, and then for the *sins of the people; for he needeth not offer sacrifice for his own sins, for he knew no sins; but for the sins of the people. And this he did once, when* he offered up himself.

JST, Hebrews 11:1. Compare Hebrews 11:1

Faith is the assurance of things hoped for.

1 Now faith is the *assurance* of things hoped for, the evidence of things not seen.

JST, Hebrews 11:35. Compare Hebrews 11:35

The faithful who are tortured for Christ obtain the First Resurrection.

35 Women received their dead raised to life again; and others were tortured, not accepting deliverance; that they might obtain *the first* resurrection;

JST, James 1:2. Compare James 1:2

Afflictions, not temptations, help to sanctify us.

2 My brethren, count it all joy when ye fall into *many afflictions;*

JST, James 2:1. Compare James 2:1

Members should not regard one person more highly than another.

1 My brethren, *ye cannot* have

the faith of our Lord Jesus Christ, the Lord of glory, *and yet have respect to* persons.

JST, James 2:14–21. Compare
James 2:14–22

Faith without works is dead and cannot save.

14 What profit *is it*, my brethren, *for* a man *to* say he hath faith, and hath not works? can faith save him?

15 Yea, a man may say, *I will show thee I have faith without works; but I say,* Show me thy faith without works, and I will show thee my faith by my works.

16 *For* if a brother or sister be naked and destitute, and one of you say, Depart in peace, be warmed and filled; notwithstanding *he* give not those things which are needful to the body; what profit *is your faith unto such?*

17 Even so faith, if it *have* not works is dead, being alone.

18 *Therefore* wilt thou know, O vain man, that faith without works is dead *and cannot save you?*

19 Thou believest there is one God; thou doest well; the devils also believe, and tremble; *thou hast made thyself like unto them, not being justified.*

20 Was not Abraham our father justified by works, when he had offered Isaac his son upon the altar?

21 Seest thou how *works* wrought with his *faith*, and by works was faith made perfect?

JST, 1 Peter 3:20. Compare
1 Peter 3:20

Some of the spirits in prison were unrighteous in the days of Noah.

20 *Some of whom* were disobedient *in the days of Noah, while* the long-suffering of God waited, while the ark was preparing, wherein few, that is, eight souls were saved by water.

JST, 1 Peter 4:6. Compare
1 Peter 4:6

The gospel is preached to those who are dead.

6 *Because of this, is* the gospel preached to them *who* are dead, that they might be judged according to men in the flesh, but live *in the spirit* according to *the will of* God.

JST, 1 Peter 4:8. Compare
1 Peter 4:8

Charity prevents us from sinning.

8 And above all things have fervent charity among yourselves; for charity *preventeth a* multitude of sins.

JST, 2 Peter 3:3–13. Compare
2 Peter 3:3–13

In the last days, many people will deny the Lord Jesus Christ. When He comes, many natural calamities will happen. If we endure in righteousness, we will receive a new earth.

3 Knowing this first, that *in the last days* there shall come scoffers, walking after their own lusts.

4 *Denying the Lord Jesus Christ,* and saying, Where is the promise of his coming? for since the fathers fell asleep, all things *must* continue as they *are, and have continued as they are* from the beginning of the creation.

5 For this they willingly are ignorant of, that *of old* the heavens, and the earth standing *in the water* and out of the water, *were created by the word of God;*

6 *And by the word of God,* the world that then was, being overflowed with water perished;

7 But the heavens, and the earth which are now, are kept in store *by the same word,* reserved unto fire against the day of judgment and perdition of ungodly men.

8 But *concerning the coming of the Lord,* beloved, *I would not have you* ignorant of this one thing, that one day is with the Lord as

a thousand years, and a thousand years as one day.

9 The Lord is not slack concerning his promise *and coming*, as some men count slackness; but long-suffering *toward us*, not willing that any should perish, but that all should come to repentance.

10 But the day of the Lord will come as a thief in the night, in the which the heavens shall *shake, and the earth also shall tremble, and the mountains shall melt, and* pass away with a great noise, and the elements shall *be filled* with fervent heat; the earth also *shall be filled*, and the *corruptible* works *which* are therein shall be burned up.

11 *If* then all these things shall be *destroyed*, what manner of persons ought ye to be in holy *conduct* and godliness,

12 Looking *unto*, and *preparing for the day of* the coming of the *Lord* wherein the *corruptible things of the* heavens being on fire, shall be dissolved, and the *mountains* shall melt with fervent heat?

13 Nevertheless, *if we shall endure*, we *shall be kept* according to his promise. *And we* look for *a* new heavens, and a new earth wherein dwelleth righteousness.

JST, 1 John 2:1. Compare
1 John 2:1

Christ is our advocate with the Father if we repent.

1 My little children, these things write I unto you, that ye sin not. *But if any man sin and repent*, we have an advocate with the Father, Jesus Christ the righteous;

JST, 1 John 3:9. Compare
1 John 3:9

Whoever is born of God does not continue in sin.

9 Whosoever is born of God doth not *continue in* sin; for *the Spirit of God* remaineth in him; and he cannot *continue in* sin, because he

is born of God, *having received that holy Spirit of promise.*

JST, 1 John 4:12. Compare
1 John 4:12

Only men who believe in God can see Him.

12 No man hath seen God at any time, *except them who believe*. If we love one another, God dwelleth in us, and his love is perfected in us.

JST, Revelation 1:1–8. Compare
Revelation 1:1–8

John the Apostle receives the prophecies in the book of Revelation. He is visited by Jesus Christ and by an angel.

1 The Revelation of *John, a servant of God*, which *was given* unto him *of Jesus Christ*, to show unto his servants things which must shortly come to pass, *that* he sent and signified by his angel unto his servant John,

2 Who *bore* record of the word of God, and of the testimony of Jesus Christ, and of all things that he saw.

3 Blessed *are they* who read, and they who hear *and understand* the words of this prophecy, and keep those things which are written therein, for the time *of the coming of the Lord draweth nigh.*

4 *Now this is the testimony of* John to *the seven servants who are over* the seven churches in Asia. Grace unto you, and peace from him *who* is, and *who* was, and *who* is to come; *who hath sent forth his angel from* before his throne, *to testify unto those who are the seven servants over the seven churches.*

5 *Therefore, I, John,* the faithful witness, *bear record of the things which were delivered me of the angel,* and from Jesus Christ the first begotten of the dead, and the *Prince* of the kings of the earth.

6 *And* unto him who loved us, *be glory; who* washed us from our sins in his own blood, and hath made us kings and priests unto God, his Father. To him be glory and dominion, forever and ever. Amen.

7 *For* behold, he cometh *in the* clouds *with ten thousands of his saints in the kingdom, clothed with the glory of his Father.* And every eye shall see him; and they who pierced him, and all kindreds of the earth shall wail because of him. Even so, Amen.

8 *For he saith,* I am Alpha and Omega, the beginning and the ending, the Lord, *who is,* and *who* was, and *who* is to come, the Almighty.

JST, Revelation 2:22. Compare Revelation 2:22

The wicked are cast into hell.

22 Behold, I will cast her into *hell,* and them that commit adultery with her into great tribulation, except they repent of their deeds.

JST, Revelation 2:26–27. Compare Revelation 2:26–27

Those who overcome the world by obedience to Christ's commandments will rule kingdoms in the world to come with faith, equity, and justice.

26 And *to him who* overcometh, and keepeth my *commandments* unto the end, will I give power over *many kingdoms;*

27 And he shall rule them with *the word of God; and they shall be in his hands as the vessels of clay in the hands* of a potter; *and he shall govern them by faith, with equity and justice,* even as I received of my Father.

JST, Revelation 5:6. Compare Revelation 5:6

Twelve servants of God are sent to all the earth.

6 And I beheld, and, lo, in the midst of the throne and of the four beasts, and in the midst of the elders, stood a Lamb as it had been slain, having *twelve* horns and *twelve* eyes, which are the *twelve servants* of God, sent forth into all the earth.

JST, Revelation 12:1–17. Compare Revelation 12:1–17

John explains the symbols of the woman, the child, the rod of iron, the dragon, and Michael. The war that began in heaven is continued on the earth. Note the changed sequence of verses in the JST.

1 And there appeared a great *sign* in heaven, *in the likeness of things on the earth;* a woman clothed with the sun, and the moon under her feet, and upon her head a crown of twelve stars.

2 And *the woman* being with child, cried, travailing in birth, and pained to be delivered.

3 *And she brought forth a man child, who was to rule all nations with a rod of iron; and her child was caught up unto God and his throne.*

4 And there appeared another *sign* in heaven; and behold, a great red dragon, having seven heads and ten horns, and seven crowns upon his heads. And his tail drew the third part of the stars of heaven, and did cast them to the earth. And the dragon stood before the woman which was delivered, *ready* to devour her child *after* it was born.

5 And the woman fled into the wilderness, where she *had* a place prepared of God, that they should feed her there a thousand two hundred and threescore *years.*

6 And there was war in heaven; Michael and his angels fought against the dragon; and the dragon and his angels *fought against Michael;*

7 And *the dragon* prevailed not *against Michael, neither the child, nor the woman which was the church of God, who had been delivered of her pains, and brought forth the kingdom of our God and his Christ.*

8 Neither was *there* place found in heaven *for* the great dragon, *who* was cast out; that old serpent called the devil, and *also called* Satan, which deceiveth the whole world; he was cast out into the earth; and his angels were cast out with him.

9 And I heard a loud voice saying in heaven, Now is come salvation, and strength, and the kingdom of our God, and the power of his Christ;

10 For the accuser of our brethren is cast down, which accused them before our God day and night.

11 For they *have overcome* him by the blood of the Lamb, and by the word of their testimony; *for* they loved not their own lives, *but kept the testimony even* unto death. Therefore, rejoice O heavens, and ye that dwell in them.

12 *And after these things I heard another voice saying,* Woe to the inhabiters of the earth, *yea,* and *they who dwell upon the islands* of the sea! for the devil is come down unto you, having great wrath, because he knoweth that he hath but a short time.

13 *For* when the dragon saw that he was cast unto the earth, he persecuted the woman which brought forth the man-child.

14 *Therefore,* to the woman were given two wings of a great eagle, that she might *flee* into the wilderness, into her place, where she is nourished for a time, and times, and half a time, from the face of the serpent.

15 And the serpent casteth out of his mouth water as a flood after the woman, that he might cause her to be carried away of the flood.

16 And the earth *helpeth* the woman, and the earth *openeth* her mouth, and *swalloweth* up the flood which the dragon *casteth* out of his mouth.

17 *Therefore,* the dragon was wroth with the woman, and went to make war with the remnant of her seed, which keep the commandments of God, and have the testimony of Jesus Christ.

JST, Revelation 19:15, 21.
Compare Revelation 19:15, 21
God uses the word of Christ to smite the nations.

15 And out of his mouth *proceedeth the word of God, and* with it he *will* smite the nations; and he *will* rule them with *the word of his mouth;* and he treadeth the winepress *in* the fierceness and wrath of Almighty God.

21 And the remnant were slain with the *word* of him that sat upon the horse, which *word* proceeded out of his mouth; and all the fowls were filled with their flesh.